Oz Clarke's
New Wine Atlas

Oz Clarke's
New Wine Atlas

Unique panoramic maps of the world's great vineyard areas

WINES AND WINE REGIONS OF THE WORLD

PANORAMIC MAPS PAINTED BY
KEITH & SUE GAGE

HARCOURT, INC.
NEW YORK SAN DIEGO LONDON

The coastal hills of Tuscany south-east of Grosseto in the Maremma are buzzing with activity. Many producers, from Tuscany and beyond, are rushing in to buy up existing vineyards as well as suitable new land for planting.

Chardonnay vineyards belonging to Leeuwin Estate in the Margaret River region of Western Australia. Chardonnay from this high-flying winery was one of the first in Australia to exhibit Burgundian style complexity and concentration.

Detail from the panoramic map of the Heart of Mendoza, Argentina.

INTRODUCTION – SECOND EDITION

California is at the very heart of progress in the world of wine, but it doesn't forget tradition, and it carefully cossets some of the oldest vines in existence. The grapes off this 100-year-old Zinfandel vine at Lytton Springs in Dry Creek Valley are used to make superb red wine by Ridge.

I FEEL AS THOUGH I'VE COME FULL CIRCLE. My first visits to wine regions were all about vineyards. I didn't get inside many wineries, unless I had wheedled an intro – which just occasionally I managed to do. Most winery owners had more sense than to let me in – I was a student, after all, and a thirsty one. But it didn't matter. It meant that I spent the time ambling and clambering through the vineyards, dallying in them, picnicking in them, and sometimes sleeping in them. Instead of standing wide-eyed and bemused amongst the barrels in a dusty *cave*, I was outdoors acquainting myself with what really mattered – the soil, the vines, the rain, the wind and the sun.

By the time I began to write about wine, it was the 1980s – the most frantic, frenetic, frenzied decade the world of wine had yet seen, when the Old Order was stood upon its head and the New World tyros blazed their trail across the globe, convinced they had unlocked all the secrets that wine could hold, and that wherever they chose, whenever they wished, they and their bag of winemaker's tricks could create wines of genius and delight. Well, up to a point they could. But their whole focus was on the winery, not the vineyard. Interestingly, as they seemed to be winning the argument of new versus old, Europe, and France in particular, was putting together a golden decade of great vintages, based on the genius that lay in the soils and the climatic conditions of her best vineyards. Taste the classics that Europe produced in the 1980s versus the bluster and bravado of the 1980s New World offerings, and there's no doubt the old still held sway then.

But the 1990s saw a shift of emphasis again. No longer was I always ushered straight to the winery to admire the forest of stainless steel and the barns full of barrels, and regaled with tales of cultured yeasts and self-draining fermenters. Winemakers became less cocky, less convinced that you could achieve anything you wanted with just the right equipment, the right chemicals, and the skills to use them. New World winemakers started drawing back from the mixture of brilliant innovation and control freakery that had characterized their earlier efforts. And as the Old World quietly set about learning a few of these tricks to try on the fruit from their ancient hills and valleys, the New World realized that the key to their making wine which could equal the best in Europe lay not in the pages of the wine making manual, the sensitivity of the crusher–destemmer or the particular grain of oak the barrel maker used – it lay under their feet, in the vineyard.

It was this move back towards the vineyard that persuaded me to write the first edition of this Atlas the better part of a decade ago, and this second edition has been prompted by the astonishing rate of change that the world of wine is experiencing again. And, above all else, that change is focused on the vineyards. The number of new plantings in such places as New Zealand, Australia, Chile and North America is remarkable. Regions that hardly had a vine, like New Zealand's Central Otago, Australia's Limestone Coast or Chile's Casablanca Valley, are now fully fledged, exciting and self-confident producers creating wines of real individuality, thanks to the special nature of their climate and soil. At the same time ancient vineyard areas of Europe like the south of Italy, Portugal's Alentejo, Spain's Priorat and Ribera del Duero and Greece are being revitalized by modern methods in the winery and the vineyard. So, I've set out to re-evaluate all the vineyards of the world – some task! I've revised all the original text and written completely new sections where areas and countries warrant it; and, as well as six totally new maps, every existing map has been updated to reflect the state of the world's vineyards as they are now. In some instances, as in Australia's Clare Valley or New Zealand's Marlborough, the effects are dramatic with a doubling of land under vine.

Yet, with all this hectic change, the eternal truths of what makes wine good and special have never been more evident. Every good winemaker in every country in the world knows that the final limiting factor on wine quality is the quality of the grapes. And every winemaker knows that some regions grow better grapes than others, some areas within those regions are more suitable, some small patches of the very same field are better than others – and some growers care more about their work and will always produce the finest fruit.

And so I'm back where I began. And once more, you're far more likely to find me out amongst the vines than seated at the tasting table. Sure, I'll taste – try to stop me – but I'll taste when I have seen the vines, their soil, their place, the wine's place. If I'm in Côte-Rôtie, I want to climb to the highest point on the slope from whose grapes the juice always runs blackest and sweetest. I want to stand with my face held up to the sun, imagining how it creeps into view at dawn and fades with the evening shadows. I want to feel the poor stony soil crumble beneath my feet and touch the twisted, tortured trunk of the vine which each year struggles to survive on this barren slope and ripen its tiny crop. If I'm in Margaux, I want to tread the warm, well-drained gravel outcrops and then step off into the sullen clay swamps nearby and, with this single step, I'll know why the gravel-grown grapes are precious and the clay-clogged ones are not. I want to see the Andes water gushing down off the mountains into the fertile vineyards of Chile's Maipo Valley. I want to feel the howling mists chill me to the bone in California's Carneros, and then feel the warm winds of New Zealand's Marlborough tugging at my hair. I want it all to make sense.

And I hope this Atlas will help. I was convinced I wanted to write the first edition as soon as I saw the prototype panoramic map. It was a map of Chablis. I saw the town, the little valleys, I saw which hills were high, which were low, which faced the sun, and which were protected from the wind. I had never seen a map before that made me exult in the sense of place like this one. Suddenly it was blindingly obvious why the Grand Cru wines were riper, fatter, more intense, why the Premier Cru wines were better than basic Chablis. I had walked through all the vineyards, but this new perspective was shattering. It was as though I was hovering in a helicopter directly above the vines, able to dip down and swoop in and out of every tiny twist in the slope, through every gully, round every outcrop of rock. The roads and railways I had travelled, the rivers and hilltops I'd used for reference – all were set out before me.

What we have tried to achieve in these brilliant maps is a grand aerial tour of the world's vineyards. Focusing minutely on areas where there are particularly exciting features dictating the character of the wine, but also taking a broader regional view to put the world's great vineyards into context. And in my writing, I have tried to achieve a distillation of all the travelling I have done since student days. Some villages and their vines seem unchanged since then and may still be unchanged a hundred years from now. Has anything much really changed in the quiet communities of Burgundy's Côte d'Or, in the hamlets high up in Portugal's Douro Valley towards the Spanish border, in the friendless huddles of huts on Spain's bleak La Mancha plain? In other places, there were no vines at all when I first passed through, yet now they stretch as far as the eye can see. The North Fork of Long Island, New York, was all potatoes when I first went there. A 100-ha (250-acre) vineyard now carpets the English North Downs near Dorking, making my childhood memories of pastureland and copses of tall, dark trees seem ever so remote. Some places seem to have slipped into poverty and decline. Others have a Klondike air as the gaze of fashion turns upon them and their wines, and every available scrap of land is planted up with vines. I just hope that when the dust settles in Coonawarra or Hawkes Bay, the right vines will have been planted on the right soils by the right people. And in this age when change has come faster than ever before in the world of wine, it is equally certain that within the decade some of those now in decline will be fired by a new confidence and popularity; others now considered so chic will be struggling in the tough real world as their first flush of fame dissolves; and yet others, at this moment mere pastureland or rocky mountainside, will become flourishing vineyards producing wines whose flavours may be entirely different to anything yet achieved on this planet.

And through all this will run the constant theme: the relationship between the land and its climate, the grape varieties planted, and the commitment of the winemakers concerned.

These elements have always been intrinsically connected, yet frequently the relationship has been an insincere one because the history of wine is littered with examples of human endeavour failing to match the quality of a site. To say that a piece of land is a great vineyard site is only to say that it has the potential to produce great wine, so long as the right grapes are planted and the desire for greatness burns brightly in the breasts of the growers.

But just as the massive advances in winemaking technology made available excellent wine from areas that had never before excelled, so the dramatic progress made in vineyard management and the manipulation of the vine, enabling it to perform well in less than perfect mesoclimates, has made the definition of a great site today far more wide-reaching than ever before. Wine styles that were lauded a generation ago may not be so widely appreciated now: the rich, heady exotic Chardonnays from Australia's Hunter Valley or the Napa Valley in California that ushered in a new age of wine a mere generation ago are snubbed by many wine lovers today. The slavish attempts to ape Red Burgundy that produced so many light and feeble Oregon and New Zealand Pinot Noirs have been replaced in those areas by a robust self confidence in the different characters their Pinot Noirs possess. Wines that are lapped up with enthusiasm these days have flavours that weren't possible a generation ago. The south of Italy was derided for producing truckloads of coarse, high alcohol hooch fit only for a distant blending tank. Now the Negroamaros and Primitivos of Puglia and the Nero d'Avolas of Sicily are regarded as exciting examples of new technology marrying into old vineyards and old vine varieties. Argentina's perfumed Malbecs, South Africa's tangy Sauvignon Blancs, Canada's Icewines – none of these flavours were thought possible a generation ago.

The world of wine has moved at breakneck speed since the 1980s, and if the vineyard men and women and the winemakers, the committed wine merchants and the enthusiastic wine consumers were allowed to get on with things unhindered, all would be well. But there is a cloud on the horizon threatening the world of well-tended vineyards, well-ripened fruit and finely flavoured wines. Profit – or should I say profit as the overriding principle. Wine has never been thought of as a cash cow. But as the wealthy nations of northern Europe, North America, and Asia turn increasingly to wine as their drink of choice, often at the expense of spirits and beer, the brewers and distillers, and the venture capitalists and entrepeneurs can all smell the unlikely aroma of excessive profit in the wine world's air. As I write, vast wine conglomerates are being created crossing continents, meshing traditions and individuals into a disturbingly homogeneous whole ruled by profit, not by flavour, ruled by market share and corporate identity, not by the human passion and commitment that has created all the world's great wines so far.

Well, this Atlas stands for something I hope is more permanent than the unsightly couplings of multinational money makers and brand builders. In this Atlas I've tried to show the world of wine in all its natural, timeless beauty. A vineyard evolves. It is not about political wrangling, about special interest pleading protectionist legislation, about copywriters' fantasies or the market share of a brand. It is about a piece of soil, the sun, the wind and the rain, and the happy chance of men and women wanting to love that place, cherish it and, through their vines and the wines they make, bring it to its fullest expression. Wherever those vineyards are, whether they are great or small, famous or unknown, I dedicate this new edition of the Atlas to them and to those who care for them.

The frontiers of wine are being pushed back all the time, but you can't push much further southwards than these vineyards on Bannockburn Heights overlooking Lake Dunstan in the Central Otago region of New Zealand's South Island. This is the world's most southerly wine region, and, unless someone pushes even further south in Chile or Argentina, likely to remain so.

Author's Acknowledgements
Heartfelt thanks go to all who have helped to produce this Atlas. An illustrated work of reference is by definition a team effort – and you can't beat the team I've had! Editors, designers, cartographers, DTP experts, researchers, regional consultants (sharing their insights and expertise with great generosity) – and especially Fiona Holman, my long-standing and long-suffering editor, Nigel O'Gorman (art director) and Andrew Thompson (chief cartographer). A full list of acknowledgements can be found on page 336.

THE VINE & ITS ENVIRONMENT

The setting sun intensifies the bronzed foliage of the vines at Clayvin Vineyard in Marlborough, New Zealand, long after the harvest is over. Irrigation is crucial here; the barren hills beyond show clearly just how dry the region naturally is.

WHEN DID YOU LAST SEE A WILD VINE? The answer, almost certainly, is never. Not a European wild vine, anyway, because such vines are probably extinct. The European wild vine is a species from which cultivated vines were bred several millennia ago. The story of wine is the story of the taming of the vine. Vines, if they're allowed to, will rampage over everything in their path in their drive to find sunlight. They will produce leaves and fruit many yards from their trunks, and if you made wine from their grapes it would be thin, dilute stuff, short on flavour and high on acidity – because the vine doesn't exist to produce wine. It exists to produce grapes and reproduce itself. So when man intervenes and diverts the vine from its original purpose, he has a fair bit of work on his hands.

The grower must consider every detail of the vine's environment: the draining capability of the soil and the minerals present in it, the angle of the slope to the sun, the amount of sunshine and rainfall in that particular spot, the strength of the wind and the likelihood of frost. If he is French he will refer to the whole package – climate, soil and exposure – as *terroir*. Every *terroir* is unique, he will say, and imparts its own character to its wine. His New World counterpart would, until recently, have dismissed this as nonsense. There are mesoclimates – the climatic conditions affecting a whole vineyard – yes, and there are micro-climates, which are the conditions pertaining to the individual vine, but what really matters at the end of the day is how you make the wine.

Now that is changing. Now the buzzword in every serious New World region is – you guessed it – *terroir*. Sometimes it is merely a marketing tool: in a world awash with decent-to-good wine, *terroir* is seen as the key to distinguishing one Merlot or Shiraz from another. Of course the New World has great *terroirs*: they turn up just as frequently as in the Old World. And where *terroir* is most influential is in a marginal climate – a place where it is only just warm enough to ripen those particular grapes. Long, cool ripening seasons give subtle flavours with a good balance of fruit, alcohol and acidity. But what is cool for one vine is warm for another: even the finest *terroir* is wasted if the choice of vine is inappropriate – or if the viticulture is geared to quick results and high yields.

The vine's environment is so complex and finely balanced that to alter one part of it affects everything else. Pruning, drainage, soil type and exactly the right amount of sun and rain at the appropriate times are all vital to its development.

A warm climate may be made cooler by seeking higher altitudes; in a cool climate, however, lower altitudes don't always help, as cold air collects in the valley floor, increasing the risk of frost. Slopes are generally better than flat land, because drainage is better and they enjoy more sun. Then there is the question of which way the slope faces: in the northern hemisphere due south is marvellous, but east-facing slopes catch the morning sun, west-facing slopes the warmer afternoon sun. And while shelter from the wind makes a vineyard warmer, a breeze can dry the grapes after a shower and prevent rot.

And soil is important. In cool damp areas, free-draining, warm soils are crucial; in hot areas less so.

CASE STUDY OF A VINEYARD

St-Estèphe is in the north of the Haut-Médoc, and the deep, undulating gravel beds that mark out the best parts of the region are getting a bit sparser here. As a result there are only five Classed Growth châteaux in the commune, and vineyards here are far more likely to make Cru Bourgeois wine than Grand Cru Classé. One of these châteaux, Cos d'Estournel, is in the south of St-Estèphe, and faces Château Lafite-Rothschild (in Pauillac) across the tiny Jalle du Breuil stream that divides the two communes. The land immediately around the stream is low-lying and damp, and not planted with vines, but then the ground rises, gravel takes over again, and there is Cos d'Estournel, the best property of the commune.

The photograph on the right shows the sloping Cos d'Estournel vineyards. You can see just how dense the gravel is there. This is quite warm, heat-retaining soil and, as a result, some 60 per cent of the vineyard is planted with Cabernet Sauvignon. It drains well, but there is enough sand in it to ensure that it holds some humidity in summer to protect the vines from drought. And while the photograph doesn't show the Gironde (the river is just over a mile away), its estuary affects the climate of the whole region, softening the extremes of both winter and summer. And look how closely the vines are packed in. Growing them cheek by jowl in this way reduces yields and increases concentration. It's all part of making the vine work hard for its living.

1. BUDBREAK

Northern Hemisphere:
March to April.
Southern Hemisphere:
September to October.
In early spring the vine wakes up after the dormant winter months. Sap rises and the pruned shoots drip with 'tears'. Some varieties of vine bud earlier than others; warm, sheltered vineyard sites and warm soil will also bring vines on faster. Generally, the air temperature needs to reach an average of 10°C (50°F). The earlier the budding the greater the danger from spring frosts.

2. FIRST FOLIAGE

Northern Hemisphere:
April to May.
Southern Hemisphere:
October to November.
Shoots and leaves emerge, followed by miniature bunches of flower buds. Frost is a major danger now. Most European wine nations have dates after which they breathe easy and decide that the frost risk is finally past. In Germany they don't relax until the middle of May – after the Three Kings of May (11-13 May) and Cold St Sophie (15 May) are past.

3. FLÓWERING

Northern Hemisphere:
May to June.
Southern Hemisphere:
November to December.
Flowering lasts about 10 days, and the ideal average temperature is between 18 and 20°C (64 and 68°F). The perfect weather is frost-free, sunny, dry and still.

4. SETTING

Northern Hemisphere:
June to July.
Southern Hemisphere:
December to January.
This is when the flowers develop into miniature grapes. The success or failure of the flowering will begin to be apparent: unfertilized flowers will just drop off. In hotter climates, lack of water and excessive heat can affect set. In cool climates, wind, rain and low temperature are problems.

5. CHANGING COLOUR (VERAISON)

Northern Hemisphere:
August.
Southern Hemisphere:
January to February.
The grapes are developing well, and two months or so after flowering they begin to change colour (veraison). Sugar levels inside the grapes start to rise and the acid balance begins to change. From being small, green and as hard as bullets, the grapes soften, assuming either golden or red colouring, and grow larger: they should double in size by harvest. Dangers now are rot and mildew.

VINE PESTS AND DISEASES

Growers have to be on their guard: nature may have provided ideal conditions for their vineyards, only to hit them with a whole battery of virus diseases and pests. The photograph shows the insect currently on the Napa Valley's Least Wanted list: the Glassy Winged Sharpshooter, which spreads Pierce's Disease. This is a virus disease which kills vines, and for which treatment is so far impossible. Other unwanted virus diseases include leaf roll and fan leaf. Fungal diseases like downy mildew, powdery mildew, black rot and grey rot can be controlled by fungicides or Bordeaux mixture (lime and copper sulphate). You can tell when a grower has been using copper sulphate: the wooden posts in the vineyard will be stained a faint blue. Insect parasites, like moth caterpillars and various mites, beetles and nematodes, can all be fought with varying degrees of difficulty. But the only answer to phylloxera is to graft the vines on to resistant rootstock.

6. RIPENING

Northern Hemisphere:
August to October.
Southern Hemisphere:
February to April.
There are vine varieties suitable for both hot and cold regions and they ripen at vastly different rates. Hot-country red wine varieties would hardly even change colour by vintage time if grown in a cool German Riesling vineyard. Some vines are happy ripening fast, others will only give their best if the ripening period is as long and as cool as possible. Experts differ as to whether or not fruit flavour is improved by a long, cool ripening season: some claim the faster the better between *véraison* and actual harvest; others believe that long, sunny autumns are perhaps the most important factor in increasing flavour intensity. The aim is to build sufficient sugar in the grape, while keeping acidity in balance, and, for reds, getting the right amount of tannin and colour.

WORLD CLIMATE & VINEYARDS

This is the devastation hailstorms can cause. These vines in Mendoza, Argentina, have been stripped bare of foliage and fruit by a sudden midsummer hailstorm. Many Argentine vineyards now have protective nets against the hail that forms high in the sky above the Andes.

IF IT WEREN'T FOR THE GULF STREAM warming up the west coast of France, we'd have no Classed Growth Médoc reds. If it weren't for the sea fogs cooling down the west coast of California, we'd have no Napa Valley Cabernets. If it weren't for the cold Benguela current from the Antarctic soothing the fevered brow of the Western Cape, South Africa would be far too hot to make exciting table wines. And thank goodness for the rain-shadows of Washington State in the United States, of Marlborough in New Zealand and Alsace in France that create a long, dry autumn that lets fruit hang confidently on the vine and ripen magnificently against all odds. Thank goodness, too, for the tempering effects of Lakes Ontario and Erie on the Canada/US border. Without these huge lakes, there'd be no Ontario wine industry and no grapes would ripen in Ohio or upstate New York.

But on the other hand – damn those late spring frosts that appear out of the calm April night skies and decimate the crop in Chablis; damn the drought that creeps up unnoticed in Australia's New South Wales, stressing the hardiest vines almost beyond endurance. Damn the cyclonic storms of autumn that sweep in on Gisborne and Hawkes Bay in New Zealand and dump a month's rain in an hour on vines so tantalizingly, agonizingly close to perfect ripeness. And, for that matter, damn the damp grey clouds that sit like sullen duennas over the South Downs of England from spring to autumn, spoiling the chances of decent cricket and a decent wine vintage.

It's the world's climate in all its variety. One thing that becomes ever more evident as the debate on global warming rages is that all the climates of the world are interlinked, and whatever happens in one place will set off chain reactions that will affect conditions right round the world.

All the way through this Atlas I'll be talking about climate conditions and how they affect individual vineyards around the world. The elements of climate that are most relevant to viticulture are temperature – obviously you need a certain level to ripen grapes; variability of day and night temperatures; continentality, or the difference between winter and summer temperatures; actual sunlight; rainfall and an area's relative humidity; and wind.

The best vineyard sites have traditionally been fairly cool ones, with a measure of summer rainfall and long, dry autumns, or those with Mediterranean climatic conditions, with winter rainfall, relatively high temperatures and, ideally, moderating maritime breezes. In the Old World grape growers have slowly discovered the best conditions over the centuries. In the New World, every year brings the discovery of new and exciting sites for vines. But most wine regions are either on the cool edges of warm continents, or the warm edges of cool continents. Look at the map and you'll see what I mean.

Growers are bringing greater and greater subtlety to their understanding of climate and its effects on vines – and an increasing awareness of how difficult it is to replicate the climate of one region in another region half the world away. A pair of first-class Bordeaux producers, making wine in Chile, kicked off by trying to replicate the rainfall patterns of Bordeaux: a wet spring, followed by water stress right up to the harvest. This, they reckoned, would give wines of more Bordelais style than are commonly made in Chile. Did it? No, it did not. Not only was the resulting wine not at all like good Bordeaux, it wasn't much like good Chilean either.

The difficulty of matching one climate to another has been particularly observed by Australian researchers keen to plant finicky Italian grape varieties like Sangiovese or Nebbiolo. They have found it almost impossible – well, absolutely impossible,

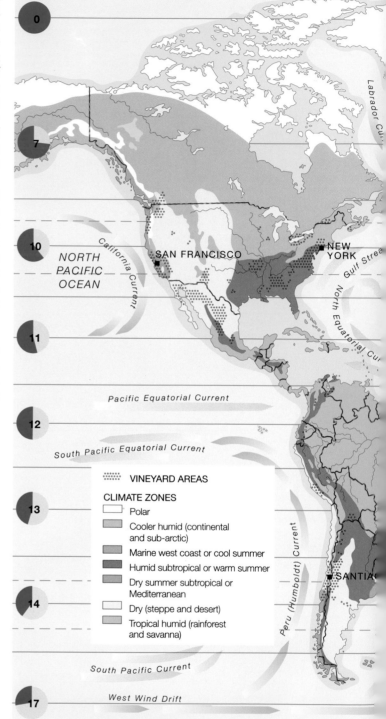

JANUARY Daylight hours

NORTH PACIFIC OCEAN

SAN FRANCISCO

NEW YORK

California Current

Labrador Current

Gulf Stream

North Equatorial Current

Pacific Equatorial Current

South Pacific Equatorial Current

Peru (Humboldt) Current

SANTIAGO

South Pacific Current

West Wind Drift

:::::: VINEYARD AREAS

CLIMATE ZONES
- Polar
- Cooler humid (continental and sub-arctic)
- Marine west coast or cool summer
- Humid subtropical or warm summer
- Dry summer subtropical or Mediterranean
- Dry (steppe and desert)
- Tropical humid (rainforest and savanna)

actually – to find exact replicas of the Tuscan or Piedmontese climates in Australia. It all boils down to a question of the relative continentality of climates; the warmth at different stages of spring and autumn, the sort of weather in the final month before the harvest, even the relative humidity in the afternoons during that month. These sorts of detail didn't matter too much when everybody was planting Chardonnay and Cabernet Sauvignon, because these grapes are so adaptable that they'll cope with pretty well any conditions you throw at them. (Making really great wine from either variety, of course, is a different matter altogether.) But now growers are moving on to trickier grapes that don't travel so easily, and life's not so simple any more.

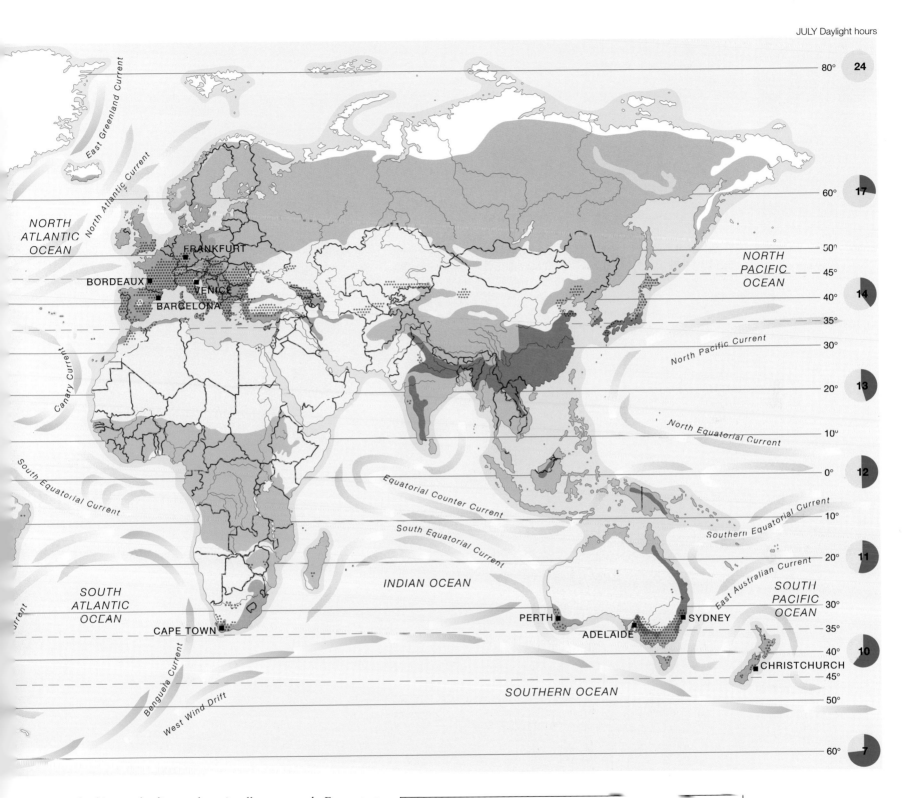

JULY Daylight hours

80°	24
60°	17
50°	
45°	14
40°	
35°	
30°	13
20°	
10°	
0°	12
10°	
20°	11
30°	
35°	
40°	10
45°	
50°	
60°	7

Just looking at the figures doesn't tell you enough. For a start, at any given latitude, the Northern Hemisphere will be warmer than the Southern, partly because of the Gulf Stream and partly because the northern land masses are greater. And yields may be higher in some New World regions not just because the soils may have higher potential vigour, but because greater sunlight in the spring encourages more flowers to form on each cluster. This can be controlled by water stress at the right moment – but what might be an optimum yield in Australia's Margaret River or Chile's Central Valley might not be ideal in Bordeaux or Tuscany.

Now that great winemaking is global, we're all learning that no one country has all the answers.

RAINFALL PATTERNS

It's not just the amount of rainfall that matters, it's the pattern. Bordeaux gets most of its rain in winter, with enough from April to August to keep the vines happy, though slightly less from August to September would be better: not for nothing is one of the standard anti-mildew sprays known as Bordeaux mixture. In San Francisco the reverse is true: lack of summer rain means irrigation is necessary, as is the case for many Southern Hemisphere vineyards. Adelaide sees far less rain than Barcelona in summer, and although Santiago, Cape Town and Perth all have some rainy winter months, their all-important growing season is extremely dry.

SITING THE VINEYARD

Burgundy's Le Montrachet could contest the title of World's greatest white vineyard, and it's just this little patch of land sloping down to the wall. Beyond the wall is Bâtard-Montrachet – nearly as good – and beyond that is the flatter Puligny-Montrachet – not nearly as good – all in the space of a few hundred metres.

So I'M A GROWER – I can choose the exact vines I want. I can survey the whole region to find the soil type that suits them. I can get all my meteorological data together, telling me precisely whether I've got a cool, warm or hot climate to contend with, and I can adjust my methods and aspirations accordingly. There's only one thing that's almost guaranteed to upset my most detailed calculations – the weather. The wretched, fickle, heartless weather. That's why, from bud-break to harvest, you can spot a winemaker by his furrowed brow and narrowed eyes. He's got stuck like that, from perpetually trying to see what's coming over the horizon.

Since I can't control the weather, I have to rely on a system of checks and balances to soften its extremes. In a cool climate, the problems are ones of frost, rain, wind and early autumns. For a start, let's be sure we have a south-facing slope. South-east and south-west are probably fine, too. But *not* north. But nothing is ever perfect, and each advantage quite often has an associated snag. For example, a supposedly ideal south-facing slope may be the warmest of all, great for ripening the grapes in a cool climate. But it will also

be where the snow melts first. In a harsh winter, snow actually keeps the ground relatively warm, and the sites which lose their protective covering of snow too early can then be exposed to damaging frost.

But planting vineyards on a slope has few disadvantages – except that they are more difficult, and therefore more expensive, to work. If I want to get twice as much sunlight onto my vines I have to plant them on a 26° (58 per cent) slope that faces the sun rather than on the flat. Conversely, if I am in a very hot climate, I can plant on an equivalent slope facing away from the sun, and get 50 per cent less sunlight. But if my slopes are so steep that I am forced to terrace them, then all my vines are effectively planted on flat land. In Portugal's Douro Valley, this isn't a problem – there's plenty of sunshine to go round – but in Germany, where every half-hour of sunshine counts, terraces are increasingly a thing of the past.

Woods near vineyards are also to be reckoned with. A good, thick wood can shelter vines from cold winds, but can also shade them from warming sunshine. A large expanse of water at the foot of a slope can reflect light back onto the vines. Conveniently, this effect is

SOLVING THE CLIMATE PROBLEM

Two very different problems nature poses are the risk of frost and the lack of water. Many marginal ripening areas run the risk of spring frosts destroying the vinebuds. One way to combat these is to operate heaters known as smudge pots on days and nights when frost threatens. These are at Nevis Bluff in New Zealand's Central Otago – the world's southernmost wine region. Mountadam estate (far right) is in the very dry Barossa Ranges in South Australia. All winter rain has to be collected into reservoirs which provide irrigation water during the growing season, without which it would be impossible to establish a vineyard.

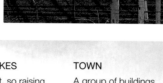

CHOOSING A SITE

SEA
Cold coastal currents can often cause temperature inversions which lead to fogs, as in San Francisco.

COAST
The area next to the coast will usually get more rain due to moisture-laden maritime breezes. However there are dry zones on the west coasts of America, Africa and Australia.

RIVERS AND LAKES
Water stores heat, so raising the temperature of the surrounding area, as well as reflecting sunshine onto nearby slopes.

TOWN
A group of buildings warms the air and helps keep the valley frost-free.

ASPECT TO SUN
Because of the inclination of the earth, south-facing slopes in the northern hemisphere and north-facing slopes in the southern hemisphere will receive more direct sunshine than others.

SLOPE ANGLE
An adequate slope is needed to gain the most benefit from the sunshine and to encourage good air circulation which prevents frosts and fogs.

SHELTER
Wooded hills provide shelter for the vines from winds.

most marked when the sun is low (in the spring and autumn), extending the growing season by a crucial few extra weeks. But water doesn't just reflect heat: as the sun heats up the earth, very useful cooling breezes come off the water. As for the sea, the Gulf Stream warms all France's west coast, including Bordeaux, while the Pacific acts as a massive air conditioner in California, Chile, Australia and New Zealand, pushing cold air far inland to regions that otherwise would be way too hot. I should remember, too, that while I may want the long ripening season given by the early springs and late autumns of a lower latitude, I may not want the high temperatures that go with it. At higher latitudes I lose the heat and the long growing season, but I gain daylight hours, so what I lose in warmth I gain in photosynthesis – which itself speeds ripening.

IDEAL VINEYARD SITES

There is no such thing as a vineyard that can excel at everything. Many big commercial vineyards in the New World prove that they are reasonable at most things, but excellence is usually very site specific, and it is usually only one or two vine varieties that shine. The Mosel Valley in Germany is cold, windswept and situated so far north hardly any grape variety will ripen there. Except one. The cold-resistant, cool-climate-loving Riesling. But even then, the site has to be exceptional. The Urziger Würzgarten site is dizzily steep, angled south and composed of a mixture of red sandstone and heat–retaining red slate. Add in the reflected warmth from the river and the result is a superb site. For Riesling. There's no point planting Syrah or Cabernet here. They wouldn't ripen.

On the other hand, there would be no point planting Riesling on the Gimblett Gravels in Hawkes Bay, New Zealand, because despite being a cool area, it's too warm for Riesling. Most of Hawkes Bay, except for Gimblett Gravels, is too cool and wet for Cabernet and Syrah. In an area that frequently has its vintage diluted and delayed by autumnal rains, the Gimblett Gravels provide some of the most free-draining conditions of any vineyard in the world as well as extra warmth. Cabernet and Syrah can ripen here virtually every year. As soon as you step off the gravels into clay, they can't.

TWO CONTRASTING VINEYARDS
Far left: The steep Urziger Würzgarten vineyard slopes down to the river Mosel in Germany. Believe it or not, there are steeper vineyards than this in the Mosel, but not many that are warmer. Riesling has been grown on this site for hundreds of years.
Left: In contrast, there were no vines at all in the Gimblett Gravels area of Hawkes Bay in New Zealand until the 1980s. Most parts of Hawkes Bay are too cool and wet to fully ripen varieties like Cabernet and Merlot, but the warm, free-draining Gimblett Gravels speed maturing sufficiently to ripen the crop.

HILLTOP
In a cool climate this may be too cold for vines.

SHADED HILLSIDE
The side of the hill facing away from the sun may, in a cool climate, be too cold to make good wine. In a hot climate it may be ideal.

INLAND
Rainfall is lower inland, particularly if there is a coastal range of hills nearby forming a rain-shadow. The climate is likely to be one of hotter summers and colder winters.

VALLEY
Frost will occur on the valley floor, and valley winds may also be a problem.

WIND-BREAK
A line of trees acts as an effective barrier to winds.

EXPOSED PLATEAU
This land is too windy for growing vines.

FLAT VALLEY LAND
On flat valley floors the soil is often too clayey and poorly drained for fine wines. However, these conditions may be overcome, as in the Napa Valley, California.

THE IMPORTANCE OF SOIL

The stony soils of Stoneleigh Vineyard in the Wairau River valley of Marlborough, on South Island, New Zealand. These free-draining soils contribute significantly to the intense flavour of the local white wines.

MY VIEW ON WHAT SOIL contributes to a wine is going to depend to a large extent upon whether I was brought up with an Old or New World wine philosophy. So, let's say I come from California. I used to think soil just held the vine upright; to me it was the climate that mattered. Now I'm coming round to the idea of 'dirt'. It's obvious now that there has to be a synergy between grape variety and place, and that the soil structure affects the development of the root system, which in turn affects flavour. I do soil analyses now before I plant, and I dig holes to look at root spread. And I'm in love with my land. You see how the slope just falls away on that hillside vineyard over there? It's the most beautiful thing. And there's a breeze there every afternoon when there won't be one anywhere else. The French call this whole soil and climate thing 'terroir'. And sure it matters. But only so that I get the best fruit that I can to then craft into the ultimate wine. *My* ultimate wine.

On the other hand I'm an Old World grower – perhaps from Alsace in France. I grow Riesling and Gewürztraminer in several Grand Cru sites, and the wines taste different from each vineyard. If I were to take up an extreme position I would say that you should be able to reconstruct the geology of the vineyard from the taste of the wine; that I want you to taste the terroir in the wine, and not even the grape variety or (God forbid) the winemaker's personality.

These positions may sound extreme, but the New World one in particular has softened significantly in the last few years, and many winemakers now point out qualities that soils give their wines. But the idea of *terroir* winning out over grape flavour is largely confined to France. They invented the concept; they're unwilling to let go.

But one thing we can agree upon is drainage. How dull. But how fundamental. You see, a well-drained soil is a warm soil, and a wet soil is a cold one. It's the temperature of the soil, much more than that of the air, that decides when a vine is going to start budding in

the spring – and that's one of the factors that decides what vines can be planted where. Soil temperature also influences a wine's acidity: cold soils give more acidic wines, since heat burns off acidity.

A well-drained soil has bigger particles: there are four basic particle sizes: coarse sand, fine sand, silt and clay. Gravel and stones, of course, are bigger still; there, water pours through very quickly, but essential nutrients are washed away and it must be fertilized before it will bear decent fruit. At the other end of the scale is clay, with particles of 0.002mm or less in diameter. Heavy clay can hold water so tightly that a vine can't get at it. Well-drained, warm gravelly soil can make more water available to the vine than a wet clay one. So in areas of heavy rain, like Bordeaux, well-drained gravelly soil has advantages over non-draining clay. Until there's a drought, you say. Well, even then a gravelly soil can be better. In poor soils (and stony soil with big particles is poor soil) the vine's roots have to plunge deeper so that in a hot, dry summer they are more likely to be able to find moisture; vines whose roots are mostly within the first metre of soil are far more likely to suffer in droughts.

But I'd hate to give you the idea that one type of soil is automatically better than another; soils that heat up quickly in the spring also get colder in the winter, and are more affected by frost; in hot climates they can reflect too much heat on to the grapes, and burn them. Small amounts of organic matter in the soil, be it gravelly or clay soil, can also help to even out water availability. And a cold clay soil can not only help to hold back an early-ripening vine, like Merlot, it can give the wine more structure and solidity, too.

Then there's the question of pH. Alkaline soils, with a pH of seven or more, tend to be young soils. They are high in calcium, from shells left behind when the sea receded, and they tend to produce wines high in acidity. Champagne's soil is like this. There's a lot of alkaline soil in Europe. But the New World, particularly

---

CASE STUDY OF A VINEYARD

There is no single soil type that is ideal for wine. And to prove it, many different soils have proved themselves perfect for particular grape varieties in particular climates. So acidic granite produces great Syrah in Hermitage and the best Gamay in Beaujolais; limestone seems to suit Chardonnay in many places, including Champagne, Chablis and the Côte d'Or; and the rich grey-blue marl of Barolo retains water and is cold – ideal for the longer, slower ripening of Nebbiolo in a warm climate. Schist can give rich, spicy reds in the Rhône's Côte-Rôtie and Portugal's Douro Valley. Clay soil reduces bouquet but gives structure to a wine, so in Alsace it is favoured for the broader, more aromatic grape varieties like Gewürztraminer, rather than for the more subtle Riesling. In Germany's Mosel Valley, steep slate slopes impart a haunting beauty to Riesling wines. However, the warm, black basalt soils of Forst and Deidesheim in the Pfalz provide Rieslings that are far more exotic and fleshy.

Clockwise, from top left: 1. Clay is not considered the best soil for growing vines. The small flat clay particles fit together closely, keeping water locked between them, and surface water tends to stagnate. One of the only advantages of a clay soil is that in a hot region it can hold enough water to sustain the vine right through a long, dry summer. This recently ploughed clay soil in Slovenia glistens with moisture in the sun.
2. The Mosel Valley's dark slate soil absorbs heat and helps the Riesling to ripen in a cool climate. In a hot climate, it could reduce acidity, but here in the Brauneberger Juffer Sonnenuhr vineyard it aids ripening and adds a minerality to the flavour.
3. Chalk soil is able to hold good amounts of water which is then released to the vine during the summer. Here in Jerez in southern Spain this is important because winters are usually wet, while summers are blisteringly hot and dry.
4. There doesn't seem to be any soil at all in these Grenache vineyards of Château de Beaucastel in Châteauneuf-du-Pape in southern France. On the surface there isn't. Instead, you have round stones called galets that absorb heat during the day and then release it after dusk pushing the grapes to super-ripeness.

Australia, has older soils and the pH may be pretty neutral, though old rocky soils can be acidic. California's Napa Valley is generally more acidic than the young alluvial gravel of Bordeaux. The wines of Napa are thus less acidic than those of Bordeaux.

So can soil affect the flavour of the wine? Yes. Stonier soils give lighter, more perfumed wines; richer soils with more clay give more solid wines. But what about particular 'mineral' flavours? Elsewhere in this Atlas, I talk about the specific smoky tang that Riesling acquires on slate soil. It's not imagination: I could pick it out for you, blind. And, although it's true that only a minute percentage of the ions from the minerals and trace elements assimilated by the vine from the soil will find their way into the finished wine, it is also true that the same grape grown by my Alsace friend on different soils will taste different. At least, it will if he keeps yields down and encourages his vines to root deep into the bedrock. Because the influence of soil on wine is most noticeable when yields are low, where the climate is marginal, and where vines are deeply rooted.

On this last point my Alsace friend will be especially vociferous. He'll stress that the right sort of viticulture for the first five years of a vine's life – dense planting and ploughing to cut the surface roots – will force the roots to search deep, down below the topsoil. That, they say, is the only way to get an expression of terroir into the wine, and if you don't work the right way in the first five years you've had it, because the root system will be established, and no matter what you do in later years, you will never get a terroir wine.

But back to California: yes, these days I want to make a terroir wine, but I want Merlot plus terroir, or Cabernet plus terroir; I don't want terroir expressed through Merlot or Cabernet, with the grape variety as a sort of neutral vector. Because at the end of the day I'm Californian, and Californian wines taste first and foremost of fruit. I suppose you could say I'm a product of my terroir. How's that?

BELOW THE VINE

1. STONES
Pebbles and stones lying on the surface help to retain heat within the topsoil. They also reflect sunlight, and therefore warmth, back onto the vines.

2. TOPSOIL
This is the main root zone, and is about 15-30cm (6-12in) thick in most soils. Topsoil is formed from a mix of weathered bedrock, organic matter from decaying plants and animals, and fertilizers.

3. SUBSOIL
This is pure, weathered bedrock, which lays the foundations for the all-important tap roots that stabilize the vine.

4. BEDROCK or PARENT MATERIAL
The bedrock is the underlying geology. Since soils are formed from broken-down and weathered rock, the bedrock has a great influence on the characteristics of a soil. The bedrock can only be used by roots if it is well-pored or fissured.

5. WATER TABLE
The water table is the level beneath which the rock is saturated with ground-water. If it is only a few yards from the surface, it can serve as a good source of water for a vine, provided it is not stagnant.

GLOSSARY OF COMMON VINEYARD SOIL TERMS

Acid soil A soil with a low pH value. These soils tend to occur mostly in wetter climates where high rainfall leaches the calcium out of the soil. The rootstock and vine variety can be chosen for their sympathy with soil pH values.

Alkaline soil A soil with a high pH value, often due to the presence of calcium (see Calcareous soil) or salt.

Alluvial deposits (alluvium) Materials deposited from rivers, usually gravels, sands and silts, such as are found in the Graves area of Bordeaux and Marlborough in New Zealand.

Basalt soil A warm dark, fertile soil, formed from volcanic rock. It is usually alkaline, being rich in calcium and sodium.

Calcareous soil A soil with a high calcium content, which comes from a limestone geology. Chalk is a form of limestone. It has a high pH (alkaline) and usually has good aeration, drainage and structure. Many vines do well, when grown on a calcium-rich soil, particularly the Chardonnay grape, as in Chablis and parts of the Côte d'Or.

Chalk A form of limestone with a characteristic white or pale colour and alkaline pH (see Calcareous soil and Limestone). It has proved good for vines growing in cooler and wetter climates, such as the Champagne region of France.

Clay The smallest size of soil particle. Soils rich in clay particles are usually cold and acidic with poor drainage, and can have a tendency to waterlogging.

Colluvial deposits (colluvium) Weathered rock and soil debris which have slid down slopes and been deposited at a lower level.

Gravel The French word for gravel, *graves*, has given its name to the Graves area of Bordeaux. Pebbles covering the ground retain heat and are freely drained.

Granite An igneous rock whose crystals are large enough to be seen with the naked eye. It can form rock masses which reflect the sun's heat, such as the hill of Hermitage.

Limestone Sedimentary rock made of calcite (calcium carbonate), typically pale in colour and with a high pH. Chalk (see Calcareous soil) is a form of limestone.

Loam A usually fertile soil, which is composed of equal proportions of clay, silt and sand particles.

Loess A layer of wind-blown silt that covers the topsoil.

Marl A sedimentary mixture of clay and limestone. Some marl contains more clay than limestone; some contains more limestone than clay.

Organic matter Humus, which is derived from living organisms, usually plants and fallen leaves, and manure.

pH A measure of acidity or alkalinity. The lower a soil's pH number, the more acidic it is. Soils that have a pH number above seven are alkaline.

Sand Large, granular soil particles, which are made up of weathered rock and quartz. A soil that contains a large proportion of sand is warm and drains freely, but is poor in nutrients and somewhat acidic.

Schist Coarsely grained, crystalline rock, which retains heat and crumbles easily. Rich in potassium and magnesium, but low in organic nutrients, it occurs most notably in Portugal's Douro Valley.

Scree The slope of debris found at the bottom of a cliff which has fallen due to erosion and weathering. It consists of various-sized fragments of rock and is usually steep.

Silt With particles larger than clay but smaller than sand, silt holds water well and is relatively fertile, as is the case in the Napa Valley.

Slate A hard rock formed from shales and clays put under great pressure. Its heat-retaining qualities provide an excellent environment for vines, sometimes passing on metallic flavours, as in the Bernkastel wines that are produced in Germany's Mosel Valley.

Terra rossa When the calcium is leached out of limestone, it can form a reddish soil, the staining coming from dehydrated iron compounds. It is usually associated with Mediterranean climates, which have very dry summers and wet winters that enable the leaching and hydrating processes to occur. However, its most famous manifestation is in the Coonawarra region in South Australia.

THE IMPACT OF WATER

Irrigation systems were in place in South America long before the arrival of Europeans. The Incas were experts at it and, by the 16th century, somewhere like Mendoza in Argentina was already using Andes snow-melt water for irrigation. With water so plentiful, most vineyards in Mendoza, like these at Trapiche, still follow the old method of channeling river water between the rows, literally flooding the vineyard.

IT'S THE HOT TOPIC of the 21st century: something so fundamental to life – and for most of us, so readily available – that we've tended to take it for granted. The factors that determined where vineyards were planted were principally soil and climate and, historically, ease of transport to centres of population – in other words, the wine-drinkers. Water didn't come into it. In Europe vines relied on rainfall, and viticultural techniques were adapted to whether rain was too plentiful or too scarce. Irrigation wasn't allowed, except for experimental vineyards or for getting young vines established.

In New World countries, where rainfall patterns do not follow the European model and where there is no such thing as a blanket ban on irrigation, if you could water your vines, you did. Even in Australia's Barossa Valley, where dry farming is the tradition, in the past you irrigated your young vines by hand until they were established enough to survive without irrigation. In Chile, you took advantage of snow-melt water pouring off the Andes in spring to get you through an otherwise impossibly dry summer. Modern techniques of computer-controlled irrigation have refined matters even further. The fact is that, today, very few of us doubt the assumption that if we want water, we can have it. We take it for granted.

This is a very complacent and comfortable picture compared with what might be the scenario in the future. We all know that the globe is warming up, and that there will be more rain for some and less for others. We also know that the world's population is increasing, and what that means is greater demand for water – not just for growing food, but for washing cars and watering golf courses, too. And while vines are relatively low users of water –

cotton and rice, for example, use around 35 per cent more, and growers in Chile's Casablanca Valley might use one litre per second to irrigate 5 hectares, while grass for cattle needs more like 1 litre per second for half a hectare – wine production worldwide is rising. If you live in California or Australia, having a vineyard near you won't affect your ability to fill your swimming pool – people take priority over vines any day. But if you want to plant a vineyard in California or Australia, the proximity of lots of houses may well affect your ability to get water rights for your vines. And in Europe, the hard line on irrigation taken by the EU is softening: irrigation is creeping into Italy, Spain, Portugal and just about everywhere else that needs a quick aqueous top-up once in a while.

Getting permission to irrigate in Europe is no longer that difficult. If a region petitions the authorities, they are unlikely to say no. Getting the water itself might, however, be trickier: all Portugal's water comes from Spain, for example, and while agreements are in place to ensure that both sides are happy, some Portuguese are pretty cynical about what might happen if push came to shove. In Spain, water is already short in Cataluña, and there is talk of diverting water from France.

In California, water availability is less of a limiting factor on planting vineyards than other environmental issues, like land use and development, and even the cutting down of oak trees and the health and happiness of endangered species. But the United States certainly has water problems, and they are not going to go away. In the south-west of the USA, there are huge aquifers filled with water from rainier periods in the globe's history, but these reserves are now being drained much faster than they are being refilled. There are plans to buy water from Canada; theoretically, Canada

---

BUYING WATER IN THE BAROSSA

Martin and Sally Pfeiffer are lucky: salinity on their Barossa vineyard, Whistler Wines, is far less serious than in some parts of the Valley and, in addition, they've managed to organise a water supply generous enough to allow for some future expansion of plantings. Even so, they've had to keep pace with a changing situation. When they bought the land back in 1982, not only did it come with a small stock dam already in place, but the Valley had no water licensing requirements at all. These days you can neither sink a bore nor dig a dam without a license – these requirements came into effect in the mid-1990s – and if you want more water than nature can provide you'll need to be a member (which means being a shareholder) in a private water scheme called Barossa Infrastructure Ltd, or BIL.

The Pfeiffers' property covers 32ha (80 acres) and so far they've planted 13ha (32 acres). Any further expansion will incur extra costs. 'A pump shed and automation control cost us A$25,000. Then there's another A$25,000 for installing and supplying water for every 10 acres of vineyard. We installed a 10-megalitre [1 megalitre = 1,000,000 litres] storage dam with a Water Resources license through the BIL scheme, and that dam cost A$20,000. Then there's the A$100,000 for costs for BIL capital, which is spread over 15 years, so that works out at A$6666 per year. In addition, there's the A$10,000 per year water usage charge for BIL water.'

So where does the BIL water come from? 'From the River Murray, which is some 80km away to the east,' says Martin. 'The company has leased water rights to access this water and, in future, it may purchase the rights.' BIL has an agreement with the state water company, SA Water, which allows it to fill a reservoir in the winter, and supply it to shareholders in the summer when the vines need it. The Pfeiffers'

membership of the BIL scheme entitles them to 10 megalitres of premium water, which is available all year round, and 10 megalitres of off-peak water, which is available only from April to October. They use the slightly cheaper off-peak water to fill the dam.

As for how much water is dripped on to the vines throughout the hot Barossa summer – well, the Pfeiffers say they normally apply around 0.5-0.75 megalitres per hectare per year for red grapes, and 1-1.5 megalitres for whites. 'Our water usage has not reduced yet, because the vines are only young and establishing deep root systems,' says Martin. 'In future years we'll be looking to reduce. But we've set aside about 20% of the Shiraz to be dry grown with no irrigation, and we'll be looking to produce a Reserve Whistler Shiraz from the 2002 vintage.'

But as always in the Barossa, there's the question of salinity. 'It's not so bad on my property,' says Martin, 'because vines and supplementary watering are relatively new to the land. But I do have some effects, particularly in the Merlot, which seems to be the most sodium- and choride-susceptible variety I have planted. Where I had difficulty establishing Merlot, I have planted salt-tolerant Ruggeri rootstock and grafted Merlot on to it.

'Salinity in groundwater varies dramatically depending on where your property is in the Barossa, and some areas within the Valley – mine, for example – have no or little groundwater. Salinity varies from 100-3500 parts per million (ppm), averaging around 1000-1200 ppm. At above 2000ppm you can see surface crusting. But even moderate salinity can reduce yields by 20 to 30 per cent – in badly affected areas vines can even die – and with salt levels slowly rising, it was important for us to have access to supplementary water.'

opposes these plans, but at the time of writing this opposition seems less than determined.

Pretty well wherever you are, if you want to take water from a river, or any source except your own rain-filled dam, you need permission. In Australia, for example, you cannot plant a vineyard unless you have previously bought a water license, and inevitably there's a price tag attached: between A$400 and A$4000 per hectare, depending on region. Water rights can be traded, too: the cost of this is relatively low for the moment, at around A$5000 per megalitre. The infrastructure of irrigation – the pumps, pipes and so on – is more expensive, amounting to about A$10,000 per hectare. In Australia millions of hectares of land are suitable for vines, but if you can't get water rights or water then you might as well forget it.

No wonder people go to extreme lengths when they see a piece of land they just know would be great for wine: when Chilean company Errázuriz found a must-have site for new vines, it pumped water from 5km (3miles) away.

NOT ALL WATER IS GOOD WATER

Water availability is, however, only part of the problem. Water quality, especially in Australia, is just as important. Australia's problem is salinity. Not all of Australia suffers in the same way: the Murray basin is the worst affected, but for 'Murray basin' read 'much of South-East Australia'. (And where does most of Australia's wine come from? Correct. South-East Australia.) If you take a look at the map on page 287, you'll see that the Murray rises in the far south-eastern corner of the country and flows more or less north-west before changing its mind and draining into the sea, south-east of Adelaide. The Murray provides most of the irrigation water for Australia's vineyards. Right now, the Murray is carrying 18.1 tonnes of salt to the sea every five minutes. Per day, that's 5212 tonnes of salt. That's just what reaches the sea. Far more is being drawn off by the irrigation pumps every single day.

Much of the Australian landmass was once an inland sea, and the water table is naturally saline. Clearance of the native trees, which grew in profusion before the first European settlers arrived, allowed the water table to rise. And, as always, we only properly understood the problem once it was too late to go back.

It was between World Wars One and Two that much of the damage was done. Huge areas of land were made available to 'soldier settlers' returning to a depressed economy – and there were government incentives to encourage them to clear it for pasture and arable farming. Well, once the scrub and forest were cleared, the topsoil simply blew away: billowing clouds of dust would hang for days over Melbourne, literally hundreds of miles away from land had been cleared up the Murray River.

And while Melbourne was coughing and spluttering and complaining about the state of its washing, back up the Murray, the saline water table was quietly creeping upwards.

Vines don't like salt. At salt concentrations of over 1200 parts per million they suffer stress, though some rootstocks, notably Ramsey and Dog Ridge, are more salt-resistant. Roots, however, are generally less affected by salt than leaves, so irrigating vines using drip irrigation, which goes straight to the roots, is much kinder and safer than applying salty water by sprinkler, which wets the leaves and quickly leads to defoliation. Australia's relentless and vital search to find ways of coping with poor water quality is the main reason that its irrigation techniques are so advanced.

There are remedies for salinity: planting native trees is one; the carrying away of salty drainage water from below the roots is another. Reverse osmosis, a technique that takes salt out of water,

is used in the Middle East but is hugely expensive. The trouble is, vines exacerbate the problem since they suck the water out of the soil and leave the salt behind, resulting in the build-up of salt.

But planting indigenous species – often the scrubby Mallee gums – means waiting for nature to do the job for you and push the salty water down beyond the reach of vines and other crops. And that's a very slow process indeed. In the past 15 to 20 years, the federal government has invested millions of dollars in reafforestation schemes, with varying degrees of success. The cheapest option of all is to wait for rain. Heavy rain will at least flush out the Murray and dilute the salt in your own dam; you can then give your vines lots of water while the quality is high, and later revert to your normal policy of giving them only enough to keep them alive.

Since grapes are such a high-value crop, producers can take their own measures and justify them economically. But in some cases wheat and sheep farmers are simply having to abandon their land – the problem is that serious. At the moment, 2.5 million ha (6.2 million acres) of Australia are already wrecked by excessive salinity. That sounds a lot. Well, it is : it's considerably larger than Wales, slightly smaller than Albania. And I can sort of hear you saying, 'well, it's not that big, then.' Okay. Projections are that by the middle of this century, 15.5 million ha (38.3 million acres) of Australia will be lost to salt. That's considerably bigger than England. That's bigger than Greece; bigger than New York State, or the states of Georgia or Illinois. Does that sound serious enough?

Salinity can be a problem in other places as well, including the South of France and even parts of Chile, where water quality is normally very good. And in Penedès on Spain's Mediterranean coast, there's a town – called Sitges (if you're thinking of visiting) – where even the tap water is salty. Just don't make tea with it.

Australia'a greatest river, right in the heart of the vineyard area at Renmark, South Australia. The Murray mops up all the water from the west side of the Great Dividing Range and then begins its extremely languid and serpentine route of 2600km (1616 miles) until it reaches the sea, south of Adelaide. By that time it hasn't got much water left, because it's all been extracted for irrigation. Well over half the vineyards in Australia rely upon the Murray and its tributaries, the Lachlan and the Murrumbidgee, for their water. Without the rivers, there would be no modern Australian wine industry.

THE MODERN VINEYARD

You can't get much more modern than this – the striking new Sileni winery in Hawkes Bay, North Island, New Zealand. In the foreground, young wines have just been planted for the first time in the virgin soil.

THIS IS THE MOMENT OF DECISION for the grape grower. He has picked the most favourable spot the landscape has to offer; he has analysed the soil and observed the climate. He has decided which vine varieties will cope best with both. Now he must plant. But before he can put a single vine in the soil, there is one more thing he must do. Virtually all the vines these days are grafted on to phylloxera-resistant rootstock, to protect them from one of the most devastating of all vine pests. But because the rootstock comes from a different vine species, it throws another element into the equation. He must choose a rootstock that is compatible with the soil, the climate and with his vines: some are more vigorous than others, some are more resistant to drought or cold and so on. So his choice of rootstock will affect the style and quality of his wine.

Then he must decide how densely to plant his vines. Higher densities reduce the yield per vine – from 5000 vines per hectare (2000 per acre) up to 10,000 (4000) is common in Europe. Vines spaced more widely develop bigger (though not deeper) root systems, and larger canopies, and can thus ripen a larger crop per vine, which can be more appropriate to certain climates and soils: Californian and Australian growers often settle for 1100 to 1600 vines per hectare (450 to 650 per acre).

Pruning, training and canopy management are all aimed at making the vine produce the optimum-sized crop. In a cool climate on poor soil, for example, the vine can ripen fewer grapes than in a warm climate on deep, rich soil, so you should prune harder to reduce the number of fruiting buds. Then you train the vine in order to make it bear its bunches of grapes where you want them: partially exposed to the sun so that they'll ripen; with good air circulation so that they won't rot; high enough off the ground to avoid frost, or low enough to benefit from the heat stored in the soil.

1. Winter pruning is the grower's most effective way of controlling yield. Here at Château Margaux in Bordeaux the pruner removes the previous year's growth, leaving only enough buds to produce a strictly limited yield.

5. In cooler parts of the world, the risk of frost lasts right through springtime. In the coolest of all, you may even risk a pre-harvest frost, too. You can lose a whole year's crop in one cold snap. Here, smudge pots blaze in the pre-dawn chill at Torlesse, in Waipara, South Island, New Zealand.

VINE MANAGEMENT

This is now accepted as fundamental to the eventual quality of the wine. The aim is to nurture a healthy plant that will deliver a crop of healthy grapes at whatever quantity and quality level the grower desires, by choosing a highly productive or a less productive clone, and planting it on a vigorous or less vigorous rootstock. To create competition and reduce crop levels, the vines can be closely planted. On non-vigorous soils, such as the Médoc gravel banks, a simple training system will suffice. On fertile, productive soils, like most New Zealand vineyard sites, training the vine through different trellising and pruning methods can transform the quality of the fruit.

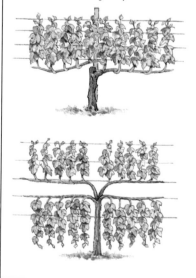

Double Guyot: This simple system is the most common one used in Bordeaux and involves training two canes along a wire, one to each side of the vine. The number of buds left on each cane after pruning will dictate the probable size of the crop.

Scott Henry: Developed by an Oregon vineyard owner, this system is popular in the New World as it increases yields and ripeness. By training the canopy vertically, the fruit is exposed more effectively to sunlight and air circulation and the canopy area available for photosynthesis is increased.

9. Irrigation is essential in many hot, dry New World vineyards. It is especially important when establishing young vines like these ones at Cowra in New South Wales. The drip irrigation system is widely used nowadays – the amount of water can be controlled carefully as each vine has its own water supply.

13. At last the grapes are ripe and ready to be picked. Increasingly this is done by machine and here at the Graham Beck winery in Robertson, South Africa, a mechanical harvester brings in the Cabernet Sauvignon. Arguments rage as to whether or not machines are as good as human pickers.

2. Chip budding, making an incision in the existing vine, as here, and grafting into it a bud of the new variety, is the quickest way of transforming an inferior vine variety into a better one.

3. Virtually all vines are grafted on to phylloxera-resistant rootstock, to protect them from one of the most devastating of all vine pests. These young vines are now ready to plant.

4. You know that winter is coming to an end in California's Napa Valley when the vineyards erupt in a blaze of yellow wild mustard, which is then ploughed in to provide nutritious organic fertilizer.

6. Several of the most important estates in Burgundy are investigating organic methods of grape-growing. In the great Romanée-Conti vineyard in Vosne-Romanée, Côte de Nuits, phacelia is planted to cleanse the soil and rid it of nematodes.

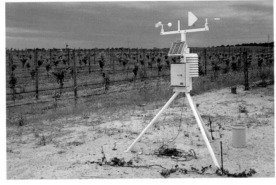

7. Predicting the weather is notoriously difficult, but collecting data on weather conditions can certainly help you make a more informed guess. This weather station is at Penfolds' new vineyards at Robe on the South Australia coast west of Coonawarra.

8. There may be restrictions on new plantings in traditional countries like France, but in Australia, if you can find water, you can plant. New plantings at Brown Brothers' vineyard at Banksdale, Victoria start to develop as the summer warms up.

10. One of the best ways to improve quality is to reduce the size of your crop by cutting off less ripe bunches. The time to do this is when the grapes change colour in mid-summer. The best bunches change colour first, so you keep those and chop the others.

11. The Okanagan Valley in British Columbia is a cool region. Usually cool regions have quite enough moisture for the vine, but the Okanagan is almost desert-dry, so Cedar Creek are providing some overhead irrigation at their Cresta Ranch vineyard.

12. Once the grapes begin to ripen, the word rapidly spreads round the bird community. Flocks of birds can devastate a crop in a matter of hours, so Tuck's Ridge in Mornington Peninsula, Victoria cover their vines with nets to keep the birds out.

14. Human pickers are definitely the preferred form of harvesting in Burgundy's top vineyards. Anne-Claude Leflaive, a top white winemaker, checks out the quality of the Chardonnay grapes from her Puligny-Montrachet Le Clavoillon vineyard.

15. These lads are happy. The sun's shining and the grapes are healthy, ripe – and harvested. Wineries often have contracts with growers for some of their grapes and here Peter Leske (right) of Nepenthe in the Adelaide Hills, South Australia clearly approves of the Cabernet Sauvignon grown by Simon Green.

16. I can feel the damp chill in the air as the vines take a well-earned midwinter rest at Trittenheim in the Mosel Valley, Germany. A cold winter is important to allow the vine a dormant period and to destroy pests and infections in the vineyard.

GRAPES OF THE WORLD

Most of the world's leading grapes end up with just one generally accepted name. However, the great Syrah or Shiraz grape has two names, Syrah being the French version and Shiraz the Australian one. Under either name it makes some of the world's most richly flavoured reds and the wines usually choose one name or the other, according to whether producers feel their style is restrained (Syrah) or rumbustuous (Shiraz).

THERE ARE THOUSANDS AND THOUSANDS of grape varieties in the world. So why does it often feel as if you're being offered a choice of only Chardonnay or Cabernet Sauvignon when you buy a bottle of wine? How come those thousands sometimes seem to have been narrowed down to two? There are several answers. Most grape varieties are used for dessert grapes or raisins, or are rarely grown, or are the wrong species for winemaking. And of the 1000 or so varieties that are at all significant for wine, only about 30 have international relevance – which leaves hundreds of obscure, but possibly excellent, local varieties to be discovered by the adventurous wine drinker.

Virtually all those 1000 varieties are of the same species, *Vitis vinifera*, the species most people mean when they refer to wine vines. And yet *vinifera* is only one branch of the vine family; there are dozens of others growing in diverse climates all over the world, from the *Vitis amurensis* of Siberia to the *Vitis cariboa* of the tropics. They all produce grapes – indeed America's first settlers made wines from the native *Vitis labrusca*, *Vitis riparia*, and *Vitis berlandieri*. The flavour of these wines has often been described as foxy, although a cross between hawthorn blossom and nail varnish might be more accurate.

You can still taste them in parts of North America, Austria and on Madeira. Some are OK – but you can see why *vinifera* won the day.

A few decades ago Chardonnay was seen as a Burgundian or Champagne grape; now it's grown in almost every wine region with aspirations. Such movements of vines are not new – merely faster than they used to be. Vine cuttings have been transported vast distances over the centuries. Missionaries took cuttings from Spain to the Americas. The Syrah of the Rhône and Australia (where it is called Shiraz) is believed to have come from Shiraz in Persia. And many of the vines we think of as Italian are, in fact, Greek in origin.

Why would people bother to take cuttings of a favourite variety to a country that probably already had plenty of its own vines? Because it has always been recognized that the crucial factor in the flavour of a wine is grape variety. Every grape has its own flavour, though most need specific climatic conditions to give their best. Thus Cabernet Sauvignon grown in too cold a climate produces thin, grassy wine; too hot and it risks being baked and raisiny. But when the worldwide movement of vines creates a chance combination of right vine, right climate and right soil, that's when classic wine styles are established.

CABERNET FRANC

To see this grape merely as Cabernet Sauvignon's less important sibling is to do it a disservice. It gives good, but not great wines as a varietal (although it is the main grape by quite a long way in Chateau Cheval Blanc, which is about as great as red wine can get). But its value as a blending grape in Bordeaux is enormous, because it is less tannic and acidic than Cabernet Sauvignon on its own. It's an early ripener, so it also does well in the cool Loire.

CABERNET SAUVIGNON

This is the world's most famous red grape because Bordeaux was the world's most famous red wine, and when local producers worldwide decided to improve their quality, they looked to Bordeaux for inspiration. Luckily Cabernet Sauvignon is up to the challenge and seems to relish travelling, almost as much as nestling on the gravel banks of its spiritual home in Bordeaux's Médoc region. Thick-skinned and slow to ripen yet rot-resistant if caught by autumn rains, it will provide deep colour, reasonable tannin, a universally recognizable aroma and flavour of blackcurrants, black cherry and plum anywhere it is grown (except in the coolest and the very hottest sites). Cabernet Sauvignon has become a byword for full-flavoured, reliable red wine.

CHARDONNAY

The world's favourite white grape is so adaptable it makes everything from light, dry sparkling wine to sweet, botrytized dessert wine, but its dry, oak-aged incarnation, based on the great wines of Burgundy's Côte d'Or, is the best known style, found from Chile to China, and from California to New South Wales. Clearly the vine is happy in a wide range of soils and climates though, as an early ripener, it buds early, which can be a problem in frost-prone regions like Chablis and Champagne. Otherwise, it is resistant to cold and yields well virtually anywhere. The wine has such an affinity with new oak (which adds a rich, spicy butteriness) that it can be easy to forget what its varietal flavour is. Unoaked, cool-climate Chardonnay is pale, appley and acidic; these flavours gradually soften towards melon and peach as the climate warms. Simple Chardonnays are made to be drunk young, and certainly most New World examples should not even be aged for a few years. But in Burgundy, Chardonnay makes one of the most long-lived of all white wines.

CHENIN BLANC

This versatile white grape is capable of producing wines that are dry or sweet, still or sparkling, and for drinking now or for cellaring for a decade or more. However, it has yet to reach great heights away from the Loire Valley in France. Here, on chalky soils and in distinctly cool climates, it can produce some of the most individual wines to be found anywhere in the world. In both dry and sweet styles, all highly acidic when young, these wines can, and should, be put away for years. In New Zealand and Western Australia, some delicious dry examples are surfacing, and in South Africa a few adventurous growers are also starting to take the grape seriously.

GEWÜRZTRAMINER

The name means 'spicy Traminer' and that spice is a smell of roses, lychees, sometimes mangoes, often with a dab of cold cream and a dusting of ginger – a nose that, as you might guess, wants plenty of acidity on the palate. But Gewürztraminer can lack acidity, and needs a cool climate to keep a tendency to high sugar levels in check. At its best in Alsace, followed by New Zealand and Italy's Alto Adige, the vine buds early and is susceptible to frosts. But if it survives these and is then affected by noble rot in a warm autumn, superb sweet wines can result.

GRENACHE NOIR

Varietal Grenache used to be very rare, yet this variety covers mile upon mile of vineyards in Spain (where it's called Garnacha Tinta), the South of France, California and parts of Australia. It is still mostly a blending grape: in Rioja and Navarra in Spain, its burly fruit fills out the rather more restrained Tempranillo. Throughout southern France, but especially in southern Rhône, its high strength, juicy, peppery character is crucial in many blends, notably Châteauneuf-du-Pape. But in Australia growers are rediscovering old vineyards of dry-farmed Grenache and making superb deep wines, and Garnacha dominates the blend in Spain's Priorat, producing super-rich monsters full of tar and figs.

MALBEC

This vine is now associated largely with Argentina, where it makes lush, damsony, violet-scented wines. Its homeland was Bordeaux, where its job was primarily to soften Cabernet Sauvignon. In Cahors' drier, hotter vineyards, Malbec (here known as Cot or Auxerrois) can produce deep, damsony wine that becomes dark and tobacco-scented with age. Chile and Australia do well with Malbec.

MERLOT

This red grape, with its rich, plummy fruit, its fondness for oak-aging and its tendency to mature in bottle relatively quickly, is a natural partner for Cabernet Sauvignon. But bottling it on its own and writing 'Merlot' on the label is currently the fastest way to sell a bottle of red wine. It has become so fashionable simply because it's so easy to drink: it is supple, luscious, low in

---

COMPOSITION OF A GRAPE

PULP
water
sugar
fruit acids
pectins

STALK
tannin

PIPS
oils
bitterness
tannin

SKIN
tannin
colour

When it comes to imparting flavour to its wine, the actual juice of the grape rarely has very much to offer. Muscat juice is sweet and perfumed – that's why we eat Muscat grapes as well as make wine from them – but most of the great wine grapes of the world are no fun at all to eat. At best, a ripe wine grape has a sugary, neutral-flavoured, colourless pulp. Much of the character for a wine comes from its skin. As the grape ripens, the skin matures: its tannins become less aggressive, its colour deepens and all the perfume and flavour components build up. The trick is to try to ripen the grape so that sugar, acid, tannin, colour and flavour are all in balance at the time it is harvested. Both the pips and the stalks are very bitter which is why modern winemakers usually de-stalk the grapes and avoid crushing the pips.

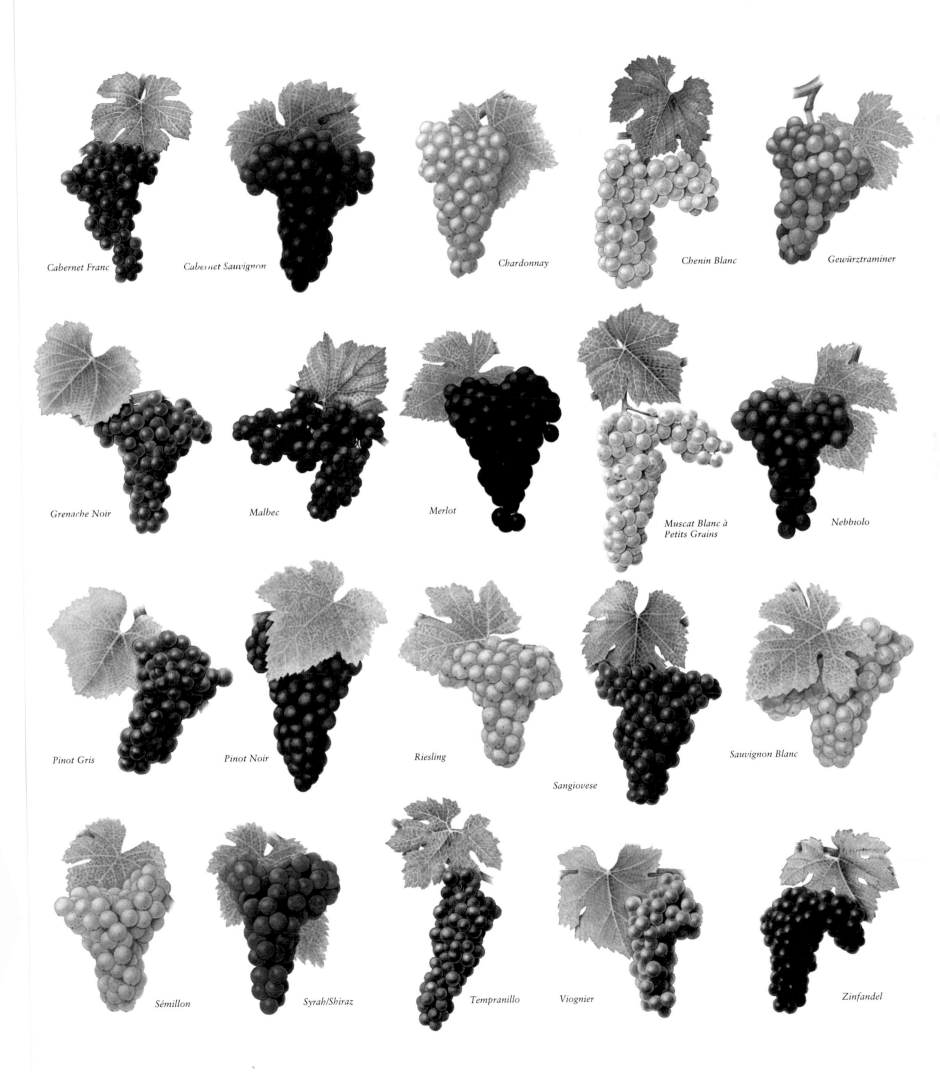

Cabernet Franc

Cabernet Sauvignon

Chardonnay

Chenin Blanc

Gewürztraminer

Grenache Noir

Malbec

Merlot

Muscat Blanc à
Petits Grains

Nebbiolo

Pinot Gris

Pinot Noir

Riesling

Sangiovese

Sauvignon Blanc

Sémillon

Syrah/Shiraz

Tempranillo

Viognier

Zinfandel

WINES & WINE REGIONS OF THE WORLD

LIST OF PANORAMIC MAPS

FRANCE

Nobody does it better – or do they? France has built her reputation on such wines as Champagne, from the cool, chalk hills of the North (main picture) and on the top wines of Bordeaux, like Château Margaux (above). But nowadays outside competition is forcing France to look to her laurels.

We've had our tiffs. I've stormed off and formed fleeting, flirtatious liaisons with other nations around the world. But true love is true love. I've always come back to France. Other countries can do some things better but when it comes to wine, no country can do so many things as well as France. My love of France, my respect for her natural genius in wine is deepened, not diminished, by contact with her rivals in Europe and elsewhere. The more I learn about wine in Chile, Australia, California, Italy, Spain or New Zealand, the more I appreciate France.

But then, France is lucky. Her geographical situation is ideally suited to many of the grape varieties that make great wine and her geological make-up has provided numerous sites perfectly suited to the measured ripening of these varieties. This combination provides a wide array of areas that achieve a precise balance between too much heat and too little, between too much rain and too little. The result is that the great varieties like Cabernet Sauvignon, Pinot Noir, Syrah, Chardonnay and Sauvignon Blanc will generally creep towards ripeness rather than rush headlong. Just as with an apple, slowly ripened fruit gives the most delicious flavour, the balance between sugar and acidity and perfume is most perfectly achieved.

Nowadays, modern vineyard technology can mimic such conditions up to a point in warmer areas, and perfect cool cellar and winemaking conditions could be created as easily at the equator as at the North Pole. But such developments are only a generation old. France's other priceless natural asset has always been her winemaking conditions. For two thousand years before the advent of refrigeration techniques, most major French wine areas were sufficiently cool by vintage time for the wines to ferment in a controlled way without artificial help, preserving the delicious, but fragile, balance of the fruit. Other great wine nations, such as Italy and Spain, the United States and Australia, had few areas that could rely on such luck.

France also enjoyed her position at the crossroads of Europe and she has a longer on-going tradition of fashioning wines to suit the export markets than her competitors round the Mediterranean. These days, it's true, newer countries and regions seem intent on stealing her thunder and proving that, whatever France can do, they can do better. Well, sometimes they can and sometimes they can't. We're in a fascinating period at the moment as France, with one eye on the New World, redefines her ideas of what makes a wine great, and what makes her wines different from all others. And my love for France? A few lovers' tiffs can't destroy the Real Thing.

BORDEAUX

TOTAL DISTANCE
NORTH TO SOUTH
144KM (89½ MILES)

BORDEAUX/BORDEAUX
SUPÉRIEUR AC

— OTHER AC
BOUNDARIES

▨ VINEYARDS   N̲

I CAN'T HELP IT. I love Bordeaux. It isn't the most friendly of wine regions. It isn't the most beautiful. Its wines can be pig-headed and difficult to understand when they are young, and some can be pretty harsh when they're still in barrel. But you know what they say about your first time. Bordeaux was my first time. My first ever wine visit, my first ever vineyards.

And Bordeaux was my first wine-tasting. And Bordeaux was my first great wine. First, first, first. I suppose it's not so strange for someone brought up in England. When I was at university, great wine was red, and great red wine was Bordeaux. Of course, we tried other wines from time to time, especially when money ran short, but if we were being treated to dinner by our richers and betters, we felt short-changed if the red wines weren't Bordeaux. Every winetasting session would always end up as a passionate discussion of the minutiae of different Bordeaux properties and vintages as we lapped up every scrap of knowledge we could. So it was only natural that one summer vacation I would optimistically jump into my Mini and, armed with a precious introduction to the late Peter Sichel at Château d'Angludet in Margaux, head off to what I hoped would be wine drinkers' nirvana.

Bordeaux is as much a story of politics and history as it is a story of wine. Look at the map. To the left I had expected great rolling hills and dales all covered in vines. Jovial bucolic cellar masters and their swains ever keen to swap a tale and share a jar. Villages and towns bustling with the busy activities of wine. I should have gone anywhere but Bordeaux. At first I found no vineyards at all.

Bordeaux was a splendid, haughtily magnificent place – well, the centre was; the rest was sprawling suburbia and industrial estates. And as I drove out towards

Margaux, the little villages seemed sullenly asleep and the land damp, low-browed and devoid of vines. I did find the vines; of course I did once I got to Margaux; I did find friendly if not exactly gregarious people, and across these broad, undulating acres, I did find some amazing châteaux – the grand houses at the centre of many estates – but the Médoc, with the best will in the world, isn't exactly a sylvan paradise. Once those vines start, that's all you get where the soil's at all suitable – vines. I found a few hills and dales around St-Émilion but even there it is mostly just a carpet of vines. The Graves isn't quite so wall-to-wall because half of its best vineyards are now buried under suburbia and an airport.

No great scenery, just vines, vines, vines. And that is the key to why Bordeaux, at the beginning of the new millennium, can claim the title of the World's Greatest Wine Region.

Look at the map again. Although there are numerous places in France, the rest of Europe, America and the southern hemisphere that can boast brilliant wines, most are produced in tiny quantities. Bordeaux has great swathes of land suited to different sorts of wine and around 200 properties producing perhaps 100,000 bottles of wine each that veers between the good and the brilliant almost every year. That's an awful lot of wine. There are several hundred more properties on slightly less favoured land whose wine can be still very good. Altogether there are about 5000 properties that bottle their own wine and another 7000 or more growers that don't, making a staggering total of between 800 and 900 million bottles of wine. Every year.

CLIMATE AND SOIL

Most of the area on the map grows vines to a greater or lesser extent, but it is only certain favoured localities that regularly achieve exceptional quality. The sea to the west gives some clues. The Gulf Stream draws in warm tropical currents up this western shore of France, crucially ameliorating temperatures near the coast. Yet the Bay of Biscay is also notoriously stormy. Only the vast stretches of Landes pine forest to the west break the salt-laden westerly winds and suck down much of the rainfall that could otherwise ruin a vintage. The consequence is a pattern of generally hot summers and long, mild autumns still only just warm enough to fully ripen the local grape varieties. But there's a fair amount of rainfall too and here's where the gravel and the limestone slopes come in.

WHERE THE VINEYARDS ARE *This map shows the greatest fine wine area of the world in all its glory. Although there are vineyards on virtually every segment of the map, with the exception of the great pine forests of the Landes that spread their protective shield along the Bay of Biscay to the west, the best vineyards are those situated close to the rivers Garonne and Dordogne, and the Gironde estuary. The important Garonne vineyards start around Langon, with the Graves region which follows the left bank up to Bordeaux. Sauternes and Barsac are clustered round the river Ciron, while the best vineyards to the south of the city are Pessac-Léognan. The Médoc runs like a tongue of land northwards from the city, with the best vineyards between Macau and St-Estèphe, close to the Gironde. Across the estuary, at Bourg and Blaye, are vineyards more famous in Roman times, and following the Dordogne east towards Libourne, Fronsac has also enjoyed greater renown. However, Pomerol, next to Libourne, and St-Émilion have never been more famous. Lesser vineyards spread out from St-Émilion, and the area between the Dordogne and the Garonne – Entre-Deux-Mers – is a source of much decent red and white wine.*

THE MÉDOC & HAUT-MÉDOC

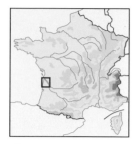

🍇 RED GRAPES
Cabernet Sauvignon is the main variety, performing brilliantly on the warm gravelly Médoc soils. Lesser varieties are the softer perfumed Cabernet Franc, Merlot planted on cooler, less well-drained soils, Malbec (in the Bas-Médoc) and the rarely used Petit Verdot.

☁️ CLIMATE
The soothing influence of the Gulf Stream sweeping along the Atlantic coast produces long, warm summers and cool, wet winters. The Landes pine forests act as a natural windbreak, sheltering the vineyards. Heavy rains can be a problem at vintage time.

🏞️ SOIL
The topsoil is mostly free-draining gravel mixed with sand, the subsoil is gravel with sand plus some limestone and clay. The best vineyards are on the gravel outcrops.

🏔️ ASPECT
Generally low-lying and flat with the main relief provided by gravel ridges and low plateaus, especially in the Haut-Médoc. Most, though not all, of the top vineyards are on very gentle rises facing east and south-east towards the Gironde estuary.

THE BEST PLACE to get a good look at the Médoc is from the middle of a traffic jam. I'd recommend about 9am or 5.30pm on a nice bright spring day, sitting patiently on the lofty span of the Pont d'Aquitaine that sweeps across the Garonne river north of the city of Bordeaux.

And look north, as far as the eye can see – out there are the great vineyards of Margaux and Cantenac; further on – from this height they should still be visible – are St-Julien, Pauillac and even St-Estèphe. Ah, bliss. Please God keep the traffic snarled up a little longer while I pause to dream.

I'm afraid dreams are your best bet. You are getting by far the best view of the land that is the Médoc, home to many of the greatest red wines in the world. But there's not much to see even from the bridge. There are the industrial estates, the sprawling suburbs, the scrubby-looking trees and the mud flats glumly following the Garonne's shores round towards Macau and Margaux. But the vineyards? Don't great vineyards need slopes and hills and precious perfect exposures to the sun? It's difficult to believe that in this flat, marshy-looking pudding of a place these unique pre-conditions exist, but they do.

The highest spot in the Médoc – all 80km (50 miles) long of it – is only 43m (141ft) above sea level. That's at the village of Listrac-Médoc, not even one of the best places. Look it up on the map on page 38. Can you spot this Mount Everest of the Médoc? Me neither. And all the best vineyards are located between 4m (13ft) above sea level (parts of Château Montrose in St-Estèphe and other good properties in Pauillac, St-Julien and Margaux creep down this close to the slimy edge of the Gironde estuary) and 29m (95ft) (Pauillac's Château Lynch-Moussas outstretches Château Pontet-Canet to reach these giddy heights). Amazingly, this pathetic 25m (82ft) spread is enough to provide growing conditions for Cabernet Sauvignon, Cabernet Franc, Merlot and Petit Verdot vines that the entire wine world envies and would give anything to possess.

Right. Let's get off this bridge – if we can – and head up towards Margaux. But keep your eyes peeled for two things – drainage ditches, and those times when you suddenly realize that the land is almost imperceptibly rising up a metre or two. You might also look right to check whether you can see the glistening waters of the Gironde because the saying is that all the best vineyards in the Médoc are within sight of the estuary. And thinking about this, I realize that there's hardly a single top vineyard without a view of the water.

Those drainage ditches are critical because, before Dutch engineers arrived in the 17th century, the Médoc was a desolate, dangerous, flood-prone swamp. The Dutch, being, I suppose, world experts on matters of drainage, dug the great channels that still slant east across the Médoc to the Gironde and created dry land where bog existed before. The slight rises in the land show where gravel ridges, washed down from the Massif Central and Pyrenees millennia ago, provide islands of warm free-draining soil rising out of the clay. Remember that the Médoc is not a particularly warm place, and that the Cabernet Sauvignon, the main grape of the region, takes a long time to ripen. It needs these deep gravel beds that warm up quickly in spring if it is going to do well in most years. Indeed in parts of Margaux, the fine gravel is mixed with white pebbles which, they say, helps the ripening process by reflecting the light on to the grapes.

I'm taking the D2 road up from Bordeaux because I never fail to thrill when the woodland sweeps aside and a broad, very gentle slope to my right displays the excellent Château la Lagune. Almost immediately I plunge into more woods, but deep in a glade to my left is the fairytale keep of Château Cantemerle whose gravel crest spreads out beyond the trees.

MARGAUX

A moment more and we're in the appellation area of Margaux, but not in its heart. There is a fair bit of sand and clay in many of the vineyards at Labarde and at Cantenac, but there are some fine properties, particularly on the south-west-facing slope round Château Brane-Cantenac. However, this is one of the thankfully few areas where the validity of the 1855 classification as a guide to the quality of the wines is questionable, although from about 1996 many of the underperforming properties have begun to get their act together. It's no good having lovely vineyards if you don't put heart and soul – and, I fear, bank balance – into the creation of great wine, and for most of the late 20th century, châteaux round here with great potential seemed to lack the will to excel. A new generation taking over, some much-needed investment, and occasionally the purchase of the property by a well-funded outsider can all turn things round, and fine Cantenac properties like Brane-Cantenac, Cantenac-Brown, Kirwan and Prieuré-Lichine are witness to this.

There is only one Classed Growth in the backwoods behind Cantenac: the Fifth Growth Château du Tertre, sitting on a knoll of gravelly soil just north of the little village of Arsac. Though the wine

---

THE 1855 CLASSIFICATION OF RED WINES

This is the original 1855 list brought up to date to take account of name changes and divisions of property as well as the promotion of Château Mouton-Rothschild in 1973. Properties are listed alphabetically, followed by their commune name in brackets.

- **Premiers Crus (First Growths)** Haut-Brion (Pessac/Graves); Lafite-Rothschild (Pauillac); Latour (Pauillac); Margaux (Margaux); Mouton-Rothschild (Pauillac) – since 1973.
- **Deuxièmes Crus (Second Growths)** Brane-Cantenac (Cantenac); Cos d'Estournel (St-Estèphe); Ducru-Beaucaillou (St-Julien); Durfort-Vivens (Margaux); Gruaud-Larose (St-Julien); Lascombes (Margaux); Léoville-Barton (St-Julien); Léoville-Las-Cases (St-Julien); Léoville-Poyferré (St-Julien); Montrose (St-Estèphe); Pichon-Longueville (Pauillac); Pichon-Longueville-Comtesse-de-Lalande (Pauillac); Rauzan-Gassies (Margaux); Rauzan-Ségla (Margaux).
- **Troisièmes Crus (Third Growths)** Boyd-Cantenac (Cantenac); Calon-Ségur (St-Estèphe); Cantenac-Brown (Cantenac); Desmirail (Margaux); Ferrière (Margaux); Giscours (Labarde); d'Issan (Cantenac); Kirwan (Cantenac); Lagrange (St-Julien); la Lagune (Ludon); Langoa-Barton (St-Julien); Malescot-St-Exupéry (Margaux); Marquis d'Alesme-Becker (Margaux); Palmer (Cantenac).
- **Quatrièmes Crus (Fourth Growths)** Beychevelle (St-Julien); Branaire (St-Julien); Duhart-Milon-Rothschild (Pauillac); Lafon-Rochet (St-Estèphe); Marquis-de-Terme (Margaux); Pouget (Cantenac); Prieuré-Lichine (Cantenac); St-Pierre (St-Julien); Talbot (St-Julien); la Tour-Carnet (St-Laurent).
- **Cinquièmes Crus (Fifth Growths)** d'Armailhac (Pauillac); Batailley (Pauillac); Belgrave (St-Laurent); de Camensac (St-Laurent); Cantemerle (Macau); Clerc-Milon (Pauillac); Cos-Labory (St-Estèphe); Croizet-Bages (Pauillac); Dauzac (Labarde); Grand-Puy-Ducasse (Pauillac); Grand-Puy-Lacoste (Pauillac); Haut-Bages-Libéral (Pauillac); Haut-Batailley (Pauillac); Lynch-Bages (Pauillac); Lynch-Moussas (Pauillac); ; Pédesclaux (Pauillac); Pontet-Canet (Pauillac); du Tertre (Arsac).

doesn't immediately show its charming side, with a little maturity du Tertre opens out into a delightful blend of blackcurrant fruit and violet perfume far more consistently than do many of the properties with higher classifications and supposedly better sites nearer the Gironde estuary.

Châteaux Monbrison and d'Angludet aren't classified at all. Yet, due to the determination of their respective proprietors, the wines they produce, from supposedly inferior soil, can easily rival many Classed Growth Margaux wines. It is possible that Margaux has even more potentially great vineyard land than Pauillac or St-Julien to the north. Thank goodness for the new generation of proprietors and winemakers doing their best to prove this could be the case.

Altogether there are five villages in the Margaux appellation totalling 1525ha (3768 acres) of vines and including a grand total of 21 Classed Growths, but the greatest Margaux vineyards begin around the village of Issan, and continue on to the little town of Margaux itself. We're on a broad plateau here, gently sloping east to the river, and the ground seems white with pebbles and even the gravelly soil is frequently a pale sickly grey. But that's excellent for the vines. The soil offering very few nutrients, the vines send their taproots deep below the surface.

As a result the wines of Margaux are rarely massive – though Châteaux Rauzan-Ségla and Margaux can be deep and chewy – yet they develop a haunting scent of violets and a pure perfume of blackcurrants that is as dry as those sun-bleached pebbles, yet seems as sweet as jam.

The Margaux vineyards continue north to Soussans, yet they become darker, the clay more evident and suddenly we dive into marshy woodland and they've gone. A matter of 5m (16ft) or so difference in the height of the land and we lose all that gravel and are left with damp cold clay. We're now in a kind of no-man's-land until we reach St-Julien about 12km (8 miles) ahead. There are vineyards here, around Lamarque and Cussac, the best being accorded the appellation Haut-Médoc, but they lack the brilliance of Margaux, crucially because the vineyards lack the depth of gravel and the drainage.

MOULIS AND LISTRAC

There are, however, two small appellations just west of Arcins that do have gravel and can produce excellent wine – Moulis and Listrac-Médoc. Neither of these villages has any Classed Growth properties, but looking at the excellent vineyard sites of Moulis in particular, you could be excused for thinking that the growers there were a little unlucky. Above all, over near the railway, around the village of Grand Poujeaux there are some splendid deep gravel ridges that would definitely have qualified for honours if they had been within the boundaries of such major villages as Margaux or St-Julien. Never mind; it allows us as wine drinkers that rare

This is not exactly what I mean when I say that the best Médoc châteaux have a view of the water. Château Pichon-Longueville just happens to have a gorgeous ornamental lake. The fairytale architecture of the château dates from 1851.

AC WINE AREAS AND SELECTED CHÂTEAUX

1. Ch. la Tour-du-Haut-Moulin
2. Ch. Lamarque
3. Ch. Malescasse
4. Ch. Clarke
5. Ch. Maucaillou
6. Ch. Poujeaux
7. Ch. Chasse-Spleen
8. Ch. Labégorce-Zédé
9. Ch. Bel Air-Marquis d'Aligre
10. Ch. Lascombes
11. Ch. Ferrière
12. Ch. Malescot-St-Exupéry
13. Ch. Margaux
14. Ch. Rauzan-Ségla
15. Ch. Palmer
16. Ch. d'Issan
17. Ch. Prieuré-Lichine
18. Ch. Kirwan
19. Ch. Desmirail
20. Ch. Brane-Cantenac
21. Ch. du Tertre
22. Ch. d'Angludet
23. Ch. Giscours
24. Ch. Siran
25. Ch. Cantemerle
26. Ch. la Lagune

MARGAUX = AC WINE AREAS

— AC BOUNDARIES

experience in Bordeaux – relatively bargain-priced wine of classic quality. The leader of this group of gravel-based wines is Château Chasse-Spleen – splendidly dark and sturdy, but beautifully ripe at its core. Other high grade wines also come from such châteaux as Maucaillou and Poujeaux.

Moulis is the better of these appellations, with a fine ridge of gravel running through its midst. Listrac-Médoc has some gravel, too, but is a crucial mile or so further away from the mild influence of the Gironde, and is located another 20m (66ft) higher. Higher vineyards are cooler vineyards and in a marginal climate like the Médoc, even 20m (66ft) makes a difference.

Whereas the Moulis wines are generally marked by an attractive precociousness, a soft-centred fruit and smooth-edged structure, Listrac wines are always sterner, more jut-jawed and less easy to love – though a greater percentage of Merlot in the blend is making them more supple these days. The quality is there all right, but the style is rather old-fashioned and reserved. Even a supremely well-equipped and well-financed property like Château Clarke, that strains every sinew to make a spicy, ripe-fruited, oak-scented 'modern' classic, is often ultimately defeated by nature, its wine demanding the traditional decade of aging that most Listracs have always needed in order to shine.

•MACAU

ST-JULIEN

You have to change gear when you cross the wet meadows and the drainage channel beneath Château Beychevelle and enter the St-Julien AC. You change down a gear to navigate the left turn and upward sweep of the road, as suddenly the vineyards surge into existence once more. But you change gear up in wine terms, up into the highest gear in the red wine world, because St-Julien and its neighbour Pauillac have more great red wines packed tight within their boundaries than any other patch of land on earth.

The St-Julien appellation is only 921ha (2276 acres) but it has 11 Classed Growths – while Pauillac has 1222ha (3020 acres) and 18 Classed Growths, including three First Growths. Here the Cabernet Sauvignon, aided and abetted by the Merlot and the Cabernet Franc (and in some châteaux, the Petit Verdot), exploits the deep gravel banks and the mellow maritime climate to produce grapes of an intensity and, above all, a balance between fruit and tannin, perfume and acid, that you simply don't find elsewhere. Add to this some of the world's highest prices for wine, which in itself is no good thing, though when the profit is re-invested in an almost obsessive care of the vineyard, superior winery equipment and row upon row of fragrant new oak barrels in which to age the wine, well, your pockets have to be deep. But you buy not only superb quality, you buy enviable consistency too.

WHERE THE VINEYARDS ARE *This map tells part of the tale of the Médoc immediately. The wide Gironde estuary provides a warming influence to the east, the pine forests to the west protect the region from salt-laden winds coming off the Bay of Biscay and draw off much of the rain from the clouds in wet weather. But the other part of the Médoc's story, the soil, isn't so apparent. All the best vineyards in the Médoc are sited on gravelly soil.*

Where there are concentrations of vineyards, as there are around the little town of Margaux, this is because the banks of warm gravelly soil that are crucial for the ripening of the Cabernet Sauvignon dominate the landscape. Where the vineyards are piecemeal, the gravel will have been largely displaced by damp clay. Such vineyards as there are on this type of soil will generally be planted with the earlier-ripening Merlot, but results are rarely thrilling.

Macau and Ludon in the south have good vineyards, but the fireworks only really start at Labarde, one of the five villages that make up the Margaux AC. The best vineyards are concentrated around Cantenac and Margaux itself. North of Soussans, the vineyards become scrappier, as the gravel banks largely disappear until re-emerging at Château Beychevelle in the St-Julien AC. Haut-Médoc is the highest AC these vineyards are permitted to claim.

West of Arcins there are two small but high quality ACs – Moulis and Listrac. There are no Classed Growths here, but there are several châteaux of high enough quality, especially on the gravel ridge around the village of Grand Poujeaux. The islands in the estuary have vineyards, but they only qualify for the basic Bordeaux AC and aren't much good. I know. I've picked their grapes. I couldn't wait to get back to dry land.

SOUTHERN
HAUT-MÉDOC

N

TOTAL DISTANCE NORTH TO SOUTH 18KM (11 MILES)

VINEYARDS

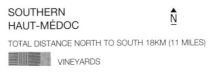

Château Beychevelle looks merely attractive from the roadway. Seen from the gardens and lawns that run down towards the Gironde, it is a stunning piece of 18th-century architecture. The villages of Margaux, St-Julien and Pauillac may consist largely of featureless vine monoculture, but the numerous enchanting and occasionally magnificent châteaux buildings do add a distinct air of romance and sophistication.

And I'm all for that, because otherwise, I'm afraid we're back to the same basics as in Margaux further south – drainage and gravel. These impoverished soils really make the vine reach deep into the earth for nutrients, and, despite modern fertilizers and certain vine clones bred for high yield making their presence felt, such infertile soil naturally keeps the volume of the harvest down.

We're in a cool climate here, remember. Gravel is a warm, well-drained soil and a small crop ripens more quickly when those autumn rain clouds start to build up out in the Bay of Biscay.

That drainage channel we drove over close to Château Beychevelle is very important, because there is a whole ridge of vineyards running westwards towards St-Laurent whose soils are a little heavier than is usual for St-Julien, and yet whose angle to the south and slope down towards the drainage channel help to produce excellent wines. Châteaux Gruaud-Larose and Branaire are the most significant of the properties here. However, for the true genius of St-Julien – of wines of only middling weight that develop a haunting cigar, cedar and blackcurrant fragrance as they age – we need to go back to the slopes near the Gironde where three gravel

MÉDOC AND NORTHERN HAUT-MÉDOC

TOTAL DISTANCE
NORTH TO SOUTH
25KM (15½ MILES)

VINEYARDS

0 km   1   2
0 miles   1

N

ESPARRE-MÉDOC

ST-SEURIN-DE-CADOURNE ▪

ST-ESTÈPHE ▪

PAUILLAC ▪

ST-JULIEN ▪

ST-LAURENT-MÉDOC ▪

WHERE THE VINEYARDS ARE   *This is the most concentrated area of fine red wine in Bordeaux. Gravel banks begin at Château Beychevelle, at the bottom of the map, and are most impressive close to the waterfront in the St-Julien and Pauillac ACs, where the best properties get the full benefit of the warm estuary and the best drainage.*

Pauillac ends very abruptly at Château Lafite-Rothschild. A drainage channel and meadow create an interlude, but then there's another low bank covered with vines and we are in the large AC of St-Estèphe. Three of St-Estèphe's five Classed Growths are found here but generally this AC has more clay than gravel, so few of the wines achieve the brilliance of Pauillac. From Blanquefort, on the northern outskirts of Bordeaux, to St-Seurin, north of the St-Estèphe AC, wines not covered by the main village ACs are allowed the title Haut-Médoc. The vineyards become patchy as suitable land is more difficult to find. North of St-Seurin are the vineyards of the Médoc AC, occasionally good but rarely thrilling.

outcrops push their way eastwards and downwards towards the estuary. Château Ducru-Beaucaillou and the three Léoville properties occupy these slopes. Great wines all.

PAUILLAC

You can't tell where you leave St-Julien and enter Pauillac, the vines are so continuous. Well, yes you can – there's another little stream helping to drain famous vineyards like Château Latour. Where the road crosses the stream, there's the boundary. And there is a change in wine style; Cabernet Sauvignon becomes even more dominant in Pauillac, the wines are darker and take longer to mature and yet have a more piercing blackcurrant fruit that mingles with the cedar and cigar box fragrance. Certainly the extra percentage of Cabernet Sauvignon deepens the colour of the wine, but is only possible because Pauillac has the deepest gravel beds in the whole Médoc, stretched out across two broad plateaux to the south and north of the town of Pauillac. And there's some iron in the gravel and a good deal of iron pan as subsoil. No one's ever proved it, but a lot of growers reckon iron in the soil gives extra depth to a red wine.

You certainly get your depth in Pauillac. Pauillac has 18 Classed Growths in its 1222ha (3020 acres) and three of the 1855 Classification's five First Growths, each playing a different brilliant variation on the same blackcurrant and cedarwood theme as well as a host of other excellent properties. Once again, the adage that the best vineyards have a view of the river holds sway, because the buffeting of tides and currents that piled up those vital gravel banks has obviously left the deepest ridges close to the estuary. But the ridges go a long way back in Pauillac, and standing on tiptoe you can still just about see the river from properties like Pontet-Canet and Grand-Puy-Lacoste. In fact, these two properties give some of the purest expressions of blackcurrant juice and cedar perfume of any châteaux in Pauillac.

Every signpost in St-Julien and Pauillac bears yet another name dripping with the magic of memorable vintages. How much longer can this parade of excellence go on? Not much longer, I'm afraid. Cruising north past Château Lafite-Rothschild, past its unusually steep, well-drained vineyards, there's one more drainage stream ahead of us, and one long slope running along its north bank.

ST-ESTÈPHE

Here we're in St-Estèphe, and despite the quality of these frontline St-Estèphe vineyards like Châteaux Cos d'Estournel and Lafon-Rochet facing Pauillac over the Jalle du Breuil stream, from now on, the gravel begins to fade and clay begins to clog your shoes. We're further north and ripening is slower here than in, say, Margaux. There's much more of the earlier-ripening Merlot planted to try to provide fleshy flavour from the clay soils. And despite the size of the St-Estèphe appellation, at 1265ha (3126 acres) only a whisker smaller than Margaux, a mere five properties were classified in 1855. The best wines are very good – full, structured and well-flavoured – but if you sometimes wonder whether they don't lack a little scent, whether they don't carry with them the vaguest hint of the clay beneath the vines, you're not wrong.

HAUT-MÉDOC

St-Estèphe marks the northern end of the great Médoc villages. Yet from the very gates of Bordeaux at Blanquefort, right up to St-Seurin-de-Cadourne, about a mile north of St-Estèphe, there are patches of land outside the main villages where a decent aspect, some good drainage and sometimes some gravel occur. Often these vineyards are interspersed with woodland, and almost all of these can carry the Haut-Médoc AC. There are even five Classed Growths within the Haut-Médoc AC, but, these apart, few wines exhibit the sheer excitement of the riverfront gravel bed wines. Good proprietors make good wine. For great wine, you need a bit more help from the Almighty.

MÉDOC

North of St-Seurin lies the Bas-Médoc (Lower Médoc), though its appellation is simply Médoc to spare the locals' egos. It's a flat but relaxing landscape covering 5431ha (13,420 acres) of vines, right up to the tip of the Médoc peninsula, though vineyards do peter out north of Valeyrac. There is much evidence of the marsh the whole area was before the Dutch started draining it in the 18th century. It's not ideal wine country, though there are a few gravel outcrops and some sandy clay. Between them they produce a good deal of decent red wine and, occasionally, as at Châteaux Potensac, Tour Haut-Caussan or la Tour-du-Haut-Moulin, something really good.

The Médoc side of the broad Gironde estuary is fringed with these little stilted fishing huts. The very edge of the shore is not planted with vines: appellation boundaries begin just slightly inland.

AC WINE AREAS AND SELECTED CHÂTEAUX

1. Ch. Tour Haut-Caussan
2. Ch. Potensac
3. Ch. Charmail
4. Ch. Sociando-Mallet
5. Ch. les Ormes de Pez
6. Ch. de Pez
7. Ch. Calon-Ségur
8. Ch. Phélan-Ségur
9. Ch. Montrose
10. Ch. Haut-Marbuzet
11. Ch. Lafon-Rochet
12. Ch. Cos d'Estournel
13. Ch. Lafite-Rothschild

14. Ch. Clerc-Milon
15. Ch. Mouton-Rothschild
16. Ch. Pontet-Canet
17. Ch. Grand-Puy-Lacoste
18. Ch. Lynch-Bages
19. Ch. Batailley
20. Ch. Haut-Batailley
21. Ch. Pichon-Longueville
22. Ch. Pichon-Longueville-Comtesse-de-Lalande
23. Ch. Latour

24. Ch. Léoville-Las-Cases
25. Ch. Léoville-Poyferré
26. Ch. Talbot
27. Ch. Langoa-Barton/Ch. Léoville-Barton
28. Ch. Ducru-Beaucaillou
29. Ch. Beychevelle
30. Ch. Branaire
31. Ch. St-Pierre
32. Ch. Gruaud-Larose
33. Ch. Lagrange
34. Ch. Belgrave

PAUILLAC = AC WINE AREAS ▬▬ AC BOUNDARIES

0 km   1   2
0 miles   1

ST-ÉMILION, POMEROL & FRONSAC

RED GRAPES
Merlot does best on the cooler, heavier clays of St-Émilion and Pomerol, with greater or lesser amounts of Cabernet Franc and Cabernet Sauvignon on gravel outcrops. There is a minuscule amount of Malbec.

CLIMATE
The maritime influence begins to moderate, producing warmer summers and cooler winters. It is drier than the Médoc with frequent, sometimes severe frosts.

SOIL
A complex pattern shows gravel deposits, sand and clay mixed with limestone. The top vineyards are either on the côtes around St-Émilion or on the gravel outcrops of Pomerol/Figeac.

ASPECT
Generally flat, especially in Pomerol, the land rises steeply in the côtes south and south-west of St-Émilion. Elsewhere the slopes are at best moderately undulating.

Pomerol is a world of small vineyards and unassuming houses that just happen to make world-famous wines. This is Le Pin, which is about as famous – and as small – as they get.

WHAT A DIFFERENCE 31km (19 miles) makes. I head east from Bordeaux on the N89 away from the prosperous, cosmopolitan city and, by the time I cross the Dordogne River into the Libournais wine region, I am in a totally different world.

The main town, Libourne, has none of the majesty and grandeur of the city of Bordeaux, no quays telling of an illustrious trading past. Although Libourne does have a quay, with wine merchants' offices huddled together beneath some willow trees at the edge of the Dordogne, it is a toytown affair compared to Bordeaux. Libourne's narrow streets and folksy market square could be in any one of a hundred towns in France.

The vineyards, too, have none of the charming sylvan air of so many of the Graves properties, carefully carved from the encroaching woodland all about, nor the proud self-confidence of the great Médoc estates. The Libournais is packed with vines: indeed, there's room for little else, so much so that in this region you get few of the copses and meadows that offer a welcome break from vineyards in the Médoc. But, unlike the Médoc, this is down-to-earth vine-growing, with nothing vainglorious or self-indulgent. St-Émilion has 5682ha (14,040 acres) of vines, yet these are divided between more than 1000 growers. Pomerol has a mere 832ha (2056 acres), and the average holding is only 4ha (10 acres). A successful Médoc property is likely to average 40ha (99 acres). So we're going to look in vain for the startling architectural follies that bring the dull Médoc landscape to life. With few exceptions, a sturdy no-nonsense farmhouse is all we'll get in the Libournais. Even the ultra-expensive, minuscule quantity super-cuvées that have become so fashionable have been sardonically termed *garagiste* or 'garage' wines with good reason.

But there are redeeming features in this region. Founded in the 11th century (though originally settled in Roman times) the town of St-Émilion is a jumble of old houses, squeezed into a cleft in the limestone plateau looking out over the flat Dordogne valley. The coarsely cobbled streets are narrow and steep and the whole town has been declared an ancient monument to preserve it for posterity. Indeed, the whole St-Émilion appellation was proclaimed a World Heritage Site by UNESCO in 1999.

And then there are the flavours. I'm almost tempted to say 'and then there is the flavour', because the joy of almost all the great wines of Pomerol and St-Émilion lies in the dominance of one grape – Merlot. Bordeaux reds are famous for their unapproachability in youth and their great longevity. That reputation has been built by the grandees of the Médoc where Cabernet reigns supreme. Cabernet Sauvignon wines are tough and aggressive when young, but Merlot wines exhibit a juicy, almost jam-sweet richness just about from the moment the grapes hit the vat. Bordeaux without tears? You want Pomerol or St-Émilion. Their best wines will age just as long as the best Médocs, it's simply that they're so attractive young that most of them never get the chance.

There is some Cabernet Sauvignon planted here – perhaps 6 per cent or so – but the lack of warm gravel soils in most of the Libournais means that it rarely ripens properly despite the climate being rather warmer and more continental than in the Médoc. Château Figeac in St-Émilion and Vieux-Château-Certan in Pomerol are two exceptions that manage to ripen it well. In Pomerol and St-Émilion, the Cabernet Franc gives far better results than Cabernet Sauvignon, especially where there is a decent amount of limestone in the soil and subsoil: the great Château Cheval Blanc has almost 60 per cent Cabernet Franc.

Though vines have been grown here since Roman times, the emergence of St-Émilion as one of Bordeaux's star turns is fairly recent and Pomerol's soaring reputation is a good deal more recent still. History and geography have conspired against both areas. The

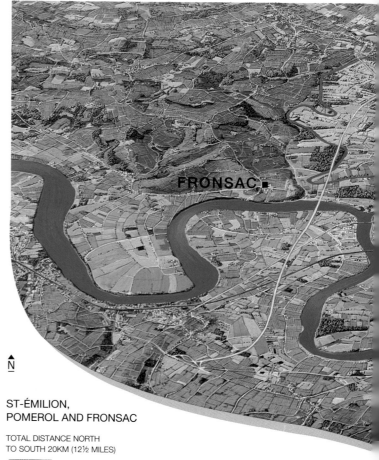

FRONSAC

ST-ÉMILION, POMEROL AND FRONSAC

TOTAL DISTANCE NORTH
TO SOUTH 20KM (12½ MILES)

VINEYARDS

majority of Bordeaux's export trade has always been carried on from Bordeaux itself. Those 31km (19 miles) may seem trivial now, but until the 1820s there were no bridges across the Garonne and Dordogne rivers between Bordeaux and Libourne. Few Bordeaux merchants felt the need to make the short but tiresome journey to the Libournais when they had the Graves and the Médoc on their doorstep. A band of Libourne merchants did grow up to ship their local wines, but they were generally regarded with disdain and Libournais wines were accorded little respect and low prices.

When the Paris–Bordeaux railway opened in 1853, with a station in Libourne, this freed local producers from the thrall of Bordeaux's merchants. Ever since, a mainstay of Libourne's trade has been the network of consumers in northern France, Belgium and Holland who happily soak up whatever wine is available, undeterred by the fact that not a single Libournais wine was included in Bordeaux's 1855 Classification.

CLASSIFICATIONS

St-Émilion is divided into two appellations: basic St-Émilion AC and St-Émilion Grand Cru AC. The latter now has its own classification system (see page 47), which includes a mechanism for promoting or demoting wines during an intended revision every decade, making it potentially one of the best systems of its kind. The classification has two categories: Premier Grand Cru Classé, divided into Groups A and B, and Grand Cru Classé. At present, despite changes in the 1996 revision, notably the promotion of Angélus and restoration of Beau-Séjour Bécot to Premiers Grands Crus Classés, there are still a number of tiny properties in the Grand Cru Classé section which would hardly achieve Cru Bourgeois in the Médoc.

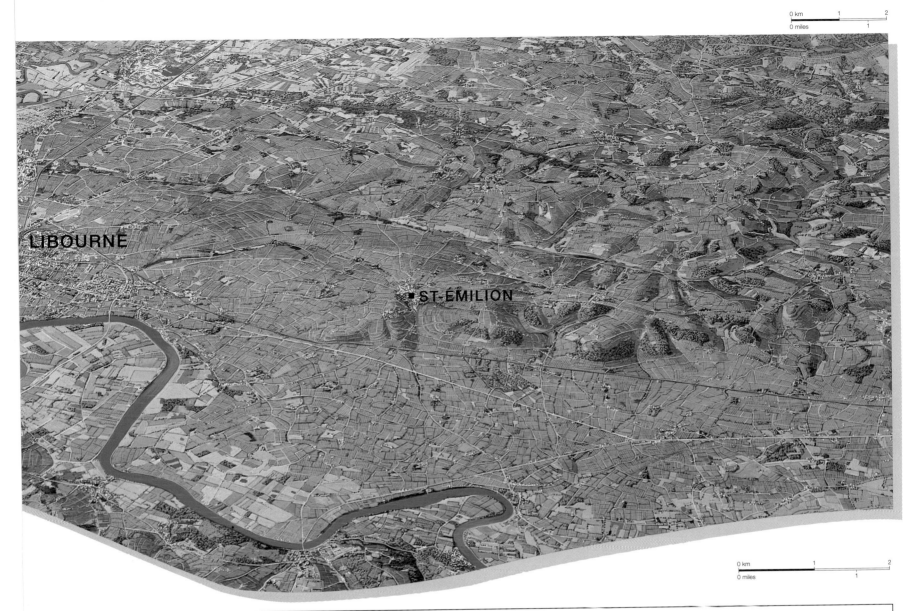

WHERE THE VINEYARDS ARE

The Libournais covers the area north of the Dordogne river. Libourne became important as the shipping port for all the wines produced on the banks of the Dordogne and is still the base for the main companies shipping St-Émilion, Pomerol and Fronsac. The slopes and hills to the west of Libourne are those of Fronsac and Canon-Fronsac. This attractive region was an obvious place for the Libourne business community to build its estates and, until the 19th century, Fronsac wines were seen as leading lights in the area. The area east of the town is now more important. Pomerol and St-Émilion also produce wines of much higher quality. From the air Pomerol appears as a uniform carpet of vines. But below the surface is an array of soil types giving different characteristics to its wines, and excellent quality overall. South of St-Émilion, a cleft in the plateau creates the south and east-facing slopes of the côtes area of St-Émilion, home of many of St-Émilion's finest wines.

AC WINE AREAS AND SELECTED CHÂTEAUX

1. Ch. Fontenil
2. Ch. Grand Renouil
3. Ch. Latour-à-Pomerol
4. Ch. Trotanoy
5. Ch. le Pin
6. Ch. l'Eglise-Clinet
7. Ch. Petit-Village
8. Vieux-Château-Certan
9. Ch. Lafleur
10. Ch. la Fleur-Pétrus
11. Ch. la Conseillante
12. Ch. Pétrus
13. Ch. l'Évangile
14. Ch. Gazin
15. Ch. Cheval Blanc
16. Ch. Figeac
17. Ch. Angélus
18. Ch. Beau-Séjour Bécot
19. Ch. Magdelaine
20. Ch. Canon
21. Ch. Belair
22. Ch. Canon-la-Gaffelière
23. Ch. Ausone
24. Ch. Valandraud
25. Ch. Pavie
26. Ch. Pavie-Macquin
27. Clos de l'Oratoire
28. Ch. Troplong-Mondot
29. La Mondotte
30. Ch. Tertre-Rôteboeuf
31. Ch. Monbousquet

POMEROL = AC WINE AREAS

━━ AC BOUNDARIES

BORDEAUX SWEET WINES

This is luscious golden wine at its most delectable. Château d'Yquem's perfectly sited vineyards flow downwards from one of the highest points in Sauternes.

WHITE GRAPES
Sémillon, the variety most prone to noble rot, is blended with much lesser amounts of Sauvignon Blanc, and sometimes a little Muscadelle.

CLIMATE
This is milder and wetter than Graves. The crucial factor for the growing of grapes for sweet wine is the combination of early morning autumnal mists rising off the Garonne and the Ciron rivers and plentiful sunshine later in the day – humidity and warmth being ideal conditions for promoting noble rot.

SOIL
The common theme here is clay with varying mixtures of gravel, sand and limestone. Both Sémillon and Sauvignon Blanc vines can do well in all these conditions.

ASPECT
The landscape ranges from moderately hilly around Sauternes, Bommes and Fargues to lower, more gentle slopes towards the river in Barsac and Preignac.

IT'S A FRUIT FARMER'S nightmare. Here I am, desperately trying to ripen my grapes in the supposedly warm days of an early autumn in the southerly reaches of the Bordeaux area – and every morning this great cloud of mist rises off the surface of the local river and creeps up the slopes of my vineyard. How can my grapes ripen in the morning sun when they're shrouded in chilly mist? How can I keep them free of disease when they're blanketed with damp fog every morning? Well, at least by the end of the morning the sun has blazed its way through the mist and burnt it all away. Heat now courses through my vineyards – but it's hardly an improvement because the hotter the day becomes, the more the humidity left over from the fog makes the air as clammy as a Turkish bath. Trying to avoid rot breaking out all over the vines is a virtual impossibility.

Which, in this case, is the whole point of the exercise. I'm talking about the vineyards of Sauternes and Barsac here. They make some of the world's greatest sweet wines. And the only way they can get their grapes sufficiently full of sugar is to encourage them to rot on the vine. But this isn't any old kind of rot: it's a very particular version called noble rot, or *pourriture noble* – or botrytis if you like. And Sauternes and Barsac are two of the few places in the world where it is a natural occurrence.

If you look at the map, you'll see the little river Ciron sneaking past Sauternes and Bommes, then turning to the north-east as its valley widens out and fills with vines, until it hits the major river Garonne between Barsac and Preignac. The Ciron is a fairly short, ice-cold river that rises from deep springs in the nearby Landes. The Garonne is much warmer, especially by the end of the summer, and the collision of two water flows of very different temperatures creates the mist, particularly in early morning, which drifts back up the Ciron valley. However, this mist just by itself is no good. Why Barsac and Sauternes are so special is that by the time those mists become daily occurrences in autumn, the Sémillon and Sauvignon (and occasionally Muscadelle) grapes in the vineyards should be fully ripe, and turning plump and golden. If the grapes are unripe, noble rot won't develop, although the closely related black rot, sour rot and grey rot will – and simply destroy the grapes.

NOBLE ROT
Noble rot is different. Instead of devouring the skin and souring the flesh inside, the spores latch on to the skin and gradually weaken it as the grape moves from ripeness to overripeness. The skin becomes a translucent browny gold but the grape is still plump and handsome. Not for long. If the warm humid weather continues, the skin is so weakened by the noble rot that it begins to shrivel. The water content in the grape dramatically reduces while the sugar, glycerine and acidity content is concentrated by dehydration. A noble-rotted grape looks horrible – wizened, maybe coated with furry fungus. It feels horrible too. Pick one and it will dissolve into a slimy mess between your fingers, the skin so weakened it can hardly contain the flesh. But persevere. Put that nasty gooey pulp into your mouth, and instead of the sourness most rotten fruit displays this is intensely, memorably, syrupy sweet, sweeter than any grape left to ripen in the normal way.

That's the magic of noble rot. This sugar level may be twice the level achieved through natural ripening. When the thick golden juice ferments into wine, the yeasts cannot work at alcohol levels much higher than 14 to 15 degrees. But that grape may have been picked with potential alcohol levels of 20 to 25 degrees. As the yeasts slow down and become comatose in their own giddy creation of alcohol all that remaining sugar stays put in the wine as natural sweetness. Great sweet wines like port and liqueur Muscat are made by adding brandy to fermenting wine to stun the yeasts into inactivity, but infection by noble rot is the classic method to produce totally natural sugar levels high enough to create such superbly liquorous sweet wine. Without attack by noble rot, the great sweet wines of Sauternes and Barsac would not exist.

The trouble is, noble rot does not attack all the grapes on a bunch at the same time, and sometimes doesn't attack them at all, even in a particularly suitable mesoclimate like that of Sauternes and Barsac. There are three stages of noble rot. The first is the 'speckled grape' phase when the grape is fully ripe and begins to exhibit speckles on its golden skin. Then there is a 'full rotted stage' when the colour quickly changes to purple brown and the grape seems to collapse in on itself. You can make good sweet wine from grapes at this stage. But if you hang on a few days longer, and if the autumn weather stays sunny and warm, the grapes reach the third 'roasted' stage – shrivelled and covered in fungus. The sugar and acid concentrations and certain chemical changes in the juice at this stage are what give the dramatic flavour of great Sauternes.

The best producers are after these 'roasted' berries. The pickers go through the vines picking off 'roasted' berries, if necessary one by one. This is time-consuming and very expensive. They have to go through the vineyards again and again as the individual grapes rot. There may be as many as ten of these *tries* as they are called, and the

---

THE 1855 CLASSIFICATION OF SAUTERNES
This is the original list but brought up to date to take account of name changes and divisions of property. The châteaux are listed alphabetically, followed by their commune name within brackets.
- **Premier Cru Superieur (Superior First Growth)** d'Yquem (Sauternes).
- **Premiers Crus (First Growths)** Climens (Barsac); Clos Haut-Peyraguey (Bommes); Coutet (Barsac); Guiraud (Sauternes); Lafaurie-Peyraguey (Bommes); Rabaud-Promis (Bommes); de Rayne-Vigneau (Bommes); Rieussec (Fargues); Sigalas-Rabaud (Bommes); Suduiraut (Preignac); la Tour-Blanche (Bommes).
- **Deuxièmes Crus (Second Growths)** d'Arche (Sauternes); Broustet (Barsac); Caillou (Barsac); Doisy-Daëne (Barsac); Doisy-Dubroca (Barsac); Doisy-Védrines (Barsac); Filhot (Sauternes); Lamothe-Despujols (Sauternes); Lamothe-Guignard (Sauternes); de Malle (Preignac); de Myrat (Barsac); Nairac (Barsac); Romer-du-Hayot (Fargues); Suau (Barsac).

WHERE THE VINEYARDS ARE *The heart of sweet winemaking in France is the strip of land that runs along both sides of the river Ciron in the centre of the map. About 2335ha (5770 acres) of vineyards spread over five communes make Sauternes, and one of these, Barsac, to the north of the Ciron, can call its wine either Barsac or Sauternes. The mesoclimate that creates noble rot is more important than the soil, which alternates between gravel and sand and clay. Barsac is relatively flat, and relies upon its proximity to the Ciron and the Garonne for the noble rot conditions to develop. The wines are particularly fragrant, but are rarely as luscious as those of the other villages. Preignac, to the south, is also fairly flat, but its major property – Château Suduiraut – is on a small hillock right next to Sauternes' greatest property, Château d'Yquem.*

All the top properties in Bommes, Fargues and Sauternes itself are spread over little hillsides. They get the benefit of noble rot in the autumn and better conditions to produce ultra-ripe grapes. The result is wines of a more intense, luscious character. The map also shows the other areas of sweet wine production in Bordeaux: Cérons and across the Garonne in Cadillac, Loupiac and Ste-Croix-du-Mont.

whole process of picking can drag on for more than two months. At the end of it all, a property like Château d'Yquem will produce perhaps one glass of wine from each vine. A top red Bordeaux property gets nearer a bottle a vine. No wonder Yquem is one of the most expensive wines in the world. It deserves to be.

Sémillon is the most important sweet wine grape, since its thick skin is particularly suited to noble rot and its wine has a propensity towards lanolin and waxy fatness when it ages. Add the lusciousness of noble rotted residual sugar and the result is smooth, rich and exotic. Most vineyards also have perhaps 20 per cent Sauvignon Blanc because it rots too and imparts an acidity and crispness that gives an exciting lift to the unctuous Sémillon. Muscadelle is occasionally used to add a honeyed texture, but is mainly planted in vineyards further from the Ciron where rot develops less well, and some extra richness is much needed. Botrytis only develops regularly in Barsac and Sauternes. Cérons, north of Barsac, makes a mildly sweet wine, though without real lusciousness, and most producers here make dry wines to sell as AC Graves. Across the Garonne are three sweet wine areas within the larger Premières Côtes de Bordeaux AC – Cadillac, Loupiac and Ste-Croix-du-Mont. In good years the wines are excellent, but noble rot develops only patchily here, and sweetness is more likely to come from shrivelling by the sun – in less than top years the wines are mildly sweet at best.

SAUTERNES AND OTHER SWEET WHITE WINE REGIONS

TOTAL DISTANCE NORTH TO SOUTH 18KM (11 MILES)

VINEYARDS

N

0 km 1 2
0 miles 1

AC WINE AREAS AND SELECTED CHÂTEAUX

1. Ch. Nairac	8. Ch. Gilette	15. Ch. Lafaurie-Peyraguey	21. Ch. d'Arche
2. Ch. Caillou	9. Ch. Bastor-Lamontagne	16. Ch. Raymond-Lafon	22. Ch. Lamothe-Guignard
3. Ch. Coutet	10. Ch. de Malle	17. Ch. la Tour-Blanche	23. Ch. Guiraud
4. Ch. Dubroca	11. Ch. Rabaud-Promis	18. Ch. Clos Haut-Peyraguey	24. Ch. de Fargues
5. Ch. Climens	12. Ch. Suduiraut	19. Ch. d'Yquem	
6. Ch. Doisy-Daëne	13. Ch. Sigalas-Rabaud	20. Ch. Rieussec	
7. Ch. Doisy-Védrines	14. Ch. Rayne-Vigneau		

SAUTERNES = AC WINE AREAS

—— AC BOUNDARIES

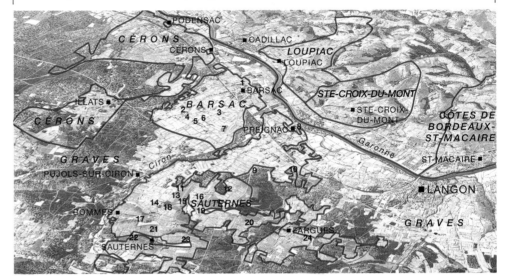

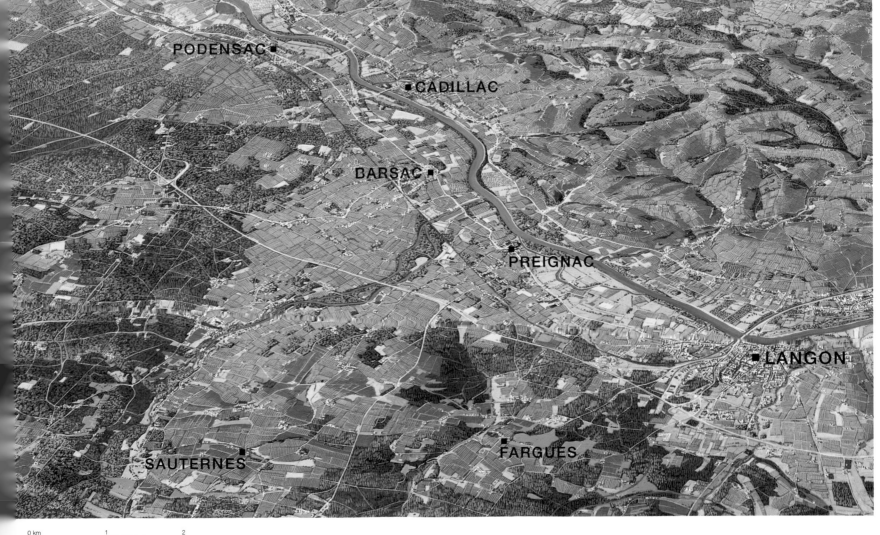

0 km 1 2
0 miles 1

REST OF BORDEAUX

SOME OF THE OUTLYING VINEYARD AREAS of Bordeaux were famous centuries ago, when the Médoc was just a marsh. And there are other areas, with little reputation so far, which could be shining stars within a generation, given a little luck and a good deal of effort and investment. The trouble is, when you lose a reputation, or when you fail to adapt to the changing tide of fashion, it's difficult to make up the lost ground. Stand on the high ground above the town of Blaye on the right bank of the Gironde estuary and you're standing among vineyards that were established by the Romans and highly regarded by the English when they were masters of Aquitaine. But Blaye wines are little regarded today. Take the ferry from Blaye across the Gironde to Lamarque, between the world-famous appellations of Margaux and St-Julien, and there you can stroll between the vines of the superstars of 20th-century Bordeaux, estates that didn't exist when the wines of Blaye were famous.

Entre-Deux-Mers: the landscape here is far more rustic and relaxed than that found in the ordered, tidy Haut-Médoc.

PREMIÈRES CÔTES DE BLAYE, CÔTES DE BLAYE

On the right bank of the Gironde Blaye is now rather a forlorn region. It is a pleasant enough place with its uplands facing the Gironde, mixing vineyards with forests, pasture and arable land, but it doesn't take an Einstein to realize that the vine plays a subsidiary role here to other agricultural pursuits. Out of about 60,000ha (148,258 acres) of agricultural land, only 9503ha (23,482 acres) are planted with vines. Of these, 87 per cent are red, and the Merlot grape dominates with 75 per cent. This makes sense.

Even if the Romans did like to sit on the quayside at Blaye watching the sun set in the west, they should have noticed that the wind got up rather too frequently and that it blew straight into their faces, rather cold and wet. Consequently many of the best vineyard sites are on fairly steep slopes, soaking up whatever sun there is and draining off the drizzle when necessary.

The Cabernet Sauvignon has a tough time ripening here but still represents 19 per cent of the red plantings. The clay and limestone soils *can* ripen Merlot, though without distinction, the reds having a rather listless, jammy quality. Most of them use the appellation Premières Côtes de Blaye rather than Blaye. A shining exception to the generally drab quality here is the imaginative, indeed inspired, estate of Haut-Bertinerie which uses 75 per cent Cabernet Sauvignon in its red – but then the owners have installed the revolutionary rapid-ripening 'Lyre' training system in their vineyards. Blaye needs more properties like Haut-Bertinerie.

Sauvignon Blanc is the dominant white grape at 42 per cent but rarely performs well without being beefed up with Colombard, which actively improves the perfume and acidity of the whites which are generally sold as Côtes de Blaye.

CÔTES DE BOURG

Bourg is a smaller area directly upstream of Blaye on the right bank of the Dordogne where it flows into the Gironde. The steep sandstone slopes and plateau with occasional patches of gravel are much more intensely cultivated with vines than the Blaye region just to the north, with 4354ha (10,759 acres) of red varieties and just 62ha (153 acres) of white. I often taste the rather brusque reds and think, well, yes, there is something there, a dark dry fruit, a hint of blackcurrant tumbled in rough earth that tells me – yes, Bourg reds could be splendid if the will and investment were there.

Recent tastings show wines with a bit more polish indicating investment in stainless steel tanks and new oak barrels, as well as reduction in yields. The good quality co-operative at Tauriac does its best and there are one or two star turns like Château Roc de Cambes showing the potential of the region.

BORDEAUX–CÔTES DE FRANCS

Côtes de Francs has got the star every small, unsung appellation needs. In fact it has three stars, and more could well follow. It's a tiny area tacked on to the eastern end of the St-Émilion satellite appellations. Indeed, growers used to sell their wines as St-Émilion. Although the region gained its own appellation in 1967, there were just a few vineyards and a fairly moribund co-operative to make use of it. No one knew why it deserved special attention.

Not quite true. George Thienpont, a relation of the owners of Vieux-Château-Certan, one of the greatest of all the Pomerol estates, could see why. He bought Château Puygueraud and Château Claverie. And the owners of Château Angélus, newly promoted St-Émilion Premier Grand Cru Classé, and the Hébrard family, formerly shareholders in Château Cheval Blanc, one of the greatest St-Émilions, could also see why. And so they bought the ancient Château de Francs.

The limestone and clay soil is good for growing vines. The mesoclimate is reckoned to be both the driest and the warmest in all Bordeaux, and the hillside slopes are all angled towards the sun, as well as being the highest in the Gironde *département*. These prescient families had the resources to invest in this unknown quantity regardless of Côtes de Francs' lack of reputation. Their wines are now showing wonderful fruit and character, and sometimes outshine many of the more famous St-Émilions just a mile or two to the west. The wines are almost all red, and Merlot is the dominant grape, but there are a few white vines as well.

CÔTES DE CASTILLON

Côtes de Castillon wines are all red, and many people say they are as good as those of the Côtes de Francs, but I'm yet to be convinced. Some of the vineyards are on flatter, clay-rich soil near the river Dordogne and, despite their good coarse fruit, the wines rarely lose that clay-clod quality. It's amazing how a certain earthiness relentlessly hounds the fruit in wines from those Bordeaux vineyards that are dominated by clay, with the exception of the rare, great sites of Pomerol and St-Émilion. Even so, the Merlot is the grape you have to have for clay here, and over two-thirds of the plantings are Merlot, with the easy-ripening Cabernet Franc making up the bulk of the rest.

When you move away from the Dordogne, northwards, you are quickly into a world of quite steep slopes, often woodland, sometimes pasture, but just as likely to be covered with a sweep of vines. There's more limestone in the clays here, and there's a fairly good limestone subsoil too. Merlot and Cabernet Franc enjoy that, and the increase in quality as you move up into the woods is easy to see. It's no coincidence that the best Castillon wines are found here and that a number of high-profile St-Émilion producers like Stephan Von Neipperg of Canon-la-Gaffelière have recently bought properties in this location. With this sort of investment and winemaking prowess there is a change in the air in Castillon. Maybe I shall have to eat my words yet!

ENTRE-DEUX-MERS

Cross over the Dordogne at the little town of Castillon-la-Bataille, remembering just for a brief moment that it was here that the English finally lost control of Aquitaine to the French in 1453, and we're in what is Bordeaux's most charming rural area – the Entre-Deux-Mers. The name means 'between two seas' and refers to the two rivers – the Dordogne and the Garonne – that make an 80-km (50-mile) long wedge from the borders of the Gironde *département* as they head north-west, getting closer and closer together until they finally join and together become the Gironde estuary just north of the city of Bordeaux. This is a landscape of charming little villages, friendly *prix-fixe* family restaurants full of good humour and rough-and-ready food. The roads dip and twist through forest, pasture and orchard, streams with nowhere much to go glint in the sun and tease and taunt you to bring your *charcuterie* and flagon of wine to the water's edge and dally the day away.

And there's lots of wine to choose from. The Entre-Deux-Mers is the great well from which most simple red and white Bordeaux is drawn. Most of it is sold under the Bordeaux or Bordeaux Supérieur title, and the most important producers are the co-operative cellars spread through the region. Some of the white wine uses the Entre-Deux-Mers appellation, and there are other small, unexceptional appellations adjoining the Entre-Deux-Mers.

Graves de Vayres in the north-west, which faces Fronsac across the Dordogne is, as its name implies, a gravelly outcrop in a zone where gravel is pretty rare. With 685ha (1693 acres) of red vines and 143ha (353 acres) of white you'd expect something a bit out of the ordinary, but in fact most of the wine is simply pleasant AC Bordeaux. Ste-Foy-Bordeaux has 847ha (2093 acres) of red and white vines in the north-east, while St-Macaire and Haut-Benauge are minor zones primarily for white wines in the south of Entre-Deux-Mers. Most growers in these appellations are quite happy to declare their wine as simple AC Bordeaux.

PREMIÈRES CÔTES DE BORDEAUX

To the south-west of the Entre-Deux-Mers, bordering the Garonne, there is a recognizable and definable leap in quality. Here in the Premières Côtes de Bordeaux appellation, which stretches in a long, narrow strip from the city of Bordeaux in the north to Langon in the south, the land rises to a majestic limestone escarpment high above the Garonne. The plateau and the flowing slopes are thick with vines, and the views across the river to the Graves and Sauternes appellations are some of the most magical in all Bordeaux.

This is an area beginning to rediscover its glorious past. Along with the Graves, these vineyards provided much of the wine that first made Bordeaux famous in the Middle Ages. Although thought of recently as an appellation making semi-sweet wines, all the action is in red and dry white (though as yet the white can only use the simple Bordeaux appellation). It may be because the views are heavenly or it may be that the vineyard sites are excellent, but there is now a lot of investment here, in modern winemaking equipment and imaginative winemaking. The reds are marked by a character that is unusually juicy and 'come-hither' for Bordeaux, while the dry whites have an extra intensity increasingly emphasized by oak-barrel maturation.

It's not inconceivable that the steeply sloping vineyards around the villages of Cadillac, Loupiac and Ste-Croix-du-Mont (all enclaves in the Premières Côtes – see also map on page 49), whose appellations are for sweet wines, will gradually convert to red or dry white wine production. It depends so much on fashion. A few good Sauternes vintages, a bit of razzmatazz for dessert wines, and the growers can make a living. When sweet wines go out of vogue they can make a better living out of dry whites, or reds.

Some of Bordeaux's top winemakers are now producing splendidly fresh, fruity wines in Entre-Deux-Mers.

Château de Barbe in the Côtes de Bourg is, at 64ha (158 acres), one of the region's largest, and finest, properties. Beyond lie the waters of the Gironde and the vineyards of Margaux.

BURGUNDY

BURGUNDY. I LUXURIATE IN THAT NAME. I feel it roll around my mouth and my mind like an exotic mixed metaphor of glittering crusted jewels, ermine capes, the thunder of trumpets and the perfumed velvet sensuality of rich red wine. And it has been all those things, because Burgundy is not just the name of a wine.

In the 14th and 15th centuries, Burgundy was a Grand Duchy, almost a kingdom, spreading up eastern France, encompassing Belgium, to the shores of the North Sea. Its power and wealth rivalled that of the throne of France itself. Burgundy was the pomp and circumstance of jewels and ermine and trumpet voluntaries, as well as the flowering of arts and architecture and the subtle but pervasive influence of some of France's greatest monastic establishments.

These may have faded, but one part of Burgundy's glorious history remains: its remarkable ability to provide the soul and the stomach with the sustenance of great food and great wine. Look at the map opposite, at the town of Mâcon, right in the centre. To the east of Mâcon lie the rich farmlands of the Saône valley packed with vegetables and fruit, but most famous for the chickens of Bresse. To the west of Mâcon as the hills of the Morvan rise up towards the central plateau of France, the small town of Charolles has given its name to the local Charollais cattle that provide France's finest beef.

And between these two extremes of mountain and plain, as the ridges slope down towards the flat valley floor, vineyards, providing every sort of wine for the feast, from the gurgling reds of Beaujolais in the south to the intense, beetle-browed giants of the Côte de Nuits reds in the north, from the round, supple Chardonnays of the southern Mâconnais to the steely-eyed austerity of Chablis in the far north. The Mâconnais and the Chalonnais also provide excellent fizz. Only sweet wines are lacking, though the sweet blackcurrant liqueur Crème de Cassis of Nuits-St-Georges goes some way towards redeeming this.

GRAPE VARIETIES

Pinot Noir has had more exasperated expletives hurled at it than just about all other great grapes put together. It is a tantalizingly difficult grape to grow successfully, its juice is tantalizingly difficult to ferment into wine, then mature to just the right age, but, ah, when it works, there's no grape like it.

The Côte d'Or is its heartland, although some is grown in the Yonne, and a fair amount in the Mâconnais and Chalonnais. It's a very ancient vine, and prone to mutation. It buds early and ripens early, but is an erratic yielder and is prone to rot. If this all sounds as if it's more trouble than it's worth, well you'd be right – were it not capable of the most astonishing marriage of scent and succulence, savagery and charm when grown by an expert in one of Burgundy's best sites.

Of the other red varieties, Gamay makes deliciously juicy wines in Beaujolais, less good ones in the Mâconnais, and is a marginal producer in the Côte d'Or. César and Tressot are two old Yonne varieties, the latter now virtually extinct.

Chardonnay is grown with such success around the world that it is easy to forget that Burgundy is where it made its reputation. It can, in the right circumstances, still produce its greatest wine here, particularly on the limestone slopes of the Côte de Beaune. However, it performs reliably well all over Burgundy. It buds early, making it prone to frost in Chablis, but it ripens early too and is a consistent yielder of generally ripe grapes. This allows it to produce lean but balanced wines in Chablis, marvellously full yet savoury and refreshing wines in the Côte d'Or, chalkier yet attractive wines in the Côte Chalonnaise and plumper, milder wines in the

The Grands Crus are the best-sited vineyards in the Chablis appellation, and produce the ripest wines.

Mâconnais. Of the other white grapes, Aligoté is quite widely grown, especially in the northern Côte Chalonnaise, and produces a sharp lemony wine, sometimes with a soft smell of buttermilk. Pinot Blanc and Pinot Gris are occasionally found.

THE YONNE REGION

The Chablis or Yonne region is, in fact, about 160km (100 miles) north of Beaune and it used to be at the centre of a vast vineyard area supplying Paris with basic *vin ordinaire*. The Yonne was one of several regions east of Paris which churned out oceans of what must have been very thin, mean reds and whites to slake the capital's thirst. None of the areas was very suitable for viticulture, and when the railways came and made possible the transport of enormous amounts of cheap wine from the Mediterranean coast, demand for these raw northern brews disappeared.

Only the very best survived, and the most famous is Chablis, centred round the little town of the same name and a few surrounding villages, where suitable mesoclimates and limestone and clay soil allow the Chardonnay grape to creep to ripeness and create highly individual wine. Elsewhere in the Yonne, mainly south-east of Auxerre, several varieties, mostly red Pinot Noir and white Chardonnay and Aligoté, are increasingly grown, but are only accorded the Bourgogne AC, the best of them like Irancy and Epineuil also using their village name on the label. Many of their grapes now go to make very good Crémant de Bourgogne fizz. The village of St-Bris now has an appellation for its Sauvignon Blanc.

CÔTE D'OR

Dijon, right at the top of the map, is at the northern end of the world-famous Côte d'Or, divided into the Côte de Nuits and Côte de Beaune, and from here, right the way south to Lyon, there is an almost unbroken vista of vines, comprising the Burgundy region. However, because we are fairly far north here, the southern warmth only begins to dominate around Mâcon, so mesoclimates of vineyards facing towards whatever sun there is are crucial for ripening grapes.

WHERE THE VINEYARDS ARE *The Burgundy region relies crucially upon the slopes of the mountains in the west to provide suitable vineyard land. The Saône Valley to the east is rich, fertile agricultural land and as such is not fit for fine wine production. You can see vineyards down by the river Saône, but they produce regional Bourgogne AC at best, and more generally vin de pays. The mountains rising to the west are the beginnings of the Massif Central that runs like a broad backbone down the centre of France. These hills and dales are generally too high and too exposed to westerly winds and rain to be warm enough to ripen grapes.*

The ridge below which the slopes drop away to the plain provides ideal protection from wind and angles the land towards the south and east to gain maximum warmth from the sun. Between Dijon and Chagny in the north lies the narrow but high quality sliver of vineyards known as the Côte d'Or and divided into the Côte de Nuits in the north and Côte de Beaune in the south. Burgundy's greatest reds and whites are produced here in these world-famous wine villages.

West of Chalon-sur-Saône the local climates become less protected and the Côte Chalonnaise reflects this with vineyards appearing only sporadically in the best sites. However passing Tournus to Mâcon, Villefranche and Lyon the warmer south allows the vineyards to spread away from the protective hills, though the finest Mâconnais whites and Beaujolais reds still come from the steep slopes to the west of the vineyards between Mâcon and Villefranche.

The inset map shows the Yonne region, a northern outpost of Burgundy, whose best known wine is Chablis.

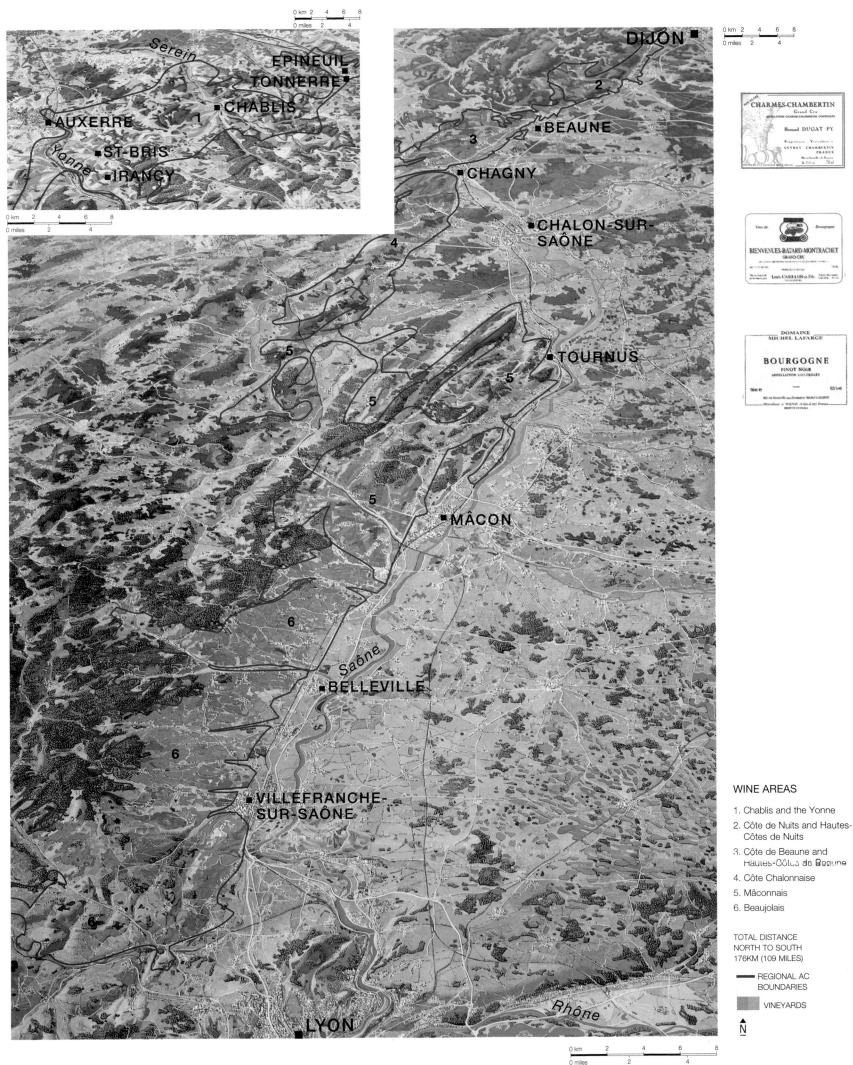

Serein

EPINEUIL
TONNERRE
CHABLIS

AUXERRE

ST-BRIS

Yonne

IRANCY

DIJON

2

BEAUNE

3

CHAGNY

CHALON-SUR-
SAÔNE

4

5

TOURNUS

5

5

5

MÂCON

6

Saône

BELLEVILLE

6

VILLEFRANCHE-
SUR-SAÔNE

Rhône

LYON

N

CHARMES-CHAMBERTIN
Grand Cru
Bernard DUGAT-PY

BIENVENUES-BATARD-MONTRACHET
GRAND CRU
Louis CARILLON et Fils

DOMAINE
MICHEL LAFARGE
BOURGOGNE
PINOT NOIR
APPELLATION CONTROLEE

WINE AREAS

1. Chablis and the Yonne
2. Côte de Nuits and Hautes-
Côtes de Nuits
3. Côte de Beaune and
Hautes-Côtes de Beaune
4. Côte Chalonnaise
5. Mâconnais
6. Beaujolais

TOTAL DISTANCE
NORTH TO SOUTH
176KM (109 MILES)

REGIONAL AC
BOUNDARIES

VINEYARDS

CÔTE DE NUITS

 RED GRAPES
Pinot Noir is the only grape allowed in non-generic wines.

WHITE GRAPES
Among the few Côte de Nuits whites Chardonnay is the main grape, though some of the best examples use Pinot Blanc.

CLIMATE
This is sunnier in the growing season than Bordeaux but the autumns are cool and the winters long and cold. Spring frosts and hail can cause problems. The Hautes-Côtes are less protected from the prevailing westerly winds and can get heavy rain.

SOIL
The Côte d'Or is basically a limestone ridge where weathering has produced a stony scree-like limestone and clay topsoil, especially on middle slopes, which provides the best drainage for the vines.

ASPECT
The top vineyards are situated on the middle slopes at 250–300m (820–984ft) where the steeper gradients, as well as the soil structure, facilitate drainage. The south- or south-east-facing aspect of the best sites also enhances exposure to the sun and therefore ripening in these northern vineyards.

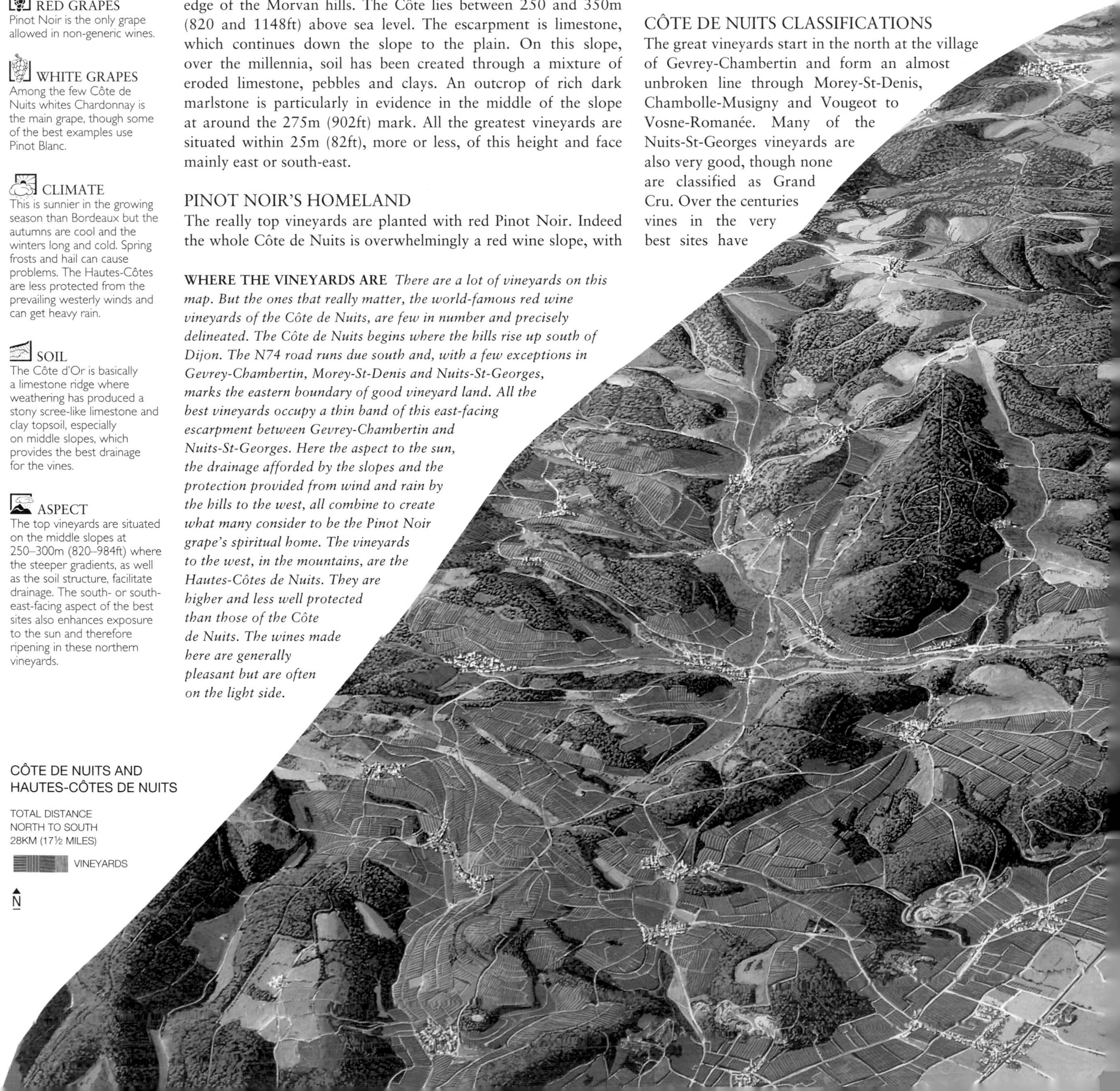

CÔTE DE NUITS AND HAUTES-CÔTES DE NUITS

TOTAL DISTANCE NORTH TO SOUTH 28KM (17½ MILES)

 VINEYARDS

N

MY FAVOURITE PLACE in the Côte de Nuits, one of the world's greatest vineyard regions, isn't the most famous. It's in the village of Prémeaux, just to the south of the town of Nuits St-Georges. Here you can step off the N74 road into the vines right below the marvellous Clos Arlot vineyard. At this point, the Côte de Nuits is little more than 90m (295ft) across, one side to the other. Admittedly this is the narrowest part, but the point is that the Côte de Nuits, which includes many of the most famous red wine names in the world, is a mere sliver of land snaking its way in and out of an east-facing escarpment that marks the eastern edge of the Morvan hills. The Côte lies between 250 and 350m (820 and 1148ft) above sea level. The escarpment is limestone, which continues down the slope to the plain. On this slope, over the millennia, soil has been created through a mixture of eroded limestone, pebbles and clays. An outcrop of rich dark marlstone is particularly in evidence in the middle of the slope at around the 275m (902ft) mark. All the greatest vineyards are situated within 25m (82ft), more or less, of this height and face mainly east or south-east.

PINOT NOIR'S HOMELAND
The really top vineyards are planted with red Pinot Noir. Indeed the whole Côte de Nuits is overwhelmingly a red wine slope, with

WHERE THE VINEYARDS ARE *There are a lot of vineyards on this map. But the ones that really matter, the world-famous red wine vineyards of the Côte de Nuits, are few in number and precisely delineated. The Côte de Nuits begins where the hills rise up south of Dijon. The N74 road runs due south and, with a few exceptions in Gevrey-Chambertin, Morey-St-Denis and Nuits-St-Georges, marks the eastern boundary of good vineyard land. All the best vineyards occupy a thin band of this east-facing escarpment between Gevrey-Chambertin and Nuits-St-Georges. Here the aspect to the sun, the drainage afforded by the slopes and the protection provided from wind and rain by the hills to the west, all combine to create what many consider to be the Pinot Noir grape's spiritual home. The vineyards to the west, in the mountains, are the Hautes-Côtes de Nuits. They are higher and less well protected than those of the Côte de Nuits. The wines made here are generally pleasant but are often on the light side.*

just a little rosé being made at Marsannay in the north, and a few bottles of rare white being made at Morey-St-Denis, Nuits-St-Georges, Vougeot and, most famously, Musigny at Chambolle-Musigny. Otherwise Pinot Noir rules. White grapes prefer impoverished, easy-draining limestone soils, and in the Côte de Beaune to the south there are various instances of limestone dominating the slopes. But here in the Côte de Nuits, limestone merely seems to temper the rich marl soil and reduce its fertility. Over-fertile soil never produces great wine, but this mixture seems just right.

CÔTE DE NUITS CLASSIFICATIONS
The great vineyards start in the north at the village of Gevrey-Chambertin and form an almost unbroken line through Morey-St-Denis, Chambolle-Musigny and Vougeot to Vosne-Romanée. Many of the Nuits-St-Georges vineyards are also very good, though none are classified as Grand Cru. Over the centuries vines in the very best sites have

consistently ripened earlier than those too high up the slope or on flatter ground at the bottom. So a minutely accurate system of vineyard classification has evolved. The Grands Crus are so carefully and jealously delineated that every single row of vines is separately assessed. The same goes for the second rank of vineyards, the Premiers Crus.

There are numerous instances of certain rows of vines being excluded from the higher appellation and condemned to the third tier – the village appellation. Even so, the village AC is still only applied to decent land, which almost always lies between the N74 and the escarpment to the west. Some vineyards, in the north at Brochon and Fixin, and in the south between Prémeaux-Prissey and Corgoloin, use the collective appellation Côte de Nuits-Villages. Less suitable land, such as the flatter vineyards to the east of the N74 (better suited to cattle and vegetables), is relegated to regional or generic appellations – Aligoté, Bourgogne, Bourgogne Passe-Tout-Grains and Bourgogne Grand Ordinaire – a good deal more Ordinary than Grand.

But the good Côte de Nuits Burgundies are very grand indeed. Red wines from a cool area like Burgundy should be delicate, not monumental, but that relatively rich soil, sloped east and south-east, can, when the summer is warm and the grape grower careful to limit his yield, produce wines of disturbing, heady brilliance. These can often be dark and brooding when young, especially those from Gevrey-Chambertin, but may break out into glorious exotic scents as they age, in particular at Vosne-Romanée and Chambolle-Musigny, finally maturing into a state of delectable decay, when all the savagery, sweetness and scent melds into a dark, ripe autumn richness of quite astonishing beauty. From the

Some of Burgundy's top vineyards are surrounded by a wall, or clos in French. Clos St-Jacques, above, is perhaps Gevrey-Chambertin's best Premier Cru.

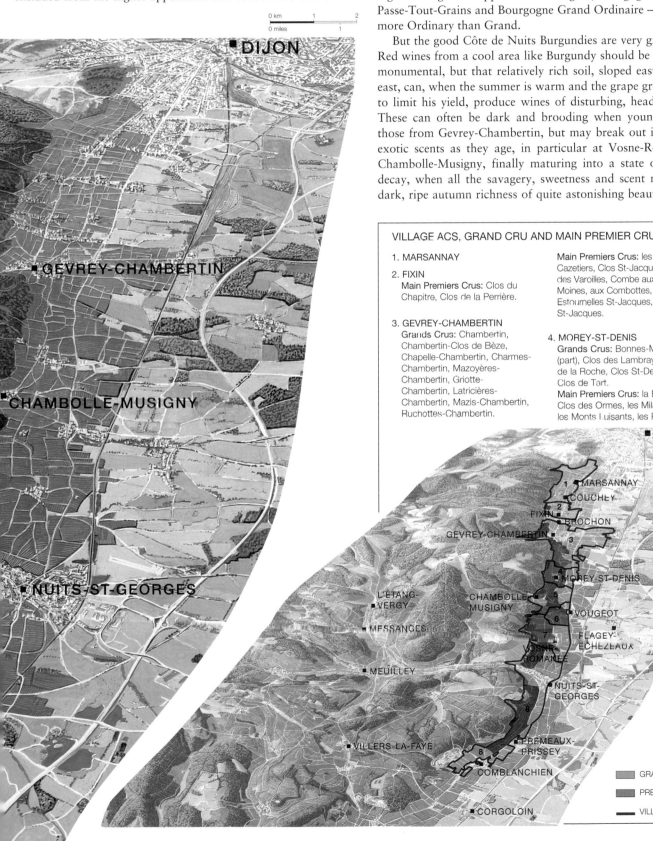

VILLAGE ACS, GRAND CRU AND MAIN PREMIER CRU VINEYARDS

1. **MARSANNAY**

2. **FIXIN**
   Main Premiers Crus: Clos du Chapitre, Clos de la Perrière.

3. **GEVREY-CHAMBERTIN**
   Grands Crus: Chambertin, Chambertin-Clos de Bèze, Chapelle-Chambertin, Charmes-Chambertin, Mazoyères-Chambertin, Griotte-Chambertin, Latricières-Chambertin, Mazis-Chambertin, Ruchottes-Chambertin.

   Main Premiers Crus: les Cazetiers, Clos St-Jacques, Clos des Varoilles, Combe aux Moines, aux Combottes, Estournelles St-Jacques, Lavaut St-Jacques.

4. **MOREY-ST-DENIS**
   Grands Crus: Bonnes-Mares (part), Clos des Lambrays, Clos de la Roche, Clos St-Denis, Clos de Tart.
   Main Premiers Crus: la Bussière, Clos des Ormes, les Milandes, les Monts Luisants, les Ruchots.

5. **CHAMBOLLE MUSIGNY**
   Grands Crus: Bonnes-Mares (part), Musigny.
   Main Premiers Crus: les Amoureuses, les Baudes, les Charmes, les Cras, les Fuées, les Sentiers.

6. **VOUGEOT**
   Grand Cru: Clos de Vougeot.

7. **VOSNE-ROMANÉE**
   Grands Crus: Grande-Rue, Richebourg, la Romanée, la Romanée-Conti, Romanée-St-Vivant, la Tâche, and (in the commune of Flagey-Échézeaux) Échézeaux, Grands-Échézeaux.
   Main Premiers Crus: les Beaux Monts, aux Brûlées, les Chaumes, Clos des Réas, Cros Parantoux, aux Malconsorts, les Suchots.

8. **NUITS-ST-GEORGES**
   Main Premiers Crus: aux Boudots, aux Bousselots, les Cailles, aux Chaignots, Clos des Argillières, Clos Arlot, Clos des Corvées, Clos des Forêts-St-Georges, Clos de la Maréchale, Clos des Porrets-St-Georges, les Damodes, aux Murgers, aux Perdrix, les Porrets-St-Georges, les Pruliers, la Richemone, Roncière, les St-Georges, aux Thorey, les Vaucrains, aux Vignes Rondes.

GRAND CRU VINEYARDS

PREMIER CRU VINEYARDS

VILLAGE AC BOUNDARIES

Looking eastwards from the vineyards of Nuits-St-Georges over the town. The autumnal gold of the vine leaves complements the glistening tiles on the church spire.

best growers, the nuances of flavour detectable in wines from vines only yards apart offer a marriage between the hedonistic and the intellectual that hardly any other wines ever manage. From a bad grower or merchant, there are few bigger, nor more expensive, disappointments than a thin, lifeless wine masquerading under these great names.

VILLAGES OF THE CÔTE DE NUITS

If you look at the top of the map on pages 58-59, you can hardly spot a vine. There used to be loads of vineyards to Dijon's south-west, but the city's suburban sprawl has swallowed them up. In any case, they were mostly planted with Gamay to make cheap quaffing wine for Dijon, not classy Burgundy. Chenôve still has a few vines on the slope just north of Marsannay, but Marsannay is the first serious village. It used to be famous for rosé, but is now an increasingly useful supplier of good, perfumed, though lightweight reds and some pleasant whites. The slopes at Couchey, Fixin and Brochon might look pretty suitable for vines: they grow Pinot Noir, but little of great excitement ever comes to light. Fixin's heavy clay soils can give good sturdy reds in a hot year.

The real fireworks start at Gevrey-Chambertin. Here the rich marl soil comes properly into play, with red clays peppered with stones, and outbreaks of rich subsoil through a thin layer of topsoil on the higher sites. The narrow east- and south-east-facing slope under its protective forest brow continues almost unbroken between Gevrey-Chambertin and Nuits-St-Georges. Here the Pinot Noir really shows what it can do.

Those village names, by the way. Over the centuries, the best Côte d'Or villages found that they had one vineyard above all whose wines people sought. The village of Gevrey had Chambertin,

the village of Chambolle had Musigny, and so on. So, to grab a little reflected glory from their greatest vineyard – and a little more profit from allying their less exciting wine with that of the star performer – wine producers hyphenated the vineyard name to that of the village for their wines.

So. Back to Gevrey-Chambertin. This village distinguishes itself with nine Grands Crus – the most of any Côte d'Or commune – safely protected from the wet westerlies by the Montagne de la Combe Grizard. The lesser vineyards spread down to and, unusually, across the N74, where a pebbly subsoil is supposed to provide enough drainage. Maybe. The potential for riches at every level in Gevrey is high but the variation among producers is dramatic. It's a problem of popularity. Chambertin, which can be so sensuously savage at its best, is one of France's most famous reds. Wines with Chambertin in their title are not difficult to sell.

Morey-St-Denis is a good deal less famous, but the vineyards are just as good. There are five Grands Crus, on slightly steeper slopes with a little more limestone in evidence and, indeed, one steep, infertile site – Monts Luisants – that is famous for a beefy white. The reds, led by Clos de la Roche, have a sweet, ripe, fruity depth and a chocolaty softness.

Chambolle-Musigny is set into a little gully in the hillside, so there is a brief loss of protection for the vines and the Grand Cru, Bonnes-Mares, ends abruptly north of the village. The other Grand Cru, Musigny, doesn't commence till the south-east-facing slope begins again near Vougeot. At its best, Chambolle-Musigny can be hauntingly perfumed.

The chief wine of Vougeot is the 50-ha (124-acre) walled Grand Cru, Clos de Vougeot. This runs right down to the N74, on to considerably lower and more alluvial soil than any other Grand Cru. Add to this 80 different proprietors all eager to exploit the famous name, and you have a recipe for some decidedly rum bottles of Clos de Vougeot. At its best, though, it is fleshy and rich.

Directly above the fine, higher vines of Vougeot are those of Grands Crus, Échézeaux and Grands-Échézeaux. Their parent village, Flagey, is in fact down in the plain, and they are considered to be part of Vosne-Romanée. Lucky them, because the other six Vosne Grands Crus, especially La Tâche and La Romanée-Conti, are the most famous and expensive of all Burgundies. Intoxicating in their spice and heady scent, thrilling in their depth of dark fruit, they really do lead the way. The red clays spattered with pebbles undoubtedly put the other Vosne Grands Crus and Premiers Crus on a special level.

Nuits-St-Georges might seem hard done by to be Vosne's neighbour – it has no Grands Crus at all. Instead it has 38 Premiers Crus. In the valley to the west the protective curtain is broken, and many of the vineyards are on flat alluvial soil. But south of Nuits down to Prémeaux, the slopes steepen, narrow, and veer back towards the south-east. Here great wines are made, Grands Crus in all but name.

THE HAUTES-CÔTES DE NUITS

Up in the hills behind the Côte de Nuits slopes, planted in carefully selected sites, are the vines of the Hautes-Côtes de Nuits appellation. In warm years, the Hautes-Côtes de Nuits vineyards with the best aspect and drainage can make light, pleasant, mostly red, wine from Pinot Noir. But the word 'Hautes' or 'high' is important. We're far north here for a major red wine area. Red grapes usually need more heat to ripen than white – and the higher you get above sea level, the cooler the sun's rays become and the more exposed you are to wind and rain. That makes for thin wine most years.

CÔTE DE BEAUNE

I'M NOT A GREAT RESPECTER of traditions and reputations just for the sake of them. In the world of wine, I often think that there are more ill-deserved reputations and baseless traditions than the other way round. But I have to say, the first time I trekked up the narrow lane from the main road (the N6) at the village of Chassagne-Montrachet, patted the crumbling stone wall on the left rather gingerly with my hand, and then sneaked into the vineyard of le Montrachet, my heart was thumping with excitement.

Le Montrachet is quite possibly the greatest white wine vineyard in the world. But why? I tasted the grapes from its vines, then crossed the lane to taste the grapes of Bâtard-Montrachet – another of the great Grand Cru vineyards – only 9m (30ft) lower down. They were different. Le Montrachet's grapes seemed to have more intensity, more vibrant personality before they'd even been picked off the vine. I clambered over the wall above le Montrachet to the adjacent Chevalier-Montrachet vineyard. It's a matter of a couple of yards, but the stony soil of Chevalier gives more austere grapes, which in turn gives leaner, haughtier, yet still superlative wine.

Since then, on other occasions I've scratched away at the soil of le Montrachet, and know that it is stonier and less rich than that of its neighbours, except for the ultra-stony Chevalier-Montrachet. I've noticed how the slope is just that little bit steeper as it gently changes angle from an easterly to a south-easterly aspect. I've felt my face warmed by early morning sun, in the midst of its vines. I've sweltered under blazing midday sun; and in high summer, late into the evening, as the surrounding vineyards are cooling in the shade, I've felt the sun's rays still streaking towards me across le Montrachet's tiny clump of vines, as it sinks into a dip in the hills.

Mesoclimate. The perfect conjunction of soil, angle of slope, and aspect to the sun, providing just that bit more chance for these northern grapes to ripen to perfection. In every commune on the Côte d'Or the endlessly changing geological and climatic conditions create little plots of vineyard, some only a few hectares broad, that give wines of more power, personality or finesse than those of their neighbours. This is what makes the Côte d'Or so fascinating, yet so exhausting a region to get to know.

Whereas the most famous wines of the Côte de Nuits, directly to the north of the Côte de Beaune, are all red, most of the world-renowned wines of the Côte de Beaune are white. And that's down to those mesoclimates again. In fact, 75 per cent of the Côte de Beaune wines are red. The fertile, red-tinged soils and, periodically, the marl that is such a feature of the Côte de Nuits, occupy the majority of the slopes, and in these cases Pinot Noir predominates. But the slopes here are less extreme, and the red Côte de Beaune wines, even from the one red Grand Cru vineyard of Corton, right next to the Côte de Nuits, have a rounder charm and less savage power than those of the Côte de Nuits itself. Wines from Aloxe-Corton, Beaune, Volnay and, in a rougher way, Pommard, are all marked by perfume rather than by power.

The whites at their best, however – from Chardonnay grapes planted where limestone dominates the darker clays – are marked by virtually every characteristic you could ask of a dry white wine. I say dry, because there is no sugar left in wines like Corton-Charlemagne, Meursault, Puligny-Montrachet, Chassagne-Montrachet, or the host of others that the different villages make. Yet the honey and butter lusciousness, the cream, the wafted scent of grilled nuts still warm from the fire, the cinnamon and nutmeg spice that ripples through the orchard fruits – all these flavours, plus the taut backbone of mineral, of herb, of smoke from a forest glade, are there. I can remember bottles like these drunk twenty years ago as clearly as if my glass were being refilled in front of me this very minute.

What is equally exciting is that, if you seek out good producers, you really can taste the difference in wines which come from neighbouring patches of vines. The Burgundian system of delineating each vineyard plot with distinctive characteristics is the most comprehensive in the world. Meursault-Perrières does have stonier soil than its neighbour Meursault-Charmes; the wine is tauter, it promises more, and will perhaps give more sublime satisfaction in time. That's how it should be. And fairly frequently, that's how it is.

RED GRAPES
Pinot Noir is the only permitted grape in non-generic wines.

WHITE GRAPES
Chardonnay is the official grape, though there may still be some Pinot Blanc and Pinot Gris.

CLIMATE
The slopes are gentler here, providing less shelter from the westerly winds, so rainfall is higher than further north and heavy rain can be a problem. The temperatures are marginally milder than in the Côte de Nuits.

SOIL
The soil structure is basically similar to the Côte de Nuits, but with limestone outcrops more in evidence and these are often where the best vineyards, such as le Montrachet, are sited.

ASPECT
These are some lower slopes and more gentle gradients than in the Côte de Nuits but the south- to south-east-facing aspect of many vineyards is even more critical here.

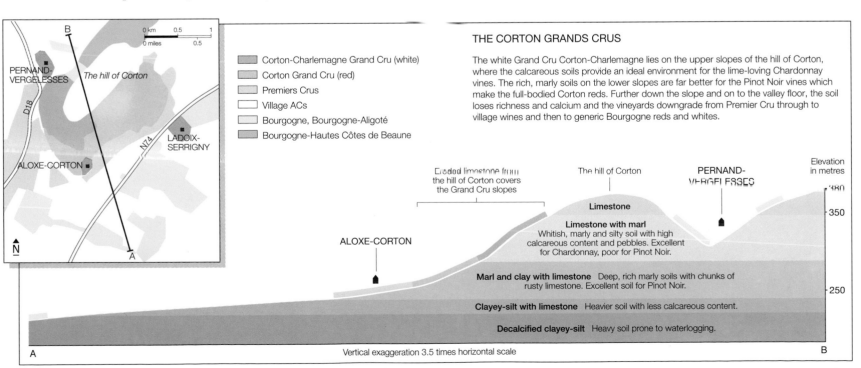

THE CORTON GRANDS CRUS

Corton-Charlemagne Grand Cru (white)
Corton Grand Cru (red)
Premiers Crus
Village ACs
Bourgogne, Bourgogne-Aligoté
Bourgogne-Hautes Côtes de Beaune

The white Grand Cru Corton-Charlemagne lies on the upper slopes of the hill of Corton, where the calcareous soils provide an ideal environment for the lime-loving Chardonnay vines. The rich, marly soils on the lower slopes are far better for the Pinot Noir vines which make the full-bodied Corton reds. Further down the slope and on to the valley floor, the soil loses richness and calcium and the vineyards downgrade from Premier Cru through to village wines and then to generic Bourgogne reds and whites.

PERNAND-VERGELESSES
The hill of Corton
D18
N74
LADOIX-SERRIGNY
ALOXE-CORTON
N
0 km 0.5 1
0 miles 0.5
B
A

Elevation in metres

Eroded limestone from the hill of Corton covers the Grand Cru slopes

The hill of Corton

PERNAND-VERGELESSES

Limestone

Limestone with marl Whitish, marly and silty soil with high calcareous content and pebbles. Excellent for Chardonnay, poor for Pinot Noir.

ALOXE-CORTON

Marl and clay with limestone Deep, rich marly soils with chunks of rusty limestone. Excellent soil for Pinot Noir.

Clayey-silt with limestone Heavier soil with less calcareous content.

Decalcified clayey-silt Heavy soil prone to waterlogging.

380
350
250

Vertical exaggeration 3.5 times horizontal scale

The entrance to the Hôtel-Dieu in Beaune, scene of the annual Hospices de Beaune charity wine auction. Ornate tiled roofs such as this are found all over Burgundy.

CÔTE DE BEAUNE CLASSIFICATIONS

As in the Côte de Nuits, the top vineyard sites are given the status of Grand Cru, but the procession of Grands Crus at around the 275m (902ft) mark isn't repeated in the Côte de Beaune, and there are only two groups of Grands Crus – one in the north, at Aloxe-Corton, and one in the south straddling Puligny-Montrachet and Chassagne-Montrachet. Apart from these two, the best vineyards for both red and white wines are Premiers Crus. The same detailed examination of the vines, row by row took place to determine the status of a plot of land because, in this cool area, the slightest nuance can make the difference between great and merely good wine. An almost imperceptible dip in the field, a scarcely registered change in slope angle or exposure to the sun, a brief streak of clay running across a limestone ridge – all these tiny details combine to form the great imponderable the French call *terroir*. And of all the French areas to take *terroir* seriously, the Côte d'Or, with its obsessive classification, is the most passionate.

Below these levels are the village appellations, and though many of these are on flatter, alluvial land, the quality is still pretty good. Sixteen villages can use the title Côte de Beaune-Villages for their reds, rather than their own village name, but these days this option is rarely exercised except by merchants keen to make up a blend. Côte de Beaune is a tiny red and white appellation from a slope west of Beaune. The least good vineyards only qualify for the Bourgogne, Bourgogne Passe-Touts-Grains or Bourgogne Grand Ordinaire ACs.

VILLAGES OF THE CÔTE DE BEAUNE

The Côte de Beaune really begins with the great hill of Corton, and three villages share its slopes – Ladoix, Aloxe-Corton and Pernand-Vergelesses. This impressive, proud crescent of vines swings right round from east to west with the pale, weathered limestone soils of Corton and Corton-Charlemagne producing white wine right up to the forest fringe at 350m (1148ft). The lower slopes produce round, succulent red Corton; in general the east-facing slopes are best for red, the west-facing for white.

Savigny is tucked into the valley just north-west of Beaune with less protected and, indeed, some north-facing vineyards, but its reds and whites are generally good. Beaune is more famous and the style of its wine is more traditionally soft and mellow; excellent red and white Premiers Crus reach down towards the town itself. Pommard and Volnay have steep, uneven slopes climbing up into the scrub-covered hills. They jig in and out, creating numerous different aspects to the sun, affording erratic protection for the vines. This means that the mesoclimate becomes particularly important, especially for the demanding Pinot Noir which dominates Pommard and Volnay. These are often jealously delimited by wall enclosures.

The heart of the Côte de Beaune runs from Meursault to Chassagne-Montrachet. Here, between 240 and 300m (788 and 984ft), with a few fine vineyards as high as

350m (1148ft) round the hamlet of Blagny, the Chardonnay revels in the spare stony soils and the limestone outcrops jutting to within inches of the surface, delights in the dips and curves of the east- to south-east-facing slopes and produces a fascinating array of brilliant flavours. All are minutely but recognizably different, and every one, when created by a serious producer, is a triumphant vindication of the notion of *terroir*. At Chassagne-Montrachet the soils become heavier again, spreading south-west to Santenay and then trailing away further west to Maranges, and more red than white is grown once again.

HAUTES-CÔTES DE BEAUNE

You can see numerous vineyards in the hills behind the Côte de Beaune. These are included in the appellation Hautes-Côtes de Beaune. It's a heavenly part of Burgundy, with twisting country lanes, ancient avenues of trees, and a tranquillity conducive to relaxing with the very best of Burgundies. But these slopes are a crucial 50 to 100m (164 to 328ft) higher than those of the Côte de Beaune, are less perfectly angled to the sun and less protected from wind and rain. They produce pleasant light reds and whites when the weather's warm – just right for a picnic in one of the high meadows.

WHERE THE VINEYARDS ARE *The Côte de Beaune is less of a single strip of land directly beneath an escarpment than the Côte de Nuits. In the Côte de Beaune there are several large re-entrants into the hills harbouring major vineyard sites; the vineyards themselves slope more gently and expansively towards the plain, and the soil structures are far less homogeneous, veering between austere barren limestone and rich marly limestone. With the exception of Volnay, whose delicate reds come largely from light, stony soils, it is the heavier soils that produce red wines. The lighter, limestone-based soil produces peerless whites such as at Puligny-Montrachet, Chassagne-Montrachet and Meursault. The hill of Corton at the top of the map is unusual in that it has two Grands Crus, one for red and one for white wine. Historic Beaune is regarded as the wine capital of Burgundy. Excellent villages like St-Aubin, St-Romain and Auxey-Duresses are less well-known and less popular. The vineyards right up in the hills to the west are the Hautes-Côtes de Beaune.*

CÔTE DE BEAUNE AND HAUTES-CÔTES DE BEAUNE

TOTAL DISTANCE
NORTH TO SOUTH
25KM (15½ MILES)

▨ VINEYARDS

N

VILLAGE ACS, GRAND CRU VINEYARDS AND MAIN PREMIER CRU VINEYARDS

1. **LADOIX**
   Grands Crus: Corton (part), Corton-Charlemagne (part).

2. **PERNAND-VERGELESSES**
   Grands Crus: Corton (part), Corton-Charlemagne (part).
   Main Premiers Crus: Ile des Vergelesses, les Vergelesses.

3. **ALOXE-CORTON**
   Grands Crus: Corton (part), Corton-Charlemagne (part).
   Main Premiers Crus: les Chaillots, les Maréchaudes, les Valozières.

4. **CHOREY-LÈS-BEAUNE**

5. **SAVIGNY-LÈS-BEAUNE**
   Main Premiers Crus: aux Guettes, les Lavières, aux Serpentières, les Vergelesses.

6. **BEAUNE**
   Main Premiers Crus: les Avaux, les Boucherottes, les Bressandes, les Cents Vignes, Champs Pimont, le Clos des Mouches, le Clos de la Mousse, Clos du Roi, les Cras, les Epenotes, les Fèves, les Grèves,

les Marconnets, les Teurons, les Toussaints, les Vignes Franches.

7. **POMMARD**
   Main Premiers Crus: les Arvelets, les Boucherottes, Clos Blanc, Clos de la Commaraine, Clos des Epeneaux, les Grands Epenots, les Petits Epenots, les Pézerolles, les Rugiens-Bas, les Rugiens-Hauts.

8. **VOLNAY**
   Main Premiers Crus: les Angles, Clos de la Bousse d'Or, les Caillerets, Champans, Clos des Chênes, Clos des Ducs, les Santenots, Taille Pieds.

9. **MONTHELIE**
   Main Premiers Crus: les Champs Fulliot, les Duresses, sur la Velle.

10. **MEURSAULT**
    Main Premiers Crus: les Charmes,

les Perrières, les Genevrières, les Gouttes d'Or, le Porusot. Certain red wines can also be sold as Volnay or Blagny.

11. **AUXEY-DURESSES**
    Main Premiers Crus: Climat du Val, Clos du Val, les Duresses.

12. **ST-ROMAIN**

13. **PULIGNY-MONTRACHET**
    Grands Crus: Bâtard-Montrachet (part), Bienvenues-Bâtard-Montrachet, Chevalier-Montrachet, le Montrachet (part).
    Main Premiers Crus: le Cailleret, le Champ Canet, Clavaillon, les Combettes, les Demoiselles,

les Folatières, la Garenne, les Pucelles, les Referts, la Truffière.

14. **ST-AUBIN**
    Main Premiers Crus: le Charmois, la Chatenière, en Rémilly.

15. **CHASSAGNE-MONTRACHET**
    Grands Crus: Bâtard-Montrachet (part), Criots-Bâtard-Montrachet, le Montrachet (part).
    Main Premiers Crus: les Baudines, la Boudriotte, Cailleret, les Champs Gains, les Chaumées,

les Chenevottes, Clos St-Jean, les Embasées, la Grande Montagne, les Grandes Ruchottes, les Macherelles, la Maltroie, Morgeot, la Romanée, les Vergers.

16. **SANTENAY**
    Main Premiers Crus: Beauregard, le Clos des Mouches, le Clos de Tavannes, la Comme, Grand Clos Rousseau, les Gravières, la Maladière, Passetemps.

17. **MARANGES**

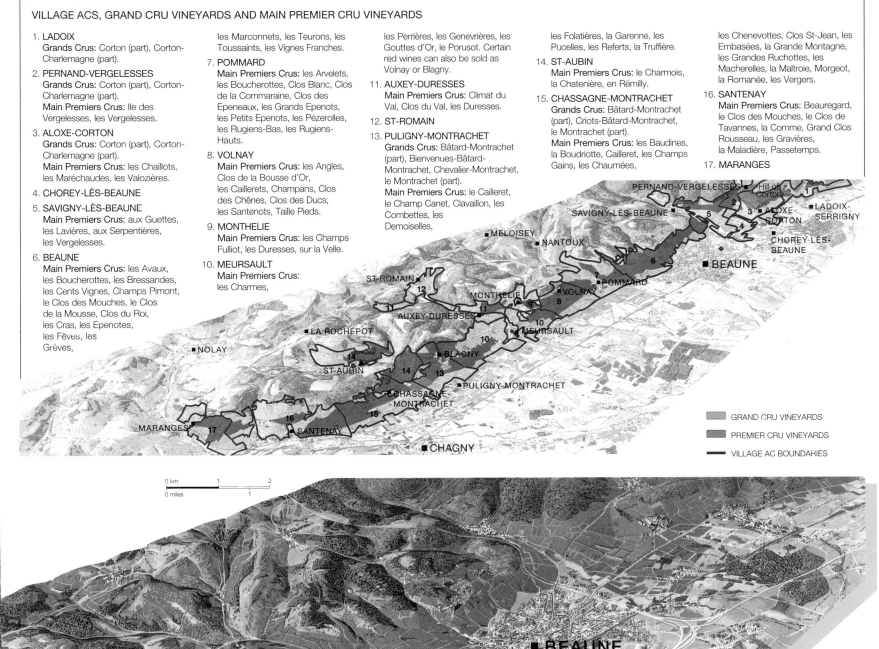

GRAND CRU VINEYARDS
PREMIER CRU VINEYARDS
VILLAGE AC BOUNDARIES

BEAUJOLAIS

**NORTHERN
BEAUJOLAIS**

TOTAL DISTANCE
NORTH TO SOUTH
23KM (14 MILES)

▓▓▓ VINEYARDS

▲
N

0 km   1   2
0 miles   1

I LIKE TO THINK OF BEAUJOLAIS as a state of mind rather than a place dependent on contours, kilometres and map references. In my mind this is a magical haven of hills, of a bucolic way of life far removed from the drab conformity of city life. That doesn't need a map of time and place, just a vaguely remembered sketch of the head and heart. I would still rather take the map below and say, do you see how that track rises from Chiroubles up to the forest rim above the village? Well, scramble up there and you can picnic in blissful solitude. Or do you want the best view out over the fat, prosperous Saône Valley and on, to the snowy peaks of the Alps?

Or would you like the most succulent frogs' legs in France, and juicy-pink *entrecôtes*, washed down with fragrant Côte de Brouilly straight from the jug? Follow me. Yes, I like to pretend that Beaujolais is all about dream-time hills, romantic peasant life. But it isn't. And perhaps it never was, because in the days immortalized by Chevallier in his famous novel *Clochemerle*, Beaujolais was a beautiful, but poverty-stricken region. Its job was to provide the basic jug wine of Lyon, France's second city. The Lyonnais had monumental thirsts, but were used to paying little for their tipple.

BEAUJOLAIS NOUVEAU
Things all changed with the advent of Beaujolais Nouveau. What a stroke of genius. Beaujolais has been drunk as young as possible in Lyon since the vineyards were first planted. But first the Parisians caught on to the idea, in the 1950s, then the British joined them in the 1970s, then the Americans, then the Japanese… By the 1980s Beaujolais Nouveau had been sold and oversold as the concept of the first wine of the year's harvest, released on the third Thursday in November, gushing, purple-pink and hardly old enough to have forgotten the flavour of the grape upon the vine. This euphoric state couldn't last forever, and few of the traditional Beaujolais markets, like Northern Europe, now take much notice of Nouveau Day. With the result that much of the prosperity of the region has faded as producers try to find a new way forward for Beaujolais – a wine that lives and dies by its joyous youthful fruit.

There was a time that only Beaujolais could do this. Now almost every country in the wine world has become adept at producing its own versions of bright, easy drink-me-quick reds.

For commercial reasons, Beaujolais has always been included as part of Burgundy even though its geology and climate are different. Its vineyards produce some 47 per cent of Burgundy's total volume of wine. But the dominant grape here, and the only one used for Beaujolais, is Gamay, barred from all but the most basic wines in the rest of Burgundy because of the raw, rough flavours it tends to produce on alkaline soils. But in Beaujolais the soils are different, and here the Gamay can produce bright, juicy-ripe glugging wine difficult to beat for sheer uncomplicated pleasure. This should be particularly so in the gently rolling, southerly vineyards nearest Lyon, where rich clay and limestone soils grow the light, easy reds sold simply as Beaujolais or Beaujolais Nouveau. But yields are far higher than they used to be and so many of the wines lack the fruit and perfume that made Beaujolais famous in the first place.

THE BEAUJOLAIS METHOD OF FERMENTATION
If we think of Beaujolais Nouveau as merely some modern marketing man's creation, well it is and it isn't. The hoopla of

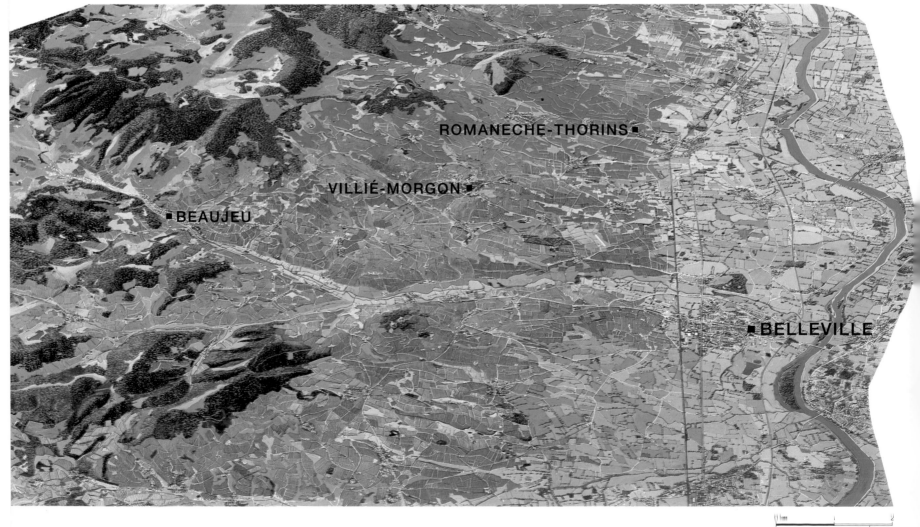

ROMANECHE-THORINS ■

VILLIÉ-MORGON ■

■ BEAUJEU

■ BELLEVILLE

Nouveau Day in November can often obscure details like whether we actually *like* the wine. But the release of the first wine of the vintage has always been a cause for merrymaking throughout wine regions the world over. Far from being a modern phenomenon, the Nouveau celebrations take us right back to the heart of tradition! They may have been hijacked by marketing men but they've been there ever since the first wine harvest. However, not all red grapes are suitable for the Nouveau treatment. Luckily Beaujolais' Gamay grape naturally has a bright strawberry and peach flavour that is accentuated when vinified by the Beaujolais method.

Grapes are harvested by hand and then, instead of being crushed, whole bunches are piled into a vat. Those at the bottom break, the juice seeps out and begins to ferment as usual, warming the vat and giving off carbon dioxide that rises like a blanket to the top. This encourages the unbroken grapes to begin to ferment inside their skins. Since the colouring and flavouring components in the skin are next to the flesh, this 'whole grape fermentation' or carbonic maceration extracts these elements, yet doesn't extract much of the bitter tannin near the surface of the skin. After four to seven days the grapes split, spilling their dark, fruity, but not bitter, juice into the vat. This mixes with the traditionally fermented juice at the bottom of the vat to create a red wine strong on perfume and colour but low in tannin. This juice is drawn off and the rest of the grapes are pressed. This pressing gives rather more tannin, but thanks to carbonic maceration, colour and fruit perfumes still dominate. This method is used with varying success all around the world by people wanting to create reds to drink very young.

WHERE THE VINEYARDS ARE *This map shows the northern part of the Beaujolais region, yet covers all the most important vineyard sites: these are the ten Beaujolais Crus and most of the 39 communes making Beaujolais-Villages. To the west of the railway line in the rolling hills with vineyards facing in all directions, it's a virtual monoculture of vines, while in the east the flat Saône valley is almost entirely farmland. As you head west, the flatter, reasonably fertile but less well-drained soils make straightforward Beaujolais; the gentler slopes make Beaujolais-Villages; while all the top Beaujolais Cru vineyards lie on the steeper, inhospitable granite outcrops from the Monts du Beaujolais where Gamay performs at its best until around 400m (1312ft), when ripening becomes a problem even this far south and vineyards revert to Beaujolais Villages once more.*

THE BEAUJOLAIS CRUS

The northern part of Beaujolais – covered by the map below – contains the potentially superior vineyards. The most important of these are the ten Beaujolais Crus, or 'growths', which account for 25 per cent of all Beaujolais; each has its own appellation contrôlée. The Cru vineyards are reckoned to produce wine with an identifiable character, and most have a granite subsoil, which is rarely associated with fine wine – Hermitage in the Rhône valley, south of Lyon, being a notable exception.

St-Amour is the most northerly commune, actually sharing its vineyards with the Mâconnais St-Véran appellation. Going south come Juliénas, Chénas and Moulin-à-Vent, all capable of producing well-structured wines. The perfumed wines of Fleurie and Chiroubles come next, followed by Morgon, whose best wines develop a delightful cherry perfume. Régnié, with its sandy soils, is the newest Cru, though so far it has not really justified its right to be a Cru, but Brouilly, the largest Beaujolais Cru, and Côte de Brouilly can produce delightful gluggable wines.

BEAUJOLAIS-VILLAGES

Thirty-nine other communes, mostly in the north of the region between Vaux-en-Beaujolais and St-Amour-Bellevue on the border with the Mâconnais region, qualify for Beaujolais-Villages status. This appellation is for wines that are better than basic Beaujolais but supposedly less fine than Crus. But what do we mean by fine?

Frankly, we're not after the longevity and complexity that may characterize the greatest reds from Bordeaux, Burgundy or the Rhône. What we want is the uncomplicated cherub-cheeked, red-fruit ripeness and spicy blossom perfumes of the best ordinary Beaujolais. But we want those fruits to be riper, those perfumes more heady, and the wine's soft-centred, smooth consistency to leave lingering trails in the memory long after the flavour fades.

These are the blessings of youth. There is hardly a Brouilly, a St-Amour or a Chiroubles that should be aged for even as long as a couple of years. An occasional bottle of Morgon, Juliénas, Fleurie or, particularly, Moulin-à-Vent does begin to resemble a charming mild-mannered Côte de Beaune Burgundy after five to ten years' age, but these are the exceptions. But, as in the rest of Beaujolais, yields are generally too high even in these top vineyards, and a grape like the Gamay can only aspire to class if yields are kept low.

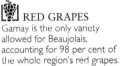

Beaujolais is almost the only place in the world that can produce memorable wine from the Gamay grape. These grapes are from the Côte de Brouilly Cru.

RED GRAPES
Gamay is the only variety allowed for Beaujolais, accounting for 98 per cent of the whole region's red grapes.

WHITE GRAPES
A tiny amount of Chardonnay and other varieties is used for the little white wine made here.

CLIMATE
Warmer and sunnier than northern Burgundy, the region is partly protected by the Monts du Beaujolais from prevailing westerly winds.

SOIL
The most important aspect is the granite subsoil which influences all the northern zone and on which Gamay thrives. Further south nearer Lyon, the soil is richer, primarily clays and limestone, and is less suited to Gamay.

ASPECT
The vineyards lie between 150 and 500m (492 and 1640ft) and face all directions. Fleurie and Moulin-à-Vent have many south-east-facing vineyards which are protected by the hills to the north-west.

NORTHERN BEAUJOLAIS

1. Juliénas
2. St-Amour
3. Chénas
4. Moulin-à-Vent
5. Fleurie
6. Chiroubles
7. Morgon
8. Régnié
9. Brouilly
10. Côte de Brouilly

BEAUJOLAIS-VILLAGES AC BOUNDARY

BEAUJOLAIS CRUS BOUNDARIES

CHAMPAGNE

🍇 RED GRAPES
Pinot Noir and Pinot Meunier account for just under three-quarters of all Champagne grapes.

🍇 WHITE GRAPES
Chardonnay accounts for a little over one-quarter of the vineyards.

☁ CLIMATE
Cold, wet, continental climate but the northerly latitude gives more daylight hours in the growing season than Provence. Rain and late spring frosts are the main enemies.

▨ SOIL
Shallow topsoil as little as 15cm (6in) in places covering subsoil largely of chalk up to 200m (656ft) thick.

◩ ASPECT
Mainly east- and south-east-facing vineyards, that lie between 100 and 200m (328 and 656ft) high, and are protected by thickly wooded hilltops.

North-facing Pinot Noir vines above Verzenay on the Montagne de Reims. Why Pinot Noir should ripen so well in such a spot is by no means clear.

THEY WEREN'T PAYING THE AREA round Reims and Épernay north-east of Paris any compliments when they called it Champagne. They weren't thinking of glittering first night parties, of dandies and dancing girls, the hectic celebrations of a Grand Prix winner or the tingling joyful tension of a lover with warm words in his mind and brave deeds in his heart.

The word 'Champagne' comes from the Latin *campania* meaning 'open, flat countryside', and I sometimes feel this is a positive understatement as I urge the car onwards. Driving through the pale, lonely plains to the east of Reims, the sea of corn enlivened by an occasional steepling grain silo, I feel more as if I were in the depths of the Oklahoma prairie than trying to make a dinner date in the heart of one of the world's greatest wine regions. As I plough through the flat sugar-beet fields of the Pas de Calais, still saturated by squalls from the English Channel, past the giant slag heaps of long-dead coal mines and once more out on to the chalky windswept plains to the north of Reims, I don't scent the slightest possibility of any vines ever ripening under such inhospitable conditions. It is simply too cold, too windy, too rainy for growing grapes.

And they don't. This whole expanse of north-eastern France is a desolate, underpopulated province of broad cornfields and dark forbidding forests, which experienced some of the fiercest fighting in World Wars One and Two. And in what many historians reckon may have been the bloodiest battle ever to take place, Attila the Hun was finally turned back east of Reims near Châlons-en-Champagne.

CLIMATE AND SOIL
But in this flat landscape there is one brief eruption of low hills – a grouping of cliffs, slopes and valleys of ancient chalk. These hills do provide just the amount of protection and privileged mesoclimate that the grape vine needs. Take a look at the map. The Montagne de Reims is one of these. The Côte des Blancs is another. The cleft where the Marne river pushes its way westward towards Paris is a third. And little pockets like the Côte de Sézanne and the Aube (see page 73) further south can also provide suitable conditions for ripening the vine. Just.

Yet this knife-edge between ripeness and unripeness is what gives the wine of Champagne its peculiar suitability to form the base for a sparkling wine. And the cold autumns and icy winters that grip the whole region in a joyless embrace are what, by chance, created the now famous bubbles in the first place.

High acidity is crucial in the base wine for a good fizz. If you can lengthen the ripening time of the fruit as much as possible so that it only creeps to maturity in the golden days of autumn, you are going to retain high acidity, yet have physically mature grapes. The flavours that these give are infinitely superior to those obtained from grapes grown in warmer climates simply picked early. All you then get is green, raw unripeness. You can't make great wine out of that.

In the few favoured vine-growing mesoclimates of Champagne, the annual mean temperature is about 10.5°C (51°F), a half degree above what is generally regarded as the minimum required to ripen any high-quality grape variety, although training the vines close to the ground will increase the temperature somewhat. The number of hours of sunshine in the growing season are actually as high in Champagne as in the considerably warmer vineyards of Alsace. But whereas Alsace, sheltered behind the Vosges mountains, has much higher temperatures and less rain due to its continental climate, Champagne's days are cooled by the damp Atlantic breezes that sweep in unhindered from the west.

And those winds often bring rain – and at the wrong time too. Although the total annual rainfall is lower than in regions like Bordeaux, Burgundy and the Loire, nearly 60 per cent of it falls in the summer and early autumn, with July and August being particularly hard hit when the rain causes mildew and rot among the ripening grapes. But this is where the importance of the right soil comes in. With the exception of the southerly Aube, Champagne's vines are planted on a thick chalk subsoil. The topsoil differs within the region – the Montagne de Reims has a kind of brown coal lignite and some gravel, the Vallée de la Marne has far more sand, and the Côte des Blancs has clay – but this topsoil is frequently so thin that the chalk keeps breaking through.

The chalk is porous and fissured, holding enough water to nourish the vine but not drown it. The vine roots burrow into the soft, almost spongy, stone thus anchoring the plant against climatic extremes above ground. Since the chalk is so close to the surface, it is relatively warm, and indeed, may even reflect sunlight back on to the vine, aiding the grapes' final struggle for ripeness as autumn drifts towards winter.

VALLÉE D

■ CHÂTEAU-
THIERRY

Marne

FROM STILL WINE TO SPARKLING
This rather sombre scenario means that wines with truly ripe, sun-filled flavours simply aren't part of the Champagne repertoire, although historically the region's reputation was based on still red wines. These must have been pretty feeble and thin and I'm glad I didn't have to rely on them for washing down my Sunday roast. But highly acidic grapes, picked just as winter set in, would have fermented slowly and inefficiently. As the freezing winter air filled the wine cellars, the yeasts would simply have become

VILLENAUXE-
LA-GRANDE

CHAMPAGNE

── CHAMPAGNE AC BOUNDARY

TOTAL DISTANCE NORTH TO SOUTH 140KM
(87 MILES)

▨ VINEYARDS

N

too cold to go on with their job: they'd have packed it in and gone into hibernation. In the days before central heating they'd have lain dormant until the following spring had warmed the cellars up and – hey presto – they'd have finished off their fermentation with a final brisk burst of bubbles to emerge as still wines.

The English and the Parisians used to buy a lot of Champagne wine. Since young wine was prized more than old, until modern times it would be shipped to them in barrel during the winter. Once the spring came, it would begin bubbling again.

Traditionally much effort was put into ridding the wines of their bubble, but in England, in the carefree period after Charles II's Restoration in 1660, and in the pleasure-mad days in France that followed the death of Louis XIV in 1715, a vogue developed for frivolous sparkling wines that may have upset connoisseurs of those times, but has ensured Champagne's fame ever since. No-one then understood exactly why the fizziness came and went. The English managed to preserve the bubbles rather longer into the summer because they had developed particularly strong

Nearly all Champagne is a blend of different vineyards – and usually all the better for it.

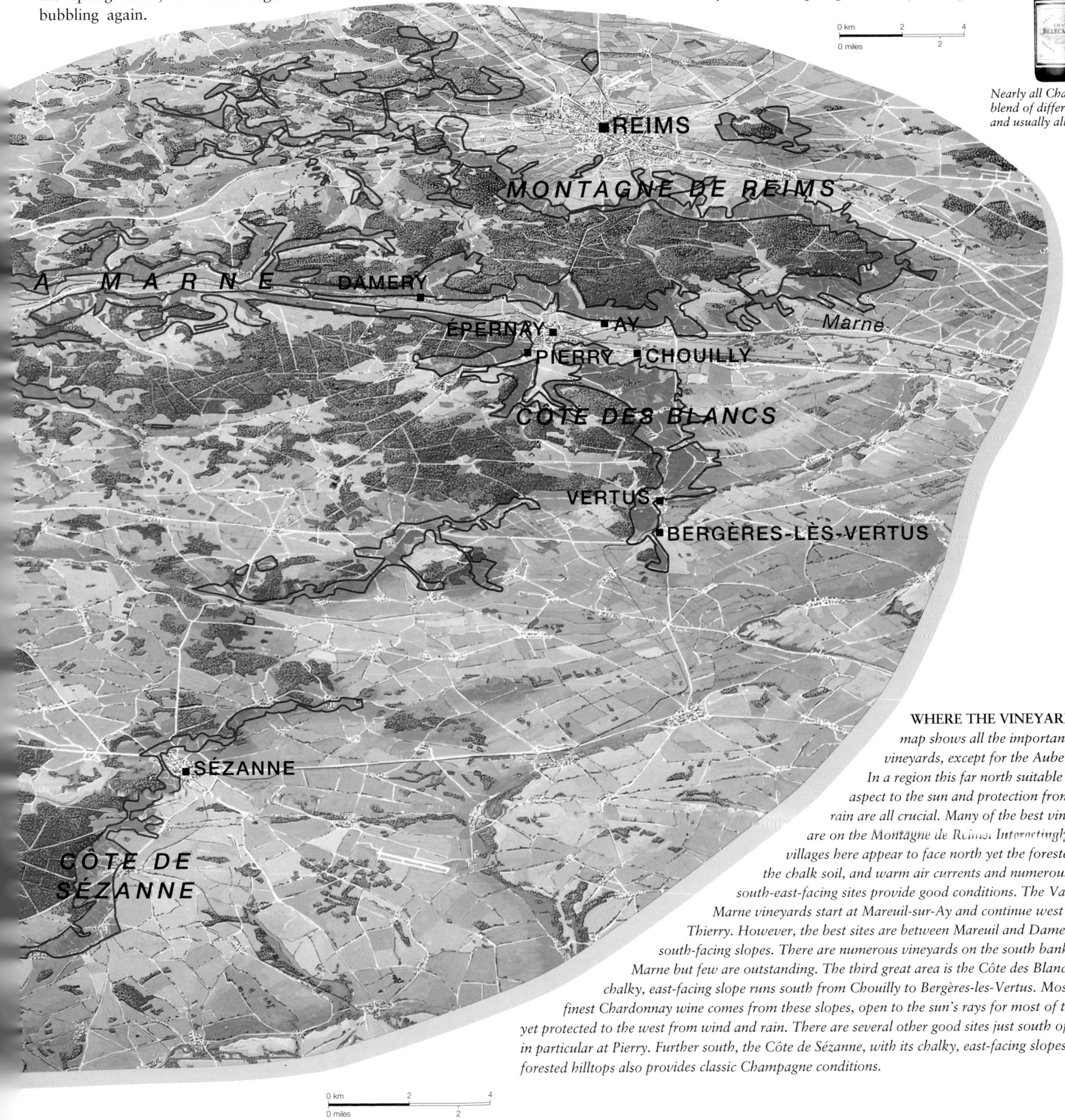

REIMS

MONTAGNE DE REIMS

A MARNE DAMERY

ÉPERNAY AY Marne

PIERRY CHOUILLY

CÔTE DES BLANCS

VERTUS

BERGÈRES-LÈS-VERTUS

SÉZANNE

CÔTE DE SÉZANNE

WHERE THE VINEYARDS ARE *The map shows all the important Champagne vineyards, except for the Aube (see page 73). In a region this far north suitable soils, good aspect to the sun and protection from wind and rain are all crucial. Many of the best vineyard sites are on the Montagne de Reims. Interestingly, many villages here appear to face north yet the forested hilltop, the chalk soil, and warm air currents and numerous east- and south-east-facing sites provide good conditions. The Vallée de la Marne vineyards start at Mareuil-sur-Ay and continue west past Château-Thierry. However, the best sites are between Mareuil and Damery, on steep south-facing slopes. There are numerous vineyards on the south banks of the Marne but few are outstanding. The third great area is the Côte des Blancs. This chalky, east-facing slope runs south from Chouilly to Bergères-les-Vertus. Most of the finest Chardonnay wine comes from these slopes, open to the sun's rays for most of the day, yet protected to the west from wind and rain. There are several other good sites just south of Épernay, in particular at Pierry. Further south, the Côte de Sézanne, with its chalky, east-facing slopes and forested hilltops also provides classic Champagne conditions.*

glass bottles and they used cork rather than rags soaked in oil as a stopper. Bottles would still burst, but not half as often as did the weaker French bottles. Gradually, in the latter part of the 17th century the English, and the French – led by Dom Pérignon, who was in charge of the cellars at Hautvillers Abbey between 1670 and 1715 – worked out how to control the fizz and then how to start it going again in a still wine.

The reputation of Champagne is based on this last achievement. By adding a little yeast and sugar to a still wine and then corking the bottle tightly, the wine re-ferments in the bottle and the bubbles dissolve, waiting to burst forth when the bottle is opened. This is the traditional 'Champagne method' of making sparkling wine and is used across the world for top class bubbly. Others have since improved upon Dom Pérignon's methods for creating a reliable sparkling wine, but he was perhaps more important for formulating other principles that are now accepted as fundamental to quality in Champagne. Above all, he saw the need to restrict yields to achieve ripeness, and to blend together the wines of different vineyards and communes to produce the best end result.

THE CLASSIFICATION OF CHAMPAGNE VINEYARDS

In the marginal climate of Champagne, there are few vineyard sites that can produce an attractive, multi-faceted wine in most years. However, the three grape varieties used for Champagne, each grown on different sites, can contribute a more rounded flavour to a final blend. Older 'reserve' wines held back from the previous year may also be added for extra flavour. As a result, Champagne is usually a blend of different wines, often from all over the region, and most of it is sold as non-vintage. A vintage is 'declared' only in especially good years, and the wines made from a selection of the best grapes. The so-called 'de luxe' cuvées are also blends from different vineyards, unless they come from a single grower.

Merchant houses – the most important are in Reims, Épernay and Ay – and co-operatives handle most Champagne production, buying grapes from the growers based on a guideline price per kilo, determined by a tribunal of officials, growers and producers and renegotiated every three or four years. Prices are fixed by a system known as the *échelle des crus*, or 'ladder of growths' whereby villages, rather than individual vineyards, are classified according to quality on a scale ranging from 100 per cent down to 80 per cent. There are 17 villages accorded the title Grand Cru, and these receive 100 per cent of the agreed grape price per kilo. The 41 villages with Premier Cru status receive between 90 and 99 per cent. All the other less-favoured villages receive between 80 and 89 per cent.

GRAPE VARIETIES

Not only are some vineyards better than others, but they are also better suited to particular grape varieties. Three varieties are grown in Champagne – two red, Pinot Noir and Pinot Meunier, and one white, Chardonnay. The total vineyard is 31,458ha (77,732 acres): Pinot Noir covers 11,935ha (29,491 acres); Pinot Meunier 10,873 ha (26,867 acres); and Chardonnay 8650ha (21,374 acres).

Just south of Reims is the Montagne de Reims with vineyards on its northern, eastern and southern slopes. Pinot Noir dominates these vineyards, especially those in the Grand Cru villages, and much of the backbone for the Champagne blends comes from these grapes and from those grown in the Aube region. Pinot Noir is also used for the rare still wines of Champagne such as Bouzy Rouge which is light but perfumed with strawberry fruit.

Chardonnay dominates the chalky, east-facing slopes of the Côte des Blancs south of Épernay. The other particularly successful areas for Chardonnay are the village of Villers-Marmery at the eastern end of the Montagne de Reims, and the Côte de Sézanne to the south. Chardonnay from the northern sites adds zest and lively, lean fruit to the Champagne blend, while that from the less chalky Côte de Sézanne is likely to add a creamy, honeyed roundness. Blanc de Blancs Champagne is from 100 per cent Chardonnay.

Pinot Meunier is the Champagne workhorse. In general it is planted in the lower-lying vineyards because it buds late, thus avoiding the worst of the frost. Most villages grow some, with the exception of the top Côte des Blancs communes, and Bouzy in the Montagne de Reims. It is particularly prevalent west of Épernay in the Vallée de la Marne where the valley vineyards are susceptible to frost. Blended with the other two varieties it can add a pleasant, mildly perfumed quality that softens the more austere, slow-developing characteristics of Pinot Noir and Chardonnay.

THE CHALK OF CHAMPAGNE

There is a thick, billowing seam of chalk that runs across northern France to Calais and across southern England. This is the subsoil for the Champagne vineyards. There are two main sorts: micraster, found on the lower slopes and the plain, and belemnite, found in all the best vineyards and on the upper slopes. Chalk has a perfect balance between porosity and water retention and is able to nourish vines equally well in dry or wet years. Its brilliant whiteness helps the soil's ability to reflect sunlight back on to the vines, and chalk retains heat well, vital factors in such a northerly vineyard region. Chalk is also alkaline, which in turn produces grapes with high acid levels – perfect for sparkling wine. In addition, the region's *caves* or cellars, dug deep into the chalk, mainly in the towns of Reims and Épernay, are cold and damp, providing an ideal environment for storing bottles while the Champagne inside undergoes its second fermentation. This is because the slower the yeasts set to work, the smaller the bubble and the more persistent the fizz in the finished wine.

The cru vineyards The best vineyards are found on the chalk slopes covered with downwash material from the upper slopes. The high proportion of calcium in the chalk prevents the vines from taking up iron and this is compensated for by the perennial use of fertilizers.

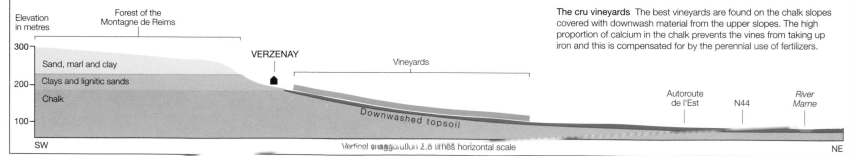

THE AUBE (CÔTE DES BAR)

Lying well south of Troyes, the former capital of the Comtes de Champagne, the vineyards in the Aube *département* have long been hampered with the problem that they are situated in the Champagne region but only just, and in the Burgundy region, well almost. The first scattered outposts of Burgundian vineyards begin across the departmental border at Chatillon-sur-Seine less than 20 kilometres (12 miles) away and the Aube's gently rolling landscape feels quite different to the heart of Champagne around Épernay a good 110km (70 miles) to the north. At least now the A26 *autoroute* between Reims and Dijon slices between the two main Aube towns of Bar-sur-Aube and Bar-sur-Seine so that we can see the region's dual personality for ourselves.

As it happens, the Aube's vineyards are a lot closer to the Chablis vineyards (only 40km/25 miles to the south-west) than any of the main Champagne districts, and they also lie on soil similar to Chablis' but the Burgundians rejected all overtures from the Aube growers. When the Marne growers further north (i.e., in the classic districts of the Montagne de Reims, the Vallée de la Marne and the Côte des Blancs) started to delimit Champagne's boundaries at the beginning of the twentieth century in an attempt to control the quality of the grapes being used some of the Aube growers petitioned for their region to be included within the Champagne-producing area. The Aube was only included as an official Champagne district after several years of violent resistance by the Marne growers and until 1927 when the Champagne *appellation* came into being, the Aube had to be content with the demeaning title of 'Champagne Deuxième Zone'. In other words, it was thought of as inferior.

Although increasingly untenable, this is an attitude that you still come across in a few of the more snobbish *grande marque* houses based in Reims and Épernay, even though they use Aube grapes in their non-vintage brands. However, partly because some of the leading winemakers from the big houses are increasingly open about the merits of the region, these days there is less ill-informed prejudice against the Aube vineyards. In fact, this area, nowadays also called the Côte des Bar, is one of Champagne's most important sources of full-flavoured, ripe Pinot Noir grapes. Nearly 85 per cent of the Côte des Bar's 6800 hectares of vineyards are planted with Pinot Noir, and it thus accounts for very nearly half (48 per cent) of Champagne's supply of this variety.

Despite past schisms, the links between Burgundy and the Côte des Bar are more than just close proximity. The Côte des Bar soils are the same as Chablis', the best sites having Kimmeridgian limestone clay subsoils, and there's a good smattering of Portlandian limestone, Chablis' other soil, as well. Even the weather has more in common with Chablis than with Champagne. Greater maximum heat in the Côte des Bar is balanced by more extreme cold and the general effect is of riper, rounder, slightly raspberryish, yet earthy fruit.

This slightly red fruit flavour is especially marked in a local oddity, the Rosé des Riceys. This is a still rosé wine, aged in cask, and made only in the warmest years. Although the cask-aging drives out any richness, there is a core of curious sweetness as though you'd left a punnet of raspberries to wither and shrivel in a hot desert wind.

Although more growers bottle their own wine today, most Côte des Bar wines either head north for blending into the Champagnes produced by the biggest houses or are sold by the large co-operative, the Union Auboise at Bar-sur-Seine, whose Devaux Champagne blend puts many a *grande marque* to shame.

Vines and sunflowers share the slopes at Essoyes in the Aube, or Côte des Bar, a source of round, early-maturing Champagnes ideal for softening the more austere wines from elsewhere in the region.

WHERE THE VINEYARDS ARE *The Aube or Côte des Bar is the least known of Champagne's four main districts, but in many ways it is the most attractive to explore. While the principal Champagne districts to the north around Épernay are affected by breezes sweeping in unhindered from the Atlantic, the Côte des Bar has a more continental climate and is particularly prone to frost. The landscape resembles the outlying areas of Chablis more than the main Champagne areas themselves. Most of the land is broad and rolling but there are also low, wooded hills with relatively steep slopes and, where the aspect is broadly south-facing, patches of vines planted among pasture and other crops. The best examples are to the east of Bar-sur-Seine, along the valley to Champignol-lez-Mondéville and Urville, and beneath the forest between Polisy and Les Riceys. North-east of Bar-sur-Seine, in this cool part of France, the land flattens out and becomes far too exposed for grapes to ripen.*

Aube

BAR-SUR-AUBE

URVILLE

CHAMPIGNOL-LEZ-MONDÉVILLE

BAR-SUR-SEINE

POLISY

ESSOYES

Seine

LES RICEYS

—— CHAMPAGNE AC BOUNDARY

TOTAL DISTANCE NORTH TO SOUTH 44KM (27 MILES)

VINEYARDS

N

ALSACE

RED GRAPES
Pinot Noir is the only red grape, occupying about 9 per cent of the plantings.

WHITE GRAPES
Riesling is the most widely planted, followed by Pinot Blanc, Gewurztraminer and Sylvaner in almost equal amounts, then Pinot Gris, whilst Muscat trails far behind. Negligible amounts of Chasselas are used in Edelzwicker, and Chardonnay in Crémant.

CLIMATE
Despite the northerly latitude, the region benefits from plentiful sun and low rainfall caused by its location in the rain shadow created by the Vosges mountains.

SOIL
The region divides into three main zones – mountain, mid-slopes, and foothills and plains. The best sites are on the middle slopes which are limestone based with marly clay and sandstone topsoils.

ASPECT
The vineyards are sited between 170 and 420m (558 and 1378ft) with the best sites on the well-drained, sheltered steep middle slopes.

There are 50 Grands Crus in Alsace; Rangen de Thann, just to the west of Cernay in the south, produces remarkable wines.

YOU ONLY HAVE TO STAND in the middle of the steeply sloping vineyards to the west of Colmar to realize there's something special about Alsace. Over to the west, dark clouds pile ominously above the mountains; yet here, where the Riesling and Gewurztraminer vines climb gamely up towards the wooded brows of the Vosges eastern foothills, the sky is as clear and blue as dreams, the sunshine is warm and mellow, the air is pure and sweet with the perfume of flowers and alive with the twittering chatter of insects. In these vineyards, grapes for some of the most heady and exotic wines in Europe ripen in the summer sun.

The vineyards of Alsace sit in a rain shadow created by the Vosges mountains that rise high above the Rhine Valley. Most of the rain brought by the westerly winds falls over these mountains and forests. By the time the clouds reach the vineyards they have just enough rain left to cast a few refreshing showers on the vines and then evaporate into the warm air. Alsace is almost as far north as vineyards can go in France – only Champagne is marginally further north. Yet that rain shadow allows Colmar to be the second driest spot in France, beaten only by Perpignan, down on the Spanish border. Perpignan cooks under torrid skies. Not so Alsace. Perpignan produces rough-and-ready hot-climate reds; Alsace, because of cooler northern temperatures, allied to day after day of clear skies, can provide the ripeness – and therefore the higher alcoholic strength – of the warm south but also the perfume and fragrance of the cool north.

The enigma goes much further than climatic conditions. Politically Alsace has been caught between two inimical philosophies. The Rhine is southern Germany's great waterway. Nowadays it forms a natural frontier as it runs northwards from Basel on the Swiss border but, in less peaceful times, the river, and the flat farmland on both its banks, formed an obvious battleground whenever the French and Germans went to war. The frontier then was seen as the Vosges mountains to the west, on whose eastern foothills all Alsace's vineyards are planted. Prussia gained control of Alsace in 1870, France won the region back in 1918; by 1940 Alsace was again under German occupation, before finally reverting to France in 1945.

After several generations of confused national identity, the region has settled into a reasonably contented dual personality. The Alsatian people maintain proudly, even ferociously, that they are as French as any Frenchman can be. Yet most of the names of their villages are German and the villages themselves look as though they've stepped off the set of some German operetta; most family surnames are German (though Christian names are often French), and the local Alsace dialect has far more in common with German than French.

ALSACE

TOTAL DISTANCE
NORTH TO SOUTH
88KM (54½ MILES)

▬▬▬ ALSACE AC BOUNDARY

▨ VINEYARDS

▲
N

SÉLESTAT ■

■ COLMAR

■ GUEBWILLER

■ CERNAY

■ MULHOUSE

STRASBOURG

OBERNAI

Rhin (Rhine)

BREISACH
AM RHEIN

WHERE THE VINEYARDS ARE *Notice how almost all the vineyards hug the foothills to the left of the map, sometimes sneaking way up into the valleys that snake down from the forest-covered mountains. There are vineyards on the valley floor that stretch across to the river Rhine, but none of them are of any note. The Vosges mountains on the far left of the map attract most of the rain from the clouds blown in from the Atlantic by the prevailing westerly winds. This causes a narrow but beneficial rain-shadow over the vineyards in the lee of the hills, creating far warmer and drier conditions than usual in so northerly a region. The best vineyards in the area lie at a fairly consistent altitude, between 200 and 350m (656 and 1146ft), on fairly steep, well-drained soil, slanting south-east to south, making the most of the available sunshine.*

GRAPE VARIETIES AND WINE STYLES

The grape varieties that make Alsatian wine are, for the large part, German too. Her two most famous grapes – Gewurztraminer and Riesling – though enthusiastically planted in Germany and much of Central Europe, are conspicuous by their absence in any of France's other appellations controlées. Sylvaner doesn't appear elsewhere in France; Pinot Gris and Pinot Blanc are tolerated at best in a very subordinate role in Burgundy. Only the red Pinot Noir, Burgundy's best red grape, and the white Muscat, planted in the fortified wine appellations around the Mediterranean, have genuine legitimacy in France. In Germany, however, Riesling, Gewurztraminer, Pinot Blanc (known as Weissburgunder) and Pinot Gris (known as Ruländer or Grauburgunder) and even Sylvaner, in the Franken and Rheinhessen regions, are regarded as producing most of that country's greatest wines.

The dual personality of Alsace is reflected by the wines too. Alsace's French grape varieties take on a Germanic perfume, while the German grapes proudly distance themselves from the flavours one would find over the border in Germany itself.

Traditionally the difference has been more marked with Riesling because nearly all Germany's great Rieslings were sweet, whereas all those of Alsace were dry. Nowadays, Germany makes increasing amounts of dry Rieslings, many very good, but they are generally taut and lean as well as subtly scented. Alsace's best Rieslings, on the other hand, are fat and round in the mouth, yet marvellously dry, streaked with cold lime pith acidity, yet thick with glycerine ripeness. Alsace Riesling does best in the hillier Haut-Rhin in the south of the region on sheltered sites with sandy-clayey loams that warm up quickly in the spring.

The two countries' other wines are also distinctive. Germany's Gewurztraminer is generally made with a certain fat sweetness and perfume. Alsace goes for the perfume of freshly plucked tea roses and the ripeness of lychee and mango. Gewurztraminer needs a long, ripening season and loves Alsace's sunny, dry weather which continues well into the autumn. Germany's Ruländer is attractively honeyed and sweetish, though it is also appearing in a full oaky style under the Grauburgunder label, whereas Alsace Pinot Gris revels in spicy, musky, honeyed and exotic flavours. Most Alsace Pinot Noir is pale and floral, whereas Germany is making a number of Spätburgunders with impressive Burgundian depth. Alsace Muscats have a light, dry grapy perfume rather than the heady but weighty hothouse flavours preferred in the Muscats from France's far south.

Kaysersberg: the 'Hansel and Gretel' architecture found in Alsace could fool anyone into thinking they were in Germany. They wouldn't be far wrong – Germany is just over the Rhine to the east.

APPELLATIONS AND CLASSIFICATIONS

▪ **Alsace AC** The general AC covering the whole region. It appears on all labels. Any of the permitted grape varieties may be used. Currently, there is no intermediate level between AC and Grand Cru, but work is being done on a Premier Cru and there's talk of a 'Villages' level, too.

▪ **Alsace Grand Cru AC** This AC covers certain special vineyards (see page 79), and is allowed only for wines made from Gewurztraminer, Muscat, Pinot Gris and Riesling.

▪ **Crémant d'Alsace AC** This AC is for sparkling wine produced over the whole region and made in the traditional method usually from Pinot Blanc or Riesling.

▪ **Vendange Tardive** Late-harvested wine made from very ripe Gewurztraminer, Riesling, Pinot Gris and occasionally Muscat.

▪ **Séléction de Grains Nobles** A higher category than Vendange Tardive made from even riper grapes of the same varieties.

HEART OF ALSACE

THOUGH ALSACE'S WINE REGION stretches north to the border with Germany at Wissembourg and south almost to Mulhouse, a distance of about 110km (68 miles), virtually all the finest wines come from a central section of vineyards in the Haut-Rhin *département* west of Colmar, a miraculously preserved medieval market town which is rightly called the Wine Capital of Alsace. Good wines are made in the north of Alsace, in the Bas-Rhin *département*, but they rarely have the ripeness or intensity of those from the vineyards of the Haut-Rhin, which lie further south.

The vineyards that twist in and out of the folds in the Vosges eastern foothills are dotted with magical little villages that make you rub your eyes in disbelief at their unspoilt charm. And they're not some kind of Walt Disney copy – these are real working villages. Those tilting gabled houses are inhabited by the people who tend the vines and make the wine; those rickety wooden doors do lead down to cellars that have housed the vats and barrels for hundreds of years.

The vineyards on these slopes also date way back, as the Romans had planted most of the lower foothills with vines by the 2nd century. There are specific vineyards like Goldert in the village of Gueberschwihr and Mambourg in Sigolsheim, whose documented reputation stretches back to the eighth century, when Alsace was ruled by the Franks, and these ancient vineyards now form the core of the present Grand Cru system of wine classification in Alsace.

GRANDS CRUS

Grand Cru means 'great growth' and is intended to apply to particular patches of land that have traditionally produced the finest grapes. A similar system in Burgundy has produced famous names like le Montrachet and Chambertin which have, for centuries, enjoyed global renown. However, hardly any of the Alsace Grand Cru names are known except to a few devoted fans, and it wasn't until 1983 that a provisional list of Grand Cru sites was produced. Alsace's turbulent history has much to do with this, since it takes a fair bit of time to build the reputation of a Cru, and in the critical 19th and 20th centuries, when areas like Burgundy and Bordeaux were advancing their fame, Alsace was concentrating on expanding its vineyards into the flat, over-fertile soils of the plain nearer the Rhine in order to produce cheap wines.

After World War Two, when Alsace finally reverted to France, the winemakers determinedly set out to achieve appellation contrôlée status for their region and decided to do so by concentrating their efforts on the single appellation – that of Alsace, which was finally granted only in 1962 – but with the different grape names prominently displayed on the best wines to indicate what flavours the drinker should expect. This labelling by grape variety may seem commonplace now, because of the influence of New World wines, but it was novel in France, where more and more precise delineation of the origin of a wine was at the heart of the appellation system.

The people with the power to market and promote Alsace as a wine region of quality were the big merchant houses and, since their objective was to produce large quantities of wine at various but consistent levels of quality, they needed to blend from numerous different vineyards and hardly ever named the actual vineyard site, preferring to promote their own names as brands. This worked well enough, but in the 1980s, when export markets like Britain and the United States became increasingly interested in single-vineyard wines from the top European wine regions, conflict between the merchants, the growers, and indeed the co-operatives became inevitable. Despite owning large tracts of Grand Cru vineyards, the leading merchant houses of Beyer, Trimbach and Hugel are most unwilling even now to put vineyard names on their wines and, indeed, they do not market Grand Cru wines, preferring to emphasize their companies' reputations instead.

Their position is understandable and not solely self-interested, because houses like Hugel have been most influential in promoting the quality classifications of Vendange Tardive for wines from super-ripe grapes, and Sélection de Grains Nobles for wines from grapes affected by noble rot. However, the concept of superior vineyard sites is crucial in marginal vineyard regions where only the most favourable mesoclimates can truly excel. Good drainage and a good aspect to the sun are vital in any vineyard area at the limits of the vine's ability to ripen.

At present there are 50 Grand Cru sites covering 8 per cent of Alsace vineyards, but they represent only 4 per cent of Alsace's total wine production. Basic maximum yields are lower than for simple Alsace wines, but are still high at 55hl/ha and serious growers never reach these figures. Current law states that only four 'noble' grapes planted in these sites are entitled to the Grand Cru appellation – Gewürztraminer, Riesling, Pinot Gris and Muscat (and all have to be unblended); but in future each local area may be allowed to nominate other varieties that perform particularly well in a given site. There is no doubt that many of the best sites, exploited by the best growers, do produce unique personalities in the wine that dominate varietal character, especially in Rieslings. Those Grands Crus that genuinely deserve a special reputation, and whose vines are tended with care and respect, will eventually establish top reputations for themselves and be able to charge top prices. But there are still numerous wines sporting Grand Cru labels that offer nothing special. But then, Alsace is still in the throes of re-organizing its classification system.

Currently, there is no intermediate level of quality between the great 'Grand Cru' vineyards and the simple Alsace AC. Work is now being done on establishing a group of Premier Cru vineyards, below Grand Cru, and these might eventually cover 2000–3000ha of land. There is also talk of a 'Villages' classification between Premier Cru and AC. And if all this sounds familiar, you're right. Burgundy operates just such a system and, from a good producer, it gives a reliable pointer to relative quality levels.

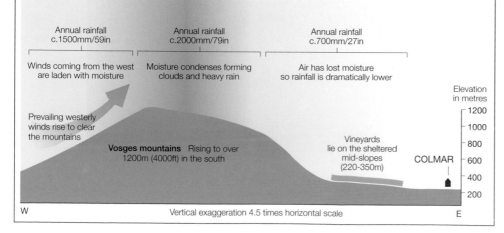

THE CLIMATE OF ALSACE

Alsace can muster enough sunshine to ripen grapes because of the Vosges mountains which run from north to south for about 65km (40 miles) in the west of the region. These mountains create a narrow but beneficial rain shadow over the vineyards in their lee. The prevailing westerly winds bring moisture-laden air in from the Atlantic. The Vosges are the first major obstacle which the air reaches and as it rises to pass over the mountains it cools and the moisture condenses and falls as rain, leaving the eastern slopes dry and sunny.

Annual rainfall c.1500mm/59in

Annual rainfall c.2000mm/79in

Annual rainfall c.700mm/27in

Winds coming from the west are laden with moisture

Moisture condenses forming clouds and heavy rain

Air has lost moisture so rainfall is dramatically lower

Prevailing westerly winds rise to clear the mountains

Vosges mountains Rising to over 1200m (4000ft) in the south

Vineyards lie on the sheltered mid-slopes (220-350m)

Elevation in metres
1200
1000
800
600
400
200

COLMAR

W

Vertical exaggeration 4.5 times horizontal scale

E

0 km   1   2
0 miles   1

WHERE THE VINEYARDS ARE *There is not a single top-quality Alsace vineyard that doesn't rely on the protection of the Vosges mountains. The reason that most of the very best Alsace vineyards are in the central block of foothills between Bergheim and Gueberschwihr is that the Vosges mountains are at their highest and broadest at this point. Further north, the mountains are substantially lower and do not provide such an efficient rain-shadow. Good wines are made in the northerly Bas-Rhin region of Alsace, but they rarely have the ripeness or intensity of those from the vineyards of the Haut-Rhin shown here. The map clearly demonstrates how the vines sweep up towards the wooded hilltops, yet peter out towards the flat valley floor. If you look at the location of the Grands Crus, all of them are either in the lee of the hills or else, as in the case of Froehn and Mambourg, on large outcrops of steeply sloping land away from the foothills. The excellent drainage and the favourable aspect to the sun provided by the slopes are crucial, particularly in a vineyard area such as Alsace, which is at the limits of the vine's ability to ripen.*

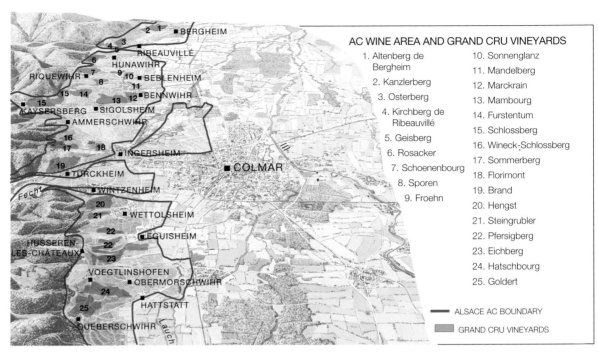

AC WINE AREA AND GRAND CRU VINEYARDS

1. Altenberg de Bergheim
2. Kanzlerberg
3. Osterberg
4. Kirchberg de Ribeauvillé
5. Geisberg
6. Rosacker
7. Schoenenbourg
8. Sporen
9. Froehn
10. Sonnenglanz
11. Mandelberg
12. Marckrain
13. Mambourg
14. Furstentum
15. Schlossberg
16. Wineck-Schlossberg
17. Sommerberg
18. Florimont
19. Brand
20. Hengst
21. Steingrubler
22. Pfersigberg
23. Eichberg
24. Hatschbourg
25. Goldert

▬▬ ALSACE AC BOUNDARY

▓ GRAND CRU VINEYARDS

0 km — 1 — 2
0 miles — 1

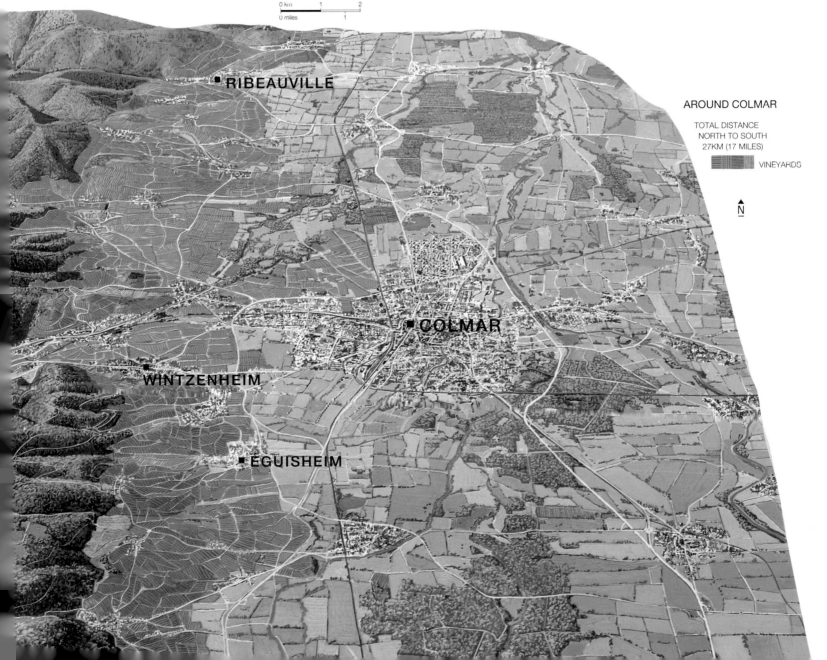

AROUND COLMAR

TOTAL DISTANCE
NORTH TO SOUTH
27KM (17 MILES)

▦ VINEYARDS

▲
N

THE LOIRE VALLEY

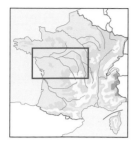

I SOMETIMES WONDER WHETHER the Loire River is just too long for its own good. It starts brightly enough, cascading and splashing out of the Ardèche gorges only 50km (31 miles) west of the Rhône at Valence, full of purpose and vivacity. Gambolling and churning its way northwards, it seems to be tiring even as it reaches the site of its first decent vineyards – those of the Côtes du Forez and Côte Roannaise, both of which make a very passable imitation of good Beaujolais from the Gamay grape. But by the time the river gets to Pouilly and Sancerre, sites of its first world-famous wines, the initial breezy seaward flow has slowed to a walk.

As the river makes its great arc northwards to Orléans past the haunting Sologne marshes, and then loops wearily south and west, through Blois, Tours, Angers, Nantes and finally to the Atlantic at St-Nazaire, the walk slows to an amble, the motion of the water so listless that the valley seems caught in a reverie, completely unconcerned about reaching its destination on the turbulent shores of the Bay of Biscay. Great gravel banks push through the river's surface, children paddle in the shallows, parents picnic and gossip on the warm pebbles (mind you, in winter it's a different story with treacherous currents and a tendency to flood). It doesn't seem as though the lazy summer Loire has the character to be a great wine river, home of some of the most thrilling and individual wines in France. But behind its dozy exterior, the Loire Valley does have exactly the character required.

GRAPE VARIETIES

The Loire is predominantly a white grape region, producing enormous quantities of wine from Melon de Bourgogne – one of the world's most neutral white grape varieties. As its name suggests, the grape was originally from Burgundy, but it is no longer grown there and is far more famous as Muscadet. Its virtue, when grown in the maritime climate near Nantes, is that it retains freshness, which makes it an exceptionally good partner to the local seafood.

Sauvignon Blanc needs a relatively cool climate if it is to express its trademark pungency, its bright green, grassy, gooseberry freshness and slightly smoky perfume. In Sancerre and Pouilly, in the hands of a good winemaker, Sauvignon Blanc excels at such

The Loire Valley was the playground of the Valois kings and the French court in the 15th and 16th centuries. Château de Chenonceau on the river Cher is just one of many outstanding Renaissance palaces built during the golden age of French culture.

mouth-tingling crispness. But Loire Sauvignon Blanc can also be associated with a pungent 'cat's pee' smell, a sure sign that the fruit was not ripe when picked. Sauvignon needs its green streak; the skill is in marrying that with proper ripeness.

Chenin Blanc needs warmth – it's raw and harsh when unripe. Few other places in the world take Chenin Blanc seriously, but here in the Loire Valley it can reach heights undreamed of elsewhere. The *tufa* soil (a type of chalky limestone) keeps acidity levels high, enabling the greatest dry and sweet Chenins to last for decades, when they mature to a honeyed, minerally richness. Chenin is used for everything from sparkling wines to botrytized sweet ones. While most dry Loire Chenin Blanc is made for drinking young, those from Vouvray and Savennières age brilliantly. Still Vouvray can, in fact, be searingly dry when young and needs aging – often at least two decades or more. Then there's the mildly sweet *demi-sec*, with its gorgeous nuances of honeysuckle and quince. And when the autumn is kind and lasts long, then great sweet wines are made, from grapes that have either been affected by noble rot or dehydrated by heat.

Cabernet Franc, used largely as a seasoning grape in Bordeaux, is the main red wine grape grown in the Loire. In Bourgueil, St-Nicolas-de-Bourgueil and Chinon, its mouthwatering perfume and smooth texture makes some of France's most lovely red wines. At its best, Cabernet Franc has an unmistakable and hugely appealing raspberry fruit and a summery tang of blackcurrant leaves. Delicious young, its wines can also be very long-lived. It is used for rosés, too.

Pinot Noir, the great grape of Burgundy, is grown in the Loire in Sancerre and Menetou-Salon where, in ripe years, it makes wines with good fruit and structure. Most red Sancerre, however, is made to be drunk young. Some Pinot Noir goes into rosé production.

Gamay makes fresh, juicy Beaujolais-like reds and rosé wines designed to be drunk young. The Teinturier Gamay (red-fleshed, as opposed to the Gamay Noir à Jus Blanc) is also grown in Touraine, but its wines are robust, solid and unaromatic.

PAYS NANTAIS

Since the river's flow can be so mild, let's begin by looking at the vineyards at its western seaward end, and then push our way upstream aided by the brisk westerly winds, to Sancerre and Pouilly, several hundred miles away. Well, I have to admit these wines of the Pays Nantais, as the western section is called, are indeed the mildest, the least memorable of the entire river. But they are also some of the most famous, for this is the home of Muscadet and the four Muscadet appellations, which between them now constitute the second highest volume of French wine production after Bordeaux Rouge.

Muscadet is famous because it is so irreproachably, ultra-gluggably anonymous. At best it has a quenching freshness, a hint of lemon and pepper, a hint of apricot, and if you're lucky, a hint of cream. But we're talking about hints here – the one thing Muscadet never does is taste of a good deal of anything. And that is the basis for its success.

Muscadet isn't the name of an area: it's the local name for the Burgundian grape variety of Melon de Bourgogne. Because this was the only variety in the Nantes region to survive the devastating frosts of 1709–10, it was enthusiastically adopted by local growers. For more than two centuries the Muscadet, and its more acidic neighbour the Gros Plant, did an excellent job of providing cheap, light white wine to accompany the superb local seafood.

But Parisians eat seafood too – from autumn to spring there are oyster stalls all over Paris' *boulevards* – and they adopted Muscadet as their seafood wine. Then, during the 1970s and '80s the export

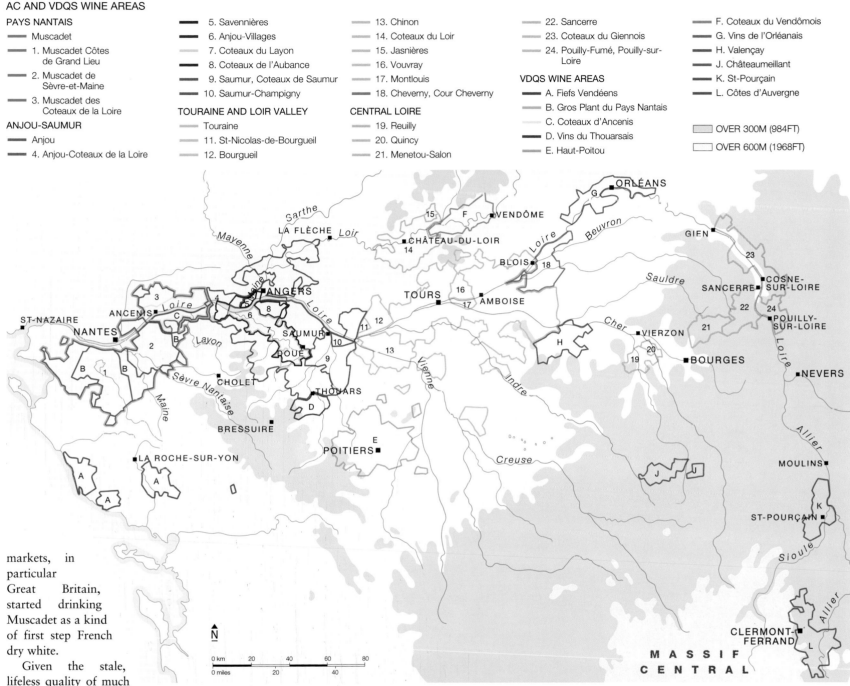

markets, in particular Great Britain, started drinking Muscadet as a kind of first step French dry white.

Given the stale, lifeless quality of much cheap Muscadet, it would be easy to say that this mirrored the sluggish brown estuarial waters of the river as it oozes through St-Nazaire. But Muscadet need not be a poor drink – it is only the exploitation of an easily remembered name by greedy merchants that makes it so. Good Muscadet, especially from the delightful jumbled rolling countryside of the Sèvre-et-Maine area south-east of Nantes, can be an absolute charmer – relatively neutral in taste, but with a streak of grapefruit and pepper assertiveness and a mild creaminess too.

Because of the innate neutrality of the grape, the best examples are left on their yeast lees, and are undisturbed before being bottled directly off the lees – thereby capturing a little of the yeasty creaminess and also some of the natural carbon dioxide in the wine. These wines are labelled 'sur lie' and their blend of freshness, neutrality and soft texture make them the perfect seafood wine. The tangy, acid Gros Plant du Pays Nantais, from the flat vineyards whipped by the salty ocean gales to the south-west of Nantes, can

equal Muscadet as the perfect accompaniment to seafood. And if I had to choose one city in France in which to enjoy brilliant seafood, Nantes would take some beating.

ANJOU-SAUMUR

We need to head upstream – past Ancenis, where, surprisingly, the Alsace grape Pinot Gris makes a little, vaguely sweet wine under the title Malvoisie – before we really begin to discover the fascinating variety that belies the river's somnambulent appearance. This brings us to Anjou, with its plantations of the thoroughly difficult, exasperating, but sometimes majestically rewarding Chenin Blanc grape variety.

Much of Anjou isn't ideal for the vine – remember that the Loire Valley is as far north as the vine can ripen on the west coast of France, and most of Anjou is planted with cereal crops and vegetables, which are able to withstand the wind and rain better than

any grape vines can. Those vines planted away from the various river valleys on exposed land are unlikely to produce anything but the most basic wine, generally the palest of pale whites – or a pale pink from various struggling reds. This explains why much of the cheap Anjou Rosé to be found skulking among the pink wines on every merchant's shelf is so poor – the grapes are grown on exposed sites that would be better suited to cabbages, and they just never ripen.

But there are sheltered vineyards, usually facing towards the south-west, ideally planted on limestone or slate soils, that can produce some absolute stunners. Most brilliant of these, and most unexpected, are the sweet Chenin wines (see below) that emerge from the folds of the river banks along the Layon Valley, and to a lesser extent, the Aubance Valley, both of which are formed by southern tributaries of the Loire river.

Generally, however, the Chenin Blanc makes medium or dry wines in Anjou. The climatic feature that allows the grapes to ripen at all along the cool Loire Valley is a generally warm early autumn that, with luck, pushes the late-ripening Chenin Blanc to a decent level of maturity. The most famous of these whites is the dry Savennières, perched on the north side of the Loire, just to the west of Angers, a gaunt, austere wine with the distant beauty of an ice maiden. Most of the rest of Anjou's whites come from vineyards spread across the fields south of the Loire. The regulations allow for up to 20 per cent of Chardonnay and Sauvignon Blanc in the blend, but increasingly producers prefer to use just Chenin Blanc, making sure it is properly ripe before picking it.

But for those grapes that fail to ripen properly, there is still a haven: in the eastern part of Anjou, bordering on Touraine, is Saumur, one of France's chief production centres for sparkling wine (see box, facing page). The soils around Saumur are more chalky than in the rest of Anjou, which encourages a certain leanness in the wines. This, combined with cool ripening conditions, often produces just the sort of acid base wine that sparkling wine manufacturers like.

Red wines are less successful in most of Anjou because the largely clay soils don't ripen the grapes sufficiently, but there are pockets of decent Gamay and Cabernet Franc – the best of these Cabernet Franc vineyards claiming an Anjou-Villages appellation – while the Saumur-Champigny vineyards to the south-east of the town can make delightful fragrant reds of varying weights.

SWEET WINES OF THE LAYON VALLEY

Across from Savennières the Layon river joins the Loire, and it is along the Layon's northern banks that the Chenin grape produces some of the finest sweet wines in France. Even so, it is often a long wait to achieve the necessary overripeness, but good sites allied to meticulous producers can manage it on a regular basis.

Most great sweet wines are made when the grapes are attacked by the noble rot fungus. For the last few miles before the two rivers join, the influence of both causes morning mists to form along the Layon and its little tributaries. This humidity rising from the streams in warm autumns provides perfect conditions for the development of noble rot, which, as in Sauternes (see page 48), helps to concentrate the grapes' sweetness to a remarkable degree. A combination of climate, the Chenin Blanc grape and those growers with nerves of steel means that sweet wines can be made here even in the most difficult of years. These luscious wines can be utterly magical.

In particular at Quarts de Chaume and Bonnezeaux, a perfect sheltered south to south-west exposure allows grapes every chance

Right: the castle and fortifications of Chinon stand proudly above the Vienne, a tributary of the Loire, but the river meanders lazily past, and the sandbanks make a perfect perch for a local fisherman.

The river Layon is a tributary of the Loire: Chenin Blanc from vineyards along its banks is rich and sweet.

to ripen, then rot. Even so, noble rot doesn't happen uniformly. Often the pickers have to comb the vines again and again, picking the grapes that have nobly rotted, sometimes grape by grape, and leaving the rest to develop the welcome fungus.

Coteaux du Layon covers 25 communes in the Layon Valley. Coteaux du Layon-Villages covers six of the best seven villages between Faye d'Anjou and St-Aubin de Luigné. Coteaux du Layon-Chaume applies to the best village in the valley. Quarts de Chaume and Bonnezeaux are the two Grands Crus with perfect conditions and slopes for when the autumn weather holds.

Both the Coteaux de l'Aubance and the Coteaux de la Loire make reasonable sweetish white wines.

TOURAINE

The best Loire reds come from Touraine, a few miles to the east where the breezes seem to soften and the air to mellow. Touraine *appellations* St-Nicolas-de-Bourgueil, Bourgueil and Chinon use the Cabernet Franc grape to create gorgeously refreshing, tangy reds – wonderful young, but also capable of staying fresh for decades.

However, I have to admit that when I'm in Touraine, I find it difficult to concentrate on the wines, because there are more spectacular castles here than anywhere else in France. These bear testament to the Valois kings who, from the 15th century onwards, used Touraine for rest and relaxation. Many châteaux are open to visitors and, though I don't normally have time for sightseeing, I have seen a few of these beauties, Chenonceau, Amboise and Azay-le-Rideau among them.

And in any case, the only other famous wine in Touraine is Vouvray. Cheap Vouvray is a peculiarly nasty sulphurous brew of no virtue whatsoever. But the appellation has been undergoing a revival. From a committed producer the dry, medium, sweet, or fizzy white wines of Vouvray can be a revelation, each of them fit for sipping on the balustrades of some of the most grandiose châteaux.

Vineyards are spread sparsely through the rest of Touraine, and as we follow the Loire up past Blois to Orléans, they become almost non-existent. Given that Orléans is the vinegar capital of France, this may be no bad thing, and it certainly makes one wonder what the local wines used to be like. Yet a tiny wine industry does survive here, and from one or two producers, including Clos St-Fiacre who make an excellent Chardonnay (here called the Auvernat), the wine can be rather good. This is also the hang-out of several producers of a pleasant, pale, smoky pink wine called Gris Meunier – from the Pinot Meunier grape, famously used in the Champagne blend. The strangest things do crop up along the Loire Valley.

CENTRAL VINEYARDS

As we turn south from Orléans up the Loire past the minor wine towns of Gien and Cosne, to the mainstream appellations of Sancerre and Pouilly-Fumé – regarded by many as the quintessential Sauvignon Blanc styles – we come across a few plots of Chasselas. This is basically an eating grape – indeed it was grown for the dining-tables of Paris in the 19th century – though it is used for wine in Alsace, Germany and Switzerland. Chasselas makes wine of just about no discernible character and yet here, in the fancy vineyards of Pouilly, in a world crying out for good Sauvignon Blanc, you still find the odd plot of Chasselas. Weird, but most of Pouilly is more than capable of looking after itself, making high-quality, high-priced Sauvignon.

Sancerre across the river also concentrates on Sauvignon whites. Recently, though, top Sancerre producers have been paying increased attention to Pinot Noir, a traditional variety in the area.

By reducing yields they have produced some remarkably full bodied reds, showing how dilute most other red Sancerres are.

Menetou-Salon adjoins Sancerre and makes delicious Sancerre lookalikes (white, rosé and red) but a bit cheaper. Going further west still, past the historic town of Bourges, brings you to Reuilly with its light reds and rosés. But Reuilly, along with its neighbour Quincy, are much better at making good, snappy Sauvignon whites, filled with the aroma of gooseberries and green grass.

UPPER LOIRE

We could continue up the river, eyes peeled for any signs of life beneath its placid surface, for another 160km (100 miles) and more until, past Roanne in the Loire gorge, it finally shows fitful signs of life. But if we do, we won't find too many vines trailing down to the water's edge. There's little wine of consequence produced between Pouilly and Roanne, except for some made around St-Pourçain close to the Allier, a Loire tributary.

Honest Gamays from the Côte Roannaise plus the occasional rosé are helped by association: the famous Troisgros restaurant at Roanne often serves the bright, Gamay red as its house wine. Past the Loire gorge, the Côtes du Forez red is similar in style – but it doesn't have a world-famous local chef to trumpet its charms.

THE SPARKLING WINES OF THE LOIRE

It would be easy to look upon the Loire Valley sparkling wine industry simply as a mechanism for soaking up large amounts of otherwise undrinkable local wines, since most of the best sparklers are made from a very acid base wine. But this wouldn't be fair, any more than it would be fair to describe Champagne in those terms. Although in a warm year the late-ripening Chenin Blanc can make excellent still wine, in the all-too-frequent cool years this high acid variety simply doesn't get ripe enough. So a cool year provides the perfect material for sparkling wines.

The best sparkling wines are made by the traditional method (as used in Champagne), that is, with a second fermentation in the bottle, and tend to come from cool vineyards of limestone-dominated soils and subsoils. Both Saumur and Vouvray, which produce the two most important sparkling wine appellations in the region, are predominantly limestone areas. Vouvray and its neighbouring appellation of Montlouis use only Chenin Blanc for their fizz and, if you give the bottles a few years to soften, they attain a delicious nutty, honeyed quality, yet retain the zing of Chenin acidity.

Saumur Mousseux is usually based on Chenin but may include other varieties like Chardonnay, Sauvignon and Cabernet Franc. Saumur Mousseux made from 100 per cent Chenin is often too lean, so the addition of Cabernet, and Chardonnay in particular, brings a very welcome softness. Crémant de Loire, an appellation created in 1975 covering Anjou and Touraine, stipulates lower vineyard yields and requires 150kg (330lb) of grapes to make one hectolitre of juice, rather than the 130kg (287lb) permitted for Saumur. This lower yield of juice means the grapes are not pressed so savagely and so the bitter elements present in the skins and pips are not extracted. The appellation also stipulates a longer aging period before release, giving a gentler foaming mousse and attractive hints of yeast and honey. The wines are generally superior to Saumur, but the title of Crémant de Loire sounds rather generic and catch-all, and so it hasn't had the success it deserves.

Occasionally in Saumur you'll find a Cabernet Franc-based fizzy red, grassy and full of fruit, ideal for picnic glugging by the riverbank.

ANJOU-SAUMUR

RED GRAPES
Groslot is used for rosé,
mainly Cabernet Franc and
a little Cabernet Sauvignon
for the reds. Gamay is also
planted in Anjou.

WHITE GRAPES
Chenin Blanc is the main
grape, with increasing amounts
of Chardonnay and Sauvignon
Blanc.

CLIMATE
A mild maritime climate
moderated by the influence
of the Gulf Stream produces
warm summers and mild
autumns and winters. Ripening
can be a problem.

SOIL
In Anjou the soil is
predominantly dark slate,
schist and clay with areas of
more permeable shale and
gravel which favour the
Cabernet grapes. Much of
Saumur is limestone
characterized by pale outcrops
of a chalky freestone known
as *tuffeau blanc*.

ASPECT
In this area of low hills specific
aspect to the sun is vital for
ripening. The best sites are
on the steeper slopes and
face south-west, south or
south-east.

SINCE 1985, ANJOU HAS HAD A DECENT RED WINE in which to incorporate its name – Anjou-Villages AC – from a grouping of 46 Anjou villages south of Angers deemed to have better than average vineyard sites. Only Cabernet Franc and Cabernet Sauvignon may be used for Anjou-Villages and, by a lucky coincidence, the 1988, '89 and '90 vintages were excellent, giving the appellation a great start, while the last five vintages of the 20th century were equally good. The dry, fruity wines need at least three to four years aging.

These hinterland villages spread across the indeterminate rolling agricultural land running from west of Angers across to Saumur, and centred on Brissac-Quincé, needed all the help they could get to make decent wine. The sweet wines of the Layon Valley (see page 83), the small, high-class, dry white appellation of Savennières, west of Angers, and the sparkling and red wines of Saumur are among the several enclaves of high-quality wine in Anjou. Despite these,

WHERE THE VINEYARDS ARE *The border between Anjou and the Muscadet region of Nantais is just to the west of the map and these wild, open acres enjoy the mixed blessing of a maritime climate. They avoid the extremes of temperature of a continental climate and, in general, enjoy a reasonably balmy autumn, but they also get the damp, westerly winds that drive inland from the Bay of Biscay. Some Coteaux de la Loire is grown in these vineyards, but it's hard work. Then see how dramatically things change where the Layon river joins the Loire at Chalonnes.*

On the Loire's north bank, suddenly there are sufficient plateaux to protect vineyards beneath them – and Savennières immediately benefits from this protection. The Layon meanders in to join the Loire from the south-east. Its northern banks have ridges of hills and forests to protect the vines and allow the long autumn ripening that the grapes need to make great sweet wine (see page 83). The land becomes wooded and undulating from here, right across to Saumur. This creates myriad mesoclimates where even a late-ripening variety like Chenin Blanc has a chance to build up sugar. At Saumur in the east of the region we are into the chalky freestone subsoil which also dominates Touraine and gives excellent conditions for white grapes.

the image of the province has been relentlessly dragged down for decades by the mediocrity of most Anjou Rosé and the over-sulphured, off-dry Anjou Blanc.

The drift away from rosé wines by the drinking public forced the Anjou winemakers to rethink. Many of the vineyards in Anjou are too exposed, and the soil is too cool and moist for them to be able to produce anything special, and, apart from ripping up their vines, growers have little choice but to continue growing the uninspiring Groslot for rosés or late-ripening Chenin for whites.

The trouble is, much of Anjou isn't particularly suited to grape-growing – the great open spaces full of cereals and sunflowers and vegetables bear witness to that. But modern methods of viticulture and winemaking can and do help. There is a small amount of Anjou-Gamay made by the Beaujolais method of fermentation – carbonic maceration (see page 68). It makes a fairly rustic, but juicy, purplish red, much of which is drunk as Primeur in November, just after the vintage.

For the Cabernet-based wines the problem is how to get enough colour and flavour from grapes that rarely ripen fully in Anjou without risking bitter, tannic harshness from unripe skins and pips. The solution is to lower the yields, de-leaf and, for top producers, to pick selectively. Micro-oxygenation is also being used to extract colour and flavour. Similarly the best white producers concentrate on getting their Chenin Blanc ripe and using stainless steel and cold fermentation. Some also ferment in new wood. There is, however, a big gap between the best and the worst, and more than ever, you need to look for the producer's name rather than the appellation.

SAVENNIÈRES

The one dry Anjou white which has always been revered, if not exactly fêted, is Savennières. The vineyards don't amount to more than 60ha (148 acres) looking out over the islands and channels of the wide Loire towards the mouth of the Layon river, but they can produce the Loire's best dry whites. When this appellation was granted in 1952 the permitted yield was set artificially low, and the

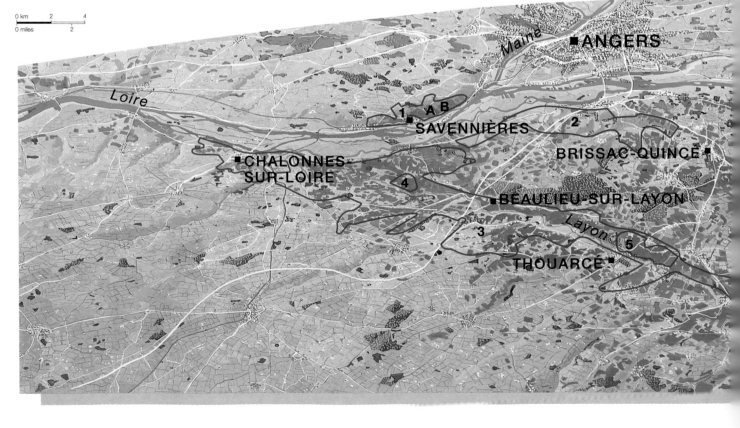

minimum alcohol level extremely high, because the wine was then generally sweet, and good sweet French wines always have very low permitted yields and ambitiously high minimum alcohol levels.

Today, Savennières is almost always dry, and the restrictions are a mixed blessing. On the slate and clay soils, high alcohol is only possible most years because of the low yield, and it is this rare, high ripeness level from the tricky Chenin grape that gives Savennières wine the ability to age and improve for a generation or more. There are two small Grands Crus – Coulée-de-Serrant, which makes the subtlest and most refined wine and la Roche-aux-Moines, whose wines are lighter but also extremely good – whose steep slopes rising up from the Loire (see right) and excellent exposure to the sun further intensify the taut, but fathoms-deep, flavour of these wines.

SAUMUR

Saumur is important both for its sparkling white wines and its Cabernet Franc reds. The soil changes as you head south-east from Angers to Saumur. The dark clay, slate and schist of Angers has been replaced mostly by limestone, especially a layer of chalky freestone called *tuffeau blanc*. This freestone layer is over 50m (164ft) thick in places, and not only provides a completely different subsoil for vines, in particular along the south bank of the Loire where the red grape vineyards are situated, but it also offers the perfect medium for wine cellars. This rock was quarried to build many of the region's châteaux and the excavations left behind numerous caves which have been adapted over the centuries for growing mushrooms, aging wine or even as dwellings.

Champagne in north-eastern France is founded on chalk, its vines grow on chalk, and its wines mature in cool, underground chalk cellars. It is very similar in Saumur, where there are reckoned to be 1000km (620 miles) of underground passages and cellars. Sparkling Saumur is based on Chenin grapes, but both Chardonnay and Sauvignon Blanc are allowed to constitute up to 20 per cent of the blend as they are in still Saumur Blanc. Up to 60 per cent of red grapes are permitted in white sparkling Saumur and 100 per cent in the rosé. Interestingly, there is also an occasional, rare sweet Chenin called Coteaux de Saumur produced at the eastern end of Anjou.

Still Saumur Rouge is based on Cabernet Franc, though Cabernet Sauvignon and the rare Pineau d'Aunis can also be used. On Saumur's chalky soils the Cabernet Franc grape does best, producing light but often attractively grassy reds, and, in the small Saumur-Champigny area, especially on the freestone plateaux east and south-east of the town, this is often married to a keen, mouthwatering blackcurrant and raspberry fruit.

Savennières' top two vineyards – Coulée de Serrant in the foreground and la Roche-aux-Moines with its château in the distance – lie on steep slopes above the Loire.

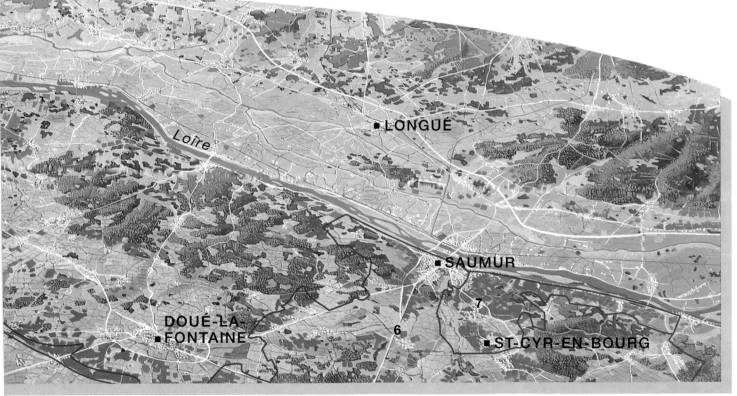

AC WINE AREAS

1. Savennières
   A. la Roche-aux-Moines
   B. Coulée-de-Serrant
2. Coteaux de l'Aubance
3. Coteaux du Layon
4. Quarts de Chaume
5. Bonnezeaux
6. Saumur
7. Saumur-Champigny

TOTAL DISTANCE NORTH TO SOUTH 40KM (25 MILES)

━━━ AC BOUNDARIES

▦ VINEYARDS

SANCERRE & POUILLY

RED GRAPES
Such reds as there are will be produced from Pinot Noir.

WHITE GRAPES
Sauvignon Blanc is king here, occupying the best sites throughout the region. There is a little Chasselas on inferior sites in Pouilly. Some Pinot Gris is used in Reuilly for rosé.

CLIMATE
As the maritime influences wane, summers are longer and warmer, winters cooler and drier. Frost can be a problem early in the year. Shelter from the prevailing north-east wind is important.

SOIL
The soil here is limestone-based with the shallow, pebbly, Kimmeridgian formations of Sancerre producing the best vineyards. Flinty deposits in Sancerre and Pouilly are supposed to affect the wine's flavour.

ASPECT
The hills rise to around 350m (1148ft). Deep crevices in the slopes produce favourable south and south-westerly aspects.

I'M ALWAYS HEARTILY GLAD to see the great mound of Sancerre looming up in front of me on the banks of the Loire. At last. A landmark in the featureless centre of France, a reference point I can relate to. I've approached Sancerre from all directions, but usually from the empty, disorientating acres of waterways and marshland which make up the Sologne, the setting for Alain-Fournier's wonderful novel, *Le Grand Meaulnes*.

This area, more than any other, conveys the sense of isolation that pervades France's lonely heart. And then up looms the hill of Sancerre: beautiful buildings, ramparts, a town square full of bustle and bars and restaurants – and a view. After so much flat land, a view across the low valleys, the exposed ridges of chalk, or up the lazy course of the Loire river as it sidles past from the south – any kind of view – and then I'm back into the square for a seat in the sun and a glass of cold, crisp white wine. Sancerre. Although the price of Sancerre has risen and its quality has just as frequently dipped as popularity has taken its toll, it is still, for me, the epitome of thirst-quenching, tangy, tingly fresh, dry white wine.

In fact there is a family of five white wines (six, if we include the rare Coteaux du Giennois from a few miles downstream) that use the Sauvignon Blanc grape to excellent effect. This little patch of France also produces red and rosé wines, but it is the palate-teasing white from the Sauvignon Blanc that made the region famous, and that still produces its best wines.

WINE AREAS

Sancerre is the biggest and most important of these appellations, covering 14 communes on the west bank of the Loire, the best of which are clustered beneath the steep slopes close to the town of Sancerre itself. Pouilly-Fumé is a white-only appellation on the Loire's east bank, a couple of miles upstream from Sancerre. Its wines are of equal quality but sometimes they have slightly more weight, a little more coffee-bean smokiness and a little less gooseberry crunch.

Menetou-Salon makes red, white and rosé from ten different communes in the charmingly haphazard countryside between Sancerre and Bourges. Its whites, from the Sauvignon grape, are of a similar standard to Sancerre and are always cheaper. Quincy is a small appellation on sandy gravel just west of Bourges, producing white Sauvignon wines with a marked, but attractive, gooseberry

WHERE THE VINEYARDS ARE *Look at that tiny town of Sancerre, perched on its hill, and surrounded by a tight little clutch of slopes and valleys as the limestone rears briefly but dramatically out of the dull, flat farmland of the centre of France. The steep south-facing slopes of these hills are crammed with vineyards. Then look across the river Loire and down a mile or two towards Pouilly. From a landscape of bland cereal fields and meadows, suddenly there is a rash of vineyards. These two vineyard areas make similar wine which is seen by many as the most perfect example of the tangy, grassy-gooseberry dry styles that are the hallmark of good Sauvignon Blanc the world over.*

Both wines are only this good because of the soil type and the mesoclimate. The open spaces of this part of France would usually not be warm enough to ripen Sauvignon, or Pinot Noir, which Sancerre uses for rosé and red. Limestone is the basis for the soil, though Pouilly, around St-Andelain, and St-Satur north of Sancerre have a good deal of flint that is supposed to influence the flavour of the wine. Indeed, you should be able to recognize a good Pouilly Fumé by its smoky, flinty whiff.

Pouilly's vineyards slope gently south and south-west and are warmed by the Loire. Sancerre's best vineyards, in Bué, Chavignol, Verdigny and Menétréol, cling to those crevices cut into the limestone hills that offer protection from wind and rain and full exposure to the sun. Chavignol is also famous for a goats' cheese called Crottin.

aggression. A couple of miles further west is the even smaller Reuilly, which makes good whites on its chalky soil, adequate reds, and surprisingly good pale rosés from Pinot Gris and Pinot Noir. One of the local growers rejoices in the name of Olivier Cromwell, but there are no other outward signs of anti-royalist feeling.

All of these smaller appellations are now benefiting from the rise in popularity of Sancerre and Pouilly-Fumé. However, this rise is extremely recent. Until the 1950s, these were country wines no-one had ever heard of. Luckily, a merry band of Parisian journalists and restaurant-owners, enjoying a few jaunts from the capital, took to these sharp, tangy whites gulped down with their lunch on the banks of the Loire. Sancerre and Pouilly-Fumé consequently became chic first in Paris, and then throughout the world.

Yet Sancerre and Pouilly weren't even white wine areas to start with. The present increased interest in red Sancerre is a reminder of the situation before the phylloxera bug destroyed the vineyards in the late 19th century. In pre-phylloxera days, because of the area's proximity to Paris, the fields were intensively farmed and mostly packed with high-yielding, low-quality vines whose vast volumes of hooch disappeared down a million uncritical Parisian throats. A further 2000ha (4942 acres) or so made reasonable red from Pinot Noir. After the phylloxera scourge, Sauvignon Blanc was chosen as the grape variety to replant, both because it was a high yielder, and because it was easier to graft onto phylloxera-resistant rootstocks.

Pinot Noir was generally replanted only in the less suitable, exposed, north-facing plots in Sancerre, and not at all in Pouilly. There are now about 1600ha (3954 acres) in Sancerre, and about

SANCERRE AND POUILLY

TOTAL DISTANCE
NORTH TO SOUTH
18KM (11 MILES)

VINEYARDS

N

0 km 1 2
0 miles 1

600ha (1483 acres) in Pouilly. Though one or two Sancerre producers now give some of their good land to Pinot Noir, most of the best sites are planted with Sauvignon Blanc. I'm sure this is correct. Sancerre Pinot Noir rarely achieves more than a rather wispy cherry fragrance although some are more serious; Sancerre and Pouilly Sauvignon Blanc, on the other hand, can mix hedgerow and meadow scents with memorable intensity. They can reek of freshly roasted beans in a coffee shop on a December morning. They can have a thrilling new cut grass, blackcurrant leaf and gooseberry attack that taunts your taste buds. They can – but over-popularity often undermines their quality.

In Sancerre, the best wines come from the villages near Sancerre town, usually from the steep south-facing slopes. Shelter from wind and exposure to sun are all-important, often more so than the different types of soil. Even so, soil does matter – the more limestone the better, in general, and the Kimmeridgian limestones and clay that produce the best Chablis reappear here and give very perfumed wine.

There are also patches of limestony gravel and a few scattered outcrops with flints. In Pouilly the vineyards cover less land, but are more dense and compact. The same limestone-dominated clays constitute most of the vineyard land, but there is also a patch of flinty, silex soil near St-Andelain which is sometimes said to be responsible for weightier, correspondingly more minerally wines.

AC WINE AREAS

POUILLY = AC WINE AREAS

—— AC BOUNDARIES

The great hill of Hermitage looms above the town of Tain and produces some of the most powerful red wines in France as well as a small amount of long-lived dry white.

capable of producing majestic reds and intriguing whites, which are able to stand the test of time as well as any other French wines. The red wines manage to combine a rough-hewn, animal power with a sweetness of fruit and wildness of perfume. This may be less academically correct than great Bordeaux and less sensually explicit than great Burgundy, but it catches you unawares and spins you in a dizzy pirouette in a way that no other red wine can.

White Hermitage lacks the immediate charm and fragrance of all France's other great white wines, and may seem fat and sulky almost before it's bottled, and its pudgy sullenness is surely no candidate for making old bones. I don't think many Rhône winemakers can explain it either, but good white Hermitage, often made solely from the Marsanne grape, but generally with a little Roussanne added, appears to get a second, third, and even a fourth wind, and seems to get younger as its red brother gets older. It can develop a leaner, fresher, flinty mineral tone, but it never loses its rich, ripe core of honey, nuts and buns, streaked with spice and topped with crystal sugar.

The Hermitage hill only has 126ha (311 acres) of vines, and on the map you can see how wonderfully exposed to the sun these are. The locals say the sun always sets last on these granite slopes of Hermitage, but it's obvious that the sun rises there first as well! The generally granite soils and the numerous terrace walls heat up in the warmth of the sun's rays, and help promote the ripening of the grapes. The drainage is clearly excellent and the Mistral wind will blow away any excess moisture in any case – yes, Virgil would have liked Hermitage.

Over two-thirds of the Hermitage vines are red Syrah. The burliest, most virile red wines come from the most forbidding granite plots, Les Bessards and Le Méal.

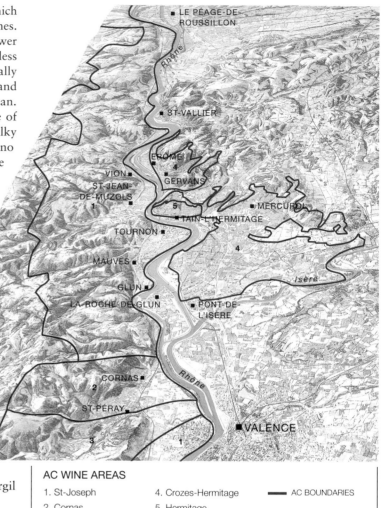

AC WINE AREAS

1. St-Joseph   4. Crozes-Hermitage   ▬ AC BOUNDARIES
2. Cornas   5. Hermitage
3. St-Péray

CROZES-HERMITAGE

All round the Hermitage hill, to the north, east and south, is the large appellation of Crozes-Hermitage. This is increasingly one of the Rhône's most satisfying red wines (although there is also some white) because the smoky, dark-fruited character of the Syrah is well to the fore, and the wines are ready for drinking when still quite young. Two styles come from Crozes-Hermitage's expanding 1230ha (3039 acre) vineyard. The granite slopes of Gervans and Erôme produce structured, finely tannic wines with some mineral and red fruit in their texture. The more clay soils of Les Chassis, the plain near La-Roche-de-Glun, give more overtly fruit-filled wines; these are bursting with exuberant blackcurrants and have softer tannins. Most growers make a fruity wine for drinking inside four years or so, and select a more wood-raised cuvée for longer keeping and greater complexity.

ST-JOSEPH

The St-Joseph appellation, on the other hand, has suffered from expansion. It was originally based on a single hillside – the south-east-facing terraces you can see between Tournon and Mauves. The first expansion was on to the steep terraced hillsides of six communes on the west bank of the Rhône between Glun and Vion, totalling less than 100ha (247 acres) of fine vineyard land. In 1969 the appellation was expanded again to include 25 communes beginning opposite Valence in the south, and running a good 65km

(40 miles) north, right up and into Condrieu. Many of the new vines were planted on the Rhône's flat, fertile banks, and the reputation of the wonderfully perfumed, fruity reds and the weighty, ripe whites from the original granite slopes was sadly eroded by the newcomers. The appellation exploded to as many as 640ha (1581 acres), and could have grown much further before sanity prevailed in the early 1990s, when further vineyard expansion was curbed. Now the terraces above Mauves, Tournon and St-Jean-de-Muzols are being restored, and with them will come the restoration of St-Joseph's reputation as one of France's most delightful rich, fruity, perfumed and approachable reds.

CORNAS AND ST-PÉRAY

Cornas should be immune from expansion fever. The name Cornas means 'burnt earth' and applies to the steep amphitheatre of Syrah vines that cups the little village of Cornas in its suntrap palm. That almost claustrophobic shell of south-east-facing vines, protected even from the destructive Mistral winds that roar up the valley from the south, is a cauldron of heat in summertime. The Cornas vineyards produce the blackest, most torrid red wine in the Rhône, perhaps in the whole of France, its dark, essential flavours wrested from deep inside the earth.

Yet even here expansion looms. The use of higher-yielding Syrah clones unable to produce the dense black tarry liquid that marks out great Cornas, and the gradual increase of low-lying plantings of vines to a present total of 90ha (222 acres) do threaten Cornas'

WHERE THE VINEYARDS ARE *Right at the heart of the map is the hill of Hermitage. Towering over the little town of Tain, it may not appear awe-inspiring from this angle, but I can assure you that, from the bottom of the vineyard slopes, it is. The hills immediately north and east of Hermitage are in the Crozes-Hermitage appellation. To the north, Gervans' granite slopes produce good reds, and the sandy slopes at Mercurol to the east are good for whites. On the flatter lands to the south much expansion and mechanization, including machine harvesting, is taking place. Traditionalists abhor this, but the resulting wines can be good.*

The heart of the St-Joseph appellation is the terraced cliff-face between Mauves and Tournon, but 25 communes are allowed to make St-Joseph on the Rhône's west bank. The wines where terraces are used should be exciting, unlike those from bulges of flat alluvial land where the river curves. Part of this has been planted with vines for St-Joseph too, but the wines deserve no more than Côtes du Rhône status.

At the bottom of the map is the sun-soaked amphitheatre of Cornas where the black-blooded Syrah excels in producing monumental tarry reds. Below Cornas are the beautifully exposed slopes of St-Péray, wasted on producing largely mediocre still and sparkling whites. It's my guess that we would see some outstanding red wines from here if Syrah were ever planted.

TOURNON

TAIN L'HERMITAGE

VALENCE

role as provider of France's most famously old-fashioned red. Luckily there's a long way to go yet, as I still haven't come across a Cornas light enough for me to see through.

Directly south of Cornas you can see another range of beautifully exposed vineyard slopes. They look as though they would continue to paint the brilliant tapestry of dark, heady Rhône reds from the great Syrah grape, yet in fact they are planted with white Roussanne and Marsanne, and 45 per cent of their wine is a gently sparkling wine made by traditional methods. St-Péray is a curiosity, certainly, but efforts to raise the quality of the

still wine have started, including the involvement of new wave growers like Jean-Paul Colombo. Wagner apparently ordered a hundred bottles of the fizzy stuff to help him break through a writer's block in the middle of composing *Parsifal*. It's a matter of opinion whether or not the St-Péray did the trick.

Already, houses for people commuting to the nearby towns are being built among the vines to capitalize on the magnificent view of the river valley. Now, if they were allowed to plant Syrah on these splendid slopes, I'd almost support a move to expand the Cornas appellation!

0 km   1   2
0 miles   1

**NORTHERN RHÔNE –
ST-JOSEPH TO
CROZES-HERMITAGE**

TOTAL DISTANCE
NORTH TO SOUTH,
50KM (30 MILES)

 VINEYARDS

N

SOUTHERN RHÔNE

I
N THE NORTHERN RHONE you need to look upwards if you want to understand the unique qualities of the best vineyards, soaring towards the sky at crazy angles. But in the southern Rhône, you need to look down at your feet. The best vineyards here are virtually flat, but covered with stones so closely packed that there is no soil in sight. In the south's top wine area, Châteauneuf-du-Pape, it is almost as difficult to keep your balance as it is on the sheer slopes of Côte-Rôtie. The reason is not steepness, though, but smooth white and rust-coloured stones, often as hot to the touch as an oven door, which slither beneath your feet at every step. These act as a natural storage heater and rainwater sieve and allow the low-yielding vines to give a wine as heady and alcoholic as any in France, yet which is packed with perfume and fruit richness.

The south is far more dominated than the north by red wines, and these are almost always blends. The Grenache grape, which doesn't figure at all in the north, is the dominant variety, and this is usually blended with Cinsaut and Syrah, and maybe Carignan and Mourvèdre as well. Châteauneuf-du-Pape can be a blend of 13 grape varieties – eight red and five white. Three of the red grapes – Counoise, Vaccarèse and Muscardin – are virtually extinct elsewhere, but have excitingly unusual personalities whose potential heights are only just beginning to be explored. It is as if the great southern reds scoop their flavours off the herb-covered hillsides and the hot stony tracks, pluck them from the sizzling sky and then boil them together like candy. Grenache Blanc and Clairette are the chief white varieties.

WINE AREAS

Between Valence, in the northern Rhône, and Montélimar, the nougat capital of France, there is a gap of 44km (27 miles) in which there is hardly a vine. From Montélimar southwards, however, the vine increasingly becomes the dominant crop, grown on all types of terrain apart from the over-fertile alluvial flatlands down near the river Rhône itself. The sun beats down so relentlessly during a typical southern Rhône summer that extra exposure to its rays seems

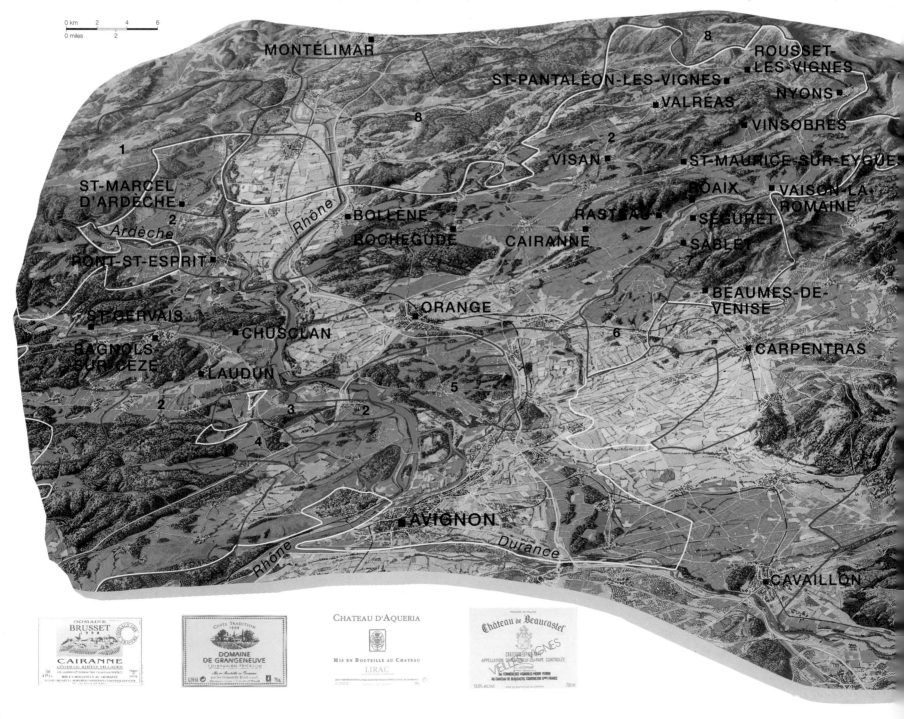

pointless. However, there are some sloping vineyards – the best ones being in villages like Gigondas, Vacqueyras and Cairanne in the eastern foothills. The best Châteauneuf vineyards are on a plateau – and such conditions do help these places' ability to super-ripen their grapes. The soil types in the major Rhône villages are also varied, and they affect the ability of different varieties to ripen. The Mistral wind is combated by windbreaks and by training the compact vines low in bush form, although more modern training on wires is becoming common in lesser appellations to allow mechanization.

CÔTES DU RHÔNE & CÔTES DU RHÔNE-VILLAGES

Côtes du Rhône is a blanket appellation covering vines from Vienne in the north to Avignon in the south. Eighty-five per cent of all the wine made between these two points is simple Côtes du Rhône and most of it comes from the sprawling vineyards that straddle the Rhône from St-Marcel-d'Ardèche and Bollène to south of Tavel. It is overwhelmingly red and, along with basic Bordeaux and Beaujolais, is France's favourite red quaffer. Generally it is a decent drink, but happily more single estates and reliable merchants like Guigal are raising the tempo a bit.

Côtes du Rhône-Villages supposedly applies to the wines of superior communes that will graduate to their own appellations, but so far only two – Gigondas and Vacqueyras – have done so. This leaves 16 communes that can add their own name to 'Côtes du Rhône-Villages' on the label. There are another 54 communes that grow Villages wine, but that may not use their own commune name on the label. The Villages growers must accept a tighter control over their choice of

grape varieties, yields per hectare and minimum alcohol levels. In the top Villages this is probably worthwhile, but in the more anonymous communes, growers frequently choose to stick with straight Côtes du Rhône regulations and accept the lower price for fewer restrictions and a higher yield.

Grenache is the chief red variety and provides a rich, heady heart to the wine. For this you need dry, stony soil and a little inclination to the sun, as in the best Villages on the eastern slopes. The Syrah grape can overripen in many parts of the southern Rhône, but find it some moister, cooler soil and it will add a gorgeous dark-fruited, serious depth to the flightiest of reds. Most of the top Villages like Cairanne have good chunks of moist clay soil gently sloping towards the plain. The late-ripening Mourvèdre adds a crucial, almost rasping, herb-leaf perfume and wild berry fruit to the more corpulent Grenache. Rich clay soil in a warm, protected spot suits it just fine.

WHERE THE VINEYARDS ARE *Speeding through the flat, fertile plains on the valley floor towards the Mediterranean, it is easy to lose sight of the grandeur of this southern part of the Rhône Valley. With a mirage of an azure sea, glistening bronzed bodies and the perfect beach-side restaurant filling your mind, it is perfectly possible not to give this sprawling, arid landscape a second thought. But this map shows the Rhône Valley's majesty as it eases into the final stretch on its trip to the Mediterranean. To the west are the tumbling hills and hidden valleys of the Ardèche, where very tasty vins de pays are made. To the east are the splendours of Mont Ventoux and the sub-alpine foothills. These create high, fertile valleys whose vast wine potential is gradually being exploited by the Côtes du Ventoux and Côtes du Lubéron appellations.*

The best vineyards are a lot less scenic, and only start appearing between Montélimar and Bollène, with the Coteaux du Tricastin and the beginnings of the Côtes du Rhône. Most of the best Côtes du Rhône-Villages communes hug the eastern slopes between Bollène and Carpentras and the very best ones huddle under the jagged fangs of the Dentelles de Montmirail. But there are some decent villages across the Rhône below Pont St-Esprit, notably St-Gervais. Further south both Lirac and Tavel are high class but the heart of the southern Rhône, however, is Châteauneuf-du-Pape, south of Orange. With an increasing number of top-quality estates Châteauneuf is one of France's top red wines today

RED GRAPES
Grenache is the most important of the many red varieties, followed by Syrah and Cinsaut, then Carignan and Mourvèdre, but there are many minor varieties.

WHITE GRAPES
Whites are far less important than reds: the main grapes are Clairette, Grenache Blanc, Bourboulenc, Roussanne and also Muscat.

CLIMATE
The region enjoys a true Mediterranean climate: hot dry summers and warm wet winters. The planting of windbreaks helps mitigate the force of the Mistral blowing chill blasts down the valley from the Alps.

SOIL
This huge area has a wide variety of soil types, ranging from the heavy clays of the upper slopes of Gigondas to the stony alluvial deposits of the plains around Châteauneuf-du-Pape.

ASPECT
Unlike more northern wine areas of France, ripening the grapes properly this far south is not a problem, and many of the best vineyards, for example those of Châteauneuf-du-Pape, are on the flat land of the valley floor.

AC AND VDQS WINE AREAS

1. Côtes du Vivarais VDQS
2. Côtes du Rhône-Villages
3. Lirac
4. Tavel
5. Châteauneuf-du-Pape
6. Vacqueyras
7. Gigondas
8. Coteaux du Tricastin
9. Côtes du Ventoux
10. Côtes du Lubéron

    CÔTES DU RHÔNE AC BOUNDARY

—— AC AND VDQS BOUNDARIES

RASTEAU = CÔTES DU RHÔNE-VILLAGES COMMUNE

TOTAL DISTANCE NORTH TO SOUTH 152KM (94½ MILES)

    VINEYARDS

9

★APT

10

★PERTUIS

Durance

N

0 km   2   4   6
0 miles   2

LANGUEDOC-ROUSSILLON

LANGUEDOC-ROUSSILLON IS THE MOST COMPLETE wine region in France. It is also the most abused. And it is the largest, in all providing one-third of France's vineyard acreage, and yet it does not have one single world-famous wine style to show for it. It is one of the most old-fashioned, hidebound, reactionary parts of the French wine scene, and at the same time it is France's most exuberantly modern, most outward-looking, most international. Contradictions are at the heart of Languedoc-Roussillon. Let's look at a few of them.

I'm standing picking away at a strange, pinkish soil flecked with slivers of stone, crumbly, hardly able to prevent itself from disintegrating into dust. This is one of the most idiosyncratic and most perfect vineyard soils in France causing Bordeaux's greatest experts to collapse into paroxysms of excitement. It's in a tiny valley west of Montpellier in the Hérault Valley. It has no appellation contrôlée. When Aimé Guibert bought the property in 1971 there had never been a vine planted there. Now, 30 years later, his Mas de Daumas Gassac reds and whites are regarded as some of the greatest wines in France. They still have no appellation contrôlée and are sold as Vin de Pays.

Aimé Guibert remains the leading light, but every year sees more passionate, imaginative winemakers arrive in the South of France determined to create great wine their own way, outside the traditional strictures of the grand appellations where innovation is

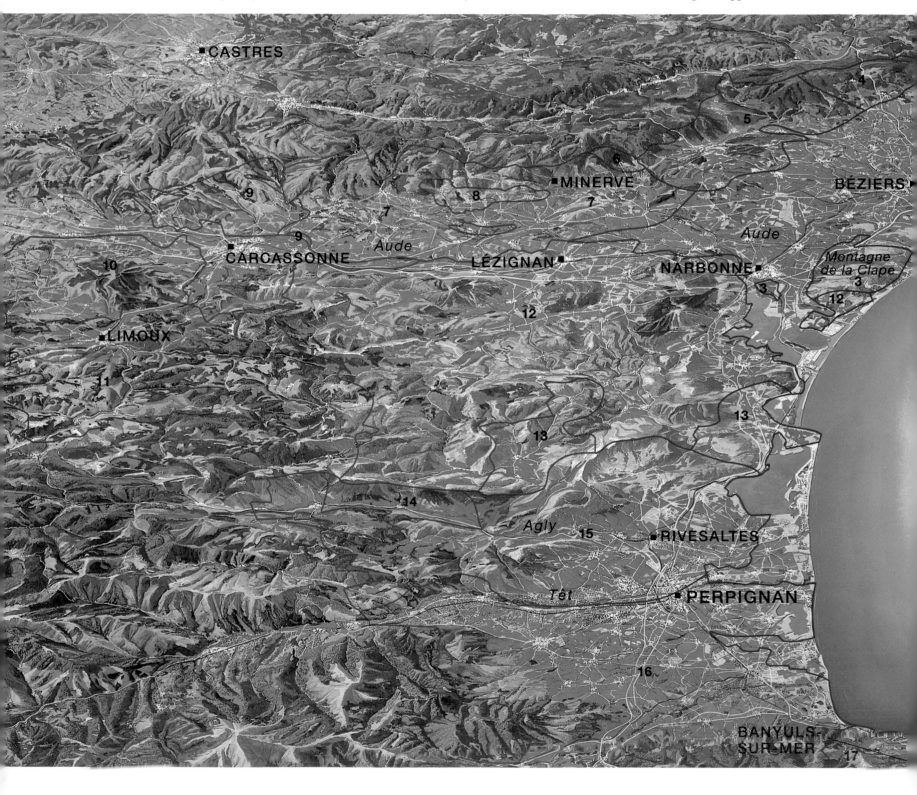

generally stifled and rules are strictly to be obeyed. Most of these innovators are French, many of them refugees from such traditional and hidebound regions as Bordeaux and Burgundy, where types of vine variety and methods of growing grapes are strictly circumscribed. But people come from much further afield, from as far as California and Australia, seeking to put their New World ways to work in an Old World setting. In France, the Languedoc is the only alternative.

If we now head south-west across country, every second village we come to will have a co-operative winery. If we find one in ten where the wine is not stale and flat I should be surprised, but 20 years ago we would not have found one in 50. Still, it's not a

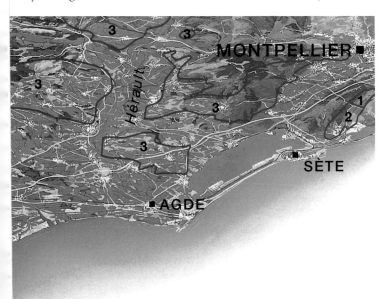

WHERE THE VINEYARDS ARE *Just about the only place on this map where there are no vines is along the ridge of mountain to the north. The higher you go, the cooler it is. But these mountains protect the vineyards from the northerly winds during the day, and at night, the warm air that has risen from the lowlands is pushed back downhill by the mountain air, dramatically cooling the foothill vineyards and ensuring balanced flavours in the fruit. Sea breezes temper the heat close to the coast, but the Mediterranean influence is basically very warm. Further west, this influence lessens and the climate cools and dampens as more temperate Atlantic influences take over. Most of the vineyards higher above sea level are on infertile, stony soil and are best suited to low yields of intensely flavoured black grapes. The lowlands areas are showing themselves highly suitable for the production of fresh whites and light reds.*

AC, VDQS AND VDN WINE AREAS

1. Muscat de Mireval VDN
2. Frontignan VDN, Muscat de Frontignan VDN
3. Coteaux du Languedoc, Clairette du Languedoc
4. Faugères
5. St-Chinian
6. Muscat de St-Jean-de-Minervois VDN
7. Minervois
8. Minervois la Livinière
9. Cabardès
10. Côtes de la Malepère VDQS
11. Blanquette de Limoux, Crémant de Limoux, Limoux

TOTAL DISTANCE NORTH TO SOUTH 144KM (89½ MILES)

12. Corbières
13. Fitou, Rivesaltes VDN, Muscat de Rivesaltes VDN
14. Côtes du Roussillon-Villages, Maury VDN
15. Côtes du Roussillon-Villages, Rivesaltes VDN, Muscat de Rivesaltes VDN
16. Côtes du Roussillon, Rivesaltes VDN, Muscat de Rivesaltes VDN
17. Collioure, Banyuls VDN

— AC, VDQS AND VDN BOUNDARIES

■ VINEYARDS

N

0 km 2 4 6 8
0 miles 2 4

co-operative we're after. It's a modern winery at Servian, north of Béziers. Here at Domaine de la Baume, the property of Australian giant BRL Hardy, they're turning out crisp, scented dry whites and balanced fruity reds. The grapes come either from the 22-ha (54-acre) estate or from local growers and the varieties are anything but regional – Chardonnay, Sauvignon Blanc, Merlot and Cabernet Sauvignon, and what about that 70/30 Viognier-Chardonnay blend they made one year? The point is, with modern technology and know-how anything is possible in this sun-kissed corner of France. That's why the Aussies are here, not further north in Bordeaux.

Is it local, though, or international? Well, the idea is international. But the *laissez-faire* attitude that characterizes the non-AC areas of Languedoc-Roussillon mirrors Australia. So does the hot sun, the dry earth and a reputation that owes nothing to the past but everything to the present and the future. What is 'local' when nothing but mediocrity or worse had ever characterized the vineyards whose grapes Domaine de la Baume now turns into pretty decent grog?

This is one side of what is so exciting in Languedoc-Roussillon. Innovation, excitement, lack of restrictions when transforming lead into gold. But there is another side. The side of some of the most ancient wines in France, some of the most ancient and distinctive styles, relying on ancient grape varieties like Carignan, Grenache, Syrah or Mauzac rather than Cabernet Sauvignon or Chardonnay.

If we go north from Béziers to Faugères, the road rises away from the plain towards the looming mountains of the Cévennes. The land is bleak but beautiful as we cut across through empty, twisting country lanes curling round the low slopes of the mountain range; the soil is barren, smothered in rock and stone, and only olive trees and vines survive.

But there are vineyards that go back to the 9th century at least, when monasteries planted these hills with vines knowing that only poor soil gives great wine. Good soil gives good fruit and vegetables. At Faugères, at St-Chinian, across the base of the towering Montagne Noire to Minerve, capital of the Minervois where the heretic Cathars were besieged during the Albigensian Crusade in 1210, but where vineyards had been established more than 1000 years before by the Romans, on and on, across the wide Aude Valley into the giddy mountain passes of the Corbières, last holdout of the Cathars, but planted with vines by the Romans too. These are great vineyards that have suffered centuries of neglect but that may justly be thought of as the true cradle of French viticulture, along with those of Hermitage.

Nowadays there is a ferocious, proud revival going on in these upland vineyards, and in many other parts of Minervois, and in Coteaux du Languedoc zones like la Clape, the rocky scrub-strewn mountain south of Narbonne that once used to guard its harbour mouth, in the days when Narbonne was the First City of Roman Gaul, and which is one of the coolest growing zones in the Midi. The wines are generally red, often still based on the Carignan grape, but old Carignan vines in poor stony soil can give excellent wine, especially when the blend is abetted by Grenache, Syrah, Cinsaut and Mourvèdre.

There are other great historic wines too. Limoux, high up in the Aude Valley south-west of Carcassonne, claims that its sparkling wine Blanquette de Limoux or Crémant de Limoux – based on the Mauzac grape which gives it its striking 'green-apple skin' flavour – is the oldest sparkling wine in the world. Certainly its wines were well-known in 1388 and the locals have set the date of their discovery of how to make them sparkle at 1531, more than a century before Champagne claims to have discovered the process.

New vineyards in Collioure, just north of the border with Spain. These vines are almost certainly destined to produce heavyweight red table wines, rather than fortified wines, in line with current fashion.

🍇 **RED GRAPES**
There is a huge variety of grapes: traditional (e.g. Carignan, Grenache, Cinsaut, Syrah) and international (Cabernet, Merlot).

🍇 **WHITE GRAPES**
Whites are less important, but include Grenache Blanc, Mauzac, Clairette, Muscat, Bourboulenc, Chardonnay, Viognier and Sauvignon Blanc.

☁ **CLIMATE**
The summers are hot and dry, winters cool and wet, with temperatures decreasing with increasing altitude. The chilly Mistral from the north, and mild sea breezes help cool the vines, and some varieties such as Carignan are drought-resistant.

▨ **SOIL**
This huge area displays a great diversity of soil types, some highly localized. Broadly they encompass the shale and marly limestone of the hills overlaid with clay in the best sites, red pebbly lateritic soil, and gravelly alluvial terraces among others.

⛰ **ASPECT**
The rugged landscape provides numerous and varied sites for vine-growing, the broadly west-east orientation of the valleys combining protection from the north with good southern aspects.

GERMANY

The heart and soul of German wine. An amphitheatre of golden-leaved vines, a tranquil river and a little village huddled on its banks. The sloping vines are those of the great Piesporter Goldtröpfchen vineyard in the Mosel Valley. And sundials – Sonnenuhren in German – are often placed in top vineyards, facing south to catch the sun.

If ever there were a country whose vinous treasures need cosseting, whose ability to thrill depends upon an annual dance along a climatic knife-edge, it is Germany. No country's growers must take greater risks to create the brilliant wines upon which their reputation relies. No vineyard sites need to be more carefully chosen for maximum exposure to sun and minimum exposure to wind, frost and rain. And in no other country are the most famous names betrayed more shamefully by vineyards with no right whatsoever to be associated with them.

Vineyards like those of the Mosel-Saar-Ruwer are pretty well as far north as you can go and still ripen any of the classic grapes. But the genius of the Riesling grape is that, if you allow it to ripen slowly through long, cool summers, and are lucky enough to have a balmy autumn, it is capable of a sublime balance between fruit acidity and fruit sweetness that is unique in the world – even at ridiculously low alcohol levels and scarily high levels of acid. Add a little noble rot and the result is even more remarkable.

Yet this is only possible on special sites. These should be as lovingly delineated and protected as are far less special sites elsewhere in Europe. Instead, such action was deemed elitist back in 1971, when Germany's current wine law was passed, while Germany's international reputation has been ruined by a misguided attempt at popularism in providing large amounts of innocuous, cheap wine. On the label there is no obvious difference between Piesporter Goldtröpfchen (see left) – one of Europe's great natural vineyard sites – and Piesporter Michelsberg, a name covering any wine from numerous inferior villages in the area. Bernkastel is a great wine village with some superb sites, yet wine from the whole Middle Mosel can call itself Bereich Bernkastel. What began as an attempt to simplify and update traditional practice has become one of the main reasons Germany's fine wine reputation is defiled. But there is hope: the best Rheingau sites now have an official classification – Erstes Gewächs. Other regions are evolving unofficial classifications, hoping that these, too, will become law.

One of the greatest changes in recent years is a growth in the awareness of terroir – something that the best growers have always understood. The other is the shift to red. In 1991 just 12 per cent of Germany's vineyards were planted with red grapes; in 2001 the figure is 24 per cent. And while most of these wines are not of much interest to drinkers outside Germany, there is a notable minority of growers making exciting reds, mostly from Pinot Noir, which the Germans call Spätburgunder.

MOSEL-SAAR-RUWER

 **RED GRAPES**
There is a tiny amount of Spätburgunder.

 WHITE GRAPES
All the great Mosel wines come from Riesling. Müller-Thurgau is the other important grape.

CLIMATE
The Mosel is damp and cool but there are sheltering hills and dams along the river have improved the mesoclimates. The Saar and the Ruwer are cooler still.

SOIL
Different types of slate predominate in all areas apart from the Upper Mosel, which is largely limestone.

ASPECT
The Mosel has many south, south-east and south-west-facing vineyards. The Saar flows north and has fewer ideal sites; the Ruwer's vineyards face mostly west-south-west. Vines are planted at 100–350m (328–1148ft).

YOU KNOW THAT FEELING. You look out of the window in the morning at blue skies. The trees are impossibly green and the river below the town glitters in the sun. You throw on jeans and a T-shirt and hurry out – and seconds later you hurry in again. You want a sweater, or two. This is May in the Mosel and it's cold.

Then you leave the town and cross the river – and you take off one of the sweaters. You're in the vineyards now, on the lowest slopes where the river reflects all that early morning sun back on to the vines. It's dazzlingly bright. It's not warm, precisely, but it's warmer, and you can see the town across the river, still in shadow. The vines around you are soaking up all the sun they can get, and you feel guilty about your shadow, spoiling the morning for at least three vines. You scramble up the slopes – and I mean scramble. It's so forbiddingly high and steep here that you wonder if Mosellaners are born with different legs to the rest of us. Each vine is tied to its own 2.5m (8ft) pole, and has its branches pulled back and down to spread the leaves to the sun; you can hang on to these poles as you climb, if you like, because they're embedded in solid rock. At the top of the slope you're glad of that second sweater again. It's cooler up here and the wind whistles round your ears.

This chilliness is the essence of the Mosel. In the best stretch, the Middle Mosel, where the river has carved out sheltered, steep slopes that face south, south-east or south-west, Riesling has an immensely long ripening time: between 120 and 150 days, compared with 105 to 115

for Cabernet in Bordeaux. These warm spots are responsible for the fame of the entire river. Elsewhere, and in inferior sites, vineyards are starting to fall out of cultivation: in 2001 there were 10,445ha (25,809 acres) of vineyards, a decrease of about 2000ha (4942 acres) in a decade.

The Mosel enters Germany from France and for almost 40km (25 miles) it runs north along the border with Luxembourg. Here in the Upper Mosel, slopes are gentle, and the river much narrower than it becomes later on – and thus less able to

KOBLENZ

KOBERN-GONDORF

WINNINGEN

Rhein

Mosel

1

COCHEM

ZELL

2 2 2

TTLICH
2

TRABEN-
TRARBACH

Mosel

BERNKASTEL-
KUES

PIESPORT

N

TOTAL DISTANCE
NORTH TO SOUTH
122KM (82 MILES)

VINEYARDS

QUALITY WINE REGION
AND BEREICHE

MOSEL-SAAR-RUWER

1. Bereich Burg Cochem
2. Bereich Bernkastel
3. Bereich Saar
4. Bereich Ruwer
5. Bereich Obermosel
6. Bereich Moseltor

BEREICH
BOUNDARIES

WHERE THE VINEYARDS ARE

I sometimes think it's a wonder that the Mosel ever reaches its confluence with the Rhine at all. The river has so many twists and turns on the way, trying first one direction and then another, and all because it keeps bumping into rock. The Mosel, over the millennia of its existence, has nudged and eased its way between walls of solid slate, and in doing so it has revealed some of the most diverse and perfect mesoclimates for the vine to be found in any wine region anywhere in the world.

Look at the way the vineyards hug the river and at the great amphitheatres of vines around Bernkastel-Kues: if there's a sun-trap along these banks, it will be thick with vines. And then look at the way the vineyards occasionally sprawl away from the water, on to flatter land or north-facing slopes. Are those vines going to be as good? The simple answer is, no, they're not. From the late 1960s to 1990, some 5000ha (12,355 acres) of these inferior vineyards were planted with grapes like Müller-Thurgau, Bacchus, Ortega and Optima, but these areas are gradually reverting to farmland.

throw the sun's warmth back on to the vines. The Mosel has an average width of only 7.5m (8 yards), although the main stretch from Trier up to Koblenz is wider. The slopes in the Upper Mosel are even a different colour: composed of shelly limestone, sandstone and red marl, they're softer and warmer in colour than the harsh, dark grey slate that takes over further downstream.

The Elbling has been the main grape here since Roman times: it makes dry, brisk, acidic wines that seldom manage higher quality than QbA and are a godsend to the Sekt industry. Kerner gives high yields and is one of the reasons (along with 21 per cent Müller-Thurgau, 8 per cent Kerner and tiny amounts of Bacchus, Grauburgunder, Optima, Ortega, Weissburgunder, Dornfelder and Spätburgunder) why Riesling, while covering 54 per cent of Mosel-Saar-Ruwer vineyards, only yields 30 per cent of its wines. These are all, apart from Dornfelder and Spätburgunder, white grapes.

Red grapes don't ripen easily here: it's too cold. This coolness is recognized in law: Mosel-Saar-Ruwer wines require lower Oechsle readings at all QmP levels except *Trockenbeerenauslese* than do the wines of warmer regions like the Rheingau. Mosel-Saar-Ruwer Riesling Kabinett can have an Oechsle reading of 67°, for example, compared to 73° in the Rheingau. Yet the lightness and fragility of Mosel wines is deceptive and they can last and improve for years.

The six Mosel-Saar-Ruwer Bereichs, going north, are Moseltor on the French border; Obermosel (Upper Mosel); Saar and Ruwer – two tributaries; Bernkastel – the whole of the Middle Mosel; and Burg Cochem (formerly Zell) between Zell and Koblenz, covering the Lower Mosel (Untermosel). Generally the Upper Mosel is cooler and windier than the Middle Mosel, though increasingly exciting wines are being made at the best sites here. In the northerly Lower Mosel, the Hunsrück hills press in close to the river leaving little room to live, never mind cultivate vines. Even so, there are some excellent sites here – steep, terraced slopes of sandy rocks that are even harder than the Devonian slate of the Middle Mosel. The villages of Winningen and Kobern-Gondorf would be better known were they closer to the clutch of famous villages further upstream.

This Riesling Spätlese from the Brauneberger Juffer Sonnenuhr, a perfectly sited south-east-facing vineyard, will need at least 10 years in bottle to show at its best.

MIDDLE MOSEL

THE SUNDIALS GIVE THE CLUE. In the Middle Mosel the most famous are at Wehlen, Zeltingen and Brauneberg, and they're right in the middle of the vines. The vineyards take their name – *Sonnenuhr* – from these intruders that squat in their midst. And what can you guess about a vineyard that has a sundial in it? It gets a lot of sun – which is so precious to vines in this northerly latitude that the towns and villages lie across the river on the shady side.

The tortuous bends of the Mosel specialize in such ideal sites. Vineyards rise to 200m (656ft) above the river, and beech and fir forests take over on the hilltops where it is too windy and cool for vines. The forests are home to wild boar, though, and boar are partial to grapes: one grower douses his fences in Lancôme's *Magie Noire* to keep them away.

The river is wider here than at any other point (broadened even more by the locks built since 1951) and that means more sunlight and warmth reflected back on to the vines, and more botrytis, too, since it means more early-morning fogs.

Sometimes, as at Wehlen, the town huddles on the north-facing bank and the sunny opposite bank is nothing but a wall of vines. Sometimes we find a twin town like Bernkastel-Kues linked by a bridge but the vines of the great Doctor vineyard press right to the back door of the gabled houses.

What's less ideal is when a town's north-facing slopes are also planted, and when an *Einzellage* name includes not only the south-facing slopes but also the much chillier north-facing ones, and even the flat ground by the river. These places were only planted with vines, mainly Müller-Thurgau, from the late 1960s to about 1990.

0 km   1   2
0 miles   1

ENKIRCH TO KLÜSSERATH

TOTAL DISTANCE
NORTH TO SOUTH
22KM (13½ MILES)

VINEYARDS

N

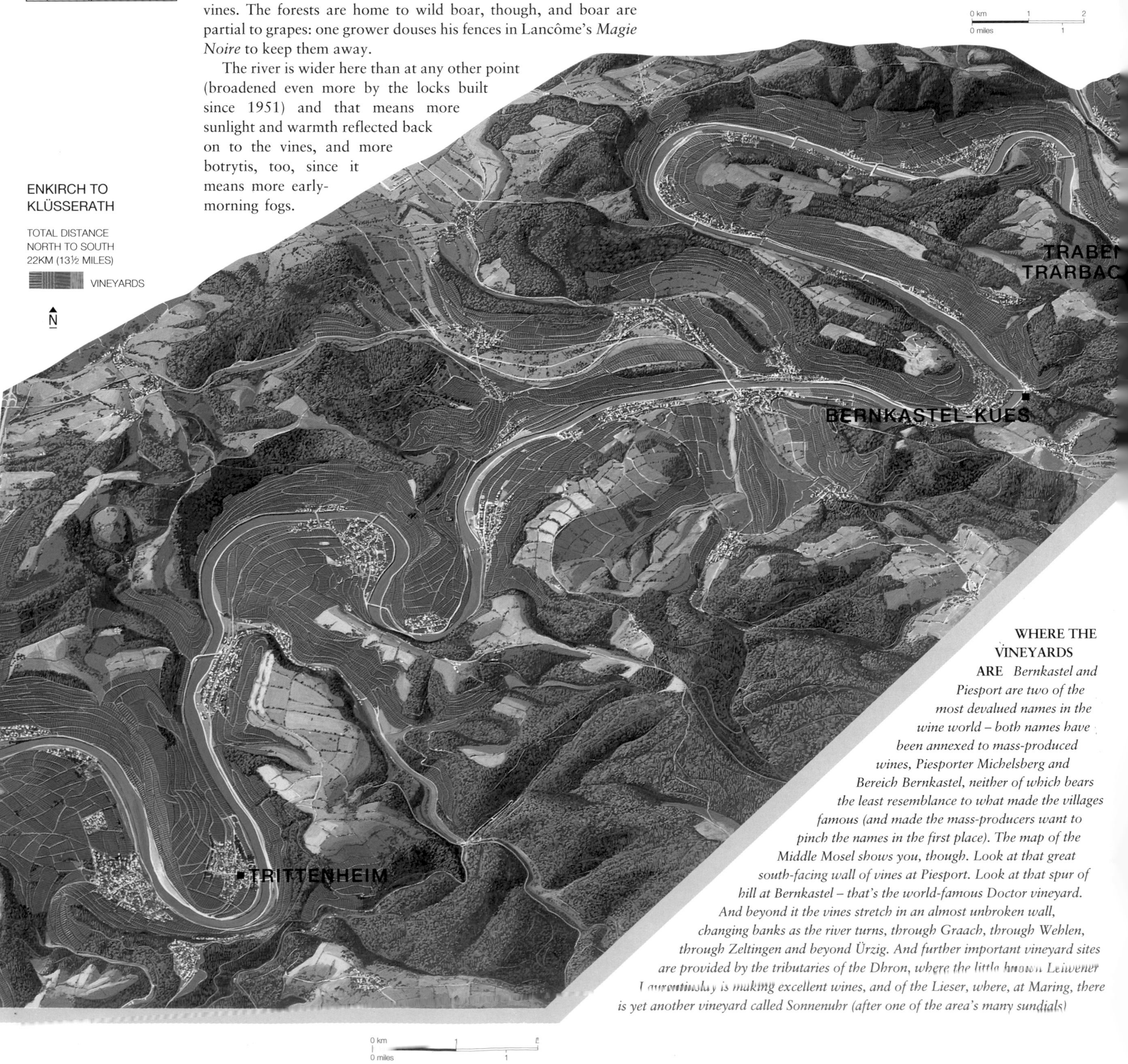

TRABEN-TRARBACH

BERNKASTEL-KUES

TRITTENHEIM

WHERE THE VINEYARDS ARE *Bernkastel and Piesport are two of the most devalued names in the wine world – both names have been annexed to mass-produced wines, Piesporter Michelsberg and Bereich Bernkastel, neither of which bears the least resemblance to what made the villages famous (and made the mass-producers want to pinch the names in the first place). The map of the Middle Mosel shows you, though. Look at that great south-facing wall of vines at Piesport. Look at that spur of hill at Bernkastel – that's the world-famous Doctor vineyard. And beyond it the vines stretch in an almost unbroken wall, changing banks as the river turns, through Graach, through Wehlen, through Zeltingen and beyond Ürzig. And further important vineyard sites are provided by the tributaries of the Dhron, where the little-known Leiwener Laurentiuslay is making excellent wines, and of the Lieser, where, at Maring, there is yet another vineyard called Sonnenuhr (after one of the area's many sundials).*

0 km   1
0 miles   1

Fruit trees were the original crop, and German wine would be in a better state if they were still there. Müller-Thurgau covers 21 per cent of the Mosel-Saar-Ruwer vineyards – less than in most German regions, but yields are far higher than the 30 to 40hl per hectare a top grower might take from old Riesling vines on the old, sloping terraces of, say, Zeltingen. Where terraces have been smoothed out by the Flurbereinigung programme of vineyard reshaping, the vines are often younger and yields are higher, perhaps 90hl/ha – though even Riesling will go up to 120hl/ha if it is allowed to (and encouraged with nitrogen fertilisers).

For the best growers, and in the best villages, the names of Middle Mosel and Riesling are synonymous. There's less agreement on what constitutes the Middle Mosel: the most conservative view has it beginning upriver at Trittenheim and continuing as far as Ürzig. But there are excellent sites both upriver and downriver of these points, for example the Bruderschaft site behind the village of Klüsserath. Downriver the top sites – like Kröver Steffensberg, Wolfer Goldgrube and Enkircher Batterieberg – become fewer.

MOSEL SLATE

The keys to the Middle Mosel are not just warmth and exposure: these enable the sun to ripen the grapes, but it is the soil that flavours them. The soil in the Middle Mosel is Devonian slate, dark and heat-absorbing, dry and instantly-draining, which decomposes into a thin topsoil that in the past was constantly replenished by the simple method of pulling chunks from the hillsides, breaking them up and scattering the shards. Nowadays this is too expensive, but because of slate's low pH it may be necessary to fertilize with lime every couple of years. Stand on these slopes and you'll feel them soft and flaky under your feet. The sun glints on the slate fragments and they slide as you move, bouncing down between the vines. Slate gives a particularly smoky taste to Riesling, a tang that, once tasted, is never forgotten. And when it rains the rain pours straight through like water through a sieve. More absorbent soil would hold the water, and in so doing would be washed down the slope. (More absorbent soil would also mean more water in the grapes and more risk of rot: free-draining slate is one reason why growers in the Mosel can pick so late.) Since Bernkastel gets twice as much rain as Geisenheim in the Rheingau, it's just as well that it can cope.

All the best Mosel vineyards are perilously steep, teetering above the river. This is the great Brauneberger Juffer.

WINE STYLES

Where the topsoils are thinnest, wines are more elegant; deeper soils make fuller wines. Ürzig gives spicy wine, particularly from its Würzgarten (spice garden) site and excels in dry years; so does Graach, where the slate is deep and rich in weathered clay-like soil. Erden has lighter soil and prefers wet years; Wehlen's best vineyards are at the base of the slope where it's 2°C warmer than at the top. Bernkastel gives smoky wines, rich and concentrated. But rich is a relative term in the Mosel. It's a region of *Kabinett* and *Spätlesen*, and sometimes *Auslesen* wines. A Mosel *Beerenauslese* is a rare bird, and even when the grapes are ripe and nobly-rotten enough, it won't have the lusciousness of a Rheingau. It's a paradox of the Middle Mosel that such a forbidding-looking place yields such delicate wines – but they're wines with a shining core of steel.

SELECTED VINEYARDS

1. Enkircher Batterieberg	14. Bernkasteler Doctor
2. Wolfer Goldgrube	15. Lieserer Niederberg-Helden
3. Kröver Steffensberg	16. Brauneberger Juffer Sonnenuhr
4. Erdener Treppchen	17. Brauneberger Juffer
5. Erdener Prälat	18. Wintricher Ohligsberg
6. Ürziger Würzgarten	19. Piesporter Goldtröpfchen
7. Zeltinger Sonnenuhr	20. Piesporter Domherr
8. Wehlener Sonnenuhr	21. Trittenheimer Apotheke
9. Graacher Josephshöfer	22. Trittenheimer Leiterchen
10. Graacher Himmelreich	23. Trittenheimer Felsenkopf
11. Graacher Domprobst	24. Leiwener Laurentiuslay
12. Bernkasteler Lay	25. Klüsserather Bruderschaft
13. Bernkasteler Alte Badstube am Doctorberg	▬ BEREICH BOUNDARIES

ERDENER PRÄLAT

The Middle Mosel's Erdener Prälat vineyard, located between the river Mosel and high cliffs above, provides ideal conditions for the Riesling grape. It became a single vineyard around the end of the 19th century, hived off from the Treppchen next door because its extraordinarily warm mesoclimate consistently produced riper grapes, although the higher parts are cooler than lower down. Add to this a perfect south-facing exposure, a high stone content in the iron-rich, red slate soil which retains heat and reflects warmth back onto the vines along with some old vines and the result is one of Germany's top vineyard sites.

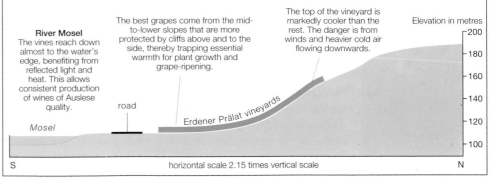

River Mosel The vines reach down almost to the water's edge, benefiting from reflected light and heat. This allows consistent production of wines of Auslese quality.

The best grapes come from the mid-to-lower slopes that are more protected by cliffs above and to the side, thereby trapping essential warmth for plant growth and grape-ripening.

The top of the vineyard is markedly cooler than the rest. The danger is from winds and heavier cold air flowing downwards.

Elevation in metres

road

Mosel

Erdener Prälat vineyards

S — horizontal scale 2.15 times vertical scale — N

THE RHINE VALLEY

THE RHINE (RHEIN) IS ONE OF THE MOST European of rivers. It rises in Switzerland and flows west along the northern border with Germany. At Basel it leaves Switzerland behind and turns north to form the border between France and Germany for some 170km (106 miles) before setting off through the heartland of Germany. But Rhine wine is universally understood as being German. And if you wanted to get to grips with the nature of German wine, you could do a great deal worse than take a trip up the river from Basel to Bonn.

In fact, to understand German wine at all you have to look at Germany's river systems: it is the rivers that make viticulture an industry, and not just a hobby, in most of these cool climate regions. Even given that the Riesling is a grape that can resist the cold better than most; even given the long autumns that enable it to go on ripening well into October; in spite of all this, the growing of fine grapes in the more northerly vineyards of Germany would be a matter of chance, of reliance on the vagaries of the climate, if the rivers were not there to even up the odds a little. What the rivers do is temper the extremes of climate. They keep frosts at bay and, by reflecting sunlight and warmth, give the vines on their banks an added advantage. In addition, over the millennia they have carved deep gorges out of the rock through which they pass. Those steep banks, when planted with vines, catch all the available sunlight.

In the far south of the Rhine Valley (south of this map, and stretching up to meet it from the Swiss border) are the vineyards of Baden, one of the few places in Germany warm enough for you to wander alongside a vineyard and pull cherries or apricots from the trees. The Kaiserstuhl area of Baden is the warmest wine region in Germany, and the central part of the Pfalz is warm, too – warmer than much of Baden.

Baden faces Alsace across the Rhine and uses many similar grapes such as the Pinot family, Riesling and Gewürztraminer, though sadly the most common grape is the dull Müller-Thurgau. At Baden-Baden the Baden vineyards stop for a bit, and then continue on our right as we go northwards – while on our left, on the other side of the Rhine, the Pfalz begins.

THE PFALZ

The Pfalz is really a northerly continuation of Alsace. The south of the Pfalz has never been considered to be as good quality as the north and taken overall it still isn't. It's a region of small-scale growers' co-operatives and one of the main sources of Liebfraumilch. But it is also home to some growers of ambition and great imagination, and some of the most exciting wines in Germany are emerging from these slopes – even if the vineyard names are still relatively unknown compared to those of Deidesheim, Forst and Ruppertsberg in the Mittelhardt. These are what made the Pfalz famous – and they're all between Neustadt and Bad Dürkheim on the map.

So let's take a walk westwards over the wide agricultural plain, towards the wine villages north of Neustadt. It's quite a long way from the river – so far that the Rhine can't really be given much credit for the quality of their vineyards. Instead, it's the Haardt mountains, a continuation of Alsace's Vosges mountains, in the foothills of which the Pfalz vineyards shelter, that make a warm climate even warmer. Riesling is on the increase here: there's now 21 per cent Riesling in the Pfalz and 18 per cent Müller-Thurgau.

RHEINHESSEN

But as we wander away from the hills, heading north-east across the gentle slopes of the Rheinhessen, the Riesling all but disappears. Instead there's Müller-Thurgau and Silvaner, plus Kerner and Scheurebe and a few others – and watch out as you cross the roads, or you'll be mown down by the tankers of simple, grapy, mass-produced wine on their way to the Liebfraumilch cellars. Only when we reach the riverside towns of Oppenheim, Nierstein and Nackenheim, and we find ourselves overshadowed by the rust-red hills of the Roter Hang, are we again in serious wine country. The soil here is sandstone and decomposed red slate, and the hills rear high enough to offer good south-east exposure across the Rhine – though still only a mere handful of growers take advantage of this.

RHEINGAU

We'll cross the river here, over to the right bank, and take a bus through the suburbs of Wiesbaden. We're now in the Rheingau, where we'll find many of Germany's most famous (but also, all too often, most underperforming) wine names. This, traditionally, is the culmination of the Rhine. The vineyards are crammed in on the foothills of the Taunus mountains between the river and the forest. As you go west from Wiesbaden the slopes get higher and steeper; the river reflects all the available warmth back on to the Riesling vines (because it is virtually all Riesling here, though there's a bit of Spätburgunder) and the wines can be some of the weightiest, fieriest, most complex examples to be found.

MITTELRHEIN AND AHR

West of Bingen the Rhine resumes its northward course. There are fewer vineyards here in the Mittelrhein than there were 50 years ago; fewer even than ten years ago. The best vineyard sites are often tucked away in the side valleys, and the Sekt industry, with its need for light, lean wines, relies heavily on grapes from this region.

At Koblenz the Mosel joins the Rhine, and after that there is only one more wine region to go before Bonn. The tiny Ahr Valley, though, can spring surprises. Most of its wine is red, or at least pink; it used to be mainly sweetish, though dry wines are more in vogue now. At Bonn the Rhine vineyards stop. The local drink north of here is beer: the hop can ripen where even the hardy Riesling fears to tread.

WHERE THE VINEYARDS ARE *This is a bird's eye view of the greatest of Germany's wine regions (apart from the Mosel-Saar-Ruwer), and it also contains some of the most commonplace. The latter sprawl flatly across the centre of the map; the great ones are tucked into the corners, where you could easily miss them if you didn't know what you were looking for. The Rhine with its tributaries, the Nahe, Main and Neckar, is the artery of German wine; indeed before the advent of motorways it was the main artery of Germany itself. Even today it carries a heavy industrial traffic of barges as well as pleasure-boats, while clustered on its banks at irregular intervals are villages with some of the most famous names in German wine.*

On the lower lefthand side of the map are the Haardt mountains; the vineyards on their eastern foothills, sloping down to the plain, are the best parts of the Pfalz. Go north from there, to Bad Kreuznach on the Nahe, and you can just make out the remarkable vineyard slopes to the west of the town. And just north of the Rhine, where it heads westwards at Wiesbaden, and the wooded Taunus mountains take us off the map, that 32-km (20-mile) long strip of vineyards along the Rhine between the forest and the river is the main stretch of the Rheingau.

In contrast, look at the rich farmland enclosed within the great bend of the river at Mainz. This is the Rheinhessen region which produces soft, sweetish wine often sold in bulk, with one small exception, the band of the Rheinfront between Nierstein and Nackenheim. The vine shouldn't be allowed to take life too easily: this map shows the difference.

Pfalz wines are often rich and dry, with more alcohol than those from vineyards further north.

Assmannshausen's beautiful vineyards, sloping down to the river Rhine on its north bank, are unusual in that they are best known for red wines from the Spätburgunder (Pinot Noir) grape.

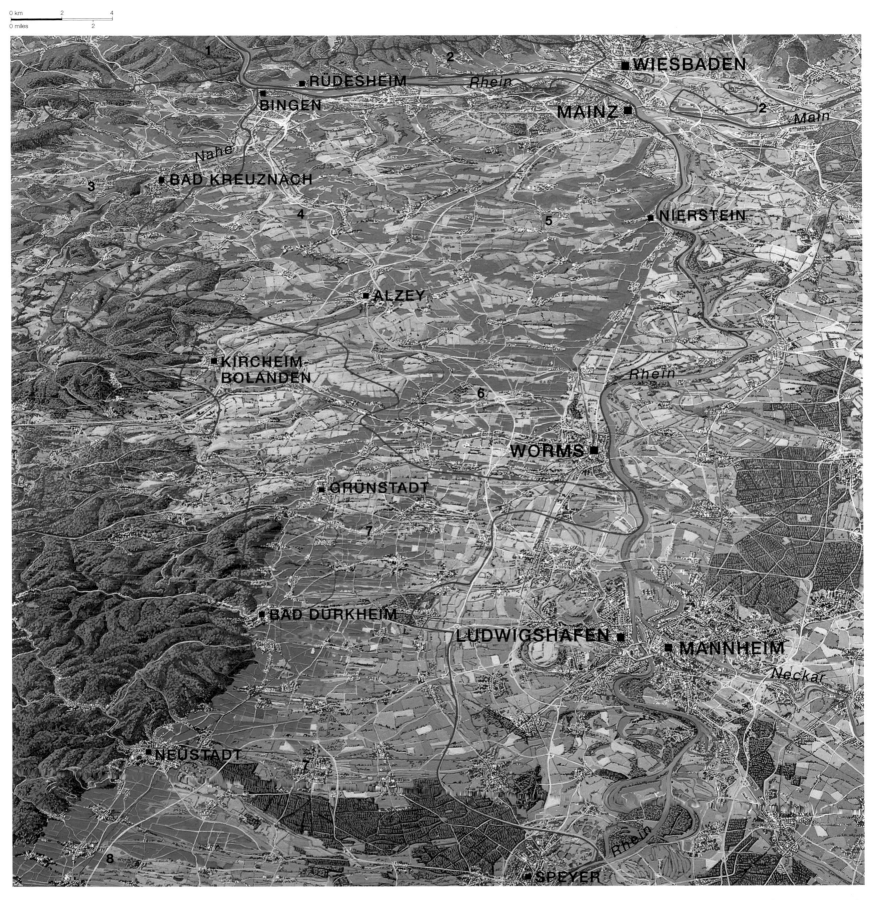

0 km 2 4
0 miles 2

QUALITY WINE REGIONS AND BEREICHS

MITTELRHEIN

1. Bereich Loreley

RHEINGAU

2. Bereich Johannisberg

NAHE

3. Bereich Nahetal

RHEINHESSEN

4. Bereich Bingen

5. Bereich Nierstein

6. Bereich Wonnegau

PFALZ

7. Bereich Mittelhaardt/
Deutsche Weinstrasse

8. Bereich Südliche
Weinstrasse

0 km 2 4
0 miles 2

TOTAL DISTANCE NORTH TO SOUTH 89KM (55 MILES)

━━━ BEREICH BOUNDARIES

▨ VINEYARDS

PFALZ

RED GRAPES
Spätburgunder (Pinot Noir) and Portugieser are grown at Bad Dürkheim.

WHITE GRAPES
Mainly a white wine region, the Pfalz has important plantings of Riesling (21 per cent). Müller-Thurgau is now down to 18 per cent. Kerner and Silvaner are other important white varieties.

CLIMATE
This is Germany's sunniest and driest wine region and it is almost as warm as Baden.

SOIL
The soils are very varied, including loam, weathered sandstone (especially near the Haardt mountains), shelly limestone, granite and slate. The Südliche Weinstrasse has heavier, more fertile soils than the northern Mittelhaardt.

ASPECT
Vines are planted either on the plain or on the gentle east-facing slopes of the Haardt mountains up to 250m (820ft).

Many of the Pfalz vineyards are on the flat but Schloss Wachenheim's vineyard slopes downward from the castle crag.

DIE PFALZ – IT EVEN SOUNDS RICH and ripe and spicy. If you had to guess, you might say it was a land of fertile soil and good living, of rich food and rich wine to match. And you'd be right. In fact, if you imagined something along the lines of Alsace you'd also be right, because if you were to head due south off this map, you'd soon find yourself crossing into France. The hills would be the same and so would the river, (the Rhine), flowing northwards at some distance from the hills. Many of the grapes would be the same and many of the growers would have Germanic names, but the language and the flavours, would be different.

The Haardt mountains, which rise up to the west of the Pfalz vineyards and shelter them, are simply a northerly extension of the Vosges. The soils are mixed as in Alsace and the villages as picturesque, full of life-size gingerbread houses. Yet something happens to the wines as you cross from France into Germany. Even though today they are largely dry, they are still indefinably German, just as Alsace wines, though made from Germanic varieties, are indefinably French. Any doubts that a winemaker's character is crucial to the wines are dispelled on that short trip from Pfalz to Alsace. The Pfalz is divided into two Bereichs, the Mittelhaardt/ Deutsche Weinstrasse north of Neustadt and the Südliche Weinstrasse to the south. Traditionally, the best wines come from the north.

SÜDLICHE WEINSTRASSE

The Südliche Weinstrasse was long viewed as the home of fat, overcropped wines that quickly flopped over into blowziness. More recently it was the source of much Liebfraumilch: like the Rheinhessen, this part of the Pfalz has flattish, easily worked vineyards and a large proportion of high-yielding grapes like Müller-Thurgau and Kerner. But times have changed, and those quiet, rural villages in southern Pfalz are gaining a reputation for being among the most exciting regions in Germany. Ambitious growers are determined to make themselves a name for quality, while the collapse of the market for Liebfraumilch and lookalikes is having its effect. Yes, high-yielding vineyards are still there, but the discovery that field-grafting works in the warm Pfalz climate means that good growers should soon be grafting over to higher quality clones and varieties.

Generally it is even more fertile here than further north. Yields can be high, often too high, from the heavy, lime-rich soils. When it comes to grapes, think spiciness. There is not much Riesling, therefore, but Weissburgunder, Pinot Gris (alias Grauburgunder) and, particularly in the far south, Gewürztraminer. Silvaner, too, is spicier here than elsewhere and Müller-Thurgau can be a veritable pot-pourri. The best growers, of course, take only fairly low yields from their grapes, ferment them dry, and then often break what used to be an unwritten rule of German winemaking – they age their Pinot family wines in new oak. But then oak suits the Pinot family well, so long as it is applied with a light hand.

Gentle slopes (or no slopes at all) are usual for high-yielding vineyards, but top ones, even in the South, are sloping, sometimes steep. In Südliche Weinstrasse are small farmers who are only part-time vine-growers (an average vineyard holding in the whole Pfalz is less than a hectare); the big wine estates are in the Mittelhaardt.

THE MITTELHAARDT/DEUTSCHE WEINSTRASSE

Even though this is where the best Pfalz wine is made, results are still mixed: the vineyards sprawl over the sandy river plain, and there's plenty of bulk wine made here, too, but the stars are the string of villages from Neustadt north to Wachenheim. Neustadt is not

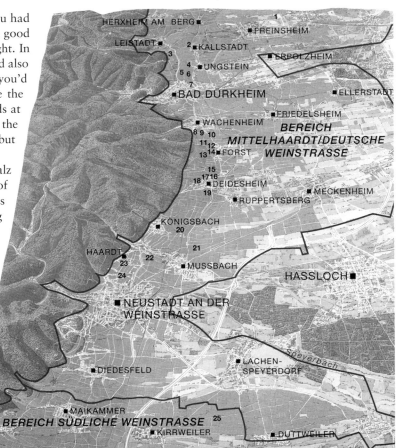

SELECTED VINEYARDS

1. Freinsheimer Goldberg	15. Deidesheimer Kalkofen
2. Kallstädter Saumagen	16. Deidesheimer Grainhübel
3. Kallstädter Annaberg	17. Deidesheimer Hohenmorgen
4. Ungsteiner Weilberg	18. Deidesheimer Leinhöhle
5. Dürkheimer Spielberg	19. Ruppertsberger Reiterpfad
6. Ungsteiner Herrenberg	20. Königsbacher Idig
7. Dürkheimer Michelsberg	21. Mussbacher Eselshaut
8. Wachenheimer Belz	22. Gimmeldinger Mandelgarten
9. Wachenheimer Rechbächel	23. Haardter Herrenletten
10. Wachenheimer Goldbächel	24. Haardter Bürgergarten
11. Forster Pechstein	25. Kirrweiler Mandelberg
12. Forster Jesuitengarten	
13. Forster Ungeheuer	
14. Forster Kirchenstück	▬ BEREICH BOUNDARIES

particularly hilly. The vineyards continue on sandy-soiled slopes through Ruppertsberg, suddenly steepening at Deidesheim. The vines are planted up to 250m (820ft) and they're sheltered by hills; here the Rhine is really too far away across the plain to make any great difference. We're in Riesling country now; in the best parts of the Mittelhardt Riesling covers around 70 per cent of the vineyard. Nowhere else in the Pfalz is it so important: in fact, overall it only accounts for 21 per cent, though the proportion is creeping up, while Müller-Thurgau's 18 per cent is shrinking.

At Forst the soil is varied by an outcrop of black basalt which makes already warm soil even warmer; not surprisingly, growers that don't have any basalt often import it, to the particular benefit of the Mariengarten and Kirchenstück vineyards and those in Deidesheim. The subsoil is water-retentive clay, which seems to give the wines their fascinating backbone. But Forst's secret isn't just soil. The vineyards are perfectly sheltered by the hills of the Haardt –

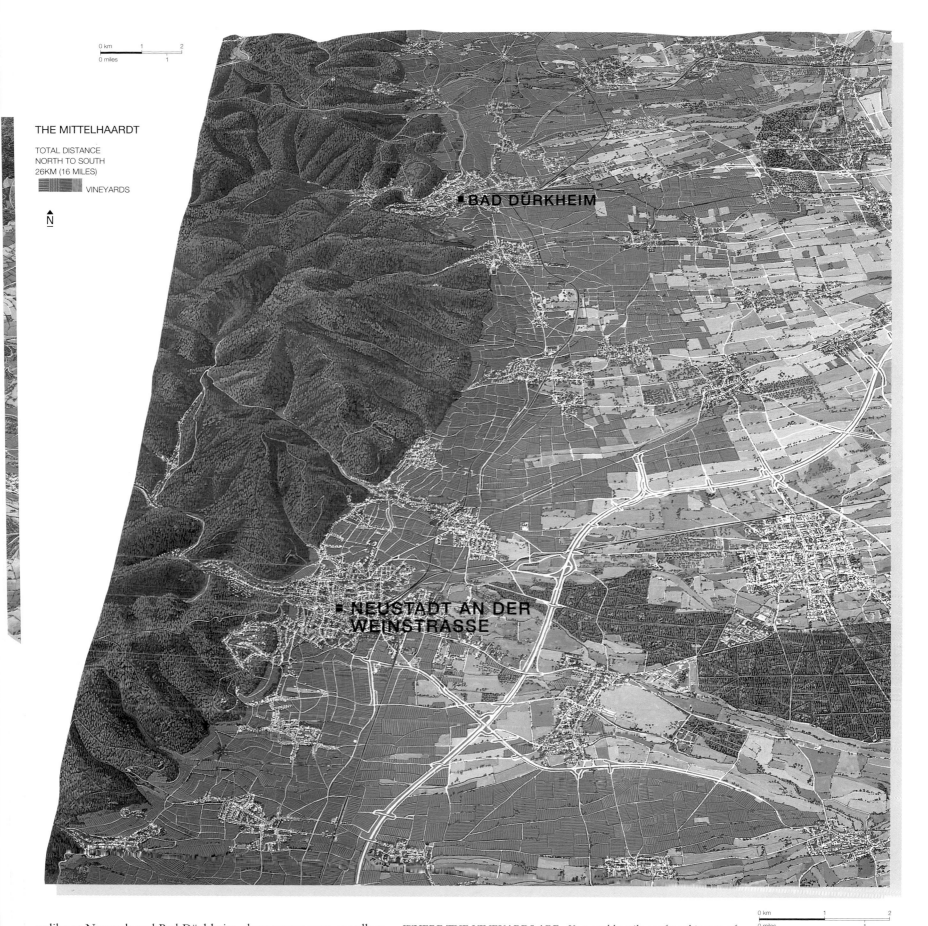

N

■BAD DÜRKHEIM

■ NEUSTADT AN DER WEINSTRASSE

0 km   1   2
0 miles   1

unlike at Neustadt and Bad Dürkheim, there are no gaps or valleys here. So while Forst has no steep slopes for vines, it has other compensating factors. The Kirchenstuck and Jesuitengarten are perhaps the most famous sites in the whole of the Pfalz.

Most of the great vineyards here and in Wachenheim are 100 per cent Riesling but, at Bad Dürkheim, except in the best sites, red grapes like Spätburgunder and Blauer Portugieser are favoured. The region's reputation is fairly recent: until the end of World War Two Pfalz wine was generally bottled elsewhere, much blended with Mosel wines. The Pfalz has been reinventing itself ever since.

WHERE THE VINEYARDS ARE *You could easily confuse this map of the Pfalz with that of Alsace. There's that same narrow, sheltered strip of vineyards, the same spilling of vines on to the plain towards the Rhine, and the Haardt mountains, a northerly continuation of Alsace's Vosges mountains, can be seen stretching away to the west. Even though the southern Pfalz proves time and time again that flat or flattish vineyards can make excellent wine, there is a clear distinction in the Mittelhaardt, the area shown on the map, between the plain and the hills. The plain, with its intensive farming and higher yields, is home to bulk wines and Riesling is concentrated on the east-facing slopes north of Neustadt.*

WEINGUT
Dr. Bürklin-Wolf
1999
PECHSTEIN
FORST

VALAIS

RIDDES TO LEUK

TOTAL DISTANCE NORTH TO
SOUTH 12KM (7½ MILES)

▨ VINEYARDS

Fᴏʀ ᴀ ᴡɪɴᴇ ᴇɴᴛʜᴜsɪᴀsᴛ, the train from Geneva to the Simplon Pass into Italy has to be one of the greatest journeys in the world. Heading out along the idyllic north shore of Lake Geneva to Lausanne, the Vaud vineyards crowd in on the track. Turning east and south past Vevey and Montreux on to Yvorne and Martigny, the tranquil beauty of the lake is matched by the increasing grandeur of the mountains and the strips of vineyards reaching down into the valley floor.

At Martigny the railway track does a right-angle turn to the left, and stretching up to Sion and Sierre are the south-east-facing slopes of the Bernese Alps. Glue your face to the lefthand windows of the train. I don't know anywhere else where the monoculture of the vine is more beautiful or more startling. Vines seem to climb vertically up the spectacular mountain faces, tiny villages perch on plateaux cut off from every other manifestation of life except their vines and, even in the height of summer, the great mountain peaks glow with luminous snow as this Alpine suntrap bakes its perfectly exposed vines to a quite remarkable degree of ripeness. Past Sierre, the vines need to seek nooks and crannies to ripen fully and at Visp, just before the Simplon tunnel, a little narrow gauge railway trails off up to Zermatt past the death-defying terraces of Visperterminen, the highest vines in Europe at 1100m (3609ft).

But you have to step off the train and actually trek up the mountainsides themselves to understand fully quite how remarkable these vineyards are. And it's only by braving the elements in person that the unique character of the Valais vineyards makes sense. The sun and the steep angle of the vineyard slopes you can gauge from the train. The wind, you can't. And however perfect those slopes, they still wouldn't be able to ripen grapes at these altitudes without the wind. This wind is called the Foehn – and it is Switzerland's godsend. It blows up the valleys from the Mediterranean south, and it blows east–west along the Rhône Valley, crucially raising the temperature, and helping the grapes to ripen.

GRAPE VARIETIES AND WINE STYLES

This Rhône is, of course, the same Rhône that produces massive, tannic Syrah reds a long way downstream in France. Here, though, 58 per cent of the wines are white, from Chasselas (here called Fendant), Sylvaner, Marsanne (alias Ermitage), Pinot Gris (alias Malvoisie), Arvine, Amigne, Muscat, Riesling and a few others, including increasing plantations of Chardonnay.

The reds are principally from Pinot Noir and Gamay, often blended into that Valais speciality, Dôle, which must be a blend of at least 80 per cent of these two varieties. Blends from less ripe grapes can be sold as Goron. Pinot Noir is also sometimes bottled on its own. Sometimes it's perfumed and good, and generally speaking Valais reds are the fullest-bodied in Switzerland. There's even some Syrah, and while the Swiss can sometimes overdo the hype here, there are a few genuinely very good examples – as good even as a decent St-Joseph from the northern Rhône.

Some of the vines here, like Petite Arvine, are found nowhere else in Switzerland. They thrive in the Valais because this long gorge, where the Rhône flows approximately south-west for about 50km (31 miles) and then north-west into the more isolated vineyards of the Bas Valais, is one of the sunniest parts of the country, with 2100 hours of sunshine per year. Most of the vineyards are on the right bank, facing south and catching all the sun. It's dry, too, with between 400 and 700mm (16 and 28in) of rain per year – in fact, since the soils are light and well-drained it's sometimes rather too dry for comfort, and irrigation has to be used. The vignerons used to have little canals called *bisses* cut into the hillsides to carry melted snow down to the vines, but now you're more likely to see the draped hoses of drip irrigation.

You might think that getting any water up or down these mountains would be a feat of engineering, but the Swiss, to judge from their vineyards, are good at engineering. Some of these slopes have gradients of as much as 85 per cent, and there's no way you can cultivate anything except ivy on a slope that steep. So the mountains are terraced, with the neatest dry stone walls I've seen anywhere. Even the supporting walls tower high above your head: the Swiss have taken mountains and they've fortified them. Now, if that's not devotion to the vine I'd like to know what is. It also requires an enormous communal effort. There are 5231ha (12,926 acres) of vines in the Valais, and 22,700 owners; that's not many vines each. Only about 700 owners bottle their own wine; the rest take their grapes to the co-operatives or sell to the merchant houses, and the wines are sold mostly by grape name or by style. Village names, with the exception of a few like Sion, the capital of the Valais, don't feature all that much.

Sion is famous for its Fendant (or Chasselas), a variety which, rather like the Riesling, reflects the character of its soil in its flavour. Sion is schist; elsewhere in the Valais there is limestone

The vineyards of the Valais are some of the most inspiringly beautiful in Europe and their steep terraces angled towards the sun produce surprisingly alcoholic wine. These vineyards are at Chamoson.

[Map showing MONTANA, SALGESCH, LEUK, SIERRE, Rhône]

WHERE THE VINEYARDS ARE

The map shows the main part of the Valais, the broad expanse of south-facing vineyards on the north bank of the Rhône from Riddes to Leuk. Eight-five per cent of the Valais' vineyards are in this stretch. The vineyards here are dwarfed by the mountains: altitudes that sound fantastically high when compared to other vineyards elsewhere in the world look pitifully low compared to peaks that are snow-covered all the year round. But look how the vineyards creep just a little bit higher into the warmer side valleys and how the flatter land on the valley floor has only a few vineyards. Instead there are orchards – the Swiss are fond of fruit brandy to polish off a meal.

On the south bank of the Rhône and further west off the map, where the river takes an abrupt turn for the north-west, there are a few vineyards, but these are found in small pockets, rather than in a continuous band – a reflection of their less good exposure. But look how all the vineyard land twists in and out, ducking round an outcrop here, nudging the water's edge there and then drawing back as the sun and the shadows and the changing soil alter the balance for the vine. Deciding which vines to plant in which spots in an area like this has taken the growers centuries of trial and error.

in a long stretch from Leuk in the east to Leytron and Saillon in the west, with the greatest concentrations of limestone at Leuk and Sierre. West of Saillon, at Fully and Martigny, there is hardly any limestone, which makes these prime areas for Gamay. And at Saillon and the villages to the east, Leytron, Chamoson and Ardon, there is gravel. The growers have put it there themselves as it retains the heat admirably and reduces water evaporation. Chamoson also has the largest alluvial cone of the region which provides good conditions for Sylvaner, here called Johannisberg. Leuk, set in a position where it catches all the sun, makes good Dôle; Salgesch (Salquenen in French) also makes good reds. Val d'Anniviers, facing Sierre, is the home of a local speciality, Vin des Glaciers, made originally from the now all-but-extinct Rèze grape, but nowadays usually from Arvine and other white varieties. The wine is aged at high altitude in a modified solera system.

But there are two other parts of the Valais. There is the Bas Valais, the stretch of the river leading to Lake Geneva (Lac Léman), where the vines face mostly west or south-west. But even including the vineyards in Martigny and Entremont, the region can boast only 217ha (536 acres) of vines – just four per cent of the total. Then there are the vineyards east of Sierre, the traditional dividing point between the German-speaking Haut-Valais and rest of the Valais – and they really are *haut*. There are only 150ha (371 acres) of vines here, but they include the ones at steepling Visperterminen.

RED GRAPES
Pinot Noir is found throughout the Valais and takes up over 60 per cent of the vineyard area. Gamay is the other main variety. The Valais has Switzerland's only plantings of Humagne Rouge.

WHITE GRAPES
Nearly half the vineyards are given over to Chasselas (called Fendant in the Valais), with Sylvaner being restricted to the best vineyards. There are also small amounts of other varieties, including Chardonnay, Pinot Gris (called Malvoisie here) and the indigenous Amigne, Arvine, Humagne Blanc and Rèze.

CLIMATE
The Valais is Switzerland's sunniest wine region. It is always windy, and the Foehn wind helps to raise the temperature. Rainfall is low.

SOIL
The soil is generally light and well-drained and warms up rapidly. There is limestone, gravel, schist, as well as various alluvial cones along the Rhône.

ASPECT
Vines grow as high as 1100m (3609ft) at Visperterminen; elsewhere they grow to 750m (2460ft), mostly on south-facing slopes overlooking the Rhône. The slopes are usually terraced and irrigated.

ITALY

The Chianti vineyards of Rampolla in Tuscany near Panzano, left, and newly picked Nebbiolo grapes from Roberto Voerzio in Barolo country in Piedmont, above. For many years these two regions and styles of wine were the twin poles of quality in Italian red wines. Now, I'm happy to say, they are being challenged by new ideas all over the country.

Italy. What an exasperating country. No other nation can so easily fill my eyes with tears at the sheer beauty of its human achievements, yet no other country makes steam shoot from my ears in fury at the wholesale squandering of nature's gifts. But, I wonder, is it possible to have it any other way? There are countries where you can easily understand the potential and range of their wines, good or bad. Reliable, conformist, unlikely to let you down. Unlikely to thrill you either. Italy's not a bit like that. Some of her most famous vineyards produce some of her worst wines. Some of her greatest wines had no legal standing at all until 1995. The DOC system, set up in 1963 to try to make sense of the anarchy that was Italian wine, has spent as much time enshrining mediocrity and protecting incompetence as it has promoting and preserving quality and regional character. In an area such as Tuscany, where great wine names like Chianti and Vino Nobile di Montepulciano had come to be meaningless, the region's innovative, quality-conscious producers were forced to go outside the law rather than submit to regulations that had nothing to do with excellence and everything to do with political expediency.

And yet, and yet. From the northern terraces in the snowy embrace of the Tyrolean Alps to the southern islands that are mere specks on the horizon within hailing distance of Africa, Italy has more continuous vineyard land than any other country. Italians are also the world's leading drinkers of wine, but they still have enough spare to be the world's main exporter of wine too. The Apennine backbone running down the centre of the country means that increasing sunshine can almost always be countered with altitude. The surrounding seas provide calm, soothing maritime influences to all the wine regions except those of the far north. And most of the grape varieties are Italian originals.

It all sounds like a wine paradise on earth. Well it hasn't been, not recently, maybe not ever, as generation after generation failed to make the best of this bounty. But Italy now swarms with enthusiastic, talented young vine growers and winemakers passionate in their desire to test just how good her wines can be. The timing is perfect. The new wave of wines across the world has been based largely on French role models and French grape varieties. But the 21st century has brought with it a hunger for new directions and new flavours. Italy, with her maverick mentality, her challenging wine styles and her jungle of grape varieties, is at last ready to take on the role of leadership she has avoided for so long.

THE WINE REGIONS OF ITALY

Gaja is arguably Italy's most famous producer. Sperss is a top Barolo vineyard but Gaja has chosen to use the less restrictive Langhe regional denomination.

VINES AND ITALY SEEM TO GO TOGETHER. Indeed, given the amount of wine that Italy produces, a first-time visitor to the country might expect every imaginable nook and cranny to be planted with vineyards. But they'd be wrong. There are vast tracts of vines in Italy, but these tend to be concentrated in a few regions: Piedmont (Piemonte) in the north-west, Veneto and Friuli in the north-east, Tuscany (Toscana) and Emilia-Romagna in west central Italy, Marche and Abruzzo in the centre-east, Puglia in the south and the islands of Sicily and Sardinia. In between you often don't see a vine.

Even so, there are more vines growing in Italy than in almost any other country on earth and when you remember how long Italy is, it's obvious that enormous differences of wine styles are going to appear from the far north to the deep south. In the Alpine valleys of the Aosta Valley you are far closer to London than you are to the tiny island of Pantelleria, which almost touches the African shores of Tunisia. And from the Alps to Sicily runs the great giant spine of the Apennines. Indeed 80 per cent of the country is hilly or mountainous and the endless twists and turns provide a vast array of beautifully exposed slopes on which the vine can bask. Their altitude is important too. While the northern Alpine slopes allow wines of delicate crystalline purity, as we head south their craggy heights are crucial in tempering the blazing southern sun.

Proximity to water is also vital, and Italy's long thin body means that many vines benefit from the cooling effects of the Adriatic and Tyrrhenian seas on the eastern and western flanks. Inland lakes like Lake Garda in the north-east create local climates that greatly influence wine styles. And then there are the rivers. From the Adige, tumbling out of the Dolomites in the north-east, to Piedmont's Tanaro creating the boundary between the Roero and Langhe hills, on to the Po bisecting northern and central Italy, to Tuscany's Arno and Lazio's Tiber. In some cases, these rivers serve to moderate the climate, but with others, most notably the Po, they provide fertile valleys in which the vine performs like an athlete on steroids.

Given the great climatic and topographical diversity, it is hardly surprising that Italy has such a wide range of native grape varieties, most of which are suited only to their local growing conditions.

The Nebbiolo, for instance, only seems to flourish in Piedmont, and nowhere better than on the limestone rich soil of the Langhe hills; the white Moscato grape, though grown throughout the peninsula, excels in the white, chalky soils around Canelli in Piedmont's Monferrato hills.

Further east, around Verona, the white Garganega and red Corvina flourish in the Dolomite foothills, while in the hills along the Slovenian border, international varieties like Pinot Grigio and Sauvignon do battle with natives like Tocai Friulano and Ribolla. On the eastern coast the Montepulciano grape holds sway, but attempts to transport it across the Apennines to Tuscany have been thwarted by the cooler climate there. Sangiovese, however, produces meagre wines on the eastern coast, but in Tuscany rises to great heights. It is planted throughout the peninsula, as are Barbera and the white Trebbiano, the latter still being Italy's most widely planted white grape, accounting for almost 10 per cent of all the vineyards. But while Barbera and Sangiovese can produce great wines in the right sites, Trebbiano is prized only for its resistance to disease and prodigious yields, and is today rapidly losing ground.

Moving south, we encounter varieties first brought to the peninsula by the Greeks 3000 years ago – Negroamaro, Uva di Troia, Aglianico, Gaglioppo and Greco di Tufo – all of which perform brilliantly in southern conditions. When northern varieties like Sangiovese and Trebbiano are planted in the south they ripen as early as August and, as a result, produce wines of ineffable neutrality, but the native southern grapes, more accustomed to the hot summers, have a much longer growing season, which allows them time to develop interesting and complex perfumes and tastes.

The islands, too, have their own varieties. In Sicily the Nero d'Avola is unrivalled, while in Sardinia, evidence of Spanish domination in the Middle Ages is still to be found in grape varieties like the red Cannonau (Spain's Garnacha) and Carignano (Cariñena) and the white Vermentino (said to be a strain of Malvasia). Here, as elsewhere in Italy, the importance of matching these grape varieties with suitable terrain and climate cannot be underestimated.

THE CLASSIFICATION SYSTEM FOR ITALIAN WINE

Italy's wine laws evolved out of the chaos of the 1950s and in 1963 the Italian government set up a system of *denominazione di origine*, or denomination of origin, which was based loosely on the French appellation contrôlée system. Until recently only about 10 per cent of the enormous Italian wine harvest was regulated by wine laws. This is now changing as new wine laws passed in 1992, known as the Goria law, continue to incorporate more wines into the various categories.

QUALITY CATEGORIES
Wine is divided into two categories – quality wine (DOCG and DOC) and table wine (IGT and VdT).
- **Denominazione di Origine Controllata e Garantita (DOCG)** This top tier of Italian wine started off as a tighter form of DOC, as a way of recognizing the finest Italian wines. There were more stringent restrictions on grape types and yields and the wine had to be analyzed and tasted by a special panel before being granted its coveted seal. Although set up in 1963 the first DOCG was not granted until 1980 and even by 2001 only 21 wines had been granted DOCG status. It acknowledges the evident superiority of wines like Barbaresco, Barolo, Brunello di Montalcino and Vino Nobile di Montepulciano.

- **Denominazione di Origine Controllata (DOC)** This level applies to wines made from specified grape varieties, grown in specified zones and aged by prescribed methods. To a certain extent the DOC rules serve to preserve existing traditions which have more of an eye to quantity than quality at the expense of progress, and do not always guarantee good quality. Nearly all the traditionally well-known wines are DOC, and new ones are added to the list each year. In the 1970s and '80s there was a huge increase in wines in the VdT category, many of which outshone the DOC wines, which led to the introduction of IGT in 1992.
- **Indicazione Geografica Tipica (IGT)** This is a higher level of table wine and designed as an Italian version of the successful French *vin de pays* category. The wines can use a geographical description on the label followed by a varietal name. Perversely, because some individual producers have become disillusioned with the DOC laws which restrict their originality and initiative, some of Italy's greatest wines carry the humble IGT designation.
- **Vino da Tavola (VdT)** This is the most basic classification and no geographical or varietal distinctions can be made on the label. Particularly cunning is the prohibition of the mention of vintage, forcing most producers upward at least into the IGT category.

MAIN DOCG/DOC WINE AREAS

VALLE D'AOSTA

PIEMONTE
1. Gattinara DOCG
2. Ghemme DOCG
3. Barbera d'Asti
4. Roero, Roero Arneis
5. Dolcetto di Dogliani
6. Barolo DOCG
7. Barbaresco DOCG
8. Dolcetto d'Alba
9. Asti DOCG, Moscato d'Asti DOCG
10. Brachetto d'Acqui DOCG
11. Gavi DOCG

LIGURIA
12. Rossese di Dolceacqua
13. Cinque Terre

LOMBARDIA
14. Oltrepò Pavese
15. Lugana
16. Franciacorta DOCG
17. Valcalepio
18. Valtellina Superiore DOCG

TRENTINO-ALTO ADIGE
19. Alto Adige
20. Teroldego Rotaliano
21. Trentino, Trento

VENETO
22. Bardolino
23. Bianco di Custoza
24. Valpolicella, Recioto di Valpolicella
25. Soave, Recioto di Soave DOCG
26. Breganze
27. Prosecco di Conegliano-Valdobbiadene
28. Piave

FRIULI-VENEZIA GIULIA
29. Colli Orientali del Friuli
30. Collio Goriziano
31. Friuli Isonzo

EMILIA-ROMAGNA
32. Colli Piacenti
33. Lambrusco DOCs
34. Colli Bolognesi
35. Albana di Romagna DOCG
36. Sangiovese di Romagna DOCG

TOSCANA
37. Carmignano DOCG
38. Vernaccia di San Gimignano DOCG
39. Chianti Classico DOCG
40. Chianti DOCG
41. Bolgheri
42. Brunello di Montalcino DOCG
43. Vino Nobile di Montepulciano DOCG
44. Morellino di Scansano

UMBRIA
45. Orvieto
46. Torgiano Rosso Riserva DOCG
47. Montefalco Sagrantino DOCG

MARCHE
48. Verdicchio dei Castelli di Jesi
49. Rosso Conero
50. Rosso Piceno

ABRUZZO
51. Montepulciano d'Abruzzo

LAZIO
52. Frascati

MOLISE

CAMPANIA
53. Greco di Tufo
54. Taurasi DOCG
55. Fiano di Avellino

BASILICATA
56. Aglianico del Vulture

PUGLIA
57. Castel del Monte
58. Brindisi
59. Salice Salentino
60. Primitivo di Manduria

CALABRIA
61. Cirò

SICILIA
62. Malvasia delle Lipari
63. Etna
64. Faro
65. Alcamo, Bianco d'Alcamo
66. Marsala
67. Moscato di Pantelleria

SARDEGNA
68. Carignano del Sulcis
69. Cannonau di Sardegna, Vermentino di Sardegna
70. Vermentino di Gallura DOCG

PANORAMIC MAPS OF ITALY

Barolo and Barbaresco *pages 158–159*

Alto Adige *pages 162–163*

Veneto *pages 164–165*

Friuli-Venezia Giulia *pages 166–167*

Chianti Classico *pages 172–173*

Brunello di Montalcino *pages 174–175*

Vino Nobile di Montepulciano *pages 176–177*

Bolgheri *pages 178–179*

OTHER MAPS

North-West Italy *page 155*

North-East Italy *page 161*

Central Italy *page 169*

Southern Italy *page 180*

Sardegna *page 182*

Sicilia *page 183*

BAROLO & BARBARESCO

RED GRAPES
Nebbiolo rules supreme in both Barolo and Barbaresco, but it needs careful siting. Dolcetto and Barbera are more accommodating.

WHITE GRAPES
Although considered chiefly a red wine area, Moscato, Chardonnay and Sauvignon Blanc also thrive here.

CLIMATE
The continental climate is tempered by air currents flowing along the Tanaro Valley, bringing slightly cooler summer temperatures and allowing formation of autumn fog which causes Nebbiolo's slow ripening.

SOIL
The soil is generally fertile with calcareous bluish-grey marl in the west, and an iron-rich sand and limestone conglomerate in the east.

ASPECT
Most vineyards here face south-west to south-east on steep to very steep hills. The Barolo vineyards, at 250 to 450m (820 to 1476ft) are higher than those of Barbaresco, which lie at between 200 and 350m (656 and 1148ft).

I USED TO THINK THAT BURGUNDY was the most difficult wine to understand until I visited Barolo and Barbaresco. Before that, and despite the urging of friendly Italophiles, I had failed to find the magic they purported to divine in a glass of Barolo. All I found was a hard, tannic wine, its fruit eviscerated by long aging in large, old oak casks. Throughout the 1980s, I searched many times for the complexity and greatness said to reside in the Nebbiolo grape. More often than not, though, I ended up in need of a dentist, my teeth and gums suffering from the full-frontal assault of tannin and acidity. But as the decade progressed things changed. My doubts, and Nebbiolo's wall of tannin, seemed to crumble at the same rate. In 1986, when the 1982s were released, I first glimpsed something of the magic of the Nebbiolo. By the time I tried the '85s in 1989, I knew that the producers were bottling the wine in time to capture those perfumes of roses, liquorice, violets, mint, cherries and game.

As the wines improved, the differences between producers became more marked. Previously the stylistic variations had been masked by tannin and oxidation. Now I began to find that the new approach in the vineyards brought lower yields with better ripeness and riper tannins. In the cellar, the extraction of better tannins meant less aging in barrel and more in bottle, which in turn ensured greater freshness, releasing the many beautiful notes Nebbiolo is capable of sounding.

Soon afterwards, I visited the town of Alba for the first time, keen to discover the source of these striking notes. First stop was Barolo. Alba lies on the banks of the Tanaro river, and the first slopes of the Langhe hills rise up from the narrow plain just south of the town. The road out of Alba is straight, but once you reach the small town of Gallo d'Alba it begins to twist and climb. It then splits into three, heading off towards Serralunga d'Alba, Castiglione Falletto and Monforte d'Alba, or La Morra and Barolo. Being a moderate soul, I took the middle road and began climbing towards Castiglione Falletto. I got a sore neck, and almost drove into the ditch several times, as I tried to get my bearings and distinguish the south- and south-west-facing slopes. Those vineyards with the finest exposure are planted with Nebbiolo. Those with an easterly or south-east aspect are planted with Dolcetto and Barbera, or with white grapes like Chardonnay.

As the road evens out, you get a spectacular view of the whole of Barolo. To your right are the La Morra and Barolo vineyards, while to your left are those of Serralunga. Snow-capped mountains loom behind the hilltop town of La Morra and the lighter, whiter chalky soil of the vineyards that stretches below seems to reflect the snow.

The soil in the western part of Barolo is a Tortonian calcareous marl, while in the east, there is Helvetian marl with higher levels of lime and iron. Because of Nebbiolo's sensitivity to soil, the wines from the former tend to be lighter and more fragrant than the powerful, tannic wines that characterize Serralunga. The spur running through Castiglione Falletto to the southerly vineyards in Monforte d'Alba produces wines that combine the power of Serralunga with some of the grace of La Morra and Barolo.

Barolo's 1250ha (3088 acres) are split between some 1200 growers. Such fragmentation results in as many different approaches to winemaking as there are plots of land, producing a confusing picture. Old-timers remember when Nebbiolo, the last grape to be harvested in the Langhe, would be left in its fermentation vat, in contact with its skins, until after Christmas. The resulting wines were so tough that they needed aging in large *botti* (casks) for anything up to ten years before the tannins had softened enough for the wine to be bottled. But by that time the wine would have oxidized.

In the 1960s, changes took place as younger producers like Renato Ratti, Angelo Gaja and Aldo Conterno travelled to France and saw a different approach to winemaking. Fresher and softer wines were the aim, though disputes raged about how to achieve them. Some proposed little contact with the skins and even less with oak; others suggested substituting small oak barriques for large *botti*; others simply said, reduce yields and clean up your act in the cellar. Top producers split into traditionalist and modernist camps. But the complexity of the zones and of Nebbiolo itself, and the approach of different growers, defies such a simplistic solution. And in Barbaresco, where lower vineyards and a closer proximity to the Tanaro mean a warmer mesoclimate and an earlier harvest, the wines are, in any case, different in character.

However, debate has been healthy. Not only are the wines much better than they were 15 or 20 years ago, but the growers have established themselves as a great force in the region. In the

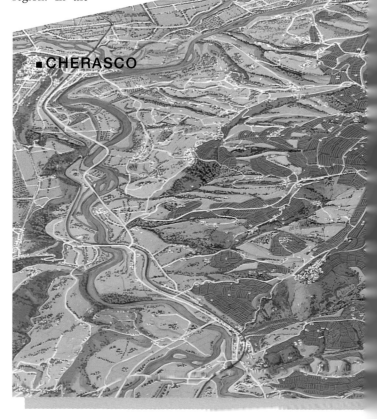

■ CHERASCO

BAROLO'S TERRA BIANCA

Barolo's famous *terra bianca*, or white earth, is a milky calcareous marl bearing reflective and alkaline qualities. To the west of the town of Barolo, near the impressively sited Castello della Volta, the younger Tortonian soil is bluish in colour from magnesium and manganese, which stimulate growth and flavour, producing elegant, early drinking wines. The land to the east has the older Helvetian soil, more beige-yellow in colour from rust, producing powerful, long-lasting reds. Between these, running north-east from the town, is the Cannubi ridge (*connubio* means marriage or union), with the perfect combination of soil producing wines with the finest characteristics of both areas, the strength and staying power of the east mixed with the finesse and delicacy of the west. Owning vines here is a mark of prestige.

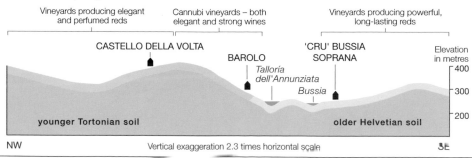

Vineyards producing elegant and perfumed reds

Cannubi vineyards – both elegant and strong wines

Vineyards producing powerful, long-lasting reds

CASTELLO DELLA VOLTA

BAROLO

'CRU' BUSSIA SOPRANA

Elevation in metres

Talloria dell'Annunziata

Bussia

400

300

200

younger Tortonian soil

older Helvetian soil

NW

Vertical exaggeration 2.3 times horizontal scale

SE

0 km   1   2
0 miles   1

past, merchants would buy wines from numerous growers and blend them together to make a wine of a house style. Improvements in the vineyard and cellar have led to a new emphasis on the wines of individual communes and, within these communes, single vineyards. Specific terms such as *Bricco* (hilltop), *Sorì* (slope), and *Vigna* (vineyard) now appear on labels – with a grape like Nebbiolo, the importance of provenance cannot be overstated. The future looks bright and growers are trying non-Italian varieties like Syrah, Cabernet Sauvignon, Sauvignon Blanc and Chardonnay. But success has brought conservatism.

Many younger growers think there is only one way to make a good Barolo: early picking and short maceration followed by barrique-aging, all too often resulting in those subtle grape aromas being overwhelmed by those of toasty oak. It would be sad if this resulted in a lack of diversity, and I can only hope there is no slowing down in the experimentation which, in the past couple of decades, has improved these wines beyond all recognition.

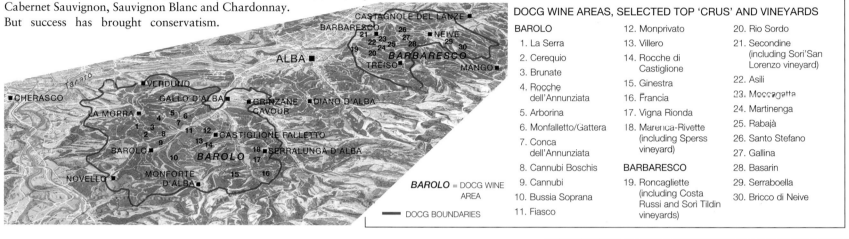

DOCG WINE AREAS, SELECTED TOP 'CRUS' AND VINEYARDS

BAROLO

1. La Serra
2. Cerequio
3. Brunate
4. Rocche dell'Annunziata
5. Arborina
6. Monfalletto/Gattera
7. Conca dell'Annunziata
8. Cannubi Boschis
9. Cannubi
10. Bussia Soprana
11. Fiasco
12. Monprivato
13. Villero
14. Rocche di Castiglione
15. Ginestra
16. Francia
17. Vigna Rionda
18. Marenca-Rivette (including Sperss vineyard)

BARBARESCO

19. Roncagliette (including Costa Russi and Sorì Tildin vineyards)
20. Rio Sordo
21. Secondine (including Sorì San Lorenzo vineyard)
22. Asili
23. Moccagatta
24. Martinenga
25. Rabajà
26. Santo Stefano
27. Gallina
28. Basarin
29. Serraboella
30. Bricco di Neive

BAROLO = DOCG WINE AREA

――― DOCG BOUNDARIES

BAROLO AND BARBARESCO

TOTAL DISTANCE NORTH TO SOUTH
23KM (14 MILES)

▨ VINEYARDS

0 km   1   2
0 miles   1

N

WHERE THE VINEYARDS ARE *These are the slopes producing two of Italy's most famous wines – Barolo and Barbaresco. Barolo winds its way through a string of steep to very steep hills south-west of Alba and, as autumn fogs close in during October, the particular vineyard site assumes great importance. The Barbaresco hills are directly south of the Tanaro which warms the area slightly and ripens the Nebbiolo a little earlier than in Barolo. Between these two are many more vineyards, but none that have the right balance of altitude, aspect and soil type to suit the Nebbiolo grape to perfection, so other grapes are preferred.*

NORTH-EAST ITALY

SOAVE, VALPOLICELLA, PINOT GRIGIO. Each of these wines, virtually synonymous with Italian wine as a whole, is produced in north-east Italy – yet this is perhaps the least Italian of any part of the country. To the north is Austria, to the east Slovenia, and both have contributed to the diversity of culture, peoples, food and wine that exists in north-east Italy. Names of winemakers like Gravner and Haas hardly evoke images of pasta and Chianti, but the vagaries of 20th-century politics have made them Italian, though perhaps not quite as Italian as pasta and Chianti, I admit.

North-east Italy is a region that has been at the crossroads of Europe since at least Roman times. Merchants, scholars and soldiers coming from the north or east would pass through this part of the country on their way to Rome, Florence or Milan, as would the great traders of Venice, the city that controlled much of the world's commerce in the 14th and 15th centuries. Each of these visitors left a legacy that we are enjoying today. The Malvasia grape of Friuli was undoubtedly brought back from Greece by Venetian merchants, as perhaps was Ribolla, which today can still be found on the Ionian island of Kefallonia (as Robola). And the French varieties so prevalent here, Chardonnay, Cabernet and Merlot, owe their presence not to the fact that they fell off a passing bandwagon in the past decade, but that they were brought from France by horse and cart in the wake of the Napoleonic invasion almost two centuries ago.

All the best Valpolicella vines are grown on hillside sites to the north-west of Verona.

Even earlier than that, other 'foreign' varieties were being planted in what is today part of north-east Italy: before the early part of the 20th century both Friuli-Venezia Giulia and the Alto Adige were part of the Austro-Hungarian Empire. The hills of Friuli were filled with varieties like Riesling, Müller-Thurgau and, later, Sauvignon Blanc and the Pinots Blanc and Noir (called Pinot Bianco and Nero in Italy). Wines made from these grapes were particularly highly regarded by the Habsburg court in Vienna. Such a ready market for their wares gave the grape growers of Friuli an early incentive to produce quality, though this was rudely removed when the region joined Italy in 1919.

The quality of the wines from the North-East shot back up to its previous peak when, in the 1960s and 1970s, increasing wealth among the people of prosperous cities like Milan and Venice created a clamouring market for the varietals from the hills of Collio and the Colli Orientali. The same factors – climate, soil and grape variety – that produced the wines enjoyed by the Habsburg monarchs successfully came back into play.

Alto Adige – or Süd-Tirol as most of the inhabitants prefer to call their region to this day – wasn't at all happy to be detached from Austria in 1919 as part of the peace treaty. They were even less happy as the determined attempt to Italianize their towns and villages by Mussolini meant great train-loads of immigrants from further south in Italy being dumped on their doorsteps. Place names were Italianized and the Tirolean German that had been spoken for hundreds of years was banned.

Nowadays this mountain province seems a charming and contented place, but there is even still a simmering undercurrent of Tirolean nationalism, and the majority of the people still prefer to speak German, and follow Austrian customs. One benefit of being detached from Austria could perhaps be seen in Alto Adige's tourist industry as German, Swiss and Austrian holidaymakers crowd through the Brenner Pass and fill the locals' coffers with gold. But an adverse side-effect of this is that the majority of Alto Adige's vineyards grow red grapes in an area that would seem brilliantly suited to high-quality whites.

It's those tourists again. With traditions of very light, mild reds in their own countries, they have encouraged the wholesale plantation of the Vernatsch or Schiava grape to produce enormous volumes of semi-red wine of completely forgettable quality. But the white wines are gaining ground both in Italy, which suffers from a shortage of fresh, fragrant whites, and abroad. And South Tyrol reds from Cabernet, Merlot, Pinot Nero and the local Lagrein are being taken increasingly seriously.

North-east Italy is protected from cool north winds by the Julian pre-Alps to the north. From the hills just outside Gorizia the snow-capped peaks of this protective barrier can be seen standing guard on the border with Austria. In the east, the tree-covered hills were once bisected by the southern reaches of the Iron Curtain, while to the south lies the Adriatic, its gentle waters providing a moderating influence on the continental climate that would otherwise prevail here. The hills of Gorizia and Collio are the source of the best wines in this region: rich and perfumed varietals like Pinot Grigio, Tocai Friulano and Pinot Bianco that often stake competing claims to the title of Italy's best dry white wine – and rightly so.

Moving further west, away from the hills and onto the plains, the soil becomes more fertile, the vines more prodigious and the wines increasingly insipid. This trend continues and reaches its lowest point in the Piave Valley. The Piave, one of the two great rivers in the north-east (the other is the Adige), flows from the Alps through an alluvial plain in the eastern Veneto into the Adriatic north of Venice. Its fertile plain produces a great deal of the bulk

wine used to pad out the blends of the Veronese merchants to the west, and a fair amount of the light, lean but refreshing mealtime reds glugged and forgotten in the cafés and restaurants of Venice.

THE VENETO

Bordered to the south by the Po river and to the west by Lake Garda, the Veneto accounts for about 10 per cent of Italy's wine, ranging from the gushing torrents of Piave to the intense trickles that emerge from the hills of Valpolicella. As well as Valpolicella, historically one of Italy's best-known red wines, the region is also home to Soave, Bardolino, Breganze, Bianco di Custoza and huge amounts of Pinot Grigio (see pages 164–165).

The best wines of the Veneto, including the Classico (or hilly) areas of Soave and Valpolicella, come from the chain of hills that rises from the northern rim of the Po Valley. The valley itself is the home of most of the basic stuff that makes the region such an important player in the wine mass-market. Important in volume, that is, not in quality. Very little of the valley floor Soave or Valpolicella deserves its name. The heat here in summer is unbearable, the temperatures often rising higher than those in the low-lying Salento peninsula 900 km (560 miles) to the south. It is only as you move into the hills that relief from the heat is granted, not only for people but also for vines. The cooler night time temperature up in the hills is one of the factors behind the finer wines produced here.

In the hills on the western shores of Lake Garda, the shimmering leaves of olive trees give a rare Mediterranean touch to this northerly region. While most of north-east Italy labours under the hot summers and cold winters that characterize a continental climate, the proximity of Lake Garda moderates the winter temperatures here so that this is the most northerly point in Europe that the olive is cultivated.

FRIULI-VENEZIA GIULIA

The vineyards of Friuli-Venezia Giulia may be a great deal closer to the Mediterranean, with many of the vines planted on low land running down towards the Adriatic and the Gulf of Trieste, but they don't feel balmy too often. With the Julian and the Carnic pre-Alps directly to the north there is a non-stop seesaw of air currents between the cold, wet mountains and the sea that keeps the region mild and damp by Italian standards, with fairly continual breezes (see pages 166–167).

TRENTINO-ALTO ADIGE

The Mediterranean influence quickly recedes once past the northern shores of Lake Garda. The same glacier that carved the lake also cut an almighty swathe through the Dolomites to the north. The result – the Adige river and its valley – is for the most part cast in shadow by the steep, granite walls of the mountains. This fertile valley runs south from the border with Austria, taking in Alto Adige and Trentino. For political purposes, the region is known as Trentino-Alto Adige, but the two have little in common. A strong Germanic influence remains in Alto Adige but grapes like Riesling, Sylvaner and Müller-Thurgau are slowly giving way to Chardonnay and Pinot Grigio and, though Schiava (Vernatsch to the locals) remains the most widely planted variety – thanks to an Austrian affinity for the light, innocuous reds that this variety excels in producing – it too is steeply on the decline.

The snow-dusted Dolomites often serve to convince people that this is an area to which the term 'cool-climate viticulture' must be applied. Anybody checking the temperature chart in an Italian newspaper in July will know that this need not be the

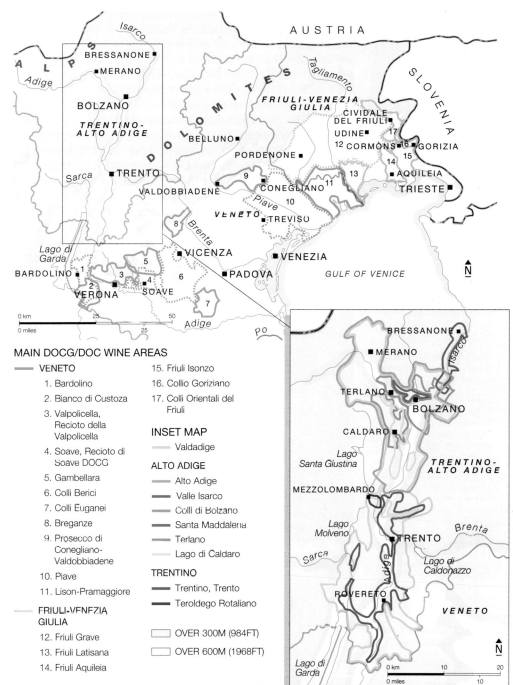

MAIN DOCG/DOC WINE AREAS

— VENETO
1. Bardolino
2. Bianco di Custoza
3. Valpolicella, Recioto della Valpolicella
4. Soave, Recioto di Soave DOCG
5. Gambellara
6. Colli Berici
7. Colli Euganei
8. Breganze
9. Prosecco di Conegliano-Valdobbiadene
10. Piave
11. Lison-Pramaggiore

— FRIULI-VENEZIA GIULIA
12. Friuli Grave
13. Friuli Latisana
14. Friuli Aquileia
15. Friuli Isonzo
16. Collio Goriziano
17. Colli Orientali del Friuli

INSET MAP
— Valdadige

ALTO ADIGE
— Alto Adige
— Valle Isarco
— Colli di Bolzano
— Santa Maddalena
— Terlano
— Lago di Caldaro

TRENTINO
— Trentino, Trento
— Teroldego Rotaliano

☐ OVER 300M (984FT)
☐ OVER 600M (1968FT)

case: Bolzano is often the hottest place in the whole country. As elsewhere in Italy, altitude can play an important role in moderating extreme temperatures but, unfortunately, too many of the vineyards here are on the valley floor. One reason Trentino wines often seem flat and dull is that so many of the vineyards are on fertile valley floor land; most of the valley floor in Alto Adige is given over to apples.

At their best, Süd-Tirol wines are fragrant and intense, but often lack the weight that the same varietals display in other parts of Italy, a factor local producers attribute to their northern European approach to viticulture. If by northern European they mean a desire to produce more litres of wine per vine than nature intended, as in so many of Germany's vineyards, then I'd have to agree. But the great German vineyards produce wines of superb intensity. It's the same in Alto Adige and Trentino: where there's a will to excel, the vineyards and the grape varieties are all there waiting to be pushed to the limit (see pages 162–163 for more detail).

Superb red, it is made unusually from just one of the Valpolicella grape varieties, Corvina.

VENETO

IT IS LIKELY THAT one of your first experiences of Italian wine was a bottle of Veneto wine. It could have been Soave, Bardolino or Valpolicella, or Bianco, Rosso, Merlot or Tocai del Veneto, or even a Pinot Grigio, Chardonnay or Cabernet. For not only does the Veneto produce a vast array of wines, it also churns out a huge volume, from the shores of Lake Garda in the west to the Piave Valley in the east, from the Alpine foothills in the north to the dull flatlands of the Po valley to the south. Quality varies from anonymous whites and weedy reds to a few outstanding wines produced in the Valpolicella and Soave Classico zones in the hills that flank Verona.

Although, by and large, greater Italian reds are found in Tuscany and Piedmont, no other region makes such a range of styles at a such a decent average level of quality and charges relatively so little for them. The wine styles, from native grapes in the west like red Corvina and white Garganega, to international stars like Chardonnay and Pinot Grigio, Cabernet and Merlot, are generally soft, accessible and reassuringly recognizable, while consistent quality comes from the presence of one of Italy's wine schools at Conegliano in north-east Veneto. The school has trained a generation of winemakers who have transformed the region's bountiful crop into clean, faultless wines. And, even if it may be coupled with anonymity, this consistency has been popular.

Names like Valpolicella and Soave are world famous and, seen as good-value wines in the 1960s, they soon helped forge Italian wine's cheap-and-cheerful image. Despite this image, the Classico vineyards of both zones, up in the Alpine foothills that spring suddenly from the northern lip of the vast Po Valley, remain the finest in the region, in terms of current quality and future potential. But both Classico zones must be distinguished from the wines of

the plains which can only use the straight Valpolicella and Soave names. On the plains the soil is more gravelly, irrigation is more widely used and yields are higher. The wines, particularly those of Valpolicella, are consequently a pale shadow of those from the stony, limestone hills of the Classico zones.

In Soave Classico, the Garganega grape is king. Traditionally supplemented with Trebbiano di Soave to add perfume to the wines, it may now be blended with Chardonnay or Sauvignon, though most top producers stick to Garganega. Soave wines from the best producers have an attractive purity of fruit and understated perfumes, and are never better than when drunk with fresh seafood. The sweet Recioto version, from dried grapes, is now a DOCG.

The quality of Soave has increased more rapidly than that of Valpolicella Classico in recent years, though from a lower base, and the potential for quality in the latter zone far outstrips that in Soave. The steep slopes of the Valpolicella Classico zone, the climate of which is tempered by its proximity to Lake Garda, are ideally suited to the Corvina and Corvinone grapes. Unfortunately, Corvina became diluted by lesser grapes in the post-war years. The high percentage of Molinara used and the fact that the vines are traditionally trained high in a pergola form that usually leads to excessive yields and a further dilution of quality are why many people think of Valpolicella as a light red wine. But that image is fading as more and more growers bring out outstanding table wines like Allegrini's La Poja and La Grola.

Indeed in sites where the proportion of Corvina Classico is high, or where good viticulture is practised, the wines have marvellous depth and intensity, and can rival a good Chianti for concentration. Traditionally, such concentration has been achieved

VALPOLICELLA CLASSICO AND VALPANTENA

━━━ VALPOLICELLA DOC BOUNDARY

VALPOLICELLA CLASSICO = VALPOLICELLA ZONES

━━━ VALPOLICELLA ZONAL BOUNDARIES

TOTAL DISTANCE NORTH TO SOUTH 16KM (10 MILES)

▦ VINEYARDS

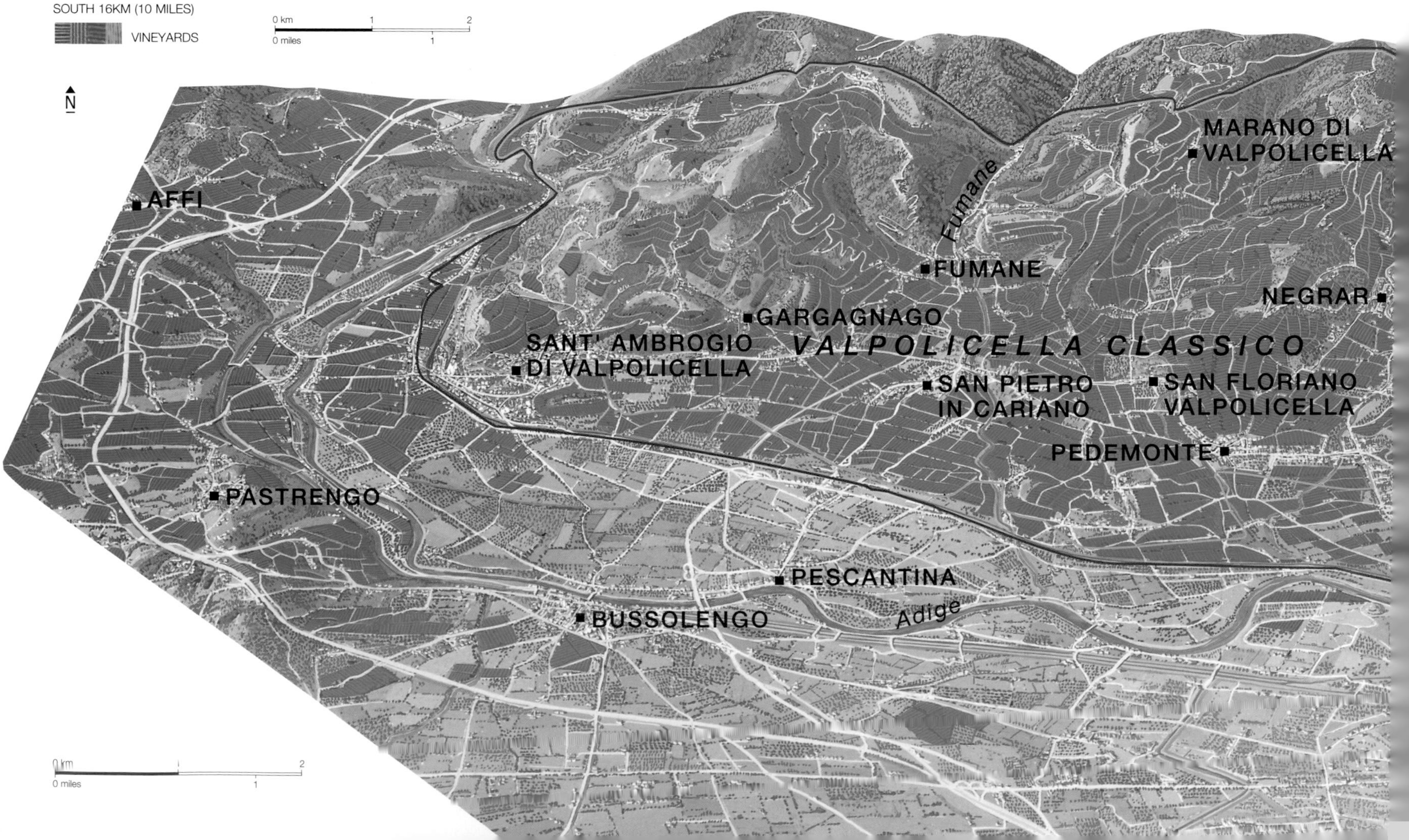

0 km   1   2
0 miles   1

N

MARANO DI VALPOLICELLA

AFFI

Fumane

FUMANE

NEGRAR

GARGAGNAGO

VALPOLICELLA CLASSICO

SANT' AMBROGIO DI VALPOLICELLA

SAN PIETRO IN CARIANO

SAN FLORIANO VALPOLICELLA

PEDEMONTE

PASTRENGO

PESCANTINA

Adige

BUSSOLENGO

0 km   1   2
0 miles   1

by refermenting the young wines on the skins of the dried grapes used in the production of Amarone and Recioto. These refermented wines, known as *ripasso*, have better alcohol and weight than the younger wines and are often smoother with higher viscosity, since the refermentation releases more glycerine into the wine as well as increased concentration and complexity.

The great wines of Valpolicella, however, are the dry Amarone and sweet Recioto. The grapes (primarily Corvina) are picked early and laid out on mats to dry until any time from the December to the February following the vintage. This drying process concentrates sugars, acids and flavours, and the resulting wines – rich, intense and alcoholic – are, at their best, unique in the world of wine.

To the west of Valpolicella, across the Adige in the western corner of Veneto, the glacial shores of Lake Garda are carpeted with vines. Here, a similar mix of red grapes to those in Valpolicella are used to make Bardolino, which is lighter in style than its more illustrious neighbour, thanks to the glacial soil. The white wine of

the zone is Bianco di Custoza which can be surprisingly characterful blend of Garganega, Tocai, Trebbiano and Cortese grapes. Garda is a catch-all DOC for a range of wines in the provinces of Verona and Mantova and Brescia across the border in Lombardy.

East of Valpolicella, again in the Alpine foothills, is the Breganze DOC. North of Vicenza it incorporates a diverse range of varietals including Tocai, Pinot Grigio, Pinot Bianco, Vespaiolo, Merlot, Cabernet and Pinot Nero. Further east, around Conegliano, the Prosecco grape makes a soft, creamy fizz that charms the tired palates of Venice. South of Vicenza, the volcanic hills are home to the Colli Berici and Colli Euganei DOCs, where a similarly wide range of varietals is used to make wines that have, at their best, more intensity than Breganze achieves. In the far eastern Veneto, hills give way to the broader plains of the Piave valley, which produces a boundless source of Merlot and Cabernet. Beyond Piave, astride the border with Friuli, the Lison-Pramaggiore zone makes reliable wines from Cabernet, Merlot, Tocai and Pinot Grigio.

WHERE THE VINEYARDS ARE *The best Valpolicella vineyards are in the steep hills north of Verona in the Classico and Valpantena and Val d'Illasi zones. The altitude in these hills ranges from 100 to 400m (328 to 1312ft) above sea level and the soil is full of limestone pebbles. The Classico zone consists of three main valleys: Negrar, Marano and Fumane. All the valleys are open to the north and act as funnels for the cool wind that blows off the Lessini mountains to the north. Fumane is the most open of the three valleys, and as a result it receives more light, which helps the grapes to achieve greater ripeness, producing wines that are more robust in style. Marano is the most closed valley and, because far fewer of its vineyards have southerly exposures, the wines are lighter and finer, and tend to have a higher level of acidity. Negrar has some of the best vineyard sites (Jago and Moron) in the whole Classico zone, but a higher percentage*

of Molinara in the vineyards here tends to obscure the true quality of the sites which, at their best, produce fine, powerful wines that age wonderfully. To the west, Sant'Ambrogio is classified as a semi-valley and its vineyards are more exposed to the moderating effect of nearby Lake Garda (just off the left of the map) than to the northerly winds.

To the east, Valpantena and Val d'Illasi (off the map) are the only valleys that have similar climatic and soil conditions to those in the Classico zone. The cool breeze blowing down the Valpantena helps to produce supremely elegant wines, the best of which has always been from Bertani, whose estate at Grezzana has some outstanding vineyards. Dal Forno, considered by some to be Valpolicella's greatest producer, though his vineyards are far from the Classico zone, is the best-known producer of the Val d'Illasi.

 RED GRAPES
Corvina, Molinara and Rondinella are used for Valpolicella and Bardolino. Merlot and Cabernet are popular in the Veneto.

WHITE GRAPES
Garganega is grown everywhere but is best known in Soave. Trebbiano di Soave, a superior sub-variety of Trebbiano, is widely used for blending, and Prosecco makes sparkling wines of great popularity.

CLIMATE
The influence of Lake Garda and protection of the Alpine foothills combine to produce a generally mild climate, but the plains can be hot in summer. Hail is a constant problem.

SOIL
Around Lake Garda is a mixture of moraine, sandy gravel and clay. Further east there is calcareous clay and limestone. Piave has sand and clay over gravel with finer loam near the Adriatic.

ASPECT
The best vineyards are on hillsides as the plains are too fertile for good quality wine production.

FRIULI-VENEZIA GIULIA

TUCKED INTO THE NORTH-EASTERN corner of the country, stretching from the plains of the eastern Veneto to the borders with Austria and Slovenia, Friuli is a relative newcomer to united Italy as it was, until 1919, part of the Austro-Hungarian Empire. Perhaps because of this, the locals take a view of themselves as hard-working, constant northerners who are different from their more fickle, flighty neighbours elsewhere in Italy.

There is a certain truth in this as far as making wine goes. Over the past couple of decades, Friuli white wines (which account for approximately two-thirds of DOC production in the region) have become a byword for modernity and consistency. Seventy-five per cent of all wine produced here is entitled to DOC status (the national average is 10 per cent). Thanks to its Austro-Hungarian legacy and its proximity to Eastern Europe, Friuli has a wide range of both imported and native grape varieties. And, as an added bonus, it has some outstanding vineyard sites, mainly in the Collio and Colli Orientali hills. Friuli's northern borders are defined by the Julian and Carnic pre-Alps, which make up just over 40 per cent of the total land area. These inhospitable peaks

hold no prospects for the vine, although, as well as forming a stunning backdrop to the vineyards, they do trap the cool wind, the Bora, that blows off the Gulf of Trieste. The Bora blows from the south across the rest of Friuli, which is comprised largely of the Venetian Plain and the gentle hills along the Slovenian border which are home to the Collio Goriziano and Colli Orientali zones. The cool Tramontana wind that blows off the mountains from the north also moderates the climate.

The two zones, though geographically identical, are divided by provincial boundaries. The sandstone and marl hills are flecked with limestone, the soil being nicely friable, well-drained and easy to work. Terraces, known as *ronchi*, have been carved into the hills in order to pander to the vine's temperamental nature and to make work easier in the vineyards.

The numerous cultural influences to which Friuli has been subjected over the centuries have resulted in a multitude of primarily white grape varieties of German, French, Italian and Eastern Europe origins. Riesling and Traminer perform well – though, rather like a beetroot-red northerner on a sun-drenched beach, they seem to hanker for the cooler reaches of their

0 km   1   2
0 miles   1

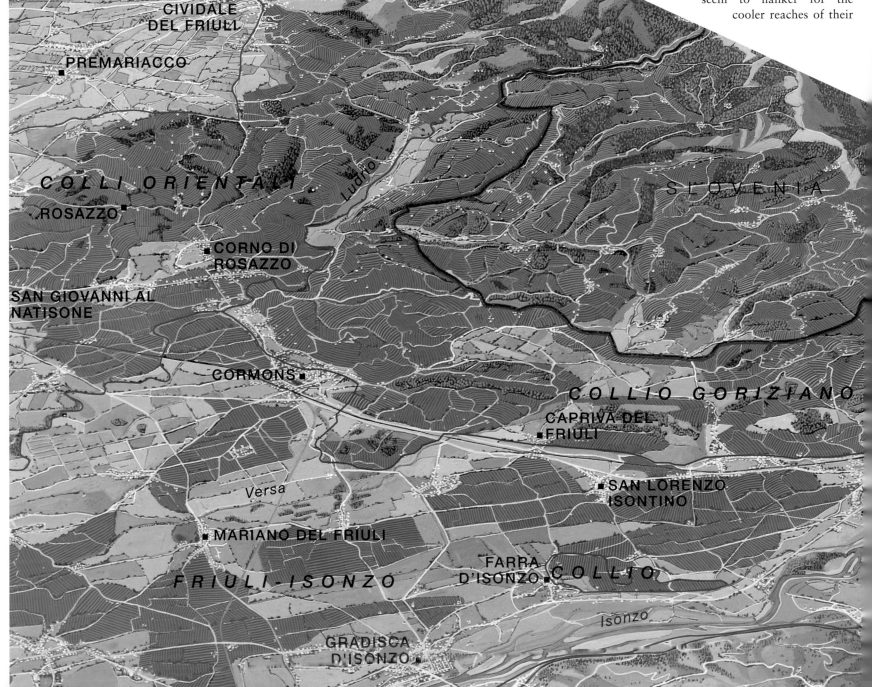

CIVIDALE DEL FRIULI

PREMARIACCO

COLLI ORIENTALI

Ludrio

SLOVENIA

ROSAZZO

CORNO DI ROSAZZO

SAN GIOVANNI AL NATISONE

CORMONS

COLLIO GORIZIANO

CAPRIVA DEL FRIULI

Versa

SAN LORENZO ISONTINO

MARIANO DEL FRIULI

FARRA D'ISONZO

COLLIO

FRIULI-ISONZO

Isonzo

GRADISCA D'ISONZO

German homeland. Pinot Grigio, Pinot Bianco, Chardonnay and Sauvignon have had no such problem adapting – reflecting, perhaps, the greater similarities that exist between the growing conditions in France and northern Italy.

The native Ribolla Gialla is currently enjoying something of a revival, although its waxy nature and tangy acidity do not endear it to palates with a greater affection for the richer, more rounded styles of Australian and Californian wines, while the Tocai Friulano can produce some of the most interesting of Friuli's dry whites.

Other natives include Picolit and Verduzzo, both of which are highly regarded locally for the quality of their sweet wines, but their erratic quality means we rarely see them off their home patch. Of the reds, Refosco dal Peduncolo Rosso can, at its best, be as much of a mouthful to drink as it is to pronounce, while Schioppettino produces lighter wines. Neither, however, produces wines of the stature of the whites.

In Collio and Colli Orientali, producers like Mario Schiopetto and Vittorio Puiatti began producing fresh, modern varietals in the 1960s when the rest of the peninsula was still churning out wines that bore a greater resemblance to poor-quality sherry. Others, like Jermann, Gravner, Livio and Marco Felluga, Abbazia di Rosazzo, La Castellada and Radikon followed, making this a rare area in Italy where small growers and merchants outnumbered the large merchants and co-operatives.

Their success was immediate though it must be said, easy, while the rest of Italy lagged behind. These largely unoaked whites very firmly emphasized the primary fruit aromas of the varietal and were supported by a viscous richness on the palate derived from the warm growing conditions and low yields. Such wines were immeasurably more characterful than those made from

Trebbiano or other grapes elsewhere in Italy. As a result, Friuli in general, and Collio and Colli Orientali in particular, acquired this great reputation for quality, something that was reflected in the prices the wines fetched. Despite (or perhaps because of) these prices, the wines soon came to be seen as rather one-dimensional and, in an attempt to add complexity, growers like Gravner began experimenting with oak and a partial malolactic fermentation.

As you move on to the plains, the quality and price both descend, and the differences between the zones become far less pronounced. In the far west, the Friuli Grave zone produces more red than white wine. The soil on this large alluvial plain consists mainly of gravel, which results in reds of decent weight and colour. A great deal of this wine is sold in bulk, though there are some attractively herbal Merlots and some rather weedy Cabernets. However, as elsewhere in north-east Italy, Pinot Grigio and Chardonnay are on the increase.

Red wines also predominate between Grave and the Adriatic, in the Latisana zone. Here, however, the soil is more fertile, and the wines lack the weight that the best in Grave can attain, though they are usually eminently drinkable. A similar drinkability prevails east of Latisana in the Aquileia zone, but in Isonzo, situated between Aquileia and Collio, more intensity creeps into the wines as the hills begin rolling towards Gorizia.

In all areas, the grape mix is similar to that in Collio and Colli Orientali. The region's predilection for the varietal has proved a very useful marketing tool, but times change, and all over Italy producers are jumping on the varietal bandwagon, often with considerable success, and frequently at lower prices. If Friuli wants to hold on to its pre-eminent spot in Italian whites in particular, we'll want to see a wider diversity of styles and a greater intensity of flavour to justify those prices.

RED GRAPES Red varieties are no longer predominant in the region but Merlot still counts for one-third of vineyard plantings. Cabernet Franc is losing ground to Cabernet Sauvignon, and Refosco is also in decline.

WHITE GRAPES Tocai Friulano remains the most planted white grape, but Chardonnay, Pinot Bianco, Pinot Grigio and Sauvignon are on the increase. Picolit and Verduzzo are two ancient Friuli varieties.

CLIMATE To the north, the Carnic Alps have the heaviest rainfall in Italy but generally the Friulian climate is mild and fine. The coastal plains can be hot and dry in the summer.

SOIL Hillside vineyards are often planted on crumbly marl and sandstone. Elsewhere soils range from clay, sand, and gravel to the alluvial deposits of the Isonzo river, and famous limestone formations of the Carso.

ASPECT The best vineyards lie on well-sited slopes between the Alps to the north and the Venetian plain to the south and west.

WHERE THE VINEYARDS ARE *Thanks to modern technology, excellent raw materials and some fine vineyard sites, Collio and Colli Orientali are considered to be Italy's best white wine zones. Two-thirds of Collio's best sites are said to be in Slovenia and, as a result, many grapes are transported across what used to be the border with the Iron Curtain.*

In Collio, north of Gorizia along the border with Slovenia, the chalky vineyards on the lower-lying hills, 100 to 150m (328 to 492ft) above sea level, give wines of great intensity, especially around San Floriano and Oslavia. To the west, between Gorizia and Cormons and especially on the slopes west of Capriva, the wines combine richness and perfume. It is here that many of the best producers (among them, Schiopetto, Jermann and Puiatti) are situated.

South of Cormons the soil consists of more gravel than limestone, and we move into the Isonzo zone. The climate, though, is similar to Collio's and some producers, notably Gianfranco Gallo of Vie di Romans and Alvaro Pecorari of Lis Neris, are showing that the wines can have similar stuffing, if slightly less refinement than the best Collio can offer – but only if the approach to viticulture is equally rigorous. North of Cormons, the slightly cooler climate gives Collio wines with more delicate aromas.

Colli Orientali is merely a north-easterly extension of Collio and virtually all its best vineyards are along the border of the two zones, around Rosazzo.

CIVIDALE DEL FRIULI TO GORIZIA

COLLIO GORIZIANO = DOC WINE AREA

— DOC BOUNDARIES

TOTAL DISTANCE
NORTH TO SOUTH
24KM (15 MILES)

 VINEYARDS

N

0 km 1 2
0 miles 1

CHIANTI

CHIANTI CLASSICO: GREVE TO SIENA

TOTAL DISTANCE
NORTH TO SOUTH
28KM (17½ MILES)

▨▨▨ VINEYARDS

N

THE AREA OF CHIANTI SEDUCED ME from the first second. I alighted from the train at Florence station, marvelled at the city and then, within a few hours, headed off south into the hills of what I now know were the northern reaches of Chianti Classico. But the wine? Well my first mouthful of gushing, prickly sour red-fruited wine on that trip – from an unmarked bottle in some farmer's field by the side of a silent road – that was a revelation. Yet the vast majority of Chianti wine that I drank until at least the mid-1990s tottered between dull and disgraceful. The change in quality and attitude at the end of the 20th century and the start of the new millennium has been nothing short of remarkable.

Chianti first came to prominence around the beginning of the 13th century. At the time, Florence was the banking capital of the world. Its bankers – the Medici and Frescobaldi families, among others – funded the wayward campaigns of most of the rulers of medieval Europe and became rich in the process. This wealth spilled out of the city into the countryside, where the great villas and estates that now lure tourists to these verdant hills in summer were developed into agricultural properties. Because of the rocky soil, only the olive tree and the vine flourished, yet its products were greatly appreciated in affluent Florentine society.

This wealthy market provided the impetus to the development of Chianti as a quality wine zone. By the beginning of the 15th century, Chianti's name was already established and, as has happened the world over when a certain area attains fame, others tried to pass off

their usually inferior products as the real thing. This led, in 1716, to the Grand Duke of Tuscany mapping out the borders of the zone in an attempt to prevent fraud. While delimiting the area, the Grand Duke also pushed the borders north from their original area towards Greve and Panzano. Such elasticity, however, did little to staunch the flow of ersatz Chianti that increased towards the end of the 19th century, when Chianti enjoyed a boom thanks to the shortage of wine created by phylloxera. By this time, virtually every Tuscan red wine, no matter what its provenance or history – and some, like those from Rufina, Carmignano and Montepulciano, had histories every bit as noble – was being sold as Chianti.

There were many, then, who argued that some legal definition was required to protect the name of Chianti, but this was generally ignored in the rush for sales. It was only several decades later, during the slump that inevitably followed the boom, that people began to think along these lines. This resulted in the Dalmasso commission, whose report in 1932 led to new boundaries being established.

The original zone was doubled in size to take in the lower-lying, clay-clogged hills closer to Florence and was renamed Chianti Classico. This new name distinguished it from the six new Chianti zones that were created by appending to the name a broad geographical designation. In most cases, this was simply a matter of mopping up all the vineyards in a particular province like Florence or Siena that weren't already covered by another zone. It is an

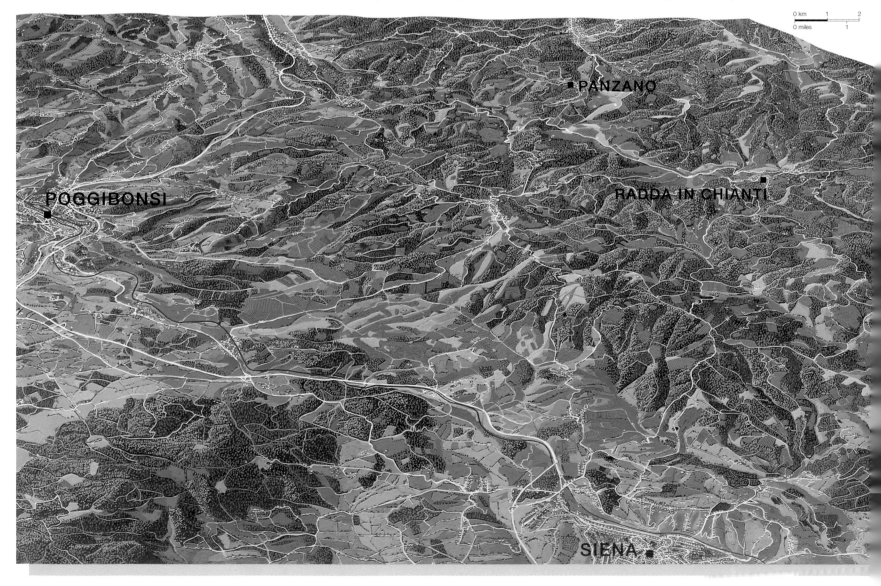

0 km 1 2
0 miles 1

PANZANO

POGGIBONSI

RADDA IN CHIANTI

SIENA

idiotic basis upon which to define a wine, yet it was confirmed by the DOC laws of 1967, reaffirmed when the DOCG was introduced in 1984 and remains in practice to this day.

In the province of Siena, for instance, any appropriate grapes grown outside the Sienese part of Classico, or beyond the borders of the Montepulciano and Montalcino zones, are entitled to the name Chianti Colli Senesi. Never mind that the zone covers a wide variety of soils and mesoclimates, it's just that the area fits neatly into the politically defined borders of the province of Siena. Similarly in Florence, all areas under vine not covered by Rufina, Pomino, Carmignano, Montalbano and Chianti Classico is delimited as the Chianti Colli Fiorentini, despite the fact that this takes in two such diverse zones as the Val d'Arno and the Val d'Elsa. Now whether you believe in the sanctity of *terroir* or not, it is manifestly stupid that wines produced in such distinctive zones as these should bear the same name. By extending the name of Chianti over vast tracts of Tuscany, from the green rolling hills of central Classico to the arid Sienese slopes, from the cool reaches of Rufina to the low-lying vineyards of the Colline Pisane, the Italian authorities have succeeded not only in confusing the adventurous wine drinker, but also in robbing the growers of their individual identities.

There are something like 7000 growers in the seven Chianti zones and it is likely, given the diversity of soil, altitude, climate and, to a lesser extent, varietal composition, that there are as many

different styles of wine. Even within Classico, altitude varies between 150 and 550m (492 and 1800ft), resulting in great temperature variations. The vineyards in the central Classico hills are higher and cooler than those on the coast, one factor that gives finer, more perfumed wines.

Proximity to forests, valleys or rivers throws another complicating variable into the equation. Those vineyards on the western flank of Classico, for instance, produce fuller wines than do their neighbours several miles nearer the central part of the zone, largely because of the warmth generated by the Val d'Elsa. In the Rufina zone, on the other hand, the cool breeze funnelled down the Sieve Valley from the Apennines sets this tiny area apart, creating a unique mesoclimate and a distinctive style of wine.

But through all the variations in climate, soil and altitude within the Chianti zone there is one constant factor: the Sangiovese grape (see page 170). This grape forms the mainstay of Chianti, being used on its own in some of the best wines, or blended with native varieties like Canaiolo and Colorino, or international ones like Merlot and Cabernet, in others. In lesser wines, white grapes such as Trebbiano and Malvasia still occasionally find their way into the blend, remnants of the lean times in Tuscany when they were used to boost production and render the wine lighter, and ready for drinking sooner. As vineyards are replanted, however, their numbers are diminished, at least among the quality producers.

WHERE THE VINEYARDS ARE *This map shows the southern half of the Chianti Classico zone and the three communes – Radda, Castellina and Gaiole – that comprised historic Chianti, the area noted for the quality of its red wines since the 13th century. In 1932 the zone was extended to take in the lower-lying hills that spread further north towards Florence, but generally, the best vineyards are still in these southern Sienese hills. Soils vary greatly within the zone and this, along with Sangiovese's chameleon-like character, results in wines that range from aristocrats to peasants. The clay of Greve and the northern part of the zone gives way, in Panzano, to galestro,*

a friable, shaly clay that, along with the limestone alberese, *which begins to appear also at this point, provides the ideal growing conditions for the Sangiovese grape. Both* galestro *and* alberese *dominate the vineyards of Radda and Gaiole and in the south, around Castelnuovo Berardenga, the potent mixture of tufaceous rock and galestro gives some of the greatest wines of Chianti at estates like Felsina. Yields from these sites are invariably low.*

In the past 15 years, in the search for quality, many estates, including Fontodi, Rampolla and Isole e Olena, have replanted their higher vineyards, which had been abandoned in the 1960s and 1970s in favour of lower-lying, more easily worked sites.

RED GRAPES
The most important grape is Sangiovese (locally also called Sangioveto). Canaiolo Nero and Colorino are also sometimes used in Chianti as well as increasing amounts of Cabernet and Merlot.

WHITE GRAPES
Trebbiano is widely planted, but rapidly decreasing in importance. Malvasia del Chianti is also in decline as Chardonnay and Sauvignon Blanc become more fashionable in varietal wines.

CLIMATE
The central hills of the Chianti Classico zone are cooler and more temperate than the coast. Hail can sometimes be a problem in summer and the occasional frost can be quite severe and damaging.

SOIL
Stony calcareous soils are varied by parcels of limestone, sand, clay and schist. In the heart of Chianti Classico the shaly clay known as galestro gives wine with notably good body. The Colli Senesi and Colli Aretini zones have clay and towards the coast the soil becomes lighter and sandier.

ASPECT
The region is characterized by sloping vineyard plots among woods and groves of olives. Altitude plays a key role in determining the style and quality of Chianti produced.

CHIANTI CLASSICO DOCG WINE AREA AND SELECTED ESTATES

1. Badia a Passignano (Antinori)
2. Poggio al Sole
3. Vecchie Terre di Montefili
4. Querciabella
5. Villa Cafaggio
6. La Massa
7. Castello dei Rampolla
8. Fontodi
9. Casa Emma
10. Isole e Olena
11. Monsanto
12. Castello della Paneretta
13. La Brancaia
14. Castellare
15. Rocca delle Macie
16. Castello di Fonterutoli
17. Terrabianca
18. Castello di Volpaia
19. Montevertine
20. Poggerino
21. Badia a Coltibuono
22. Riecine
23. Castello di Ama
24. Rocca di Castagnoli
25. Cacchiano/Rocca di Montegrossi
26. Ricasoli/Castello di Brolio
27. San Giusto a Rentennano
28. San Felice
29. Fattoria di Felsina

— DOCG BOUNDARY

BRUNELLO DI MONTALCINO

RED GRAPES
Brunello is another name for the Sangiovese of Chianti. Some producers have also made experimental plantings of Merlot and Cabernet for use in alternative wines.

WHITE GRAPES
Moscato Bianco is grown to produce Moscadello di Montalcino. Chardonnay and Sauvignon Blanc are also beginning to be planted.

CLIMATE
The temperate hill climate benefits from the influence of the Tyrrhenian Sea, while nearby Mount Amiata offers protection from storms.

SOIL
The best vineyards are on the prized *galestro* (shaly clay). Elsewhere sandy clay is often combined with limestone.

ASPECT
The longest-lived wines come from the relatively cooler, higher vineyards found on the four major slopes which dominate Montalcino. Further plantings have recently been made on lower-lying terrain.

Castello di Argiano is on the lower slopes of Montalcino – you can see the higher slopes behind the castle – and this contributes to the rich, ripe fruit quality of its wines.

LEAVING BEHIND THE WOODED HILLS of Chianti and the ancient towers of Siena, and heading south towards Rome, I could be forgiven for thinking that I have seen the last of Tuscany's vines. The hills of the Val d'Orcia are parched brown, the heavy, clay soil proving more suitable to the cereals swaying in the southerly breeze than to the vine. The horizon is open, with only a few gentle hills occasionally providing relief from an otherwise unbroken vista.

Then, just past Buonconvento, I turn to my right and, as the road winds uphill, clay gives way to *galestro*, vines replace wheat and, at 600m (1968ft) altitude, I arrive in Montalcino, the town famed for its Brunello, Italy's longest-lived and, some would say, greatest wine. This is a town that lives on and for wine. On the main street, there is a wonderful bar, the Fiaschetteria, serving any number of Brunellos by the glass, as well as a wide selection of other wines. Since extended aeration used to be regarded as vital for drawing out the aromas of Brunello, you could well strike lucky with some sullen old brute finally cracking a smile after a couple of days open behind the bar. With modern Brunellos, I'd want one opened on the day I drank it.

The renown enjoyed by Brunello is a rather recent development. Indeed, it was only in the 1960s that whispers reached the outside world of wines of incredible longevity from the cellars of one producer in Montalcino called Biondi-Santi. The legendary 1891, tasted by few but lauded by all, put first Biondi-Santi and then Montalcino on the map. A legend was created, and the prices of Biondi-Santi wines climbed higher than Mount Olympus. Some producers, able to sell their wines at half the price (still double what the better bottles of Chianti fetched), were happy to let Biondi-Santi make all the running. Others, keen to jump on the bandwagon, planted vineyards, increasing the area under vine from less than 100ha (247 acres) in 1968 (soon after the Biondi-Santi-drafted DOC regulations came into force) to over 1300ha (3212 acres) today.

Despite this growth the legend lives on, but there is no doubt that Montalcino is a zone with a great vocation for viticulture. Rising from a sea of clay, it is ringed by a protective wall of valleys – the Ombrone to the west, the Orcia to the south and east – and mountains, with the forbidding face of Mount Amiata standing guard on Montalcino's southern flank. These protect the vineyards from nasty weather and help to make the Brunello zone the most arid of all Tuscany's wine areas, with about 500mm (20in) of rainfall a year. But cooling breezes blowing off the sea, a luxury neither Chianti nor Montepulciano enjoy, provide a bit of relief.

The dry, hot climate brings the grapes to maturity quicker than in Chianti or Montepulciano. There are years when producers in Montalcino have their grapes safely in the fermenting vats, while their colleagues to the north are still struggling to complete the harvest amid the onset of autumn rains. In overly hot years, however, the wines of Montalcino can be brutish in character, and lacking any of the gentler tones found in the best Chiantis.

Perhaps because of their stature, Montalcino wines have traditionally been aged in large old oak barrels for a protracted period in order to temper their ferocious tannins. A compulsory wood-aging period of four years was inserted into the DOC law in 1966, recently reduced to two years in oak before release, though the total aging period remains over four years. This lengthy period may have been fine a generation or so ago when tastes were different, but in today's market it all too often results in the wines' freshness perishing under the onslaught of wood. True, Biondi-Santi's great old wines (made as recently as 1975 and 1964) were able to withstand this aging, and their high acidity also enabled them to age well in bottle. But what about the lighter years, when elegance is prized above structure? Four years in oak would kill

whatever elegance the wine may initially have had. There are those today who reckon that even two years is too long in wood in a light vintage, and that the total of four is absurd – why shouldn't the consumer take responsibility for bottle-aging the wines, they demand, as in the case of Bordeaux? Relaxing of regulations would more closely reflect the already widely diverging styles of Brunello, though since Brunello was never meant to be an easy mouthful, traditionalists already feel they've moved far enough.

WINE STYLES

Brunello's original claim to greatness was based on the wine's longevity (and an inflated price), and the so-called classic style – as exemplified by Biondi-Santi – is still made by producers in the centre of the zone where the soil is *galestro*-rich and the vineyards are relatively high, at 400–500m (1310–1640ft) above sea level.

On new estates in the north-west and north-east of the zone, producers like Castiglion del Bosco, Caparzo and Altesino have planted vineyards on clay soils not previously cultivated with vines. Though these wines are good, they often need to be given polish by adding a little something from vineyards around Sant' Angelo in Colle in the south or from the *galestro*-rich ones around Montosoli.

This diversity of wine styles illustrates the limitless number of masks the old trouper Sangiovese has at its disposal. As part of the myth management process, Montalcino producers, led by Biondi-Santi, propagated the theory that their particular sub-variety of Sangiovese, called Brunello, was distinctive from, and superior to those found elsewhere in Tuscany. But independent research showed that there were numerous clones of Sangiovese in

WHERE THE VINEYARDS ARE
As Montalcino has expanded, areas not previously cultivated have come under vine, and there is now a much greater diversity of wine styles than ever before. What might be termed the classic Biondi-Santi style lives on, not only at the family's Il Greppo farm, but also among other producers in the high central section around Montalcino. Here the soil has more galestro *than clay, which, combined with the higher altitude, results in wines that have more acidity and a leaner, steelier fruit than those from lower-lying vineyards nearer the zone's perimeter. This style is best exemplified by Costanti's Colle al Matrichese estate and, when they are good, Biondi-Santi.*

In the south around Sant'Angelo Scalo, a different style is produced. There is more clay and limestone in the soil, and warmth from the nearby Val d'Orcia gives richer wines with a lower acidity that tend to be fleshier and more accessible when young, yet ceding none of their aging ability.

MONTALCINO

N

TOTAL DISTANCE NORTH TO SOUTH
19KM (12 MILES)

 VINEYARDS

0 km   1   2
0 miles   1

Montalcino vineyards, so the growers adopted a new position, claiming that Brunello was a local name for the Tuscan grape stemming from the fact that, in the hot, arid Montalcino summers, the grapes often acquired a brownish hue at ripening, hence Brunello, or 'little brown one'. Moves by California growers to cash in on Montalcino's success by labelling their wines 'Brunello' have since forced the Italian growers to renounce Brunello as a grape name, and today it is officially viewed by them as just a wine.

However that may be, the sole use of Sangiovese for their wines did make the producers of Montalcino unique in Tuscany. But now that others in Chianti and beyond are adopting the same approach and improving the quality of their raw materials, the Montalcino producers are having to fight to retain their pre-eminent position.

Realizing that selling their wines at high prices brings with it a certain responsibility with regard to quality, as far back as 1984 they set up a 'junior' DOC called Rosso di Montalcino, followed in 1996 by a much broader and more inclusive DOC called Sant' Antimo. These 'junior' DOCs have proved particularly successful, not only in maintaining the generally high standard of quality but also in giving a modern and more attractive range of red wines to widen the choice in Tuscany. And of course if you can sell the wine younger, you get your money earlier.

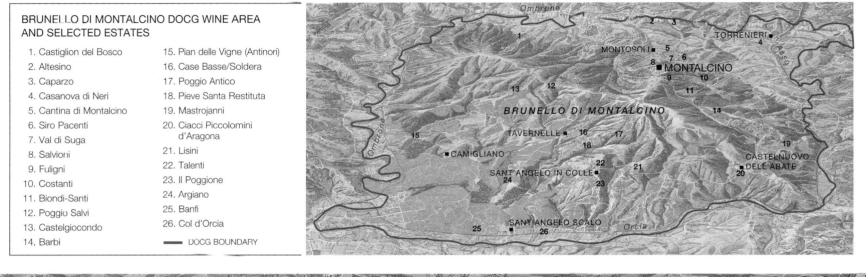

BRUNELLO DI MONTALCINO DOCG WINE AREA AND SELECTED ESTATES

1. Castiglion del Bosco
2. Altesino
3. Caparzo
4. Casanova di Neri
5. Cantina di Montalcino
6. Siro Pacenti
7. Val di Suga
8. Salvioni
9. Fuligni
10. Costanti
11. Biondi-Santi
12. Poggio Salvi
13. Castelgiocondo
14. Barbi
15. Pian delle Vigne (Antinori)
16. Case Basse/Soldera
17. Poggio Antico
18. Pieve Santa Restituta
19. Mastrojanni
20. Ciacci Piccolomini d'Aragona
21. Lisini
22. Talenti
23. Il Poggione
24. Argiano
25. Banfi
26. Col d'Orcia

—— DOCG BOUNDARY

VINO NOBILE DI MONTEPULCIANO

RED GRAPES
Sangiovese, under the name
Prugnolo Gentile, is king.
Canaiolo is allowed to 20
per cent, as are Cabernet
Sauvignon and Merlot.

WHITE GRAPES
A blend of Chardonnay and
Sauvignon Blanc make the
best whites. Trebbiano and
Malvasia are becoming less
popular, except for Vin Santo.

CLIMATE
Quasi-continental with hot
summers and cold winters,
mitigated to a modest extent
by the proximity of Lake
Trasimeno.

SOIL
Predominantly the classic
albarese with prized *galestro*
(shaly clay), but in parts with a
higher proportion of sand.

ASPECT
The majority of the Vino
Nobile vineyards face east or
south east, occasionally at
altitudes up to 550m (1800ft).

THE TOWN OF MONTEPULCIANO (and let's be quite clear – we are not talking about the grape Montepulciano, which is barely grown in Tuscany) is one of the most seductively attractive in all of Italy. Steeped in history and personality, Montepulciano was the home town of Lorenzo de' Medici's favourite poet, Poliziano. It stands in a commanding position on a steep hill, and from its medieval walls you can gaze out over rolling vineyards and olive groves and a distant blue horizon – a view that probably hasn't changed for centuries.

Montepulciano (from the Latin *Mons Politianus*) is situated 40 minutes' drive east of Montalcino in the province of Siena and is the most inland of Tuscany's classic zones. It has the most continental climate and its vineyards are at a generally higher altitude than those of its rivals. Like Montalcino, it is a zone which runs on Sangiovese – here called Prugnolo Gentile, though this historic name is retained mainly for marketing purposes as the Sangiovese clones grown here are, for the most part, the same as those cultivated in Montalcino and Chianti.

Montepulciano was a papal favourite as far back as the 14th century and much of its production used to be run by the local nobility – hence the denomination Vino Nobile di Montepulciano DOCG. In 1680 Francesco Redi (poet and physician to the Dukes of Tuscany) went so far as to hail Montepulciano 'of every wine the king', an accolade that other wine-producing zones of Tuscany, let alone the rest of Italy, might dispute today. But by the end of the 1970s, if not much earlier, this 'king' had lost most of his royal trappings, and was left with 'nobility' in name only. By then, the grandly named Vino Nobile had descended to the humble level of ordinary Chianti.

As with Chianti, local rules let winemakers put a hefty proportion of white grapes into the blend – almost a third was allowed and 10 per cent was mandatory – more than enough to ruin any red wine with pretensions to class. Worse still, the wine had to contain at least 10 per cent Canaiolo (an inferior red variety) and its excessive aging processes were conducted in old barrels, finally killing off any quality or freshness that might have survived to that point.

The granting of DOCG status in 1980, although it seemed a travesty at the time, turned out to be just the stimulus the winemakers needed to get their act together. While the new law still allowed white grapes into the blend, and required Canaiolo, it seemed more flexible and the best producers, in time-honoured Italian tradition, started to ignore the law's stupidities and began writing their own script. This led to the development of wines made with 100 per cent Sangiovese, or Sangiovese blended with Cabernet or Merlot, all officially illegal until further changes to the law were made.

Perhaps the first producer to rise from the ashes and gain an international reputation was Avignonesi. This company became known not only for a classier version of Vino Nobile, but also for more international style wines like Grifi – a now defunct super-Tuscan blend of Sangiovese and Cabernet and Il Marzocco (Chardonnay). It also produced the most sought-after Vin Santo of all Tuscany (theirs is a non-botrytized sweet wine, barrel-aged and produced in tiny quantities).

TORRITA DI SIENA

GRACCIANO

MONTEPULCIANO

N

MONTEPULCIANO

TOTAL DISTANCE NORTH TO
SOUTH 13KM (8¼ MILES)

VINEYARDS

0 km 1 2
0 miles 1

The key to Vino Nobile's revival, though, lay in the taming of tannins and acids which, while making the wine one of Tuscany's longest-lived (before they started adding white grapes), also made it impossibly tough when young. Since the early 1990s techniques learned from the French – in the vineyard, during fermentation and in the aging process (particularly the use of barriques) – have enabled more and more producers to make wines which are concentrated and full of extract, yet approachable within two to five years of vintage.

Today's Vino Nobile is not yet on a par with either Montalcino or Chianti Classico, the former doing a better job with pure Sangiovese and the latter, if you include the IGT super-Tuscans, putting out superior blends as well as varietals. There are, on the other hand, fewer producers here, and far fewer that have a quality track-record. But the

signs are very encouraging and the feeling is that Vino Nobile di Montepulciano is finally coming back into its own at the outset of the 21st century. As in Montalcino nearby, the introduction of the Rosso di Montepulciano DOC as essentially a second wine has given producers the chance of improving the selection for the grander Vino Nobile wine.

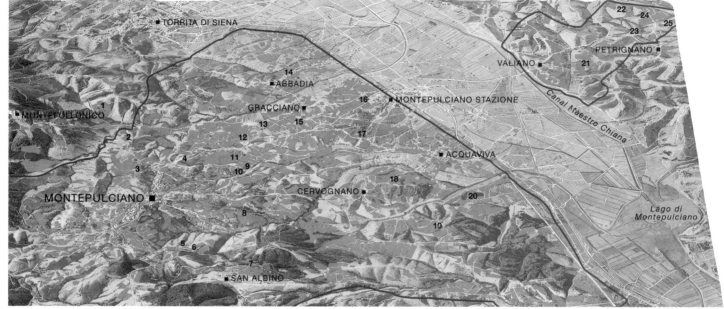

VINO NOBILE DI MONTEPULCIANO DOCG WINE AREA AND SELECTED ESTATES

1. Innocenti	9. La Casella	18. Boscarelli
2. Contucci	10. Valdipiatta	19. Del Cerro
3. Canneto	11. La Ciarliana	20. Bindella
4. Redi (Vecchia Cantina)	12. Il Macchione	21. Lodola Nuova
5. Salcheto	13. Fassati	22. Avignonesi
6. Paterno	14. Villa Sant' Anna	23. Trerose
7. Le Casalte	15. Lombardo	24. La Calonica
8. Dei	16. Poliziano	25. La Braccesca
	17. Romeo	▬ DOCG BOUNDARY

WHERE THE VINEYARDS ARE *Climbing up its hillside in a regal manner, the town of Montepulciano, with wonderful palaces, churches and cellars, is without question 'noble', even if the wine which enjoys the title has only recently began to show signs of being worthy of the name.*

It is worth walking up to the grand central piazza at the top of the town, remembering that the wine and other goodies get better and cheaper the higher you go. From the top of the town you'll also be able to see many of the better Montepulciano vineyards fanning away across the gently undulating slopes to the north and north-east – that is, after you've stopped gazing in awe at the beautiful Tuscan vista spread out on all sides beneath you.

From the town, at a height of 500m (1640ft), the vineyards drop away toward the Chiana Valley, usually facing south-east. They come to a halt to the west of the river at about 250m (820ft), where sunflowers and cereals take over on the flatter land. On the far side of the valley, beyond the autostrada, the land begins to rise again, and around the medieval hill village of Valiano is a small enclave of vineyards, which are included in the DOCG, and several superlative wine estates.

BOLGHERI

RED GRAPES
Primarily Cabernet Sauvignon for the top wines with some Cabernet Franc, Petit Verdot and Syrah. Merlot is increasing and Sangiovese declining.

WHITE GRAPES
Traditionally the quality white grape here is Vermentino, but Chardonnay and Sauvignon Blanc are making progress.

CLIMATE
It is significantly hotter here on the low-lying coast than inland Tuscany, but with mitigating sea breezes.

SOIL
The key to Bolgheri's quality is drainage, helped by the gravel and sand mixed in with the marl.

ASPECT
Most vineyards are on very gently rising ground facing west and south; there are a few hillside sites.

In 1974, A SIX-YEAR-OLD SASSICAIA WINE won an astonishing victory over an assortment of illustrious Bordeaux Grands Crus in a tasting organised by *Decanter* magazine. It put Bolgheri on the map. Before that no-one would have dreamt that a Cabernet, let alone a great one, could conceivably hail from central Italy, nor that a high quality wine of any sort could be produced from the once-malarial, low-lying Tuscan coast known as the northern Maremma or Costa degli Etruschi. Nor had anyone ever heard of the quiet village of Bolgheri, in the province of Livorno, other than a few artists and tourists, or horse-lovers keen to admire the fine beasts reared and trained on the vast properties of the della Gherardesca and other noble families.

Bolgheri itself is an insignificant parish or '*frazione*' of the commune of Castagneto Carducci, a zone named after a pretty hilltop town a few kilometres to the south. The fact that the region's prototype wine, Sassicaia, comes from an estate situated near Bolgheri is no doubt the reason for the honour of DOC being bestowed on the *frazione* rather than the commune. Bolgheri DOC wines can, in fact, come from anywhere in the commune of Castagneto, except the part nearest the sea, west of the Via Aurelia. But the influence of Sassicaia and Bolgheri extends much further, spreading along the coast northwards to Montescudaio, in the province of Pisa, and south to Suvereto-Val di Cornia in Livorno.

The land near the sea is flat, rising gradually until you reach the first slopes of the Colline Metallifere, a few kilometres inland,. The DOC vineyards are both on the flat and on slopes and some producers, including the producers of Sassicaia, make wine blended from grapes grown in both terrains. Soils contain varying amounts of marl, sand and gravel, the drainage is similar to that of Bordeaux and the climate, which one might have thought impossibly hot for Bordeaux grapes, is modified by the nearness of the sea. And there are plenty of umbrella pines, cypresses and even eucalyptus trees to break up the sometimes brisk breezes whipping off the water.

In terms of a history, this wine zone hasn't really got one. It was known largely for rosés made principally from Sangiovese. This grape ripens well here (some say too well) producing a jammy, blowsy product, unless care is taken in both vineyard and winery. Some excellent Sangiovese reds now come from Bolgheri: Michele Satta's Vigna al Cavaliere is an outstanding example. But once the Marchesi Incisa della Rocchetta – of Sassicaia fame – along with their advisers, Giacomo Tachis and Professor Emile Peynaud, had shown Bolgheri to be ideal for Cabernet, it was to Bordeaux varieties that growers turned, to a rising crescendo of applause.

First to take the plunge in the early 1980s was Lodovico Antinori (brother of Piero, and cousin of Niccolò Incisa of Sassicaia through their della Gherardesca mothers). Lodovico planted Cabernet Sauvignon, Cabernet Franc, Merlot and Sauvignon at his Ornellaia estate. He showed the world how well both Merlot (the wine is called Masseto) and Sauvignon Blanc (Poggio alle Gazze) could perform here. His brother Piero followed suit at Tenuta Belvedere with a Cabernet/Merlot blend, Guado al Tasso. And a few years ago another big name, Angelo Gaja, from Piedmont, also bought an estate in Bolgheri – Ca' Marcanda.

The Bolgheri DOC, approved in 1994, has a broad scope: its red wines are based on Cabernet Sauvignon (up to 80 per cent) or Merlot or Sangiovese (70 per cent), topped up with other varieties. Bolgheri Sassicaia, for example, is a blend of 80 per cent Cabernet Sauvignon and 20 per cent Cabernet Franc (interestingly, this is the first Italian estate wine to have its name attached as a sub-zone to a DOC). Whites can be based on Sauvignon, Vermentino or Trebbiano (to 70 per cent), with the remainder being other white grapes, such as Chardonnay or Viognier.

BOLGHERI AND MONTESCUDAIO

TOTAL DISTANCE NORTH TO SOUTH 22.5KM (14 MILES)

VINEYARDS

N

Cabernet Franc vines, just outside the fortified village of Bolgheri, belonging to Tenuta dell'Ornellaia. Count Lodovico Antinori, a member of the famous Tuscan wine dynasty, established the estate in the 1980s to create world-class Bordeaux-style reds. In 2002, he sold it to a partnership of the Californian Mondavi family and the Tuscan Frescobaldis.

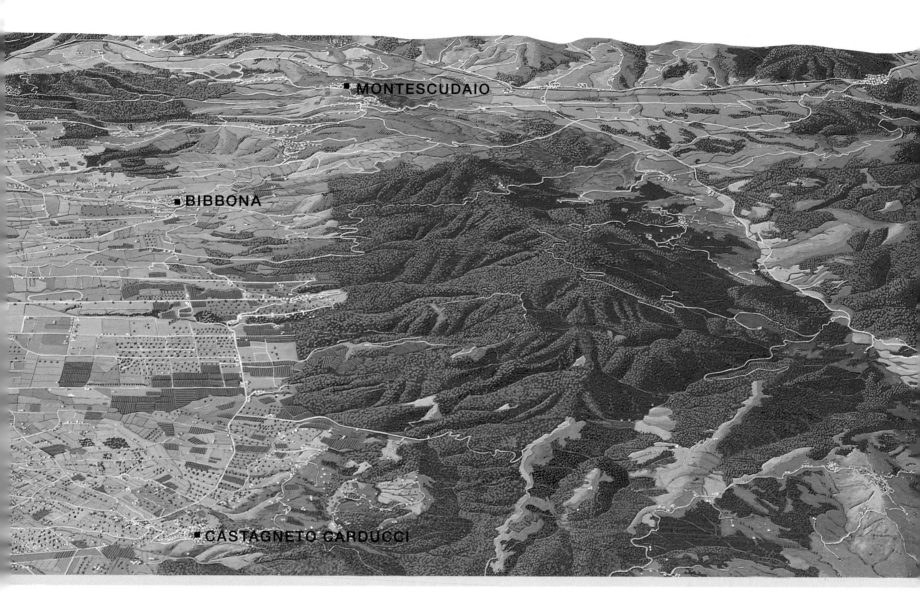

MONTESCUDAIO

BIBBONA

CASTAGNETO CARDUCCI

WHERE THE VINEYARDS ARE *It was years before I worked out what was so special about Bolgheri and its more inland neighbour, Montescudaio. The landscape between Livorno and Piombino along this part of the Tuscan coast is of such unrelenting drabness that there had to be something else – and luckily there is.*

Lack of any significant grape-growing and winemaking traditions and no restrictive regulations about which grape varieties could be used were a crucial part of the area's success. But the poor, infertile soils of those vineyards huddled up against the hills (the 1-hectare patch of rocky hillside that was the first Sassicaia vineyard is actually several kilometres up into the hills) are also important.

Sea breezes moderate the strong Tuscan summer sun, yet yields on these generally poor soils are so low that ripening is usually two to three weeks ahead of central Tuscany. There aren't many producers, even today, despite the number of local success stories – the area's estates are large and the amount of land suitable for viticulture is limited.

Montescudaio's vineyards, like the earliest tiny Sassicaia vineyard, are mostly some 300m (985ft) above sea level, and the altitude and sea breezes allow a remarkable array of white grapes to flourish, as well as some exciting reds.

DOC WINE AREAS AND SELECTED ESTATES

MONTESCUDAIO
1. Poggio Gagliardo
2. La Regola
3. Merlini

BOLGHERI
4. Tenuta San Guido (Sassicaia)
5. Sassicaia vinoyard
6. Tenuta Guado al Tasso (Antinori)
7. Guado al Tasso vineyard
8. Le Macchiole
9. Tenuta dell'Ornellaia
10. Ca' Marcanda (Gaja)
11. Grattamacco
12. Michele Satta

BOLGHERI = DOC WINE AREA
— DOC BOUNDARIES

SPAIN

Green and gold, the colours of Spain: vast expanses of arid cereal land punctuated by the bright fresh green of vines. These are the vines of Bodegas Nekeas, one of Navarra's most forward-looking wineries. Above are 60-year-old Tinto Fino vines at harvest time, their grapes carefully laid in small modern plastic boxes, before being taken to the Dominio de Pingus winery in Ribera del Duero, one of Spain's top red wine regions.

The late 1990s provided a dramatic turnaround in the quality of Spain's long-neglected wines, and also in the international perception of the many Spanish regions that had long been overshadowed by the indomitable duo of Jerez and Rioja. A drastic modernization of winemaking technology has finally allowed regions like Priorat, Ribera del Duero, La Mancha, Rueda and Toro to muscle into the limelight with potent fruit-driven wines with the impact and style to convert the modern consumer.

Spain is basically far hotter and drier than its more famous wine neighbour, France, so the variation in local climates is less and the range of grapes that find conditions ideal is limited. It has taken her a long while to appreciate the need to search out mesoclimates influenced by altitude and by maritime cooling conditions. And it has taken her some time to realize that hot-climate grapes like Garnacha, Cariñena, Tempranillo, Verdejo and Monastrell can produce delicious flavours if approached with up-to-the-minute New World technology and attitudes.

The lush, hilly north-west is heavily influenced by cool, damp Atlantic conditions and the fragrant whites and tangy, juicy reds are marvellously individual. Further south along the Duero river are some of Spain's most exciting reds and whites.

Andalucía in the south-west doesn't have much to offer in terms of table wines, but the fortified wines of Jerez and Montilla-Moriles can be among the world's greatest. Málaga's fame has faded since the 19th century, but occasional bottles still show how exciting her wines can be. The large area of the Levante stretching between Alicante and Valencia and the vast plateau of La Mancha and Valdepeñas inland, to the south of Madrid, used to be synonymous with cheap, coarse flavours that filled the flagons of forgettable international brands owned by brewers and distillers. Yet the enormous potential for low-priced, attractive wine is at last being realized as the giant wine companies modernize their wineries, their techniques and their desire to please.

The north-east has traditionally been seen as the quality wine capital of Spain, with famous reds and whites from Rioja and Penedès, and Cava sparklers. But here, too, the winds of change are blowing, and areas like Navarra, Somontano, Campo de Borja and Costers del Segre are making thrilling contributions to the new, exciting Spain. After a long wait in the shadows of nations like Italy and France, the 21st century could finally be Spain's century.

CATALUNYA

It's almost like crossing the border into another country. With its separate language (Catalan) much in evidence, its thriving capital city of Barcelona and an independence of spirit unmatched anywhere else in Spain, Catalunya is like a little kingdom of its own. Catalunya has always been a prosperous place, and Cava, Spain's traditional-method sparkling wine, and the mould-breaking winemaker, Miguel Torres, have contributed to that wealth.

Catalunya has a great deal of rugged mountain landscape: the Pyrenees dominate the north region, and mountains hem in the Mediterranean coast all the way south. The coastal zone, where many of the vineyards are situated, some even within sight of the glistening sea, enjoys a mild Mediterranean climate but, as you travel inland towards the border with Aragón, the climate becomes more continental, with hotter summers and colder winters.

PENÈDES DO WINE AREA

TOTAL DISTANCE NORTH TO SOUTH 39.5KM (24½ MILES)

━━━ DO BOUNDARY

 VINEYARDS

0 km   1   2
0 miles   1

N

PENÈDES
The Penèdes DO provides the widest variety of wine styles in this part of Spain. More than 30 years ago it was no better known than any other of the Catalan wine areas, but that was before Miguel Torres returned from winemaking studies in France in 1961 to work at the family bodega at Vilafranca del Penedès in the heart of the region. Since then he has brought a host of international grape varieties into the extensive Torres vineyards –

not just Cabernet Sauvignon and Chardonnay but also Riesling, Gewürztraminer, Muscat d'Alsace, Sauvignon Blanc and Pinot Noir – as well as using vine-trellising systems, higher planting densities, organic methods and mechanical pruning quite unknown in Spain before. Not only a pioneer in the vineyard, Torres has experimented in the bodega – earlier bottling of red wines, temperature-controlled stainless steel fermentation, single-variety wines and blending local Parellada and Tempranillo with international varieties are just a few examples.

The Torres influence is not confined to Penedès – in neighbouring Conca de Barberá the Milmanda (Chardonnay) and Grans Muralles (Catalan varieties) vineyards make sought-after wines. The only pity is that Catalunya in general has failed to progress along the path set out by Torres a generation ago, though the whites still stand out for their perfume and finely-balanced fruit. About 90 per cent of Penedès wine is white, mainly from Xarel-lo, Macabeo and Parellada (the best for quality), and Chardonnay has been allowed since 1986. Some of the whites, particularly from those from Chardonnay, Sauvignon and the aromatic varieties, can be individual and exciting. As a result of the Cava boom, red wine has been rather neglected in Penedès. Poor winemaking far too often mars what seems to be good quality fruit, and even the mould-breaking Torres reds no longer lead the pack.

SANT SADURNÍ D'ANOIA ■

VILAFRANCA DEL PENEDÈS ■

■ EL VENDRELL

VILANOVA I LA GELTRÚ ■

■ CALAFELL

MEDITERRANEAN SEA

0 km   1   2
0 miles   1

Penedès is the most important region for Cava production (see page 189) and Cava companies now own one-fifth of the Penedès vineyards. Many of the big name producers are based at Sant Sadurní d'Anoia, where several make still wine as well as sparkling. Winemaking in Penedès revolves around two regional centres, Sant Sadurní d'Anoia and Vilafranca del Penedès – you'll see signs for bodegas in every lane and alley surrounding the residential areas of both these towns. The wealth and expertise generated by the prosperous Cava industry have kept Penedès way ahead of the rest of Catalunya, but Penedès' problem is that it is so well known for Cava, and Torres is so famous as a brand, that the region itself lacks identity.

OTHER CATALAN WINE AREAS

One important development is at Lleida, in the parched wastelands between Barcelona and Zaragoza. Here the Raïmat winery, owned by the Raventós family of the giant Codorníu group, rises from the scrub. It was the force behind the granting of a DO in 1988 to several patches of vineyard in the area, now called Costers del Segre. Raïmat owns over 1800ha (4448 acres) here, over one-third of the total DO plantings, which are irrigated and include Chardonnay, Cabernet Sauvignon, Tempranillo, Pinot Noir and Merlot. None of the region's traditional wines were previously up

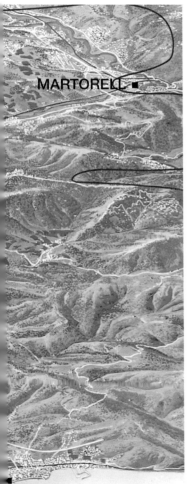

WHERE THE VINEYARDS ARE *The map shows the heart of Penedès, around the towns of Sant Sadurní d'Anoia, the thriving centre of Cava production, and Vilafranca del Penedès, where Torres has its ultra-modern vinification plant.*

The Penedès vineyards are arranged in three tiers, moving up in steps from the coastline, and these provide a wide range of growing conditions.

The strip of hot, flat coastal vineyards is known as the Bajo Penedès. The vineyards here are planted traditionally with Moscatel but hardy red varieties that can cope with the blazing summer sun are taking over.

Across the ridge of hills in the broad valley around Vilafranca del Penedès is the Medio Penedès, where 80 per cent of the Penedès vineyards are found. It's still fairly hot here but a mixture of varieties (mainly Xarel-lo and Macabeo for Cava but also some red ones) benefit from the cooler, higher altitude, between 250m (820ft) and 500m (1640ft) above sea level.

Further inland and higher still, up to 800m (2625ft), is the Penedès Superior with a climate almost as cool as Bordeaux. When you climb higher there's not much in the way of villages but the scattered vineyards are highly prized. Here are found the high-quality white grapes, mostly aromatic Parellada for Cava, but also experimental plantings of international varieties such as Chardonnay, Gewürztraminer, Muscat and Riesling.

MARTORELL ■

SITGES

to much but Raïmat's wines, both still (especially the Chardonnay, Cabernet Sauvignon and Tempranillo) and sparkling, have shown excellence is possible in these unpromising conditions.

Right up in the north of Catalunya the tiny Empordà-Costa Brava DO hugs the border with France, squeezed in by the Mediterranean and the Pyrenees. Here the mountains come almost down to the sea and the lower foothills are covered in vines. But it isn't all a holiday-making idyll along this beautiful rocky coastline – you'll notice the vines here are firmly tied to stakes, standing up bravely against a dreaded wind locally known as *tramontana*, which can blow for days on end. The wines here are mostly reds from Garnacha and Cariñena and the whites come from Macabeo and Xarel-lo. Nevertheless, along with many other areas of Catalunya such as Pla de Bages, new international grape varieties, mainly Cabernet Sauvignon, Merlot and Chardonnay, are creeping into the vineyards.

Further south in Catalunya the wine regions cluster around Barcelona and Tarragona. Down by the coast near Barcelona is Alella, rapidly becoming a victim of expanding urbanization. As the city grows, so the poor Alella vineyards, which are capable of producing rather tasty fresh white wines, disappear under new buildings. The DO was extended in 1989 to include land at higher altitudes so that Alella now runs from the coast inland to the foothills of the Cordillera Catalana. The new areas are cooler because they are higher, and are based on a limestone bedrock in the shelter of the mountains. Down on the coast the vines are mainly Garnacha Blanca; in the new, higher vineyards you'll find Pansa Blanca (Xarel-lo) and quite a bit of decent Chardonnay.

For spectacular mountain scenery head for Priorat and Terra Alta, relatively inaccessible inland areas in Catalunya's south. Weave round their precipitous twisting roads, and you're sure to emerge green and shaky for the experience – but it's worth it. These are among the most dramatically situated vineyards in Europe. Rugged mountains form a backdrop to the small terraced vineyards cut into the steep hillsides and interspersed with almond and olive trees.

Priorat has a special soil known as *llicorella* which glints with mica particles: its heat-retaining qualities help create monstrously powerful and alcoholic red wines. A group of new producers moved into the area around the village of Gratallops in the heart of Priorat in the 1980s, planted French varieties such as Cabernet Sauvignon alongside the native Garnacha and Cariñena, introduced modern winemaking techniques and new French oak barrels and created a new style of Priorat which took the world by storm. As a result of these rare, expensive wines Priorat was promoted to DOC in 2001 (the only region other than Rioja to be awarded Spain's highest wine category). Terra Alta, literally 'high land', had little contact with the rest of the country until the beginning of the 20th century, and it shows. The southernmost DO in Catalunya, it is chequered with green vineyard oases nestling between the mountains.

Elsewhere in Catalunya, the DOs fan out towards the dusty Tarragona plain. The large Tarragona DO sprawls around the city of the same name to a radius of 30km (18 miles). The Falset sub-region, bordering Priorat and enjoying the same advantages of low-yielding vineyards and a slightly cooler climate, now makes reds of real quality and was promoted to its own DO of Montsant in 2001. Conca de Barberá sits in a natural basin protected by the rolling Tallat, Prades and Montsant mountain ranges. The area produces vast amounts of hazelnuts and almonds, as well as much of the base wine for Cava. It is also the home of Torres' Milmanda and Grans Muralles vineyards.

Old Garnacha vines after harvest planted near Gratallops, the heart of Priorat, in intensely stony, schist soils (llicorella).

RED GRAPES
Garnacha Tinta, Cariñena, Monastrell and Tempranillo (locally called Ull de Llebre) are the main traditional grapes, with increasing amounts of Cabernet Sauvignon, Merlot, Syrah and even Pinot Noir.

WHITE GRAPES
Macabeo, Garnacha Blanca, Xarel-lo and Parellada are the chief varieties, with decreasing amounts of Malvasía. New wave whites use Riesling, Muscat, Chardonnay, Gewürztraminer and Sauvignon Blanc.

CLIMATE
Coastal Catalunya enjoys a Mediterranean climate and it becomes drier and more extreme further inland.

SOIL
This varies, depending on whether you are in the rugged mountainous areas or nearer the coast. There is some limestone in the northern coastal regions. The Penedès lowlands have sand, while the highlands have clay. Quartzite and slate make up a special soil called *llicorella* in hilly Priorat and parts of Conca de Barberá.

ASPECT
There are low-lying vineyards on the coast at between sea level and 200m (656ft), while inland the vines can be set into terraces on the sides of steep foothills, up to 800m (2625ft) in Priorat and Terra Alta, or on alluvial river valley floors, as in Tarragona.

RIOJA

 RED GRAPES
Tempranillo is the most important variety, followed by Garnacha Tinta and a little Mazuelo and Graciano. There is some experimental Cabernet Sauvignon.

WHITE GRAPES
Viura (Macabeo) is the main white grape. There are tiny amounts of Malvasía and Garnacha Blanca.

CLIMATE
The Sierra de Cantabria protects most of the vineyards from the Atlantic weather, and for the most part, Rioja is sunny and temperate. Rioja Baja, to the south-east, has a Mediterranean climate and is hotter and more arid.

SOIL
Rioja Alavesa has yellow calcareous clay soils, as do parts of Rioja Alta. Rioja Alta and Rioja Baja are mainly alluvial silt, with ferruginous clay on the higher ground.

ASPECT
Vines are planted on relatively high ground in the Alavesa and Alta sub-regions, usually between 400 and 800m (1312 and 2625ft). In the Baja the ground slopes down to nearer 300m (985ft) and the vines are planted on the flat, fertile valley floor.

I THINK WE SOMETIMES FORGET what life was like before Rioja. Even I have to keep reminding myself. But I can remember the wonderful flavour of strawberry and blackcurrant swathed in soft, buttery vanilla of the first Rioja reds I tasted. So soft, so enjoyable. Red wine wasn't supposed to be this irresistible, this easy to understand. In the days before the New World wine revolution taught us that it was OK to have fun with fine wine, Rioja was preparing the way. And as such it was effortlessly Spain's leading table wine. It's still the most famous, but despite being granted Spain's first supposedly superior DOC classification, the 1990s were a fraught time for the region with too much inferior land planted, overproduction common and made worse by the introduction of irrigation in the late 1990s, and seesawing prices. It has to be said that too many Riojas on sale today are characterless and overpriced and do the region – and Spain – no favours.

Rioja was originally the name for the basin of land formed by the small Oja river which flows into the Tirón near Haro. The Tirón eventually joins the Ebro river, and it is a chunk of the much larger Ebro valley that Rioja has come to stand for – the part that lies 100km (62 miles) south of the Atlantic and is bounded by mountains to north and south. It would be easy if the autonomous region of La Rioja corresponded to the Rioja DOC winemaking region, but parts of La Rioja have no vines in them at all, while the Rioja DOC veers off across the regional boundary into both País Vasco and Navarra and, on a few hundred acres, Burgos.

The Rioja DOC is divided into three sub-regions: Rioja Alavesa lies north of the Ebro in the province of Alava in País Vasco; Rioja Alta is in the west and lies entirely within the province of La Rioja; Rioja Baja lies to the east of Logroño, taking in land on both sides

WHERE THE VINEYARDS ARE *The map shows the western half of the Rioja DOC, the Rioja Alavesa and Rioja Alta sub-regions – the flatter, more arid Rioja Baja begins further east of Logroño. The Alavesa vineyards are north of the Ebro river and extend from the foothills of the Sierra de Cantabria down to the river. The Rioja Alta vineyards lie to the south of the river, with one small enclave north-east of Briones on the other side. The whole DOC is closely concentrated on the Ebro valley, the mountains forming a dramatic backdrop along the northern edge and protecting the vineyards from the Atlantic weather to the north. Note how dense the vineyards are in this part of Rioja where vines are the most important crop. Much of the valley floor land used to be farmland, and cannot produce top quality grapes. Small vineyard plots are common – 85 per cent of the vineyards are owned by a total of 14,000 growers.*

of the Ebro, as well as the Navarra and Burgos enclaves. Logroño, Rioja's capital city with a population of 120,000, lies just west of the point where the three sub-regions meet, roughly halfway along the 120-km (75-mile) west-to-east stretch of the Rioja DOC.

Although Rioja is relatively close to the sea, the mountain ranges, especially the Sierra de Cantabria, protect its northern edge and shelter the vineyards from the cold Atlantic winds, and you can find yourself standing in warm sunshine among the vines, while in the distance, clouds gather threateningly over the mountain tops.

RIOJA ALAVESA AND RIOJA ALTA
The Rioja Alavesa vineyards start at 800m (2625ft) above sea level, among the foothills of the Sierra de Cantabria and descend in terraces down to the steep north bank of the Ebro river at just below 400m (1312ft). Cross the Ebro and you are in Rioja Alta, which mostly follows its south bank – apart from the Sonsierra, an important enclave on the north bank. These two sub-regions aren't radically different from one another, the line between them simply follows provincial boundaries rather than soil types, say, or climate differences, which would make more sense from a wine viewpoint.

We're still on fairly high ground, especially in the south of Rioja Alta where the land climbs to 700m (2300ft) above sea level again. Despite the mountains' embrace, cool breezes meander in from the Atlantic, moderating summer temperatures and creating frosty winters. In general, the further east you go, the warmer and drier the climate. Haro's average annual temperature is 12.8°C (55°F), in Logroño it's just over 13°C (55.4°F) and, further east in Alfaro, at the extreme end of the DOC, it jumps again to 13.9°C (57°F).

RIOJA ALAVESA
■ LABASTIDA
HARO ■
OLLAURI ■
■ BRIONES
SAN ASENSIO ■

THE SOILS OF RIOJA

Rioja has three main types of soil. The best wines come from clay with limestone soil found all over the Rioja Alavesa sub-region and in some parts of Rioja Alta. This yellowish-looking soil is densely planted with vineyards and Tempranillo flourishes here in the limestone, producing grapes with high acidity and a rich concentration of flavours. The second type, ferruginous clay, is found south of the Ebro in pockets of land on higher ground within larger areas of alluvial soil, the third Rioja soil type. Ferruginous clay produces good, sturdy wines with high levels of alcohol. Large parts of Rioja Baja and Rioja Alta are alluvial silt, much of it too fertile for good-quality grapes. Wines from this soil type tend to be high in alcohol and are used mostly for strengthening wines of lighter quality from the Alavesa and Alta.

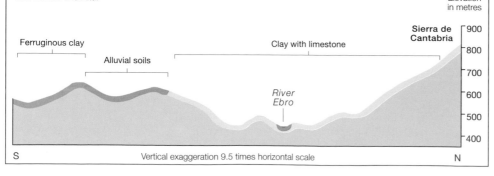

Ferruginous clay
Alluvial soils
Clay with limestone
Sierra de Cantabria
River Ebro

Elevation in metres
900
800
700
600
500
400

S
Vertical exaggeration 9.5 times horizontal scale
N

0 km   1   2
0 miles   1

Some of the region's most delicately scented and elegant red wines come from the yellow calcareous clay soils of Rioja Alavesa, which extend into Rioja Alta. Rioja Alta's more varied soils include patches of ferruginous clay and alluvial silt, and tend to produce firmer wines (though traditionally, Rioja producers have put little emphasis on soil types – the style of wine has long been more a product of aging in the winery than of *terroir* – and I'd say it was time for a rethink). Both sub-regions are widely planted with Tempranillo, the great grape of red Rioja, which thrives on chalky and clay soils and in the relatively cool climate. Rioja Alta also has a little Garnacha Tinta – great for heady Rosado – but the principal growing area for this variety is the third sub-region, Rioja Baja.

RIOJA BAJA

East of Logroño, the lower-lying Rioja Baja has a much warmer Mediterranean climate than the rest of Rioja and parts are even classified as semi-arid. Vines compete for space on the fertile, alluvial clay with red peppers, artichokes, asparagus. Garnacha Tinta does well here and in a long, hot autumn reaches high levels of ripeness, making chunky, fat wines of up to 15 per cent alcohol. Tempranillo is increasingly grown in the higher, hillier areas.

RED AND WHITE RIOJA

Much Rioja red is a blend from all three sub-regions, and a blend of different grapes. Once, over 40 varieties were grown here, but today DOC rules allow just seven. Tempranillo accounts for over half of all plantings; it is responsible for the graceful strawberry flavour of red Rioja and is well suited to long aging. Garnacha Tinta is added to flesh out the blend, and there may be a splash of Graciano and

Mazuelo, too. There are experimental plantings of Cabernet Sauvignon – not yet officially recommended – and some would also like to see Syrah approved. The myriad combinations offered by the different sub-regions and varieties allow merchant bodegas to blend a unique house style. A little white Viura was traditionally added to help the acid balance and lighten the colour; this sometimes still happens in the Alavesa. White Rioja is made largely from Viura.

The vines are densely planted and pruned in bush shaped *gobelet* style to protect them from the elements. A few decades ago a jumble of varieties were all grown and harvested together. Now each variety is planted and picked separately, often in small plots that characterize the region. And if the patches of low-lying bush vines tell you you're in Rioja, so will the coopers. There can be few winemaking regions in the world that use so much oak. The casks (generally 225-litre *barricas*) are traditionally American oak, with its butter and vanilla flavours, but French is increasingly used.

Rioja joven sees little or no wood, and some fresh, unoaked whites are made, but much of the red wine is *Crianza*, released in its third year having spent a year in oak, or *Reserva*, released in its fourth year after at least a year in oak and two in bottle, or *Gran Reserva*, traditionally made only in exceptional years, and not released until its sixth year, after least two years in oak and three in the bottle. White Crianza must have spent six months in cask.

RIOJA ALTA AND RIOJA ALAVESA

TOTAL DISTANCE NORTH TO SOUTH 24KM (15 MILES)

RIOJA ALTA = RIOJA SUB-REGION

━━━━ RIOJA DOC BOUNDARY

━━━━ SUB-REGIONAL BOUNDARIES

▦ VINEYARDS

N

0 km   1   2
0 miles   1

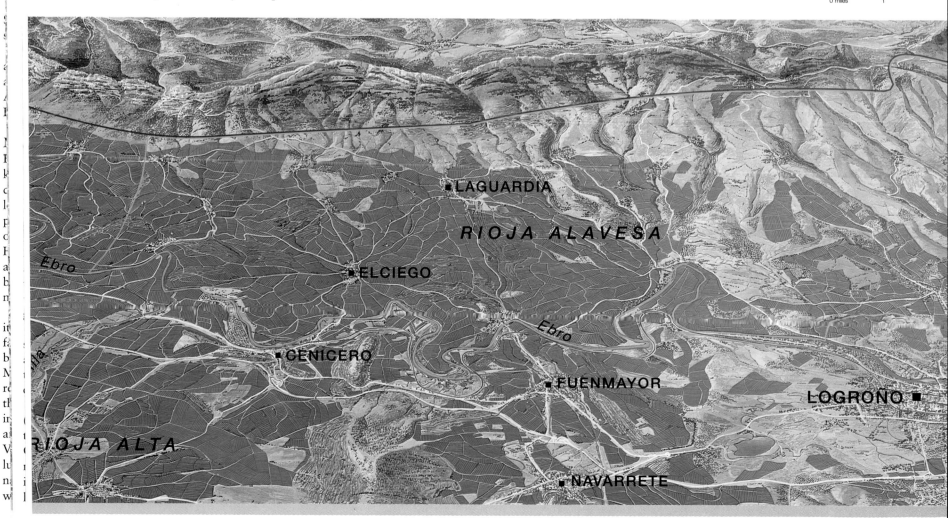

PORTUGAL

Portugal at its most traditional: terraced vineyards in the Douro Valley (left), and painted tiles at the railway station at Pinhão, one of the main towns of the Douro Valley. For centuries the steepness of the slopes has meant that everything has to be done by hand. However, the terraces shown to the right of picture are new ones, cut into the hillsides wide enough to accommodate a small tractor.

It isn't so long ago that I would have approached Portugal's table wine world with exasperation at lost opportunities easily outweighing the pleasure I gained from its occasional triumphs. There seemed to be so much potential from its myriad native grape varieties, and yet the producers seemed supremely unconcerned about what we foreigners might like to drink. Well, that's half the story. She did have some wines that we liked to drink – and which were always intended for export – the great fortified wines of port and Madeira were invented by traders, largely from Britain; the medium-sweet, lightly sparkling rosé wines of Mateus and Lancers were created after World War Two with the export market very much in mind. The rest of Portugal's wines, however, were mostly lapped up by the domestic market along with countries like Brazil and Angola which had strong Portuguese connections.

This has meant that many wine producers have begun only recently to bring their methods and machinery close to accepted modern standards. But it also meant that the rush to uproot old vine varieties and replace them with international favourites like Chardonnay and Cabernet only happened on a very small scale. For which we should give thanks because Portugal is a jewel house of ancient vine varieties. In a world of increased standardization, Portugal is a beacon of individuality. Careful application of modern methods to these varieties, far from spoiling their character, is demonstrating just how good they are. Portugal has been through several Golden Ages as a fortified wine producer. Its Golden Age as a table wine producer is only just beginning. As it is, Portugal, with the tempering influence of the Atlantic affecting all her coastal regions, already offers a fascinating array of wines. These range from the fiercely acidic yet fragrant Vinho Verdes of the Minho in the north, through the majestic ports and succulent soft reds of the Douro Valley, past the rudely impressive reds of Bairrada and the potentially magnificent reds and whites of Dão, and on to the areas of the centre and the south, where the transformation from simple bulk producer merely satisfying local thirsts to international player creating some of the most original and thrilling flavours in Europe has been astounding. Much poor wine is still made, especially in the Estremadura and the tourist honeypot of the Algarve, but in the low hills of Alenquer, in the broad acres of the Ribatejo inland from Lisbon, in the area around Setúbal to the east and in the torrid plains of the Alentejo, good whites and great reds are beginning to appear, and frequently there isn't a Chardonnay or Cabernet Sauvignon vine in sight.

THE WINE REGIONS OF PORTUGAL

IMAGINE TWO GLASSES OF WINE standing side by side. The first, a Vinho Verde, is almost water-white with a few rather lazy bubbles clinging to the side of the glass. It smells vaguely citrous and it knocks you sideways with its acidic rasp. Then on to the second, a port, with its deep impenetrable colour. A heady aroma of super-ripe fruit wafts from the glass and its rich flavours warm and soothe, conjuring up images of a homely winter's evening by the fireside. It is hard to believe that the two wines, with at least ten degrees of alcohol separating them, come from the same country, let alone adjacent regions, but Vinho Verde and port live cheek by jowl in the north of Portugal. It's not as if we're talking about a large area. Port and Vinho Verde cohabit in a country that is little more than 160km (100 miles) wide. You're driving along, you turn a corner and you go from one wine region to the next, just like that.

That's the beauty of Portugal. For such a small country she has a strong regional feel and the climate plays a vital role in this. With its prevailing westerly winds, the Atlantic Ocean exerts a strong influence on the coastal belt, but this diminishes sharply as you journey inland. As you cross a mountain range, grey rain-bearing clouds scudding inland from the sea suddenly disappear. Taking a straight line across the north of the country, climate statistics illustrate this dramatic change. The Atlantic coast north of Porto is drenched by over 1200mm (47in) of rainfall a year. This rises to 2000mm (79in) on the mountains inland, a figure comparable with Bergen on the fjord coast of Norway. Then in the rain-shadow to the east of the mountains the figure falls progressively to as low as 400mm (16in) near the frontier with Spain, drought conditions by any standard. Between these two extremes is the heart of the Douro valley with around 700mm (28in) of rainfall, the perfect climate for ripening the grapes that make port, Portugal's most famous wine.

As you travel across Portugal, the landscape, architecture and traditions change dramatically too. As mountains rise and subside, the temperate maritime climate with its lush vegetation gives way further south and east to more extreme temperatures and arid scrub. Sturdy grey granite houses built to withstand wind and rain become flimsy shelters painted white to reflect the burning sun.

This regional identity is reflected in the breadth of Portugal's wines. Two fortified wines, port and Madeira, are world-famous. Others like Setúbal and Carcavelos, popular in the 19th century, virtually gave in to the commercial pressures of the 20th century. Apart from light, spritzy Vinho Verdes, the north of the country also produces reds that are earning very different reputations for themselves. The Douro's best reds have a luscious, perfumed, soft-textured depth; Bairrada demands a sterner reaction to her aggressive, but impressive wines; and Dão is now showing why it was so well regarded generations ago. Modern vinification methods produce some increasingly attractive fresh whites. In the centre and the south ripeness is the key, with healthy red grapes that would be the envy of many a cool-climate Frenchman being turned into wines packed with ripe berry-fruit flavours. It is here that Portugal shows the most promise, having attracted the attention of several international winemakers.

But long-standing traditions, often deeply rooted in rural culture, are only reluctantly cast aside. Nowhere is this better illustrated than in Portugal's rather muddled vineyards. In the past, the same grape variety was frequently christened with four or five names depending on where it was planted. The Portuguese authorities (egged on by the EU) have banged a few heads together and decided on a principal name for each of Portugal's grape varieties. For example Castelão Francês, once variously known as João de Santarem and Periquita, is now simply known as Castelão. It won't really affect the smaller farmers, as many have no idea what grapes they have growing in their haphazard vineyards. But it will have an impact on the larger growers, most of whom have now replanted their vineyards with each variety carefully delineated.

Following examples set elsewhere in the world, the Portuguese have set out on a varietal path. Varieties like the deeply coloured, scented Touriga Nacional, traditionally planted in the Douro and Dão, are now appearing on wine labels up and down the country. Likewise Tinta Roriz (which also still travels under the name of Aragonez and is better known outside Portugal under its Spanish name of Tempranillo), Trincadeira, Tinto Cão and Castelão – all unfamiliar names on the international circuit. Portugal has woken up to the potential of these grapes to make world class wines.

Although less significant, some native white grapes have also come to the fore. In Vinho Verde there is the triumvirate of Alvarinho, Loureiro and Trajadura, each of which is being made into varietal wines. Then there's Bical, Fernão Pires and in southern Portugal Arinto, a variety that hangs on to its crisp acidity in spite of the warm sun. Red or white, the future's bright in Portugal.

The Portuguese only began to sort out their chaotic vineyards in the mid 1980s after the country joined the EU. Much has changed since. Impressive mountain-breaching roads now link remote inland regions with the coastal centres where most of the country's population lives. The result is that the new stainless steel wineries in land-locked regions like Dão and the Douro are now a commute from Porto; in the past the journey would take half a day.

Quinta do Crasto have led the way in creating exciting new Douro table wines, often from single-grape varieties: this is Touriga Nacional.

THE CLASSIFICATION SYSTEM FOR PORTUGUESE WINE

Portugal's wine laws have been in a state of flux ever since the country joined the European Union in 1986. That's the polite way of describing the chaos that has resulted from bureaucrats in Brussels meeting bureaucrats in Lisbon. The new wine regions are now beginning to settle into a framework, but recent shenanigans rather detract from the fact that Portugal mothered the modern appellation system over two centuries ago. After a period of fraud and scandal in the fledgling port industry, in 1756 Portugal's forward-thinking prime minister, the Marquis of Pombal, drew a boundary around the Douro vineyards to protect the wine's authenticity – one of the world's first examples of vineyard delimitation. Nothing more happened until the early 20th century, when several other wine regions were similarly demarcated. The situation then remained static until after the 1974 Revolution, when Bairrada's vineyards were finally awarded demarcated status. On joining the EU, Portugal's wine classification was brought into line with that of other EU countries.

QUALITY CATEGORIES

• **Denominação de Origem Controlada (DOC)** This top tier replaced the Região Demarcada (RD) category in 1990. It parallels the French Appellation d'Origine Contrôlée (AC, AOC) and is being expanded as newer regions make the grade.

• **Indicação de Proveniência Regulamentada (IPR)** Intermediate category of regions which entered the statute books in 1989/90. There were over 30 at the outset, most of which have now been promoted to DOC.

• **Vinho Regional** This is an increasingly important category, particularly in the south where wines are often made from grapes grown over a wide area. These large regions parallel the French regional *vins de pays* and allow similar flexibility, making them more popular with winemakers than many of the more obscure DOCs and IPRs.

• **Vinho de Mesa** The most basic category: table wine.

WINE REGIONS

A journey around Portugal's wine regions can hardly ever be whistle-stop. From the Minho province that marks the border with Spain in the north-west to the Algarve in the south may be just under 650km (400 miles) as the crow flies but there are over 30 officially recognized wine regions in between, as well as a tier of Vinhos Regionais (VR) or regional wines that cover most of the country. Almost everywhere you go in Portugal, apart from the highest mountain peaks where viticulture is simply not feasible, it seems that someone somewhere is making wine.

The largest region is Vinho Verde which covers the entire soggy north-west of the country, including the lower reaches of the Douro valley. The Douro region itself, delimited both for port and table wine, begins 80km (50 miles) or so upstream and extends east to the Spanish border. In the granite mountains immediately to the south, the Dão spreads over three river valleys, the vineyards climbing into the foothills of the Serra da Estrêla, Portugal's highest mountain range, which rises to a lofty 1993m (6539ft). Bairrada, with its tannic red wines, occupies the flat coastal strip between the misty Aveiro lagoon and the ivory-towered university town of Coimbra.

Stretching along the rolling coastal hills to the south, Estremadura (known as the *Oeste* or 'west') is a colourful region making bulk wines for the thirsty local market. For many years the area was best known for its historic enclaves of Bucelas, whose white wines were drunk by Wellington's army during the Peninsular War nearly 200 years ago, and Colares, with its centenarian, phylloxera-free vines growing in the sand. More recently, the town of Alenquer has lent its name to a new enclave, which is being taken seriously by a number of forward-thinking single estates.

The Tagus or Tejo river, which flows into the Atlantic near Lisbon, marks the divide between the hilly north and the great plains of the south. Inland the Ribatejo region spans the broad river valley, its fertile alluvial soils producing fat, juicy tomatoes and large crops of ripe grapes. The Setúbal peninsula south-east of Lisbon (Lisboa) is one of the few Portuguese regions to embrace foreign grape varieties, which have found a niche on the limestone slopes of the Serra da Arrábida. East and south the undulating Alentejo plain sweeps to the Spanish border with vineyards concentrated around the small whitewashed towns of Portalegre, Borba, Granja-Amareleja, Moura, Redondo, Reguengos and Vidigueira, not forgetting Évora – the regional capital. Last, and probably least, on the Portuguese mainland, the Serra de Monchique separates the Alentejo from the Algarve whose warm maritime climate is ideal for sun-seeking tourists, but few winemakers have yet exploited it.

But there's more to Portugal than the mainland, or *continente* as it is known. The Portuguese are custodians of a number of volcanic Atlantic islands, which their early navigators were the first to discover. Vines were introduced to the Azores by Portuguese settlers in the 15th century. Two islands in this remote archipelago, Pico and Graciosa, exported fortified wines, but the industry was all but wiped out by oidium and phylloxera in the 19th century. Madeira, 1100km (680 miles) south-west of Lisbon, has been home to a flourishing wine industry ever since it was first discovered in the 15th century, and by the end of the 17th century there were already 30 wine shippers on the island. It too suffered oidium and phylloxera but the wine industry underwent a slow and painful recovery. The island's humid subtropical climate and the manufacturing process of heating the wine sets it apart from the rest of Portugal; the process of modernization is slower and more difficult, too.

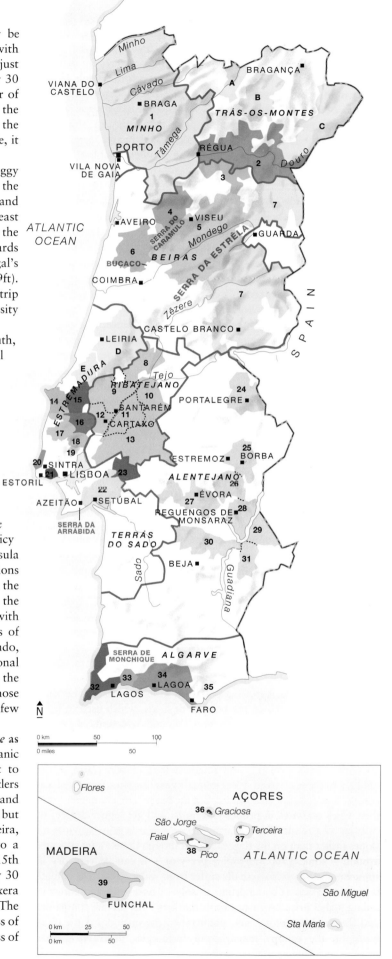

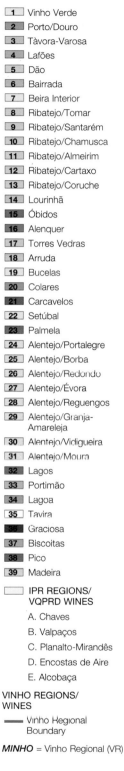

DOC REGIONS

1	Vinho Verde
2	Porto/Douro
3	Tàvora-Varosa
4	Lafões
5	Dão
6	Bairrada
7	Beira Interior
8	Ribatejo/Tomar
9	Ribatejo/Santarém
10	Ribatejo/Chamusca
11	Ribatejo/Almeirim
12	Ribatejo/Cartaxo
13	Ribatejo/Coruche
14	Lourinhã
15	Óbidos
16	Alenquer
17	Torres Vedras
18	Arruda
19	Bucelas
20	Colares
21	Carcavelos
22	Setúbal
23	Palmela
24	Alentejo/Portalegre
25	Alentejo/Borba
26	Alentejo/Redondo
27	Alentejo/Évora
28	Alentejo/Reguengos
29	Alentejo/Granja-Amareleja
30	Alentejo/Vidigueira
31	Alentejo/Moura
32	Lagos
33	Portimão
34	Lagoa
35	Tavira
36	Graciosa
37	Biscoitas
38	Pico
39	Madeira

IPR REGIONS/
VQPRD WINES

A. Chaves
B. Valpaços
C. Planalto-Mirandês
D. Encostas de Aire
E. Alcobaça

VINHO REGIONS/
WINES

—— Vinho Regional
Boundary

MINHO = Vinho Regional (VR)

PANORAMIC MAPS OF PORTUGAL

The Douro Valley *pages 212–213*

Madeira *pages 216–217*

THE DOURO VALLEY

RED GRAPES
Up to 80 varieties are permitted, but Touriga Nacional, Touriga Franca, Tinto Roriz and Tinta Cão have been identified as the four best varieties.

WHITE GRAPES
Varieties for white port include Codega, Rabigato, Gouveio and Viosinho.

CLIMATE
The humid Atlantic climate in Oporto is ideal for aging port. Further east it is more arid.

SOIL
Port vines are only planted on schistous soils.

ASPECT
The Douro is famous for its steep terraces which follow the narrow river valleys.

TAKE MY ADVICE and leave the car behind. I'm not suggesting it because of the port but because going by train is much the best way to see the Douro. Yes, there's a smart new road linking the Douro with Porto, the city that has given its name to 'Vinho do Porto' or port wine, and it will get you to Pinhão in half the time taken by the train – but what's time? The train offers one of the great railway journeys of the world. The little single-track line runs alongside the river for much of the journey, so if you want a pre-taste of the Douro – the winding, contoured terraces, the high, perching villages, the tethered fishing boats – this is the way to do it. But before you set off, look down from the two-tier bridge that links Porto and Vila Nova de Gaia on the opposite bank. You'll see the black roofs of the port lodges and the waterfront lined with *barcos rabelos*, boats which once brought the young wines downstream, before the river was dammed in the 1970s, on an unnerving journey through the rapids. Thank goodness for the train.

The Douro vineyards are between 80 and 200km (50 and 125 miles) upstream from Porto. As you leave the murky suburbs and the sea mist behind, the train passes through chaotic Vinho Verde country with characteristic tall crops growing beneath pergolas of vines. About an hour into the journey the Douro comes into view and from there on to the end of the line the train snakes alongside the river. It's not uncommon for passengers to sit with the door open on the steps of the carriage and there are places along the track where you can almost dangle your feet in the still waters.

The train rounds a bend and the landscape changes. Hard grey granite gives way to flaky, silver-coloured schist. This is where the port vineyards begin, today as they did in the mid-18th century when Portugal's prime minister, the forward-thinking Marquis of Pombal, first drew a boundary around the Douro Valley vineyards to protect the authenticity of port wine.

The Douro DOC divides unofficially into three sub-regions. The most westerly one, Baixo Corgo, is centred on the town of Régua. Here the climate is cooler and wetter than further upstream and the wines from here tend to be lighter and less substantial – ideal for young rubies and light tawnies that supply the insatiable French taste for cheap port. Indeed, half of all port comes from the Baixo Corgo. The train pauses at Régua but it is worth continuing upstream as far as Pinhão. This is the heart of the Cima Corgo sub-region, and from Pinhão's station you can see Cálem's Quinta da Foz, Ferreira's Quinta do Seixo, Dow's Quinta do Bomfim and Royal Oporto's Quinta das Carvalhas. The Pinhão valley is where you'll find Quinta do Noval and properties belonging to Taylor, Warre and other famous shippers. As the train climbs towards Tua more celebrated names come into view, including Croft's Quinta da Roêda and Graham's Quinta dos Malvedos.

Upstream from Tua the vineyards cease for a while. A massive outcrop of granite squeezes the river into a forbidding gorge. The railway disappears into a tunnel only to reappear once again among terraced vineyards carved from the schist. This, the most easterly of the three sub-regions, is known as the Douro Superior. It has attracted port shippers like Cockburn, Ferreira and Ramos Pinto who have pioneered vineyards on the relatively flat land

WHERE THE VINEYARDS ARE *This map of the Douro Valley shows the Cima Corgo and part of the Douro Superior sub-regions where the best port vineyards are located. The finest tawny, vintage and late bottled vintage ports are sourced from the Cima Corgo where all the major port shippers have large vineyard holdings. The little town of Pinhão is surrounded by steep terraces of vines, with some of the most famous names in port emblazoned on the high retaining walls shoring up these terraces. Vineyards are graded officially from A to F according to 12 different factors, among them altitude, aspect, locality and soil. Nearly all the best A and B grade quintas are within sight of the Douro or one of its tributaries, the Tedo, Távora, Torto and Pinhão. The higher vineyards around the towns of Sabrosa, Alijó and São João da Pesqueira are awarded lower grades (C, D, E and F) and a much smaller proportion of their production is made into port. They can, however, produce good table wines with lighter body and higher acidity than are needed for port: there can be two to three weeks difference in ripening between high sites like São João da Pesqueira and vineyards down by the river.*

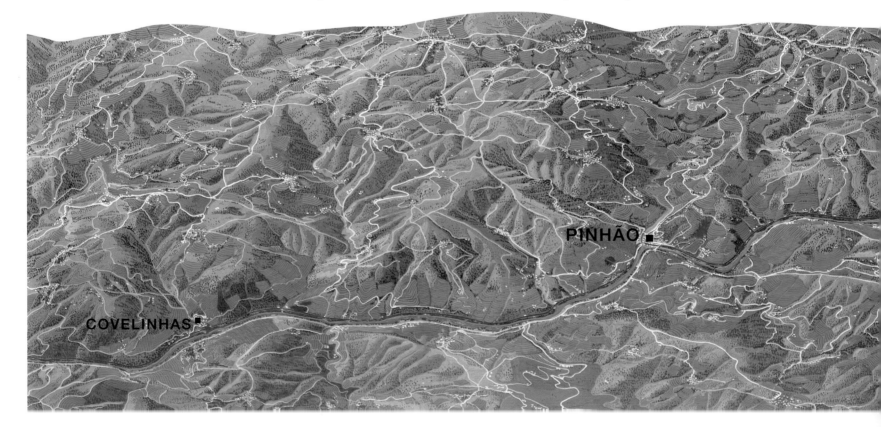

PINHÃO ■

COVELINHAS ■

towards the Spanish frontier. The train crosses the river and two of the grandest of all vineyard properties can be spied: first Taylor's Quinta de Vargellas, then Symington's Quinta do Vesúvio, both of which have their own railway stations. Beyond here the landscape begins to look increasingly arid and vineyards tend to be planted on high land out of sight of the river. Just before the train reaches the end of the line Quinta do Vale do Meão appears, former home of Portugal's legendary red wine, Barca Velha. Production has since moved to a new property, Quinta da Leda, away from the river. At Pocinho the driver shunts the engine to the other end of the carriages and the train returns to Porto.

Few visitors, however, get this far. To most of us the Cima Corgo around Pinhão is the epitome of port country: steep schist slopes with vineyards facing north or south, east or west: there's no shortage of heat here. The shortage, instead, is of water. The lower slopes are more schistous and retain water well, as do the old, pre-phylloxera terraces, the ones with hand-built dry-stone walls that need constant maintenance. Irrigation is being discussed and, used properly, could improve quality. In the Douro Superior the climate is the most constant, but the climate in the Pinhão and Torto valleys is better balanced with slightly more rainfall. Further upriver, irrigation could definitely help improve the balance. The

remote Douro Superior is where the landscape departs from the stereotype. Go within spitting distance of the Spanish border and you'll find vineyards that are rolling rather than mountainous – and vineyards that are mechanized. (Mechanization here in the Douro really only means perhaps pre-pruning by tractor and then finishing by hand.) The trouble is that labour costs are rising, so technology is aimed at replacing even the labour used for treading grapes – with robots. But no-one can change the soil.

To plant in dense Douro schist you must break up the rock to a depth of 1.5m (5ft) to give the roots a chance. After five years the roots reach the bedrock where finding water gets easier. The soil is pretty homogeneous throughout the valley: there are pockets of other soils, but schist rules. What varies here and makes one wine different from its neighbour is exposure, altitude and climate. That, and of course winemaking.

SELECTED QUINTAS

1. Qta. de Nápoles	6. Qta. da Boa Vista	11. Qta. das Lages	16. Qta. do Noval
2. Qta do Crasto	7. Qta. do Porto	12. Qta. de la Rosa	17. Qta. da Cavadinha
3. Qta. da Água Alta	8. Qta. da Côrte	13. Qta. da Foz	18. Qta. de Terra Feita
4. Qta. de São Luiz	9. Qta. do Seixo	14. Qta das Carvalhas	19. Qta. do Cruzeiro
5. Qta. do Panascal	10. Qta. do Bom Retiro	15. Qta. do Bomtim	20. Qta. do Passadouro
			21. Qta. de Santo António
			22. Qta. da Roêda
			23. Qta da Gricha
			24. Qta. dos Malvedos
			25. Qta do Tua
			26. Qta. de Vargellas
			27. Qta. dos Canais
			28. Qta. do Vesúvio

– – UNOFFICIAL SUB-REGION BOUNDARY

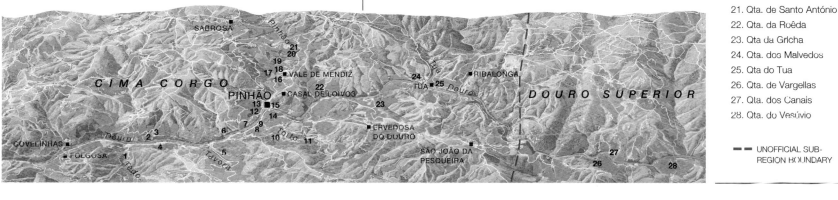

SÃO JOÃO DA PESQUEIRA

FOLGOSA TO VESUVIO

TOTAL DISTANCE
NORTH TO SOUTH
17 KM (11 MILES)

VINEYARDS

CENTRAL & SOUTHERN PORTUGAL

 RED GRAPES
Castelão is found throughout the region, along with Tinta Miuda in Estremadura and Trincadeira in the Ribatejo and Alentejo. Some Cabernet Sauvignon and Merlot in the Ribatejo and on the Setúbal Peninsula.

WHITE GRAPES
Arinto has the potential for good wines. Fernão Pires is widely planted in the Ribatejo, where there is also some Chardonnay. Roupeiro and Antão Vaz are the best white grapes in the Alentejo and there is Muscat on the Setúbal Peninsula.

CLIMATE
The influence of the Atlantic is important in the west. Inland, the arid Alentejo can be very hot in summer.

SOIL
Estremadura has calcareous clay and limestone, Ribatejo clay, sand and fertile alluvial soils and Alentejo granite, limestone and red clay.

ASPECT
The Ribatejo and Alentejo plains contrast with the hillier Torres Vedras, Alenquer and Arruda areas.

João Portugal Ramos is one of a new breed of winemaker/consultants, concentrating on single varietal wines.

THE MUDDY TEJO or Tagus river flows south-west through central Portugal dividing the country into two roughly symmetrical halves. Just north of the river the mountains subside and as you drive south the roads straighten out and the patchwork of poor, intensively farmed smallholdings of the north gives way to vast estates or *latifúndios*, some of which cover thousands of acres of low-lying plain.

ESTREMADURA

This strip of rolling countryside, stretching from Lisbon's populated hinterland along the wild and windy western Atlantic coast, is known colloquially as the Oeste (pronounced 'wesht', a rather drunken-sounding version of the word 'west' which is what it means). Although Estremadura produces more wine than any other single region in Portugal, until recently there were few wines of any quality. It has been divided into several DOCs but, apart from Alenquer, few are going to hit the headlines. Most of the wines emanate from a number of huge co-operatives which have benefited from significant investment since Portugal joined the European Union. Although Estremadura produces little that could be classed as truly fine, it is the source of some large volumes of simple, easy-to-drink red and white wine.

The picturesque towns and villages are considerably more memorable than most of the wines. Lush, high-yielding vineyards are predominantly planted with bland white grape varieties which used to produce large quantities for distillation, but now find their way onto the local market as wine. Ripening can be difficult in this relatively cool maritime climate and red wines, made predominantly from the ubiquitous Castelão grape, often taste mean and thin.

But there is hope for the Estremadura region. A number of properties around Alenquer are making increasingly good red wines from grapes like Touriga Nacional and Tinta Roriz as well as Cabernet, Merlot and Syrah. Quinta de Pancas, Quinta da Cortezia, Quinta do Carneiro, Quinta do Monte d'Oiro, Quinta das Setencostas and Casa de Santos Lima are names to look out for. The region has also been taken by storm by José Neiva who, through DFJ Vinhos, is making large volumes of very drinkable wine, predominantly with quality conscious export markets in mind. Manta Preta and Grand'Arte are two of Neiva's many brand names bottled under the Vinho Regional Estremadura designation.

Two tiny enclaves in Estremadura are worth a special detour. The windswept, seaside vineyards of Colares just 35km (22 miles) west of the centre of Lisbon grow in the sandy soil on the clifftops, their roots anchored in the clay below. This sand protected the vines from the phylloxera louse which attacked vineyards throughout Europe in the 19th century. Consequently, the local Ramisco vine is one of the only European varieties that has never been grafted onto phylloxera-resistant American rootstock. Cultivating vines in the sand is difficult and expensive today and the region has been in slow decline for the last 30 years. Still, the few gnarled old vines that remain are a pilgrimage for incurable wine romantics who like to sample these strangely wild, tannic reds within sight and smell of the great ocean.

Inland, shielded from the damp, misty Tagus estuary by a low range of hills, the Bucelas region produces dry white wines from two grape varieties, the Arinto and the aptly named Esgana Cão meaning 'dog strangler'. Both grapes, especially the latter, retain plenty of natural acidity in a relatively warm climate producing crisp, dry white wines that became popular in Britain in the nineteenth century under the title 'Portuguese Hock'. Mention that name to a Brussels legislator today and it would send him into paroxysms. Carcavelos, a rich, raisiny, fortified wine with a nutty,

port-like length, enjoyed a moment of glory in the 18th century, but it's hard to find any vineyards today. With the relentless expansion of Lisbon along the Tagus estuary, most of the Carcavelos vineyards have disappeared under roads and blocks of apartments.

RIBATEJO

Journeying inland, the broad Tagus Valley, known as the Ribatejo, serves the capital as a kitchen garden. Ripe, fat tomatoes, curly beans, maize and grapes compete for space on the fertile alluvial flood plain which is regularly irrigated by the swollen river. Like neighbouring Estremadura it has been subdivided into a number of smaller sub-regions, but the whole of the Ribatejo has been raised to DOC with the confusing designation of 'Ribatejano' permitted for wines that fall into the Vinho Regional category (mostly those made from international grape varieties).

Ribatejo wines reflect their soils. The fertile alluvial flood plain alongside the Tagus known as the *leziria* yields large volumes of light insubstantial red and white wine. Away from the river the wines from the *charneca* or heathland are more substantial, particularly towards the south-east of the region where they tend to resemble those of the Alentejo.

Although the Ribatejo is still dominated by large co-operatives, there are a number of single quintas making increasingly good wines. Casa Cadaval, Falcoaria, Quinta da Lagoalva and Quinta do Santo André are all labels to look out for. Australian winemaker Peter Bright (of Bright Brothers) sources Sauvignon Blanc, Chardonnay, Cabernet and Merlot for much of his wine from the giant Fiúza estate and makes wines with more than a hint of the New World. DFJ's José Neiva prefers to focus on wines made from native grapes: the honeyed white Fernão Pires, the rich red Castelão and spicy Trincadeira.

SETÚBAL PENINSULA

Two elegant suspension bridges span the Tagus linking the north bank of the river to the densely populated Setúbal Peninsula on the south. After a while, Lisbon's tall suburbs finally subside and you find yourself travelling through a forest of fragrant umbrella pines growing on the warm, sandy plain. Around Setúbal to the south, the rugged Arrábida hills rise out of the plain and then shelve steeply to the Atlantic. The region around Setúbal, now officially delimited as Palmela DOC and Vinho Regional Terras do Sado after the river just to the south, is home to some of Portugal's most enterprising winemakers making wines from a wide variety of Portuguese and foreign grape varieties. The two leading companies are the internationally minded J P Vinhos (formerly known as João Pires and famous for its dry Muscat) and José Maria da Fonseca, who make a series of powerful reds as well as some superb Moscatel de Setúbal.

The large fishing port of Setúbal at the mouth of the Sado lends its name to an unctuous, raisiny fortified wine made mainly from Muscat grapes from vineyards on the limestone hills behind the city. In recent years this traditional sweet Muscat has been upstaged by other wines from the region, including the light, dry, João Pires Muscat, first made in 1981 from a surplus of Moscatel grapes, and Quinta de Bacalhôa, a ripe, minty red made from a Bordeaux blend of Cabernet Sauvignon and Merlot. Chardonnay also seems to be well suited to the north-facing limestone soils of the Arrábida hills and the warm maritime climate.

But foreign grape varieties still have some way to go before they oust native grapes like Castelão (still unofficially known as 'Periquita') which thrives on the broad, sandy plain around the walled town of Palmela. José Maria da Fonseca's raspberryish

Vines as far as the eye can see in the Arruda region of Estremadura, north of Lisbon. Traditionally just producers of bulk wine, many parts of the Estremadura are rapidly modernizing, with some impressive results.

Periquita is one of Portugal's best known red wines and they also produce some excellent *garrafeiras* (reserve wines) labelled with curious code names like 'CO' and 'TD'.

ALENTEJO

After a brief stop at Fonseca Successores' old winery in the main street at Azeitão, it's time to head east. After a few miles batting down a long straight road – what a change after the winding roads of northern Portugal – the landscape begins to change and a giant, undulating plain unfolds before our eyes. This is the Alentejo. Golden wheat fields extend for almost as far as the eye can see, dotted by deep evergreen cork oak and olive trees that provide shade for small nomadic herds of sheep, goats and black pigs. Green in spring, the landscape turns an ever deeper shade of ochre with summer temperatures that frequently soar over 40°C (104°F) and rainfall that barely reaches 600mm (24in) a year. The open vista is broken only by the occasional dazzling whitewashed town or village and perhaps the jagged outline of a ruined castle on the crest of a low hill.

At first glance, vineyards don't seem all that prominent but as we approach a town rows of vines stretch out before us. Until fairly recently cork was the Alentejo's main connection with wine and cork oaks, stripped of their bark, are a common sight. Now eight small enclaves have earned the right to Alentejo DOC plus their own name: Borba, Evora, Granja-Amareleja, Moura, Portalegre, Redondo, Reguengos and Vidigueira. The entire province, stretching from the Tagus in the north to the Algarve in the south, has been designated Vinho Regional Alentejano.

The Portuguese used to deride the Alentejo as 'the land of bad bread and bad wine'. Conventional wisdom dictated that climate was against it. It seemed healthy, fault-free wine was impossible when the summer temperatures were high enough to force the indolent locals indoors out of the relentless sun. This wasn't helped in 1974 when the south was the most determined and aggressive part of Portugal in overthrowing the dictatorship. Having been a land primarily of absentee landlords – unlike the Douro where relationships between landowner and worker were close and the revolution was a positively gentlemanly affair – the peasants and workers relished occupying the large estates. Unfortunately they weren't interested in making them work, even on a co-operative basis. But now, with a bit of gleaming stainless steel technology, the Alentejo has begun to prove that it can produce fine wines, especially reds from evenly ripened native grapes.

Among the red grapes, Trincadeira and Aragonez are the best performers and both the white Arinto and scented Roupeiro manage to hang on to good, crisp natural acidity in spite of the heat. A number of properties are also experimenting with Syrah. The best Alentejo vineyards are over to the east, not far from the Spanish border – Cartuxa near Évora, Quinta do Carmo and Quinta da Moura at Estremoz, Esporão near Reguengos and Cortes de Cima at Vidigueira are just five Alentejo properties which deserve to be singled out for their wines. Co-operatives at Borba, Redondo and Reguengos make wine on a larger scale, but are turning out some sound, full-flavoured reds.

ALGARVE

The title 'land of bad wine' should probably have passed to the Algarve where two large co-operatives bottle headaches for the tourists that flock here each year. Cliff Richard has shown what can be done by planting vines and producing something pretty serious, and José Neiva is also in the region. Lagoa makes an intriguing dry aperitif wine aged like *fino* sherry under a veil of flor.

MADEIRA

RED GRAPES
Tinta Negra Mole is Madeira's most widely planted variety.

WHITE GRAPES
White grapes all planted in fairly small quantities: Sercial, Verdelho, Bual and Malvasia.

CLIMATE
A warm, damp subtropical climate means that oidium and botrytis can be a problem. Rainfall varies from 3000mm (118in) inland to about one-third of that on the coast.

SOIL
The soil is volcanic. The pebbles of basalt have often weathered red.

ASPECT
The vineyards are planted on terraces up to 1000m (3280ft) in the south of the island and lower down in the north.

IT'S DIFFICULT TO GET a really good look at Madeira. The early Portuguese navigators who saw a bank of black cloud billowing over the Atlantic thought that they had reached the end of the world and steered well clear. Approaching the island's precarious airport today with a view of dark, cloud-covered mountains on one side and the ocean on the other, you could be forgiven for thinking the same.

There are two ways to appreciate Madeira when you have safely reached land. First of all, clamber down to the rocky shore that passes for a beach, turn your back on the sea and stare inland. Behind the subtropical shoreline with its decorative palms and exotic flowers, tiny shelf-like terraces stack up the mountainsides until they seem to be subsumed in the clouds. Then drive up one of the tortuous roads from the coast to Pico de Arieiro which, at 1818m (5965ft) above sea level, is nearly the highest point on the island. On the way you pass through a belt of dank mist, only to emerge in bright sunlight before the summit. From here you can see volcanic peaks poking through the cloud, but on a rare clear day you might glimpse the ocean.

On the face of it Madeira is an unlikely place to make wine. This humid, subtropical island 700km (435 miles) from the coast of North Africa has long, warm winters and torrid summers and a mean annual temperature in Funchal of 19°C (66°F) – hardly the temperate clime of the world's best wines. But Madeira wine certainly has individuality and there's no lack of finesse in a glass of venerable Malmsey. The answer is that the character of Madeira comes from the aging process: it may be wrong to say that the geography of the island has little effect, but when viticulture is geared to high yields of barely ripe grapes from vines under 15 years old, as it is here, you cannot expect even the faintest whiff of *terroir* to show through.

Like so many of the best inventions, Madeira wine came about almost by accident. Soon after the island was discovered, it became an important supply point for ships en route for Africa and the east. Wine was one of many goods to be taken on board and a generous drop of local brandy was added to prevent it from spoiling on its long voyage. The pitching and rolling across the tropics seemed to suit Madeira and it often tasted better when it reached its destination than at the start of the journey. The taste caught on and demand grew for *vinho da roda*, wine that had crossed the equator and back.

As Britain and the United States emerged as important customers for Madeira in the 19th century, merchants looked for ways to simulate the long but costly tropical sea voyages that had proved to be so beneficial to the wine. They built *estufas*, store rooms with huge vats heated by fires to produce the maderized aromas and flavours that the world had become accustomed to.

But Madeira's isolated island economy has suffered from a catastrophic cycle of boom and bust. The boom began in the eighteenth century when demand for Madeira began to outstrip supply. It lasted until the 1850s when oidium (powdery mildew) reached the island and spread rapidly through the vineyards encouraged by the warm, humid climate. Eventually, sulphur dusting of the vine leaves was found to cure the problem, but not before the island's monocrop economy had been devastated.

Worse still, 20 years later phylloxera struck, destroying entire vineyards in its wake. Shippers left the island, and the wine trade never really recovered.

Bananas replaced vines as the island's most important crop and the vineyards that remained were planted with disease-resistant hybrids which produced large amounts of dreary wine. In 1913 a number of shippers merged to form the Madeira Wine Association,

PORTO MONIZ

RIBEIRA DA JANELA

ATLANTIC OCEAN

SEIXAL

SÃO VICENTE

CALHETA

SERRA DA ÁGUA

JARDIM DA SERRA

PONTA DO SOL

CÂMARA DE LOBOS

RIBEIRA BRAVA

CABO GIRÃO

MADEIRA

TOTAL DISTANCE
NORTH TO SOUTH
21.5KM (13½ MILES)

 VINEYARDS

N

0 km   1   2
0 miles   1

precursor of the Madeira Wine Company which produces most Madeira today, as well as controlling half the exports. Few of the shippers own any vineyards, and land is now too expensive to buy. Instead they buy their grapes from myriad tiny smallholdings perched on little terraces, or *poios*, carved out of the mountainsides; with approximately 4000 growers owning only 1800ha (4448 acres) of vines, the average vineyard holding is tiny, covering only about half a hectare and the largest single vineyard on the island is less than 4ha (10 acres). This is hardly conducive to good or progressive viticulture.

Along with vines most farmers grow other crops, including bananas, avocados, lemons and, especially in the east of the island, willow for baskets and other tourist items. The warm, damp climate means that the vines have to be trained off the ground so as to lessen the risk of fungal diseases and this makes backbreaking work in the vineyards as the labourers duck beneath the lattice of straggly vines to apply treatments or harvest the grapes.

Agriculture is only really possible on Madeira because of the high annual rainfall on the inland mountains – more than three times as much as falls in Funchal down on the coast. This water is diverted into a complex network of over 2000km (1243 miles) of manmade channels called *levadas* which ensure an even distribution to every tiny property.

Most Madeira goes to the French market, for cooking rather than for drinking. It is made from the versatile, but dull local red *vinifera* grape, Tinta Negra Mole. The pale, pinky-red wine is fortified with grape brandy and heated in an *estufa* to between 40° and 50°C (104° and 122°F) for a minimum of 90 days. The cheaper wines made in this heavy-handed manner often smell and taste coarse and stewed and are a poor imitation of the real thing.

The finest Madeiras, usually produced from one of four top-quality or 'noble' grapes: Sercial, Verdelho, Bual and Malvasia are, are made without any *estufagem* or artificial heating at all. They age slowly on *canteiros* or racks under the eaves in lodges in the island's capital, Funchal.

Warmed naturally by the sun, they gradually develop a unique pungency and intensity of flavour. Having been subject to this long, slow, controlled maturation, fine Madeira stands the test of time like no other wine.

Traditionally, different styles of Madeira have been distinguished from each other by the grapes from which the wines were made, and the styles range from dry to sweet. Of the four traditional 'noble' grape varieties, Verdelho and Malvasia are the most planted, and there are smaller amounts of Sercial and Bual. However, all the noble grapes together comprise anywhere between seven and 20 per cent of the total: nobody knows the true figure.

Sercial likes the coolest vineyards and grows on the north side of the island and at the highest altitudes in the south. With a lower accumulation of sugar it makes the driest wine with a distinctly sharp, acidic tang. Verdelho is also planted on the cooler, north coast, but in slightly warmer locations and it ripens more easily than Sercial, producing a wine that is softer and medium-dry. Bual is found growing on the warmer, steamy south side of the island where it produces richer, medium-sweet wines.

Finally, Malvasia (better known in English as Malmsey) grows in the warmest, low-altitude locations on the south coast, like the spectacular vineyards at the foot of the island's highest cliff, Cabo Girão. The darkest and sweetest Madeira, a good Malmsey will be raisiny and smoky, still retaining a characteristic tang of acidity which prevents the wine from cloying.

The productive American hybrid grapes which crept into the vineyards, following the destruction of the island's best vineyards by phylloxera, can no longer be used for bottled wine and most Madeira now comes from Tinta Negra Mole. Madeira producers have been obliged to comply with EU legislation which states that a varietal wine must be made from at least 85 per cent of the variety named on the label.

A replanting programme is currently underway in the Madeira vineyards to increase production of the four 'noble' varieties which are in short supply, but for the moment most Madeira blends are labelled only with the terms *seco* (dry), *meio seco* (medium dry), *meio doce* (medium-sweet) and *doce* (sweet or rich).

Terraces are the only way of cultivating land in Madeira. Here vines rub shoulders with cabbages and other crops.

BLANDY'S
B.B.
MADEIRA
WINE
Established
1811

Sercial 1910

Produced & bottled by
MADEIRA WINE COMPANY S.A., FUNCHAL
Produce of the Island of Madeira (Portugal)

22% Vol.   e 75cl./750ml.

HENRIQUES&HENRIQUES
EST⁰
1850
SOLAR
MADEIRA
MALMSEY
Aged 15 in Oak
YEARS
PRODUCT OF PORTUGAL

SANTANA

FAIAL

PORTO DA CRUZ

MACHICO

SANTA CRUZ

FUNCHAL

WHERE THE VINEYARDS ARE

Agriculture on this small, densely populated island is confined to the narrow coastal fringe, where banana plants compete with vines and other crops for precious space in the tiny terraced fields. Vineyards tend to be concentrated around the capital, Funchal, on the warmer south side of the island, where the best Malvasia and Bual vineyards are situated. In recent years, bananas have ousted vines from some of the best land above the picturesque fishing village of Câmara de Lobos. There are plots of Sercial at Jardim da Serra ('mountain garden') lying at around 900m (2952ft) above the south coast, but grapes for the drier styles of wine come mainly from the cooler vineyards clinging to the near-vertical slopes on the north side of the island. Here, the spectacular vineyards have to be protected from the fierce northerly winds by high bamboo and broom windbreaks.

ENGLAND & WALES

Wine production in england and wales is no longer the domain of retired army officers, hobbyists and eccentrics. Although today's winegrowers still have to contend with apathy from the home market, a government which gives little help and the reliably unreliable weather, they are a much more professional bunch than they were 20 years ago. Many of the vineyards set up in the 1960s and '70s either no longer exist or just concentrate on grape-growing, leaving the winemaking to those better at it. Today's industry leaders, such as Valley Vineyards, Chapel Down Wines, Denbies and Three Choirs, are as commercially run as any in the world. Many of the most successful winemakers have benefited from experience abroad and are well aware that their wines have to compete on the shelf with those from around the world.

While vines are planted as far north as Leeds, most lie below a line drawn from the Wash to the Bristol Channel. The counties of Kent, East Sussex and West Sussex are the most heavily planted. Vineyards in Britain are at the northern extreme of wine production and only possible due to the tempering influence of the Gulf Stream. The summers lack the heat that vines like, and yields are well below those achieved in Continental vineyards. But with the right varieties and correct growing techniques, ripening grapes is not a problem and good wines are now consistently produced.

In the vineyards, the various subsoils include limestone, gravel, chalk (south Kent), clay (Essex, north Kent) and Kimmeridgian clay (Dorset). However, more important than soil is a microclimate that allows the grapes to ripen and the best sites are on sheltered south-facing slopes below 100m (328ft).

The grape varieties grown are those able to ripen in this marginal climate – mostly German crosses developed for cool climates. Müller-Thurgau is the most widespread, accounting for roughly 13 per cent of total plantings, although this has fallen considerably since the 1970s. Then comes the neutral early cropper, Reichensteiner; then comes Seyval Blanc, a French hybrid whose natural disease resistance makes it a favourite among growers and which can make some of England's best wines, both still and

sparkling; next comes the aromatic Bacchus – not unlike Sauvignon Blanc – and then Schönburger, a bit like a light Gewürztraminer.

The style of white wines varies more between wineries than between regions, and depends on factors such as the ripeness of the grapes and winemaking techniques. The best are delicate and aromatic, with flavours of apples, grapefruit, elderflower, grapes and hints of smoke, with enough ripeness and depth to balance the crisp acidity. Wines from varieties such as Bacchus, Reichensteiner and Schönburger can be drunk young and one vineyard, Three Choirs, produces a 'nouveau', released in November after the harvest. In the past, sweetness was sometimes added to counter excess acidity, but that is changing. Clean, grapy fruit has replaced clumsiness in the better wines, with residual sweetness being retained from fermentation, rather than added later. Some excellent late-harvest botrytized dessert wines are also made. Sparkling wines, too, are improving rapidly, with suitable clones of Chardonnay and Pinot Noir being increasingly used to make top quality products. The best whites, both still and sparkling, can be long lived.

Ripening red varieties can be a problem, but today, with better varieties and techniques, including the use of top quality French and American oak *barriques*, results can be impressive. Although grown less widely than whites, red varieties are becoming more popular with Rondo (a newish German cross), Dornfelder and Pinot Noir being the most widespread. The best are produced by Chapel Down, Denbies and Valley Vineyards.

In 1992, a Quality Wine Scheme was hastily brought into operation in an attempt to prevent the EU introducing a planting ban. The scheme (which has been followed by a Regional Wine Scheme equivalent to the French *vin de pays*) is not universally admired. The fact that hybrids like Seyval Blanc and Rondo, which are capable of producing some of the country's best wines, are excluded from the Quality Wine Scheme has not made it very user-friendly – and some producers have opted out completely. So, as with virtually every wine region, the best guarantee of quality is the producer's reputation.

● SELECTED VINEYARDS

1. Astley
2. Frome Valley
3. Three Choirs
4. Sugar Loaf
5. Llanerch
6. St Augustine's
7. Camel Valley
8. Beenleigh Manor
9. Sharpham
10. Wylye Valley
11. Beaulieu Abbey
12. Danebury
13. Northbrook Springs
14. Wickham
15. Priors Dean
16. Bothy
17. Boze Down
18. Chiltern Valley
19. Valley Vineyards
20. Nutbourne
21. Nyetimber
22. Denbies
23. Ridgeview
24. Breaky Bottom
25. Hidden Spring

26. Davenport
27. Chiddingstone
28. Penshurst
29. Battle Wine Estate
30. Sandhurst
31. Chapel Down Wines
32. Tenterden
33. Biddenden
34. Leeds Castle
35. Bearsted
36. Barnsole
37. Great Stocks
38. New Hall
39. Mersea
40. Carters
41. Warden Abbey
42. Shawsgate
43. Bruisyard

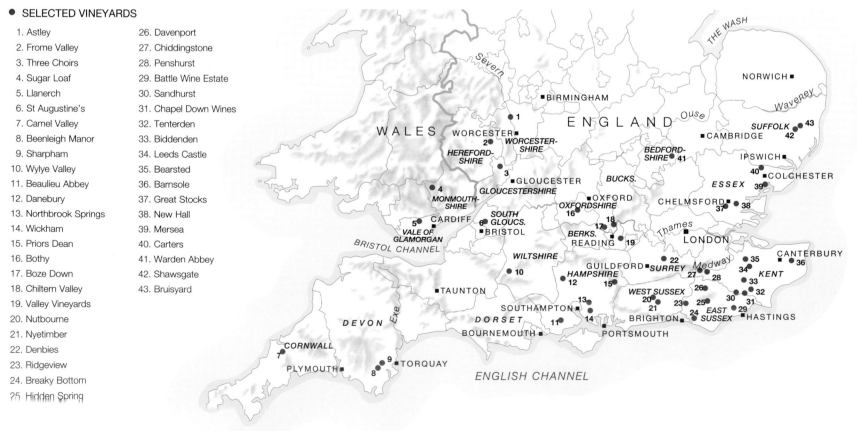

CZECH REPUBLIC & SLOVAKIA

When Czechoslovakia was one nation there was a pretty natural divide: Slovakia made the wine, the Czechs brewed the beer. Yet this divide is simplistic. Slovakia generally has better conditions for viticulture; indeed in the far east of the country, some of the original villages for the famous sweet Hungarian wine, Tokaji, lie within its borders. But the Czech vineyards of Morava are almost as good. Nevertheless, if I had to choose the wines from either country that have given me most pleasure, they would be the violet-scented, damsony St-Laurent, the boudoir-perfumed Irsay Oliver and the crackly, peppery, celery stick Grüner Veltliner – all from Slovakia.

Despite the gluggability of that St-Laurent – and the occasional Frankovka – both countries are better suited to white, rather than red wine production. There's huge potential for quality here: the latitude is virtually the same as that of Alsace and many of the best wines have the same spicy fatness; most companies are run on a refreshingly human scale; and Australian and French winemakers, there to advise, say that the winemaking equipment in several cellars is pretty good.

After the division of the country into two in 1989, Slovakia found itself with two-thirds of the former nation's vineyards. Nonetheless, talk to the café drinkers of Prague (Praha) and they all swear that the best wines come from the Morava region on the Czech side of the border. Well, Prague cafés may be very seductive places in which to drink, but I'll stick with Slovakia for now, especially as the flying winemakers there are making a fair go of raising standards without sacrificing individuality.

Both countries enjoy a settled continental climate: warm and dry in the growing season, with cool, dry autumns and little variation between regions, though Slovakia is slightly warmer. If we start in the west, most of Čechy's 500ha (1235 acres) of vineyards are clustered round the Elbe (Labe) and its tributaries. These wines, seldom seen outside the region, resemble their Sachsen counterparts across the border in Germany, being dry with marked acidity – you begin to see why most people drink the beer. Moving south-east, Morava's 11,500ha (28,416 acres) of vineyards are planted in the valleys of the Dyje, Svratka and Morava rivers, which flow into the Danube (Dunaj). The grapes are mainly Grüner Veltliner, Müller-Thurgau, Welschriesling, Ryzlink Rynsky (Riesling) and Pinot Blanc for whites, and the spicy, plummy, St-Laurent and Lemberger for reds. The wines from around Znojmo have a good reputation, and sparkling wines are made in Mikulov and Bzenec.

Slovakia's 20,000ha (49,420 acres) of vineyards are located mainly around the Váh, Nitra and Hron tributaries of the Danube. The vines are planted on undulating land around Bratislava or on the foothills of the Tatry mountains, although there are several smaller vine-growing regions as you travel east along the border with Hungary, each producing perfumed whites such as Irsay Oliver, Veltliner and Riesling, and light reds (with white vineyards dominating red by three to one). Slovakia's most important producer is the state winery at Nitra, while Western investment is improving quality in the smaller wineries to the south and west, such as Gbelce and Hurbanovo near the Hungarian border at Komárno. The grape varieties grown here are virtually the same as the Czech ones, with the addition of some tasty Grüner Veltliners, the fruity Frankovka red and the local Ezerjó and Leányka. In Tokai, at Slovakia's eastern extreme, Furmint, Hárslevelü and Muscat Ottonel are said to produce wines of similar character to the more famous Tokaji wines of neighbouring Hungary.

The loss of the Soviet market in the late 1980s meant that the wineries need more than ever to export to the West. Governmental organization seems to have progressed slightly more quickly in the Czech Republic than in Slovakia, but foreign companies – and indeed domestic wine producers – are still waiting for the dust to settle before investing.

SLOVAKIA WINE REGIONS

17	Malokarpatský
18	Južnoslovenský
19	Nitriansky
20	Stredoslovenský
21	Východoslovenský
22	Tokai

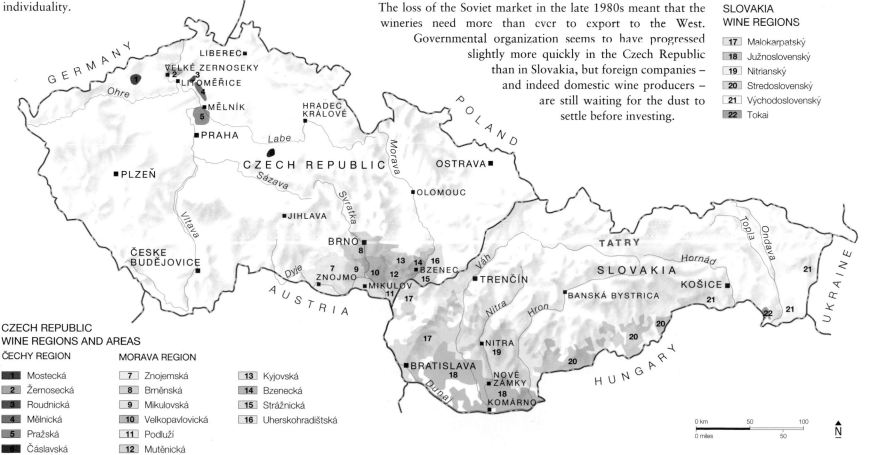

CZECH REPUBLIC WINE REGIONS AND AREAS

ČECHY REGION

1	Mostecká
2	Žernosecká
3	Roudnická
4	Mělnická
5	Pražská
6	Čáslavská

MORAVA REGION

7	Znojemská
8	Brněnská
9	Mikulovská
10	Velkopavlovická
11	Podluží
12	Mutěnická
13	Kyjovská
14	Bzenecká
15	Strážnická
16	Uherskohradišťská

HUNGARY

Vines high above Lake Balaton looking down towards the castle of Szigliget. The warmth of the lake and good sandy/volcanic soil combine to produce some of Hungary's best white wines, the most exciting being from the Szürkebarát and Kéknyelu.

I THINK I'VE ONLY DONE IT ONCE. Given a perfect score to a wine: 20 out of 20. A 1957 Tokaji. Somehow this bottle had escaped the process of homogenization that the Hungarian wine industry suffered after the Soviet invasion of 1956. Of all Eastern Europe's nations, Hungary's traditions were the proudest and most individual, and they died slowly under the Soviet system of state-run farms and wineries.

In the 1960s, fine reds were still being released under the Bull's Blood or Egri Bikavér label. Indeed it was international distributors clamouring for the rights to such a marketable name that encouraged the authorities to debase what was a splendid wine. At the end of the 1960s, you could still find marvellous yet fiery whites, golden in colour, almost viscous lanolin in texture, with sparks of spicy perfume darting in and out of their dry, but mellow fruit flavours like fireflies on your tongue. Historic white wines such as Hárslevelű (meaning 'linden leaf') from Debrő, an old wine region now part of Mátraalja, and Szürkebarát (Pinot Gris) and Kéknyelű from Badacsony, fell into a sleep through the 1970s and '80s. The 1990s saw a reawakening of Hungary's pride and energy and the rebirth of Hungary as a great wine producer began again at breakneck speed.

Moving into the new century the initial spurt has given way to steady, but solid progress. The wine export boom in the 1990s was led by international grape varieties – in particular Chardonnay, Sauvignon, Cabernet and Merlot – and the country enthusiastically welcomed the Antipodean 'flying winemakers'. But top Hungarian winemakers are emerging, determined to put New World principles into practice, as well as to rediscover Hungary's great past: they are set to produce gorgeous wines from both international and indigenous varieties. The Tokaj (Tokajhegyalja) region has already attracted multinational wealth and expertise. Other regions, well stocked with international grape varieties, plus a clutch of marvellous indigenous ones, are ideally placed for the 21st century.

White wines (58 per cent) dominate, but red plantings are growing. There are now 80,000ha (197,677 acres) split into 22 regions. Most of the country's output – easy-drinking styles made from Olasz Rizling and Kékfrankos grapes – comes from the Great Plains (Alföld) between the Danube (Duna) and Tisza rivers, where the sandy soil is suitable for nothing but viticulture. Hungary's climate is similar to much of inland Europe, warm and dry, with altitude bringing the only variation. However, the vineyards around Lake Balaton enjoy the tempering effect of central Europe's largest lake.

AROUND LAKE BALATON
On the north shore, Badacsony and Balatonfüred-Csopak produce some of Hungary's best whites. They benefit from well-drained soil – a mix of sand and volcanic rock – and gain heat from the sun's reflection off the lake. Badacsony produces good to excellent Olasz Rizling (Welschriesling), Szürkebarát and Traminer, as well as its own local variety, the spicy but increasingly rare Kéknyelű. East of Badacsony, Balatonfüred was a vineyard and spa town in Roman times. The vineyards, on the south-facing lower slopes of the Bakony hills, are planted with 60 per cent Olasz Rizling, more's the pity.

Dél-Balaton on the southern shore of the lake is one of the country's newest regions. Labelled as Balaton or Balatonboglár, the wines are mainly whites made from familiar varieties such as Chardonnay, Sauvignon Blanc, Olasz Rizling, Rhine Riesling and Traminer, as well as less well-known Irsai Olivér and Királyleányka.

You may find a Chasselas-based sparkling wine, as well as the occasional red made from Merlot, Pinot Noir, Cabernet Sauvignon, Kékfrankos, Zweigelt and Kékoportó. Heavy investment is paying off with definable quality increases.

THE SOUTH
Better for reds is Villány-Siklós, down on the Croatian border, with its loam and limestone soil. The eastern (Villány) end of the region produces lovely, juicy, soft red wines made from Kékoportó, Kékfrankos, Cabernet Sauvignon and Merlot, while Siklós is better for whites: Chardonnay, Olasz Rizling, Traminer and Hárslevelű.

The Mecsekalja region around the city of Pécs has Chardonnay and good Olasz Rizling, while Szekszárd has its own Bikavér as well as Ovörös – old red wine – made mainly from Kékfrankos, popular in Hungary but rarely seen abroad.

THE NORTH-EAST
The south-facing vineyards of Eger are famous for Egri Bikavér (Bull's Blood of Eger), once a hearty blend of Kadarka, Kékfrankos, Cabernet Sauvignon, Kékoportó and Merlot. While vinous anaemia may have diluted much of the current output, especially where Kadarka has been replaced, good examples can still be found, particularly those made by winemakers Vilmos Thummerer and Tibor Gàl. And new stringent regulations controlling varieties, release and quality are correcting the overall situation.

There are interesting white wines made from Leányka, Hárslevelű and Cserszegi Füszeres, but the increasing presence of Chardonnay and Olasz Rizling means that these are becoming harder to find.

In the foothills of the Mátra mountains, the Nagyréde co-operative has a reputation for reds and rosés made from Kadarka, but the best wines have been whites made by international winemakers like Hugh Ryman and Kym Milne.

THE NORTH-WEST
Mór's speciality is the Ezerjó grape (*ezerjó* means 'a thousand good things'), whose wines have been described perhaps rather damningly by Jancis Robinson as 'Hungary's nearest answer to the fragile charms of Muscadet'. I have a sweet Ezerjó in my kitchen right now which is anything but fragile.

To the north, Ászár-Neszmély is best known for white wines, including Olasz Rizling, Chardonnay and Irsai Olivér.

TOKAJI WINE

Wine from the region of Tokajhegyalja is truly the stuff of legend. A Commission for Hungarian wines was set up in St Petersburg to ensure regular supplies for the Tsars, and bottles of the precious nectar were kept by the bedside to revive ailing monarchs. The communist regimes of the 20th century succeeded in removing most traces of greatness from the region by blending the top wines with the mediocre, achieving something which, while perfectly drinkable, was hardly remarkable. New ownership is beginning to restore much of the wine's former glory.

The wine has been produced since the middle of the 16th century and in 1700, 56 years before the demarcation of the Douro vineyards in Portugal, the Rákóczi family, one-time princes of Transylvania (now part of Romania), made the first appraisal of the Tokaji vineyards, which were spread out between 28 villages north-west of the town of Tokaj at the confluence of the Tisza and Bodrog rivers. A subsequent classification in 1804 defined three Great First Growths, followed by First, Second, Third and Unclassified Growths. The three Great First Growths were all on the slopes of Mount Kopaszhegy or 'Bald Mountain' near the village of Tarcal, north-west of Tokaj. Of these, only Mézesmály remains, the rest having been amalgamated with various other First Growth areas.

Most of the vineyards are on south-east to south-west-facing slopes, but what makes the great vineyards great is their soil. Vineyards with fast-draining loess north-west of Tokaj, near Tarcal and Mad, are considered the best. The other Tokaji soils are largely stony clays. Vines on loess ripen faster and give the richest, most aromatic wines. Those on clays tend to produce wines of higher acidity (and possibly longer life). The best vineyards have slopes of 15 per cent or more, the middle part of the slope being the best.

The region is sheltered by the Carpathian mountains to the north-east, while warm winds off the Great Plains maintain a reasonably high temperature. Indeed, drought at vintage time can be a problem. Mists rising from the Bodrog river in autumn encourage the onset of noble rot in the Furmint grapes, which make up around two-thirds of a typical Tokaji with the balance being the sugar-rich Hárslevelű and Muskotály (Muscat Ottonel).

The botrytized grapes, known as *aszú*, spend about a week in a bucket, during which time an unctuous juice known as *eszencia* seeps out. This precious fluid is so rich in sugar that, even with special strains of yeasts, it can take years to ferment. Pure Eszencia is usually used to bolster lesser wines, but bottles do appear occasionally. In spite of all that sugar, Eszencia does not taste hugely sweet – colossal acidity levels balance it out nicely. But it's so thick it's virtually impossible to drink – you almost have to chew it.

After the removal of the Eszencia, the remaining grapes are mashed to a syrupy paste, and then added to dry base wine. The quality of the wine is determined by the number of *puttonyos* (30-litre tubs) of paste added to each *gönc* (136-litre barrel) of dry wine. Two-*puttonyos* wine is never made; three, four and five are reasonably easy to find; six is only made in good years. The 'Aszú Eszencia' available today is about an eight-*puttonyos* wine, while 'Szamorodni' (literally 'as it comes') is a wine to which no *aszú* has been added, and can come as either a sweet (*édes*) or dry (*száraz*) wine. Neither form is particularly attractive, having a rather sherry-like character that cries out for sweetening from the *aszú* grapes.

After the grape paste has steeped in the base wine for around a week, the wine is racked off to begin its long, slow fermentation in barrel. In the past, the state-owned casks were not always topped up and the oxidized styles that resulted became the norm. Now, non-oxidized styles are taking over, allowing the botrytized flavours of the wine to shine through. In addition, a flor-like fungus attacks the wine, giving it further complexity. The resulting flavours – a perfumed cocktail of apricots, marzipan, blood oranges, smoke, spice, tea and tobacco – do take some getting used to, but they are certainly unique in the world of wine, and Tokaji clearly deserves a place among the world's great sweet wines.

Most Tokaji is sweet, and its intensity is measured in puttonyos. *Five* puttonyos *wine, such as this one, is very sweet but by no means the sweetest.*

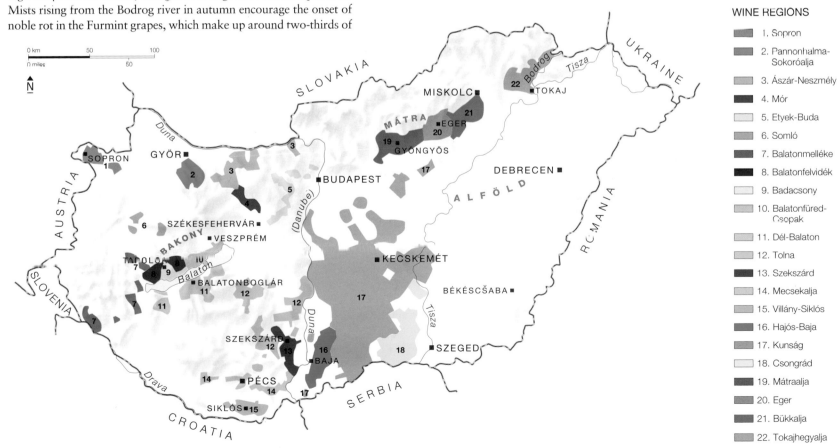

WINE REGIONS

1. Sopron
2. Pannonhalma-Sokoróalja
3. Ászár-Neszmély
4. Mór
5. Etyek-Buda
6. Somló
7. Balatonmelléke
8. Balatonfelvidék
9. Badacsony
10. Balatonfüred-Csopak
11. Dél-Balaton
12. Tolna
13. Szekszárd
14. Mecsekalja
15. Villány-Siklós
16. Hajós-Baja
17. Kunság
18. Csongrád
19. Mátraalja
20. Eger
21. Bükkalja
22. Tokajhegyalja

ROMANIA

Lᴛʜᴏᴜɢʜ ꜱᴜʀʀᴏᴜɴᴅᴇᴅ ᴏɴ ᴍᴏꜱᴛ ꜰʟᴀɴᴋꜱ by people of Slavic origin, the proud brown eyes of the Romanian burn with a definite Latin fire. The capital Bucharest, even after the ravages of Ceauçescu and subsequent turmoil and unrest, still has much of the ambience and architecture that earned it the soubriquet 'Little Paris'. It comes as no surprise, then, to learn that grapes have been grown in the country for more than 6000 years.

Romania covers much the same latitudes as France, but its climate is very different, being generally continental, with hot summers and cold winters. The Black Sea exerts a moderating influence, while the Carpathian mountains act as a barrier to cooler weather systems from the north. In general, the northern regions of the country, especially Moldavia and Transylvania, favour white wine production, while the best reds come from the south, from Muntenia and Dobrogea.

Major replanting programmes, both at the end of the 19th century after phylloxera, and in the 1960s under the communists, have meant that Romania now produces more wine than any other Balkan state, and has the fifth-largest area under vine – 253,000ha (625,154 acres) – in Europe (after Spain, France, Italy and Portugal). The first set of replantings introduced French varieties to the country, notably Cabernet Sauvignon, Merlot and Pinot Noir. The second was mainly of the indigenous varieties. As a result, Romania now has some of the best raw materials in Eastern Europe, in the form of mature, reasonably healthy vines of a wide range of familiar and unfamiliar grape varieties, and some superbly sited vineyards.

Such a state of affairs should have led to a major Romanian assault on the world wine market, but the political situation hinders progress, while the wine industry here desperately lacks investment. However, one British wine-shipper, Halewood International, is investing in Romania's potential and has bought several wineries in the Dealul Mare area, which may help improve quality and consistency. German investment has taken a shorter-term route, shipping wines that hide their Romanian origin. Vinexport, formed in 1990, a body owned ten per cent by the state, 40 per cent by the wineries and 50 per cent by companies in England, Germany, Holland and Denmark to promote and market Romanian wine, is involved with some 80 per cent of Romania's exports.

Modern winemaking, along with winemaking expertise from abroad and new equipment, is beginning to make a difference, but bottle shortages, conflicting tax regulations and limited ownership of local companies don't help. Neither do local tastes. Romanian wine drinkers take the age of a wine as a sign of quality, and tannin as a defect in reds as well as in whites. Their preference for strong sweet wines, especially reds, needs to adapt if the production of wines attractive to world markets – and currencies – is to become the order of the day. Having said that, there's no doubt that where temperature can be regulated and where there is some residual sugar, the whites can certainly be good, if not great. Dessert styles, whether botrytis-affected or not, can be excellent. The tendency to high acidity means that wines of 30 years old or more still taste remarkably fresh, although more fruit flavours might be welcome.

WINE REGIONS AND MAIN SUB-REGIONS

TRANSYLVANIA
1. Târnave
2. Sebeş-Apold
3. Alba Iulia
4. Aiud
5. Lechinţa

MOLDAVIAN HILLS
6. Cotnari
7. Iaşi
8. Huşi
9. Tutova
10. Bujoru
11. Zeletin
12. Nicoreşti
13. Iveşti
14. Panciu
15. Odobeşti
16. Coteşti

MUNTENIA-OLTENIA
17. Dealul Mare
18. Stefaneşti
19. Samureşti
20. Drăgăşani
21. Segarcea
22. Vânju Mare-Orevita

BANAT
23. Dealul Tirolului
24. Buziaş
25. Recaş

CRIŞANA-MARAMURES
26. Minis-Maderat
27. Simleul Silvaniei

DOBROGEA
28. Sarica-Niculitel
29. Istria-Babadag
30. Murfatlar

DANUBE TERRACES

SOUTHERN ROMANIA

The same could be said for much of the red wine, where softness is the desired attribute, and there is frequently a degree of sweetness, although this is disappearing. Warm fermentations bring out jammy characteristics in many, and long aging in oak does nothing to promote freshness. Some offerings are particularly rustic. The fruit could be of sufficiently high quality to mask winemaking defects but, infuriatingly, just as we are starting to see wines that are made to reasonably modern standards, they've started ripping all the grapes off the vines before they're ripe. The new dawn has produced a trickle of correct but fruitless wines, and I rather pine for the old-fashioned versions which at least were packed with flavour.

GRAPE VARIETIES

Of the native grape varieties, herby, rustic Fetească Neagră is the best red, producing deep-coloured, robust wines that are full and fruity when young, but which can age for decades. Babeaşcă Neagră and Crimpiosa produce lighter wines, while Cadarca (the same as Hungary's Kadarka) is used for more basic glug in the west of the country.

For dry whites, the spicy, grapefruity Fetească Albă and Fetească Regală are the most interesting grapes, while the ubiquitous Riesling is always the inferior Riesling Italico, rather than Rhine Riesling. The best sweet wines usually come from Grasă and Tămîioasă (both Alba and Româneasca) – Tămîioasă is the Romanian name for Muscat and it is known as the frankincense grape due to its aroma – while Traminer, Tămîioasă Ottonel (Muscat Ottonel) and Kékfrankos, here known as Burgund Mare, are used for wines of all degrees of sweetness and quality.

Most successful of the international varieties are Cabernet Sauvignon, Pinot Noir and Merlot for reds, Chardonnay and Pinot Gris for whites. An increasing number of plantings that were thought to be other varieties are, on closer inspection, turning out to be Sauvignon Blanc which means, happily for the growers, that both demand and price are increasing.

ROMANIA'S WINE REGIONS

Wine legislation introduced in 1998 has delineated high-quality areas and set out the rules. Basic wines, outside the classification system, are termed *vin de masa*. Fifty named regions produce superior quality (VS) wines, similar to the French vins de pays. Wines from a controlled area of origin are DOC; top-of-the-range wines are DOCC, with quality grades similar to German ripeness categories: wines from fully ripe grapes are labelled DOCC-CMD; late harvested grapes, DOCC-CT; nobly rotten grapes, DOCC-CIB – a strange hybrid of French and German ideas of classification.

The appellations fall within eight main wine regions. Moldavia, in the north-east, is predominantly white wine country. At Bucium, near Iaşi, whites made with Aligoté and Traminer can be especially good. Merlot is the best of the reds, demonstrating a minty, eucalyptus character, and sparkling wines are also made. Nicoreşti is known for its Babeaşcă Neagră, and the Pinot Noir from Coteşti has a good reputation. But a sweet wine known as the pearl of Moldavia is the region's pride and used to be Romania's most famous wine. Cotnari is a sweet, botrytis-affected white which at one time enjoyed the same prestige as Hungary's Tokaji. Cotnari is sheltered from the cold east winds by a range of hills. It enjoys warmth and mist, and the harvest continues as late into the year as November. In good years, sugar levels can reach 300g per litre, and the wines, bursting with raisin, honey and orange peel flavours, taste fantastic and can last almost indefinitely.

Murfatlar, with 2000ha (4942 acres) of vineyards in the centre of the Dobrogea/Black Sea region, produces some of Romania's best reds, full and fruity. The 210 days of sunshine a year are tempered by cool winds from the nearby Black Sea, permitting an extended growing season. Long, warm autumns encourage the development of noble rot in the Tămîioasa, Pinot Gris and Chardonnay grapes, producing the prized sweet wines. Once Romania gets itself sorted out, there is every reason to hope that this could become a really classic vineyard region. As good as Bordeaux, or Coonawarra, or Sonoma? Why not?

Muntenia's main wine district, Dealul Mare, in the foothills of the Carpathian mountains, is one of the largest – at 14,500ha (35,829 acres) – and most important regions, where the warm climate allows the production of good, and not excessively tannic, red wines. It is particularly known for Pinot Noir, Cabernet Sauvignon and Merlot. There is a sporadically brilliant white wine made in Pietroasa to the east, whose vines thrive in the calcareous, stony soil, and whose Tămîioasa grapes are often affected by botrytis.

Stefaneşti, on the Argeş, produces reasonable dry and sweet white wines, as does Drăgăşani on the left bank of the Olt. The Cabernet Sauvignon from the Olt's opposite bank at Sambureşti is highly regarded.

Transylvania's premium wine area is Târnave, surrounding the Târnava Mare and Târnava Mică rivers. The high altitude means a cool climate, although the rivers act as a tempering influence. White grapes predominate, and Traminer makes particularly good wines at several levels of sweetness.

In the west, Banat produces a large output of drinkable whites and everyday reds but, so far, it has not excelled itself in either colour.

The label design may seem a bit dated, but Cotnari wine was once famous throughout Europe and is still an intensely sweet impressive mouthful.

Romania has suffered much turbulence in the last generation, but Transylvania, caught in the crook of the Carpathian mountains, has survived better than most. This tranquil street in the town of Ernea is in the Tarnave region where the Feteasca and Traminer grapes make fresh, fragrant whites, both dry and sweet.

WESTERN BALKANS

THE WESTERN BALKAN STATES – torn by civil war in the early 1990s and still troubled in many areas – are working hard to rebuild their wine industry and infrastructure. The good news is Slovenia is now well-established as a separate nation, and should soon be able to realize her considerable potential.

The western Balkans lie roughly across the same latitudes as Italy, with similar viticultural conditions, and yet the two wine industries share few characteristics. Austria, due north of Slovenia, provides more of a comparison with its aromatic, sometimes sweet, wines. And strong links in wine styles cross from Hungary to parts of Croatia and Slovenia.

The large area of Croatian vineyards are now recovering following the war, with many being replanted. They can be split geographically into two distinct areas. Inland Croatia or Kontinentalna Hrvatska runs south-east along the Drava tributary as far as the Danube. This is mainly white wine country, growing Traminer, Welschriesling (here known as Graşevina), Muscat Ottonel and Pinot Blanc, often on terraces. The best wines are said to come from the slopes of Baranja, in the Danube Valley north of Osijek, and known as 'The Golden Hill' since Roman times. Along the strip of coastal Croatia – Primorska Hrvatska – the sun, sea and rocky soil combine to produce good reds, particularly those made from the characterful and ageworthy Plavac Mali grape. The best-known wines are Postup and Dingač from the Peljesac peninsula

and Faros from the island of Hvar, although Plavac of varying quality and sweetness is produced all along the beautiful Dalmatian coast. Plavac Mali leapt to unexpected renown during the 1990s when it was thought that Californian Zinfandel was in fact Plavac Mali. Now it seems that both Zinfandel and Italian Primitivo are the same as the obscure Croatian variety, Crljenak, which itself probably comes from Albania or Greece. That's what the DNA experts say, but I say this one will run and run.

West of Split, another native variety, Babic, produces a light red wine for everyday drinking. The Istrian peninsula produces Motovunski Teran, a tart, herbal-tasting red wine (the grape Teran is believed to be related to Refosco). Istria also grows Malvasia, Pinot Blanc, Merlot, Cabernet Sauvignon and Gamay. Mike Grgich, of Californian fame, has set up a small winery on the Peljesac peninsula to bring modern technology back to his homeland. This is what is needed now: more investment, more technology in vineyard and winery and a fair price for the grapes. An origin-based quality wine scheme, linked to a tasting system, is used for premium wines.

Bosnia-Herzegovina, with its Muslim traditions, has never been a strong wine-producing area. A few wines, such as the red Blatina and the dry, unusually full-flavoured white Zilavka, had built up a good reputation. But rebuilding is slow, and it's hardly a mecca for investment. If there was stability there would be some potential here. Serbia and Kosovo, thrown into disarray by the war, must now rebuild and move forward technologically. This was an area with potential. The large winemaking area of central Serbia included the vineyards of Zŭpa in the Kruševac area – some of the former Yugoslavia's oldest – which

WINE AREAS

SLOVENIA

PRIMORSKA
1. Goriška Brda
2. Vipavska Dolina
3. Kras
4. Koper

POSAVJE
5. Bela Krajina
6. Dolenjska
7. Bizeljsko-Sremič

PODRAVJE
8. Smarje-Virštajn
9. Haloze
10. Maribor
11. Srednje Slovenske Gorice
12. Ljutomer-Ormož
13. Radgona-Kapela
14. Prekmurje

CROATIA

KONTINENTALNA HRVATSKA
15. Plešivica
16. Zagorje-Medimurje
17. Prigorje-Bilogora
18. Moslavina
19. Pukuplje
20. Slavonija
21. Podunavlje

PRIMORSKA HRVATSKA
22. Istra
23. Hrvatsko Primorje
24. Sjeverna Dalmacija
25. Dalmatinska Zagora
26. Srednja i Južna Dalmacija

BOSNIA-HERZEGOVINA

HERZEGOVINA

SERBIA

SUBOTICA-HORGOS DESERT

SREM

BANAT

POCERINA

SUMADIJA-GREAT MORAVA RIVER
27. Beograd
28. Mlava River
29. Oplenac
30. Jagodina

TIMOK VALLEY
31. Krajina
32. Knjaževac

NISAVA AND SOUTHERN MORAVA RIVERS
33. Aleksinac
34. Toplica River
35. Niš
36. Nišava River

37. Leskovac
38. Vranje

WESTERN MORAVA RIVER
39. Cacak
40. Kruševac

MONTENEGRO

MONTENEGRO

KOSOVO

KOSOVO

F.Y.R.M. (MACEDONIA)

PELAGONIJA-POLOG

POVARDARJE

PCINJA OSOGOVSKE

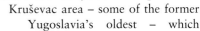

ranked among Serbia's finest. Red grapes predominated, particularly the native Prokupac, which was often blended with Pinot Noir and Gamay. The poor soils of Kosovo were only good for viticulture. Reds predominated: Pinot Noir, Cabernet Franc, Prokupac, Merlot and Gamay. Whites included Welschriesling, Rhine Riesling and Zilavka.

Macedonia is the latest casualty in this troubled Balkan region. Sad, because Macedonia's mild winters and dry subtropical summers are ideal for viticulture. The best wine is red, made from Kratosija and Vranac.

In Montenegro, red Vranac, with its bitter cherry flavour, predominates. The best-known vineyards are those in the sparse, pebbly soil on the southern and south-western slopes surrounding Lake Skadar. A similar quality system to Croatia applies.

SLOVENIA

The relative calm of the new independent Slovenia, established in 1991, is testimony to the common heritage of the Slovenian people. This thriving economy is hotly tipped for the next extension to the EU. Wine has always been part of its heritage. It comes as no surprise to discover Roman writers praising the wines from the Devin area of Kras in the first century AD. Today, Slovenia has around 24,600ha (60,786 acres) of vineyard – up from 24,000ha (59,303 acres) in 1995 – with more designated for development. This is far less than the 50,000ha (123,548 acres) at the end of the 19th century, when the country was part of the Austro-Hungarian empire.

A well-policed quality wine scheme allows only the best wines to be bottled and exported. These normally carry a seal of approval. A drive towards quality is still needed for Slovenia to fulfil its potential.

The country has three defined wine districts and the style of each looks to its neighbour. Littoral (or Primorska) touches the Adriatic for a stretch of the coast around Koper and extends north along the Italian border. This is hilly country with a *karst* plateau – a limestone region with many underground caves and passages formed by the dissolution of the rock – and many of the vineyards lie in the valleys between the mountains and the plateau. The proximity of the Alps tempers the Mediterranean climate. The most famous vineyards of this area straddle the rather artificial border around Dobrovo, Nova Gorica and the area called Goriška Brda or Collio Goriziano in Italian. Grapes such as Refosco (known here as Refosk or Teran), Ribolla (Rebula), Tocai Friuliano (Tocay) and Picolit (Pikolit) highlight the shared culture between this region and neighbouring Friuli-Venezia Giulia. Also grown are Malvasia, Muscat Blanc à Petit Grains (for dessert wines), Chardonnay, Sauvignon Blanc, Pinots Blanc and Gris, Merlot, Cabernets Franc and Sauvignon and Barbera. Vipava's indigenous white specialities are Zelen and Pinela. The white wines from Koper can also be good. For Slovenians the most noted wine is the red Kraski Teran, made from Refosco grapes grown around Sezana in the Kras region, where *terra rossa* (literally, 'red earth') overlays the *karst*. Vipava and Brda are forward-looking areas with go-ahead co-operatives.

The country's best whites come from Posavje, the Sava Valley, in the south-east. This is the meeting point of three different weather systems – alpine, continental and Mediterranean – resulting in a climate with showers in spring, hot summers and warm sunny autumns. High sugar levels are possible, and a recent development has been the production of Eiswein in the Metlika district. The vineyards, mainly on steep slopes, grow Laski Rizling, Traminer, Sauvignon Blanc, Chardonnay, Pinot Blanc, Sipon (Hungary's Furmint) and Silvaner. Rumeni Plavac, a white relation

of Dalmatia's Plavac Mali, is grown around Bizeljsko, although its lack of character often means that it is blended with grapes such as Laski Rizling. The speciality of the Dolenjska region is the light red Cviček, and other reds and rosés are made from Blaufränkisch, Zametovka (or Kîlner Dark), Blauer Portugieser, Pinot Noir, Cabernet and Merlot.

Podravje, or the Drava Valley, has similar climate, grape varieties and winemaking practices to those of the Austrian Steiermark region just across the border, producing young, fresh, tangy whites. Best known is Ljutomer Laski Rizling, once, as Lutomer Riesling, the top-selling wine in the UK, although the Gewürztraminer (known here as Traminec), Sauvignon Blanc and Chardonnay are much better. The semi-sweet 'Tiger Milk' is made from Bouvier, or Ranina as it is locally known. In Gorna Radgona, Pinot Blanc can be used to make sparkling wines by the traditional method.

In many ways the success of Lutomer Riesling, and the consequent flow of hard currency into the region, did as much harm as good. Lutomer Riesling was initially an extremely enjoyable full, soft, rather fruity white. It was the first white wine to cross my lips, and in fact it was usually the only white wine we had in the house when I was a kid. But, as its success grew, rather than use the profits to create ever larger amounts of good wine, the quality got worse and worse. Those of us who had enjoyed it did increasingly violent U-turns to avoid it, and inevitably, its success faded and with it the whole reputation of the old Yugoslavia as a producer. This was quite unfair, but Lutomer's place in the easy dry white pantheon was then taken by Liebfraumilch – initially a pleasant, fruity German wine that was wildly popular. As Liebfraumilch's quality slumped, the whole of Germany's reputation in the export markets suffered exactly the same way as Yugoslavia's had done.

The vineyards of the Drava Valley in eastern Slovenia are squashed in between those of Hungary and Austria and closely follow the contours that weave in and out of the wooded hills. The prospect of mechanization here is very distant indeed.

BULGARIA

I'VE HAD A LOVE-HATE RELATIONSHIP with Bulgarian wine right from the beginning. The first tasting I did was when Jancis Robinson asked me at zero hour minus one minute's notice to 'guest edit' the *Which?* wine monthly newsletter for her. We organized a tasting of Bulgarian wines. These were some of the first samples to hit British shores, at the very beginning of the 1980s. There were some remarkable hefty, violent, scabrous reds – strange, soupy and thick on the tongue. But there was fruit there too, a proud, rip-roaring essence of blackcurrant, quite unlike the delicate, lacy perfume of old Bordeaux, quite unlike the bright, keen flavours of Chilean Cabernet.

The reds were infinitely preferable to the whites, whose blend of searing acidity, reckless sulphur and building-site dust made them painful to the lips and dangerous to one's sanity. Since then, although the red wines still easily outshine the whites in Bulgaria, the flavours have changed. The stentorian old Cabernets are no longer so impressive, but the bright young Cabernets and Merlots are infinitely better.

One gets the sense that in the 1980s, Bulgarian Cabernet Sauvignon was made for an export market that was starved of new and exciting affordable flavours. New World offerings then came along in the 1990s and filled the gap just as the Bulgarian success story of the 1980s fell into disarray. Free market reforms followed, in particular, land reforms which gave Bulgarian wineries the opportunity to buy their own vineyards. Hopefully, rationalization, positive restructuring and control over the huge variation in fruit quality bode well for the future, but progress is still painfully slow.

Although Bulgaria has been cultivating vines for 3000 years, its immediate past doesn't stretch back much past the end of World War Two. Between 1396 and 1918, Turkish Islamic domination brought winemaking to a commercial halt. Hillside plantings were established after the end of Turkish rule but it was the Soviet decision that Bulgaria should be a massive modern vineyard to supply the USSR that triggered the planting of all the fertile flatland vineyards that now mark out Bulgaria. And it was some canny

WINE REGIONS AND CONTROLIRAN WINE AREAS

DANUBE PLAIN
1. Novo Selo
2. Lozitza
3. Svishtov
4. Roussenski-Briag
5. Pavlikeni
6. Suhindol
7. Lyaskovets

BLACK SEA
8. Kralevo
9. Khan Krum
10. Novi Pazar
11. Varna
12. Preslav
13. Strandja

EAST THRACIAN VALLEY
14. Sungulare
15. Slaviantzi
16. Sakar
17. Stambolovo

WEST THRACIAN VALLEY
18. Asenovgrad
19. Brestnik
20. Oriachovitza
21. Rozova Dolina

STRUMA VALLEY
22. Harsovo

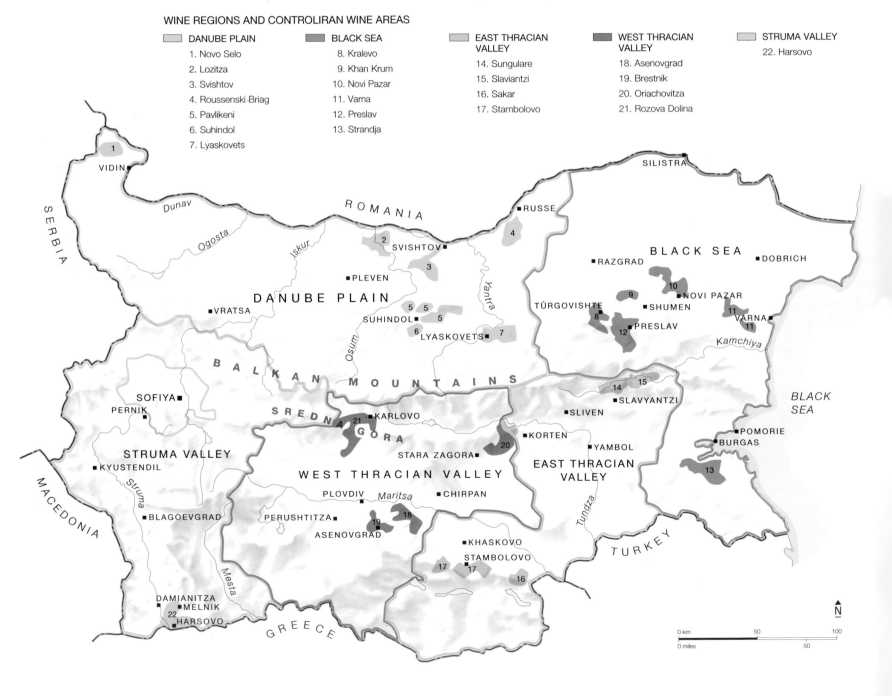

bartering with American cola companies that gained her the vast acreage of international grape varieties upon which she has made her export reputation.

The grape most readily associated with Bulgaria, and which is the country's most widely planted, is Cabernet Sauvignon. The wines first appeared in the West in the early 1980s, and they were a revelation at that time – unassuming, but tasty and affordable. Since their debut the easy, ripe, plummy, well-priced Bulgarian offerings arguably have done as much as anything from Australia or California to establish the variety as the world's most famous red grape.

Those first Bulgarian wines, rich, creamy and blackcurrant, with some oak and some bottle age, were virtually identikit pictures of what wine drinkers were seeking, and we lapped them up. In a rush to provide us with more of what we were clamouring for, production increased and quality slipped. It may just be nostalgia, but all these years later, current releases still don't seem as good as those first Suhindol Cabernets from the late 1970s.

Merlot can also be good, particularly from Stambolovo. Gamza (the same grape as Hungary's Kadarka) is vigorously fruity when young, but can age to a meaty richness, while the similarly sturdy, plummy Mavrud also produces wines of character. Pamid is the most widely planted native variety, but generally its wines are thin and lacking in character, though modern winemaking may yet produce bright gluggers from this variety. Much better is the Shiroka Melnishka Losa, usually just called Melnik, a powerful, fruity red wine which takes to oak aging very well.

Native white varieties include Dimiat, which manages to maintain a fairly aromatic, soft-centred character even from quite high yields, and Red Misket, a musky, grapy variety which one might think had some relation to the Muscat family but it doesn't. Rkatsiteli is the most widely planted white, and there are also significant amounts of Chardonnay, Ugni Blanc, Sauvignon Blanc, Riesling, Muscat Ottonel and Aligoté.

While the reds have thrived, the whites have been, on the whole, disappointing. The reds have been developed along French lines, and have been able to cope with some pretty rudimentary winery conditions. The whites initially followed Germanic models, with Riesling and Welschriesling being prominent. But Germanic models require positively aseptic conditions to succeed. In Bulgaria, grapes were frequently unhealthy and the wineries simply not clean enough: even today, sulphurous brews outnumber attractive drinks, although there is now a handful of perfectly good 'international' Chardonnays being made.

There are now 110,000ha (271,806 acres) under vine, and 70 wineries, 19 of which are exporting. The 16 main wineries all have major technological investment programs in place. The largest company, Boyar Estates, has amalgamated wineries at Yambol, Schumen, Sliven, Rousse and Korten under one umbrella, in addition to acquiring 1000ha (2470 acres) of vineyards. Early lessons from flying winemakers have been learned. Quality and consistency are apparent. Winery capacity and grape production at last match! But the wines have still not re-established any real individuality, rather than just a vague and acceptable modernness. The next step must surely be movement up the quality ladder and the creation of regional pyramids of quality for specific wines.

The wine laws are already in place. Country wine corresponds to France's *vin de pays*, varietal wine is more strictly controlled (made from a single grape variety), while premium wine is better still. DGOs are quality wines from a Declared Geographical Origin, divided into sub-regions, districts or towns, or villages. At the top of the tree are the Controliran wines, of which there

are currently around 30. These are made from specified grape varieties grown in certain DGOs.

The scheme works reasonably well, though as with France's appellation contrôlée system, many of the Controliran wines are nothing special. Indeed, some of Bulgaria's most appealing bottles are those bearing the humble country wine tag. In addition, those which conform to special aging requirements can claim the titles Reserve or Special Reserve. Since excessive aging in old oak is one of Bulgaria's problems, these wines are rarely worth seeking out. The move towards early-release Young Vatted Cabernets and Merlots is good news.

WINE REGIONS

The Black Sea region is known for some of Bulgaria's best modern whites. Around Shumen, there are important wineries at Novi Pazar, Preslav and Khan Krum.

Reds and whites are made in roughly equal amounts in the Danube Plain Region, although the reds are the real gems. Suhindol's best-known wine is the Cabernet Sauvignon, although the Merlot and Gamza are also good. Suhindol was the first Bulgarian area to become famous with its Cabernet Sauvignon. New technology and judicious use of oak have restored the quality in recent years. Ready to snatch the crown for Bulgaria's top wine when the quality at Suhindol slipped were the Cabernet and Merlot from the foothills around Rousse in the north-east of the region. The wines come in young, fruity carbonic maceration styles, sold abroad as Young Vatted Cabernet Sauvignon and Young Vatted Merlot as well as deeper, darker oak-aged versions. Another decent Cabernet comes from the Svishtov region on the border with Romania.

Cabernet Sauvignon is also important south of the Balkans in the West and East Thracian Valleys, both on its own or blended with Merlot or Mavrud. That from Plovdiv is good, although nearby Assenovgrad produces a better version, as well as impressive chunky Mavrud. The vines are planted in rich black and red carbonated soils on gentle slopes chosen for their low susceptibility to frost.

The hilly districts of Sliven, Oriachovitza and Stara Zagora, just south of the Balkan mountains, are also sources of good Cabernet Sauvignon. The vineyards enjoy a sheltered southerly exposure and the soils are mostly well-drained sand and clay. Sliven also produces a very drinkable, clean Chardonnay and a fine cheap blend of Merlot and Pinot Noir. In the hilly regions of the south, Merlot from Stambolovo can be excellent, with the special Reserve releases sometimes being Bulgaria's best wines. The Merlot from Sakar is also good, as is the Cabernet Sauvignon.

The Struma Valley is the warmest area in the country. The continental climate is modified by warm air rising from the Struma river and has a distinctly Mediterranean feel, although the altitude prevents temperatures from rising too high for viticulture. This is the home of Melnik, a variety which thrives on the clay and sand soils around Damianitza and Harsovo: a wine to watch. Even in such warm conditions, Melnik ripens late, and autumn rains can give rise to problems with rot before harvest in October.

Experiments are under way, particularly with Melnik, to produce new strains of grape designed to require a growing period two to three weeks shorter than other varieties, so that they can be harvested before the rains begin, thus avoiding damage to the crop. Cabernet Sauvignon, Merlot, Rkatsiteli and Muscat Ottonel are also important. Further north, the wineries in and around Kyustendil produce small amounts of Rkatsiteli, Pamid and Cabernet Sauvignon.

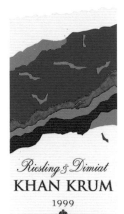

Bulgaria has several tasty indigenous grape varieties. Mavrud makes powerful, plummy reds.

GREECE & EASTERN MEDITERRANEAN

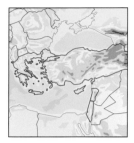

T HIS REGION HAS BEEN MAKING WINE FOR THOUSANDS OF YEARS. Heavy, oxidized wines that pleased local drinkers are rapidly disappearing in favour of modern, clean wines. The best are very good, though the rest have a long way to go yet. The country which is leading the charge is unquestionably Greece, where a new generation of winemakers and grapegrowers, many of them trained in France, California or Australia, have looked in horror at the decay of a wine culture stretching back thousands of years and resolved to do something about it. Technological upgrading of wineries has been matched by the revival of old vineyards and the creation of new ones, especially in the relatively rare cooler parts of the country. But above all, these modern Greeks have a vision of the flavours they want to achieve, and a reassuring pride in Greece itself. Many of the newer estates, that could have just planted a swathe of Cabernet and Chardonnay, have in fact covered the majority of their vineyards with native varieties, and the wines are modern, but marvellously original too. Established companies such as Boutari, Kourtakis and Tsantalis, together with a new band of small, quality-minded producers – Gaia, Gentilini, Gerovassiliou, Hatzimichalis, Constantin Lazaridi, Papaïoannou, Strofilia and the younger members of the Boutaris family – are upping the quality stakes.

NORTHERN GREECE

Along the wine roads of Makedonia, the Xinomavro grape is responsible for the dark, spicy powerful Naousa and, when blended with Negoska, the softer, rounded Goumenissa. The best producers of Naousa are Boutari, Tsantalis, Chrisohoou and Kyr-Yianni. In Goumenissa, Aïdarinis is a winery to watch. On the Chalkidiki peninsula, Tsantalis leases vineyards from the Mount Athos monastery and produces red wines that blend the native Limnio with Cabernet and Grenache. Evanghelos Gerovassiliou, a former pupil of Bordeaux's Professor Peynaud, is Greece's most respected enologist; he now has his own eponymous state-of-the-art winery in the rolling hills near Epanomi. Terrific Rhône-like reds and a fine Condrieu-style Viognier are among his impressive offerings.

CENTRAL GREECE

Other parts of Greece make equally good wines, particularly the Hatzimichalis estate north-west of Athens where a diverse collection of grape varieties is grown. The Cabernet Sauvignon, Merlot, Chardonnay, and the Ambelon Estate white – 100 per cent Robola – are all good, if a little pricy. Robola plays second fiddle to the Savatiano grape further east on the island of Evvoia. Savatiano is the source of most retsina, which gets its particular character from Aleppo pine resin added during fermentation. Love it or loathe it, retsina when fresh and young is a brilliantly individual drink, but retsina sales are falling fast, both domestically and internationally.

The Ionian island of Kefallonia is best known for its dry white Robola. Most exciting are the Gentilini wines made by Gabrielle Beamish. Her Classico white, reminiscent of Australian Semillon, with its crisp lemon acidity and mineral perfume, is a blend of Robola and another local grape, Tsaoussi, together with small amounts of Moschofilero and Muscat. The Fumé is an oak-aged blend of Chardonnay and Sauvignon Blanc.

PELOPONNISOS

The best wine of the Peloponnese (Peloponnisos) is the dark, spicy Nemea, made from Aghiorghitiko. Vineyards are found between 250 and 800m (820 and 2600ft) with the best ones on slopes below the plateau of Asprokambos. (Wines from Antonopoulos, Cambas, Gaia, Kokotos, Papaïoannou and Skouras are worth seeking out.) Further west, the aromatic white Moschofilero produces Mantinia, one of Greece's most promising whites; those produced by Cambas, Achaïa Clauss and Spyropoulos are especially good. Elsewhere in the Peloponnese, Patras dry whites are made from rather dull Roditis – but the Kouros brand from Kourtakis is good. The two *vins doux naturels* – Muscat of Patras and Mavrodaphne of Patras, made mainly from the red Mavrodaphne grape supplemented by Korinthiaki, can be deliciously exciting, especially when aged.

GREEK ISLANDS

In the Aegean, Crete (Kriti) produces an awful lot of awful wine, but Kourtakis has begun to produce remarkable reds from ungrafted vines as well as crisp clean whites. Boutari also has a decent white. Better wines can found in Rhodes (Rodos), particularly the Muscat, although better still is the Muscat from Samos. The unfortified Samos Nectar from the Samos co-op is a marvellous mouthful. The white wines from the volcanic island of Santorini (Thira) are made from the Assyrtiko and Aidani grapes, with the vines trained like coils of rope to resist the wind. They have the minerally grip and tang of Sémillon matching an intense baked-apple fruit (especially Gaia's Thalassitis), a magnificent old-fashioned sweet *vin santo* is also produced.

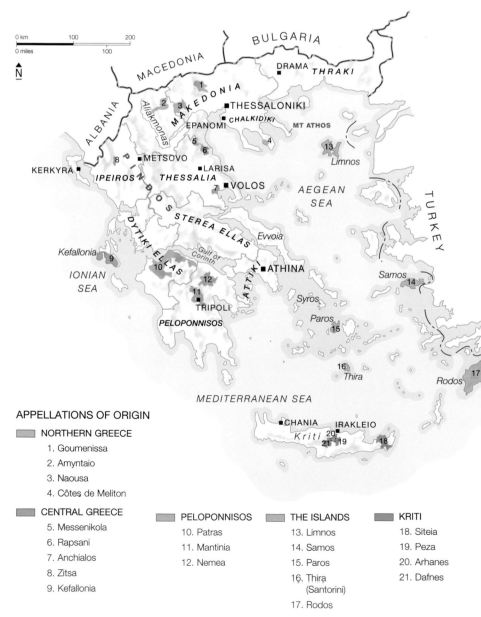

APPELLATIONS OF ORIGIN

NORTHERN GREECE
1. Goumenissa
2. Amyntaio
3. Naousa
4. Côtes de Meliton

CENTRAL GREECE
5. Messenikola
6. Rapsani
7. Anchialos
8. Zitsa
9. Kefallonia

PELOPONNISOS
10. Patras
11. Mantinia
12. Nemea

THE ISLANDS
13. Limnos
14. Samos
15. Paros
16. Thira (Santorini)
17. Rodos

KRITI
18. Siteia
19. Peza
20. Arhanes
21. Dafnes

TURKEY

Only three per cent of the huge acreage of Turkey under vine is used for wine production; the rest is table grapes. Turks who do drink – and 99 per cent of them, being Muslim, are not supposed to – do so for the effect, rather than the flavour, and the oxidized, high-alcohol style of many wines find few devotees in today's wine world.

Most famous of the red wines is Buzbag from Eastern Anatolia, made from the native Öküzgözü and Bogazkere grapes. It can be good, or just awful. Turkey's better producers include Diren from Tokat in Eastern Anatolia, Kavaklidere near Ankara and Doluca in Thrace: here modern technology, French oak barrels and local and international varieties come together in a very drinkable way.

LEBANON

Quality is improving all over the Lebanon; modernization has even gripped Château Ksara, Lebanon's oldest and largest winery. Its new releases of such modern wines as Chardonnay Cuvée du Pape, the Cabernet-Cinsaut-Syrah mix Réserve du Couvent or indeed the straight Cabernet, are a world removed from what they were offering only a few years ago.

The other most important wineries are Château Musar and Château Kefraya, both of whose vineyards lie on the east-facing slopes of Mount Barouk, overlooking the beautiful Bekaa Valley. The high altitude, over 1000m (3280ft) above sea level, keeps temperatures low. Clos St Thomas is a high-quality smaller producer in the valley whose top red is stunning.

Kefraya's best-known red is 70 per cent Cabernet Sauvignon plus Syrah, Mourvèdre and Grenache, but I prefer the young Turkish Delight-scented les Bretèches – a Cinsaut-Cabernet-Syrah mix – or the seriously impressive top-of-the-line Cabernet-Syrah Comte de M. Kefraya's whites are also greatly improved, using Ugni Blanc, Clairette, Bourboulenc and Sauvignon Blanc.

Château Musar, established in 1930 by Gaston Hochar, is the most internationally famous of the Lebanese wine producers and was for a long time the shining star in Lebanon's wine sky. The red, based on between 50 and 80 per cent Cabernet Sauvignon, the balance being largely Cinsaut, and only released after its fifth year, used to be a thrilling, exotic, kasbah-scented mishmash of flavours, unlike any other. But while Lebanon's other wineries have moved ahead, Musar seems to be somewhat stuck in a time warp. Musar Blanc is also full-bodied and is a blend of the local Obaideh and Merwah – Chardonnay and Sémillon lookalikes respectively.

ISRAEL

Most of Israel's best wines to date have come from the Galilee region, which counts the Golan Heights as its best sub-region. The Golan Heights Winery makes good dry whites under the Yarden and Gamla labels, and also produces Yarden bottle-fermented sparkling wines. The vineyards, in the foothills of Mount Hermon, are on well-drained soils over basalt and other volcanic rocks, hence the success of the winery with Cabernet Sauvignon, Merlot, Muscat, Chardonnay and Sauvignon. The altitude keeps daytime temperatures below 25°C (77°F).

Israel's oldest and largest producer, Carmel, makes 55 per cent of the total output, but in the 1990s numerous new boutique wineries opened, making good use of modern technology, but often producing tiny quantities. Some of Israel's most promising wines now come from Castel in the Judean Hills, Galil Mountain in Galilee and Tishbi in Shomron. Let us hope the continuing conflict in this area does not stall innovation and expansion.

CYPRUS

The Cypriot wine industry is still recovering from the triple whammy of the collapse of the Russian wine market, the banning of the name 'sherry' from the island's fortified wines, and 14 years of drought, which dramatically reduced the annual crop to 500,000 hectolitres. Not surprisingly ETKO, the oldest producer on the island, is now investing in mainland Greece. But the other effect has been that the large companies – ETKO, KEO, LOEL and SODAP – have been forced to take quality more seriously.

Native grape varieties, Mavro (black) and Xynisteri (a white grape better and more subtle than Mavro), still cover around 85 per cent of vineyard plantings, but there are now small but significant amounts of international varieties being grown, generally on the slopes of the Troodos mountains, where the melting snow provides much-needed water for irrigation in this parched island. For the first time we are seeing varietal wines being made in Cyprus, and early efforts with grapes like Cabernet Sauvignon and Sémillon are impressive. Commandaria, Cyprus's dark, sweet and often fortified wine, is still the most famous wine from the island. It is made with sun-dried Mavro and Xynisteri grapes, and aged in solera systems.

The Bekaa Valley was once the frontline in Lebanon's civil war. These vineyards belong to Château Kefraya, an important producer.

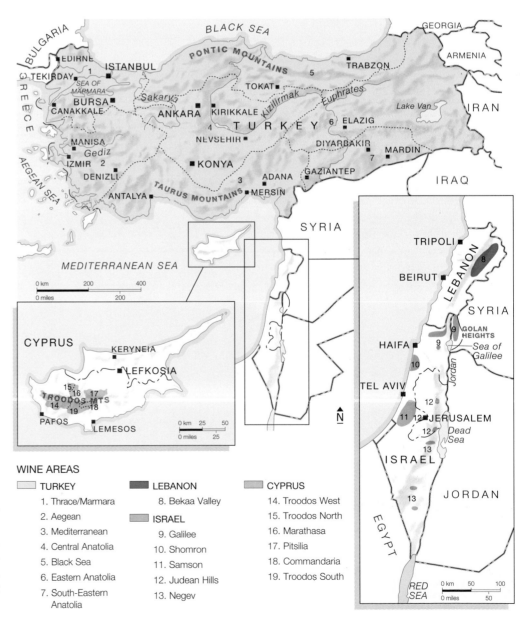

WINE AREAS

TURKEY	LEBANON	CYPRUS
1. Thrace/Marmara	8. Bekaa Valley	14. Troodos West
2. Aegean	ISRAEL	15. Troodos North
3. Mediterranean	9. Galilee	16. Marathasa
4. Central Anatolia	10. Shomron	17. Pitsilia
5. Black Sea	11. Samson	18. Commandaria
6. Eastern Anatolia	12. Judean Hills	19. Troodos South
7. South-Eastern Anatolia	13. Negev	

NORTH AMERICA

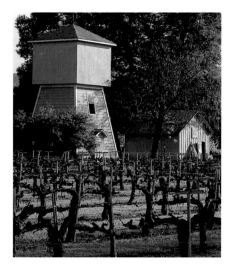

A vineyard doesn't need to be centuries old to be famous. Bien Nacido (left) in the Santa Maria Valley was only planted in 1973 but various wineries, especially Au Bon Climat, whose winery is in the background, have made a string of great wines from its Pinot Noir, Chardonnay and Syrah grapes. Napa Valley is full of ultra-modern wineries, but a little history remains like this old water tower (above) at Franciscan Vineyards' Oakville Estate.

An event in Paris on 26 May 1976 proved to be a watershed in North America's winemaking history, the date with destiny the country had been heading towards since 1619 when Lord Delaware had tried to establish a vineyard of French wine grape varieties in Virginia. That sounds pretty sensationalist, I know, but that day has had a more far-reaching effect on the world's perception of fine wine than any other in the modern era.

Stephen Spurrier, a young British wine merchant, held a tasting in Paris for the most finely tuned French palates of the day. Ostensibly a Bordeaux and Burgundy tasting, it also included a few Californian wines, which the French judges then proceeded to denigrate in pretty condescending terms.

Except that this was a blind tasting. The wines they were denigrating turned out to be French, some of the top names in Bordeaux and Burgundy. The wines they were praising as typical examples of great French wines... weren't. The top white was Chateau Montelena Chardonnay 1973 from California's Napa Valley, which trounced wines from vineyards in Burgundy planted a thousand years before. The top red was Stag's Leap 1973 Cabernet – only the second vintage of this Napa Valley wine – which beat off the challenge of wines like Bordeaux's Château Haut-Brion and Château Latour which had the benefit of being rooted in hundreds of years of history.

Until that moment, France had reigned supreme in the world of wine, and had generally behaved as though its hallowed wines had a God-given right to be the best. No more. The astonishing victory at the blind tasting gave Americans the confidence to believe that they could match the best of the Old World, but on their own terms, and it inspired the other nations of the world that now produce world class wines – ranging from Australia and New Zealand to South Africa, Chile and others – to do the same.

It also fashioned the approach taken by many Americans to making wine. With the exception of the bulk producers, there are winemakers in California, Oregon, Washington, Texas, Virginia, New York – and now Ontario and British Columbia in Canada, too – who take 'the best' as their goal, the top wine as their role model, and buy the finest equipment to achieve their aim. Sometimes sheer ambition is their downfall. But more often their efforts sing with the excitement of a new industry turning the tables on old, revered institutions, and the whole world has cause to be grateful for that.

NORTH COAST

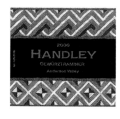

Iᴛ's ᴀ ɢᴏᴏᴅ ɪᴅᴇᴀ to start with Mendocino way up in northern California, because we're going to have to get used to the wild fluctuations in climate that afflict – or bless, depending on how you look at it – every single coastal wine region down to Santa Barbara. Up in Mendocino are some of California's hottest high-quality vineyards (I'm excluding the bulk-producing San Joaquin or Central Valley regions), best suited to grand, old-style, rip-roaring, throaty Zinfandel reds. But there are fog-draped, drizzly, chilly sites in Mendocino as well, that can just about coax Chardonnay and Pinot Noir to some sort of ripeness, and that make the eyes of a winemaker from the windswept Champagne region of northern France well up with tears of homesickness.

MENDOCINO AND LAKE COUNTY

The climatic variations found in Mendocino are all to do with those cold air currents rising up from the Pacific Ocean, and their accompanying fogs. The Anderson Valley which slices north-west through the towering redwood forests, feels them right to the bone. This is fascinating backwoods country, with vastly contrasting vineyard conditions, depending upon whether you are above or below the fog line. It is perhaps the most dramatic of Mendocino's various vineyard areas.

Up on the ridges above the valley, way above the fog line at between 400 and 700m (1300 and 2300ft), are some great old Zinfandel vineyards, their origins dating back to the sites that were first planted by Italian immigrants back in the closing decade of the 19th century. With a surfeit of sun, but cooled by their elevation above sea level, these mature vines give some thrilling flavours. New plantings of Zinfandel, Pinot Noir, Syrah and Merlot are also going on in the new AVA – known as Mendocino Ridge – for the scattering of vineyards in the west of the county sited at least 370m (1200ft) up.

Down below in the valley, though, things couldn't be more different. Even the early pioneers in the 1970s planted cool-climate grapes like Gewürztraminer and Riesling, and all the recent action

Flowers Winery vineyards at Cazadero, in the cool Sonoma Coast region. The netting is to stop birds eating the grapes.

is to do with Pinot Noir and Chardonnay destined for sparkling wine that has proved to be some of California's best and is uncannily similar to Champagne itself in character.

But generally most of Mendocino just sits and sizzles in the heat. Whereas further south in California I talk endlessly about how gaps in the Coast Ranges allow maritime breezes into the interior to cool everything down, up in the north in Mendocino, none of the little river valleys reach far enough inland to make much difference, because the Coast Range mountains here are 600 to 900m (1970 to 2953ft) high. And at that height, you are not going to get even a sniff of cooling breeze coming in from the Pacific. Indeed, the main valley here runs north-south, carved out by the Russian River (though the Russian River Valley AVA wine region doesn't appear until further south, in Sonoma County), which has to head right down to Healdsburg before it can

0 km 2   4
0 miles 2

WHERE THE VINEYARDS ARE

On this map you only catch sight of a sliver of the Pacific Ocean to the west, and a tiny inlet or two of San Pablo Bay to the south, but keep a good eye on those two splashes of water: they're crucial to an understanding of the vineyards that lie north of San Francisco. Also take a note of the Coast Ranges. These are the mountains that run down to the edge of the Pacific. In general, they're not particularly high, but they are high enough to act as a barrier to most of the fog and icy wind that would otherwise sweep in from the ocean.

On the other hand, the areas inland from the sea would be far too hot for growing good wine grapes were it not for some cooling influence. And this is provided by the sea. In Mendocino County, the Anderson Valley; in Sonoma County the Russian River Valley; and in Sonoma, Napa and other counties east, the Golden Gate gap allows fog and cold air to be sucked in to the warm interior day by day. Without this effect, there would be no fine wine industry in California. With this effect, we have cool vineyards near the sea, gradually warming as the maritime influence weakens further inland.

Areas cut off from the maritime influence, like Potter Valley and Clear Lake, rely on altitude to keep their vines cool. There are also areas that rely upon altitude to moderate the heat as they are above the fog line. Howell Mountain, Atlas Peak, Spring Mountain, Mount Veeder and Sonoma Mountain are the best known.

find a low enough gap in the Coast Ranges to force a way through to the sea. Up in Mendocino, we're at the river's source. So the maritime influence which affects things further downstream has been pretty well played out, and the whole upriver basin is simply left to bake.

The results are strong, ripe reds from the north around Ukiah – mainly from Cabernet Sauvignon and Zinfandel, but there are also encouraging results from Italian and Rhône varieties. Following the Russian River south, the red wines are still quite hefty; and the beginnings of cooler conditions produce some fair whites down by Hopland. To the north of Ukiah, the Redwood Valley produces good whites and some excellent reds, while Potter Valley, further inland, is that bit warmer, but its elevation helps in providing cool nights. McDowell Valley, east of Hopland, is a high, sloping benchland that still has ancient planting of Grenache and Syrah, and is also getting good results from Viognier and Marsanne.

Further east is Lake County, where vineyards around Clear Lake, mostly at sites above 400m (1300ft), experience scorching days with ice-cold nights, and produce both red and white fruit of considerable intensity.

NORTH SONOMA
If Mendocino is relatively simple to understand, Sonoma County, directly to the south, is the most complex but also the most intriguingly satisfying of the other main wine counties north of San

SELECTED AVA WINE AREAS

1. Mendocino Ridge	6. Clear Lake	11. Napa Valley
2. Anderson Valley	7. Sonoma Coast	12. Carneros
3. Mendocino	8. Northern Sonoma	
4. Potter Valley	9. Guenoc Valley	
5. McDowell Valley	10. Sonoma Valley	

CALIFORNIA NORTH COAST AVA BOUNDARY

——— OTHER AVA BOUNDARIES

TOTAL DISTANCE NORTH TO SOUTH
139KM (86 MILES)

VINEYARDS

RED GRAPES
Certain districts are associated with particular grape varieties, such as Dry Creek Valley Zinfandel, Napa Cabernet and Carneros Pinot Noir. Merlot also features.

WHITE GRAPES
Chardonnay is most widely planted. Sauvignon Blanc shows regional variations in style. There is also Pinot Blanc, Gewürztraminer and Riesling.

CLIMATE
The two-season climate of short, mild winters and long, dry, hot summers is dramatically influenced by summer fogs coming off the Pacific.

SOIL
An extraordinary variety of soils ranges from well drained gravel and loam to infertile gravel and rock, volcanic ash with quartz and sandy loam.

ASPECT
Hill slopes are favoured for important vineyard sites, though much of the Napa Valley is flat.

N

[Map labels: UKIAH, Russian River, LAKEPORT, Clear Lake, HOPLAND, CLOVERDALE, HEALDSBURG, CALISTOGA, Lake Berryessa, Russian River, SANTA ROSA, SEBASTOPOL, PACIFIC OCEAN, SONOMA, NAPA, PETALUMA, NOVATO, San Pablo Bay, VALLEJO]

0 km 2 4
0 miles 2

Francisco. Again, the dominant factor is the cooling effect of sea fogs and breezes, both as they push inland through the Russian River Valley, and as they flow off the northern slopes of San Pablo Bay at the southern end of the county – although, obviously, different soils, different elevations and different exposures to the sun also count.

Coming south from Mendocino on Highway 101, the Alexander Valley opens out north of Cloverdale; it's warm here, and both Zinfandel and the Rhône varieties ripen easily. However, the valley doesn't really begin to show its form until you get south of Geyserville. The broad fertile swathes of gravelly loam encourage vines to run riot, but modern methods of pruning, trellising and yield restraint now produce wonderfully soft-edged, yet mightily flavoured Cabernets that are a joy in youth and yet age with grace. Of slightly more concern are the swathes of high-yielding Chardonnay that carpet much of the southern section around Jimtown. One wonders quite who is going to buy it all. The small Knights Valley AVA, further east on the road to Calistoga in the Napa Valley, used to be very much a one-horse domaine – Beringer bottled a delicious fruity Cabernet from Knights Valley grapes, but apart from that the area was a vinous backwater. It isn't now. Much former pastureland is now strewn with vines and the big

players like Gallo have significant plantings here. Chardonnay is much more important than it was. The most encouraging sign is that there are some significant plantings on the low-yielding hillsides, rather than just on the valley floor.

Dry Creek Valley was planted with Zinfandel by Italian immigrants during the 1870s and it is still Zinfandel, in the breezeless, baking northern half of the valley, that makes Dry Creek special and gives you a feeling that the old rural America is still hanging on in here, amid the ever increasing dominance of the large companies. On both sides of the river are deposits of reddish rocky, gravelly soil, well-drained but able to retain the higher than average rainfall the valley receives. Cabernet is encroaching on these sites, but it is the Zinfandel that makes me want to shout for joy. On the valley floor, well-drained gravels produce surprisingly good Sauvignon Blanc and Chenin Blanc and, at the cooler southern end of the valley, some fine Chardonnay is grown.

It's really only south of Healdsburg in the Russian River Valley AVA that Sonoma County changes from a warm environment with a few cooling influences to a cool environment with warm patches, especially in the areas affected by the river. Technically, it should be too cold for Zinfandel along this stretch of the Russian River, but some marvellous examples crop up, frequently in vineyards that

NORTH SONOMA

TOTAL DISTANCE
NORTH TO SOUTH
32KM (20 MILES)

VINEYARDS

N

also grow superb Pinot Noir – no, don't ask me why, but you get the same paradox in Australia, where fine Shiraz and Riesling can grow in neighbouring fields. There's also lovely Gewürztraminer (albeit too little), Syrah and Merlot. Intensely flavoured Sauvignon Blancs (most notably from Rochioli) perfectly capture the grape's freshly cut hay and citrus peel aromas and, now that Sauvignon is becoming trendy in the US – thanks to the arrival of superb examples from New Zealand, patches of land with proven Sauvignon performance are going to be in demand.

But it is for Chardonnay and Pinot Noir that the cooler reaches have become famous. The Chardonnays have tropical fruit flavours backed by healthy oak and really fill your mouth. Most are naturally high in acid, so winemakers generally put them through malolactic fermentation. Yet, thanks to a long growing season, they maintain their pinpoint fruit character without ever being flabby.

RUSSIAN RIVER VALLEY

Russian River Valley has been seen as one of the premier appellations for Pinot Noir in California for more than a decade. At first, these wines grabbed our attention for their ripeness and boldness, a style far removed from the delicate, pretty examples that areas like Carneros were striving for at that time. Yet today there's been something of a U-turn. Areas like Carneros, Santa Maria and Anderson Valley in California, and Willamette Valley in Oregon to the north, are achieving richer, more succulent styles, just as the Russian River growers seem on the whole to be easing back. The typical Russian River style based on sweet black cherry fruit is being replaced by wild strawberry and a whiff of Coca Cola – sounds strange, but it's not uncommon in good Pinot Noir. Does it work? Yes it does, and so long as the wines retain their delightful lush texture, I'm pretty happy with what is yet another manifestation of Pinot Noir's increasing brilliance on the West Coast of America. If this implies Russian River is just about

Pinot – well, it isn't. Chardonnay for a start is renowned here. This is the heart of the fruit that goes into famous brands like Sonoma-Cutrer, and as you crisscross the areas west of Healdsburg and Windsor, you get a sense of insatiable thrust for more and more Chardonnay. But there's Zinfandel too – brilliantly different, juicier, fresher than much other Zin, because those fogs travelling up the Russian River Valley from the sea have cooled things sufficiently to allow the grapes up to two weeks extra ripening time on the vine.

The early morning mist is still clearing from the ancient Lytton Springs Vineyard in Dry Creek Valley. Ridge use the fruit for a famous Zinfandel, but there's also some old Carignan as well as some Petite Sirah.

WHERE THE VINEYARDS ARE *It doesn't look like much, that little thread of Russian River Valley in North Sonoma, curling in from the west, but even a small gap like the Russian River Valley can let enough cold maritime winds and fogs creep inland to have a dramatic cooling effect on what would otherwise be an extremely hot growing environment.*

There are now vineyards planted so far out west they are within sight of the coast, that are producing exciting Pinot, Chardonnay and sparkling wine. The vineyards you can see here, at the extreme left of the map, are for sparkling wines; follow the river east and you will come to Green Valley, whose vineyards are still strongly affected by fog and wind; these produce both sparkling wines and good Chardonnay and Pinot Noir.

The climate is a little warmer looking across to Santa Rosa, although surprisingly Pinot Noir can still be excellent in places, as can Zinfandel. The Chalk Hill area to the east has shown form with Chardonnay and with Sauvignon Blanc. Healdsburg is the hub for two other areas. Dry Creek Valley is an excellent warm region lying in a short, north-west-running valley. And to the north of Healdsburg, Alexander Valley provides some of the most approachable Cabernets in California.

AVA WINE AREAS, SELECTED WINERIES AND VINEYARDS

1. Fritz
2. Ferrari-Carano
3. David Coffaro
4. Duxoup
5. Preston
6. Frick
7. Marietta Cellars
8. Geyser Peak
9. Quivira
10. A Rafanelli
11. Pezzi King
12. Dry Creek
13. Lambert Bridge
14. Gallo-Sonoma
15. Nalle
16. Lytton Springs (Ridge)
17. Clos du Bois
18. Murphy-Goode
19. Robert Young Vineyard
20. Upper Barn Vineyard
21. Seghesio
22. Robert Mueller
23. Simi
24. Jordan
25. Belle Terre Vineyard
26. Stonestreet
27. Chalk Hill Winery
28. Siduri
29. Iron Horse
30. Marimar Torres

For further wineries, see RUSSIAN RIVER VALLEY map on pages 242–243

DRY CREEK VALLEY = AVA WINE AREA

━━━ AVA BOUNDARIES

•••• ALEXANDER VALLEY AVA BOUNDARY

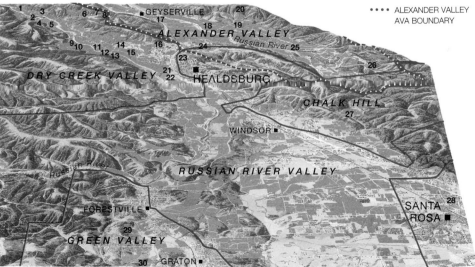

0 km 1 2
0 miles 1

Vineyards in the Russian River Valley. The green of the pine forest implies a cool climate and, indeed, the vines are cooled by breezes running up the river valley from the Pacific.

RUSSIAN RIVER VALLEY

VINEYARDS

TOTAL DISTANCE NORTH TO SOUTH 24KM (15 MILES)

0 km   1   2
0 miles   1

N

There's an interesting debate going on in Russian River just now. The AVA that was mapped out in 1983 was basically political. The growers now want to redefine it according to grape-growing conditions – and in particular to limiting it to those areas affected by fog. This would remove chunks of Alexander Valley and Chalk Hill, as well as adding other traditionally foggy stretches. Hopefully the growers will get their way, because many politically motivated AVAs make no sense. If accepted, it will be the first time an existing AVA has been redefined and will open the door for numerous other areas to put a proper vineyard-sensitive definition on the books. The whole concept of 'Appellation' in California will be greatly enhanced.

Green Valley is a sub-AVA south of Forestville, and is even cooler – a prime site for Chardonnay, Pinot Noir and sparkling wine. Interestingly, examples of Pinot Noir from here are darker in colour than the rest of Russian River Valley, with more intense acidity and greater concentration. The sparkling wines, aided by these slow-ripening tasty grapes, are full and fleshy, but age extremely well.

SONOMA COAST

The Sonoma Coast appellation is a mish-mash that covers all of Russian River, along with parts of Sonoma Valley and Carneros. This boundary definition came about, as did several other AVAs in California, through political grandstanding. Basically, it means that the appellation has no signature style, although there are a few sites that display special characteristics with Pinot Noir. The vineyards around the town of Cazadero, only a few miles inland

from the Pacific Ocean, are among the most prized in Sonoma. At a height of some 350 to 450 metres (1150 to 1475ft) above sea level, they are above the fog line, enabling the grapes to ripen fully in the bright sunlight. Yet the proximity to the ocean means very cool temperatures, which can make optimal ripening a problem in certain years.

These struggles allow for deeply coloured – well, purple really –, massively concentrated Pinot Noirs that are Californian versions of Chambertin. Flowers Winery is the leading estate here, while the Hirsch Vineyard has been the source for remarkable Pinot Noir for several of Sonoma's finest estates. But the State's trendsetters are also flooding in to the region. Marcassin's Chardonnays and Pinot Noirs, grown on a site 460m (1500ft) up but only one bluff in from the sea, are producing thrilling flavours, and Pahlmeyer and Marimar Torres are heading towards the coast, and Failla-Jordan, whose owner makes wine for Turley in Napa Valley, has even planted Syrah. Not all the vineyards are as high as 460m (1500ft) – Coastlands to the south, for instance, is significantly lower – and not all the vineyards are quite so close to the sea – it's a 11-km (7-mile) hike from the new Torres Dona Margarita site – but over the next few years, we're going to see some remarkable wines from the gullies, bluffs, creeks and forest glades that make up the Sonoma Coast region.

SONOMA VALLEY

The Sonoma Creek rises south-east of Santa Rosa and the Sonoma Valley AVA stretches southwards, taking in the lower slopes of the Mayacamas mountains, and bordering the Carneros AVA down

WHERE THE VINEYARDS ARE *The Russian River Valley AVA is fairly compact, but there are still marked differences in climate and terrain. In summer the great heat of the Californian sun is tempered by chill coastal air and fog drawn through the gap in the hills north of Forestville. Vineyards nearest the gap are the coolest and allow Pinot Noir to excel. The Green Valley, also affected by fog, is ideal for sparkling wine. Gravelly outcrops along the river toward Healdsburg yield most of the best sites, but others in the hills near Graton are also good. And on low ridges north-east of Windsor, Chalk Hill offers conditions that give first-rate whites.*

HEALDSBURG

WINDSOR

FORESTVILLE

GRATON

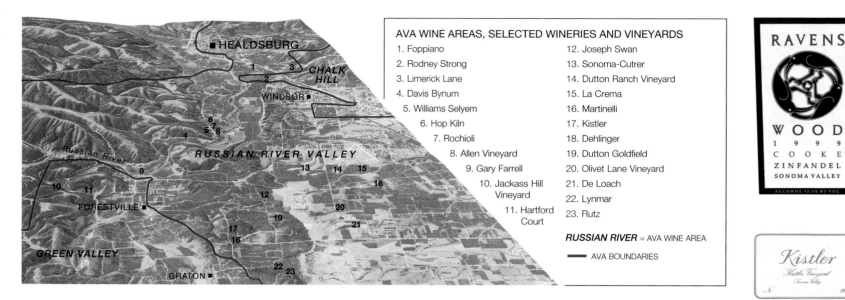

AVA WINE AREAS, SELECTED WINERIES AND VINEYARDS

1. Foppiano
2. Rodney Strong
3. Limerick Lane
4. Davis Bynum
5. Williams Selyem
6. Hop Kiln
7. Rochioli
8. Allen Vineyard
9. Gary Farrell
10. Jackass Hill Vineyard
11. Hartford Court
12. Joseph Swan
13. Sonoma-Cutrer
14. Dutton Ranch Vineyard
15. La Crema
16. Martinelli
17. Kistler
18. Dehlinger
19. Dutton Goldfield
20. Olivet Lane Vineyard
21. De Loach
22. Lynmar
23. Rutz

RUSSIAN RIVER = AVA WINE AREA
━━━ AVA BOUNDARIES

towards San Pablo Bay. From Santa Rosa south to Kenwood, some of the cooling fog and ocean air from Russian River can still be felt, but the more powerful tempering forces are the fog banks and wind that have roared through the Golden Gate gap at San Francisco, howled across Carneros and still had enough chilly life in them at Kenwood to see off any fog from the north.

This double influence does make for unpredictable, if cool, conditions, particularly south of Glen Ellen, where the Mayacamas and Sonoma mountains crowd in on the valley from the east and west. Good Chardonnay, Pinot Noir and Merlot are grown in these cooler climates – as you might expect with Carneros nudging the southern border. Zinfandel, which you might not expect, also performs well here; these versions are pure blackberry as opposed to the rich raspberry jam and dates of Dry Creek Valley.

Conditions change dramatically when you climb above the fog line. On the west-facing slopes of the Mayacamas, the greater intensity of afternoon sunshine produces deep-fruited, dark-hearted Cabernets and Zinfandels. Sonoma Mountain is also above the fog line, but has more vineyards angled east-to-north-east to avoid direct exposure to the midday and afternoon rays. With relatively warm nights due to the fogs on the valley floor pushing warmer air up the mountainsides, equally intense, but more thrillingly fragrant and soft-hearted Cabernets and Zinfandels are produced, as well as a famous Chardonnay at McCrea vineyard south-west of Glen Ellen.

CARNEROS

Carneros extends right across the bottom of the map on pages 244 to 245; to its south is the San Pablo Bay and, over its border to the north east, is the city of Napa. It is one of the most important vineyard areas in California. In the search to make wines of a supposedly European delicacy and finesse, Carneros was singled out as long ago as 1938 by Californian wine wizard André Tchelistcheff, but the region had been growing vines for maybe a century before that. It was the very un-California-ness that attracted Tchelistcheff – small crops and small grapes struggling manfully to survive in difficult soil, with not enough rain, and with fog and wind a virtual certainty throughout the growing season.

The Carneros wine region slithers across the southern end of Napa and Sonoma, the Mayacamas and Sonoma mountains splaying their feet into a series of rumpled hummocks that gradually subside into San Pablo Bay. Farmers have always known that this was

difficult soil to grow anything on, and traditionally most of it was consigned to grazing. With the lowest annual rainfall in both Napa and Sonoma counties – usually about 560mm (22in) – and a shallow, silty soil, often only a couple of feet above impenetrable, dense clay, few people felt inclined to plant anything in the area.

And then, when the search for a cool-climate vineyard began, they were converted. The Golden Gate gap at San Francisco is the only place that the Pacific Ocean actually breaches the Coast Ranges, to form the long enclosed sea of San Francisco Bay and San Pablo Bay. And as the fogs and the winds are sucked inwards by the baking heat of the inland valleys, the first land they come to is Carneros. Fogs blanket Carneros on summer nights. These clear by late morning to be replaced by bright sunshine – and then up comes the afternoon breeze, merely strong or positively howling depending on the conditions that day. The net result of this combination of hot sun and clammy fog is a very long, cool ripening period, from early March until well into October. The wind cools the vines, but its strength can also cause the vines' photosynthetic system to shut down temporarily, delaying ripening. This is almost too much for most grape varieties, but remember, even if the warmth of Carneros is not hugely different from somewhere like Chablis in Burgundy, we're at latitude 38° North here: that's the equivalent of the toe of Italy in Europe. This means that the intensity of sunshine, warm or not, is much greater in southern Italy than it is in northern France. And it's the same in Carneros. These conditions are ideal for zingy, crisp Chardonnays and tartly refreshing sparkling wines and, of course, expressive Pinot Noirs. While these Pinots were delicate wines at first, the introduction of new clones plus careful canopy management to ensure riper fruit, has resulted in a bigger, meatier and, frankly, much more exciting style.

There is the occasional Cabernet and some fine Syrah emerging from Carneros as well, particularly from vines that are set back from the Bay, but the newest star is Merlot. Just as Pomerol is better suited for Merlot than Pauillac or St-Julien in the Haut-Médoc, so too does Carneros suit this variety. Two factors are at work here: cooler temperatures and clay soils. Merlot likes both and the examples from here, as opposed to those from the middle of the valley, have greater intensity and higher acidity. Black cherry flavours and soothing textures dominate these wines, instead of the simple raspberry or cranberry fruit and, frequently, rough unripe edges, that characterize Merlot from the warmer reaches of the valley.

As virtually every inch of available land in Napa Valley seems to be under vine, growers are always on the lookout for new sites. South and east of the city of Napa, thousands of acres have been planted around American Canyon. Cool temperatures and gently rolling hillsides make the area ideal for Merlot and Chardonnay, as these grapes, used by many of the valley's premium producers, add structure and backbone to final blends. Less reassuring are plantings in the low-lying land west of Napa River as it approaches the Bay and also down towards the naval base of Skaggs Island, on land that seems barely better than swamp.

NAPA VALLEY
The Napa valley runs north-west to south-east for only about 48km (30 miles), but the difference in conditions along this short distance is dramatic. Calistoga, at the head of the valley, has a daytime climate hot enough to ripen every known red variety, and is only saved from being a cauldron in which to bake the life out of its fruit by the ice-cold air that drains down the high mountains, hemming it in on three sides. Yet down at the mouth of the valley is Carneros, chilled by fogs and gales, only able to ripen its cool-climate Pinot Noir, Merlot and Chardonnay because of the brief bursts of sun that separate the morning fogs from the afternoon wind.

And throughout most of the valley, it is still the climatic conditions that govern what types of grape are grown and what wines excel, rather than the soils and their exposure to the sun. There are, in fact, more soil types in Napa, I'm told, than in the whole of France, and some committed growers are trying to match grape variety with soil conditions as they replant. But, with a few brilliant exceptions, such as the well-drained fans of soil around Rutherford and Oakville, much of the soil on the Napa Valley floor

NAPA VALLEY, SONOMA VALLEY AND CARNEROS

TOTAL DISTANCE NORTH TO SOUTH 49KM (30 MILES)

VINEYARDS

N

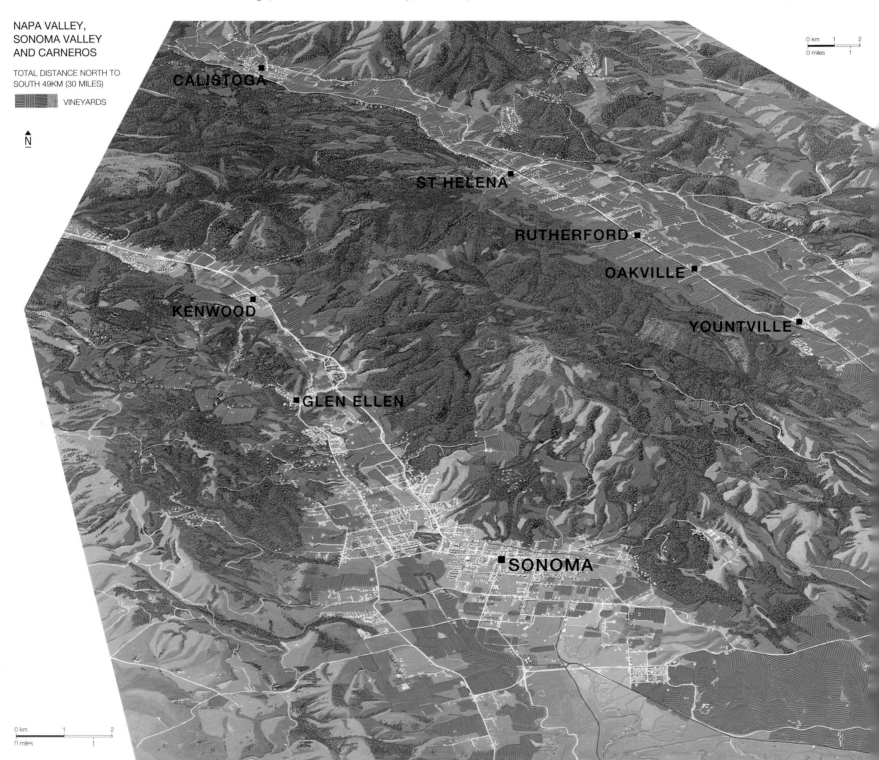

is heavy, clayish, over-fertile and difficult to drain, and certainly unfit to make great wine. There's no shame in this, because much of Bordeaux's great Médoc region cannot spawn a decent grape. The only shame is in pretending that this isn't so. The trouble is that the wines made from the good soil have been so good that every man and his dog wanted a piece of the action. When two Napa wines, a Chardonnay and a Cabernet Sauvignon, won the famous 'Judgement of Paris' tasting in 1976 against Grand Cru white Burgundy and Premier Cru Bordeaux, Napa· became a promised land – for those with ambition and money.

Vineyards were planted and wineries sprang up like mushrooms after rain; a couple of dozen wineries at the end of the 1960s had become over 300 by the beginning of 2000. And, sadly, this traffic jam of growers and producers, many blending grapes and wines from sites all over the valley and outside it as well, led to a blurring of personality and a dilution of recognizable flavours. But a clutch of fine vintages at the end of the 1990s and beginning of the 2000s, and a greater maturity among winemakers who initially were slavishly following college textbook winemaking methods, rather than allowing themselves and their grapes free rein, has begun to signal an upturn in Napa quality.

Brilliant conditions do exist in the Napa Valley, and there are more committed owners and gifted winemakers at work today than ever before, but as quality reaches an all-time high, the chief point of distress is that prices are at an all-time high too. So let's see where they grow their fruit. We'll work from north to south. And we'll stick to the valley floor first, and then look into the mountains where some of the most exciting fruit is grown.

Calistoga at the head of the valley has a touch of the frontier town about it, with a more rough-hewn feel than the other wine towns and villages, and I always head here to try to dissolve some of the black Cabernet tannin off my teeth with draughts of local ale. But it has good vineyards too. One or two mesoclimates like Storybook Mountain to the north-west of Calistoga produce startling Zinfandel; otherwise, the rocky outcrops and sandy loams produce good results with Cabernet and Merlot.

This is one of the most expensive wines produced in America. Harlan Estate's Napa Valley red is made from the Bordeaux varieties.

WHERE THE VINEYARDS ARE *So many great Californian vineyards are packed into the flatlands of Sonoma, Carneros and Napa and up on the surrounding mountains, that I hardly know where to start. But I'll try. Let's begin with Carneros at the bottom of the map. To the south, just off the map, is San Pablo Bay, whose roaring winds and billowing fogs affect all the vineyards. Their cooling influences extend up the Sonoma and Napa Valleys, lessening as they go. In the north-west are Sonoma Mountain's fine vineyards and, directly north, the Mayacamas mountains boast equally good sites. East of the Mayacamas, Spring Mountain, Mount Veeder and Howell Mountain all have fine, high-altitude vineyards. There are also excellent sites in Stags Leap and on the hills near Napa itself.*
Vines carpet the valley floor, from cool Napa right up to warm Calistoga, while the most famous sites are at Oakville and Rutherford.

NAPA ■

AVA WINE AREAS, SELECTED WINERIES AND VINEYARDS

SONOMA VALLEY AVA

1. Matanzas Creek
2. Landmark
3. St Francis
4. Chateau St Jean
5. Kenwood
6. Kistler Vineyard
7. Laurel Glen
8. Benziger
9. Kunde
10. Wellington
11. Arrowood
12. B R Cohn
13. Monte Rosso Vineyard
14. Carmenet
15. Ravenswood
16. Buena Vista
17. Gundlach-Bundschu

NAPA VALLEY AVA

18. Storybook Mountain
19. Chateau Montelena
20. Diamond Creek
21. Reverie
22. Clos Pegase
23. Araujo/Eisele Vineyard
24. Cuvaison
25. Sterling
26. Schramsberg
27. Barnett
28. Robert Keenan
29. Philip Togni
30. Cain Cellars
31. Stoney Hill
32. El Molino
33. Burgess
34. Viader
35. Dunn
36. Liparita
37. La Jota
38. Seavey
39. Neyers
40. Green & Red Vineyard
41. Bryant Family Vineyard
42. Harrison
43. Chateau Potelle
44. Mayacamas
45. Mount Veeder
46. Hess Collection
47. Havens
48. Newlan
49. Monticello
50. Altamura
51. Jade Mountain
52. Luna
53. Atlas Peak
54. Pahlmeyer
55. Robert Biale

CARNEROS AVA

56. Durrell Vineyard
57. Sangiacomo Vineyard
58. Gloria Ferrer
59. Richardson
60. Artesa
61. Truchard
62. Domaine Carneros
63. Carneros Creek
64. Acacia
65. Saintsbury
66. Bouchaine
67. Kent Rasmussen

For further wineries, see HEART OF NAPA map on pages 246–247

NAPA VALLEY –
AVA WINE AREA

── AVA ROUNDARIES

---- CARNEROS AVA BOUNDARY

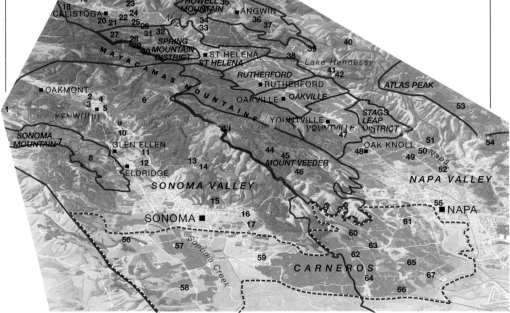

Just above St Helena, the Napa Valley changes direction: instead of running east-south-east, it alters to something more like south-south-east and keeps this orientation more or less until Carneros. As it begins to broaden out, vineyards stretch right across the valley floor, though the best, like Spottswoode and Grace Family, are still tucked into the base of the mountain slopes on either side.

The only time when there seems to be a general consensus about valley floor conditions being truly excellent over one great swathe rather than just in dribs and drabs, is at Rutherford and Oakville. All the great original Cabernet Sauvignon vineyards were planted here, some of them over a century ago, mostly on the so-called Rutherford Bench. Two alluvial fans spread out at Rutherford and at Oakville, though Rutherford attached its name to the Bench first. They are well-drained in Napa terms, though also heavy enough to hold moisture during summer, and they slope just perceptibly towards Highway 29, which is crucial for drainage. Whether or not these soils go beyond the road is one of those arguments to keep lawyers and pedants happy for generations. Suffice to say that Napa Valley Cabernet made its reputation on fruit from these Rutherford and Oakville acres.

But was it just the soil? I personally think the soil gets heavier and more cloddish east of the road, but fine Cabernets still turn up from sites not only east of the road, but east of the river too. Nevertheless, the Rutherford Bench and Oakville vineyards do seem to have struck the right balance between water-holding and drainage, between vigour and restraint, for the climatic conditions of this particular part of the Napa Valley. Imprecise, sure. But there's more than a century of experience that says it's so. This imprecise but definable balance of elements affecting the grape is what the French would call *terroir*. It took them quite a while to work it out, too.

Oakville and Rutherford are separate AVAs, and while there are fine examples of Chardonnay and Sauvignon Blanc made here, Cabernet is what both do best. As more new money has been invested in replanting and research, a separate style is starting to emerge from these districts. Rutherford, being further north, is slightly warmer and produces wines that feature black cherry and black olive fruit and a dusty, grainy, tannic flavouring, known as Rutherford Dust.

Oakville, being cooler, gets more hangtime in the vineyards, consequently producing riper wines that display a wider and wider array of black fruits. It is these flavours, from estates such as Screaming Eagle, Opus One and Harlan, that have created such a stir over the last decade. However, even within Oakville, two styles emerge. As the district runs the entire east-west length of the valley, wines vary according to where the grapes are grown.

The vineyards on the east side that receive the hotter afternoon sun (Dalla Valle) produce wines that are riper and softer in tannins than those from the west side. Wines from this cooler mesoclimate (Harlan, Far Niente) are tighter and not as sumptuous on release. These wines also show more herbaceousness and often a slight mintiness in the aroma, at least partly due to the effect of the prominent eucalyptus trees in the area.

When you drive past the bluffs in the middle of the valley, just north of Yountville, you're driving past a barrier to the fog and wind that brings about a discernible dip in temperature to their south. Yountville is decidedly cooler than Oakville and it gets even cooler down by the town of Napa. They do grow reds here, but the most impressive results are from Chardonnay.

The Mayacamas Range to the west is a collection of gaunt, thinly populated peaks, where coyotes, rattlesnakes and wild deer are as likely to impede your progress as people. But they do harbour some smashing vineyards, especially on Mount Veeder, Spring Mountain and, further north off our map, Diamond Mountain. We're talking primarily incisive, focused, powerful red wines from low-yielding volcanic soils at heights that can go past 600m (1970ft).

Stags Leap District spreads out onto the valley floor towards Yountville and up the sides of several small hillocks about a mile away from the eastern mountains proper, and produces Cabernets that are rich and pinging with fruit, yet artfully balance tannin and acidity. Many of California's wine regions have acquired their fame through relentless marketing efforts. Stags Leap is famous because its wines taste better. Higher up the eastern mountains are Atlas Peak, Chiles Valley, Pope Valley and above them all, Howell Mountain, whose vineyards have been famous since the 19th century and whose coppery red volcanic soil, exposed to the sun but cooled by its altitude of 420 to 600m (1378 to 1970ft) regularly produces some of the sturdiest but most deliciously scented reds in Napa.

0 km 1 2
0 miles 1

ST HELENA

RUTHERFORD

OAKVILLE

YOUNTVILLE

HEART OF NAPA

TOTAL DISTANCE
NORTH TO
SOUTH 18.5 KM (11½ MILES)

VINEYARDS

N

0 km 1 2
0 miles 1

You know spring is near when the mustard begins to flower. These vines, that are framed by the low ranges of the Mayacamas Mountains, are in the Rutherford area of the Napa Valley, which has been prime Cabernet territory over the last 70 years or so. The flat, benchland soils are deep and well drained, giving rich wines with lovely black cherry fruit, touched with a supple spiciness.

WHERE THE VINEYARDS ARE

The heart of the Napa Valley is really California's promised land for one great variety – Cabernet Sauvignon. The character of the wines can be refreshingly diverse, depending on whether the grapes come from the valley floor or from the surrounding mountain slopes.

On the valley floor, conditions become gradually warmer as you head north-west, away from the fogs and cold winds. Yountville's cooler conditions can produce fine Chardonnay, but Oakville and Rutherford, appreciably warmer and with well-drained vineyard sites, have long been famous for Cabernet Sauvignon.

Mount Veeder, Spring Mountain and Diamond Mountain provide a fascinating array of steeply angled, low-yielding sites on volcanic soils, well above the fog belt, but cooled by altitude. Stags Leap is a famous Cabernet stronghold, benefiting from just enough of the cool breezes off San Pablo Bay, while the grapes planted on its wide, well-drained alluvial fan ripen to perfection.

AVA WINE AREAS, SELECTED WINERIES AND VINEYARDS

1. Colgin	18. Niebaum-Coppola	33. Opus One	48. Paradigm
2. Grace Family	19. Grgich Hills	34. Harlan Estate	49. Cardinale
3. Vineyard 29	20. Beaulieu Vineyard	35. Oakford	50. Lokoya
4. Duckhorn	21. Conn Creek	36. Martha's Vineyard	51. Dominus
5. Newton	22. Frog's Leap	37. Far Niente	52. Domaine Chandon
6. Beringer	23. Caymus	38. To Kalon Vineyard	53. S. Anderson Vineyard
7. Cafaro	24. Bacio Divino	39. Etude	54. Shafer
8. Spottswoode	25. Mumm Napa	40. Saddleback	55. Silverado Vineyards
9. Merryvale	26. ZD	41. Groth	56. Pine Ridge
10. Abreu	27. Staglin Family	42. Miner Family	57. Stag's Leap Wine Cellars
11. Flora Springs	28. Swanson	43. Silver Oak	58. Chimney Rock
12. Heitz Cellars	29. St. Supéry	44. Rudd	59. Clos du Val
13. Livingston	30. Cakebread	45. Plumpjack	
14. Whitehall Lane	31. Robert Mondavi	46. Dalla Valle	
15. Franciscan	32. Turnbull	47. Screaming Eagle	
16. Joseph Phelps			
17. Quintessa			

NAPA VALLEY = AVA WINE AREA

━━━ AVA BOUNDARIES

NORTH CENTRAL COAST

RED GRAPES
Cabernet Sauvignon, Pinot Noir and Zinfandel are widely planted, while the minor varieties include Petite Sirah and Merlot.

WHITE GRAPES
Chardonnay and Sauvignon Blanc are ever-present, along with some Chenin Blanc, Riesling and Pinot Blanc.

CLIMATE
This ranges from cool and foggy when influenced by San Francisco and Monterey bays, to dry and very hot. Strong, incessant winds can also represent a threat to the vineyards. Rainfall is low.

SOIL
A wide variety of soils includes gravel, stones of considerable size, clay and loam, with occasional granite and limestone outcrops. These can be mixed, even within single vineyards.

ASPECT
Vineyard exposure is very important in order to ensure the correct ripening of the grapes. Elevation varies widely, which causes great differences in the influence of fog, wind and sunshine.

THERE AREN'T MANY OF MY FAVOURITE VINEYARDS that I can say I prefer to visit at night, but Ridge, high in the Santa Cruz Mountains, is one of them. Climb to the top of the rise above the tasting room on the night of a full moon. As the moon hangs heavy in the vast night sky, its cloak of silver stars spreadeagled across the purple blackness, the dark crags of the forested mountain peaks pierce the pale night light to the west. And to the east, 600m (1970ft) below me, lies the bustling city of San Jose, so far below that the brilliant city lights are just twinkling patterns on the valley floor. The sullen drone of its cars and businesses fades to silence halfway up my mountain slope, and away to the north, San Francisco Bay glows with a faint pewter sheen.

Ridge is the most famous of the wineries that are sprinkled sparsely around San Francisco Bay itself. There used to be many more, but as the Bay area's urban sprawl reaches further into the hinterland, few wineries or vineyards have been able to resist the temptation of the easier profits to be gained by selling up to housing developers. But that doesn't mean the companies have all gone out of business. They haven't. They've simply moved their vineyard interests further south. This North Central Coast region divides neatly into the old regions of Livermore, Santa Clara and Santa Cruz, where wineries outnumber vineyards, and the great new tracts of land centered on Monterey County, where wineries are few and far between, but contract vineyards can stretch as far as the eye can see.

You have to use your imagination in the Livermore Valley to see it as one of the original great vineyard sites of California. Getting there, either from the north or the south, is a seemingly endless trek through industrial parks and housing subdivisions that don't let up till you're right in the vineyards themselves, glancing nervously at the nuclear facility to one side and the futuristic wind generator farms to the other. But Livermore is a fine vineyard site, albeit one that has its back to the wall as the start of the new millennium decides its land is more useful for houses and factories. There are still about 650ha (1600 acres) of vines, mostly owned by the Wente family who are staunchly leading a fight against urbanization. It is relatively warm, because hills to the west block off most of the chill Pacific winds, and the gravelly Médoc-like soils promise good results from grapes like Cabernet Sauvignon. Curiously, reds are not that special, but white Bordeaux specialities – Semillon and Sauvignon Blanc – can be outstanding.

Santa Clara County's vines have been pushed relentlessly south by San Jose's suburbs, and it is really only around Gilroy that you get a sense of a wine culture still hanging on. Gilroy is the self-dubbed 'garlic capital of the world' and, boy, can you smell it when you stop on Highway 101 to fill up with gas. But good fruit is grown to the east of the town and wineries pay good money for Pinot Noir, amongst others. If you turn west off 101 and head up through the Hecker Pass, you'll find remnants of the old farmgate Italian wineries that used to pepper Santa Clara and Santa Cruz counties, and you'll find scrubby patches of bush vines of varieties like Grenache, that are at last beginning to be appreciated.

Santa Cruz County is important for its wineries, rather than its vineyards, though locals estimate there may be 160ha (395 acres) or more of vines sprinkled through the majestic forested hills that rear up on this Pacific Coast between San Francisco and the resort of Santa Cruz. Some of these vines – as those belonging to Mount Eden, David Bruce and, of course, Ridge – produce stunning wines, but much fruit is bought in from other areas. It is impossible to characterize the Santa Cruz conditions: vineyards range in height from over 600m (1970ft) high down to fog level, and their aspects can be east, south, north or west facing; the only relatively consistent features are the soil, which is largely infertile, impoverished shale – keeping yields low and contributing to the startling flavours in many of the local wines – and the likelihood of an earthquake disturbing your slumbers: the San Andreas Fault lies right alongside Ridge's winery.

Startling flavours were nearly the undoing of the other part of the North Central Coast – the vast, flat, supremely fertile, dark-soiled acres of Monterey County. The 'Monterey veggies' these unripe, green flavours were called, and since, as I head down for Santa Cruz, I pass through Watsonville, Prunedale, Castroville, Salinas and so on – towns which variously proclaim themselves World Capital of the artichoke kingdom, or prunes, or broccoli, lettuces and pretty well anything else a starving vegetarian might crave – I suppose I shouldn't be too surprised.

The Salinas Valley, in Monterey County, does have every reason to proclaim itself the Salad Bowl of America, and most of its flat valley floor is given over to intensive vegetable and fruit cultivation. However, as long ago as 1935, experts were suggesting it would be a good area for planting grape vines

MAIN AVA WINE AREAS

- •••• Central Coast AVA
- ▬ 1. San Francisco Bay
- ▬ 2. Livermore Valley
- ▬ 3. Santa Cruz Mountains
- ▬ 4. Ben Lomond Mountain
- ▬ 5. Santa Clara Valley
- ▬ 6. San Ysidro District
- ▬ 7. Pacheco Pass
- ▬ 8. Mount Harlan
- ▬ 9. Cienega Valley
- ▬ 10. Lime Kiln Valley

- ▬ 11. San Benito
- ▬ 12. Paicines
- ▬ 13. Monterey
- ▬ 14. Carmel Valley
- ▬ 15. Santa Lucia Highlands
- ▬ 16. Chalone
- ▬ 17. Arroyo Seco
- ▬ 18. San Lucas
- ▬ 19. Hames Valley
- ▢ OVER 500M (1640FT)
- ▨ OVER 1000M (3280FT)

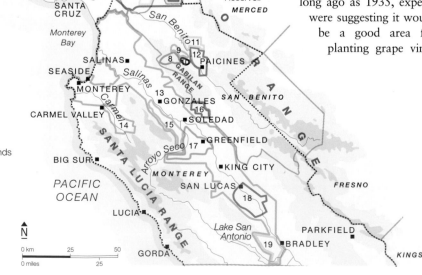

and, when vineyards in the Bay area were squeezed by urban development in the late 1950s and 1960s, big companies like Masson and Mirassou upped sticks and headed south to the Salinas Valley, planting like fury as they came.

Monterey County now has 18,700ha (46,200 acres); one vineyard alone near King City is 14 by 8km (9 by 5 miles). The only problem is they mostly planted the wrong grapes, and in the wrong places, and in particular, too many red grapes, too near the sea.

Let me explain. The first point is, as usual in California, the influence of the Pacific Ocean. Monterey Bay is about 56km (35 miles) wide and acts as an enormous funnel at the mouth of the Salinas Valley. Its waters stay a chilly 13°C (55°F) all year round. Looking south-east up the valley, the Santa Lucia mountains lie between the ocean and the valley, virtually without a break along their 138km (86 mile) length.

On the inland side, the Gabilan mountains are much more broken up, with large gaps leading through into the Central Valley. The Central Valley bakes daily under the sun, its hot air rises creating a thirsty vacuum, which then sucks the cold Monterey Bay air up the valley with sometimes terrifying ferocity. The closer to the sea, the colder and more violent the wind. It's cold enough to destroy any vine's chance of ripening, and it's violent enough to rip the branches off a tree, let alone a young vine trying to set its first crop. A lot of those first vines never even got as far as boasting a single grape.

As we move further up the Salinas Valley, the winds become milder and warmer. At Gonzales, you can just about ripen white grapes, you can ripen most red grapes by Soledad and Greenfield, and by King City, with the wind dropping to a pleasant breeze, you can ripen anything, although, so far, nobody's been thrilled by the result. There is very little rainfall throughout the valley – an average of 250mm (10in) a year – and, with the eternal sunshine, some growers claim that the valley has the longest ripening period in the world. With budbreak as early as February due to the mild winters, and an autumn that can linger on into December, they may well be right, though you'll hear the same claim from growers in Edna Valley and Santa Maria Valley further south (see page 250).

But where's the Salinas River? Right under your feet. In fact, the Salinas River is California's largest underground river and is fed by the Santa Lucia, Gabilan and Diablo ranges. Given that the soil is mostly deep, free-draining silt and sandy loam, I can see why the early pioneers saw it as a paradise for the vine. But the vine is a greedy plant, and the early plantations suffered from massive over-irrigation, leading to vigorous vines pushing out forests of foliage – and producing grapes of a decidedly green vegetable flavour that made wines with an equally vegetal taste. If we wine-enthusiastic humans were going to gain any benefit from this paradise, we were going to have to take the vine firmly in hand.

Vineyard management now, at the start of the new millenium, is far more advanced. The areas too close to the sea have been abandoned to the vegetable farmers. The cooler areas, a bit further inland, are left to white grapes, irrigation is properly controlled, and areas away from the valley floor have been developed for higher quality whites and reds – indeed, all the really exciting wines so far have come from these sites. Facing north-east towards Gonzales and Soledad are the Santa Lucia Highlands slopes. Thanks to a few growers – mainly the irreverent Gary Pisoni – this AVA has become one of the state's most revered for Pinot Noir. Once again, it's the passion of the Pinot Noir enthusiasts that pushes back the limits in California, while the producers of the easier-to-grow, easier-to-sell Merlot and Cabernet are more likely to settle contentedly in the mainstream. The wines

here share a meaty, spicy, muscular character that is attracting wineries from Sonoma, Napa and Santa Barbara to buy this fruit. Carmel Valley and Arroyo Seco have some favoured spots; and high up in the Gabilan range, both Chalone and Calera make world-class Pinot Noirs and a variety of whites in splendid limestone isolation.

A gruff old Frenchman, André Noblet, the legendary winemaker at Domaine de la Romanée-Conti at Vosne-Romanée in the heart of Burgundy, would murmur 'limestone, limestone' under his breath in response to the endless questions from callow young Americans about his marvellous wines, and the magic ingredient that made them so special. This belief in the power of limestone so devotedly held by Burgundy's top winemaker, provided the spur for Calera and Chalone, which are now two of California's most famous – and most individual – wines.

Limestone isn't easy to find in California, but is at the heart of the greatest sites in Burgundy – places where finesse usually wins over power. In the 19th century a roving Frenchman called Curtis Tamm searched along the Californian coast for years for limestone soil to make sparkling wine. He finally found what he wanted on a parched wilderness 600m (1970ft) up in the Gabilan range below the Pinnacles peaks, the site of present-day Chalone. A dozen miles north, 670m (2200ft) up on the north-east-facing slopes of Mount Harlan, Josh Jensen established Calera on limestone soils that he first had to clear of virgin scrub.

This being California, neither winery manages to make wines of Burgundian delicacy, but what they do achieve is something more exhilarating – the savage, growling, unfathomable, dark beauty of the great red wines of Burgundy's Côte de Nuits. In land that deserves a desert rating for its aridity, the grape yields are tiny (as they have to be with Pinot Noir), the methods of winemaking are traditional to a fault and, as is the case of their Burgundian role models, the Chalone and Calera Pinot Noirs are of an unpredictable yet brilliant magnificence.

Vineyards seem to stretch for ever in the Salinas Valley in Monterey County. These are at Soledad. The milk cartons in between the vines protect new plantings from rodents and, when summer comes, sunburn. The soil is very fertile and crops are planted between the rows to provide competition for the vine.

This label proudly boasts that Chardonnay grapes for this wine were grown 610m (2000ft) above the valley floor, in the Santa Cruz Mountains.

SOUTH CENTRAL COAST

RED GRAPES
While Cabernet Sauvignon has greater acreage in Santa Barbara, Pinot Noir is better suited to local conditions. In San Luis Obispo, Cabernet and Zinfandel are planted extensively.

WHITE GRAPES
Chardonnay is widely planted, with lesser amounts of Sauvignon Blanc, Riesling and Gewürztraminer.

CLIMATE
Differences are huge, being largely related to the influence of the Pacific sea fogs.

SOIL
Alkaline sandy and clay loams, with some rich limestone.

ASPECT
Paso Robles vineyards are on a valley floor, sheltered by mountains. Santa Maria has half its vines on benchlands above the fog line.

Mondavi's Byron Vineyards, in Santa Maria Valley. A part of the vineyards – the Nielson Block – was planted in 1964 and is the oldest commercial planting in the valley.

I'M AFRAID I ONLY GET TO SEE PASO ROBLES, the northernmost wine region of the so-called South Central Coast, if I'm in a hurry. There it is, straddling Highway 101 right at the source of the Salinas River; it seems easy enough to get to. But there's another road southwards from Santa Cruz and Monterey. Highway 1. Hugging the coastline, dipping and diving in and out of the cliff face and soaring up above the crashing ocean waves, and – I'm a 60s boy remember – traversing Little Sur, Point Sur and Big Sur. What am I supposed to do? Hurry down boring old 101, or bask in the glory of this wild Pacific coast?

Well, I take Highway 1, don't I? Not a vine in sight, and no passing places. I once left Santa Cruz to try to make a lunch appointment in Santa Barbara County. Unwisely, but inevitably, I took Highway 1. And I got behind a band of six camper vans, laden with spaced-out hippies dawdling contentedly down the coast, drinking in every second of the majesty of Big Sur and its stuff of dreams. Lunch? I just about made dinner. Luckily my host was a dreamer, a romantic – and an ace winemaker. He understood.

Paso Robles, though, is a good wine area. Right next door to the rather underperforming San Lucas region, it should really be taken as the southern outpost of North Central Coast rather than the northern outpost of South Central Coast. I know, I know. Does it really matter? No. Do I care? No. It's just another example of the AVA system doggedly following political boundaries, rather than geological ones. Paso Robles is the high point in the Salinas Valley that runs north-west through Monterey County to the sea. And its hot, dry climate is the natural progression from foggy and cold at the seaward end to baking and arid at its head as the influence of Monterey Bay's chilly waters is finally dissipated under the burning sun. But the San Luis Obispo County line crunches across the map about 14km (8 miles) north of Paso Robles, so Paso Robles is in South Central.

Never mind that a 460-m (1500-ft) high pass has to be traversed to get down to the sea level of San Luis Obispo. Nor that San Luis Obispo's reputation is for some of the coolest-climate fruit in the whole of California, as the fog and sea breezes chill Edna Valley and Arroyo Grande so successfully that some of the most Burgundian Chardonnay in the state comes from Edna Valley, and some of the most characterful Pinot Noir comes from Arroyo Grande. Well, that's the way it is. So let's turn back up 101 as it heads away from the sea at San Luis Obispo and climbs to the hot inland gaps at Paso Robles.

There are several reasons why Paso Robles makes an increasing amount of red wine. It is divided from the Pacific to the west by the 900-m (2950-ft) Santa Lucia Range. Even the California fogs and sea winds can't get over that, although a stiff breeze sometimes works its way up to Templeton along Highway 46 and even causes ripening difficulties for Cabernet in one or two spots south of Templeton.

To assist the last gasps of ocean breeze puffing up the valley from Monterey or along Highway 46, you've got altitude. The vineyards are at between 180–300m (590–985ft), though the small, cool York Mountain area west of Paso Robles reaches 500m (1640ft) above sea level. And being protected from the maritime influence means that the temperature plummets at night. In the scorching months of July and August, the difference between day and night temperatures is usually over 28°C (50°F). That's great for the flavour of the fruit. And it is fruit quality that makes Paso Robles exciting. That, and a willingness to break the stranglehold of Cabernet Sauvignon. Paso Robles does have a lot of Cabernet, almost 2833ha (7000 acres) out of a total of 8094ha (20,000 acres) of vineyard. Cabernet grows mostly on its east side, on river terraces and the rolling grassland of the Estrella Prairie to the north east, but it has a joyous ripe quality and minimal tannic intrusion that makes for some of California's eminently approachable examples.

The limestone soils to the west are home to numerous old Zinfandel plantings, and both sides of the valley are becoming more interesting for their plantings of Rhône and Italian varieties. The creation of an estate to grow Rhône varieties near Adelaida to the west of Paso Robles by the Perrin Brothers, who own Château de Beaucastel in Châteauneuf-du-Pape, is a clear indication that things are getting exciting down here. Interestingly, it was their Rhône-style whites which shone first, as the brothers discovered that a headstrong area like the Paso Robles takes a few vintages to reveal how to grow the grapes and make the wine.

WHERE THE VINEYARDS ARE *This map shows in dramatic manner the way that the sea's influence makes great vineyards possible in California. The sea may look nice and blue on the map, but more likely it will be covered with a thick blanket of fog during the summer and, wherever there is a break in the mountains for a river to force its way to the sea, this blanket will stream inland for between 16 and 32km (10 and 20 miles). But that wouldn't have looked so nice, so we chose a rare sunny summer's day.*

Right at the top of the map, look how dry and parched the land seems to be around Paso Robles. It is parched, and the vineyards here are only slightly cooled by air currents from the Salinas Valley to the north and the odd breeze from the west, that comes up from the sea through what is known as the Templeton Gap. Most of the vineyards are in the dry lands, east of Paso Robles, but there are some excellent sites in the wooded hills to the west.

However, near San Luis Obispo, Edna Valley and Arroyo Grande are both strongly influenced by maritime cool, and the vineyards just east of Arroyo Grande are some of the coolest for Pinot Noir in the state. It's far too cold for vines west of Santa Maria, but south and east, the conditions are perfect. Many people think this may prove to be one of California's top vineyard regions for Chardonnay and Pinot Noir – and I'm one of them. Lompoc is also too cold, but a few miles east along the Santa Ynez Valley are some of the best cool-climate vineyards in California, gradually warming up as the valley opens out at Santa Ynez and Los Olivos.

EDNA VALLEY AND ARROYO GRANDE

On into the real San Luis Obispo, and the areas of Edna Valley and Arroyo Grande. Neither is big, neither is well known, but both are exceptional. Edna Valley's forte is Chardonnay, and I can vividly remember the first example I tried. It was a 1979 or 1980 – it's not important, really – from Edna Valley Vineyards, made by Dick Graff, winemaker at Chalone. It was dry yet luscious, lean yet viscous with a heavenly savoury quality: butter melting on toast or hazelnuts lightly grilling over a log fire. Such wine was rare enough from Puligny-Montrachet; from California, it was a revelation.

Sparkling wine used to be the strong point for Arroyo Grande, but as sales of domestic bubbly have been less than buoyant, much of that production has shifted to still Chardonnay and Pinot Noir. Of the two, Pinot Noir is the star varietal in Arroyo Grande; the ripe plum and black cherry fruit and fine structure make this one of the state's most underrated regions for the grape.

The climate has much to do with the quality of Pinot Noir here. While it is obviously warmer than Burgundy's Côte d'Or, it is cool and temperate by Californian standards, with an early February budbreak and flowering, yet a long, gentle ripening period and,

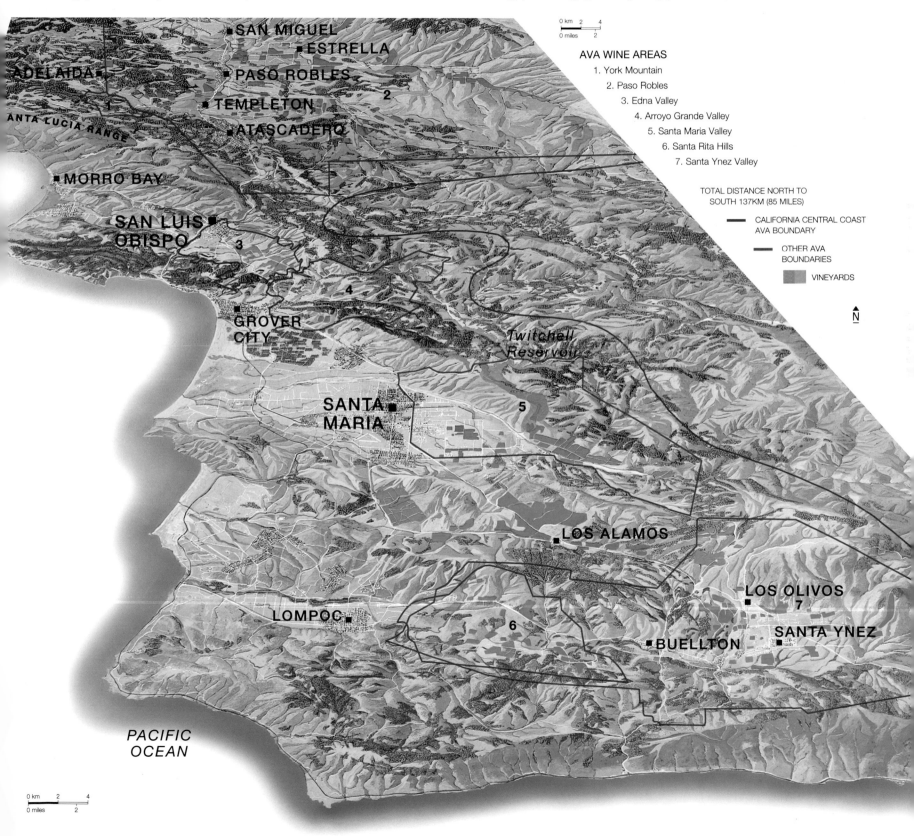

AVA WINE AREAS
1. York Mountain
2. Paso Robles
3. Edna Valley
4. Arroyo Grande Valley
5. Santa Maria Valley
6. Santa Rita Hills
7. Santa Ynez Valley

TOTAL DISTANCE NORTH TO SOUTH 137KM (85 MILES)

—— CALIFORNIA CENTRAL COAST AVA BOUNDARY

—— OTHER AVA BOUNDARIES

VINEYARDS

This wine isn't shy of telling us how good it is – 'Incredible Red' it's called. With some reason, because Peachy Canyon in warm Paso Robles does produce powerful Zinfandel.

interestingly, the morning fogs become more frequent in autumn, making the grapes susceptible to noble rot – which, for Chardonnay, adds that touch of magical richness in the finished wine as harvest sometimes lingers on as late as November.

Arroyo Grande also has marine deposits in its soil, which improves fruit quality, along with a fair bit of clay loam. Laetitia, which bought out sparkling wine producer Deutz, has the area's vineyards that are nearest to the ocean, planted with Pinot Noir, Chardonnay and Pinot Blanc. The highest part of the valley is hot enough to ripen Zinfandel – from a patch of vines planted in 1879 – and in between, excellent Pinot Noir and Chardonnay are grown by Talley Vineyards. All in the space of less than 16km (10 miles).

SANTA MARIA VALLEY

Onward down the 101, and over another county line into Santa Barbara County, and the Santa Maria Valley region. I'm beginning to pine for Highway 1 and Big Sur again, because this is monotonous country. As I swoop into the wide valley, the dusty anonymous town of Santa Maria sprawls away to my right, and to the left, inland, it looks like yet another sub-'East of Eden' lettuce prairie spreading gloomily away to the distant hills. It may not look much, but the Santa Maria Valley is one of California's most important fine wine regions, in particular producing Chardonnay that frequently puts better-known vineyard areas north of San Francisco to shame, as well as exciting Pinot Noir and Syrah.

There are several parallels with the development of Monterey's Salinas Valley further north. During the 1960s and 1970s, as demand for wine boomed, various farmers decided to give grapes a try, and planted what rapidly became vast spreads of grapes grown almost entirely for purchase by wineries in other regions which were desperate for a decent supply. This was fine while the demand for grapes outstripped supply, but the 1980s saw a serious over-supply situation develop, just as the region was finally proving its worth and the reputation for Santa Maria Chardonnay and Pinot Noir was rocketing. With banks and insurance companies repossessing the land, but not at all keen to get into the grape-growing business, three of California's most important quality wineries – Mondavi, Beringer and Kendall-Jackson – put their money where their mouths were and snapped up vast tracts of prime vineyard land to stop any of their rivals getting their hands on it. We consumers have been the beneficiaries of greatly improved Chardonnays from these three players. So, as in the Salinas Valley, most of the vineyard land is owned in large blocks, and there are very few local wineries. But in terms of quality, Santa Maria has won hands down over the Salinas Valley so far.

Sea fogs play a part, yet again. Santa Maria must be one of the least pleasant of all wine towns to live in – it gets on average 87 days a year of heavy fog, generally in the late summer to autumn period. The late summer is particularly bad when deep, cold ocean currents well up and are carried landward as the summer

SANTA MARIA AND SANTA YNEZ VALLEYS

TOTAL DISTANCE
NORTH TO
SOUTH 45KM
(28 MILES)

VINEYARDS

N

SANTA MARIA

LOS OLIVOS

BUELLTON

SOLVANG

progresses, and are pushed southwards along the California coast. By August these cold currents are icing up the shoreline as far south as Santa Barbara County. The wet off-shore winds are cooled right down and head inland to meet warm inland air head on – *et voilà* – fog. Loads of it.

But remember we're a long way south here. The sun is incredibly powerful; glance up at the hilltops on both sides of the Santa Maria Valley and they are scorched and windswept. So the fog may ooze in from the sea, but it is burnt off by the sun. Yet as soon as that happens, cool ocean breezes take up the slack. So there's loads of sun, but it is always being tempered by the ocean.

The average summer temperature is only 24°C (75°F), but the crucial thing is that the heat peak is at 1.30pm, after which up come those chilly ocean breezes that get to work sparing the grapes from the danger of roasting under a hot afternoon sun. (North of San Francisco in the better-known areas of Sonoma and Napa counties, the heat peak is often about 4pm.) Add to that an early budding and flowering in Santa Maria – and, because of the more southerly latitude, a long, reliable autumn giving the grapes extra time to hang on the vine – along with the odd touch of noble rot again, and you've got Chardonnay nirvana if it's handled properly.

Mostly it is. The soil here is a mix of sandy loam and marine limestones which don't encourage foliage vigour, and lead to yields that can be as little as two or three tons an acre – that's low for California. Most of the vines are managed extremely competently by farmers who know that – stuck in the middle of a not very attractive nowhere as they are – quality is everything. With average rainfall running at between just 300 and 380mm (12 and 15in) a year, irrigation is essential, but so far, it hasn't been abused.

Most of the 2000ha (4940 acres) or so of vineyards lie on a curious ledge to the north of the Santa Maria river, though there are a few excellent properties quite close to Santa Maria township on the south side of the river. Chardonnay is the clear favourite, but Pinot Noir can be spectacular (from Au Bon Climat and others) and the Bien Nacido ranch was one of the earliest sites in California to show superb results with the Rhône varieties Syrah

and Viognier. And a few miles further south, over the Solomon Hills, there are considerable plantings – of about 3050ha (7539 acres) – in Los Alamos, an area without an AVA, but with a good reputation for Chardonnay and for Pinot Noir.

SANTA YNEZ VALLEY

While the Santa Maria Valley goes from ultra-cool to, well, mild at best, the Santa Ynez Valley goes from equally cool to hot, so much so that it's hot enough for Cabernet Sauvignon, Merlot and the Rhône varieties to ripen easily in the upstream vineyards. But whereas the Santa Maria Valley is very broad-mouthed, rapidly narrowing as it turns from west to south, Santa Ynez is narrow near the sea, opening out and fragmenting inland above Solvang.

The whole feeling of the valley, only a short distance north of the city of Santa Barbara, couldn't be more different from that of Santa Maria. There are numerous small estates, fine homes, ancient trees and paddocks sporting handsome stallions. It's wealthy country with more than a sprinkling of Hollywood and Los Angeles glamour about it, and this can't have hindered its entry into the limelight during the 1970s as the source of California's supposedly finest Pinot Noirs.

In fact, those early Pinot Noirs were pretty weird, but underlying the maverick winemaking there was a core of exciting fruit, most of all from the mean, shaly soils of the Sanford & Benedict Vineyard 11km (7 miles) west of Buellton, and 29km (18 miles) from the coast. Located at between about 25 and 40km (15 and 25 miles) from the sea, this area is known as the Santa Rita Hills, and has been planted with Pinot Noir and Chardonnay by more than a dozen of the county's finest producers. A combination of north-facing slopes avoiding the direct strong afternoon sun along with fog and sea breezes shrouding the vines have convinced some that this may be the greatest site for Pinot Noir in the whole of California. How many 'greatest sites' does that make, you may ask. I don't know, but the wonderful thing is that when it comes to Pinot Noir and excellence, so many people care.

Machine-harvesting is common in California, but many producers prefer to trust human pickers. These vines are at Sanford's La Rinconada vineyard, near Buellton in the Santa Ynez Valley.

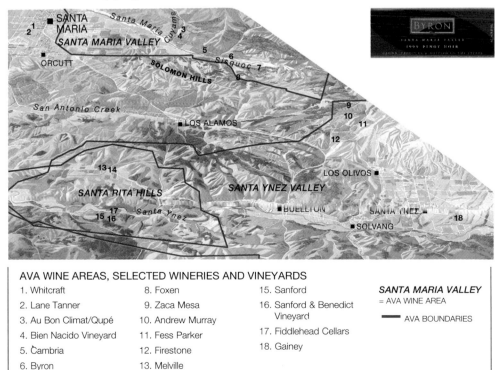

AVA WINE AREAS, SELECTED WINERIES AND VINEYARDS

1. Whitcraft	8. Foxen	15. Sanford
2. Lane Tanner	9. Zaca Mesa	16. Sanford & Benedict Vineyard
3. Au Bon Climat/Qupé	10. Andrew Murray	17. Fiddlehead Cellars
4. Bien Nacido Vineyard	11. Fess Parker	18. Gainey
5. Cambria	12. Firestone	
6. Byron	13. Melville	
7. Rancho Sisquoc	14. Babcock	

SANTA MARIA VALLEY = AVA WINE AREA

— AVA BOUNDARIES

SANTA YNEZ

0 km   1   2
0 miles   1

CENTRAL & SOUTHERN CALIFORNIA

ISUPPOSE I SHOULD APOLOGIZE for allowing the region that produces four out of every five bottles of California's wine less than a full page to itself, but the trouble is, there's not a lot to say about most of the wine, and there's not a lot to say about most of the region. A minute proportion of the wine actually proclaims its provenance as California's Central Valley – or, more correctly, the San Joaquin Valley – and my chief problem in driving around the interminably flat, sunbaked and over-irrigated land is trying to stay awake.

Yet the valley is a triumph of agro-industry, even if glamour is signally absent, and indeed an air of moody secretiveness hangs over not only the massive wine complexes, but the other enormous vegetable and fruit concerns that dominate the landscape. The Central Valley is not a place to linger in; strangers don't receive too warm a welcome down here.

Technically, there are two parts to the Central Valley – the San Joaquin Valley and the Sacramento River Valley – and there is a significant difference between the two, because around Sacramento, and pushing just a little south towards Lodi, the cool maritime breezes can still make their way up through the gap the Sacramento River has forged in the Coast Ranges. At Lodi, at Clarksburg below the daunting levees of the Sacramento River delta, and in parts of Solano County just above San Pablo Bay, interesting table wines can be produced.

However, the awesome vastness of the Central Valley starts south of Lodi. This is where a substantial amount of the United States' vegetables and fruit are produced, as well as the massive majority of its wine. There are wineries that would dwarf oil refineries, producing more than many serious wine-producing nations. Gallo has four plants, with a combined output of about 6.3 million hl (138 million gallons) per annum. Chile's current annual output is only around 5.5 million hl (120 million gallons), and Australia's around 8 million hl (176 million gallons).

The vineyards run right down to Bakersfield, a distance of 370km (230 miles) and the deep fertile soils can spread as wide as 110km (70 miles) between the Coast Ranges and the Sierra Nevada. There is almost no moderating influence for the overpowering heat, and there's precious little rain, but two

We're looking at some of California's highest vineyards at Lava Cap winery. Vines here in El Dorado County, up in the foothills of the Sierra Nevada, are planted as high as 1000m (3300ft), almost at the limit of grape-growing.

reservoir and canal systems based on 19th-century irrigation schemes draw off all the water from the Sierra Nevada range for hundreds of miles making rain irrelevant.

Few producers have made a name for quality wine, although, given the torrid conditions, there have been some high-quality fortified wines created. Andrew Quady at Madera makes the best of these, and his imagination was fired by a batch of Zinfandel grapes from Amador County in the Sierra Foothills in the early 1980s. If the Central Valley can seem like a new millennium nightmare, the attractive Sierra Foothills towns can just as easily seem like a delightful leftover from more than a century ago.

SIERRA FOOTHILLS

This is where the great goldrush began in 1848 and, just as gold fever gripped the nation in Australia, so it did in California. Gold miners have massive thirsts and, by the 1870s, there were more than 100 wineries, largely in El Dorado and Amador counties. Some of the ancient Zinfandel vines still bear fruit and, though more fashionable varieties have made their mark, and Sangiovese, of all things, is now attracting attention, dark, alcoholic, massively flavoured Zinfandels are still what the Sierra Foothills does best.

The vineyards can be as high as 900m (2950ft) around Placerville in El Dorado, but are likely to be just over 300m (985ft) in the main Amador area of the Shenandoah Valley and anywhere from 450 to 750m (1476 to 2460ft) in Fiddletown.

The highest vineyards attract rainfall of up to 1150mm (45in) a year, the lower ones less than 760mm (30in). Differences between day- and night-time temperatures are similarly more extreme in the higher vineyards, helped by night-time mountain breezes and the tail end of maritime breezes off San Francisco Bay. But in the ripening season, daytime temperatures usually hover between 27 and 38°C (80 and 100°F) and the resulting mix of tannin and intensity of fruit makes for some of California's most impressive and traditional wines.

SOUTHERN CALIFORNIA

South of Santa Barbara, the coast takes a long lurch eastward, and the effects of the ice-cold waters are largely lost. There is only one more vineyard region of significance along this coast – Temecula. Situated 38km (24 miles) inland to the south-east of Los Angeles, it's a strange spot. Its high elevation – 430m (1400ft) – gives it a welcome cool edge and the mild Pacific breezes also help, but even so, this far south, you'd expect red wine to be the major player. In fact, almost all Temecula's best wine is white.

As in the Livermore Valley, east of San Francisco Bay, urban expansion is squeezing the vineyard areas, although local politicians and property developers regard vineyards as part of the lifestyle they are trying to promote. Disastrously, though, the area has been hit by a deadly vine ailment called Pierce's Disease. The bacterial infection has no known cure and is spread by the glassy-winged sharpshooter. While researchers race to find ways to combat the disease, vine damage has been so significant over the last few years that the future of Temecula viticulture is in question.

Pierce's Disease has, in fact, been present in California for over 100 years, and even the leading areas of Napa and Sonoma accept losses. Temecula's sad notoriety is based upon it being the entry point for the glassy-winged sharpshooter, brought over from Florida on ornamental plants. With no known predators on the West coast and an ability to travel considerable distances per day, all of California's vineyards are at risk. The Central Valley already has infestations, and the probability is that the insect and its deadly disease will travel inexorably northwards.

SOUTHERN & MID-WEST STATES

NEW MEXICO LIKES TO CLAIM that it is the original winemaking state of what is now the USA and, I must say, there's no reason why it shouldn't. The conquistadores headed up from Mexico along the Rio Grande – and it makes sense to me that they'd have planted vines to rectify the extremely haphazard supply of hooch from Spain. They'd have found it tricky, though. Rainfall is very sparse – as little as 200mm (8in) a year around Albuquerque – and the height of the Rio Grande Valley, rising to 2000m (6560ft) at Santa Fe, not only makes for savage winter frosts, but also extremely cold summer nights and, consequently, very acid grapes.

Nowadays, all these factors are considered to be advantages when trying to grow grapes with good flavours. Irrigation water is now readily available, winter frosts can be countered by piling up earth round the vines as protection and, without the high-altitude cold, it would be too hot to grow decent *vinifera* grapes. Wineries like Anderson Valley produce remarkably good Cabernet Sauvignon wine, but that ability to ripen grapes in the relentless sun yet preserve high acids has, not surprisingly, led to some excellent fizz being made by producers such as Gruet, Domaine Cheurlin and Mont-Jallou.

The high altitude has also attracted winemakers to Colorado, at about 1200m (3940ft) up along the Grand Valley of the Colorado River, where a clutch of wineries make intense, rather piercing *vinifera* wines for a chic and well-heeled holiday crowd, as well as Colorado Cellars' Alpenglo – a sweetish Riesling given a sunset hue by adding a tiny amount (1.5 per cent to be precise) of red Lemberger juice. High altitude is also what makes decent wine possible in Arizona. Plantings here go as high as 1460m (4800ft): Callaghan Vineyards at Elgin, near Tucson exploit the relentless sunshine tempered by mountain coolness and dramatic differences between day and night temperatures to produce not only memorable reds based on Zinfandel, Syrah and the Bordeaux varieties, but also thrilling white blends based on anything from Riesling to Viognier.

But the slumbering giant of south-west wine is Texas. I've been tasting these wines since the boom-time days of the 1983 vintage, when the volume of production was doubling every year, and you could catch vintners like Bobby Cox of Pheasant Ridge making gobsmacking assertions like, 'If half the cotton fields on the high plains around Lubbock were planted to grapes, we could produce as much wine as all of France'.

I'm sure you could, Bobby, but you'd have to make sure the stuff tasted decent if you weren't going to oversee the biggest bust in viticultural history. And the trouble throughout the 1980s was that ambitious vineyard developments simply weren't matched by good winemaking skills. From the biggest vineyard to the smallest – well, relatively smallest; this is Texas after all – I didn't taste one exciting wine, and most ranged from dreary to worse.

Somehow you would expect Texans to be able to conquer all their problems simply through money, effort and sheer self-belief. Perhaps, therefore, it is humbly reassuring to realize that establishing a wine culture is considerably more complicated than that. There do seem to be several areas that are suitable for viticulture. The High Plains near Lubbock in north-west Texas, at around 1200m (4000ft) above sea level, have dramatic shifts between day and night-time temperatures, deep, fairly loose, limestone soil and low humidity, yet a reasonable amount of rainfall. The West Texas Mountains are surprisingly cool. And the

Texas Hill Country around Austin is, indeed, vaguely hilly, and there's a fair amount of decent limestone and sandy loam soil there as well as some cool mesoclimates.

Scattered sparsely through these vast and isolated regions and Dallas-Fort Worth in the north-east are a mere 30 or so wineries, almost all miles, if not hundreds of miles, from their nearest winemaking neighbour. From these, good Cabernets, Chardonnays, Sauvignon Blancs and Rieslings emerge from time to time, but I expect Texan flavours to be brash and assertive – and these aren't. What the wines are, though, are cleaner and more correct than they were before. Maybe they're in the transitional phase of correctness before daring to start expressing themselves. In which case, they really should ring up some of their colleagues in Colorado, New Mexico and Arizona to see what a bit of daring and conviction will achieve. After all, we expect nothing less from Texans. In general, the rest of the south finds it pretty difficult to grow decent grapes. But that doesn't mean that they haven't had a damn good try. Napoleon's soldiers planted Cabernet Sauvignon vines in Alabama when they were left at a loose end after the French defeat at the Battle of Waterloo. Mississippi, which kept Prohibition on the statute books until as recently as 1966, understandably hasn't been a hotbed of activity, and indeed many other southern states still have local by-laws restricting or even forbidding the sale of alcohol. But there is still a wine industry, and in several of the states, they've made a virtue out of necessity by championing non-*vinifera* wine.

Scuppernong isn't exactly a poetic title for a grape variety, but it is the leading member of the Muscadine varieties of *Vitis rotundifolia* that manage to survive the humidity and heat on the Gulf of Mexico and round to the southern Atlantic seaboard. These are massive vines – a single wild Scuppernong vine can cover an acre – and the grapes, which can be 2.5cm (1in) in diameter, grow in loose clusters, so resisting the rot that is the scourge of tightly bunched *vinifera* grapes down here. The wine flavour is musky and distinctly fruity, and was the basis for Virginia Dare – for some years after Prohibition the bestselling wine in the US. I have to say, when I've been down in the Gulf, I find the humidity such a challenge that Cabernet Sauvignon is the last thing on my mind, but a chilled tumbler of Scuppernong makes a really pleasant drink.

Even so, there are some *vinifera* plantings. The magnificent Chateau Biltmore in North Carolina has a 32-ha (80-acre) vineyard. Swiss, Germans and Italians planted vines in Arkansas in the 19th century and, particularly around Altus in the state's north-west, vines still do well. Further north, Missouri actually had the first AVA granted – for Augusta in 1980 – though most of the state's wineries grow hybrids and *labrusca*, rather than *vinifera* grapes. And all the states bordering the Great Lakes in the north have some sort of wine industry.

Even Minnesota and Wisconsin squeeze a few wines out of mainly hybrid vines. Indiana has a mix of hybrid and *vinifera* plantations struggling along. But Michigan and Ohio do better than that. Michigan is the USA's fifth biggest wine producer, and though a lot of it is hybrid and *labrusca*, there's a healthy clutch of wineries on the south-eastern shores of Lake Michigan, as well as some delicious Riesling from the Leelanau peninsula further north.

In the 19th century, Ohio used to grow more grapes than California and, while those days are long gone, the conditions that prevail along the south shore of Lake Erie and on the offshore islands to the north of Sandusky, aided by the warm waters of this shallow lake, are good enough to produce some excellent Chardonnay and Riesling as well as those hybrids and *labruscas*.

This looks more like a blasted heath than a vineyard, but these high-altitude vines near Elgin, Arizona produce excellent grapes.

Arizona Zinfandel: Callaghan's mountain vineyards, mixing bright sunshine with cool temperatures produce startling, intense reds and whites.

PACIFIC NORTHWEST

IT'S HARD TO IMAGINE TWO more totally different wine regions than those of Washington's Columbia River Valley and of Oregon's Willamette Valley. The Willamette Valley has a gentle, long-settled rural quality, with quietly prosperous, self-contained families that run back generations tending the farm. It's more like New England than the next-door state to California, or more like one of the bucolic counties of Old England, such as Gloucestershire or Herefordshire.

The Columbia Valley is a desperate desert of a place – wild, empty, and far too savage for most people to settle in, however hardy they are. And through this inhospitable desperado's backyard runs the great Columbia River and, here and there along its banks, are vast spreads of green gardens sprouting in the desert. Not people, not nice friendly communities, gabled barns and paddock fences – just the raw bones of fields and crops, against an eerie wilderness of bleached sagebrush ranges.

Yet both owe their existence to the same geographical phenomena. And both owe their rise from obscurity to international renown to a desire to prove that California and its particular styles of wine, based in the 1960s and 1970s upon big, ripe, assertive flavours, weren't the only valid American styles, and maybe weren't even the best.

The best place to read the geological tale is in Ted Jordan Meredith's *Northwest Wine* (out of print but available in libraries), where the author makes the activities of the earth's plates, volcanoes and rivers over millions of years sound as fresh and immediate as a news report. I'll just précis the story – but it's a vital story since the activities of the tectonic plates in America's Pacific Northwest are still visible today. Remember Mount St Helens exploding in 1980? That was the tectonic plates in action.

What has been happening for millions of years in the Pacific Northwest is that the Oceanic plate has been crunching up against the Continental plate and sinking beneath it, at the same time depositing sedimentary layers on the Continental crust and pushing it upwards.

This uplift has pushed the Willamette area above sea level and created the Coast Ranges, which ward off just enough of the cold Pacific influences to make the Willamette Valley an ideal cool-climate vineyard area. Meanwhile, the Oceanic plate keeps on pressing inland, deeper and deeper below the Continental plate, until it melts. And about 160km (100 miles) inland the molten basalt forces itself upwards creating the series of volcanic peaks known as the Cascades.

As the Mount St Helens eruption showed, this process is ongoing, and parts of the volcano are only 2000 years old. The youth of the Cascades explains the majestic soaring beauty of the major peaks and the overall height of the range, often reaching 3650m (12,000ft). Almost all the ocean influences – the breezes, fogs and rain – get stopped by this mountain barrier. To its east is the virtual desert of the Columbia River basin – endless sunshine, almost no rain. All it took was human ingenuity to harness the Columbia's mighty flow for irrigation and you had one of the world's great unnatural vineyards.

There's a lot more to the story than this – massive floods of lava sweeping across thousands of square miles of landscape at some 50km (30 miles) an hour; these enormous lava flows being buckled into ridges as the west coast itself moves northward; vast glacial floods up to 300m (985ft) deep scouring the landscape during the last ice age. If you want to get excited about geology and geography, the Pacific Northwest is the place to do it. And it explains the almost primeval desolation of so much of the land east of the Cascades.

THE FIRST VINEYARDS

The Willamette Valley has been settled since the first migrants arrived along the Oregon trail, and parts of the Columbia, the Yakima and Snake River valleys have been exploited agriculturally for the best part of a century, but none had been exploited for classic wine grapes. Western Oregon was reckoned to be too cool and damp for *vinifera* varieties. The Columbia Valley in

This may not look like a vineyard yet, but these plastic 'grow-tubes' accelerate the growth of new vines by as much as a year. This is a new vineyard of Sangiovese vines at Kiona Vineyards in Washington's Yakima Valley. Sangiovese – more at home in central Italy – is proving a tricky variety to get right in the United States.

eastern Washington was simply too far over the Cascades from any sizeable market and, although moderating winter influences did come from the Columbia River, these weren't always able to combat periodic bouts of intense winter frost, as freezing weather from Alaska got caught in the Columbia River basin.

And yet, beginning in the 1960s and continuing through the 1970s, these two totally different wine regions grew and flourished together. Oregon's cool, wet Willamette Valley was sought out by Californians keen on cool-climate grapes like Pinot Noir, Riesling and more recently Pinot Gris, and by refugees from the big, brash California way of living.

In Washington State in the early 1960s, a group of university professors founded a little wine company (Associated Vintners) to produce homemade wine from some *vinifera* grapes they'd located in the Yakima Valley. At the time, the state was suffering from archaic liquor laws and its wine industry was based on cheap, sweet fortified wine made out of *labrusca* grapes. Within a decade the company – now renamed Columbia – was fashioning new vineyards out of the sagebrush along the Yakima and Columbia rivers, together with a big new operation based on a Yakima growers' co-operative called Chateau Ste Michelle, owned and generously financed by US Tobacco. Chateau Ste Michelle came here looking for an alternative to the wine regions further to the south – land was expensive and egos were big in the California of the 1970s.

Columbia and Chateau Ste Michelle studied the figures for eastern Washington and saw a healthy bottom line, based not on cheap bulk but on high-quality wine, grown in controlled conditions at a latitude similar to that of Bordeaux.

With slower ripening fruit, and the combinations of long sunny days and chilly nights giving higher acids than California, yet ample sugar, Washington wine producers realized that perhaps they could approach the European ideal of a balanced wine more easily than their California colleagues, and they have based their business on this argument ever since.

The European card has worked for both states. Oregon's Eyrie Vineyard's 1975 Pinot Noir equalled Burgundy's greatest reds in a 1979 'Olympiad' held in Paris, and since then Pinot Noir has been Oregon's greatest achievement. However, some 35 years after the first planting of Pinot Noir in the Willamette Valley, consistent success has not yet been achieved. Which is fair enough. It's a very marginal climate. It took Burgundy a thousand years to get sorted. Thirty-five years is early yet.

Washington's first great success came with Riesling, but the market moved quickly on, and first Semillon and Sauvignon and now Chardonnay dominate white plantings. But the market moved again – to red – and now Merlot and Cabernet with Syrah in hot pursuit are making all the running. The red varieties have taken to Washington conditions with enthusiasm, and give fruit of a powerful, individual style. Not all the wines have so far matched fruit quality, but each

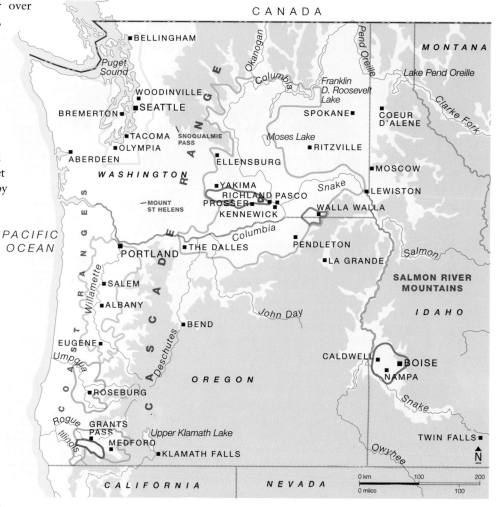

year produces more star performers. Yakima and Columbia flavours needed taming. Sorting out how to grow the fruit wasn't difficult, but Washington, like Oregon, learns with each vintage how to make the best wine from some of America's best vineyards.

IDAHO

There is a third member of the Pacific Northwest wine family – Idaho. Idaho's winemaking tradition actually goes back to the 19th century, when European immigrants brought winemaking ambitions with them, and an Idaho wine won a prize at the 1898 Chicago World Fair. But Idaho was a keen prohibitionist state, and for most of the 20th century the potato saw off the grape without too much difficulty. But there's something catching about the wine bug. Idaho now has over 445ha (1100 acres) of vineyard planted with 11 varietals, and 13 wineries producing varietal wines.

Even so, if it weren't for fruit farms wanting to diversify, Idaho wouldn't seem a perfect spot for a wine industry. The Snake River does allow some moderating maritime influence to flow up from the Columbia Valley, which is necessary, because the Idaho vineyards are high, at 600m (1970ft) above sea level. They enjoy hot bright summer days, but intensely cold nights – and are continually at risk from frost. Many of the best wines have been made from grapes grown in Washington, but even though the daytime temperatures can be hot, the very cold nights and the foreshortened, high-altitude growing season leave me wondering whether homegrown grapes can ever really ripen fully here. There is some extremely good Idaho sparkling wine, however – but then, the best sparklers tend to come from not fully ripe grapes.

Andrew Will is one of Washington's top winemakers, but his winery is on the forested Vashon Island west of Seattle. His Merlot grapes, however, come from some of the state's best vineyards east of the Cascade Mountains.

WASHINGTON STATE

RED GRAPES
Merlot is the main grape, followed by Cabernet Sauvignon, Syrah, Cabernet Franc and Sangiovese. The hardy Lemberger is popular in the Yakima Valley.

WHITE GRAPES
Riesling was the first success in Washington State. Semillon and Sauvignon Blanc are now out-planted by Chardonnay. Viognier and Pinot Gris are gaining in popularity.

CLIMATE
There can be very dramatic contrasts between summer and winter temperatures. The region west of the Olympic Mountains has a maritime climate with high rainfall. East of the Cascades, the pattern is continental and some areas are semi-desert.

SOIL
Most of the Columbia Valley is basaltic sand with some loess and occasional river gravel. The Yakima Valley has sandy soils with low water retention, making irrigation essential.

ASPECT
Vineyards are few and far between. All plantings have been made on either low ridges, the south-facing slopes of hills, or near rivers. The most important factor is avoiding damaging winter cold, rather than excessive summer heat.

YOU'VE GOT A CHOICE for the most unlikely, inhospitable vineyard site ever. The Australian Outback. Or the moon. You get both in the Columbia River Valley basin, to the east of the towering Cascade Range in Washington State, up in the cold, foggy Pacific Northwest corner of the United States. But there are two vastly different landscapes in Washington State: the part where people live, make money, support football teams and go to the opera is cool and foggy, lies to the west of the Cascades and is open to the influence of the northern Pacific Ocean that, in 1579, had Sir Francis Drake reeling, beaten back by 'the most vile, thick and stinking fogges'. They're still there, around Puget Sound, Seattle and the mouth of the Columbia River.

But take Interstate 90 south-east out of Seattle, away from the leafy suburbs, through the Snoqualmie Pass and over the Cascades into the head of the Yakima Valley at Ellensburg. You'll feel you've moved to a completely different world of clear, dry mountain air, barren ridges and uneasy civilization. Here you have a choice. Take Interstate 90 further east across the Columbia River, across Moses Lake way across to Ritzville. You wanted moonscape? You've got it. Windswept sagebrush ranges, like the great hunched backs of vast animals, spread out over the plain, and as signs of habitation get less and less, the vast sky loses its charm and starts to threaten you with its emptiness. You find yourself nervously checking your fuel gauge every ten minutes. Then the plains flatten and spread, lifeless, inhospitable, useless. That's eastern Washington.

But take the right turn just after Ellensburg and head south. Sure the mountain ridges are still as desolate and gaunt as you could wish, but you'll suddenly see the Yakima Valley open out beneath you, a brilliant splash of dappled greens like a lush turf carpet laid on a sun-bleached earthen floor. Someone wasn't too clever with the carpet shears, though: the neatly defined edges are erratically cut, and the fertile greens come to razor-sharp edges, then nothing but parched bleached uplands, the hills like the vertebrae of some giant fossilized lizard. This is eastern Washington too. That spread of bright green is

agro-industry at its most intense, the jagged edges marking out the limits of irrigation water rights. Without human resourcefulness there'd be little more growing here than out in the empty vastness towards Ritzville and beyond.

Eastern Washington is desert. The curtain of volcanic peaks making up the Cascade Range runs north to south only 80km (50 miles) east of Seattle, and continues to rise inexorably towards the Rocky Mountains of Idaho and Montana. Nothing much grows there except firs. But there's one vast bowl gouged out between the mountains and skirted by the mighty Columbia River as it hurls its mighty flow against the Cascades, turns unwillingly south until, aided by the extra volume of the Snake and Yakima rivers, its torrent forces its way back west and out to the ocean.

This is the Columbia River basin, all 60,000 square km (23,000 square miles) of it. And among the millions of empty acres lie 11,730ha (28,985 acres) of vines. They're not here by chance, but because the Cascade Range, rising to 3650m (11,975ft), creates a virtual rain-shadow to its east, guaranteeing minimal rainfall and maximum sunshine. Not maximum heat though.

WHERE THE VINEYARDS ARE *You're looking here at one of the most remarkable landscapes in the world of wine. Without human effort, this whole vista would be a drab, sun-parched expanse, only saved from being a wilderness by the mighty Columbia River to the right, and the Yakima River running across the map left to right. Irrigation has changed the Yakima valley into a prolific grower of vegetables, fruit and, today, wine grapes.*

Most of the valley floor is taken up with orchards and crops other than grapes – but look at those watercourses that appear to be running across, rather than down, the hills. Those to the north, in the Rattlesnake Hills, are the Roza and Sunnyside canals, the one to the south running across the base of the Horse Heaven Hills on the other side of the valley is the Satus number 2 pump canal. These take off water from the Yakima and its tributaries and pump it to the hillside properties where nearly all the wine grape vineyards are found. These hills are two examples of the buckled basalt ridges that crop up in the Columbia River basin and afford protection from severe Alaskan weather patterns, as well as south-facing slopes for vines.

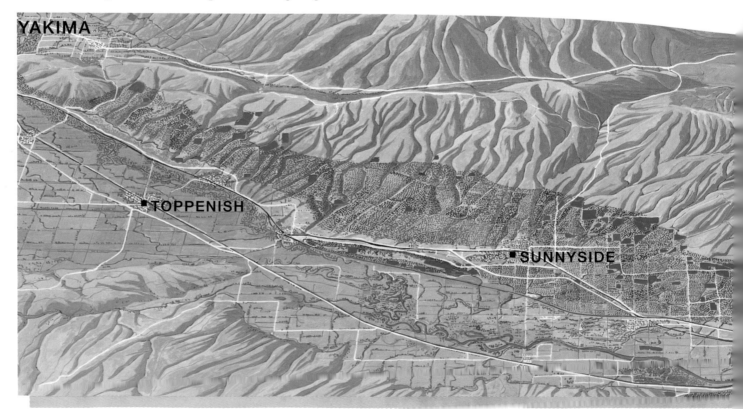

YAKIMA

TOPPENISH

SUNNYSIDE

0 km   4
0 miles   4

Columbia Valley can get incredibly hot, but all its vineyards are in mesoclimates that are warm at best. Yet being so far north – most vineyards are between 46° and 47° North – you can get up to two hours more sun daily than in California's Napa Valley. Vital, as it's photosynthesis, powered by sunlight, that ripens grapes, not blasts of midday heat. And, since this is a continental climate, temperatures plummet at night. So you get grapes full of sugar because of long, sun-filled days, yet chilly nights keep acids high…the perfect recipe for wine grapes.

One more thing – there's almost no rain. So you irrigate. The Columbia is America's second river in terms of volumes of water shifted. The Yakima and Snake Rivers are two other significant performers. On the Columbia and Snake Rivers, vineyards are either planted right on the banks to reduce the very real threat of winter and spring frosts, or on low, south-facing ridges close to the water. Irrigation is simply a case of obtaining water rights.

Most of the Yakima valley floor, protected by hills to the north-east and south-west, is taken up with horticulture other than vines. But vineyards occupy the irrigated low ridges, especially on south-facing patches of the Rattlesnake Hills east of the city of Yakima.

Washington's wine industry used to be based on orchard fruits, *labrusca* vines and a few plantations of varieties like Müller-Thurgau in the west near Seattle. Several major wine concerns are still based there, including the two biggest, Chateau Ste Michelle and Columbia. But 99 per cent of the state's grapes are grown east

of the Cascades in the Columbia Basin. Although the whole of Washington's acreage under vine is only one third that of the Napa Valley, the state has the second largest planting of classic *vinifera* varieties in the United States after California. Figures are approximate, since new plantings keep coming. The overall AVA is Columbia Valley. This encompasses all the vineyards east of the Cascades, though Yakima Valley and Walla Walla can use their own names if they choose. Yakima has about 4455ha (11,000 acres) of wine grapes, Walla Walla less than 485ha (1200 acres) and the rest of Columbia Valley under 6800ha (16,800 acres). There are also about 4ha (10 acres) of vines way up near Spokane. West of the Cascades only adds another 14ha (35 acres) of *vinifera* vines, the best of these being on the Oregon border near Portland.

Initially, Washington was seen as white wine country because of its relatively cool climate, but long sunlight hours have started to produce superb Merlots as the vines mature, and the rare Lemberger makes excellent crunchy reds in the Yakima valley. Reds now dominate – just – with Merlot leading in acreage and plantings of Syrah rapidly increasing. Both Riesling and Semillon positively shine, while Chardonnay flares brightly in places such as Woodward Canyon, but is more often pleasant than exciting.

Leonetti makes Washington's most sought-after Merlot – its succulent fruit showing the great potential of Columbia Valley fruit.

AVA WINE AREAS, SELECTED WINERIES AND VINEYARDS

1. Sagelands
2. Hyatt Vineyards
3. SilverLake
4. Tefft Cellars
5. Harrison Hill Vineyard (DeLille Cellars)
6. Paul Thomas
7. Washington Hills/Apex
8. Chinook
9. Hogue Cellars
10. Hedges Cellars
11. Klipsun Vineyards
12. Kiona

YAKIMA VALLEY = AVA WINE AREA

— AVA BOUNDARIES

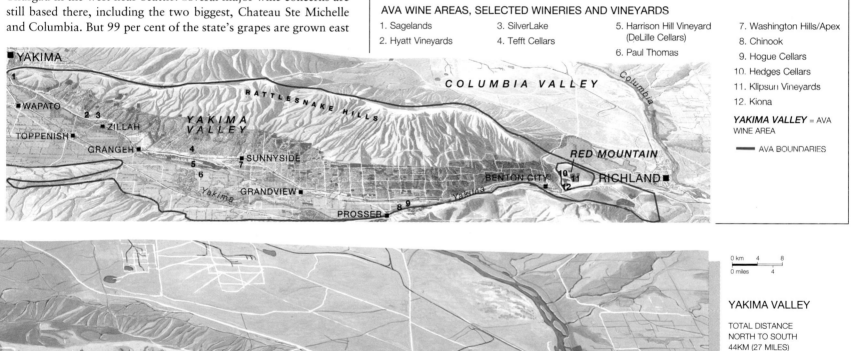

YAKIMA VALLEY

TOTAL DISTANCE NORTH TO SOUTH 44KM (27 MILES)

▦ VINEYARDS

0 km 4 8
0 miles 4

▲ N

OREGON

RED GRAPES
Pinot Noir rules in Oregon, especially in the Willamette Valley, but Merlot is also present, as well as small amounts of Cabernet Sauvignon and Zinfandel.

WHITE GRAPES
Pinot Gris and Chardonnay are dominant with Riesling a distant third. Sauvignon Blanc, Gewütztraminer and Müller-Thurgau have a following.

CLIMATE
The lower Willamette Valley is cooler than the upper part, which in turn is cooler than Umpqua, itself cooler than Rogue Valley down on the Californian border. Frequent rainfall in the north declines in a similar sequence. The Rogue Valley acts as a heat trap, with long hot spells, but sunshine is generally less reliable than in California.

SOIL
In the Willamette Valley, particularly the 'red' Dundee Hills, the soil is of volcanic origin and rich in iron. The Rogue Valley is more mixed with some granite.

ASPECT
Most vineyards are planted on slopes, to avoid spring frosts and to make the most of summer sun, but the Rogue Valley also has plantings on the valley floor.

There wouldn't have been an Oregon wine industry if it weren't for the bloody-mindedness of its pioneers. But by pioneers, I don't mean the settlers who followed the Oregon trail out west in the 1850s or the first wave of Californians who trekked north a bit later and began planting grapes just over the state line. No. I'm talking about the second wave of Californians. The 1960s wave, which has continued to this day and results in many of Oregon's wineries being owned by people who, for whatever reason, couldn't hack California any longer and decided to head north.

Nowadays, there's good reason to forsake the easy life in California for the damp, cool Oregonian hills. Thirty years of pioneering winemaking has finally proven that Oregon can make some remarkable wines, quite unlike anything that is being produced in California.

Forty years ago a betting man wouldn't even have offered odds on such a dumb proposition. But a few 1960s kids took the gamble all the same. Although California's astonishing growth didn't begin before 1966 at the earliest, when Robert Mondavi set up shop, the University of California at Davis already boasted the most important winemaking and vineyard management course in the nation. The aim of the course was then – and to some extent still is – to teach students how to raise huge crops of healthy grapes in warm climates, and how to avoid foul ups, rather than encouraging them to strive for something difficult and unique.

But a few of the graduates didn't simply want to head off to warm fertile valleys and effortlessly produce copious amounts of adequate wines. Above all, they had visions based on two great European wine styles that California had never mastered: the stylish Rieslings of the Rhine and Mosel valleys in Germany, and the classic Pinot Noir red wines of Burgundy. One of the Davis professors is said to have told David Lett, a young student passionate about Pinot Noir, 'You'll be frosted out in the spring and fall, rained on all summer and you'll get athlete's foot up to your knees.' Given that Oregon's own State University was warning that quality *vinifera* wine varieties would not ripen, you did have to be pretty pig-headed to give Oregon a go. Richard Sommer of Hillcrest and David Lett of Eyrie were just that. First Richard Sommer established a Riesling vineyard in the Umpqua Valley in southern Oregon, then David Lett headed further north for cooler, more unpredictable weather – more like Burgundy, in fact. That's exactly what Lett wanted, and exactly what he got.

PINOT NOIR RULES

The reputation of Oregon has been made on Pinot Noir. Lacking local expertise, many grape growers did turn to the University at Davis and, in general, they got advice on methods of cultivation and ground preparation, and choice of clones, especially in the case of Chardonnay, that might have suited California, but that weren't relevant to the situation in Oregon. Big winery mentality simply didn't suit Oregon because, of all the American wine regions, Oregon is based on small family units. Five acres, ten acres, maybe twenty-five is typical, anything much bigger is rare. The whole state production is still only about a tenth of that currently being produced by the Robert Mondavi Winery alone in California, and there is a homespun air even to the most successful wineries.

The parallels with Burgundy don't end there. The sun often doesn't shine, and rain frequently falls before the grapes are ripe. And in Oregon, as in Burgundy, mesoclimate is everything in the battle to ripen grapes. Uniquely, among the great red varieties, Pinot Noir needs cool spots rather than hot ones.

Let's look at the Willamette Valley first, since almost all the well-known Oregon wines come from here. The long valley stretches from north-west of Portland to just below Eugene, with the Coast Ranges to the west and the Cascades to the east. The crests of the rather haphazard Coast Ranges allow a fair amount of maritime influence through, usually in the form of cloud cover and damp, cool air. While the latitude may be similar to that of Bordeaux, the daytime summer temperatures are actually slightly warmer on average, but the nights here are considerably cooler.

Though its wine history is very short, a surprising number of sub-regions are already staking a quality claim. Almost all of these are based on small ridges of hills running down the west side of the Willamette Valley, which afford protected south and south-east-facing slopes. The Tualatin Valley has a group of good, primarily white, vineyards in the north, and there are good vineyards almost within Portland's suburbs. Heading south, the east-west Chehalem Mountains grow some of Oregon's finest fruit; the Dundee Hills with their red volcanic soil are the most heavily planted, while the Eola Hills, south of McMinnville have also produced top material.

The climate slowly warms as you head south, and so, though there are vineyards right down as far as Eugene, the real cool-climate action is between the Tualatin River and the Eola Hills.

WHERE THE VINEYARDS ARE *This map shows less than half of the Willamette Valley, but the northern half of the valley does include nearly all the important quality vineyard sites. If you think the Willamette landscape looks a bit cool and green to be a major wine region, you'd not be far wrong – it is chilly and damp here. That's why there are no grand swathes of vines; the growers here have to search out the few little pockets of land that will manage to ripen their grapes.*

Virtually all of the vineyards are on low hillsides, facing south-east to south-west. It's a marginal climate in the Willamette Valley. The Coast Ranges to the west of the valley cut off most of the foggy, wet Pacific influence, but can't exclude it completely. The Cascades to the east cut off the worst of the continental winters that could otherwise kill the vines.

The most important grouping of vineyards is on the Dundee Hills, just to the south-west of Newberg. Here are many of the original plantings, as well as recent additions like Domaine Drouhin, established by Robert Drouhin from Burgundy in the late 1980s. North-west of Newberg, the Chehalem Mountains have good, well-protected sites. There are some vineyards right up next to Portland, but the other important area on the map is in the north-west, where the Coast Ranges offer good protected sites. At the top-left corner is Montinore, Oregon's first large-scale vineyard development.

NORTH WILLAMETTE

TOTAL DISTANCE
NORTH TO SOUTH
32KM (20 MILES)

 VINEYARDS

0 km   1   2
0 miles   1

The Umpqua Valley, squeezed between the Coast Ranges and the Cascades, is warm enough to grow fair Cabernet Sauvignon alongside Pinot Noir. On the California border the Rogue Valley sites, though higher than 300m (1000ft), are still fairly warm. The Illinois Valley, cooled by Pacific influences, can take even longer than the Willamette to ripen its fruit. In the north-east, bordering Washington State along the Columbia River, there are now irrigated plantings of a similar character to the Washington vineyards on the far bank of the river.

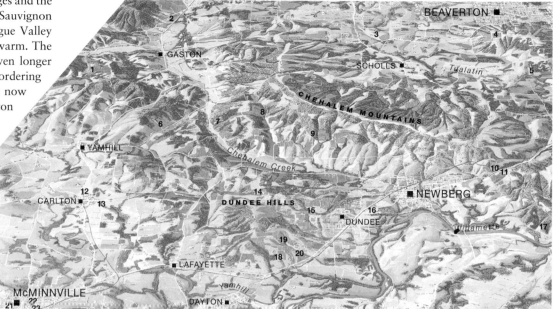

SELECTED WINERIES

1. Elk Cove	9. Adelsheim	17. McKinlay
2. Montinore	10. Rex Hill	18. Sokol Blosser
3. Oak Knoll	11. Chehalem	19. Domaine Drouhin
4. Cooper Mountain	12. Ken Wright	20. Archery Summit
5. Ponzi	13. Domaine Serene	21. Panther Creek
6. WillaKenzie	14. Erath Vineyards	22. Torii Mor
7. Beaux Frères	15. Cameron	23. Eyrie
8. Brick House	16. Argyle	

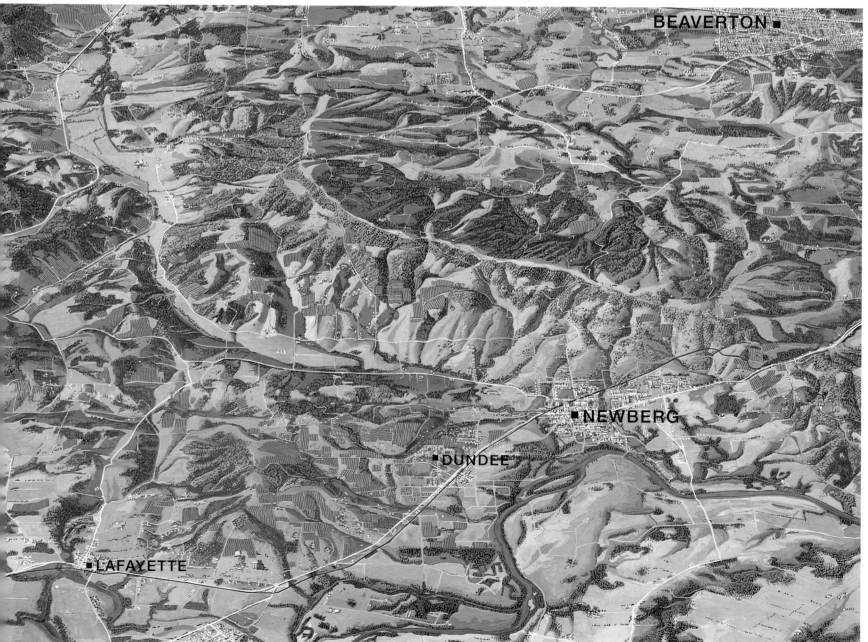

EAST COAST

THE EAST COAST IS WHERE the American wine industry started, but it took a long time to work out how to make anything half-decent. America must have seemed to be a winemaker's paradise, when the first settlers arrived to find fat, juicy grapes hanging off the trees at every turn in New England and Virginia. But, as early as 1606, a certain Captain Smith was complaining that while they might be good to eat, these native varieties made horrendous wines.

In 1619 Lord Delaware brought over French vine cuttings and French vignerons to try to emulate French wines. No go. The vines simply died in droves, and the vignerons weren't any more successful at making a drinkable wine out of the native vines than the original guys. Moses 'the Frenchman' Fournier was having a go on Long Island and Peter Stuyvesant, governor of what was then called New Amsterdam, was planting vines on Manhattan. And his successor helped French Huguenot settlers to plant vineyards futher north up in the valley of the Hudson River. But nothing worked.

The chief problem was phylloxera. This is a tiny aphid that preys on the roots of vines, sucking out their sap and eventually killing the vine. It is endemic throughout North America, and so domestic varieties of vine evolved that could thrive even in soils that were seething with phylloxera. The imported European vines, from the *Vitis vinifera* family, had no such tolerance and immediately succumbed. The only legacy they left is that some of these doomed vines may have cross-bred with native species. These resultant so-called hybrids gained an immunity to phylloxera's depredations and, at the same time, ameliorated the strange, sickly, sweet-scented yet sour-edged fruit of the local grape varieties, in particular those of the *Vitis labrusca*.

This is probably how the first well-known American hybrid – the Alexander or Cape – came into being, and this led on to such varieties as Isabella, Catawba and Concord in the early 19th century. These hybrids produced good crops and could cope with the East Coast's fierce north-eastern winters without rotting in the humid, sticky summers, but, unfortunately, they produced wine that was, well, barely drinkable at worst, with a flavour usually referred to as 'foxy' – the sickly-sweet *labrusca* parentage still showed and it was a long way from any wine aroma familiar to drinkers of *vinifera* wines. But if it was made into 'sherry', 'port' or sparkling wine, it was really quite palatable.

Throughout the 19th and 20th centuries, a reasonably thriving wine industry grew up on the East Coast, led by New York State. It was dominated by wine made from hybrids such as Concord. During the years of Prohibition, between 1920 and 1935, this reliance on Concord served the industry well. The grapes and their juice could be sold for eating or drinking just as they were.

If you had to print such helpful instructions on what were called 'grape bricks' (blocks of pressed grapes) as 'To prevent fermentation add one-tenth per cent Benzoate of Soda' – well, sometimes you just happened to forget, and then sometimes the damned thing did ferment. And it seemed such a waste to throw it

AVA WINE AREAS

— OHIO

1. Isle St George
2. Grand River Valley
3. Loramie Creek
4. Ohio River Valley (also in Kentucky, Indiana and West Virginia)

— WEST VIRGINIA

5. Kanawha River Valley (also in Ohio)

— VIRGINIA

6. Rocky Knob
7. North Fork of Roanoke
8. Monticello
9. Northern Neck George Washington Birthplace
10. Virginia's East Shore
11. Shenandoah Valley (also in West Virginia)

— MARYLAND

12. Linganore
13. Catoctin
14. Cumberland Valley (also in Pennsylvania)

— PENNSYLVANIA

15. Lancaster Valley

— NEW JERSEY

16. Central Delaware Valley (also in Pennsylvania)
17. Warren Hills

— NEW YORK STATE

18. Lake Erie (also in Pennsylvania and Ohio)
19. Finger Lakes
20. Cayuga Lake
21. Hudson River Region
22. Long Island
23. North Fork of Long Island
24. The Hamptons

— CONNECTICUT

25. Western Connecticut Highlands
26. Southeastern New England (also in Rhode Island and Massachusetts)

— MASSACHUSETTS

27. Martha's Vineyard

☐ OVER 500M (1640FT)

▨ OVER 1000M (3280FT)

away, so you simply drank it. It may not have tasted all that good, but in the era of bathtub gin, who really cared what it tasted like?

It wasn't until a few tentative moves in the 1960s, followed by a slow push first towards quality hybrids and then towards classic European *vinifera* grapes grafted onto American rootstocks, that things began to really hum. New York State has been the leader in this movement, but a surprising number of other states have managed to produce attractive *vinifera* wines before the fading sunlight and icy air of Maine kill off the grape's chance of ripening in the north, or the humid climes of South Carolina and Florida rot it on the vine to the south.

New Hampshire grows a few vines, and Massachusetts grows rather more, with the most attractive efforts produced so far being those wines made from grapes grown on the island of Martha's Vineyard – proving that the sea's tempering influence does allow *vinifera* vines to survive at such a northern latitude.

Rhode Island claims a similar climate to Bordeaux – but then an awful lot of maritime vineyard regions do. I wouldn't go that far, but good mesoclimates do abound here, the sea helps moderate the extremes of climate, and certainly Sakonnet Vineyards has produced some pretty fair Chardonnay.

Connecticut benefits from the mild influence of Long Island Sound. There are wines made upstate, but the climate gets pretty continental away from the maritime influence, and all the best ones I've had, like Chamard Chardonnay, have come from vines grown down near the Sound.

Skirting round New York State, New Jersey is struggling to put her past as a *labrusca* producer behind her, and West Virginia produces some wine up in her north-east corner, but the important wine-producing states, after New York State, are Pennsylvania, Virginia and Maryland.

Maryland's chief claim to fame is Boordy Vineyards, where Philip Wagner planted America's first French-American hybrids – just as resistant to the cold winters, the scorching summers and the phylloxera as the American versions, but with a much more European flavour. Until recently, most of the best East Coast wines came from these hybrids – Vidal and Chambourcin are two of the best known – and though there are an increasing number of *vinifera* success stories from wineries like Boordy and Basignani, producers such as these generally continue with their share of hybrids. Overall, however, Maryland has not yet lived up to the potential it showed in the 1980s and it has been largely surpassed by its neighbours, Pennsylvania to the north and Virginia to the south.

Pennsylvania divides its vineyards between the shores of Lake Erie in the north-west, where long, but cool days suit some of the northern European varieties like Riesling and Pinot Noir, and the south-east, in the Lancaster and Cumberland valleys, where a new generation of winemakers are having particular success with Chardonnay, though the hybrid, Chambourcin is also producing surprisingly good dark-coloured reds from wineries like Chaddsford and Naylor.

Some winemakers say south-east Pennsylvania reminds them of Burgundy, but Virginia, which shares the same sweep of mountain slopes that run down to the west of Washington DC, actually offers a more realistic comparison. This was where Captain Smith tried and failed to make wine from vinifera varieties in the 17th century, and where Thomas Jefferson, a great admirer of Bordeaux wines, suffered the same fate in the 18th on his estate at Monticello.

Things got so bad, that in 1960 Virginia grew only 6.5ha (16 acres) of vines – and all for table grapes. Now there are some

650ha (1600 acres) of vines, more than two-thirds of which are *vinifera* varieties with Chardonnay leading the way. That almost goes without saying, since to build up a cellar-door trade you have to offer a Chardonnay, and Virginia is perfectly placed not only for Washington D.C. but also for a thriving tourist trade – even colonial Williamsburg has its own winery now. Luckily Chardonnay has taken well to Virginia. But that hasn't stopped people experimenting, not only with obvious choices like Riesling, Merlot or Cabernet Franc, but also with such long shots as Viognier and Barbera.

Things still aren't easy, however. Phylloxera may have been conquered, but the warm climate still poses a constant threat. With most of the vineyards being planted inland on the eastern slopes of the Blue Ridge Mountains, away from the tempering effects of Chesapeake Bay, and with a latitude similar to that of southern Italy and southern Spain, the winemakers are lumbered with all the classic problems of a continental climate – cold winters, spring frosts, tremendous heat and possible excessive humidity and summer rainfall. Even the soils are by no means perfect, consisting largely of fertile red clays and clay loams.

But they do manage a certain amount of success. By planting the vineyards at mostly between 335 and 460 metres (1100 and 1500ft) up on slopes, the grape-growers can provide drainage for excess water and good air circulation. This is vital in order to combat spring frosts and to reduce the incidence of grape rot when the humidity starts to climb. Wide spacing of vines and an open trellis canopy also help to circulate air and minimize rot.

Some of the more cold-sensitive *vinifera* varieties find the winters too harsh in Virginia, but the Riesling, Sauvignon Blanc, Chardonnay, Cabernet and Merlot, from wineries like Barboursville Vineyards, Linden, Tarara, Horton, White Hall, Valhalla and even Williamsburg, down on sandy soils near the coast, point the way to Virginia challenging New York for East Coast quality in the not-too-distant future.

The aromatic grape varieties do well in New York's cool conditions. This highly perfumed Gewürztraminer is from the Finger Lakes in northern New York State.

It would be impossible to grow grapes this far north in New York State were it not for a group of deep glacial lakes, called the Finger Lakes after their long, thin appearance. This is Seneca Lake, the deepest at 193m (632ft), and able to store heat so effectively that the vintage can sometimes continue until November.

NEW YORK STATE

RED GRAPES
Native American and hybrid varieties continue to dominate, with Concord accounting for 75 per cent of total plantings, plus Baco Noir and De Chaunac. *Vinifera* vines include Cabernet Sauvignon, Merlot, Cabernet Franc and Pinot Noir.

WHITE GRAPES
Chardonnay is the leading *vinifera* variety, followed by Riesling, Gewürztraminer and Sauvignon Blanc. However, these are overshadowed in volume by such hybrids as Aurora, Seyval Blanc, Cayuga and Vidal Blanc.

CLIMATE
The Finger Lakes have a short, humid growing season, followed by severe winters. The Hudson River is milder, while Long Island benefits from the moderating influence of the Atlantic Ocean.

SOIL
Soils are varied. By Lake Erie there is gravelly loam and around the Finger Lakes calcareous shale. The Hudson River has shale, slate, schist and limestone. Long Island is sandy with silt and loam.

ASPECT
The Allegheny plateau traps the warmth of Lake Erie. Finger Lakes vineyards are on slopes to avoid frost and the steep Hudson River Valley is an efficient conduit for warm Atlantic air.

I KNOW THEY SAY THAT LONG ISLAND is the closest vineyard area to New York City, but it depends on when you visit. Don't do it in June, or July, or August, or any time when it's sunny, or weekends – and don't drive. If you do, you'll need to leap out of bed before dawn, slam the hire car into 'drive', hare through the Midtown Tunnel, out through Queens on Interstate 495 and in no time – well, even obeying the speed limit, in about an hour-and-a-half – you should be at Riverhead, with time for some leisurely vineyard visits. Except for me it didn't work out like that: I visited in summer. Four hours to Riverhead, every appointment missed, and then the long drive home. Too much sea and sand. Too popular.

Well, that's Long Island for you. It's the reason everyone rushes there as soon as the sun comes out. It's also the reason that it is seen increasingly as America's answer to its quest for a Bordeaux-like wine region. It's got similarities, I'll grant you, and is making a good stab at Cabernet and Merlot, although most of its best wines are Chardonnays, as is often the case on the East Coast. And the vineyards laying claim to a slice of Bordeaux's glory are virtually all on the North Fork. The South Fork has the Hamptons: they throw better parties there, the houses are bigger, the limos longer, but in wine terms its soil is rather heavy, leading to waterlogging when summer and autumn rains get excessive. Its spring frosts can strike as late as May, prevailing winds are cooler and the ripening period is two or three weeks shorter than on the North Fork. Makes you wonder why the socialites didn't choose the North Fork.

Long Island is New York's newest wine area. A few vines were planted here in the 17th and 18th centuries, but nothing really happened until 1973 when Alex and Louisa Hargrave uprooted a vegetable patch at Cutchogue, a couple of miles up the North Fork from Riverhead, and planted vines. So? So the vines they planted were the French classics of Bordeaux and Burgundy, together with Riesling. Until then New York's reputation, such as it was, had been based on native American vines and French hybrids: a few plantations of classic *vinifera* grapes existed upstate. Everyone said they couldn't survive the bitter winters and short, fiery summers.

WHERE THE VINEYARDS ARE *We're looking at a tiny sliver of land here. Riverhead to Southold is a mere 19km (12 miles), and Jamesport north to Long Island Sound is only 5km (3 miles). But dotted about among the scarcely undulating fields, full of lush market produce, are about 400 ha (1000 acres) of vineyards that many experts think will prove to be some of the best in the USA. Indeed you can narrow things down even more to the area around Cutchogue, where most of the best vineyards are and which people have begun whispering about as the Médoc of America.*

There are some vines on the South Fork of Long Island, but the North Fork clearly has better potential; the South Fork's soils are heavier, the climate is a little cooler and the risk of spring frosts catching you unawares lasts a little longer. Long Island's soils were formed by retreating Wisconsin glaciation about 10,000 years ago, but the North Fork's thin claw has grabbed the freest draining, more gravelly and sandy soils. It has also grabbed the better climate.

Stretching north-east into Long Island Sound, with Peconic Bay to its south, the North Fork is surrounded on three sides by relatively warm water. The prevailing westerlies reach the North Fork after blowing across the Sound. This helps to create a mild growing period of up to 230 days, although the relative air humidity requires fairly strict anti-fungal spray regimes as does the likelihood of late season rain. The climate during September and October mirrors that of Bordeaux, and winemakers in the North Fork can experience the same heartbreak that a sudden downpour in the middle of harvest causes their French counterparts.

But if they really want to be thought of as this transatlantic Médoc, they're going to have to get used to dreams of 'Vintage of the Century' turning to ashes far more frequently than they become glorious reality.

This didn't bother the Hargraves. They realized that the waters of Long Island had a moderating effect on the North Fork, cooling the summer heat and warding off the worst of the north-east winter cold. They'd also found that the gently undulating farmland around Cutchogue – sitting on deep sand and gravel subsoils – was ideal for decent drainage and reasonable water retention. And their thoughts turned to Bordeaux, and to the Médoc especially, which juts out into the Bay of Biscay on its tongue of low-lying land. They checked the growing season temperatures and found that, though the season starts a little later than in Bordeaux, slightly warmer summer temperatures bring both areas' grapes to ripen at much the same time, between mid September and mid October. And the well-drained soil means that a slightly higher rainfall isn't that much of a problem and lessens the chance of late season rot.

But it hasn't been an easy ride. Fungicide sprays are crucial to control rot caused by the humidity. The soils are more fertile than those of Bordeaux's best properties and pruning and trellising must be adapted accordingly. And New York City has been slow to take Long Island's wines to its heart. I remember on an early trip trying to persuade the city's gastronomic glitterati of Long Island's brilliant potential. I might as well have been extolling the friendly nature of the Great White Shark to a group of scuba divers. But at last, the quality of Long Island Chardonnay, the fine Merlots, Cabernets and, occasionally Sauvignon Blancs and late-harvest Rieslings, have become hot enough in the Big Apple that on a recent trip, every restaurant I ate in boasted at least one Long Island wine.

In the past few years, Long Island's wine industry has been transformed. The Hargraves sold their winery in 1998 to an Italian count. Then Kip Bedell sold his to a movie mogul, and Jerry Gristina cashed in for millions from a telecoms executive. I hope this infusion of capital and new plantings – the area under vine had reached about 1000 hectares (2500 acres) in 2000, all of it *vinifera* – will lead to higher quality, rather than profiteering. The area is an attractive weekend destination and it's certainly worth trying some of that Chardonnay with the famous local lobsters.

RIVERHEAD

0 km   1   2

But other parts of the State have a longer grape-growing tradition and contribute the bulk of the volume that makes New York the main state for grapes after California. The Lake Erie region has 7700ha (19,000 acres), yet no one's heard of it because most of its vineyards grow Concord, which makes great grape juice but pretty duff wine.

The Finger Lakes region also relies upon the effects of water in tempering a climate that would otherwise be far too harsh for wine grapes. Its 11 thin, deep lakes, running north to south just below Lake Ontario, were gouged out of rock by glaciers in the last Ice Age. The three biggest – Keuka, Seneca and Cayuga – have the majority of the region's total 4200ha (10,400 acres) of vineyards, and Cayuga now has its own separate AVA designation. Initially, the region was seen as suitable only for native varieties and hybrids, but a visionary called Konstantin Frank believed that vines such as Riesling and Chardonnay could survive icy winters if grafted on to sufficiently hardy rootstocks. He eventually proved his point (using rootstock from a convent in Quebec) and there are now increasing numbers of delicate, delicious white wines being made on the shale-dominated soils. Leading producers such as Fox Run and Lamoreaux Landing now make some delicate Pinot Noir, spicy Cabernet Franc and juicy Merlot but, in general, reds still struggle to ripen fully. The lower altitude and greater depth of Seneca and Cayuga lakes, allowing a slightly longer protection from frost, are regarded as the best sites.

The Hudson River Valley, directly north of New York City, has the longest unbroken grape-growing tradition in the USA. Only recently have the 400ha (1000 acres) of slate, shale and schist soils begun producing good *vinifera* wines, including of some the State's best Chardonnay and Pinot Noir, as growers realized that the steep Pallisades through which the Hudson flows south act as a conduit for warming maritime influences from the Atlantic Ocean.

AVA WINE AREA AND SELECTED WINERIES

1. Palmer
2. Paumanok
3. Macari Vineyards
4. Pellegrini
5. Galluccio Estate/Gristina
6. Castello di Borghese/Hargrave
7. Peconic Bay
8. Bedell
9. Pindar
10. Lenz

NORTH FORK = AVA WINE AREA

⸺ AVA BOUNDARY

NORTH FORK OF LONG ISLAND

TOTAL DISTANCE NORTH TO SOUTH 23KM (14 MILES)

▦ VINEYARDS

The Okanagan Valley is one of Canada's top resort areas and vines have to share the land with holidaymakers. Here Quails' Gate Vineyard slopes down to the holiday homes and jetties on Okanagan Lake, just below Kelowna.

longer of sunshine per day during high summer than the vineyards in California do. Not as hot, maybe, but it's sunshine, not heat, that builds up the sugar in those grapes. No wonder that a strip of land just south-west of Oliver in this southern stretch has been called 'The Golden Mile', and that it is packed full of vineyards that are sprouting Cabernet Sauvignon, Cabernet Franc and Merlot, proving that you can ripen reds like these above the 49th Parallel. And they do taste special. Those very hot days are followed by very cool nights up here by the Columbia Mountains. High acids are the result, and this, combined with high sugar levels makes for some very interesting wines.

Of course, there are a few problems. About every ten years or so, an almighty winter freeze threatens to destroy your vines. And despite the torrid high summer conditions, winter closes in very fast here come mid-October. You can't let the grapes hang around for extra flavour, as you can in somewhere like New Zealand. If you're not intending to make Icewine, those grapes have simply got to come off – ripe or not.

There are about 2024ha (5000 acres) of wine grapes planted, and the figure is increasing. Nearly 90 per cent of these are planted in Okanagan, with the heavier concentration south of Penticton. But there are also a few other areas to note. West of Oliver lies the Similkameen Valley, described as 'high desert cattle country' with hot, dry summers and low humidity. It sounds good for grapes, and there are already a couple of hundred acres that have been planted with vines. Down the Fraser Valley towards Vancouver, where it's cooler and wetter, there are also some vines. And, more importantly, out on the heavily wooded lumber and leisure centre of Vancouver Island, with a mild climate that is tempered by the sea, there are a number of small vineyards and wineries that cater to an eager tourist trade.

the rainfall drops right down to 152mm (6in) a year. This little region is the only part of Canada officially designated as 'desert', and irrigation is a must if vines are to survive and flourish. And think – only 152mm (6in) of rain a year. That means clear skies. That means endless summer sunshine. Correct. And being so far north, they reckon they get about 2 hours

ICEWINE

Every winter, the temperatures in the vineyards of Ontario and British Columbia drop way below freezing and frequently stay there for weeks, if not months, on end. If your grapes are still on the vine in late November and December, they freeze. This doesn't sound good. But if you gather these grapes, frozen, and take them, still frozen, to the winery and delicately press them – still frozen – you'll discover that the water which constitutes more than 80 per cent of the grape juice has turned into ice crystals, and the sugar has separated out into a thick, gooey, sludgy syrup that is ridiculously sweet. Remove the ice from the syrup and you've got the basis for one of the most distinctive flavours in the wine world – the phenomenally rich Icewine. Once or twice a decade, a few German vineyards attempt this wine style, and sell their minute production at astronomical prices. In Canada, they can make it every year.

The first Icewine was made by Hainle in British Columbia in 1973, and though British Columbia still produces a small but growing amount, Ontario now dominates production with over 300,000 litres (79,252 gallons) per year. Things really took off in 1991 at the Vinexpo World Wine Show in France, when a 1989 Inniskillin Icewine won the Grand Prix d'Honneur – although the wine was banned by the EU. Vinexpo continues to be a happy hunting ground for Icewine – in 2001, two Icewines won two trophies in the same sweet wine category – and the EU finally relented and allowed imports of Icewine as from 2001.

Harvesting frozen Vidal grapes for Icewine in mid-January at Inniskillin.

ONTARIO

ONTARIO'S 4856HA (12,000 ACRES) of vineyards lie on the shores of Lake Ontario and Lake Erie, between 42° and 43.5° North – on the same band of latitude as Corsica and the Languedoc vineyards of southern France. That sounds extremely promising for some fairly gutsy flavours, but it isn't as simple as that. Those European vineyards are strongly influenced by the perenially warm Mediterranean sea. Even in the middle of winter you can still jump into the sea at Ajaccio or Marseilles and experience, at worst, a mildly bracing immersion. Jump into the sea off Canada's 44th parallel in midwinter and you'll be nursing some extremely nasty cold bruises from the icebergs. And that's only half the story. Proximity to the sea tempers any region's extremes, but Ontario's vineyards are hundreds of miles inland. Long, numbing winters and short, searing summers would rule out any chance of winemaking – if it weren't for the lakes.

It's the lakes that make viticulture possible in Ontario, by storing up the summer heat to release it slowly though the winter, yet also providing breezes that help cool the fierce, if short-lived, summer sun. We end up with summer temperatures that are higher than both Bordeaux and Burgundy – a crucial point, because until the end of May, Ontario is appreciably cooler, and by September her temperature drops below that of Bordeaux once again. But in between, Niagara is hotter than Bordeaux in June, July and August, and it's hotter than Burgundy right up to the middle of October, when there's a dramatic drop. In the south, Pelee Island, 18km (11 miles) out in Lake Erie, has a ripening period 30 days longer than the Canadian mainland, helped by the southerly latitude and the warming effect of the shallow Lake Erie. That warming effect only lasts till winter comes. Then, the extreme shallowness of the lake means it frequently freezes over and Pelee Island is encased in ice. So, despite the potential of a much longer ripening period, vintages are erratic. Lake Erie North Shore, near Windsor, also benefits from the water's warm surface temperature and suffers less from the winter freeze.

However, the heart of Ontario viticulture – and indeed the engine room for Canadian wine in general, since it produces 80 per cent of the country's wine grapes – is on the Niagara Peninsula. The most important part of this is a narrow strip of land running for about 56km (35 miles) east from Hamilton to Niagara-on-the-Lake and comprising the south-western shore of Lake Ontario, but there's also a stretch following the Niagara River south to the Niagara Falls. It would be easy to dismiss this as one homogenous small region, but when you are in marginal conditions, little things matter, and they do here. The general view is that this slim peninsula, bounded by the two Great Lakes – Ontario and Erie – is protected from the worst of the winter weather because of the heat those great bodies of water hold. This is broadly true, but there seem to be three distinctly different parts to the Niagara vineyard region, all tightly meshed together. Right on the Lake Ontario shore, there's no doubt the continual movement of air does ward off frost, but these constant breezes also cool the air down in spring, delaying the whole development of the vine. That's fine for avoiding spring frosts, but not so good for completing ripeness, especially when you're faced with a cold October.

A mile or two south of Niagara-on-the-Lake is the Niagara Plain – it's not very big but, being further from the Lake, you lose some of the breezes and immediately encounter a problem with spring frosts. But the plus point is that the vines start to develop sooner, and the higher summer temperatures give fatter, richer flavours and an earlier harvest.

And running east-west just south of the Ontario shoreline is the Niagara Escarpment – or the Niagara Bench, as wine people like to call it. This reaches up to 175-185m (574-607ft) in height. Vineyards here are cooler than those on the Plain, but drainage is good on the slopes. It needs to be. There's a lot of fairly heavy clay loam soil mixed in with the sandy loam, and the continual air movement minimizes frost danger, and helps to balance out loss of heat by eliminating the fungal diseases that bedevil humid areas at the end of the ripening season. The wines in general have higher acidity but, year by year, become better balanced.

And which is the best? Hard to say. Some people like the St David's Bench near Niagara Falls. Others like the Beamsville Bench further to the west, past St Catharine's. Time and commitment from the growers will sort it all out.

And what types of wine will they be producing? Well, even the best hybrids are in retreat, except for Vidal, which due to its ability to produce startling Icewines with the exotic flavours of mango, guava and lychee – and yet keep the acid up – has earned itself its place. The first wave of *vinifera* plantings presumed that Ontario had to be white wine country – fair enough, and of course this was in the late 1980s to mid 1990s, when the world was mad for white. Early concentration on Riesling and Gewürztraminer was quickly superceded by the realization that you could grow the superstar Chardonnay here. Inniskillin and Chateau des Charmes led the way and everyone followed, with considerable success. But now the world wants red – and Ontario shows it can do that too – from Gamay and Zweigeltrebe right up to that talisman of New-Age red – Syrah. And, of course, there's Icewine. Where would Canada be without Icewine?

RED GRAPES
Pinot Noir seems most suited, but Cabernet Franc, Cabernet Sauvignon and Merlot and even Syrah are on the increase, though there are few sites that can ripen them successfully, and then only in the warmest years.

WHITE GRAPES
Chardonnay leads, followed by Gewürztraminer, Pinot Blanc and Riesling. The hybrid Vidal remains important, particularly for Icewine.

CLIMATE
A cool region, it depends on the moderating effect of its lakes for successful viticulture. Rainfall is moderate, and snow in December and January favours Icewine production.

SOIL
Soils range from free-draining sandy loams, gravels and sand to heavier soils with varying amounts of clay.

ASPECT
There is a mixture of flat and sloping vineyards. Those close to the shore of Lake Ontario and on the Niagara plain are basically flat. Those on the Niagara Bench reach up to 185m (607ft) in altitude and the best sites are on the relatively steep, north-facing slopes.

ONTARIO VQA WINE AREAS
— Niagara Peninsula
— Lake Erie North Shore
— Pelee Island

SOUTH AMERICA & MEXICO

THE PAN-AMERICAN HIGHWAY makes for the geographical ride of a lifetime: a great, long road running south from the US border, it takes you through a political, cultural and economic landscape of incredible diversity. Mad drivers and the impressive mountainous spine of the Andes are almost the only constants on a road which connects the heat of Mexico with the chill blasts of Patagonia. Apart from football, one of the major forces that provides any cohesion or unity on this southward trek is religion. Early missionaries propagated Christianity in the mid-16th century, beginning their journey in Mexico and spreading throughout South America. With them came the *vinifera* vine from Europe, and the traditional view is that they made wine in order to celebrate the Eucharist.

Wine for normal consumption was also made by the *conquistadores* – importing wine from back home was far too risky. Few wines reacted well to the long sea voyage across the Atlantic, even less to the hot, bumpy overland journey to the Pacific coast, followed by yet another stage by sea down to Chile and Peru. Subsequent dispersal of settlers and missionaries took winemaking from the mile-high plateau of Mexico to the Río Negro in Argentina. Various waves of largely European immigrants have had their effect on the development of both the wine industry and the culture that supports it, in particular the influence of the French in Chile and the Italians in Brazil and Argentina. These days, winemaking techniques are a blend of local knowledge and international expertise. This expertise is increasingly bringing out remarkable quality, especially in parts of Chile and Argentina, which enjoy warm, dry conditions, ideal for the vine, and are well away from the influence of the tropics.

TOPOGRAPHY AND CLIMATE

Latitude and climate are the most obvious restrictions on winemaking in South America and Mexico. From the Tropic of Cancer which bisects Mexico, to the Tropic of Capricorn which cuts across Argentina's northern border, high temperatures and humidity alternately rot the grapes or bake them, making it difficult in many places to produce quality wine. Clever use of altitude, together with stubborn persistence, do, however, create exceptions. French winemaker Michel Rolland has exploited the benefits of being over 1700m (5577ft) above sea level at Cafayate to make award-winning red Malbec and white Torrontés wine in the Argentine region of Salta, barely 150km (93 miles) from the tropics. And Venezuela, too, has made a substantial investment in tropical wine experiments.

The massive Andean chain and cooling breezes off the Pacific are the most important physical influences on viticulture. These maritime breezes help regulate excessive temperatures the length of the coast, from Baja California, down through the Ica region of Peru and on into Chile's Central Valley. In the case of Chile, the cold Humboldt Current creates an additional chilling factor, which benefits white wine areas such as Casablanca. On the eastern side of the continent, vineyards in Uruguay and parts of southern Brazil are influenced by the problematic combination of warm, wet oceanic weather off the Atlantic, and regular blasts from the cold *Pampero* wind that originates in the Argentine pampas.

The effect of the Andean mountain chain is most evident in South America's two most important wine regions: Chile's Central Valley and Argentina's Mendoza region. Just 150km (90 miles) separate the two yet, because the Andes lie between them, shielding Argentina from the moist Pacific breezes, temperature and rainfall differences are enormous. Mendoza gets almost no rain and would be a virtual desert were it not for abundant irrigation from rivers fed by mountain run-off. The Andes has had a dramatic effect on soil, too. Over the millennia, silt washed down onto the alluvial plains has created rich, fertile soils, which, as Chile demonstrates, creates ideal conditions for most kinds of horticulture. Vines love it too, but produce enormous crops if not rigorously controlled. Top wines rarely come from high yielding vines.

CHILE

In South America, Chile continues to lead the way. Since the mid-1980s, its winemakers have been returning from France, California, Australia and New Zealand, bringing with them ideas and technology. Foreign investors have been attracted by the political and economic stability, with the result that Chile now boasts more than 70 exporting wineries with a total annual export income of US$545 million, compared with US$23 million in 1988.

Like the country itself, the wine industry is squeezed into a long, narrow, north-south strip either side of the capital, Santiago, with vineyards never more than 100km (60 miles) from the coast or the Andes, and with little climatic variation, except in small valleys like Casablanca, that are open to the sea, and in areas like Bío Bío in the south. Matching grape varieties with subtle differences in soils and mesoclimates has resulted in a good range of wine styles.

MAIN WINE AREAS

- Mexico
- Venezuela
- Colombia
- Ecuador
- Peru
- Bolivia
- Brazil
- Uruguay
- Argentina
- Chile

0 km   1000   2000
0 miles   1000

ARGENTINA

Over to the east, a previously sleeping giant is at last stirring into action. Who would have thought the world's fifth largest producer of wine, with over 550 wineries in the Mendoza area alone, could have remained so quiet on the international scene for so long? The reason for this is a thirsty Argentine population, ready to drink most of what's produced, and triple to quadruple figure inflation that made any economic activity problematic. However, stability arrived in the late 1980s, when the banks found new ways to deal with the country's huge debt crisis. The hope is that all this won't have been thrown away by the debt crisis re-emerging worse than ever in 2002. Torrontés, Syrah, Malbec and Barbera – these are the grape names making Chilean winemakers nervous, as the world is now starting to hear a lot more about what Argentina has to offer.

URUGUAY

Uruguay's wine culture was developed at the end of the 19th century, mainly by Basque settlers, and it is now the fourth biggest South American wine producer. About 9000ha (22,240 acres) are planted, mostly near Montevideo, and we are just starting to see experimental plantings in other parts of the country, that may prove more suitable. Compared to Chile and Argentina, Uruguay is a small player, but could well flourish by being definably different.

BRAZIL

You look at Brazil, that vast country whose bulk seems to squeeze all the other South American states into margins of the continent and you think – there must be some ace places to plant vineyards. Well, there aren't. From Uruguay at 33° South of the equator to Venezuela at 5° North, there doesn't seem to be anywhere that isn't too humid or too hot, or both. That hasn't stopped people trying. There are 57,000ha (140,845 acres) of vines, – mostly on the Uruguayan border and just north of Porto Alegre – but even there the twin evils of damp and heat make it extremely difficult to ripen *vinifera* grapes without them rotting on the vine. I've had some decent Cabernet Franc, Gewürztraminer and Sauvignon, and the fizz isn't bad, but most vines are hybrids or American varieties that survive the conditions but don't make good wine. Brazil used to export millions of litres under the Marcus James label, but since its government failed to ratify the Uruguay round of GATT talks, exports have slowed to a trickle.

VENEZUELA

I wouldn't normally give Venezuela its own entry – surely it's far too close to the Equator to be able to grow grapes. Wrong. The vine loves Venezuela. It loves it so much that at around 10° North, near Maracaibo, it can obligingly give three crops a year – and two is perfectly normal! Labels often tell you not only the vintage but also the month – there are discernible differences in flavour and quality between each harvest. The only quality-first vineyards are in Lara State, where the Pomar winery, owned by the giant Polar Brewery, has had some success with Syrah, Petit Verdot and Tempranillo.

BOLIVIA

Bolivia is a difficult country to comment on, since her small volume of wine is nearly all consumed locally. But the vineyards appear to be good. There are about 4000ha (9884 acres), mostly near Tarija in the south-east, and they are high, mainly at 1800m (5900ft) to 2500m (8202ft). These certainly used to be the highest in the world, though new plantings near Cafayate in northern Argentina threaten to surpass even this awesome height. The word is that the grape quality is excellent.

Catena's highest Merlot vineyard is sited at an altitude of 1450m (4757ft), in Tupungato, Mendoza. Behind lies arid scrubland and the magnificence of the Andes.

OTHER SOUTH AMERICAN COUNTRIES

Peru used to have a relatively important wine industry, but its vineyards have now slumped to about 11,000ha (27,180 acres), and most of the grapes are used for distilling Pisco, the local spirit. Still, there are vineyards sprinkled down the coast of Peru, whenever a valley from the Andes breaks up the desert and allows irrigation. And just inland the Ica Valley has some important wineries, such as Tacama who have employed French specialists for decades, but I've never enjoyed the wines very much. I haven't enjoyed Cuba's wines much either. South American expert, Christopher Fielden, has tried the offerings of such places as Ecuador, Colombia and Paraguay. He left me in little doubt that I had no need to follow in his courageous footsteps.

MEXICO

Mexico ought to play a much more important role in this atlas, since the whole Central and South American wine industry, as well as that of California, stems from the Spanish arriving in Mexico and making wine from native vines. It wasn't long before they were planting imported Spanish vines and establishing wineries. The oldest winery in the Americas was established here towards the end of the 16th century, and is still going. But Mexicans have never taken to wine and, although the country has nearly 50,000ha (123,548 acres) of vines, over 90 per cent of the grapes go for brandy, or just for eating. The few quality vineyards are mostly in the Baja California peninsula, just south of the USA border, where a number of east-west valleys mimic the Californian conditions – considerable heat tempered by mists and cooling breezes, sucked in from the cold Alaska current that lies just offshore. Two companies – Domecq and L.A. Cetto – dominate production in Mexico and make some good reds from grapes like Petite Sirah, Nebbiolo, Tempranillo and Zinfandel. There is also one high quality producer on the other side of the country – Casa Madero, operating west of the city of Monterrey.

CENTRAL VALLEY/RAPEL VALLEY

RED GRAPES
Despite the valley's reputation for Merlot and Carmenère, there is still considerably more Cabernet Sauvignon. Malbec and Cabernet Franc are here too, as is Pinot Noir, especially in the east near the foothills of the Andes. Syrah is the most important new variety.

WHITE GRAPES
Chardonnay and Sauvignon Blanc are the dominant whites, but only here and there have wines been produced with good levels of natural acidity. Gewürztraminer, Semillon and Viognier are also present in small quantities.

CLIMATE
Warm and dry, even in the most westerly part of the Coastal Ranges. Only very near the Pacific is it markedly cooler. Even so, there is a range of mesoclimates determined by elevation, slope and exposure. River mists also have an influence near Chimbarongo.

SOIL
Soils are very mixed. But there is clay here as well as the usual Chilean patchwork of loam, limestone and sand. The fertile soils on the plain have been eroded from the surrounding mountain ridges, becoming more sandy and gravelly towards the river's edge. The rivers fed by Andean snows feed the high water-table, often very close to the surface. Away from the river and on low slopes, the soils are thinner and less fertile, and drip irrigation is the norm.

ASPECT
Rapel is criss-crossed by hills or mountains; there are no extensive flat areas, common to the other subregions of the Central Valley. There is only a relatively narrow break between the Andes proper and the Coastal Ranges. While many vineyards are on the river plains of the Colchagua and Cachapoal valleys, much of the recent spate of planting has been on low slopes through to quite steep hillsides.

THE FIRST COUPLE OF TIMES I VISITED THE Colchagua Valley, I had no idea I'd done so. I'd turned right at San Fernando and headed off down a river valley towards the coast. The river was called the Tinguiririca. There were vines here and there –always on the fertile valley floor – but there were far more fruit trees and maize fields, and I only remember noting one tired-looking winery before we finally got to the elegant spread of Los Vascos, about 60km (37 miles) to the west. The whole valley seemed a pleasant, rather indolent, mild-mannered place, with very little ambition to be anything else. And the name Colchagua was never mentioned.

How things change in just a few years. Now Colchagua is a powerhouse. Grape growers have decided to become wine producers. Those sleepy wineries have given themselves a radical makeover and have not only begun to produce wine infinitely finer than anything they'd ever made before, but they've also taken the lead in challenging the old belief that the Colchagua Valley's rich soil and high water-table could only produce large volume bulk. They've shown that you can make thrilling wines even with super-fertile conditions – if your vines are old enough and you're strict enough with them – but they've also led the flight to the hills, and to the sea. In other words, away from the easy life and headlong into the challenge of wresting great quality from far more taxing conditions.

Colchagua Valley is the principal, but not the only part of the Rapel Valley section of the Central Valley. And if you're looking for the Rapel River, you won't have much more luck than with the Colchagua River – it doesn't start until after Lake Rapel, outside the vineyard area to the west. The river at the top of the map is called the Cachapoal and, thank goodness, its valley is actually called Cachapoal Valley. It's less important than Colchagua, and at 9021ha (22,290 acres) it has just over half as many vines as Colchagua, but it does have some strong points.

Requínoa, huddled underneath the Andes, right to the east of the valley, is one of them. Historically this area has always produced a fresher, fruitier Cabernet Sauvignon (over half of Cachapoal's vines are Cabernet) because the proximity to the Andes brings about extreme day-night differences of temperature. Add to this free-draining gravelly soil and a very low water-table, and it adds up to superb red wine conditions, reminiscent of the Médoc in Bordeaux. A series of French and Bordeaux-financed properties in the area compound this impression.

Cachapoal's other important area is between Peumo and Las Cabras, where the river curls round a limb of the Coastal Range and heads north-west to Lake Rapel. The lake provides continuous cooling breezes, which are necessary because the sloping vineyards are well exposed to the afternoon sun, but a mixture of gravels, red clays and a high water-table produce exceptionally fresh but ripe reds. On the valley floor here, the water-table is so high that during the winter you can find crayfish in the vineyards, but, remarkably, Sauvignon Blanc thrives.

Colchagua is directly to the south of Cachapoal, separated from it by some fairly serious mountains. Again, its strength is reds. Of the 19,960ha (49,320 acres) of vines planted, almost 10,000ha (24,710 acres) are Cabernet Sauvignon and about 6000ha (14,826 acres) are other reds ranging from Merlot and Carmenère to Syrah, Zinfandel and Sangiovese. There are some decent whites, but they are generally soft and mild, betraying their fertile-soil and hot-climate origins.

But Colchagua isn't all hot. The centre of the valley floor certainly is, but to the east and west, things are less torrid. It's possible to divide the valley up into three areas, though only in very general terms. The east is the easiest. North of San Fernando, the Andes and the Coastal Range almost converge on Angostura, and there are good vineyards, old and new, on both sides of of the narrow pass. Day-night differences in temperature are very marked with the Andes and their ice-cold air so close – up to 22°C (40°F) in the ripening period – and morning fogs temper the fierce afternoon heat, allowing not only Cabernet and Carmenère to thrive, but also such unlikely bedfellows as Chardonnay and Sangiovese. South of San Fernando, Chimbarongo is renowned for its river mists drifting off the

WHERE THE VINEYARDS ARE
Of the various rivers on the map, the two most important are the Cachapoal, which enters the map from right of top centre, then curls round to reach Lago Rapel, upper left off the map, and the Tinguiririca, which sweeps across the bottom of the map, before turning north to join the Cachapoal at Lago Rapel.

The Cachapoal has two main vineyard areas. The well-drained area of Requínoa benefits from considerable day-night temperature differences by being so close to the Andes to the east. The area round Peumo, nestling against a limb of the Coastal Ranges and cooled by westerly breezes, is successful for both reds and whites.

The area irrigated by the Tinguiririca is called the Colchagua Valley. It has three main areas. To the east, there are vineyards north and south of the river between the Andes and the Coastal Ranges. The closeness of the Andes creates a day-night temperature difference of around 22°C (40°F) and the morning mists cool things still further. In the centre, round Nancagua and Cunaco, though spreading right across to Peralillo, are traditional valley-floor vineyards. These have always been exploited by Chile's wine companies as the source of soft, ripe reds from fertile soils, nourished by a very high water-table. Consequently, there are a lot of mature vines here, and today's producers are learning to make the best of them, despite the fertile conditions. But look at the hillsides, both north and south. These are difficult, steep, stony sites, quite unlike the typical Chilean vineyards, but all the best local producers are now planting them to create powerful reds. The many plantings west of Peralillo near Marchihue are mostly new, on clay-rich soils, but far enough away from the river to require bore-hole irrigation. Expect powerful reds from here too.

0 km 2 4
0 miles 2

SANTA CRUZ

0 km 2 4
0 miles 2

SELECTED WINERIES & VINEYARDS

1. La Rosa
2. Château Los Boldos
3. Larose (Las Casas del Toqui)
4. Corpora (Gracia/Porta)
5. Torreón de Paredes
6. Morande
7. Casa Silva
8. Selentia
9. Los Vascos
10. Bisquertt
11. Mont Gras
12. Santa Laura
13. Caliterra La Arboleda Winery
14. Casa Lapostolle
15. Viu Manent
16. Montes Apalta Vineyards
17. Santa Emiliana
18. Luis Felipe Edwards
19. Cono Sur

Hill juts out of the valley north-west of Santa Cruz and it too is covered, top and sides, with vines. And out towards Peralillo, those southern hills sprout one vineyard after another. A new style of Colchagua wine. A new mood. These vineyards are the exact opposite of those in the valley. There's no ground-water up there to dilute the fruit. You get breezes at that height to cool the vines. And the soils are fierce – barren and infertile, boulders as big as beasts littering the edges of the new plantations. Montes prised out 700 truckloads of boulders to plant their Apalta vineyards. First indications are a triumphant vindication of the effort. Late-ripening grapes like Syrah, Cabernet and Carmenère have produced thrilling, dense flavours from tiny yields. And at high prices. All very different to the past.

The third part of Colchagua is out towards the sea. In particular north-west of Peralillo, around Marchihue, where parched and undulating grazing land is being transformed by bore-hole irrigation. It's pretty warm here, though breezes do get through from the Pacific. Thousands of hectares are being planted, mostly with warm-climate reds, but I've already seen surprisingly fragrant Viognier as well. West of Santa Cruz, through a gap in the hills, Lolol is being touted as another top red area, with Syrah already showing form. And way out towards the coast, chilly conditions have already produced very attractive Chardonnay and Riesling, of all things. If you can produce good Riesling, it must be cool.

Viña La Rosa's aptly named La Palmería vineyard hugs the Coastal Range mountains in Cachapoal Valley.

Tinguiririca every morning and keeping the deep, stony, sandy soils and their fruit cool. Until the emergence of Casablanca, all Chile's decent Pinot Noir came from here.

But the centre of the Valley is traditionally the heart of the action. The Tinguiririca runs west from San Fernando before turning north and heading for Lake Rapel after Santa Cruz. To start with, both north and south, high hills hem the valley in creating a canyon effect. The result is a very warm area, with very fertile river soils. That's why it was so popular in the old days – you could ripen enormous crops of decent tasting wines here every year. By Cunaco the valley is widening, and the heat is only maintained because the southern range of hills swings round and heads north, deflecting the cold Pacific breezes. And something else is happening. Look closely left and right at those mountain slopes. They're not all bare any more. North of Cunaco, the great horseshoe of Apalta is cross-hatched with vines on its steep south-facing slopes. The Ninquen

■ SAN FERNANDO

N

RAPEL VALLEY

TOTAL DISTANCE
NORTH TO SOUTH 50KM
(31 MILES)

▬▬▬ VINEYARDS

ARGENTINA

MALBEC

FAMILIA ZUCCARDI

Snow-melt water from the Andes is so plentiful in Mendoza that the traditional irrigation method is simply to flood the rows between the vines. These are young vines at Norton's Luján de Cuyo property.

IN ARGENTINA, EVERYTHING SEEMS TO COME BIG – distances, hailstones and steaks all give the impression that you've arrived in the land of the giants. The wine industry is equally gargantuan in proportion: Argentina is the fifth-largest producer of wine in the world, and used to be a top consumer too, though annual consumption has now dropped to a mere 37 litres (10 gallons) per head from 96 litres (25 gallons) per head in 1979! This, more than anything, explains why Argentina is now so determined to improve the quality of its wines and succeed in the export markets.

If your local population will drink everything you make, it's not difficult to decide exports don't matter, and when you've got a very uncertain political and economic climate – inflation peaking at about 5000 per cent a year – export markets are not that keen on doing business with you in any case. Indeed, for a long time Argentina was virtually a closed society, and it wasn't till the 1990s, with important political change and some serious restructuring of the economy, that Argentina could finally start to do business on the rest of the world's terms. It's no coincidence that during the second half of the 1990s, wine quality improved dramatically, and heavyweight investors from Europe and America began vineyard and winery projects. Sadly, 2002 saw Argentina's economy lurch back into crisis, but by then the new Argentine wine fraternity was too set on its determined way to be deterred.

GRAPE VARIETIES

Back in 1557, the Spanish started planting Criolla, the pink-skinned grape used to make huge quantities of deep-coloured, oxidized white wine. Since then, the vine has spread out over a distance of 1700km (1050 miles), from the Río Negro in the south, up to the Calchaquí Valley, close to the far northern town of Salta. Now international varieties are fast replacing grapes like Criolla, Pedro Gimenez (sic) and Ceresa. Of the 209,000ha (516430 acres) under vine, about half are now planted with international varieties. Over the past three years, 33,000ha (81,542 acres) of high quality varieties have been planted. However, walk into any wine shop in Argentina, and you'll still see lines of bottles labelled Borgoña or Chablis; both are comprised of unknown blends and require little in the way of tasting notes.

Of the European varieties, the intense black, liquorice-lined Malbecs and ripe, spicy Syrahs show the most potential for red wines. Italian immigration has brought in varieties such as Sangiovese, Bonarda and Barbera, and the Spaniards have brought in Tempranillo, but their flavours traditionally have been fused together in blends. Now they are starting to appear under their own names and are showing how suited they are to Argentine conditions. Even so, Malbec is undoubtedly the grape best suited to the hot continental climate, producing wines which are packed with blackcurrants, damsons and spice – vastly superior to its French counterpart.

Of the white grape varieties, the highly aromatic Torrontés – probably a distant relative of the Spanish Malvasia family – is the most widely planted quality variety, and there's a lot of Muscat of Alexandria. Chardonnay, predictably, is rapidly increasing, but is still outplanted by such varieties as Ugni Blanc and Chenin. Viognier looks as though it may be good in the warm areas, but Argentina, with the exception of cooler areas like Cafayate, Río Negro and Tupungato, is still without question a red wine country.

The Andes form the most important physical influence on Argentine vineyards. This barrier removes all moisture from the Pacific winds, thus creating bone-dry conditions and 320 days of sunshine every year, but also providing plentiful water for irrigation. A more negative role played by the mountains helps to explain why nets are strung over many vines in the Mendoza region. High-altitude thunderstorms formed over the Andes regularly drop golfball-sized hailstones just before the harvest, and this is more of a hazard than frost.

Unlike Chile, Argentina does not have the natural barriers to protect it from phylloxera, which is now widespread in the country, but which appears to cause little concern among winemakers. Most argue that poor soils and the use of flood irrigation keep the louse at bay. In general, soils are arid and stony with very little humus, creating stressful conditions for the vines.

CLASSIFICATION OF ARGENTINE WINE

So far, Argentina is the only South American country to have a Denominación de Origen Controlada (DOC) system. It is, however, fairly new, and as yet only two areas have official DOC status – San Rafael and Luján de Cuyo, both in the province of Mendoza, Argentina's main wine-producing region. Whether more DOCs will be added currently remains in some doubt, as there is little enthusiasm for the system at present among Argentine winemakers.

In Mendoza, if you're looking for the best white winegrowing conditions, you have to head up towards the Andes foothills, using altitude as your cooling system. But if you head south of Mendoza, well south, right down to Patagonia itself, you come to the small, but highly promising Río Negro region. It doesn't look promising as you press your face against the window of the tiny plane that carries you south from San Rafael. Endless barren scrub is relieved only by minimal signs of human endeavour, and even these offer little reassurance. A settlement laid out near the Río Colorado is now nothing but rectangular scars scratched into the parched sandy soil. But then the greenery returns – the gash of fertility that marks the Río Negro. Yet again, you realize how most of Argentina would be mere desert if it weren't for irrigation. And if you climb up to the ridge on the south bank of the Río Negro, you are looking at the beginning of Patagonia, the stone–strewn, inhospitable terrain in front of you which spreads south towards Cape Horn for 2500 km (1553 miles). Turn back and look north towards the river, and you can see poplars swaying in the evening breeze, dark green fruit trees packed tight next to vineyards, and the odd cloud of dust as a rare car hurries along the unpaved roads. And below the ridge on the northern side of the valley, the reason for this verdancy – the Valle Alto irrigation channel that runs from the main town of Neuquén and waters all the plantations between the northern ridge and the Río Negro itself.

There are about 5000ha (12,355 acres) under vine here, though local producers are talking ambitiously of increasing this to 25,000ha (61,774 acres) within 10 years. The Río Negro could very easily become Argentina's best white-wine region, with its long ripening seasons and cool conditions, giving grapes that are naturally high in acidity. But for now this is primarily red-wine country, and certainly the Malbec is marvellously scented and deep in colour. As yet the best producer is Humberto Canale, who also produces good Semillon and Pinot Noir.

OTHER REGIONS

North of Mendoza, there are still substantial vineyards, but their wines are far less known than those of Mendoza itself. San Juan, directly north of Mendoza, grows about 24 per cent of the national grape crop. We don't hear much about it for two reasons. The majority of grapes there are pretty dull varieties, and most of them end up as grape concentrate. Secondly, we are only just beginning to see the emergence of private estates. Until now, most of the wine has been processed at co-operatives and has ended up in anonymous blends. However, the potential of this warm area is good, especially in the El Pedernal Valley down towards Mendoza, where there are vineyards planted as high up as 1350m (4429ft) above sea level.

The Famatina Valley in La Rioja, around Cilecito, is hot and dry, with mainly poor, sandy soil. Most grapes here are white and processed by local co-ops, which are luckily pretty good, especially with Torrontes. Clearly this is an area that suits reds, but it's a slow process trying to persuade smallholders to uproot healthy white vines and replant with red. In any case, expansion may be hindered by shortage of water, which would be a pity because there are promising sites going up to 1200m (3937ft).

North of La Rioja, Catamarca has some vineyards, including a new one at 2000m (6562ft), planted by a group led by Peñaflor, Argentina's biggest producer. It should be interesting, but the real action in the north is in Salta province, particularly in the mountain resort of Cafayate, sitting at 1700m (5577ft) in splendid isolation in the midst of what is virtually a desert. A new airport has made access easier, but I'd still recommend driving from Salta to Cafayate through the Rio de las Conchas Valley for some of the most breathtakingly beautiful mountain scenery you will ever encounter. Vineyards go well past 2000m (6562ft) here, though most are sited at around 1700m (5577ft), and the speciality of the area is a wonderfully scented version of Torrontés, though all whites are good, as is the purple–hued Malbec. The height clearly cools things down, and although temperatures can rise to 38°C (100°F), in February, they generally drop back at night to 12-15°C (54-59°F). But Cafayate gets 350 days of sun a year – so an important extra bonus for the grapes is a breeze that starts every day between 2 and 3pm and blows until about 8pm, when the sun has already gone down. So far any investment here has been hindered by the inaccessibility of the region, but as more and more producers crave cool-climate sites, this is sure to change.

Malbec is Argentina's most famous red; and Mendoza is the centre of production.

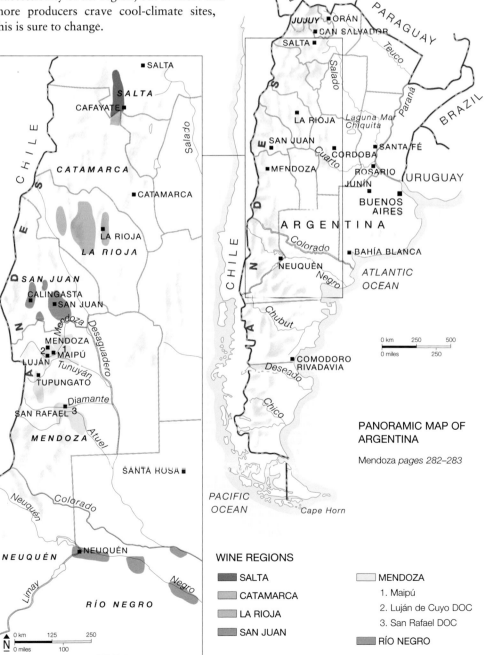

PANORAMIC MAP OF ARGENTINA

Mendoza *pages 282–283*

WINE REGIONS

- SALTA
- CATAMARCA
- LA RIOJA
- SAN JUAN
- MENDOZA
  1. Maipú
  2. Luján de Cuyo DOC
  3. San Rafael DOC
- RÍO NEGRO

AUSTRALIA

In the foreground (left) sheep graze as they have done for generations and in the background vineyards reach up from the Barossa Valley floor on to the arid slopes above Tanunda. Ancient gum trees (above) stand guard over Mountadam's vineyards in the Eden Valley, South Australia and suck what moisture they can from the parched hillsides.

Australia didn't have many advantages when it came to establishing a wine industry. There was no history of wine among the aboriginal people because there weren't any native vines. None of Australia's trading partners in South-East Asia had ever had wine as part of their culture. And it didn't seem propitious that the nation which decided to colonize the vast continent was Britain. Now, if the French, or the Italians, or the Spanish…

We forget one thing. The British weren't much good at growing grapes at home, but they were the world's greatest connoisseurs when it came to appreciating the wine of other European countries, in particular the table wines of France and the fortified wines of Portugal and Spain. Since Australia was initially settled as a penal colony, the authorities were keen to establish a temperate wine-drinking culture, rather than one based on the more savage rum. And at the end of the 18th century, when New South Wales was gradually establishing itself, Europe was embroiled in war. The idea of a British Imperial vineyard not hostage to the recurrent political crises in Europe must have seemed enticing. Well, it almost did work out like that. For considerable portions of the 19th and 20th centuries, Australia provided a steady stream of unchallenging – and mostly fortified – wines that were lapped up by Britain. But by the last quarter of the 20th century the country had embarked on a remarkable voyage of wine discovery that has placed her at the forefront of all that is best in the New Age of wine – despite having a vineyard area that is dwarfed by the major European nations.

This position has been achieved without Australia enjoying many of the perceived benefits of Europe's classic regions, most of which are poised on the cusp between not being able to and being able to ripen their fruit. Unlike Europe, the general rule in Australia is more than enough sunshine and not nearly enough rain. Traditionalists say you can't make great wine under such conditions but Australia's winemakers have turned this to their advantage, using irrigation freely and highlighting the ripeness of the grapes in a succession of sun-filled, richly textured reds and whites. Despite the very different conditions these may initially have been inspired by the best of Europe, but they have created such a forceful identity of their own that Europe now often attempts to ape the these Down Under Wonders. In the meantime, a better understanding of how to bring grapes to optimum ripeness – not over- or underripe, but just so – have led to an explosion of cool-climate wine regions on the fringes of this parched continent that challenge, but in no way imitate, the old classic regions of Europe.

THE WINE REGIONS OF AUSTRALIA

WATER, WATER, WATER. That's the story of Australia. On this vast, parched continent, finding meagre supplies of moisture is an ever-present priority, and not just for grape-growers. The nation's population, let alone any vineyard development, is limited by the availability of water and little of the rain that does fall arrives when it is most needed – during the long, hot summers. Yet Australians show amazing resourcefulness and new vineyards spring up where no-one had dreamt vines could flourish.

At the beginning of the 1980s, when its thoughts turned winewards, the country was known abroad for little more than the odd bottle of Kanga Rouge red. Since then Australia has established a reputation for approachable, yet high quality, characterful wines of every possible style that is nothing short of astonishing.

All the major states manage to find a mixture of cool, warm and roasting conditions in which to grow their wines. All the major players, that is. The Northern Territory's Chateau Hornsby near Alice Springs probably qualifies as the hottest – and maddest – winery in the universe. Queensland is pretty torrid too, though some high-altitude vineyards down on the New South Wales border like to think of themselves as coolish. Tasmania endlessly seeks patches of land warm enough to ripen grapes in a climate once condemned by its own government as too cool for grapes and about right for apples, and most of its main vineyards, based in the north of the island, find life a struggle.

WESTERN AUSTRALIA

Western Australia is a vast state, virtual desert except for its south-western coastal strip. Its wine industry was one of the first to be established in Australia, but Perth's isolation kept it largely focused on supplying the local market, with the exception of the Swan Valley, whose Houghton White Burgundy was highly successful in the eastern states. This old-fashioned, sun-baked region was best suited to throaty reds and fortified wine. But winery and vineyard expertise is now so sophisticated that remarkably good dry whites are now emerging. Even so, the most exciting wines come from the secluded vales of the Margaret River and the Lower Great Southern regions, where the continent's south-western tip turns away from the Indian Ocean towards the cold depths of the Southern Ocean.

SOUTH AUSTRALIA

South Australia was the last of the major wine states to be established in the 1840s, but more than made up for lost time. It dominates the Australian wine scene, growing the greatest tonnage of grapes, making the largest volume of wine – and housing most of its biggest wine companies. The bulk of its grapes are grown in the impressive vineyards along the banks of the Murray River where mechanization, sunshine and a plentiful supply of water from the river have created some of the most efficient vineyards in the world.

But South Australia has far more to offer than oceans of attractive, undemanding, gluggable wine. The single most important factor is that the phylloxera bug, which destroyed almost all the world's wines in the 19th century, never reached South Australia, so their vines, along with those of Chile, are planted on their own roots, not grafted. In the north, the verdant Clare Valley, scooped out of the parched grazing land that stretches away on all sides, is an unexpected but excellent producer of 'cool-climate' table wines. Not always that cool, however, because, as so often in Australia, local climates within an area provide a far broader range of styles than one would find in Europe. Clare Shiraz and Clare 'port' are just as good as delicate Clare Riesling.

The Barossa Valley is South Australia's heartland, where most of the big companies are based and much multiregional wine is processed. It is also home to some of the planet's oldest vines, and the blockbuster Shiraz and Grenache from these vines have made Barossa world famous. Eden Valley, in the hills east of Barossa, has a spectrum of wine styles, but it is the crisp, steely Rieslings that set it apart. Just south of Adelaide is the first wine area to be developed in South Australia, once famous for 'ferruginous' reds and fortified wines, which were shipped to England in vast quantities. Despite incursions from the expanding city, the area is now a major producer of high quality reds and whites.

Population explosion has never been a problem at Padthaway and Coonawarra – hardly anyone lives in this damp, forlorn corner of the state – but this has allowed the development of superb vineyards making thrilling wines, and the lack of a local populace has forced the region to become the world leader in the science of total vineyard mechanization.

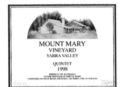

There are vines up to 140 years old in the Hill of Grace vineyard owned by Henschke in Eden Valley, South Australia. No wonder this Shiraz wine is one of Australia's most expensive wines.

THE CLASSIFICATION SYSTEM FOR AUSTRALIAN WINE

Australia's system for classifying wines on the labels of bottles for export stems from an 1994 agreement with the EU. In order to reach this agreement, it was necessary to define areas of origin, and the Geographical Indications Committee was set up in 1993 to do this. It divided the wine-producing states into a number of zones, regions and sub-regions. The complete extent of all of them is yet to be agreed and the discussions, arguments and political wranglings that always accompany such decisions will be in full voice for some years yet.

The system has to encompass certain peculiarities. The main one is the widespread use of regional blending in Australia: that is, trucking grapes from several different areas, possibly in different states, for blending together. Four major wine groups (Southcorp, BRL Hardy, Orlando Wyndham and Beringer Blass) make nearly 60 per cent of Australia's wine, and they rely a lot on blending varieties and wines from different areas, especially for their big-selling brands, such as Koonunga Hill and Jacob's Creek, which are now important players in the wine scene. Whatever the origin of a wine, however, 85 per cent of its grapes must come from the area specified, whether it is a zone, region or sub-region, and it must be made of at least the same percentage of the named grape variety.

QUALITY CATEGORIES AND GEOGRAPHICAL INDICATIONS

- **The Label Integrity Program** This system (also called LIP) was introduced in 1990 and guarantees all claims made on the label, for example, the vintage, variety and region, by making annual checks and audits on specific regions, varieties and wineries.
- **Produce of Australia** This is the most general geographical designation. Any wine sold solely under this category will not be able to have a grape variety or a vintage on its label.
- **South-Eastern Australia** This is the next level, a category which covers, in fact, most of the wine-producing areas of Australia and is widely seen, particularly on the big-selling brand name wines.
- **State of Origin** This is the next most specific category.
- **Zones** Many of Australia's traditional wine areas are being incorporated into these new zones. For example, Barossa is a zone within the state of South Australia.
- **Regions** These are the next level, for example, Barossa is divided into the regions of Barossa Valley and Eden Valley.
- **Sub-regions** Some regions are divided into sub-regions, for example Eden Valley consists of the High Eden and Springton sub-regions.

VICTORIA

Victoria's vineyards seem like they've been hurled into position with a scatter-gun. This is because they followed the Gold Rush, and when gold was exhausted odd vines were left all over the state. They can, however, produce some of the most exhilarating and distinctive Australian wines, albeit in tiny quantities. Victoria was Australia's major wine producer for most of the 19th century, until phylloxera devastated her vineyards. She has only recently reassumed her position as provider of some of the most startling Australian wines. Large amounts are produced in the Murray River area, but it's the stunning liqueur Muscats of Rutherglen and Glenrowan, the thrilling dark reds of Central Victoria, the urbane Yarra Valley and Mornington Peninsula reds and whites, and the lean, perfumed reds and whites that crop up in patches of cool vineyard land right across the state that leave their imprint on my mind.

NEW SOUTH WALES

Colonial Australia began in New South Wales (in the Hunter Valley), as did the wine revolution that propelled Australia to the front of the world stage. However, the state is a major bulk producer along the Murrumbidgee River, and a clutch of new wine regions in the Central Ranges are grabbing headlines.

PANORAMIC MAPS OF AUSTRALIA

Barossa pages 290–291
Coonawarra page 293
Clare Valley page 295
Yarra Valley pages 298–299
Hunter Valley page 303
Margaret River page 306

OTHER MAPS

South Australia page 289
Victoria page 296
New South Wales page 301
Western Australia page 305
Tasmania page 308
Queensland and Northern Territory page 309

WINE ZONES

WESTERN AUSTRALIA

1. Eastern Plains, Inland and North of Western Australia
2. Greater Perth
3. Central Western Australia
4. West Australian South-East Coastal
5. South-West Australia

SOUTH AUSTRALIA

6. Far North
7. The Peninsulas

8. Mt Lofty Ranges
9. Barossa
10. Lower Murray
11. Fleurieu
12. Limestone Coast

VICTORIA

13. North-West Victoria
14. Central Victoria
15. North-East Victoria
16. Western Victoria
17. Port Phillip
18. Gippsland

NEW SOUTH WALES

19. Western Plains
20. Northern Slopes
21. Northern Rivers
22. Hunter Valley
23. Central Ranges
24. Big Rivers
25. Southern New South Wales
26. South Coast

QUEENSLAND

NORTHERN TERRITORY

AUSTRALIAN CAPITAL TERRITORY

TASMANIA

SOUTH AUSTRALIA

RED GRAPES
Shiraz and Cabernet Sauvignon predominate, but Merlot and Grenache are also important, as is Pinot Noir, especially in the cooler sites.

WHITE GRAPES
Riesling, Chardonnay, Semillon and Sauvignon Blanc are widely planted, with some Colombard, Chenin and Verdelho, and a smattering of Viognier and Gewürztraminer.

CLIMATE
This ranges from 'cool climate' areas like the Adelaide Hills and Coonawarra, to hot, dry areas like Barossa.

SOIL
The soil is a mix of sandy loam, red loam, various clays and fertile volcanic earth. Coonawarra has an area of terra rossa over a limestone subsoil.

ASPECT
This varies widely, from the flat vineyards of Coonawarra to vines on quite steep slopes in the Adelaide Hills, the Barossa Ranges and parts of the Clare Valley.

The bleakness of Coonawarra railway station surrounded by a sea of vines and not a house in sight illustrates the remoteness of the Limestone Coast.

THEY RECKON ADELAIDE'S DRINKING WATER is some of the worst in the civilized world. I do, too. But the beer is excellent, so, apart from brushing my teeth, I don't have a lot to do with it. However, throughout the state, water – or lack of it – is a hot topic. The only part of South Australia that has enough water is the southern tip where Coonawarra almost drowns in the stuff. In the rest of the state every drop counts.

Luckily, South Australia has one massive zillion-gallon water resource – the Murray River – which follows a tortuous route for nearly 2600km (1615 miles) between New South Wales and Victoria before arcing through South Australia and trickling out into the ocean at Lake Alexandrina. The exploitation of the Murray for irrigating hundreds of thousands of otherwise uncultivable barren acres was one of the great agro-industrial feats of the 20th century, but ever increasing exploitation of this finite resource and a disturbing rise in the salinity of the soils it nourishes is causing great concern.

This was not an issue in the early 1950s when the late Max Schubert, winemaker at Penfolds near Adelaide, produced his first experimental barrels of Grange – a wine that was to transform the perception of what quality was possible in the vineyards of the 'New World', and which is now as prized and appreciated as the greatest red wines of Europe. But when he set out to create Grange, Schubert didn't have a special vineyard to hand – he merely had a vision of flavour, great scientific expertise and a bloody-minded belief that if the French could do it, so could he. This approach is not approved of by the traditionalists of Europe, who maintain, through their systems of controlled appellation of origin, that great wines only come from special rare patches of land, pinpointed after centuries of trial and error. They've had a thousand or two years to fine-tune this principle of *terroir*, which lays all the emphasis for specialness on the place, and regards the men or women involved merely as transient guardians of the flame. But they're missing half the trick.

Australia hasn't had hundreds of years during which to gradually pick and choose her favourite spots. She hasn't had a hundred generations of inhabitants whose lives revolved around the vine, developing a fine wine tradition across the ages.

Max Schubert's success at creating a great wine is proof of Australia's greatest gift to the world of wine – the belief that everything is possible. And that the art of blending suitable wines to create a delicious flavour – regardless of where the vines grew and what varieties they were – is a truly noble art. You can do it from scratch, with whatever materials suit your purpose. You just have to believe. Of course, you can't guarantee what the end result will be like, but if you follow your vision with courage and determination, you can do it.

ADELAIDE'S FIRST VINEYARDS

As with the other states, vines were planted within a year of the first settlement in 1836 and, as with Sydney and Melbourne, these first vineyards have long since disappeared under the tarmac and brick of modern Adelaide, although a small patch of the original Penfolds vineyard at Magill is still producing grapes, hemmed in by suburbia. Vineyards were fairly quickly established in the northern reaches of the city, and the influx of German settlers to the Barossa Valley in the 1840s created a vineyard and winery community that has played a dominant role in Australian wine ever since, and left it with some of the world's oldest vines.

But the first moves out of Adelaide were in fact to the south: to Morphett Vale, Reynella, McLaren Vale and Langhorne Creek. Morphett Vale and most of Reynella have now largely disappeared under the creeping tide of urban sprawl, but Adelaide is not only much smaller than Melbourne and Sydney, it is also more aware of the importance of wine to the state. Consequently the attractive neighbourhood of McLaren Vale has largely been able to resist the developers and to enjoy a burgeoning number of vineyards and wineries, both large and small.

RIVERLAND

Australia has two Californians to thank for much of the wine they drink today. The Chaffey brothers arrived in Australia at the end of the 1880s, having successfully established irrigation schemes in Californian desert conditions. They had the foresight and determination to utilize their experience to transform the annual flooding of the Murray River into the most important resource in Australian viticulture.

The headwaters of the Murray River are numerous streams fed by the melting snowfields of the Great Dividing Range. Every year the river used to bulge and burst with the thaw. The waters flooded vast expanses of empty, arid land that gratefully lapped up the moisture – but to no avail, since no-one knew how to exploit this annual bounty.

First at Renmark in South Australia, and then at Mildura further upstream in north-west Victoria, the Chaffeys built pumping stations, dams, locks and irrigation channels to harness the Murray River. As a result verdant market gardens and vineyards were planted where nothing but saltbush desert had existed before.

Both Renmark and Mildura went through tricky times but, by and large, they and the other Murray Valley regions of South Australia and Victoria flourished, and so did the Riverina region which lies on a Murrumbidgee River tributary in New South Wales. Today, the grapes for all the low-priced, but attractively fruity, red and white Australian wines the world laps up will have come from these vast mechanized, irrigated vineyards.

This large-scale irrigation has helped Australia to transform the quality of budget wine worldwide, but it is a relatively recent phenomenon. The heart and soul of the South Australian wine industry is still in the water-starved, sun-soaked fields and vales to the north and south of Adelaide.

GRANGE

It was near Adelaide that Australia's fine wine tradition began, when Max Schubert, Penfolds' chief winemaker, began work in 1951 on what was to become one of the greatest wines in the world – known first as Grange Hermitage, now as Grange.

Schubert had returned from a trip to Europe's vineyards the year before, fired up most of all by the great red wines of Bordeaux's Médoc – a fine wine area with a lot of rain, barely enough sunshine, and a predominance of the Cabernet Sauvignon grape. The region produced wine that was aged in new French oak barrels and could mature for half a century. He was determined to make the same style of wine in South Australia – where there was tons of sunshine, hardly any rain, about one shopping basket full of Cabernet Sauvignon in the entire state, and not a new French oak barrel to be found. And until his visit to Bordeaux he had had no idea that a red wine could hope to age for more than ten years at the outside.

No worries. Schubert had the vision. He decided the Shiraz grapes – the same variety as Syrah in France's Rhône Valley – were the best South Australia could offer. So he'd use these. Different flavour from Cabernet, but if he picked them early from low-yielding vines and treated them with kid gloves from the moment of picking to the moment of bottling, he reckoned he could get the result he wanted. He managed to secure a few American rather than the more traditional French oak barrels, and decided they were in any case more suitable for his Shiraz.

Ah yes, the vineyards. Well, Schubert began with some vines at Morphett Vale, south of Adelaide, and some at Magill in the foothills fringing Adelaide. They weren't famous vineyards, but he knew them, he knew their soils, their ripening patterns, and the flavour of their fruit. They served him well for the first Grange. Later he added Kalimna, in the Barossa Valley, and when Morphett Vale was sold for housing he expanded into the Clare Valley. These days, with Southcorp, Penfold's parent company, controlling a massive amount of South Australia's top vineyards, Coonawarra fruit joins McLaren Vale, Barossa, Clare, indeed any fruit that is good enough. Simple as that. If the fruit is good enough it will be considered for Grange, though recent vintages have been increasingly Barossa dominant.

Whenever someone starts to lecture me about the necessity of colonizing the world with the self-serving, protectionist appellations that stifle so much of Europe's creativity, I triumphantly raise the case of Grange. All it claims on the Grange label is 'South Australian Shiraz'. That's a proud enough statement for me. I hope it never has to change.

FLEURIEU

The region directly south of Adelaide, with McLaren Vale at its centre, is called Fleurieu. Its success right up to the 1950s was based on its ability to ripen black grapes sufficiently to create fortified 'ports' of high quality, or strapping great red table wines that boasted of their 'ferruginous' (iron-rich) character as being of medicinal quality. Generations of respectable British ladies supped happily on Tintara and Emu Burgundy, convinced they were imbibing for their health's sake. Well, well, perhaps they were.

In fact Fleurieu has proved a highly adaptable wine region. Although it is sunny, and McLaren Vale and further north is genuinely hot, most of the vineyards benefit from afternoon sea breezes cooling down the vines. Langhorne Creek on the eastern side of the Fleurieu Peninsula is positively cool and is also fairly heavily irrigated. Water is short in McLaren Vale and the Cabernet, Shiraz and even Grenache are rich and heady, but there are also surprisingly good Chardonnays and Sauvignons.

MOUNT LOFTY RANGES AND BAROSSA

Just inland from McLaren Vale you can see the southern tip of the Adelaide Hills. These head north, skirting Adelaide, to become part of the Mount Lofty Ranges, continuing up east of the Barossa Valley to Mount Pleasant, where they become the Eden Valley.

The hills more or less directly east of Adelaide, around Piccadilly, are high, even slightly damp, and they produce some exceptional 'cool-climate' whites and exciting sparkling wines. Lenswood, a little to the north, can also produce gorgeous reds. It's an area which has attracted some of the greatest talents in the South Australian wine world and, with the recent vogue for cool- rather than warm-climate sites, they make a series of remarkable wines, seemingly improving every year as their experience grows and the vineyards mature.

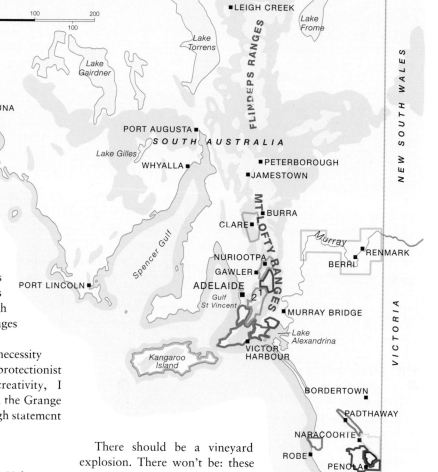

There should be a vineyard explosion. There won't be: these vineyards need irrigation and the hills are a crucial catchment area for Adelaide's water. The water may taste lousy, but thirsty citizens with votes win over vines every time.

The tale is of water right through South Australia. Clare Valley in the north might also have expanded much more than it has done if there were enough water, but rainfall is low and subterranean water hard to come by. Meanwhile, Barossa growers have paid to build a massive new pipeline from the Murray River to boost its over-burdened bore water supply and Clare will be next.

LIMESTONE COAST

Water dominates the cool far south of the state as well, but in a different way. The Great Artesian Basin stretches across the area towards the sea. The water table is so high that most of the land is far too swampy for viticulture. But there are a series of limestone ridges in the south-east of the state that offer brilliant conditions for vines. Coonawarra's exceptional qualities have been known about since the end of the 19th century, and it is now perhaps Australia's most sought after locality for vineyard land. Padthaway, 65km (40 miles) to the north of Coonawarra, is another fine region, and wherever limestone crops up we are seeing vineyards being developed – right out to the coast at Robe and Mount Benson.

However, in order to preserve supplies of drinking water to Victoria in the east, South Australia has had to accept strict limitations on how much water she extracts on her side of the state border. Even when there is water, water everywhere, someone is going to stop you doing what you want with it.

WINE REGIONS AND SUB-REGIONS

- Clare Valley
- Riverland
- Barossa Valley
- Eden Valley
- Adelaide Hills
  1. Piccadilly Valley
  2. Lenswood
- McLaren Vale
- Southern Fleurieu
- Currency Creek
- Langhorne Creek
- Kangaroo Island
- Padthaway
- Wrattonbully
- Coonawarra
- Penola
- Mount Benson
- OVER 200M (656FT)
- OVER 500M (1640FT)

Charles Melton's Nine Popes from the Barossa Valley is a pun on France's Châteauneuf-du-Pape, and the wine is a rich, ripe red based on Grenache and Shiraz – just like Châteauneuf-du-Pape.

BAROSSA

RED GRAPES
Shiraz is the star red, not only dominating current plantings, but new vineyards as well. Cabernet Sauvignon is also important, but the next most precious resource is hundreds of hectares of old Grenache and a little ancient Mataro (Mourvèdre). There are also tiny quantities of Spanish, Italian and Portuguese varieties.

WHITE GRAPES
Riesling is still the leading grape, mostly planted in the Eden Valley, but there is almost as much Semillon and Chardonnay, and a small amount of Sauvignon Blanc and Chenin.

CLIMATE
The Barossa Valley is hot, with some drip irrigation used to counteract the arid summers. The Eden Valley and the Barossa Ranges are cooler with more rain, but it's winter rain when the vines are dormant, so irrigation is often necessary.

SOIL
Topsoils are varied, ranging from heavy loam with clay, to light sand; some soils need the addition of lime to counteract acidity. Subsoils are limestone, quartz-sand and clay, and red-brown loams.

ASPECT
Traditional valley floor estates are best at producing big reds; estates in the Eden Valley at 300–400m (985–1300ft) are excellent for cooler climate styles.

JUST LISTEN TO THESE NAMES – Kaiser Stuhl, Siegersdorf, Bernkastel, Gnadenfrei – the names of wineries and vineyards in the Barossa. And listen to these names – Johann Gramp, Johann Henschke, Peter Lehmann, Leo Buring – the names of Barossa winemakers, ancient and modern. Add to these a delightful assembly of old Lutheran bluestone churches, bakeries offering *Streusel* and *Kuchen*, rather than buns and cakes, delicatessens displaying *Mettwurst* and *Lacksschinken*, and the strains of lusty-lunged choirs and brass bands at practice cutting through the still warm air of a summer's evening – and you know the Barossa is different. It's in a time warp from the early days when Lutheran settlers from Silesia (now part of Poland) travelled halfway round the world to spread themselves across this valley just to the north of Adelaide, intent upon creating a new homeland.

Scratch the surface, though, and you find a different story. These days Kaiser Stuhl and Leo Buring are mere brand names within the giant Southcorp group. Many of Australia's largest-scale and most efficient wineries now cluster round the old settler towns of Nuriootpa, Tanunda and Angaston. Indeed, today more than half of all Australia's wine is made by these big Barossa-based companies. But not many of the grapes for these wines are grown in the Barossa by the descendants of the Silesian settlers who used to provide the fruit.

It was little less than a disaster for Australian wine in the late 20th century when, one by one, the famous old Barossa wine concerns grew into nationally important operations, and two things dawned on the money-men. First, the Barossa vineyards might produce good grapes, but their yields were low and their prices were high. Second, that the reverse was true of the vast easily irrigated vineyards that were springing up along the banks of the Murray River. These might not produce exciting grapes, but they have high yields and low prices.

These large companies concluded that if talented corporate winemakers could make perfectly good wines out of these inferior grapes, why use expensive local fruit? They showed a callous disregard for the welfare of the local Barossa growers, much of whose crop, during the 1980s, they were prepared to let shrivel, unpicked, on the vine. Beady-eyed financial ruthlessness pushed Barossa grape-growing to the brink, and many ancient Barossa families cursed the men in suits who now ran the companies their forebears had created. But by the beginning of the new millennium, the pendulum had swung the growers' way. Enthusiasts worldwide realized that some of the oldest pre-phylloxera vines still alive survive in Barossa – many over a century old. The incomparable flavours these centenarians offer has meant that 'boutique' small-scale, high quality wine production now flourishes in the Barossa. The big companies are still there, and put these precious grapes to far better use than before but now, when they try to browbeat a grower, the grower has somewhere better to turn.

The Barossa Valley was settled by a mixture of German and British pioneers in the 1840s and '50s. George Angas, a Scot, was one of South Australia's most important frontiersmen. To counteract the chronic shortage of labour to work his estate north of Adelaide, he paid for three shiploads of German Lutherans to emigrate from Silesia. They arrived in the Barossa Valley in 1842 and, though Anglo-Saxon families like the Hill-Smiths of Yalumba have thrived since, settling at Angaston in 1849, it was the Germans – or Barossa Deutsch – who moulded the character of the valley. Vineyards and wine companies were established, which, by the beginning of 20th century, already led South Australian production. With the abolition of interstate tariffs and the decimation of rival Victoria's vineyards by phylloxera, South Australia fast assumed the dominant position in Australian wine, and the efficient Barossa companies were the natural leaders.

NURIOOTPA

ANGASTON

TANUNDA

LYNDOCH

BAROSSA VALLEY VINEYARDS

Vineyards were established in two main areas: the gently undulating valley floor, along the North Para River from Nuriootpa down to Lyndoch, and on the hills to the east. The valley floor is hot and dry; soils veer from infertile yellow clays to deep red loam, suited to the production of dark intense red wines. There's little rainfall, and there's little subterranean water suitable for irrigation. This seemed to satisfy all parties until the 1970s, when there was a huge swing in public taste towards fresh, fruity, white wines – not at all what the Barossa was suited to with its gnarled old Shiraz and Grenache. It becomes blindingly obvious why big companies gave up using Barossa grapes and began developing huge, mechanized vineyards on the Murray River.

The Barossa Valley as a grape-growing region might have sunk without trace. But luckily a local hero – Peter Lehmann – was around to rescue one of Australia's greatest wine heritages. He set up a company with the sole aim of saving vineyards from the plough. Now others, including giants like Southcorp and Yalumba, have joined him.

EDEN VALLEY

Up in the hills it is very different. Henschke grow brilliant Shiraz north of Eden Valley, and Mountadam has made remarkable Pinot Noir

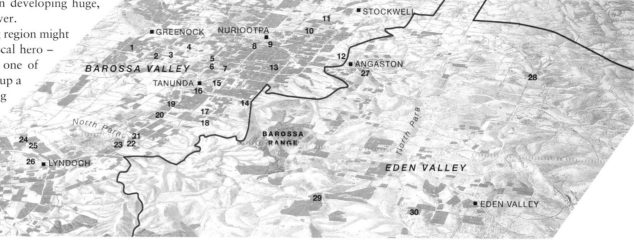

SELECTED WINERIES			
BAROSSA VALLEY	9. Elderton	18. Charles Melton	**EDEN VALLEY**
1. Greenock Creek	10. Willows Vineyard	19. St Hallett	27. Yalumba
2. Barossa Valley Estate	11. Wolf Blass	20. Grant Burge	28. Henschke
3. Heritage	12. Saltram	21. Orlando	29. Mountadam
4. Torbreck Wines	13. Haan Wines	22. Miranda	30. Irvine
5. Veritas	14. Bethany	23. Jenke Vineyards	
6. Peter Lehmann	15. Basedow	24. Yaldara	*EDEN VALLEY* = WINE REGION
7. Richmond Grove	16. Turkey Flat	25. Charles Cimicky	——— REGIONAL BOUNDARY
8. Penfolds	17. Rockford	26. Burge Family	

on the outcrops to the west, but greater height means much cooler conditions. This has made Eden Valley and the surrounding hills one of Australia's top white wine producers: the Rieslings, in particular, with their steely attack and lime fragrance are often Australia's best. Big companies increasingly use Eden Valley fruit in their top wines, and it is significant that the French giant Moet Hennessey has taken over the trailblazing Mountadam. But the true glories still come from old family operations like Henschke.

BAROSSA AND EDEN VALLEYS

TOTAL DISTANCE NORTH TO SOUTH 31KM (19 MILES)

▰▰▰ VINEYARDS

0 km   1   2
0 miles   1

WHERE THE VINEYARDS ARE *This map is a marvellous panorama of the whole Barossa grape-growing region. One of the things that always strikes me in South Australia is how seemingly insignificant the mountains are. The inaptly named Mount Lofty Ranges stretch up the right of the map, yet these ancient hills have been worn away over the millennia into hummocks of storm-smoothed rock. But they are a vital few hundred metres above the valley floor, creating cooler, windier conditions for viticulture, and since they are some of the first obstacles the westerly winds have encountered since coming in from the Indian Ocean, whatever moisture there is will drop mainly in these hills.*

As you can see, most of the vineyards have lakes next to them. These are to catch winter rains for irrigation in the dry summers, when each vine may need 5 litres (2 gallons) of water a day. Mountadam, for instance, at the bottom of the map, is a 1000-ha (2470-acre) estate, yet just 75ha (185 acres) are planted with vines. The rest is largely used as a catchment area for the 86cm (34in) of rain that falls each winter and spring.

The valley floor gets far less winter rain and almost none in summer. Not only that, subterranean water to the west of the North Para River is too salty to be of much use for irrigation. Consequently, most vineyards lie east of the river. But the dry land to the north and around Nuriootpa and Greenock can produce stunning reds from old, low-yielding vines: Penfolds' Grange is based on Kalimna fruit from north of Nuriootpa. Further south, wineries such as St Hallett, Rockford and Charles Melton are building enviable reputations. A new pipeline from the Murray River will either help top growers to maximize quality, or allow greedy producers to maximize volume. The west of the valley needs this pipeline. I'm not sure the rest does.

In the Eden Valley hills, water is less of a problem – so long as you are prepared to build large catchment dams to hold the winter rains, as precious little falls in summer. It is distinctly cooler here, due to the height of the hills themselves: most vineyards are at 400–500m (1300–1640ft) high, and produce some of Australia's top white wines.

COONAWARRA

RED GRAPES
Success with Cabernet Sauvignon make this the predominant variety now, though there is a good deal of Shiraz and Merlot, and a little Pinot Noir.

WHITE GRAPES
Chardonnay is the most widely planted variety, but there's also Riesling and some good Sauvignon Blanc.

CLIMATE
These are the southernmost, and, therefore, coolest of South Australian vineyards. The easily accessible water table gives high yields of good quality. Vintage can take place from early March to as late as May.

SOIL
An area of terra rossa (literally 'red soil'), or crumbly red loam, covers the low ridges, with both black cracking clay and sandy soils over a clay base on lower ground.

ASPECT
It is flat here – uniformly so, and with its long growing season, high light intensity and unique soil structure, it is ideal for vines.

Wynns was one of the earliest wineries in Coonawarra: this is its John Riddoch Cabernet, named in honour of the region's first grape-grower, the founder of the Coonawarra fruit colony in 1890.

MOST OF THE GREAT VINEYARDS of the world owe their presence to a river which has carved its path to the sea, creating a mixture of valley slopes and river plains that provide unique conditions for grapes to ripen. Coonawarra's uniqueness is the fact that there *aren't* any rivers: there are mountains to the east; there's sea to the west; but there are no rivers to connect one to the other.

There is a lot of water, though, falling in the mountains every winter. And it seeps, inch by inch, just below the surface across the bleak swathe of bogland that makes up the southern tip of South Australia. They call this the rump end of the Great Artesian Basin – at least, that's how I interpret their vernacular. Depending on who you talk to, the water has seeped from neighbouring Victoria or all the way from Queensland. And depending on how far the water has come, it could be thousands of years old or hundreds. Anyway, it's so pure you almost need to add salts to it to make it suitable for vines. And there's lots of it, just below the surface.

That's all very well. But what about what happens above ground? What about the climate; and, for that matter, what about the soil? So far this sounds like a graphic description of one of the world's all-time squelchy hell-holes. What's it to do with wine? Let's go back a bit. About 600,000 years.

The area was underwater then, with the shoreline marked by the Comaum Range east of Coonawarra. But two things happened. First, there was a reversal in the earth's magnetic field, followed by a slow but continual upheaval in the land that has by now raised Coonawarra 60m (200ft) above sea level. Second, about every 50,000 years, there has been an ice age and the seas have retreated. With each subsequent warm period, the seas have crept back to find the land sufficiently raised that a new beach is established, and a new ridge is built up of limestone over sandstone. There have been 12 ice ages in the last 600,000 years. There are 12 ridges between the Comaum Range and the sea – one for each ice age – running north to south, parallel to the shore. Between each ridge the land is a sullen mix of sandy soil over a clay subsoil, or black cracking clay. On the barely perceptible ridges, a thin sprinkling of fertile reddish soil sits above a tough limestone cap. Break through that cap and the limestone becomes so damp and crumbly you can poke your finger into it and waggle it about. And a yard or two further down, the pure mountain waters from the east seep slowly towards the sea.

The limestone ridges topped with *terra rossa* soil provide perfectly drained sites for vines, islands in a vast expanse of waterlogged land. And the underground water provides one of the best natural resources for irrigation that any wine area in the world possesses – that is, if the vines need it: many of the older vines' roots tap directly into the water. Given that Australia is a hot country, this should be a recipe for the efficient production of vast amounts of reliable, low cost wine.

CHILLY VINEYARDS

But there's one other thing. It's not hot in the south of South Australia. Coonawarra, 400km (250 miles) south of Adelaide, is surrounded by the chill Southern Ocean. The winters are cold and damp, with most of the rain dumping uselessly on the area during winter, often waterlogging all but the scattered limestone ridges. Springtime is squally, and often frosty too.

Summer starts out mild but dry, yet in February and March there are often hot spells that can scorch and exhaust the vines: then the bore holes pump day and night, providing life-saving irrigation. And as the grapes slowly ripen into April the weather can break into sour, joyless early winter before the harvest is in and stay unfriendly and raw until the following spring.

RED WINES

And yet some of Australia's greatest red wines are made on this thin strip of vineyard land, where the climate makes vines struggle all year but the famous red soil and subsoil cosset and spoil them. Indeed Coonawarra has been called the 'Médoc' of Australia, and its conditions do resemble those of Bordeaux.

Since its foundation as a vine-growing area in 1891, French-style reds, primarily from Shiraz and Cabernet, have dominated. But, it wasn't until the 1960s that the world began to appreciate the relatively light yet intensely flavoured qualities of Coonawarra reds. By the 1990s, Coonawarra's terra rossa acres had become some of the most sought after vineyard land in Australia.

This has led to problems and infighting. On both sides of the terra rossa ridges are heavy clay plains, where hundreds of acres are planted with vines. Some decent white wine has been produced, but such damp cold soils cannot ripen Cabernet or Shiraz. Should their wines be allowed the name Coonawarra? More to the point, to the north, west and south there are outcrops of *terra rossa* rising a metre or so above the damp clay. Should these be allowed the Coonawarra name? Well, they've been bickering since 1984 about this. A decision in 2000 gave a tight, historically accurate definition

TERRA ROSSA

The diagram shows a vine root growing in Coonawarra red earth, commonly known as terra rossa. It is one of the best soils for growing vines in Australia, and covers a north-south strip 15km (9 miles) long and 2km (1 mile) wide. Although both red top soil and limestone have excellent drainage, it is not fully understood why this soil produces such fine grapes.

1. is the rich, red-brown topsoil, a freely drained earth, about 2–50cm (¾–20in) deep.

2. is a band of hard calcrete of up to 15cm (6in) deep, a result of calcium carbonate being leached out of the topsoil and redeposited above the limestone. This layer needs to be broken up before planting to provide access for vine roots and passage through for water.

3. is a thick, free-draining limestone, an ideal environment for root nourishment.

4. is where the rock becomes saturated with ground water. The water table is unusually high in Coonawarra, at a depth of only 2–4m (6½–13ft) and the vine roots that extend deep enough can benefit from year-round water.

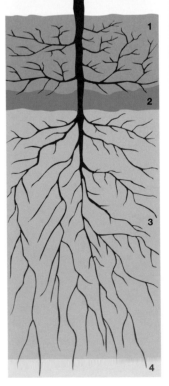

of Coonawarra. But powerful interests were excluded, so in 2001 it went to appeal – and a larger area was validated. Then, at the end of 2001, the appeal was appealed by yet another powerful local interest. So this tasteless farce goes on, and the lawyers still argue...

OTHER VINEYARD AREAS

Of course, Coonawarra is only one ridge. There are other similarly good ones: Mount Benson on the coast, St Marys, just to the west, and various sites around Naracoorte to the north, in particular Wrattonbully, produce superb quality. Also the regional title 'Limestone Coast' is already achieving significant acceptance as a general description of the cool climate wines of the whole area. And Padthaway, 65km (40 miles) to the north, produces fantastic wines. The area wasn't developed with quality in mind. In the early 1960s. it was forecast that Australian wine consumption would triple in the next 30 years. So the big companies looked for land to buy and operate cheaply. Seppelt, Hardy and Lindemans have such efficient mechanized vineyards there that they reckon to need only one person per 40ha (99 acres). Planted with all kinds of varieties, at first superb Chardonnay, and now fine Shiraz and sweet wines have propelled this featureless plot to star status.

0 km   1   2
0 miles   1

SELECTED WINERIES

1. Rymill
2. Penley Estate
3. Brand's
4. Wynns
5. Rouge Homme
6. Zema Estate
7. Mildara
8. Majella
9. Lawrence Victor Estate
10. Katnook Estate
11. Highbank
12. Leconfield
13. Bowen Estate
14. Balnaves
15. Bluk Estate
16. Hollick
17. Punters Corner
18. Peppertree
19. Parker Estate
20. Lindemans

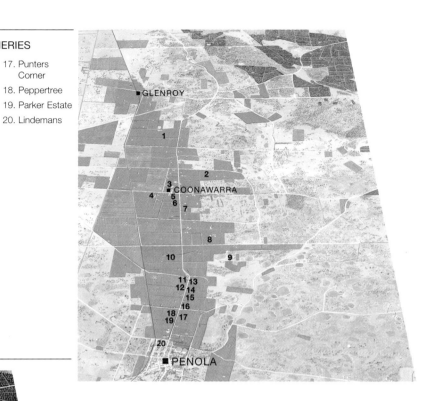

WHERE THE VINEYARDS ARE   *Well, here it is – one of Australia's most famous vineyard areas in all its glory. It is a spectacular place to grow vines, but it just so happens to be dumped in the middle of what is virtually a swamp. When the rain starts, you keep to the roads or take a pair of water-wings. Penola – the little town at the bottom of the map – is aboriginal for 'big swamp'.*

But if you take the main road north out of Penola, for about 15km (9 miles) you travel along the low limestone ridge of Coonawarra. This slight increase in altitude raises the road and a thin strip of land either side a crucial few feet above the surrounding waterlogged clay soils, and provides brilliant conditions for growing an abundance of healthy vines.

The best land has a thin covering of red-brown topsoil which lies directly over a layer of calcrete and then limestone. This terra rossa topsoil is extremely fertile, so the best quality comes from thin coverings of as little as an inch or two on top of barely perceptible rises in the land.

However, those vines you can see to the west of the railway are on black clay soils, and many of the vines stretching east are on white clay, some of which (both black and white) is little more than partially reclaimed swamp. Neither is capable of properly ripening Cabernet or Shiraz grapes.

The underground water that nourishes the Coonawarra vines is remarkably pure, but as more and more water is drawn out of the Great Artesian Basin by Coonawarra and other nearby emergent wine areas, damaging salts are likely to be leached from further inland. A water-sharing agreement between South Australia and Victoria, only 20km (12 miles) east of here, aims to limit any water extraction in the future.

COONAWARRA

TOTAL DISTANCE NORTH TO SOUTH 24KM (15 MILES)

▨ VINEYARDS

▲
N

0 km   1   2
0 miles   1

COONAWARRA

CLARE VALLEY

RED GRAPES
The main plantings are Shiraz and Cabernet Sauvignon, with some Malbec, Merlot and Grenache.

WHITE GRAPES
Riesling is the principal variety, with significant amounts of Chardonnay and Semillon plus some Sauvignon.

CLIMATE
The heat should lower acidity and send sugars soaring, but instead produces light wines, especially Rieslings, with an unexpected natural acidity and delicacy.

SOIL
The main subsoil is of calcareous clay. In the north, there's a sandy loam topsoil, in the centre, red loam, and in the south, red clay.

ASPECT
Vineyards are planted at 400–500m (1300–1640ft) above sea level, in the narrow valleys running from north to south, and in the foothills to the west. Aspects vary, with twisting contours.

One of the remarkable things about Clare Valley is its suitability for both hot-climate grapes, like Shiraz, and cool-climate ones, like Riesling. Jeffrey Grosset's Riesling is one of the best in Australia.

IT DOESN'T MAKE SENSE. Here I am, heading out of Adelaide in South Australia, the hottest and driest of Australia's major winemaking states. And I'm heading north towards the parched centre of the continent. Yet I'm looking for a famous cool-climate vineyard area – the Clare Valley. It might make a little more sense if I were heading up into the Adelaide Hills I can see to the east, since a climb of a few hundred metres dramatically cools the air, and the craggy hills also attract whatever rainfall there might be.

But I'm driving along the flat northern highway out past Gawler and Tarlee, through arid, dun-coloured cereal fields interrupted by occasional grain silos. The vista of broad, bone-dry acres peppered with doughty gums makes my tongue stick to the roof of my mouth as I ache for an ice-cold beer. And suddenly, in a dip in the land just north of Auburn, there's a field of shocking green. There are vines – the first vines of the Clare Valley – healthy, vigorous, their leaves waving gently in the breeze.

The breeze? There wasn't any breeze when I stopped back at Tarlee for a beer. There is unmistakably one now, taking the harshness out of the hot afternoon sun. And the air feels fresh, hillside fresh. Without once realizing that I was climbing at all, I've reached over 400m (1300ft) above sea level. At last some of the reasons for Clare's reputation as one of Australia's great cool-climate vineyard regions are falling into place.

Don't worry. They'll fall out of place again. Clare may have a reputation for elegant, balanced Riesling, but it also produces some of the most startlingly concentrated, brawny Shiraz in South Australia. Its 'ports' and Liqueur Tokays are pretty exceptional, for that matter. In one vineyard Riesling grapes struggle to ripen by late April. A couple of miles north-east, another vineyard harvests the port variety Touriga Nacional in February. I'll try to explain.

I've seen Clare described as a frontier town and as the 'hub of the north' in its early days. I'll buy that. After the long trek up from Adelaide, nearly 130km (80 miles) away, Clare promises to offer the last relief before the endless parched plains that stretch away to the north towards Jamestown and Port Pirie. Since the town of Clare's establishment in 1846, it has always been a focal point both for trading and for the refreshment of tired limbs and parched throats for the whole area. It's been a boom town several times. Copper was discovered nearby in 1845. Clare serviced that boom. There were massive wheat plantations established during the 1870s. Clare serviced these too. World-class slate reserves were discovered at neighbouring Mintaro, and there was a silver rush leading to the formation of the Broken Hill Propriety Co – Australia's largest company – in 1855. Once again, this small town reaped its share of the benefits.

What is left now is a traditional, well-worn market town – still quietly prosperous long after those early frenzied years – and vines. Vineyards throughout much of Australia were established to slake the thirsts of wealth-crazed pioneers in the 19th century. Those of the Clare Valley were no exception, though one distinct novelty, for Australia, was the establishment of Sevenhill Jesuit monastery in 1851. Naturally they planted vines. Just as naturally, they are still making wine.

Clare was luckier than many areas in that there was a genuine effort made to plant only the better grape varieties – and particularly Cabernet Sauvignon, Malbec and Shiraz. But then, as elsewhere in Australia, these were largely supplanted by varieties planted for cheap fortified wine and brandy in the early 20th century. However, the re-establishment of Clare Valley as a quality region during the 1950s and 1960s saw the better red varieties dominate new vineyard plantings once more, along with the white grapes Riesling and (more recently) Chardonnay.

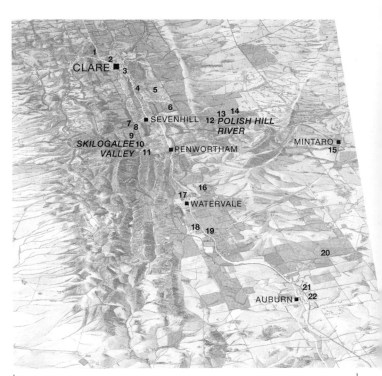

SELECTED WINERIES

1. Jim Barry Wines	9. Skillogalee Wines
2. Knappstein Wines	10. Mitchell Winery
3. Leasingham Wines	11. Killikanoon Wines
4. Tim Adams	12. Paulett Wines
5. Wendouree	13. The Wilson Vineyard
6. Sevenhill Cellars	14. Pikes Wines
7. Stringy Brae Wines	15. Mintaro Cellars
8. Waninga Wines	16. Quelltaler Estate/ Annie's Lane

17. Crabtree Wines
18. Brian Barry Wines
19. Tim Gramp Wines
20. Taylors Wines/ Wakefield
21. Grosset Wines
22. Mt. Horrocks Wines

VINEYARD AREAS

The trick was to have planted the vines in the right place. The term 'valley' isn't really an accurate description of this region. There are in fact three valley systems in Clare Valley, stretching both south and north with a watershed plateau in the middle at Penwortham. Incorporated into this are five sub-regions with differing soils at different heights above sea level – and differing mesoclimates too. Confusing, especially since Clare seems to get about as much heat as, and even less rain in the growing season than the impossibly hot Liqueur Muscat centre of Rutherglen in Victoria. Well, it does and it doesn't. Except in the valley bottom, it would be impossible to establish vineyards without irrigation. Storage dams for winter rain are the most effective source of water. And the tumbling landscape allows a wide variety of aspects to the sun, while nights are generally chilly and breezes arise to cool the vines during the day.

There is some disagreement about these cooling breezes because they have a fair way to travel inland from the sea, 50km (30 miles) to the west and south-west. It seems that, by and large, they only arise in the late afternoon, cooling the vines in the evening and at night, but not affecting the most intense heat of the early afternoon. So ripening is not hindered, but acid levels in the fruit remain high. Some locals say it is the daily fade-out, around 4pm, of the hot, northerly winds that is the crucial factor in cooling the vineyards, especially in the north-facing valleys above Penwortham.

Altitude certainly seems to help. The excellent Enterprise and Petaluma vineyards, both giving outstanding Riesling wine, are over 500m (1640ft) high, facing west over the town of Clare. The

CLARE

SEVENHILL

WATERVALE

AUBURN

vineyards of the Skillogalee Valley, south-west of Sevenhill, are not far short of 500m (1640ft) and protected from the north. Their fruit flavours are particularly fine and focused.

Soil also plays a major role. Deep dark loams below Watervale produce ripe, fat reds and whites, yet the ridge of limestone north of Watervale provides white wines with an acid bite that such a warm climate should deny. In the Polish Hill River area an acidic slaty soil seems to retard ripening by as much as two weeks and the results are surprisingly delicate structured whites and reds. A paradoxical place, the Clare Valley? It certainly is.

WHERE THE VINEYARDS ARE *Clare Valley is only 25km (15 miles) long, but a surprising number of different growing conditions exist for its near 2000ha (4942 acres) of vines. To call it a valley isn't actually accurate, as the watershed at Penwortham forms a plateau from which three river systems run, two north – including the Clare – and one south. The area, however, with its remarkably crisp, fragrant whites and elegant reds, is baffling. It seems too hot and dry. Certainly altitude is very important. None of the vineyards seen here are at less than 400m (1300ft). But Clare has one of the lowest summer rainfalls of any Australian quality wine region and could do with more. And it relies on sea breezes from the west and south-west to cool the vines and would prefer to have an uninterrupted flow.*

CLARE VALLEY

TOTAL DISTANCE
NORTH TO SOUTH
33.5KM (21 MILES)

VINEYARDS

N

VICTORIA

 **RED GRAPES**
Shiraz, Cabernet Sauvignon, Merlot and Pinot Noir predominate.

WHITE GRAPES
The main quality variety is Chardonnay, followed by Riesling, Sauvignon Blanc and Semillon, but there are also small amounts of Marsanne, Muscat Blanc à Petits Grains and Muscadelle.

CLIMATE
Coastal areas have a maritime climate. The north-east of the state, producing fortified wines, is hot.

SOIL
There is red loam in the north, quartzose alluvial soils in the Goulburn Valley, crumbly black volcanic soil at Geelong.

ASPECT
Steep, sloping, north-facing vineyards in cool-climate areas allow extended ripening. Most of the interior is pretty flat.

Morris's Old Premium, from Rutherglen in north-east Victoria, is intensely rich and will include a tiny proportion of treacly 100-year-old wine.

ROLL UP, ROLL UP to the Great Victorian Wine Show! All human life is here, with its triumphs, its tragedies, its noblest qualities and its greed. Especially greed. Swiss settlers were the first to make their mark, with toil and honest endeavour. Later, Gold Fever hit Victoria, bringing speculators with a mighty yet indiscriminate thirst. Soon after came the first attempts to harness the Murray River and turn desert into orchards and vineyards. Then came phylloxera, the world's most feared vine predator, followed by the Great Bank Crash, bankruptcies and ruin. The few remaining outposts of vines struggled for survival.

And then the new Victoria emerged. All the old vineyard areas have now been re-established. New vineyard areas have flared into life, offering a wealth of styles more diverse than any in Australia, ranging from some of the richest, most succulent fortified wines in the world made at Glenrowan and Rutherglen in the torrid north-east, down to damp, windy Drumborg in the south-west tip, where the grape struggles to ripen enough even for sparkling wine. The greatest problem is that the amounts produced of many of these remarkable wines is pitifully small and, with few exceptions, the wineries are spread thinly across the state, rather than bunched together in comprehensible regional groups. But that just makes the effort to find them all the more rewarding.

FIRST PLANTINGS

Let's have a quick look at the history first. The vine arrived in 1834 from Tasmania, of all places. Melbourne itself, at the north of Port Phillip Bay, proved ideally suited to vine-growing: not too hot, with an attractive maritime climate easing the grape towards ripeness. But the city's expansion was, obviously, always going to push out the vineyards, and the two areas that thrived were out of town at Geelong and the Yarra Valley.

Geelong is to the west of Port Phillip Bay, and is challenging vineyard land. The best sites are on outcrops of deep, crumbly, black volcanic soil, and are water-retentive but not prone to waterlogging. Although it isn't that wet, it's rarely that hot either and the cold Antarctic gales haven't crossed any landmass to reduce their chilly force when they hit Geelong. The reason Geelong did well – by 1861 it was the most important vineyard area in the State – was largely due to the settlement of Swiss vignerons who knew how to coax good flavour out of cool surroundings. They did the same in the Yarra Valley and we look at that in more depth later (see page 298).

The next wave of vineyards was established not because the land was thought suitable, but because gold was discovered there in 1851. From all over the world men flocked to the heartland of Victoria, their minds giddy with dreams of untold wealth from these extensive, easily dug lodes of precious metal. And they were thirsty too. Avoca established vineyards in 1848, Bendigo followed suit in 1855, Great Western in 1858 and Ballarat in 1859. North-East Victoria already had vines near Rutherglen, but was equally boosted by the madhouse prosperity brought by gold. Wine could be sold for as much as £5 a gallon in the goldfields – twenty times

WINE REGIONS

- Murray Darling
- Swan Hill
- Henty
- Grampians
- Pyrenees
- Bendigo
- Heathcote
- Goulburn Valley
- Rutherglen
- Beechworth
- Alpine Valleys
- King Valley
- Glenrowan
- Central Victorian High Country
- Macedon Ranges
- Sunbury
- Yarra Valley
- Mornington Peninsula
- Geelong
- OVER 200M (656FT)
- OVER 500M (1640FT)

the price it would fetch in New South Wales, southern Victoria or South Australia.

Eventually the Gold Rush died, and with it most, though not all, of the vines. But far worse was to come. Phylloxera arrived in Australia via Geelong in 1875. Geelong's vines were uprooted by government order, and so were those of Bendigo, but to no avail. Phylloxera spread through most of Victoria and by 1910 the state that was once the jewel in Australia's winemaking crown had seen her wine industry reduced to a withered rump centred on North-East Victoria, the Murray vineyards (whose founders, the Chaffey brothers, were paupered by the combination of the Great Bank Crash of 1893 and the Murray River inexplicably drying up) – plus a few vines at Tahbilk in the Goulburn Valley and at Great Western.

RED AND WHITE WINES
The rebirth of Victoria as a key wine region began with the re-establishment of vines at Geelong in 1966, but it really only began to take off in the 1980s. The result has been dramatic and triumphant. Among the wine areas to have enjoyed a resurgence, Geelong is no easier a place to grow vines in than it was 150 years ago, but it still manages to produce brilliantly focused, dark-hearted reds and attractive whites, when the sun stays out long enough. The Mornington Peninsula is still windy, but its position provides more maritime stability than Geelong, and any harsh north and north-east winds are cooled and dampened during their journey across the waters of the bay. The wines, especially the Chardonnays, Pinot Noirs and Rieslings, are light in texture but magnificently piercing in fruit intensity.

There are further cool-climate vineyards whose fruit intensity is remarkable near Portland in the south-west and at Gippsland in the south-east. Macedon, barely further north of Melbourne than its airport, combines fine sparkling wine with stunning lean but concentrated reds and whites. The central Goulburn Valley north of Melbourne is warmer and principally famous for Chateau Tahbilk whose ancient vines provide palate-crunching reds and heady but approachable whites. At Mansfield north-east of Melbourne, Delatite make beautiful reds and whites under the baleful eye of the snowfields of Mount Buller.

CENTRAL AND WESTERN VICTORIA
Scattered sparsely across the Central and Western Victoria zones are the remnants of the great goldfield vineyards. The soils are mostly poor, producing a low yield of fruit, and rainfall is generally meagre. Although there is a considerable amount of sunshine, high altitudes, at places like Ballarat, the Pyrenees and much of Great Western, moderate the heat and produce remarkable results from Shiraz, Cabernet Sauvignon, Chardonnay and even Riesling. If you think you spot a fascinating streak of eucalyptus and mint in these reds, you're not wrong – they were commenting on its presence 150 years ago. And since you'll have to make your way through miles of daunting eucalyptus forests to find most of the vineyards, you can guess where that scent of eucalyptus comes from.

MURRAY RIVER
The Murray River marks the northern border of Victoria. The majority of Victoria's wine comes from the vast, irrigated fields that fan out from the lefthand banks of the river. An increasing amount is made to a remarkably high standard. Lindemans' Karadoc, the biggest winery in Australia, processes much of the fruit, and the giant Mildara plant at Merbein, just north of the small town of Mildura, does a similar job.

NORTH-EAST VICTORIAN 'STICKIES'
There are two main regions in North-East Victoria noted for their sweet fortified wines or 'stickies': Glenrowan, where Baileys make sensational sweet 'stickies' as well as startling reds; and Rutherglen. Here a host of winemakers, young and old, make a hotchpotch of styles but, above all, the magnificent 'stickies' that leave your lips smeared and stained, your palate shocked and seduced, and your soul uplifted by their unashamed richness. At Milawa, Brown Brothers also make top-quality 'stickies', often from Rutherglen fruit, but their more significant contribution has been the revival of King Valley as a top table wine area and the establishment of Whitlands, at 800m (2600ft), one of Australia's highest vineyards.

Red soils often crop up at the site of Australia's best vineyards, and it's the same in North-East Victoria. At Rutherglen all the finest wines come from a bank of red loam soil. At Glenrowan, Baileys grow their Muscat and Muscadelle (usually called Tokay) on a deep seam of pulverized red granite soil. Both of these soils are friable, but do hold water and allow the vines to develop a massive, deep root structure. Each vine is reckoned to want up to 5l (1 gallon) a day, and Baileys, with access to water from Lake Mokoan and the Broken River, prefer to irrigate, unlike many of the Rutherglen producers, who prefer to leave things to nature and have their small crops of intensely sweet fruit to prove their point.

North-East Victoria gets no cooling sea breezes, so grapes really do bake in the heat (though cold nights help preserve acid). Muscat and Muscadelle grapes often reach 20–22 per cent potential alcohol, as they shrivel in long warm autumns. When picked, they ooze richness, and the thick juice is barely fermented before being whacked with spirit to kill the yeasts. It's then left in barrels, virtually turning to treacle as it cooks under the winery eaves for anywhere between one year and a hundred. The best, from makers like Chambers, Morris, Baileys and Stanton & Killeen, blend the bright floral grapiness of young Muscat with small amounts of thick and viscous ancient wines to give a uniquely 'sticky' experience.

Early morning mists are still lifting over the Yarra Valley. Coldstream Hills' vines slope down to Yarra Yering (on the left) and on to grazing land on the valley floor.

YARRA VALLEY

RED GRAPES
Pinot Noir is the leading red, with some Cabernet Sauvignon and small amounts of Shiraz, Merlot, Pinot Meunier and Cabernet Franc.

WHITE GRAPES
Chardonnay dominates, but Sauvignon Blanc is also important.

CLIMATE
The cool climate allows extended ripening. Wind and rain can interfere with flowering and fruit-set in December and January.

SOIL
There are two main types of soil: grey, sandy clays or clay loams and deep, fertile, red volcanic soil.

ASPECT
The angle of slope and height above sea level vary greatly, with vineyards planted at 50–400m (165–1300ft).

I CAN SEE IT NOW, 1837, AND William Ryrie breasting the hills above Healesville in the blazing afternoon sun. He'd trekked over mountain and prairie all the way down from Cooma in New South Wales. He must have been parched and exhausted. Spreading out below him was a lush valley with a glistening, if sluggish, river curling its way down the centre. As the sweet air drifted up to him, he must have thought – yes, this'll do.

Ryrie did settle in the Yarra Valley, and he laid the foundations for both its wine industry and its cattle-rearing business. The two have been at odds with each other ever since. But the beauty and serenity that must have filled his heart with exultant joy in 1837 are still there. Eagles soar overhead, kingfishers race like arrows near the river, and gum trees rear majestically over the flat parkland and way up the mountain slopes, too. It's all too easy to forget that the tranquillity of this peerless landscape has been earned and created by its inhabitants.

The first people to thank are the Swiss. Ryrie employed a Swiss assistant to prune the vines he planted and to help make the wine. In 1845 he managed to produce a Burgundy-like red and a Sauternes-like white. This sounds an improbable combination, but it may say something about the Yarra's climate that has been proven time and again in recent decades. The valley is not at all hot by Australian standards, providing rare suitable conditions for the fussy Pinot Noir. And it's relatively humid, too, encouraging the noble rot which can produce brilliant sweet Yarra wines.

The Swiss straightaway took a leading role in the Yarra Valley, and their winemaking expertise quickly created a reputation for delicacy and balance that was uncommon in Australia. They even won a *Grand Prix* – the only one for a southern hemisphere wine – at the 1889 Paris International Exhibition.

But thirty years later, phylloxera and a series of financial and natural disasters put an end to all this. Not until the 1960s did vine leaves rustle once more in the valley breezes, and it was the 1980s before the big hitters of Australian wine remembered the valley's former reputation and wondered if Yarra could do it all again.

RED AND WHITE WINES

It could and it has; indeed, it has boomed. And the remarkable thing is that the Yarra Valley has shown an ability to produce virtually every type of classic cool-climate wine within its small boundaries in a way that would make French traditionalists, hemmed in with restrictive *appellations contrôlées*, wring their hands in envy and despair. Marvellous traditional-method sparkling wines are made by Domaine Chandon, and superb Burgundian-style reds and whites are made by such outfits as Coldstream Hills, De Bortoli, Diamond Valley, Yarra Ridge, Tarrawarra and Metier. Excellent Bordeaux styles also abound, particularly at Mount Mary, Oakridge and Yarra Yering, which also excels in Rhône styles as does De Bortoli, while wonderful

sweet wines are made by producers such as Seville Estate and St Huberts. Yet none of these wines taste like their European role models. They are, in general, softer in texture, fuller of fruit, equally well-structured but easy to appreciate at every stage of their lives. This is because the challenge of Yarra's cool conditions is attracting talented winemakers, sensitive enough to want to work in harmony with nature, rather than bludgeon and straitjacket her.

Certainly the Yarra Valley is cool – in Australian terms – but it neatly cuts across the conditions that might pertain for good vintages in Bordeaux and Burgundy. Generally not quite so warm as Bordeaux but warmer than Burgundy, Yarra's temperature during the ripening season is more consistent than either of the two. Rainfall, while it can disrupt flowering in late spring, almost always stops around the end of December and, except for the odd welcome shower, doesn't usually return until autumn, after the harvest. So you can let the fruit ripen gently on the vine, the prerequisite for delicate, perfumed wine.

But all this depends on where your vineyards are. Up in the hills it is often too cold for vines. The valley floor, a broad flood plain, has boggy soil that couldn't ripen grapes. Sites to the north of the valley ripen earlier than most to the south. And, depending upon whether your sites face north or south and catch the full force of the sun or only part of it, crops at the same altitude can ripen two weeks apart.

YARRA VALLEY SOILS

The two main soil types in the Yarra Valley are very different. The southern side of the valley, to the east and south of the Warramate Hills, is primarily deep, fertile red soil. Vines are extremely vigorous here, and whites and dessert wines are the speciality. The classic Yarra soils, spreading across the centre and north of the valley, are grey sandy clays and clay loams, often directly above a heavy clay pan. Vigour is restricted, vines struggle to establish themselves and often need help from irrigation during the summer, but it's these soils that first gave Yarra vines their reputation, and most of the greatest reds and whites still come off these sites.

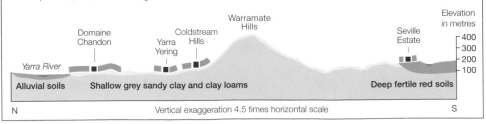

YARRA VALLEY

TOTAL DISTANCE NORTH TO
SOUTH 27.5KM (17 MILES)

VINEYARDS

N

| 0 km | 1 | 2 |
| 0 miles | | 1 |

WHERE THE VINEYARDS ARE *That's the outskirts of Melbourne in the lower lefthand corner, and the Great Dividing Range of mountains is over on the right. The Yarra Valley is beautiful, and it's only a short journey via electric train from Lilydale to the city centre. Pressure from property developers is the biggest threat to face the Yarra Valley, and a flourishing wine industry is one of the best ways to combat it. Vineyard planting here has exploded, tripling in size between 1995 and 2000 to 486ha (1200 acres), with more vines still being planted. This is great news to halt urban development, but such rapid expansion in a cool area brings poor wine as well as good.*

The vineyards originally stretched north-east of Coldstream across the grey loam soils at St Huberts and Yeringberg, and a little further west towards Yarra Glen at Yering Station. Only well-drained banks are suitable for grapes on the valley floor. There has been a great deal of development around Dixons Creek in the north of the valley, but again only on the raised ground. The land around the Warramate Hills is high enough, and as is the case in the Coldstream Hills, it is steep enough for drainage not to be a problem.

East and south of the Warramate Hills, away from the flood plain, the soil changes to a highly fertile, deep red terra rossa. This continues into the wooded hills to the south (off the map) where large developments at locations like Hoddles Creek, are producing high-quality grapes, used primarily for sparkling wine.

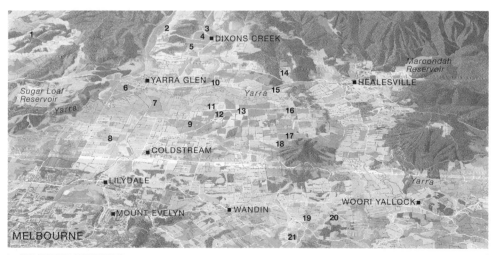

SELECTED WINERIES

1. Diamond Valley
2. Yarra Yarra
3. Shantell
4. De Bortoli
5. Fergusson
6. Yarra Ridge
7. Yering Station/ Yarra Bank
8. Mount Mary
9. St Huberts
10. Metier Wines
11. Domaine Chandon
12. Yeringberg
13. Oakridge
14. Long Gully
15. Tarrawarra
16. Eyton on Yarra
17. Yarra Yering
18. Coldstream Hills
19. Seville Estate
20. Lillydale Vineyards (McWilliam's)
21. Five Oaks

NEW SOUTH WALES

 RED GRAPES
Shiraz, Cabernet Sauvignon and Merlot are widely planted. There are also a number of other reds, of which Pinot Noir is the most significant.

WHITE GRAPES
The main varieties are Semillon and Chardonnay, but Riesling and Traminer are also significant. In Riverina, there are also substantial plantings of Trebbiano, Muscat Gordo Blanco, Verdelho and Colombard.

CLIMATE
It is hot, even by Australian standards, particularly in the Hunter Valley and Riverina. Wet, humid autumns encourage rot.

SOIL
Sandy and clay loams, along with some red-brown volcanic loams, granite and alluvial soils predominate.

ASPECT
Vines are planted on the gently undulating valley floors (Cowra, Riverina and Upper Hunter), or in the foothills of the Brokenback and Great Dividing Ranges (Lower Hunter Valley, Mudgee, Hilltops and Orange).

Unoaked Hunter Semillon, one of Australia's truly original wine styles, needs years in bottle to show at its best. Tyrrell's Vat 1 will continue to improve for a generation.

NEW SOUTH WALES is where I started my Australian wine odyssey. And I have to admit my first Australian hangover was in New South Wales, though it was the result of beer, not wine, but I wouldn't vouch for the genesis of numerous subsequent ones. It's where Australian wine started its journey, too. The very first vines to reach Australia sailed into Sydney Harbour with the First Fleet in 1788. They had been picked up in Rio de Janeiro and in the Cape of Good Hope on the long voyage out from England, and in no time the settlers had cleared some scrub by the harbour and planted vines. They weren't a great success – the humid atmosphere encouraged black spot disease, knocking out any grapes before they had a chance to ripen – but the scene had been set. All the main Australian settlements took the same line, establishing vineyards at the same time as establishing a community. And the reason usually given was to encourage sobriety. In a new, savage country where rough men became more savage and wild under the influence of fiery high-strength spirits, wine was seen as a moderating influence, a weapon against drunkenness and disorder.

These attempts in New South Wales to promote a benevolent, rosy-cheeked, wine-sipping society didn't work out too well, because there were very few places near Sydney suitable for vines. Close to the sea, the climate is too subtropical and vines routinely rotted. Further inland, around Bathurst, the cooler, high-altitude terrain looked promising, but harsh spring frosts simply made vine-growing economically unviable.

Although a few vineyards did survive near Sydney until modern times – at Camden, Rooty Hill and Smithfield – the story of wine in New South Wales is one of establishing vineyards well away from the main consumer market-place, with quality acting as the magnet drawing the attention of Sydney. This movement still continues today.

The crucial factors in New South Wales are excessive heat from the relatively northerly latitude; the presence of the sea close by; and the Great Dividing Range of mountains which separates the humid, populated seaboard from the parched, empty interior. The Great Dividing Range provides cool vineyard sites in some of its high hill passes, as well as the springs from which enough rivers flow inwards to irrigate some of the largest agro-industrial vineyards in Australia. Proximity to the sea brings with it advantages and disadvantages: the priceless bounty of cooling breezes but also the seasonal curse of cyclonic cloudbursts, frequently around vintage time.

HUNTER VALLEY
The first real success came with the Hunter Valley, which is about 130km (80 miles) north of Sydney and just inland from the major industrial city of Newcastle. Vineyards were being planted there as early as the 1820s, but it wasn't until the 1860s that the areas now thought of as best – those around the mining town of Cessnock – were planted. I cover the Hunter Valley more fully on page 302.

MUDGEE
At about the same time, pioneers pushed up into the mountains to the west of the Hunter and founded the community of Mudgee. Helped by an influx of German settlers and by a minor gold rush, vineyards were well-established by the end of the 19th century. But, as with the other New South Wales regions, the 1893 depression, then Federation in 1901 – with the lowering of trade barriers between States and the flood of cheap wines from South Australia – virtually did for the region. It wasn't until the 1960s that Mudgee began to get up on its feet again.

It all seems so idyllic here at the Broke Estate Vineyards in the Hunter Valley. The grapes ripen in the summer sun, the Brokenback mountains look on under a perfect azure sky. But the Hunter is subtropical and, more often than not, cyclonic storms will rage down the East Coast and drench the vines – normally just before harvest.

Now, its qualities are being realized. Hunter Valley wineries often used to rely on Mudgee wine for blending in the past, because the acid soils produce fat, strongly flavoured reds and whites. In addition, Mudgee's position at over 450m (1500ft) above sea level on the western slopes of the Great Dividing Range gives easily enough heat to ripen any grape variety, yet protects the vines from late summer rains. The growers were sufficiently proud of their individuality that they organized one of Australia's first appellation systems. My chief problem with Mudgee has not been with the fruit, but with the quality of the winemaking. Things look good in the vineyard, the grapes taste great on the vine, but the flavours in the bottle are solid at best and prehistoric at worst. Lack of leadership has meant lack of healthy competition. But Rosemount have transformed affairs in the last few years with a string of excellent wines. It is now up to the major players, like Orlando, as well as individual estates, to follow suit.

COWRA
Heading down off the mountains towards the interior, we come to the great irrigated vineyards of the State. The highest quality wine so far has come from Cowra on the Lachlan River, which has long been recognized as a prime source of fruit. The first Petaluma Chardonnays, beginning with the 1977, were made from Cowra fruit and immediately exhibited a fat, lush style – quite unlike the modern Petaluma Chardonnays, whose fruit is sourced in the ultra-cool Adelaide Hills. Even so, they lasted well, and their quality persuaded industry legend Len Evans to make the leap into Chardonnay when 40ha (99 acres) came up for sale in 1981. His Rothbury Cowra Chardonnay, with its rich, creamy style, became one of the winery's most successful wines.

One of the area's great virtues is its relentless reliability. The soil is sandy and free-draining, the sun shines throughout the summer, with almost no interruption from rain, and the Lachlan River provides an abundant source of irrigation water. Total reliability. But there's more. The large irrigated vineyards along the Murray River, which provide the bulk of Australia's wine grapes, are generally owned by thousands of smallholders. Their sole objective is to produce as large a crop of reasonably healthy grapes as possible, get them picked as early as they can – regardless of whether or not the grapes are truly ripe – to minimize the risk of disease and bad weather, and bank the money. Much of the region's potential is thus never realized.

But Cowra has been developed largely by major wine companies like Rothbury and Orlando's Richmond Grove, or quality-orientated, large-scale growers. With the winemakers having full control over the ripeness of crop, Cowra fruit, and Chardonnay in particular, has created what is still not that common in Australia – a totally recognizable style of its own.

RIVERINA

Riverina, in the new zone of Big Rivers, centred on the town of Griffith, way down in the scorched flatlands, is the most significant wine region in New South Wales in terms of the volume of wine it produces. Previously known as the Murrumbidgee Irrigation Area, it taps into the river system of the Murrumbidgee, a tributary of the Murray, to produce well over 100,000 tonnnes of grapes from about 5500ha (13,590 acres) of featureless land. It adjoins the large Sunraysia area which straddles the state of Victoria.

One special product of Riverina is the remarkable botrytis-affected sweet Semillon which the De Bortoli winery pioneered and others have followed. The grapes are left to hang on the vines for up to two months after the normal vintage date, and the quality often matches that of a top Sauternes from Bordeaux.

CANBERRA

With the transport efficiency of the late 20th century, Canberra – Australia's newest city, and its capital – didn't need its own vineyards unlike the cities developed in the 1800s, but that didn't stop a few impassioned inhabitants developing some in the 1970s.

Because you can't buy land freehold within the Australian Capital Territory (ACT), the vineyards have been developed just outside the ACT in New South Wales – mostly to the north-east near Lake George and to the north around Murrumbateman. The summer days are hot and dry, and not tempered by sea breezes, yet the nights are cold. The autumn, however, is cool and frequently wet. The soils and subsoils are not water retentive so irrigation is vital. Because of the cold night air moving north from the Australian Alps snowfields, sites have to be selected with care to avoid spring frosts that can occur as late as November. If this all sounds a bit negative, I'd have to say, if Canberra weren't there, these vineyards probably wouldn't be there either, but wineries like Lark Hill, Clonakilla and Doonkuna Estate have had success with Riesling, Chardonnay and, surprisingly, with Cabernet Sauvignon and Shiraz. And it is not all small-scale – BRL Hardy has installed a sizeable vineyard and 2000-tonne winery here.

OTHER VINEYARD AREAS

Although Sunraysia on the Murray River does have substantial vineyards, most of the action is across the river in Victoria. Other developments in New South Wales have been more concerned with trying to locate high-quality sites, despite challenging climatic

WINE REGIONS AND SUB-REGIONS

- Murray Darling
- Swan Hill
- Riverina
- Porricoota
- Tumbarumba
- Gundagai
- Canberra District
- Hilltops
- Cowra
- Lachlan Valley
- Orange
- Shoalhaven Coast
- Sydney
- Mudgee
- Hunter
- 1. Broke Fordwich
- Hastings River
- OVER 200M (656FT)
- OVER 500M (1640FT)

conditions. In particular, the state's winemakers hanker after a source of cool-climate fruit, with the most successful attempts being in Tumbarumba, Hilltops and Orange.

Tumbarumba in the Snowy Mountains, way down south near the border with Victoria, is producing some outstanding Sauvignon Blanc and Chardonnay, and Pinot Noir has great potential. It has red volcanic soils planted at over 750m (2500ft), and granite soils in slightly warmer, yet still cool, sites at around 550m (1800ft). The reputation of Hilltops near Young has been established by McWilliam's Barwang wines. It is warm enough for most of the New South Wales varieties, but the higher altitude and the well-drained soils encourage a slow, regular ripening season with consequently intensified fruit flavours.

There are also successful vineyards around Orange, and though we're getting back into the spring frost problems that deterred settlers in the 19th century, the region has thrived. Bloodwood Estate were the pioneers in the 1980s, and the latest development is a vast 500-ha (1235-acre) vineyard called Little Boomey at Molong. Much of the production goes to large companies such as Rosemount Estate and Rothbury, but Cabonne, who now manage the site and have a total of 900ha (2224 acres) of vineyards in the area, are developing their own wineries nearby.

Perhaps the most bizarre vineyard development is in the Hastings Valley near Port Macquarie, north of Newcastle. Here one of Australia's hottest vineyard sites combines with the highest recorded rainfall – most of it during the ripening season – but somehow Cassegrain manages to make interesting wine.

The ROTHBURY Estate

19 00 COWRA CHARDONNAY

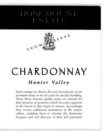

ROSEMOUNT ESTATE

CHARDONNAY
Hunter Valley

HUNTER VALLEY

RED GRAPES
Mainly Shiraz and Cabernet Sauvignon are grown, with some Merlot. Pinot Noir and Malbec.

WHITE GRAPES
Chardonnay and Semillon are the most important grapes, but there is some decent Verdelho and Traminer.

CLIMATE
The summer heat is tempered by cloudy skies. Autumn is often wet. The Upper Hunter Valley needs irrigation.

SOIL
The rich, red volcanic loams and the alluvial soils near the Goulburn River are the best. The poor-draining, heavy clay subsoils are tough going.

ASPECT
Vines are planted next to the Goulburn River in the Upper Hunter Valley. Lower Hunter vineyards are on the lower slopes of the Brokenback Range, or on the valley floor.

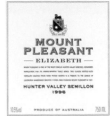

I STILL HAVE VIVID MEMORIES of the first time I realized just how special the Hunter Valley could be. Some roaming wine gypsy I knew had strayed far from his usual European pastures and ended up in Sydney. Eventually escaping with liver and limb more or less intact, he'd brought some wine back to London and decided to try it out on a group of us young whipper-snappers. Tyrrell's Vat 47 1973. A Chardonnay – well, mostly Chardonnay, with a little Semillon too, I shouldn't wonder. I can still see the astonishing day-glo, greeny-gold colour, all fiery-eyed and demanding of attention, and the sensual viscous texture of the wine that swirled lazily round the glass like a courtesan interrupted during her siesta.

And the flavour. I'd been brought up on French Chardonnay from Burgundy. I knew and understood the generally austere but fascinating, if intellectual, pleasure of those pale, oatmeal- and mineral-scented whites from the centre of France. Then there was my first mouthful of Vat 47. The explosion of peaches and honey, hazelnuts, woodsmoke and lime sent stars bursting over my palate. In that single split second I foresaw the greatness Australia could bring to Chardonnay, and Chardonnay could bring to Australia.

Yet what I was tasting was not some classic wine style, carefully honed over the generations. This was only the third vintage of the Hunter Valley's very first varietal Chardonnay. And its brilliance was even more astounding because you shouldn't really be able to create exciting wine in the Hunter at all. Ask any modern vineyard consultant about establishing a vineyard in the Hunter Valley, and he'd say you must be barmy even to consider it. So what's going on? Have all the great Hunter wines of the last 150 years been made by madmen? Or do they know something we don't?

For a start, you've got the heat against you, the rainfall patterns against you, and, except in a few charmed sites, the soils are against you, too. But, as Hunter winemakers have shown, if you're stubborn and obsessive – and, well, yes, slightly mad – you can produce wines of quite shocking individuality and quality.

UPPER HUNTER VALLEY

The Hunter Valley divides, in wine terms, into two parts as it snakes inland from Newcastle. The Upper Hunter is to the north around Denman. Its vineyards have to fight with powerful local coal-mining interests when they want to expand. Although initially planted in the 19th century, it only achieved any prominence in the 1980s and still has only two major wineries – Rosemount Estate and Arrowfield, though Barrington is also showing some form.

The area was heavily planted in the 1960s' and '70s' wine boom, mostly on rich, alluvial soil with irrigation keenly applied. But the grape most often planted was the black Shiraz, whose reaction to such fertile, high-yielding conditions was to produce limp, lifeless wine, only half-way to red. White wines fare much better under these conditions, and fleshy Chardonnays and Semillons are commonplace. But so far, only one vineyard has proven to be world-class – Rosemount's Roxburgh, a weathered limestone and basalt outcrop in the middle of pastureland between Denman and Muswellbrook. In the 1980s, early vintages of its sensational Chardonnay did more than any other wine to propel Australian Chardonnay – and therefore Australia itself – to the forefront of the New World wine revolution that was then unfolding.

LOWER HUNTER VALLEY

The drive southwards from the Upper Hunter to the Lower Hunter exposes the contradictions of this area as a grape-growing centre. You'll see more signposts to coal mines than vineyards. The black gold of coal or the white gold of Chardonnay? Until you descend into the heart of the Lower Hunter, the argument is still fierce. And

even then the area is centred around Cessnock, a town more dominated by coal than wine for most of its existence, though now the grape has pretty well won the battle of vine versus mine. Spread out to the west and north-west are numerous vines, the healthiest-looking being those that run up to the slopes of the Brokenback Range, and odd volcanic 'pimples' – ridges of weathered basalt typified by Lake's Folly and Evans Family vineyards. These red soils are fertile, well-drained and deep, and capable of producing good crops of high-quality red grapes.

The volcanic outcrops are marvellous soils, but vineyards still have to combat the heat and rain. Lake's Folly and Evans Family face south, away from the sun, and the best sites on the Brokenback slopes are those up as high as 400m (1300ft) at Mount Pleasant and the properties set back on the slopes of Mount View, west of Cessnock. These escape the warm westerlies, get a little more rain, but have the slopes to drain freely, and often ripen up to two weeks later than the vines on the valley floor.

FORMER VINEYARD AREAS

There are also some alluvial flats with sturdy-looking vines, but then you notice fields full of weary, stunted vines and great patches of barren land where you think – funny, I could have sworn there was a vineyard there. There was. But it's been ripped out after years of failing to provide a half-decent crop. The problem is that most of the good topsoil has been washed away. The thick, impermeable pug clays that remain are difficult to work and hardly support any crop, let alone the vine. Yet thousands of acres were planted in the mad Vine Rush of the 1960s on this hopeless yellow-orange clay. Rothbury Estate had a 180-ha (445-acre) vineyard here, which Len Evans, its founder and chief executive until the Mildara Blass 1998 takeover, admits was 'a total cowpat' anyway.

HUNTER VALLEY CLIMATE

Because the Hunter is relatively far to the north and close to the hotter inland zones, the climate does at first glance seem oppressive. Yet the quality of wine made here means that there must be some compensating factors. There are. Though Cessnock would appear, statistically, to get appreciably more heat than Montpellier in the broiling south of France, the warm spring and autumn temperatures – that don't actually affect the grapes' ripening – distort the figures. Heat undeniably does build up fast until early afternoon, but because the Great Dividing Range dips to the north and west of Cessnock, the warm interior sucks cold air in up the Hunter Valley. Most summer afternoons there's cloud cover over the Hunter and, in any case, being closer to the equator than Montpellier means relatively shorter summer days. The humidity is also important in reducing vine stress.

But water is a problem in the Hunter. There's not enough when you want it and too much when you don't. The annual rainfall of 700mm (27in) would be fine if it fell at the right time, but it tends to get dumped at the end of summer, often just before the Shiraz grapes are ripe. You also need good winter rains to fill the irrigation dams, since borehole water here is far too saline, but winter droughts are frequent. When rain does arrive in January and February, cyclones come in off the Coral Sea and bang up against the mountains of the Great Dividing Range, dumping their watery load on the vines. When they hit Queensland, Hunter winemakers know they've got two or three days to harvest, regardless of ripeness, before the rains reach them. You can make great Semillon from underripe grapes, fair Chardonnay, and even passable Cabernet, but you just can't transform a rain-bloated Shiraz into a classy red, and no matter how hard you try, you'll only break your heart.

WHERE THE VINEYARDS ARE *The Hunter River is just visible on the map, snaking briefly in and out of the top righthand corner. It continues to run from the west, just above the top of the map. All the original important vineyards were established on these fertile river flats. You can see just one remaining example on the bend of the river at Wyndham Estate.*

However, from the 1860s onwards, plantings shifted south and west, towards the slopes of the Brokenback Range, an isolated ridge west of Cessnock, where rich, red, volcanic loams provide that unusual combination – high quality and high volume. Occasional outcrops of red volcanic soil in the Valley also offer these conditions, as at Lake's Folly and Evans Family vineyards (see map). The south-facing aspect also helps by reducing exposure to the hot sun.

The little Mount View Range, which lies directly to the west of Cessnock, is also particularly suited to vines.

SELECTED WINERIES

1. Wyndham Estate
2. Pendarves Estate
3. Tempus Two
4. Rothvale
5. Bimbadgen
6. Kulkunbulla
7. Tyrrell's
8. Scarborough
9. McGuigan Cellars
10. Brokenwood
11. Tamburlaine
12. Glenguin
13. Rothbury Estate
14. Tower Estate
15. Pepper Tree
16. Evans Family
17. Lake's Folly
18. Allandale
19. Lindemans
20. Draytons Family Wines
21. McWilliam's Mount Pleasant
22. Petersons
23. Sadler's Creek

LOWER HUNTER VALLEY

TOTAL DISTANCE NORTH TO SOUTH
25KM (15½ MILES)

VINEYARDS

WESTERN AUSTRALIA

🍇 **RED GRAPES**
Shiraz and Cabernet Sauvignon are the main varieties, with much smaller plantings of Merlot, Pinot Noir and Cabernet Franc.

🍇 **WHITE GRAPES**
Chardonnay, Sauvignon Blanc, Riesling and Semillon are used for white wines. In addition, the Swan Valley grows Chenin Blanc, Muscadelle and Verdelho.

CLIMATE
The coastal regions have a maritime climate. Regions further inland and to the north are hotter, drier and more continental.

SOIL
Mainly brown or grey-brown alluvial topsoil, frequently fairly sandy with some gravel.

ASPECT
Vineyards are concentrated on the valley floors or gentle slopes along the coast, although there are some vines in more hilly areas along the Darling Ranges.

Sweet, loveable kangaroos at play? That's not what you'd think if you're a grape-grower; they could have just chewed all the young buds off your vines.

'WINES SHOULD BE RESPLENDENT with generosity; unless a wine can be diluted with an equal volume of water, it wasn't worth making in the first place.' This wonderful remark was made by Jack Mann, the greatest of Western Australia's old-time winemakers. He made wines in the Swan Valley, the hottest serious vineyard area in Australia and one of the hottest in the world. He admitted he never picked his grapes until the sun-baked vine simply had nothing more to offer them, and I've tasted some of the old Houghton White Burgundy wines with which he made his reputation – deep, thick, viscous golden wines, oozing with over-ripeness but aging with all the sequinned majesty of a dowager in love with a chorus boy.

SWAN VALLEY

Until the 1970s, Houghton White Burgundy was the only Western Australian wine to make any impact across the state line, and it is still one of Australia's most popular white wines. It was originally based on Chenin Blanc and contained a significant proportion of Muscadelle until the late 1980s. Now it is a blend of Chenin Blanc (50 per cent), Chardonnay (20 per cent), Semillon (15 per cent), the remainder being Verdelho, Riesling and Muscadelle.

It was about the only shooting star Western Australia had in wine between 1829, when the Parmelia landed to establish the colony, and the late 1970s, when the pioneers of Margaret River began making waves. Yet in the 19th century the Swan Valley had more wineries than any other viticultural area of Australia. As Western Australia never succumbed to phylloxera, there was a boom in plantings during the 1890s as Victoria's vineyards fell to the rapacious aphid. And as usual the discovery of gold and the attendant influx of wealth-crazed, sun-parched prospectors in need of a bit of rest and recuperation didn't do any harm either.

After World War One, numerous Yugoslavs took refuge in Perth, much as they did in New Zealand's North Island. They were doughty winemakers and loyal consumers of their competitors' wares, and dominated the local wine scene which – until the late 1960s – was almost entirely centred on the hot Swan Valley.

And we are talking roasting: the Swan has January and February temperatures that can soar to 45°C (113°F) – hotter than any other serious Australian wine region. Air humidity is very low, further stressing the vines, and summer rainfall is the lowest of any Australian wine district – though occasionally the bulk of it falls in February, bang in the middle of vintage. The Swan gets the most sunshine hours per day as well.

People bake; grapes bake. It would all be too much if it weren't for the afternoon breezes that come belting across the bay from Fremantle, swoop into the Swan Estuary at Perth and then funnel north-east up the valley, sucked across the riverside vineyards by the heat of Australia's desert heart. The best of the Swan vineyards are on river terraces of deep, well-drained young alluvial soils, often with a sandy clay subsoil to conserve winter rains for high summer, though few vineyards nowadays get by without irrigation.

All of this, despite the sea breeze, still sounds a lot more like conditions for fortified wine, rather than table wine. And many experts have predicted that the future of the Swan is in fortifieds. Yet fortifieds belong to the past, not the future of Australian wine, and as Jack Mann proved with his Houghton White Burgundy, something pretty spectacular can be achieved with table wines too.

More technologically driven winemaking, more widespread use of stainless steel, better refrigeration and the use of classier oak has made for significant improvements in the quality of the region's reds over the past decade. Excellent examples can be seen in the wines of Lamont, Talijancich, Upper Reach, Faber, Westfield and Swanbrook. The most surprising fact is that whites perform better here than reds. The reason for this becomes clearer when we look at the varieties planted. Chenin Blanc has by far the largest acreage, followed by Chardonnay, Verdelho and Semillon. Chenin's great ability is to retain acidity under virtually any conditions. Indeed, it positively courts the heat it so rarely gets in its homeland of the Loire Valley in France. Verdelho is used to make Madeira in Portugal, where it retains its attractive honeyed character, despite high temperatures. And Semillon is the best variety in New South Wales near-subtropical Hunter Valley.

Houghton makes good use of all of these and is still the major Swan producer, but, just as in the other states, when the national and export palate shifts away from overripe or fortified wine styles, so the hotter areas go out of fashion. As the Barossa and McLaren Vale in South Australia show, they can, with a few adjustments to wine style, come back into fashion again. Houghton now sources many of the grapes for its excellent whites from the slightly cooler Moondah Brook vineyard, about 60km (37 miles) north of the Swan Valley at Gingin, as well as from the much cooler Pemberton, Margaret River and Great Southern regions way to the south.

These latter two are the areas now making the running for Western Australia. Both had been considered suitable for grape-growing before. The Lower Great Southern (as it was then called) impressed Jack Mann himself between the two World Wars, and earlier still the Western Australian government had tried to get Penfolds to establish a vineyard at Mount Barker. But Western Australia is a very sparsely populated state. Until recently in Australia, unless there was a decent centre of population nearby, you couldn't establish a wine industry. Perth, with its Swan Valley, was (and is) the only sizeable city in the state.

But the wine industry in the Swan hit trouble in the 1950s. The vineyards were decaying, yields were falling and in 1955 the government called in Professor Harold Olmo (of the University of California at Davis) to find the cause. He did (it was nematodes, a root-nibbling worm, and poor drainage), and he also remarked in passing that he thought the Swan was too hot anyway. He wrote a report in which he recommended planting vines around Mount Barker and Frankland, north of the port of Albany – sites now at the heart of the Great Southern. This was easier said than done.

GREAT SOUTHERN

We're talking about a big area here – the largest recognized agricultural area in Australia – and we're talking about some fairly diverse conditions, as well as taming a wild landscape of jarrah and red gum trees and scrub. Progress was slow, the first vines didn't go in at Forest Hill (near Mount Barker) until 1966, and progress hasn't exactly been quicksilver since. Small vineyards established themselves east of Mount Barker beneath the rounded granite Porongurup Hills, west around Frankland and down near the coast, inland from Denmark and Albany.

Most of these are on gravelly sandy loams, though these soils may well be underpinned by impermeable clay subsoils, inhibiting drainage. The temperatures around Mount Barker and Frankland are fairly similar to those of the Médoc in Bordeaux – which is as cool as Western Australia gets – and this results in good, dark but lean Cabernet styles and, interestingly, lovely lean Rieslings as well.

Porongurup vineyards are cooler because the slopes are planted up to 350m (1150ft) and this can slow ripening by a good week, which serves to intensify the fruit of the Cabernets and Rieslings. Coastal vineyards between Albany and just west of Denmark benefit from cooler days and warmer nights because of the ocean's influence, though some good vineyards near Denmark face north and are sheltered from the sea. The vines also get more rain, but this is a plus in a dry state, since the extra usually falls outside the March to April harvest period. Piercing cool flavours are again the order of the day, with even some good Pinot Noir rearing its head near Albany and Denmark.

Until recently the only large vineyard in the region was the 30-year-old, 100-ha (247-acre) Westfield vineyard at Frankland, leased by Houghton and responsible for some of its most outstanding reds. Since Jack Bendat bought Goundrey in 1995, its plantings have increased at a furious rate and they now have 175ha (432 acres) under vine. Tax incentives have funded massive vineyard development at Frankland during the last five years with plantings increasing fivefold, from less than 300ha (740 acres) to more than 1500ha (3700 acres).

PEMBERTON/MANJIMUP

Situated between the Great Southern and Margaret River lie the twin regions of Pemberton and Manjimup. They are almost directly to the west of Frankland (an hour's drive away) and just south-east of Margaret River (about two hours away). It was originally established in the late 1980s as Pemberton, but personal disagreements over the name led the Geographic Indicators Committee to split the region into two – a decision that has little support among local vignerons.

There are viticultural differences between them. Pemberton is cooler, has fewer sunshine hours, more rainfall and higher humidity. Manjimup has moderately fertile gravelly sand and loam soil, while Pemberton has more fertile red loam.

No clear picture has yet emerged about which varieties most suit the area. John Gladstones recommends the Cabernet varieties, Shiraz and Chardonnay for Manjimup, and Pinot Noir and the Cabernets (especially Franc) and Merlot for Pemberton. Brian Croser of Petaluma, which owns the large Smithbrook vineyard, is confident that the Bordeaux varieties will prove the most impressive. But Bill Pannell (now at Picardy, but founder of Moss Wood, one of Margaret River's great vineyards) believes Pinot Noir and Chardonnay will make the region's reputation. For now, Cabernet Sauvignon, Merlot, Pinot Noir and Shiraz are the most important reds, while Chardonnay dominates the whites, followed by Sauvignon Blanc, and small amounts of Semillon and Verdelho.

MARGARET RIVER

More crowded, more inhabited and more organized is the Margaret River region. Here Southern Ocean influences meet those of the Indian Ocean, and the natural potential which results has already been exploited by brilliant winemakers and self-publicists alike. As it is now Western Australia's most high-profile and successful area, I talk about it separately over the page.

GEOGRAPHE

This is a diverse region covering the coastal plain near Bunbury and Capel, the dairy country round Harvey, the Ferguson Valley in the Bunbury hinterland and the orchard and farmlands of Donnybrook between Bunbury and Bridgetown. In the last decade, vineyards have been planted apace – partly fuelled by tax incentives.

The coastal strip from Capel to Harvey has fertile, brown loamy soils and a climate tempered by the sea. Merlot, Chardonnay and Verdelho do best here. The Ferguson Valley and the hills behind Harvey have vineyards 250–300m (850–1000ft) above sea level, with a more moderate climate and about 10 per cent more rainfall than those on the flat. The soil is granitic gravel over clay loam and retains water better than the alluvial sands nearer the coast. Shiraz,

Chardonnay, Semillon and Sauvignon Blanc are all promising. Near Donnybrook, vineyards occupy the gentle slopes of the Darling Ranges, where fertile soils contain granite and ironstone gravel. This warm area is particularly good for Shiraz, Cabernet Sauvignon, Zinfandel and Grenache.

The region's major winery is Capel Vale which sources fruit from throughout the state. The newly established Willow Bridge is the major player in the Ferguson Valley.

BLACKWOOD VALLEY

This small region centred on Boyup Brook, Bridgetown and Nannup has about 40 vineyards, six of which produce wines under their own label. For now, the stand-out wines are red, especially Shiraz and Cabernet Sauvignon. Chardonnay is the most widely planted white, with small amounts of Sauvignon Blanc and Semillon. The most interesting recent development is the building of a winery at Nannup by BRL Hardy to service their vineyards and growers in the south-west.

PERTH HILLS

The other small region is the Perth Hills which are, in effect, the Darling Range. These overlook Perth from 20–30km (12–18 miles) inland, and the wooded valleys have vineyards established at between 150–400m (500–1300ft) above sea-level. Sea breezes blowing in across the range's western escarpment reduce daytime temperatures; by contrast, warm sea air stops the temperature dropping too much at night. The hilly, irregular nature of the valleys creates widely differing mesoclimates that, at their coolest, ripen grapes two to three weeks later than those in vineyards in the nearby Swan Valley flats. Soils are good, with a fair amount of gravelly loam, and rainfall is high – but almost all of it is in the winter. If you've got storage dams for spring and summer irrigation, that's no problem; but if you haven't, those gravelly soils will be too free-draining to raise a crop.

WESTERN AUSTRALIA

INDIAN OCEAN

SOUTHERN OCEAN

0 km 50 100
0 miles 50

WINE REGIONS AND SUB-REGIONS

Swan District
1. Swan Valley
Perth Hills
Peel
Geographe
Margaret River
Blackwood Valley
Manjimup
Great Southern
2. Frankland River
3. Mount Barker
4. Porongurup
5. Albany
6. Denmark
Pemberton
OVER 200M (656FT)
OVER 500M (1640FT)

Leeuwin Estate in Margaret River was one of the first Australian wineries to produce world-class Chardonnay. Its Art Series Chardonnay is still superb wine.

MARGARET RIVER

THE MARGARET RIVER might never have been discovered as a fine wine vineyard area had it not been for a clutch of beady-eyed local doctors. They saw a couple of reports in the mid 1960s by a Dr John Gladstones that the Margaret River had unusually close climatic analogies with Bordeaux, but with less spring frost, more reliable summer sunshine, and less risk of hail or excessive rain during ripening.

For some reason, Australian doctors right across the nation have never been able to resist such pronouncements. First Dr Tom Cullity at Vasse Felix, then fellow doctors Bill Pannell at Moss Wood and Kevin Cullen of Cullen Wines, planted vineyards that were to form the heart of the Margaret River region right from the start. Indeed, Margaret River went on to establish itself as a remarkably versatile, if somewhat capricious, cool-climate region which was good as any in Australia. But Bordeaux? Well, yes and no.

In fact Dr Gladstones was supposed to be doing research on lupins – rather the same as Cullity and Co. were supposed to be keeping the locals hale and hearty – but his good luck was that the legendary Jack Mann at Houghton vineyard in the Swan Valley let him use a spare couple of acres of land next to the winery cellars for his lupin experiments. Lupins are all very well, but the ever-open cellar door at his neighbour's winery began to weave its magic on the doctor and distract him from his original research. The possibilities in Western Australia for fine wine, as yet barely touched upon by winemakers in the torrid Swan Valley, began to take up more and more of Dr Gladstones' time.

A visiting Californian, Professor Olmo, had already suggested in 1956 that the far south of the state, near Mount Barker and Rocky Gully, would make a high-quality vineyard site. Gladstones thought the area on the south-west coast, about 130km (80 miles) further north, between Cape Leeuwin and Cape Naturaliste, would be warmer and more predictable in weather and more flexible in the varieties of grapes that could be grown. He felt the Great Southern Region, with its cool, southerly maritime influence could indeed match Bordeaux's cooler regions, but that the Margaret River, influenced by the Indian Ocean to the west, could match the warmer Bordeaux regions of Pomerol and St-Émilion. The added advantage for Margaret River was that it was an area free of the risk of frost and rain at vintage that so often spoiled things in Bordeaux. It was these thoughts that galvanized the local winemaking doctors into action.

Yet there are problems, and the most intractable is wind. Sea breezes are crucial for cooling down vines in many areas of Australia, but these are gales we're talking about – especially in spring – when salt-laden winds power in off the Indian Ocean and can crucially affect the vine as it attempts to flower and set a crop. Given the fact that the winters are some of the mildest in Australia, vines are likely to wake up early and the early-budding Chardonnay and Merlot often get into trouble.

And then there's the wildlife. Those lovely mysterious stands of tall Karri gums are home to legions of kangaroos. Delightful, shy little roos; how we Europeans wish they were less timid so that we could feed them lettuce leaves from the palms of

NORTHERN MARGARET RIVER

TOTAL DISTANCE NORTH TO SOUTH 39.5KM (24½ MILES)

▊ VINEYARDS

N

WILYABRUP ■

■ COWARAMUP

■ MARGARET RIVER

0 km   1   2
0 miles   1

our hands. Try giving that sentimental tosh to a grape grower in springtime when the little fellas have nipped out overnight and chewed all the emerging buds off his vines. And don't talk to him about how divine those lime green parrots are fluttering and cawing among the vines. They are rapacious pests that munch away at the grapes for nourishment and then, replete with his best Cabernet Sauvignon, chew through the vine branches for recreation. And don't mention silver-eyes either, sweet little migratory birds that find the netting protecting the vines rather good for nesting in – and anyway they're tiny enough to wriggle through and devour the crop under the nets.

Such problems rarely occur in Europe – or in traditional Australian wine districts. But where new vineyards are carved from virgin land there are bound to be upsets. In such thinly populated regions as Margaret River, the relatively small areas of vines and grapes make easy targets for hungry wildlife. Interestingly, the only effective defence against the yearly silver-eye invasion is a natural one: their favourite refuelling food is the nectar of red gum blossom. When the gums flower on time, the silver-eyes relish this feast, but if flowering is late, they turn to the sugar-sweet grapes.

But it does all seem to be worth it. Across a remarkable spectrum of wines, the quality of the Margaret River fruit sings out loud and clear. These range from mighty, gum-scented Pinot Noirs to classic structured Cabernets and Chardonnays, from unnervingly French, yet tantalizingly individual Semillons and Sauvignons to positively un-Australian Shiraz and Zinfandel, and even to vintage 'port'.

WHERE THE VINEYARDS ARE *You shouldn't have too much trouble getting casual labour around vintage time in Margaret River. But be warned – it may be very casual, depending on the size of the waves, rather than the ripeness of the grapes, because that long, inviting coastline that you see on the left of the map is one of the greatest surfing beaches in the world. So don't expect the pickers to stay bent over the vines when the waves get up.*

The sea's influence, though, is one of the crucial aspects of Margaret River. That's the Indian Ocean there. It's a warm sea, and the difference between summer and winter temperatures is smaller here than anywhere else in the whole of Australia. But this isn't always a bonus: early-flowering varieties, like Chardonnay, often get lashed by westerly gales just when they are trying to set a crop, and the winds can carry salt miles inland; grapes and salt don't get on. On the other hand, those long, baking, sun-soaked autumns will ripen most varieties of grape to perfection.

The first group of vineyards, those that were established by those doctors in the 1960s, are the ones you can see in the middle of the map. They are still the most important group. It becomes cooler as you head south to below the Margaret River itself, but some of the most famous vineyards are those shown right at the bottom of the map.

At the top, inland from Cape Clairault, is the latest wave of new wineries and vineyards.

VINEYARD AREAS

There were intermittent attempts in the 19th century to plant the area, but Doctors Cullity, Pannell and Cullen really showed the way in the late 1960s and early '70s, when they planted small vineyards in the locality of Wilyabrup, about 15km (9 miles) north of the township of Margaret River, an area which still boasts the most flagship estates in the region. However, some of the highest profile estates – Cape Mentelle, Leeuwin, Voyager and Xanadu – are actually south of the Margaret River. There's also been a lot of vineyard development around Karridale in the extreme south of the region. Here summers are cooler than in the northern plots, although it also benefits from prolonged mild sunny weather into late autumn. And in the far north, around Yallingup, between Cape Clairault and Cape Naturaliste, are wineries such as Abbey Vale, Amberley, Clairault and Happs. In general average temperatures rise as you move north, and leading estates south of the Margaret River definitely produce wines of a cooler fruit flavour than those to the north.

On the other side of the Bussel Highway, in the north-east, is the former potato-growing area of Jindong. Ex-potato fields are not famous for producing high-quality grapes and the jury is still out as to whether these ones will prove an exception. But its flat land, fertile soil, plentiful water supply and moderate climate have encouraged Evans and Tate, Vasse Felix and Selwyn wineries to establish large vineyards here.

CLIMATE AND SOIL

Soils do differ, but most good vineyard sites in Margaret River are either located on gravels or sands over clay. These tend to drain well – which is fine as long as you've built plenty of dams to store your irrigation water. Of the area's annual 1160mm (46in) rainfall, just 200mm (8in) falls in the all-important growing season – between October and April – when the vines need it most. Efficient irrigation is vital.

The intensity of the fruit, and the acid and tannin structure in the wines are the best rebuttal I can think of when people suggest that you can't make great wines using irrigation. With a few outstanding exceptions, such as the excellent Moss Wood, Cullen and Leeuwin estates, in the Margaret River region you can't make great wines without it.

RED GRAPES
The main varieties are Cabernet Sauvignon, Shiraz and Merlot.

WHITE GRAPES
Chardonnay is the most widely planted variety and there are substantial amounts of Semillon and Sauvignon Blanc, which are often blended together. There is also some Chenin Blanc and Verdelho.

CLIMATE
This is a maritime climate, with a coolish growing season and a mild, wet winter. Cold Antarctic currents flowing south of the land mass, and westerly winds from the Indian Ocean cool this region and make it more temperate than Perth to the north. Sea breezes are good for preventing overheating, but bad for drying out the soil, sometimes making irrigation necessary. In spring the breezes may reach gale force, damaging early bud break.

SOIL
The topsoil tends to be sand or gravel, the subsoil is often clay loam. These subsoils have the capacity to retain water, but irrigation is still often necessary.

ASPECT
Vines are planted on low, gentle slopes, at around 40m (130ft) above sea level.

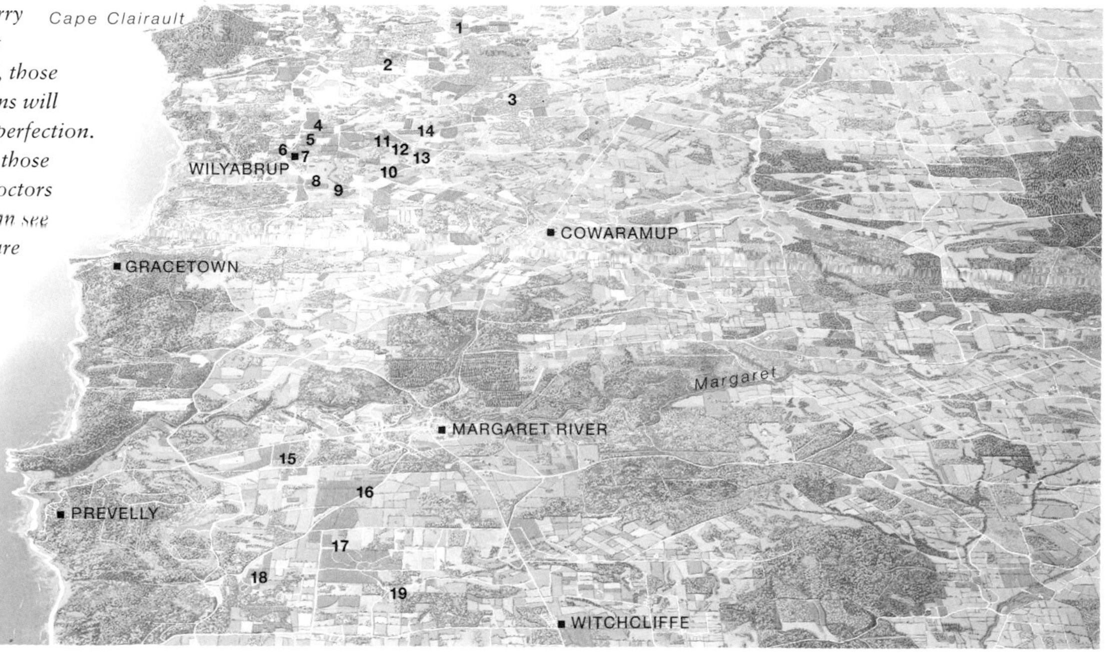

SELECTED WINERIES

1. Amberley Estate
2. Cape Clairault
3. Chapman's Creek Vineyard
4. Moss Wood
5. Evans & Tate
6. Brookland Valley
7. Pierro
8. Cullen Wines
9. Vasse Felix
10. Ashbrook Estate
11. Sandalford
12. Willespie
13. Hay Shed Hill
14. Woody Nook
15. Cape Mentelle
16. Xanadu Wines
17. Voyager Estate
18. Redgate
19. Leeuwin Estate

Map labels: Cape Clairault · WILYABRUP · GRACETOWN · COWARAMUP · Margaret · MARGARET RIVER · PREVELLY · WITCHCLIFFE

NEW ZEALAND

Ata Rangi makes Martinborough's most sumptuous Pinot Noir.

The Tutaekuri River in Hawke's Bay borders Sacred Hill vineyard. Warm gravelly soil and sheltering hills crucially aid ripening.

THE DRAMATIC TRANSFORMATION of New Zealand during the 1990s was nothing short of astonishing. From being thought of as a rather quaint, introverted nation at the far side of nowhere down towards the South Pole, New Zealand has become a vibrant, self-confident, exciting place to be. Yes, *exciting*. Has anyone but a sheep farmer ever called New Zealand *exciting* before? *Has* New Zealand ever been exciting before? I can't vouch for what the early settlers thought 200 years ago, but even the most venerable of my present-day New Zealand acquaintances are enjoying the current mood of excitement, while remaining ever so slightly bemused by it all.

And the same goes for its wine industry. Strangely, it seems to have started off well enough. A visiting Frenchman in 1840 enjoyed the local product – which he described as a 'light, white wine, very sparkling, and delicious to taste' (not bad praise from a Frenchman) – an early hint that light whites and sparklers were the styles most likely to succeed. During the 19th century, other good reports of vines and their wines surfaced from time to time but, by the 1860s, temperance societies were lobbying for laws that hedged the wine producer round with more and more restrictions, with the ultimate aim of prohibiting alcohol altogether.

There was a brief period in the 1890s when Hawkes Bay produced some supposedly good-quality wines, but districts were already starting to vote for local prohibition. Indeed, the whole country voted for prohibition in 1919, only for the result to be overturned by the narrowest of majorities, thanks to the votes of servicemen who were returning home from World War One.

Clearly New Zealand society had little regard for its wine industry, so how on earth could it flourish? It didn't. Vine diseases like *oidium* (powdery mildew) were already making life hell in the warmer, more humid areas, and phylloxera was laying waste to vineyards on all sides. Replanting, when it occurred, was either with *Vitis labrusca* – Albany Surprise was the most widely planted variety until the 1960s – or French hybrids, and the production was mostly of thoroughly mediocre fortified wines.

Good fortified wines all come from warm, dry vineyard conditions. Most of New Zealand just isn't like that. When a Royal Commission after World War Two stated that a 'considerable quantity of wine made in New Zealand would be classified as unfit for human consumption in other wine-producing countries', it was a reflection on how low the quality of New Zealand wine had sunk.

But look at the way new Zealand society treated drinking: there were restrictions on every side. You couldn't drink on trains until 1968, in theatres until 1969, at airports until 1970, or at cabaret shows until 1971. It wasn't until 1976 that caterers were allowed to serve drink, or that wineries themselves could sell a glass of wine. The first wine bar license was granted in 1979, and, good grief, sports clubs couldn't sell drink until 1980!

Although legislation against the 'demon drink' gradually eased, a whiff of disapproval still lingered over the New Zealand wine industry well into the 1980s. Close economic relations with Australia in the late 80s finally forced New Zealand to liberalize its drinking rules at much the same time as a new wave of freemarket politics was sweeping through the country and galvanizing society in general. In 1990, 'dry' areas were abolished, licensing laws were relaxed so that anyone could start a wine business if they wanted to, and supermarkets were given permission to sell wine: they now sell around half of all wine drunk in New Zealand. At last the past is being left behind – a wine past with nothing of value to cherish, a prim colonial legacy with a long expired sell-by date.

If ever there was a wine nation that should look forward and not back, it is New Zealand. Having a past that you are ashamed of can be a marvellously liberating experience. No fusty old traditions that you have to try and drag into the modern world; no cobwebby wine styles stubbornly clung to by faithful consumers. But if you are going to make a fresh start, you have to take care choosing where and how you're going to do it. New Zealand didn't get it quite right the first couple of times around.

They got the idea right – a cool climate – well, a lot cooler than their near, or rather only, neighbour Australia, in any case. And they realized that no-one in the dispirited industry itself seemed to have much idea about what to do – so they'd better call in a foreign expert. In 1895 an Italian-trained Dalmatian called Romeo Bragato arrived. He gave lots of good advice over the next few years, little of which seems to have been taken.

THE CLASSIFICATION OF NEW ZEALAND WINE

Wine labelling legislation in New Zealand has remained relatively relaxed until now. This is set to change with the introduction of a system to win international confidence by guaranteeing the geographic area stated on a wine label.

• **Geographical denominations** The broadest designation is New Zealand, followed by North Island or South Island. These will cover regional blends. Next come the 10 or so regions, such as Canterbury, followed by specific localities, and finally individual vineyards.

In the 1960s they once again decided to go for top advice, and this time to act upon it. Not unreasonably, they looked to Germany as their model. The German influence had been important in teaching Australia how to make delicious, dry Riesling wines under difficult conditions. German wine was highly thought of at the time and it seemed that a Southern Ocean Rheingau or Mosel was a feasible objective.

Dr Helmut Becker, their chosen adviser, was an excellent fellow, and a first-rate scientist. But his life's work was to prove that cross-bred grape varieties could be produced which would give the quality of Riesling without any of its drawbacks. He might have recommended wholesale plantings of Riesling, which would probably have led to many outstanding wines. But he didn't. He chose Müller-Thurgau. So the brave new dawn for New Zealand wine, which could have concentrated on creating a new Bernkasteler Doctor, instead set about creating a better Liebfraumilch. Well, they succeeded there. New Zealand Müller-Thurgau pretty quickly became the best in the world – and I wouldn't be surprised if it still is.

But the advice to go for light, Germanic white wines can be seen, in retrospect, to have been short-sighted in the extreme. It is possible superficially to equate cool South Island regions like Central Otago and Canterbury, maybe even parts of Marlborough, with some parts of Germany. But no grapes were planted in these South Island regions in the 1960s. Instead, all the plantings took place in the North Island, whose climate goes from pleasantly Burgundian in the south to subtropical in the north. Of course you can grow Müller-Thurgau in these conditions – and get massive crops of simple flavoured wine from it – but you're never going to create a drink fit for heroes.

New Zealand's heroes were late in coming. The country's social revolution was a tortuously slow affair, and long after Australian and Californian winemakers were touring the world, drinking up every wine experience they could learn from, New Zealanders were still poking about at home. It wasn't until the 1970s that visionaries like John Buck of Te Mata, or the Spence Brothers of Matua Valley began to establish vineyards, and when they did, it wasn't Müller-Thurgau they had in their sights – it was the classic grapes of Burgundy and Bordeaux.

It soon became clear that Chardonnay and Pinot Noir could ripen easily, indeed, that the North Island was mostly too hot for Pinot Noir. Buck was convinced that he could find ways to ripen Cabernet Sauvignon and Merlot in Hawkes Bay. The Spences hit lucky straight away with Sauvignon Blanc. And by 1973, the new era of New Zealand wine was finally ushered in with the planting of the first vines at Marlborough in South Island.

By 1986, there was such a glut of grapes that the government paid growers NZ$6175 per hectare to rip up their vines. Too many people had rushed into the grape-growing market and had mostly chosen to plant high-yielding bulk varieties in fertile soils. As many as 507ha (1252 acres) of Müller-Thurgau alone were grubbed up. Gisborne, Hawkes Bay, Auckland, even the brand new plantations in the South Island, lost substantial areas; all in all, a quarter of the total national vineyard area – 1517ha (3748 acres) – was pulled out.

After the vinepull, the wine industry regrouped and licked its wounds. By the end of the 1980s New Zealand was becoming known worldwide for the quality of its wines and, in particular, its Sauvignon Blancs and Chardonnays, although Riesling, Pinot Noir, Cabernet and Merlot were also making their mark.

Despite the success of other varieties it is undoubtedly the Sauvignon Blancs from those early Marlborough vines that have taken the world by storm and created a new classic wine style so thrillingly different that it has been the standard bearer for New Zealand ever since. No New Zealand wine had ever tasted like those Sauvignon Blancs from the

South Island. But then, no wine anywhere in the world had ever tasted like them. No previous wine had shocked, thrilled, offended, entranced the world before with such brash, unexpected flavours of gooseberries, passion fruit and lime, or crunchy green capsicum and asparagus spears. They catapulted New Zealand into the front rank of New World wine producers, and the gift she brought to the party was something that even California and Australia had been unable to achieve – an entirely new, brilliantly successful, wine style that the rest of the world has been attempting to copy ever since. New Zealanders now often prefer to talk of their Chardonnays, Rieslings, Merlots or Pinot Noirs, but the world is still thanking them for their Sauvignon Blanc.

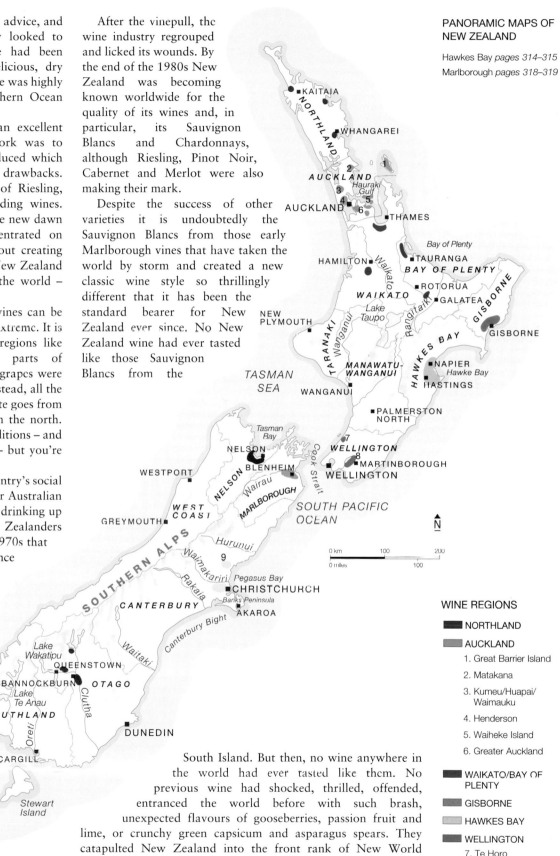

PANORAMIC MAPS OF NEW ZEALAND

Hawkes Bay *pages 314–315*
Marlborough *pages 318–319*

WINE REGIONS

■ NORTHLAND

■ AUCKLAND

1. Great Barrier Island

2. Matakana

3. Kumeu/Huapai/ Waimauku

4. Henderson

5. Waiheke Island

6. Greater Auckland

■ WAIKATO/BAY OF PLENTY

■ GISBORNE

■ HAWKES BAY

■ WELLINGTON

7. Te Horo

8. Wairarapa

■ MARLBOROUGH

■ NELSON

□ CANTERBURY

9. Waipara

■ CENTRAL OTAGO

NORTH ISLAND

RED GRAPES
Merlot has comfortably overtaken Cabernet Sauvignon, with Pinot Noir a distant third. There is also a small amount of Cabernet Franc, Malbec and Syrah.

WHITE GRAPES
Chardonnay rules, covering five times the acreage of second place Sauvignon Blanc. Müller-Thurgau is third (and falling). Next come Chenin Blanc, Semillon, Riesling and Gewürztraminer.

CLIMATE
The North Island is generally warmer than the South Island, but overall the climate in both is maritime. Rainfall is plentiful and is often a problem during the ripening season when it can lead to rot.

SOIL
Soils range from glacial and alluvial at Hawkes Bay, to loam and clay in the north, and friable gravelly silt around Martinborough.

ASPECT
Vineyard site selection is now carefully considered, after a boom period when poor varieties were planted in many unsuitable places. Most vines are found on flatlands or gently rolling hills, where too high yields are controlled by skilled vine canopy management. And growing numbers of premium-focused vineyards are appearing on sun-drenched, north-facing slopes.

WHAT'S ALL THIS ABOUT NEW ZEALAND being a cool-climate wine region? That's a bit like saying France is a cool-climate wine region: some bits are, to be sure, but some bits are as hot as Hades. And it's the same with New Zealand. Way down in the South or Central Otago it's as cool as Germany's Mosel Valley. But that's 1000km (620 miles) south of the vineyards that lie just north of Auckland. And don't try to draw any conclusion from latitude. Central Otago's latitude is 45° South, about the same as some of the warmer parts of that not particularly cold area, Bordeaux, in the northern hemisphere.

As for the furthest vineyards of the Northland, above Auckland, they're at about latitude 34° South. In the northern hemisphere 34° slices across the top of Tunisia and Algeria. Now it isn't like Tunisia north of Auckland, but there are a fair few vineyards that struggle under the sort of warm, humid conditions that verge on the subtropical, so I think I'm going to leave most of this cool-climate chat until we get to the South Island.

If you want to suggest that New Zealand is a wet-climate region, I'll go for that. With the exception of the tiny Wairarapa area near Wellington, which behaves as though it were a virtual extension of Marlborough on the other side of the Cook Strait, and perhaps Waiheke Island out in the bay less than an hour's ferry ride from Auckland, the North Island is a wet place to grow grapes.

And if you want to suggest that it is a wonderfully fertile landscape ideally suited to growing vines, I'll say, yes – fertile soils, lots of sun, lots of rain: you can grow vines the size of peach trees in no time at all. But don't expect a crop of decent grapes fit for making fine wine. The best wines come from small crops, off vines grown in dry areas with infertile, impoverished, free-draining soil, and just the right amount of sun. That's not too much of a problem in the South Island, but in the North, these conditions are few and far between. And the story of how to find such sites – and if you can't, what to do instead – is very much the story of the North Island's wine industry.

Many producers actually started out in the 19th century by growing their grapes in greenhouses. That seems a bit extreme, and could explain why hardly any wineries grew to any size during the 19th century! But the early growers may not have been so dumb. Most of the vines in the North Island do suffer from the weather, particularly around Auckland where most of the early plantings were located.

Though the latitudes should imply hot to very hot conditions, things aren't as simple as that. In Europe, the main maritime influences are the warm Gulf Stream and the warm Mediterranean. New Zealand is set alone among seas strongly influenced by the icy Antarctic currents. Strong prevailing westerly winds continually pummel the west coast. Until you get down to the central mountain ranges that protect Gisborne and Hawkes Bay on the east coast, there is no protection from the westerlies, and the rain clouds happily deposit their loads on the vineyards around Auckland and Northland.

You might get away with this if you were guaranteed a dry autumn. But that's one thing you're not guaranteed in the North Island. If the westerlies don't keep drizzling down on you, you've got the cyclonic depressions of the Pacific to think about. These are likely to move in from the east in the early autumn. Some years you'll have picked your crop, some years you won't have. These cyclonic rainstorms are a particular problem over to the east in Gisborne and Hawkes Bay, which are otherwise well-protected from westerly rain.

Lots of rain, lots of sun – all you need is fertile soil for vines to grow like jungle. Well, with a couple of exceptions in parts of

Hawkes Bay and Wairarapa, North Island soil goes from fertile to supremely fertile and that makes it very difficult indeed for quality-minded grape growers. Fertile soils rarely drain well, and they encourage large crops of grapes. Large crops take longer to ripen and – you've got it – up roll those cyclonic depressions brimful of rain just when you're not quite ready!

North Island has a history of autumn downpours, so you have to pick early even if the crop isn't really ripe. For all the negative aspects of having Müller-Thurgau as your major grape variety, it will at least provide you with adequate, mildly fruity wine at low alcohol levels from high crops. Not very ambitious, I admit, but until the 1980s, when producers began to realize something more exciting was possible, it was the mainstay of North Island vineyards.

CANOPY MANAGEMENT

Fertile soils also encourage vigorous leaf growth, and this is a serious problem if you want to progress from hybrids and Müller-Thurgau to the classic grape varieties. Excessive leaf growth shades your fruit, retarding physical maturity in the grapes and causing a lean, green streak to dominate red wine flavours even when the alcohol levels seem acceptable. For a long time, a green leafy streak of acidity was one way of identifying even the best New Zealand reds. To be honest, it can be rather a nice taste, but modern New Zealand winemakers are mostly determined to stamp it out.

Heavy foliage also reduces air movement. In the frequently damp North Island climates, this causes outbursts of bunch rot (*botrytis*) which can ruin the harvest. The desire to make wines suitable for competing in international markets, along with an increasingly demanding domestic market, forced New Zealand's wine industry to look for solutions to these problems. Led by Dr Richard Smart, New Zealand has become the world leader in developing trellising and pruning systems for fertile, warm-air, high-humidity vineyard conditions.

The results have been dramatic. For almost the first time we are seeing red wines of a fully ripe, yet memorably individual, style coming from all parts of the North Island – Auckland, Hawkes Bay, Wairarapa and even, in a few cases, from Gisborne. White wines are achieving far better ripeness without the accompanying botrytis tinge that used to be a mark of much New Zealand Chardonnay and Müller-Thurgau, and the prevailing acidity of the fruit is far better integrated in the wine. Even in cool years like 1995 and 2000, which, throughout most of New Zealand, were about as difficult as vintages can get, those vineyards using modern vineyard techniques still produced fair fruit. With the wholesale replanting necessitated by phylloxera infestation, we're seeing more and more vineyards adapting to the challenging conditions of New Zealand's North Island.

AUCKLAND AND WAIKATO

Nowhere are conditions more challenging than around Auckland. There are now very few plantings in Northland, where subtropical conditions make it difficult to ripen *vinifera* grapes before they rot on the vine. Matakana over on the Hauraki Gulf is an exception. However, the Dalmatians who came to New Zealand to work the Kauri gumfields were good old-fashioned thirsty Europeans, and many, having saved a bit of money, migrated nearer to Auckland and set up as winemakers. Almost all the traditional wine companies in Northland, as well as several of the newer ones, were founded by families of Dalmatian origin.

The hot, humid weather and the mostly heavy clay soils didn't matter too much when the chief product was fortified sherries and ports. But the swing to fine table wine production has found most of the go-ahead Auckland area wineries sourcing the bulk of their grapes from elsewhere – Gisborne, Hawkes Bay and Marlborough. Even so, there are some vineyards over by the airport to the south, rather more at Henderson just to the north, and a good deal more further up the road at Huapai and Kumeu. But finding ways to produce a balanced wine isn't easy. Availability of superior clones helps, as do de-vigorating rootstocks on these soggy clay soils, and various farming methods and trellising systems are designed to control the vines' vigour and produce healthy fruit. All these efforts are producing some outstanding estate-grown wines from companies like Kumeu River and Matua Valley, but most of Auckland's top wines are nonetheless made from bought-in grapes.

Auckland's newest wine region is in Clevedon, about 40 minutes drive south of the city in rolling, verdant farmland near the eastern coast. Here, more than ten 'lifestyle' producers have established small micro-boutique wineries with a strong focus on Bordeaux-style reds and Chardonnay. Results are variable but, at best, promising. The soils are largely heavy clay, the weather warm, and with the Tasman Sea on one side and the Pacific on the other, humidity is high, but at least that gives cloud cover against the harsh effects of the sun. If we're looking for the region's most consistently exciting estate-grown wines, we may well have to look offshore, out into the Hauraki Gulf to Waiheke Island, a paradise of a place where you can sit on the bluffs above the bay and watch the ferries plying calmly between the island's tiny quays and the bustling port of Auckland – close enough to commute, yet a world away. Vineyards were established here as long ago as 1978, but it was only in the 1990s that the tempo picked up and a swarm of hopefuls began to plant the island's slopes. They were tempted by the nagging New Zealand dream of producing great red wine from the Bordeaux varieties of Cabernet Sauvignon and Merlot. Both Goldwater Estate and Stonyridge were consistently creating deep dry reds with an uncanny Bordeaux-like structure and taste, but it was the 1993 vintage – so cold and mean in most of New Zealand, so deep and lush and intense on Waiheke Island – that persuaded doubters that this truly was an exceptional vineyard site. The remarkable thing is that Waiheke has such a warm dry climate within spitting distance of humid, rain-swept Auckland, but it does. There's very little summer rain, the soils are infertile and free-draining, and the surrounding seas create a balmy maritime climate. And it's such a heavenly place to live. Who wouldn't give it a go? There's even a vineyard out on Great Barrier Island at Okupu Beach. The guy only produces about 100 cases of wine, but hey, if he made any more, he might have to don a suit and tie and leave the reef to try to sell it. Some guys have all the luck.

The small Waikato region south of Auckland is one of the North Island's historic regions, but this rather damp, humid spot is probably better suited to dairy farming. Though there are some large vineyards here, there are few wineries, and much of the crop is made into grape juice. Even so, de Redcliffe has made some good dry wines, and Rongopai has used the warm, clammy conditions to make some superb botrytis-affected sweet wines.

GISBORNE

Heading east below the Bay of Plenty, there are several wineries – most importantly Morton Estate – but few vineyards, though there is a small vineyard on the pumice soils of Galatea to the south. But it is Gisborne, on Poverty Bay, that we are looking for. Most of the vineyards are sprawled across the Gisborne plains where a deep bed of alluvial silt supplies such fertile soil conditions that varieties like Müller-Thurgau can easily produce 30 tonnes per hectare of

acceptable fruit. But the excessive fertility isn't as suitable for higher quality varieties, since it encourages dense foliage and hefty crops that retard ripening. Chardonnay has still managed to produce high yields of decent fruit due to plenty of sunshine hours and protection from wet westerlies by the Huiarau Mountains. That protection counts for nothing, however, when cyclonic depressions form to the east in autumn. Gisborne has unacceptably high rainfall in the vintage period of February to April, a fact that has deterred most growers from trying red grapes. However, state-of-the-art vineyard management, replacement of phylloxera-infected vines with better clones, and a move into the less fertile hillside sites is turning Gisborne's reputation around. People have begun to talk of the area as New Zealand's Chardonnay capital; some of Auckland's top wineries make their best Chardonnays from selected Gisborne vineyards, and the soft, gentle, ripe quality of most recent releases shows that they may well be right.

WAIRARAPA

Hawkes Bay is way down the coast from Gisborne, and I cover it more fully over the page. But there is one more booming area – Wairarapa just north of Wellington. This is centred on the little town of Martinborough, though vineyards are now appearing on the river terraces above Martinborough, as well as further north towards Masterson. If the North Island's weak points are too much rain and excessively fertile soil, Martinborough has the answer. Surrounded by mountains to the south-west, west and north-east, the area is protected from both summer and autumn rains. And although the land down by the river flats is heavy clay, a series of flat-topped river terraces to the north-east around Martinborough are shallow gravelly silt over deep, free-draining, virtually pure gravel.

Add to this relatively cool and windy, but rainless, summers and autumns, and a bit of drip irrigation and you have positively Burgundian conditions for great Chardonnay and Pinot Noir. That, plus a splash of Sauvignon Blanc, Cabernet Sauvignon, Pinot Gris, Riesling and a handful of other varieties, is increasingly exactly what you get.

It's not just grape-growing which draws you to Waiheke Island with its warm, dry climate: the yachts in Te Whau Bay show lifestyle is equally important. But just across the water are the vineyards of Goldwater, one of New Zealand's top producers.

Few New Zealand reds get as ripe as this Hawkes Bay blend of Malbec, Merlot and Cabernet Franc from The Terraces, a tiny suntrap of a vineyard above Esk Valley's winery.

Hawkes Bay

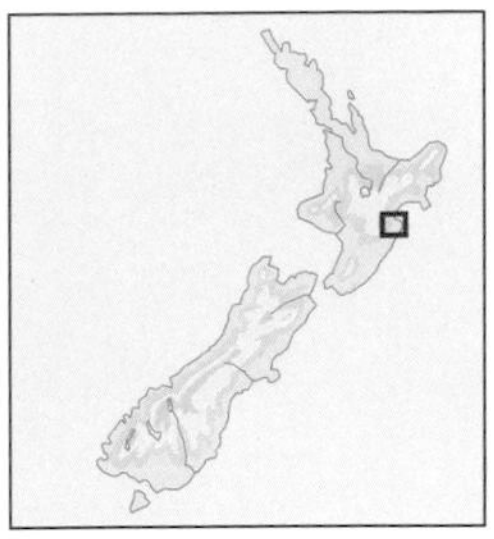

RED GRAPES
Merlot is now the most widely planted red grape, slightly ahead of Cabernet Sauvignon, and the gap is widening. Pinot Noir is a distant third.

WHITE GRAPES
Chardonnay is by far the most important white grape with Sauvignon Blanc in second place. Müller-Thurgau, though rapidly declining, is third.

CLIMATE
This is ideal for high-quality wine production. Regular sunshine ensures full ripening of the grapes and there's optimum rainfall.

SOIL
Almost all the vineyards are planted on alluvial plains, but soil types still vary from well-drained gravel and sandy loam, to fertile, heavier silty loam.

ASPECT
The best vineyards are on free-draining soils of low fertility. Most Hawkes Bay plantings hitherto have been made on flat land, but nearby limestone hills may be found superior in the future.

'WELCOME TO SUNNY HAWKES BAY' the sign says, and they're not kidding. Not long ago, I arrived here in March – straight from the heartland of Australia where I'd been boiled and bullied by the merciless sun day after day, but where Factor 30 cream had kept my face, neck and hands a hue somewhere between blancmange pink and butterscotch orange, and not a blister in sight. I had wondered, well, as New Zealand is so much cooler than Australia, will I really need sun lotion in March? But I'd slapped some on anyway and gone off to my first meeting. By late morning I was uncomfortable. By lunchtime I was hurting. By evening my hands were a welter of bright red blisters, so sore I could neither bear the sunlight on them nor soothe them with anything but cool water. Sunny Hawkes Bay? There should be a health warning.

But it's a serious point I'm making here. The sun may not feel hot, but it shines relentlessly at Hawkes Bay. New Zealand is known as the Land of the Long White Cloud, and you can see the clouds piling up near Gisborne to the north. You can watch them follow the coastline down towards Napier, yet a mile or two before the Bay, they head inland to hug the mountain range until, south of Havelock North and Te Mata, they return to the coast. More importantly, the ozone layer is presently extremely thin over the southern Pacific. I've been told that ultraviolet penetration round Hawkes Bay is higher than in any other populated area in the Southern hemisphere. It isn't known precisely what effect this has on grape ripening, whether it aids or impedes photosynthesis, the development of pigment, and the physical maturing of the grapes.

But long before ozone layers were even discovered, Hawkes Bay's blend of long sunshine hours, reasonable rainfall that usually fell at the right times, and availability of large tracts of suitable vineyard land, had made the area New Zealand's most exciting vineyard region. That was at the end of the 19th century. Various vineyards were established, mostly on good, infertile land, and mostly with classic grape varieties, and by 1913 Hawkes Bay was producing a third of New Zealand's wine. Bernard Chambers' Te Mata vineyard in Hawkes Bay was the largest in New Zealand.

However, as elsewhere in New Zealand, phylloxera, prohibition and lack of interest took their toll, vineyards were turned over to *Vitis labrusca* and hybrid varieties, and the heavy Heretaunga river flats were planted in preference to the low-yielding gravel beds. One man, Tom McDonald, kept the flame of Chardonnay and Cabernet Sauvignon flickering, though mostly in the high-yielding, unsuitable black soils of the plain. But when John Buck visited Tom McDonald in the 1960s, Tom had pointed over to the Te Mata peak and said, 'That's the best Cabernet land you'll get in Hawkes Bay – frost-free, facing north, and free-draining.'

So John bought the old Te Mata property in 1974, and released a Cabernet in 1980 that I remember to this day, and which sparked the revival of Hawkes Bay as a great vineyard area, rather than a provider of bulk grapes like Müller-Thurgau. Hawkes Bay could, once more, enter the contest for New Zealand's premier wine region. It's a battle that can't ever be decisively won, though, because other large areas like Marlborough produce such completely different styles, and tip-top areas like Nelson, Wairarapa or Waiheke Island are a fraction of its size, and so don't bear comparison. Hawkes Bay's reputation relies increasingly on its ability to fully ripen the red Bordeaux varieties – not easy in New Zealand – plus an impressive performance in the less challenging arenas of Chardonnay and Sauvignon Blanc. There is still a significant amount of planting on the heavy river flats, but Hawkes Bay's reputation depends on three different areas.

The warmest of these is Bay View and the Esk Valley. It is also the least planted, so far. Nevertheless, conditions are excellent. The bay swoops inwards north of Napier and presses up against the hills. There's not much land, but it's warm: apricot trees are all around and bud-burst comes as much as two weeks ahead of the rest of the Bay. The grapes can really fry on the terraces cut into the hillside, and red Bordeaux varieties romp to ripeness. The Esk Valley joins the sea just north of Bay View, and its well-protected, sandy alluvial soils over gravel enjoy daily sea breezes.

The heart of the Hawkes Bay revival lies in the gravel beds left behind by various rivers flowing into the Bay. Most important of

SELECTED WINERIES

1. Sileni Estates
2. Alpha Domus
3. Ngatarawa
4. Trinity Hill
5. Te Awa Farm
6. Unison
7. Stonecroft
8. Sacred Hill
9. Matariki
10. Cross Roads
11. C J Pask
12. Church Road (Montana)
13. Mission
14. Crab Farm
15. Esk Valley
16. Brookfields
17. Vidal
18. Askerne
19. Te Mata
20. Clearview

— GIMBLETT GRAVELS AREA

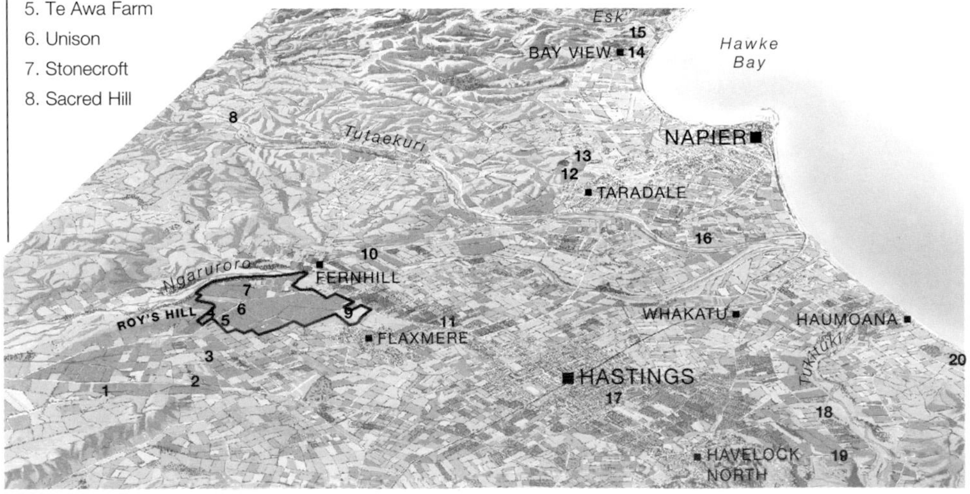

WHERE THE VINEYARDS ARE *The centre of the valley, between Hastings and Napier, is where most vineyards used to be, but with fertile soils and a high water table, quality was never good and most of the land has reverted to fruit and vegetables. One of the commonest sights now is a long line of poplars acting as a windbreak for kiwi fruit orchards. North of the airport, Bay View and the Esk Valley don't have that many vines, but Bay View is a sun-trap, and the sandy alluvial soils over gravel in the sheltered Esk Valley are excellent for grapes.*

The real action is happening along the Tutaekuri and Ngaruroro rivers. Their rushing waters have scoured parts of the valley floor clean of soil and silt until there's almost nothing but gravel left, and the rivers have also changed paths in the past, leaving great swathes of gravel ripe for vineyards. This is particularly obvious in the Gimblett Gravels area where 65 per cent of the total plantable area of 800ha (1977 acres) is now filled with vines as planting fever runs its course. The best southern sites are east of Havelock North below the Te Mata peak, where several of the vineyards for Te Mata's outstanding wines are situated, but there are also good largely unexploited sites in the Tukituki Valley, where once again, the river has scoured the land of its topsoil, leaving bare gravel beds.

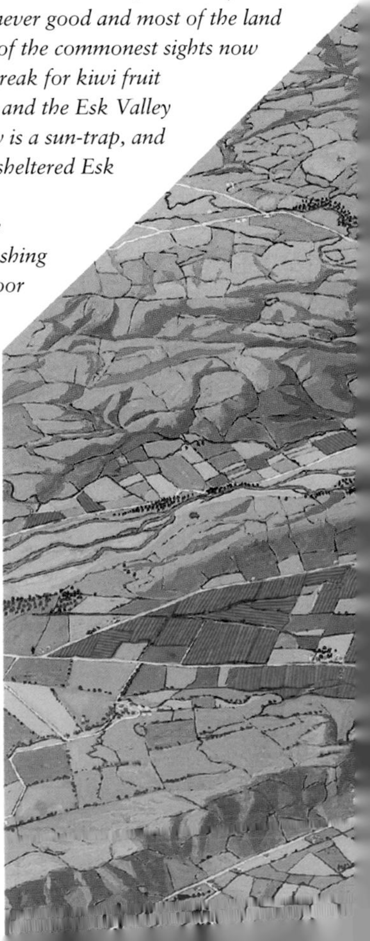

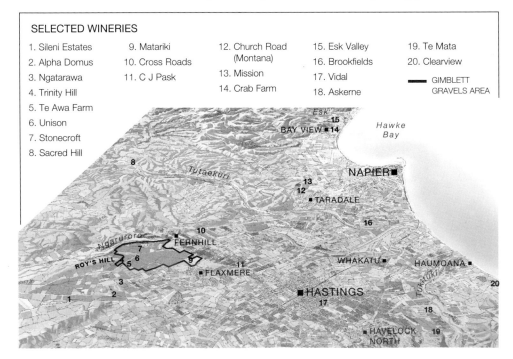

these are the Tutaekuri and the Ngaruroro. It's worth driving along and across these rivers to gaze on some of the purest gravel beds you are ever likely to see. Only the centre of Margaux in Bordeaux gets anywhere near them and yet here they stretch, mile upon mile, westwards up into the hills. Get out of the car and tramp through the vineyards next to Highway 50 and the Gimblett Road and you're walking along the old river-bed itself. Half the time there's no soil at all – just ashen gravel everywhere, with an aquifer running beneath to provide as much irrigation as you could want.

A group of 34 wineries and grape growers have banded together to define their own appellation based on an 700-ha (1730-acre) plot of this gravelly soil that produces some of Hawkes Bay's finest wines. 'Gimblett Gravels', as the new area is known, is claimed to be up to three degrees warmer than most other areas in the Bay during the day in summer and autumn. If you see 'Gimblett Gravels' on a wine label, at least 95 per cent of the grapes must be from there.

Gimblett Gravels' spokesman, Steve Smith MW, describes the area – which includes land along Gimblett Road, Highway 50, Fernhill and Roy's Hill – as 'the G-spot of Hawkes Bay'. Land prices here have increased 15-fold in the past decade. There's an air of feverish activity along the Ngaruroro at the moment as all the major players in New Zealand are planting like mad to make sure of their share of what they rightly see as Kiwi red wine heaven. Much of the land is virtually hydroponic and nothing survives without

irrigation. Indeed, the gravel can be so pure that nutrients sometimes have to put back to avoid the wines turning out with all the right technical figures, but tasting dull.

The thing about such free-draining soil is that it hands control back to the winemaker: crops can be regulated and vines trellised to maximize the sun. But the weather still comes into it. Normal weather patterns at Hawkes Bay are like Bordeaux in a good year, albeit with slightly lower maximum temperatures, but a larger spread of sunny days and less rain. You can pretty much rely on a dry warm autumn (though cyclones in 1988 and 2001 deluged the vineyards at vintage time). The real cauldron is around Fernhill where even Syrah ripens, and there's a tiny parcel of Zinfandel. As you head up the valley past Roy's Hill and west to Riverview (off the map), the cooling influence of the mountains delays budding and ripening by a good week, but means increasingly good conditions for Pinot Noir and Riesling.

The Tutaekuri river cuts its way through the hills north of the Ngaruroro and much of its course is protected from maritime winds. The same gravelly conditions exist here and also in the Tukituki Valley to the south-east and in outcrops near Havelock North and the Te Mata peak. But the south side of the bay is typically shallow alluvial soils over impenetrable pug clays. This terrain is harder to control than pure gravel, but restricts yields and can produce fine wines. Te Mata's best vineyards are either on tan-coloured, gravelly terraces ('red metal'), or loess over limestone and sandstone.

0 km   1   2
0 miles   1

HAWKES BAY

TOTAL DISTANCE
NORTH TO SOUTH
35KM (21½ MILES)

▦ VINEYARDS

N

NAPIER

FLAXMERE

HASTINGS

SOUTH ISLAND

The snow-capped peak of Mount Tapuaenuku reminds you that Vavasour's Awatere Valley vineyard is in one of New Zealand's top cool spots.

WINEMAKING IN THE SOUTH ISLAND is a lot older than you might think. It's true that when the large-scale producer Montana began planting in Marlborough in 1973 it was generally seen as the beginning of the modern industry there – the modern industry, yes, but of the centres of winemaking now spread across the island, Marlborough was the only place that hadn't had a proper wine industry before. Well, perhaps wine industry is stretching the point, since none of the original wine producers survived very long.

But Nelson, to the north-west of Marlborough, was visited in 1843 by boat-loads of Germans who, looking at the steep hills covered in virgin bush, thought the place looked too tough for them, and sailed on to Australia. Standing on the low hills running down to the sparkling waters of Tasman Bay, while a long white cloud, piled high with meringue fluff and with a base as flat as a smoothing iron, hangs motionless in the warm sky, I find it inconceivable anyone could ever want to leave this paradise. But there you go. Eventually some sort of winemaking got going there in 1868 and continued fitfully until 1939.

The French showed a bit more nerve in 1840 when they landed at Akaroa, south of Canterbury, and planted vines around their homes on the mountainous Banks Peninsula. But there are no records of them doing anything more than make enough wine for their own consumption, and when they died, so did their vineyards.

Further south, in Central Otago, was born that perennial fair-weather friend of the winemaker, a Gold Rush. It didn't spawn vineyards on the same scale as the Australian or Californian gold fevers, but there's no doubt that a Frenchman called Jean Desiré Feraud was doing good business in 1870 selling his wine and liqueurs to speculators. Yet this waned as the lustre of precious metal faded, and the island reverted to sheep, cattle and fruit – to quiet, unobtrusive, unpolluted prosperity, lost in the southern seas.

Until 1973, that is. That's when Marlborough, now New Zealand's leading wine region, was born out of nothing. At the time Montana, New Zealand's biggest wine company, was looking to expand and wanted cheap, easy land. Hawke's Bay was NZ$4800 per hectare. Marlborough was between NZ$600 and $1200 per hectare, depending on whether it was good for nothing but pasture or good for almost nothing but pasture. Montana bought 14 farms – 1600ha (3954 acres) – and before the locals had even woken up to what was happening, they had planted 390ha (964 acres) of vines, mostly Müller-Thurgau. But they took a punt and planted 24ha (60 acres) of Sauvignon Blanc – just a hunch after tasting an early New Zealand Sauvignon – but what a hunch.

Without Marlborough Sauvignon Blanc, New Zealand might still be struggling for acceptance in the World Premier League of wine. With Marlborough Sauvignon Blanc, it created a classic flavour that no-one had ever dreamed of before, and set a standard for tangy, incisive, mouth-watering dry wines as crunchy as iceberg lettuce, and as aggressive as gooseberries and lime, that the rest of the world has been trying to copy ever since.

SOUTH ISLAND'S GROWTH SPURT

Startling changes in the South Island wine industry have happened over the last generation, not least in the development of new wine regions such as Marlborough. Back in 1960 the total vineyard area for the whole of New Zealand was 388ha (960 acres) The South Island didn't have a single vine, and the most widely planted in the North Island was the *labrusca* variety, Albany Surprise, followed by a clutch of hybrids like Baco 22A and Seibel 5455.

By 1975, when there was massive vineyard expansion in the North Island, with six times as much land under vine as there had been in 1960, the first South Island vines were only just being planted. The hybrids had increased their acreage in the North Island, but the German influence was evident with Müller-Thurgau being nationally the most widely planted variety, and some 649ha (1604 acres) yielding fruit. Expansion continued at a breakneck pace and, although North Island led the way, Marlborough on South Island was rapidly proving its worth. By 1982, New Zealand's total vineyard area stood at 5901ha (14,580 acres); Auckland and Waikato still had the same area of vineyard as before, but the leaders now were Gisborne with 1922ha (4749 acres), Hawkes Bay with 1891ha (4673 acres) and Marlborough with a remarkable 1175ha (2904 acres). Small areas like Nelson and Canterbury in South Island, and Wairarapa in North Island, had now begun planting grapes, too.

The dramatic government-sponsored vinepull of the mid-1980s led to a sea-change in the industry and the significant growth since then has been entirely in high quality areas. By 2002, the total area of New Zealand vineyards, including vines not yet bearing or in the process of being planted, totalled 12,822ha (31,680 acres), with Marlborough being the largest and most important at 5228ha (12,918 acres), Hawke's Bay covering 3072ha (7590 acres) and Gisborne 1963ha (4850 acres). And new areas of high-quality vines are bursting out. On South Island, Central Otago – invisible in 1982 – now has 433ha (1069 acres) and is predicting the largest growth rate, with a doubling of production area between 2001 and 2004. Nelson now has 297ha (734 acres) and Canterbury has burgeoned to 485ha (1198 acres).

It's interesting to look at grape varieties, too. In 1970, the hybrid Baco 22A was the top variety with 217ha (536 acres). It is now officially extinct. Müller-Thurgau had 194ha (479 acres) in 1970, but by 1983 was easily the leader with ten times this amount. However, by 2002 this had dropped to 342ha (845 acres). There was no Sauvignon Blanc in 1970, but in 2002, 3086ha (7625 acres) were planted along with 3434ha (8485 acres) of Chardonnay and 1716ha (4240 acres) of Pinot Noir. White grape varieties presently

account for 65 per cent of the total planting area, but this is expected to decline further as Müller-Thurgau and other less popular white vines are grubbed up.

NELSON

Back in the South Island's early days, one of the first regions to stir was Nelson, 75km (45 miles) north-west of Marlborough. The tiny Victory Grape Wines vineyard at Stoke, a mile or so south-west of the city of Nelson, produced its first vintage in 1973, and in 1974 Hermann Seifried established what is Nelson's largest vineyard; others have since joined.

Yet development has been relatively small scale. The Waimea Plains, on flat but well-drained land running across to Rabbit Island and Tasman Bay, could have become another Marlborough, except that land prices and start-up costs are significantly higher. So much of the development has been in the beautiful Upper Moutere hills, just a few miles further to the north-west. The soils are mostly clay loam, but well-drained on these slopes, as they need to be, because Nelson is cooler than Marlborough and gets more concentrated periods of rain in autumn. Yet overall it has more rain-free days and long hours of sunshine, with the west coast taking the brunt of the westerlies. Despite the grapes ripening a week later than in Marlborough, and with the attendant risk of rain during vintage, some of the South Island's best Pinot Noir, Riesling and Chardonnay come from here.

CANTERBURY

Three hours' drive to the south from Marlborough, Christchurch sits at the heart of the Canterbury region on the shores of Pegasus Bay. The local Lincoln University began grape trials in 1973, despite the fact that all the traditional indicators said the area had to be too cold for grapes. There appears to be less heat here than in Champagne in France, hardly as much as on the Rhine in Germany and yet, and yet... One of my most vivid 'road to Damascus' tasting experiences ever was the St Helena Pinot Noir 1982, grown on an old potato field twenty minutes' drive north of Christchurch, and only its second vintage. Startling, intense, brimming with passionate fruit and heady perfume, it could have held its own with many of the Côte de Nuits' Grands Crus.

From a standing start, Canterbury suddenly became New Zealand's promised land for Pinot Noir. But it's not as simple as that: Wairarapa on North Island and Central Otago way to the south would dispute this claim, and Canterbury does have several different mesoclimates. The most regularly exciting Pinot Noirs and Chardonnays are now coming from Waipara, 40km (25 miles) north of Christchurch, where the Teviotdale range of hills protect the vines from the sea breezes and create an average temperature 2–3°C warmer than to the south around Canterbury.

Loess and gravel river terraces and their stressed low crops create a wine style that is lush and warm for Pinot Noir and Chardonnay, and thrillingly lean for Riesling. It's difficult to say if the area is really warm enough for Bordeaux varieties, but I've had some marvellous austere yet satisfying examples off the stoniest vineyards, as the grapes creep to ripeness in the long dry autumns, finally being harvested as late as May. Vines near Christchurch are battered by wind, none more so than Giesen's, which nonetheless manages to produce fabulously concentrated Rieslings, the wind's aggression being offset by low rainfall and reliably long, dry autumns. And to the south, French Farm is giving the Banks Peninsula another go, and prospectors have been seen measuring up literally hundreds of hectares further south around the Waireke River. A new north Canterbury area, around Pyramid Valley, is

another recently planted district that shows great promise. The overriding influence allowing grapes to ripen is low rainfall and free-draining soils. Long, dry summer days lead to a dry, mild autumn letting grapes hang on the vine until May – if April frosts don't strike. But then long, slow ripening is what brings flavour intensity – just like northern Europe, but without the vintage rains.

CENTRAL OTAGO

Even so, you do have to have a certain amount of heat for flavour intensity. Won't Central Otago, the world's most southerly wine region, way down near Queenstown in the heart of New Zealand's skiing region, be too cold? When you fly into Queenstown's tiny airport, wobbling between mist-wreathed mountain peaks, you feel as though you're in Scotland, not New Zealand. And the feeling remains on the ground – those raw, gaunt hillscapes are too Scottish for vines, surely? Well on paper, yes. But this is the one Continental climate among South Island's wine regions. After all, Latitude 45° South lies on the same parallel as the heart of the Rhône Valley as well as Bordeaux in the northern hemisphere. And there are hot spots here and there – on the shores of lakes, beneath sheer rock faces that reflect heat and retain it in the chilly summer nights – where heat readings rocket upwards.

This far south the summer days are very long and the rainfall frequently the lowest in New Zealand and, between December and February, the number of cloudless days with temperatures hour upon hour over 20°C (68°F) – and often peaking at over 30°C (86°F) – is exceptional. Equally important, and a major factor in the remarkable intensity of Central Otago fruit, are the fiercely cold nights. Hot days equal high ripeness; cold nights equal high acid. Result: memorable fruit flavours in the wines.

Chardonnay, Pinot Gris, Riesling and Sauvignon Blanc all show promise here, but the star is Pinot Noir. By 2004, Pinot Noir will dominate all other varieties in Central Otago, covering almost three-quarters of the region's vineyards. The Bannockburn district, a north-facing ridge riddled with abandoned gold mines, and the driest area in New Zealand, looks very exciting. The suntrap of Earnscleugh, behind Bannockburn, could turn out to be even better.

RED GRAPES
Pinot Noir is best suited to South Island's cool conditions, but Cabernet Sauvignon, Cabernet Franc and Merlot are also grown.

WHITE GRAPES
Sauvignon Blanc covers twice the vineyard area of Chardonnay, in second place. Riesling is next, followed by Semillon and a rising star, Pinot Gris.

CLIMATE
The climate is cool with abundant sunshine to help the ripening process. Autumn rainfall is low, but wind and frosts can be troublesome.

SOIL
Soil types are variable. Alluvial gravel, or alluvial silt loams over gravel subsoils, are well draining. In addition there are areas of chalky, limestone-rich loams and patches of loess.

ASPECT
Much of the vineyard land is flat and quite low lying. Nelson is more hilly with some sunny, sheltered sites.

MARLBOROUGH AND NELSON CLIMATES

Protected from the strong sea winds, Marlborough is one of the few South Island regions warm enough for large-scale viticulture. The Southern Alps dissipate the prevailing westerly winds and help to create a rain shadow in the region, reducing rainfall over the vineyards as well as cloud cover, which, in turn, increases the amount of valuable sunshine. The southern tip of North Island protects the vineyards from the cyclonic autumn storms that come in from the Pacific Ocean. The only winds that affect the Marlborough vineyards down on the flat Wairau River Valley are warm and dry and they help to boost grape ripening. Like Marlborough, Nelson also has warm summers and promisingly high sunshine hours, but as the harvest approaches there is a strong risk of damaging autumn rains.

Probably the most famous Sauvignon Blanc in the world: Cloudy Bay which comes from Marlborough in the South Island.

MARLBOROUGH

RED GRAPES
Pinot Noir is now the third most planted grape variety in Marlborough, though much of it is used in sparkling wine. Merlot and Cabernet Sauvignon are minor players.

WHITE GRAPES
Sauvignon Blanc rules with about half of the region's total vineyard area. Chardonnay is next, with Riesling well behind in third place.

CLIMATE
The climate is cool, but sunshine is abundant. Rainfall is scarce between October and April, and frost and wind can cause problems.

SOIL
Soil varies from clay to stony gravel. Very stony districts are so well-drained that irrigation is essential.

ASPECT
Generally low and flat, but the Awatere Valley benefits from protected terraces allowing maximum exposure to the sun.

I DON'T HAVE MANY REGRETS IN LIFE, but one thing I would like to have done is to see the Marlborough region in New Zealand's South Island at the beginning of the 1970s. What would I have seen? Pastureland, sheep, garlic, cherry trees, sheep, a dozy market town… and maybe some more sheep. Nothing much really. But I would like to have seen it precisely because it was so ordinary, so unmemorable, so dull. And because it didn't boast one single vine.

Now, in the new millennium, it grows more vines than any other area of New Zealand and is expanding at an exhilarating but scary rate that gives the entire region a real Klondike feel. For every vast field of vines, their lush foliage glistening in the summer sunshine, there seems to be another vast field of raw earth being straddled and stretched by posts and wires as the land is prepared for yet another carpet of vines. And there's only one reason for all this: Marlborough is such a damned good place to grow vines. In fact, I'll go further than that. It's one of the greatest places on earth to grow them, producing some of the world's most remarkable wines. And I would love to have been in on it right from the start. But is Marlborough just about Sauvignon Blanc? No, it isn't; and it isn't just about Montana either (though the company owns or controls between a third and half of Marlborough's grapes). There are other higher-profile labels, led by the brilliant Cloudy Bay – one of the world's most sought after wines – whose first vintage was as recent as 1985.

The whole spectrum of grapes has been planted as people have tried to establish precisely what limits there are to Marlborough's abilities. Well, there are limits. Like any other great vineyard area, Marlborough is not all-purpose, because then you'd have to trade memorable brilliance for overall reliability. Most of Marlborough can't do much with Cabernet Sauvignon, for example, though where the soil is rocky and well-drained and yields are kept low, warm years will ripen it. But Merlot gives good results. People thought the cool conditions were tailor-made for Pinot Noir, but the region is only just beginning to show its potential for this difficult variety. Chardonnay, too, was expected to be uniformly brilliant. It isn't. Much of it ends up as fizz but, that said, there are already some stunning luscious, buttery, intense Chardonnays.

Sauvignon Blanc was world-class virtually from its first vintage and every year new examples appear. I love Marlborough Sauvignon. You may hate it. No problem. It's that sort of wine: it demands a reaction. It would be nice if Riesling one day demanded a reaction again, because Marlborough makes superb Riesling too, usually dry, occasionally lusciously sweet. But I suspect Pinot Gris will wow them in the aisles before Riesling struggles back to centre stage.

WHERE THE VINEYARDS ARE *Well, here it is. One of the world's newest fine wine regions in all its glory. Every vine you see here has been planted since 1973. And a lot more of those wide open spaces that gaze out so invitingly from the map will be filled with vines in the next few years. But not all of Marlborough is suitable for vines. Much of the land towards the sea at the right of the map is too silty and, despite the odd gravelly patch, most of these low-lying parts are too prone to frost for successful viticulture. Indeed, spring and autumn frosts can strike right the way up the valley.*

Conditions are quite different on the two sides of the Wairau plains. In the north, near the river itself, the ground is mostly very stony and well-drained, with ample water supplies for irrigation. The land is generally flat, but there are dips which hold more fertile soil. Vines in the dips ripen more slowly than vines on the stony ridges.

The south side has more fertile, water-retentive soils, but less available water, and grapes ripen up to two weeks after those near the Wairau River. The Awatere Valley is just off the bottom right-hand corner of the map: its marginally warmer climate and extremely stony, low-yielding soil, offers the region's best conditions for ripening red grapes successfully.

Right. So where does all this flavour intensity come from? A long, slow ripening season is the key. Blenheim, the main town, often gets more sunshine hours than any other town in New Zealand. Over a ripening season, Marlborough gets about the same amount of heat as Burgundy, and slightly less than Bordeaux. But the average daily temperature is lower than either as the sunny ripening season spreads into April, or even into May, with cold nights helping to preserve acidity.

This is fine if you can guarantee a dry autumn. Almost always, you can. Most of New Zealand's bad autumn weather comes in from the Pacific in the east and is soaked up by the North Island. The southerlies get headed off by the Southern Alps, and the wet westerlies during the growing season are fended off by the mountains to the west. Rainfall from February to April is lower than in any other New Zealand wine region, while March is Marlborough's driest month. Given that it is relatively cool, it is vital that the growers have the confidence to let their fruit hang, and the dry autumns give them that (though an autumn frost occasionally wreaks havoc). A lack of rain also allows growers to minimize anti-disease programmes, with substantial cost savings.

But lack of rain means irrigation is essential. The north side of the valley has as much water as it needs from the Wairau River and its aquifers. The south side is more barren and water often needs to be pumped from the north. Nonetheless, the south needs less water than the north, as its soils are more fertile and water-retentive. The vineyards in the north are mostly shallow silt over virtual free-draining gravel. In some vineyards you can't even see the soil for the stones. Add to this a drying northerly wind aiding transpiration from the leaves, and you need irrigation alright.

South-east of Blenheim on Highway One, the north side of the

RENWICK

0 km   1   2
0 miles

Awatere Valley has a series of stony, flat-topped river terraces with the loess topsoil struggling to make itself visible between the stones. Beneath the thin topsoil there's a deep gravel subsoil before the vines reach tough but mineral-rich mudstone at the bottom. With low yields and good protection from north-westerly winds, though occasional exposure to southerly winds, Vavasour has already produced the region's best Cabernets and excellent whites too, but the area has undergone a raft of new plantings, both near the sea and up to 25km (16 miles) inland and on the more fertile southern banks, by producers who crave the marvellous pungency of Awatere fruit.

Marlborough is renowned for great Sauvignon and Riesling, and excellent sparkling wine and Chardonnay. That's not bad, I'd say. Yet people there keep asking me to predict the next flavour fad in Britain, and I'm sure they want me to say, oh, Viognier, Marsanne, Malvasia – anything they haven't got so that they can fret like mad. But Marlborough must build on what it has already achieved. As my friend the late Auberon Waugh once said, 'It's very difficult to be best in the world at anything, but New Zealand has achieved that distinction with Sauvignon Blanc. You should simply get on with the job of making more of it.' I'll drink to that.

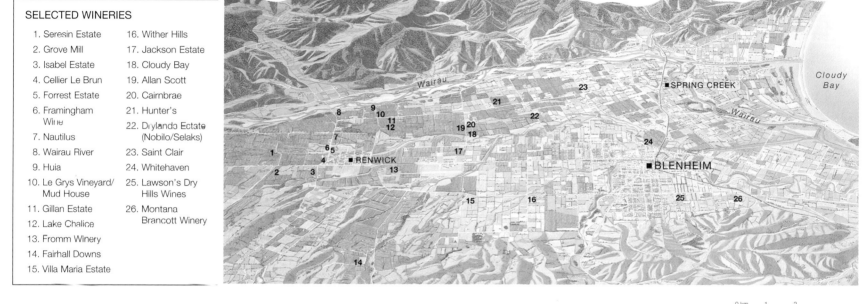

SELECTED WINERIES

1. Seresin Estate
2. Grove Mill
3. Isabel Estate
4. Cellier Le Brun
5. Forrest Estate
6. Framingham Wine
7. Nautilus
8. Wairau River
9. Huia
10. Le Grys Vineyard/ Mud House
11. Gillan Estate
12. Lake Chalice
13. Fromm Winery
14. Fairhall Downs
15. Villa Maria Estate
16. Wither Hills
17. Jackson Estate
18. Cloudy Bay
19. Allan Scott
20. Cairnbrae
21. Hunter's
22. Drylands Estate (Nobilo/Selaks)
23. Saint Clair
24. Whitehaven
25. Lawson's Dry Hills Wines
26. Montana Brancott Winery

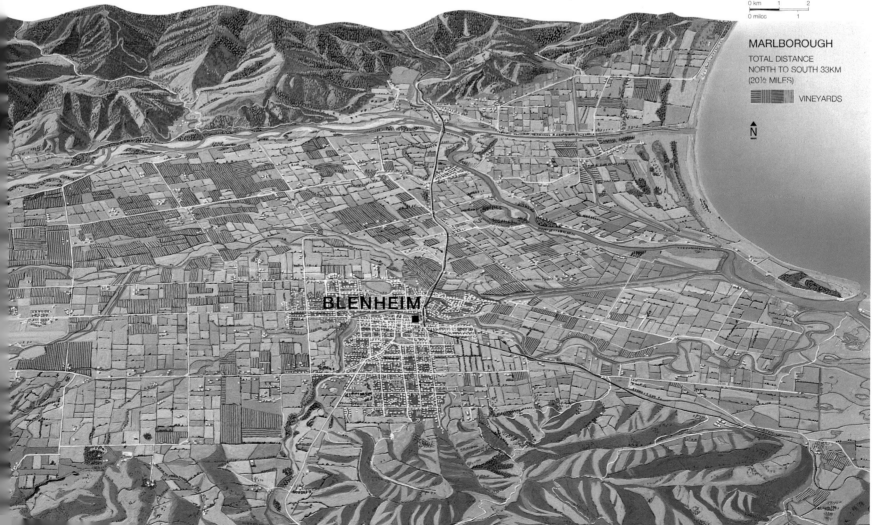

MARLBOROUGH

TOTAL DISTANCE
NORTH TO SOUTH 33KM
(20½ MILES)

VINEYARDS

SOUTH AFRICA

Fᴏʀ ᴀs ʟᴏɴɢ ᴀs I'ᴠᴇ ʙᴇᴇɴ ᴡʀɪᴛɪɴɢ ᴀʙᴏᴜᴛ ᴡɪɴᴇ – and that stretches right back into the 1980s – it's never quite seemed the right time to be writing about South Africa, her vineyards and her wines. In the 80s, it was tricky anyway, because it was difficult to find out what was actually going on. The wine industry's attitude during those last years of apartheid was extremely defensive and almost entirely controlled by giant groups like the KWV – it sounds like a secret police force but, in fact, was a little less sinister, merely an all-powerful organization of grape co-operatives that ruled most of the Cape's wine industry with a rod as hard and inflexible as Kryptonite. They and their PR outfits sold a single story – that all was well and that the oldest vineyards in the New World – we're talking a foundation date of 1655 here! – were flourishing and producing classic wines like they had always done. Well, this was tosh. Most of the vineyards were virus-infected. Most of the vines in any case were Chenin Blanc, Colombard and other grapes that basically went straight to the distillery. Not surprising, really, because hardly any of the grape growers drank wine – a brandy and Coke was the preferred tipple. And most of the winemaking was stuck in a time-warp of outdated equipment and a mentality of wine production that owed everything to the risk-averse, control-freak philosophy of the German wine schools of the 1960s and 1970s, and looked on the mould-breaking, rule-rewriting leap for freedom and flavour that marked out California and Australia with a mixture of fear and contempt. The 1980s saw more progress in technology, winery knowledge and thrilling ambition, unfettered by tradition, than in any previous decade. Winewise, the 80s were the most experimental decade of the 20th century – except in South Africa. The wine world was becoming a boisterous, babbling global village. South Africa was still the hermit on the hill.

The 1990s changed all that. With Mandela's release from jail, the winds of change finally began to blow through the Cape. There was enormous international goodwill towards South Africa in the 1990s and wine exports soared. But this success was two-edged. Few of the vineyards could do more than produce oceans of bland quaffing wine. Wines that had been stars of the previous era were now seen as outdated and stale in the bright new World of Wine. And right through the decade, a war was being waged between the reactionary old guard – unwilling to change, unwilling to cede their privilege and authority – and a new wave of youngsters who had sneaked off abroad, being made welcome for the first time in living memory by the wine producers of other countries, and had returned bristling with enthusiasm and ideas.

So, I think the beginning of the 21st century is, at last, the right time to write about South Africa. There is a mood of optimism and confidence that no longer seems arrogant – more often it is inspiring and believable. The changes being wrought in the vineyards are dramatic, yet, thankfully, lack the sense of Klondyke opportunism that concerns me in countries like Australia, New Zealand and the USA. And the wines? Transformed. Bursting with vibrant fruit, sensitively tempered by oak and actually starting to speak of a sense of place. A Sauvignon from Constantia, a Riesling from Elgin, a Pinot Noir from Walker Bay, a Shiraz from Wellington, a Malbec from Paarl Mountain, a Pinotage from Simonsberg, and a bushvine Chenin from the mountain slopes of Malmesbury. All special. All different from what the rest of the world might do with these varietals. All of them saying – this is just the beginning.

PANORAMIC MAP OF SOUTH AFRICA

Stellenbosch, Paarl and Franschhoek *pages 324–325*

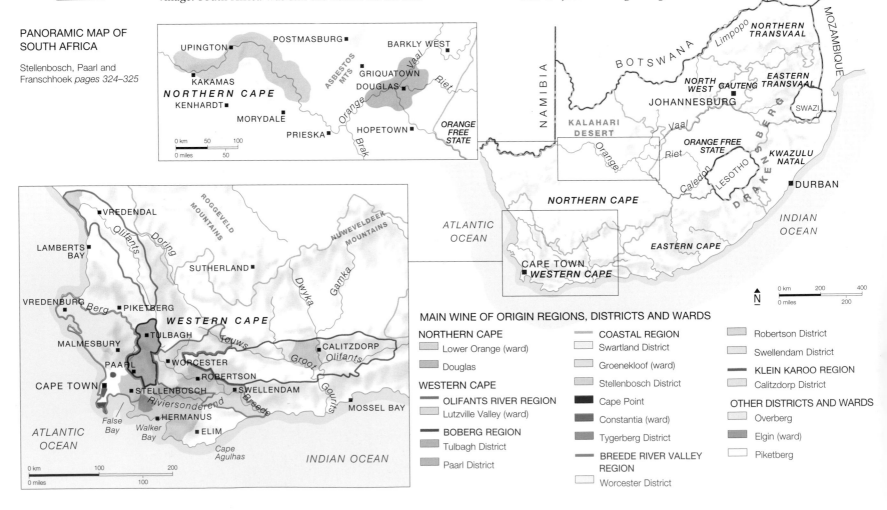

MAIN WINE OF ORIGIN REGIONS, DISTRICTS AND WARDS

NORTHERN CAPE
- Lower Orange (ward)
- Douglas

WESTERN CAPE
- **OLIFANTS RIVER REGION**
- Lutzville Valley (ward)
- **BOBERG REGION**
- Tulbagh District
- Paarl District

- **COASTAL REGION**
- Swartland District
- Groenekloof (ward)
- Stellenbosch District
- Cape Point
- Constantia (ward)
- Tygerberg District
- **BREEDE RIVER VALLEY REGION**
- Worcester District

- Robertson District
- Swellendam District
- **KLEIN KAROO REGION**
- Calitzdorp District

OTHER DISTRICTS AND WARDS
- Overberg
- Elgin (ward)
- Piketberg

And I believe it is. After a generation of being unable to decide whether they are Old World or New World in the fairest Cape, they're showing that they are precisely that – neither! Or, when it suits them, both.

THE CONCEPT OF *TERROIR*

And this mixture of new generation open-mindedness, allied to a sympathy which does lean more to France than Australia, has meant that the French idea of 'terroir' is firmly at the heart of the new South African agenda. This entails studying the geography of their country. This entails learning to match grape variety to site. It's a long process; it can't happen overnight – but, unlike in most New World countries, it's persuaded the authorities to base the demarcation of smaller areas on – wait for it – *terroir*.

Terroir? In the New World? Well, it's true that producers the world over are focusing more and more on the combination of soil, climate and exposure that go to make up the notion of *terroir*. But all too often either they're chary of admitting that that's what they're doing, or they fling the word around with all the gay abandon of a marketing department with a new toy.

In South Africa, before a new ward, as these smaller areas are called, is demarcated, there are considerations that must be taken into account. These include uniformity of soil and climate; ecological factors; the geography of the area; any existing cultural practices that may affect wine character or distinguish one area from another; existing evidence of the area's ability to produce unique wine, and the traditional name of the area. This would seem to include elements other than *terroir* – but, hang on, who really knows what *terroir* is? It's the

land, climate, but it's also all the human aspects that influence nature. And that is pretty much what this rag bag of regulations is all about. Certainly there is much more reference to *terroir* as a defining factor than there ever was when the larger districts or regions were demarcated: these were drawn up along geo-political lines. And because of that visible unifying topography, you can drive through the wards and see that they make sense.

South Africa is the world's eighth-largest wine producer, though its position of only 18th in actual vineyard area shows you how high some of the vineyard yields are – as much as 350hl (and more) per ha in the most irrigated regions like Olifants River and Orange River, though not all these dilute grapes will end up as wine. In Orange River, wine only accounts for 29 to 30 per cent of grape production: the rest is distilled, concentrated or turned into sultanas. And if you look at Stellenbosch or Paarl – well, the vines there can yield as little as 20 hl per ha, and other areas determined to improve quality – which means, fundamentally, reducing yields – include Robertson, Walker Bay, Elgin, Constantia, Durbanville, Swartland, Wellington and Franschhoek.

If you are trying to persuade a grape grower in a co-operative to reduce yield, you will have to change his entire farmer's mindset that equates success with a big crop. However, the drive for quality in the last five years is being led by a relatively new phenomenon in the Cape – a flood of new private producers. Between 1997 and 2000 about 60 new wineries started up: that's about one every 18 days. Even so, they're still a minority; co-operatives still process some 80 per cent of the crop. (Official figures for co-ops include those that have turned themselves into companies, like KWV.)

One of the glories of South Africa's vines is that you are never out of sight of the awesome mountain ranges. Here, Seidelberg's vines hug the sides of Paarl Mountain, looking across to the imposing backbone of the Simonsberg.

MOVE OVER, CHENIN BLANC

Around 60 per cent of this annual crop ends up as table wine, and white accounts for about seven out of eight bottles. Chenin Blanc is still the dominant variety, though it has dipped to under 24 per cent of vineyard area. It is followed by Colombard, with Cabernet Sauvignon, Chardonnay, Pinotage and Sauvignon Blanc now registering more strongly on the dial. Although simple, fruity white wines still account for 40 per cent of South African wine exports, the classic varieties plus Pinotage (which is not officially considered a classic variety), accounted for nearly 29 per cent of exports in 1999 and are climbing annually.

If Chardonnay and Sauvignon Blanc have levered themselves from nowhere to be a small but significant blip on the map, Cabernet Sauvignon, home-bred Pinotage and Merlot have overtaken all lesser red varieties. Shiraz, on producers' enthusiasm alone, would probably top the lot, but demand for vine material can never catch up with the irritatingly short supply. The swing towards classic, international varieties now includes small quantities of Viognier, Mourvèdre, Malbec, Nebbiolo and Sangiovese. The Cape's favourable climate, and the worldwide interest in all things Rhôneish, has also put the spotlight on the likes of Grenache, though little is currently grown here, and old bush vine plantings of Cinsaut.

WINE REGIONS

The first experimental grape plantings took place in Cape Town in 1655, and it was from just three of the vines in this experimental nursery in the gardens of the Dutch East India Company that the first South African wine was made. Virtually the whole industry has since confined itself to the south-western Cape area of South Africa from about 32° to just over 34° South, since this is the only area that can at least partially boast a Mediterranean climate. There's good rainfall in the cold wet winters, and the long hot summers, which stretch from November right through to May, would actually be too hot for really fine wines were it not, on the west coast, for the Benguela Current of chilly water that surges up from the Antarctic and sends cooling breezes inland up the river valleys, and the prevailing south-easterlies that cool down most parts east of Paarl.

Increasingly, the best wines are from growers who have selected specific sites for specific varieties, some on the slopes of the ever-present mountain ranges in order to reduce temperatures even further. Grapes tend to ripen better there because, although there are numerous soil forms – Stellenbosch alone has 20 – they tend not to be overcropped like those on the alluvial, very fertile, lower and flatter sites. But there's another point, too: growers who planted very high up discovered that because heat rises, the vines failed to go into dormancy during the winter, and that's if they avoided being devoured by the baboons who roam the peaks. So it's the mid-slopes that are now considered the most desirable, with deep, well drained soils, often of decomposed granite, and good aspects being seen as just as important as those cooling breezes.

And vineyards are moving further south: there are vines now at Elim, which is about 17km (10 miles) from Cape Agulhas, Africa's most southerly point. The vines here are planted on decomposed granite outcrops, and the plentiful and pure spring water keeps them going through the long, dry summer months. The chief problem is high humidity from the south-easterlies encouraging rot, but first results show brilliant Sauvignons and potentially fine reds.

Traditionally the best table wines have come from vineyards influenced by the cooling breezes of False Bay. Earliest and most famous are the wines of Constantia, just south of Cape Town. Spectacular sweet wines were made here in the

18th and 19th centuries, as famous as Tokaji and Sauternes. In the mid-1980s, after a long gap, the tradition of Constantia dessert wine began to be revived, but it is the cool-climate, tangy, dry whites that excite me most.

The vast majority of the top wines have always come from Paarl and Stellenbosch. Many still do, but with new areas opening up and small, quality-minded producers operating in regions previously dominated by co-operatives, competition is increasing. Those intent on finding the coolest spots have headed south-east through the Hottentots/Holland mountains. Elgin is the first area you come to, and as you drive up over the mountain pass into this bowl-shaped highland, the vegetation and the air change from warm to cool climate at a stroke. Famous for apples and pears, Elgin is increasingly producing exciting Sauvignon, Chardonnay and Pinot Noir. Keep driving south-east and you'll come to Walker Bay, and in particular the Hemelen Aarde valley, behind the cliffs at Hermanus. This is where Tim Hamilton-Russell planted in the 1970s, hoping to find South Africa's coolest conditions and re-create Burgundian Chardonnay and Pinot Noir. He, his son and his neighbours have succeeded in doing precisely that.

But it's no longer certain these conditions are South Africa's coolest. There are the Elim vineyards in the extreme south and west coast sites, cooled by fogs and breezes from the Benguela Current, are also starting to shine, most notably Darling and its subregion of Groenekloof, whose Sauvignons are startlingly tart and tasty. Durbanville Hills, its vineyards fighting a pitched battle against urban encroachment from Cape Town's suburbs, is another fine cool area. A few kilometres inland, and it warms up at every step. Co-ops dominate this landscape, but there are fine mountain slope sites at Piketberg, Riebeek and Perdeberg, where old Chenin vines share the parched soil with Pinotage, Cinsaut and Shiraz. And, as you head north to the Olifants river once again, co-ops are battling to lower yields and improve quality, while out on the coast at Bamboes Bay, yet another windy cool site begins to flex its tiny muscles.

Inland areas, such as Worcester, Robertson and the Klein Karoo, are among the warmest in the winelands, although Robertson does benefit from afternoon winds blowing up the Breede River from the Atlantic. Worcester produces the most wine of any region, much of it quaffable, easy-priced white, though some similarly undemanding reds are showing their worth. Robertson's limestone soils and good access to properly utilized irrigation have proved to be excellent for both whites and sparklers, and the move now is to see whether they can repeat their success with reds. Calitzdorp in the Klein Karoo lays claim to be the port-style capital of South Africa; with the introduction of more Portuguese varieties and greater focus on the part of the producers, some real beauties are appearing. All three regions are known for other fortified wines as well, especially sweet Muscadels.

Pinotage is South Africa's very own grape capable of making highly individual reds when handled carefully.

THE CLASSIFICATION OF SOUTH AFRICAN WINE

The Wine of Origin system, symbolized by the certificate or seal on a bottle (or other wine container), was first introduced in 1973, with major modifications in 1993. From the seal's number, the entire history of the wine can be traced back to its source, but quality is not guaranteed. Like many other New World wine countries, South Africa's labelling laws emphasize the grape variety, rather than the vineyard origin or wine style. Varietal wines for export must be made from at least 85 per cent of the named grape (or at least 75 per cent for the domestic market). To qualify as an 'estate' wine, the producer's vines must be grown on a single piece of land and the wine must be vinified, matured and bottled on the property.

STELLENBOSCH & PAARL

THE MOST ENDURING MEMORY of my first arrival in the Cape is of a colour. As I drove from the airport out to Somerset West, then turned north towards Stellenbosch along the banks of the Eerste River, a great carpet of purply crimson vines stretched out on both sides of the road, glinting in the evening sun and casting a rosy glow on to the slopes of the Helderberg that reared up to the east.

Yet that deep, dark red was nothing more than the colour of an entire vineyard region suffering from virus infection. It looked wonderful, but that crimson colour meant diseased leaves that had lost their ability to trap sunlight for photosynthesis and to ripen the crop. Some producers try to tell you that there's no longer a virus problem – but just look them in the eye and raise a quizzical eyebrow and they'll soon admit that the problem is still a major one, just as it has been in South Africa for as long as anyone can remember. Basically, the virus interferes with the natural progression of a grape towards sugar ripeness, and also the ripening of the stems and pips and the reduction in acid. This has meant that many traditional Cape red wines displayed raw green acidity and bitter tannins, and since everyone was stuck with virused vines, producers rather defiantly labelled this unappealing character the Cape Red style. But there's a new breed at work now in the Cape. The virus is now a problem to be solved, rather than endured. Better viticultural practices have shown that in cooler conditions you can coax vines to physiological ripeness and, in warm areas, good growers can actually use the virus to slow down the ripening process, allowing the grapes to hang longer on the vine and so develop more attractive complex flavours. That's the new South Africa for you. Gradually the vineyards will be replanted with virus-free material. Until this happens, they're coping.

There's another point worth mentioning amidst all this technical chat. I can't believe I've got this far without blurting it out, but this talk of lovely crimson leaves has forced my hand. The beauty of the vine leaves is nothing compared to the beauty of the land itself. The mountains that rear up at this southern tip of Africa are some of the most uplifting and majestic in the world. Almost every vineyard is within sight of them, but in Stellenbosch and Paarl they dominate your every thought, your every step, infusing you with calm and wonder – and, more mundanely, providing a rich variety of conditions in which to grow grapes. So, thank goodness for improved viticulture, then, because beneath the towering peaks of the Helderberg, Stellenbosch, Simonsberg and the Drakensteinberg mountains are some stunning vineyard sites that are at last starting to show the sort of quality at which they've always hinted.

Many of these sites are relatively warm, and have an annual rainfall of under 1000mm (40in), which is quite dry, but if your soils are right, it doesn't seem to be too much of a problem. In most of the major vineyard areas the soils are decomposed granites mixed with clay, often sufficiently deep that the vines hardly need the subsoils and shales. With the exception of super-cool areas like Elgin, that are prone to unwelcome summer rains, nearly all the rain falls in winter. The decomposed granite/clay soils, in particular, hold their water well and although many vineyards are irrigated, you can dry-farm in these conditions – especially with old bush vines – and many producers do. Which makes sense. Some wine growers see the Rhône Valley in France as having similar conditions to much of the Cape. When you drive through the

Rhône, you see mile upon mile of dry-farmed bush vines, clearly thriving in the arid conditions. Indeed, Stellenbosch is undergoing quite a bit of soul-searching at the moment. It sort of wants to believe it's relatively cool, but most of it isn't, and hopefully the tremendous quality of the new Shiraz wines now appearing will dampen the cries of the would-be cool-climate brigade.

Some areas, such as Bottelary and the Simonsberg around Kanonkop, acknowledge their warmth. Stellenbosch growers generally have to search quite hard for cooler mesoclimates, that are angled away from the sun and exposed to the maritime breezes off False Bay, directly to the south. As it happens, both reds and whites do well all over Stellenbosch, but the Simonsberg, further from the sea, is noted for richer, more muscular reds, while wines from the Helderberg, much nearer to False Bay, do tend to be finer-boned and more elegant, and some of the whites are first-class.

Well, ultra-cool climate isn't quite so trendy as it was a few years ago, so Stellenbosch and Paarl with their generally warm conditions and long established winery and vineyard infrastructure are well-placed to be the leaders of South Africa's wine world. The number of new wineries, virtually all independent, which have sprung up in the past ten years emphasises both areas' importance. The 1991 *Platter Wine Guide* listed 55 wineries for Stellenbosch and 34 for Paarl; by 2001, they had 100 and 74 respectively. This escalation has meant that individual wineries have found it increasingly difficult to stand out from the crowd. One of the answers has been to demarcate Stellenbosch and Paarl into smaller areas. And, whereas the original district boundaries were drawn up along geo-political lines, these smaller areas, known as Wards, come rather closer to the European concept of *terroir*.

THE WARDS OF STELLENBOSCH

Stellenbosch, at 43,347ha (107,110 acres), with 16,112ha (39,800 acres) under vine, covers less than a third of Paarl's area, and has a more unified look. Looking inland from False Bay, the mountains form an amphitheatre, with the Simonsberg being the furthest point from the Bay. The vineyards are dotted round the mountain slopes and straddle the lower ground in between.

The vineyards of Thelema catch the late evening sun on the Helshoogte Pass between Stellenbosch and the Franschhoek Valley.

RED GRAPES
The best red wines come from the classic grape varieties: Cabernets Sauvignon and Franc, Merlot and Shiraz. Pinotage also prospers here and there are isolated spots of good Pinot Noir.

WHITE GRAPES
Internationally popular Chardonnay and Sauvignon Blanc are widely planted. Semillon is showing great promise in various sites throughout both regions. Dry Chenin Blanc can be excellent, and both this and Riesling produce good dessert wine.

CLIMATE
The climate is Mediterranean in character, with most rainfall in winter and fairly hot, dry summers. The much-needed cooling winds of summer, known as the 'Cape Doctor' blow across the land from False Bay and the south-east.

SOIL
Stellenbosch alone has more than 20 soil forms, all of which are acidic; those in Paarl are, in general, more calcareous. Lower, flatter sites tend to be on very fertile alluvial soils.

ASPECT
Matching variety to site is what matters. Thus Sauvignon Blanc does best in cooler spots preferably south-east facing; Shiraz will be planted on hotter north-west or west facing slopes.

Mulderbosch's Sauvignon Blanc has acquired cult status since the early 1990s.

The district has five Wards and more are being considered. Many of the best-known wineries are in Simonsberg-Stellenbosch, the first Ward to be demarcated and the furthest from the cooling sea breezes of False Bay. Vineyards go up to about 480m (1575ft), where mostly white varieties are planted in decomposed granite. Deep red soils in the lower, more sheltered sites give rich, structured reds, especially from Pinotage, Shiraz and Cabernet. Bottelary Ward is warm, and vineyards run up the hillsides to about 300m (985ft) just east of Stellenbosch town. Growers here have only just started to bottle their own wines; but new producers and revitalized old ones are creating exciting flavours here. On the top of the Bottelary Hills is a vineyard trail with panoramic views of Table Mountain, Cape Town, the Hottentots mountains and the sea.

Climb over these hills and you drop down into Devon Valley, its gentle slopes forming an east-facing U-shape, down the middle of which runs a single meandering country lane that links the valley to Stellenbosch. More densely planted with vines than Bottelary, it too is mostly red wine country, though Chardonnay does well on the higher ground on the southern side of the U. Much of the soil is deep and red, and the valley has long been associated with Shiraz, though Cabernet does pretty well here. Generally wines are more restrained and less robust than those of Simonsberg or Bottelary.

As if the scenery all around here wasn't spectacular enough, if you really want to blow your mind, head for the Jonkershoek Valley. Once through the low-lying land near Stellenbosch town, you'll find yourself among towering mountains which press ever closer to the narrow,

winding road. There are only 200ha (494 acres) of vines here, almost all near the valley mouth and scrambling up to about 350m (1148ft) on the steep but cool south-facing slopes. The south-easterly winds tear down this valley and steep peaks reduce the exposure to morning and evening sun, which would explain why initially Chardonnay was the chief grape. However, despite the conditions, the more exiciting results are coming from Shiraz and Cabernet.

The last, and smallest, Stellenbosch Ward is Papegaaiberg, or Parrot Mountain. Here, urban development and a pine forest restrict vineyards to just 180ha (445 acres). To date, no wine is made in this Ward. More interesting are new developments at the northern end of the Helderberg in the Blaauwklippen Valley, where three new estates are already excelling. And, although strictly outside Stellenbosch, in the windswept Lourensford Valley, is Vergelegen, one of South Africa's top wineries.

THE WARDS OF PAARL
Paarl at 155,173ha (383,427 acres), with 17,402ha (43,000 acres) of them under vine, is by far the larger district, with a multitude of different mesoclimates, soils, altitudes and aspects. Unlike Stellenbosch, it has never claimed to be a cool area,

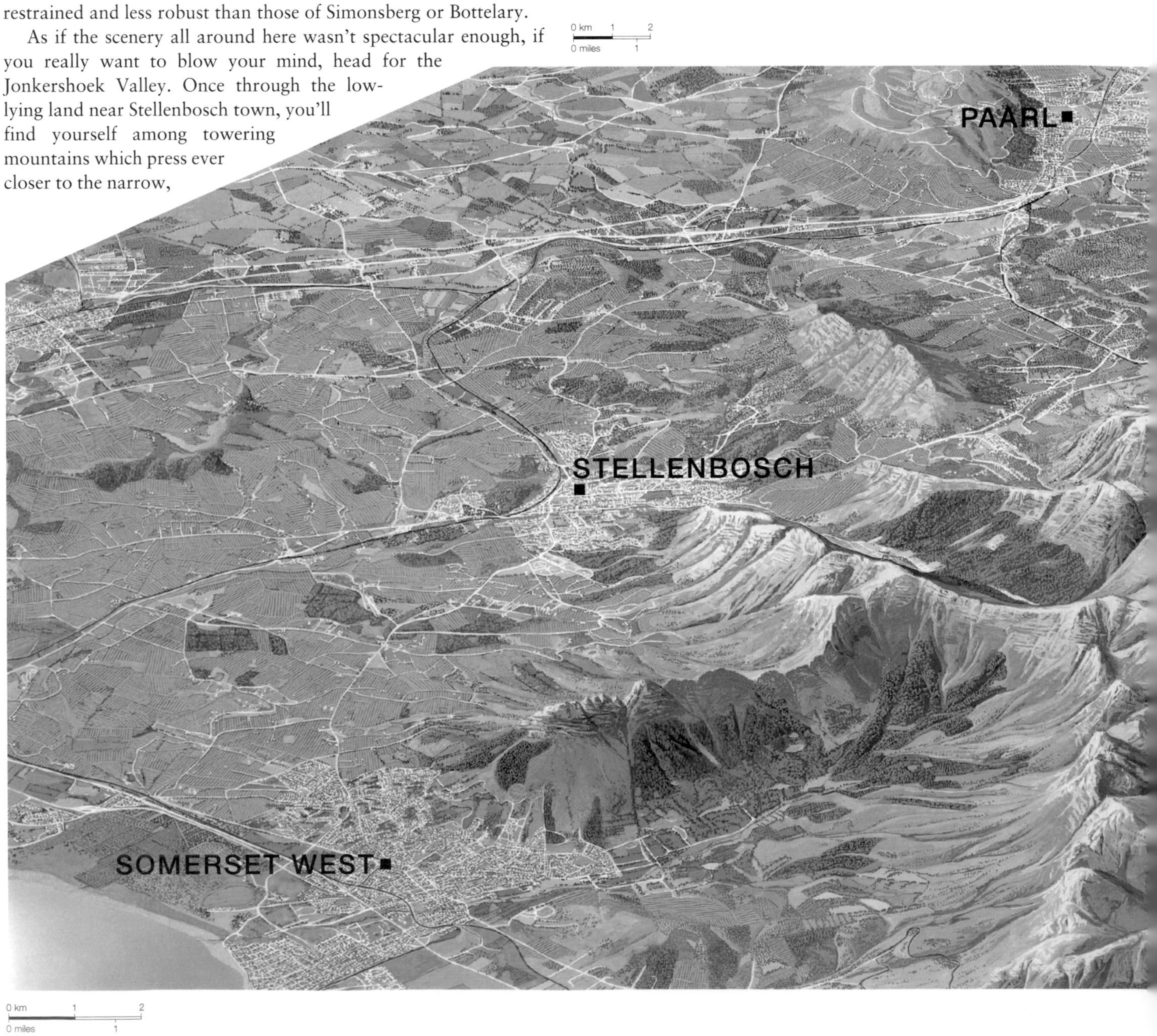

PAARL

STELLENBOSCH

SOMERSET WEST

and receives only the tail end of the False Bay breezes plus some Atlantic winds from the west. Consequently it's doing some storming stuff with the Rhône varieties and with Pinotage. But there are also spots where fragile Pinot Noir puts in a good performance.

There are currently two Wards in Paarl, with a third, Simonsberg-Paarl, being considered for the north side of the Simonsberg. Interesting idea. It's clearly got something special, because in a supposedly hot area Glen Carlou produces medal-winning Pinot Noir, while just across the valley on the south side of Paarl mountain, Fairview's Rhône and Bordeaux varieties bake to perfection in the afternoon sun. Franschhoek is the more famous Ward, a long valley barricaded by mountains, but only a small part of the land is suitable for vines. Inaccessibility, forest, otherwise unsuitable land and other fruit orchards mean that only 1500ha (3700 acres) of its 11,000ha (27,180 acres) are planted with vines. Frankly, the alluvial and sandy soil of the valley floor has produced

inferior wines for decades, but largely because, despite a spread of seemingly lovely estates, their fruit was processed at the co-op. You thought their wines tasted the same? They probably were the same. But now producers like Boekenhoutskloof are showing these soils can produce stunning Semillon and Cabernet if carefully farmed, and there's still a huge variety of north, south, east and west-facing slopes to be exploited. Plantings so far go as high as 420m (1378ft), and the chief problem is to maximize the cooling effect of the south-easterly winds that sweep down the valley without having your vines bludgeoned out of existence.

Wellington Ward is hotter, and well away from sea breezes. Its Chenin Blanc used to be a mainstay of Cape 'sherry', yet that's only half the story. There's a whole hillside of top quality, iron-rich Glen Rosa soil producing excellent reds, and the east-facing slopes of the Groenberg have some of the coolest conditions in the Western Cape – and stunning reds, of all things, to show for it.

WHERE THE VINEYARDS ARE *The most important feature on this map is down in the bottom left-hand corner, where you see False Bay. With Stellenbosch and Paarl vineyards lying at around 34° South, the sun would simply be too strong to produce fragrant, subtle wines. Even the Benguela Current, which runs along the west coast,*

barely affects False Bay. But every summer day a south-easterly wind brews up from a high pressure zone over the continental shelf at the southern tip of Africa. It's the movement, rather than the temperature, of this wind, that is so effective in cooling the vines. The next most important feature on the map are the mountains. They provide excellent sloping vineyard sites up to about 600m (1970 ft), at which point slopes generally become too steep for cultivation, and soil gives way to bare rock. But even vineyards away from the slopes are not on flat land: most Stellenbosch ones grow on some sort of undulation, even if they are described as 'valleys'. In Paarl, there are a few riverbank vineyards, but these are mostly for table grapes. And as for planting more vineyards – well, there's not a lot of suitable mountain slope land left. Heading north-west and south-east will probably be the answer.

STELLENBOSCH AND PAARL

TOTAL DISTANCE NORTH TO SOUTH
47KM (29 MILES)

VINEYARDS

SELECTED WINERIES

STELLENBOSCH

1. Hazendal
2. Kaapzicht
3. Jordan
4. Uiterwyk
5. Meerlust
6. Spier
7. Overgaauw
8. Neethlingshof
9. Hartenberg
10. Villiera
11. Meinert
12. Middelvlei
13. Simonsig
14. Mulderbosch
15. Bergkelder
16. Beyerskloof
17. L'Avenir
18. Morgenhof
19. Delheim
20. Kanonkop
21. Warwick
22. Le Bonheur
23. Lievland
24. Rustenberg
25. Thelema
26. Le Riche
27. Neil Ellis
28. Blaauwklippen
29. Vriesenhof
30. Stellenzicht
31. Waterford
32. De Trafford
33. Rust en Vrede
34. Longridge
35. Grangehurst
36. Avontuur
37. Cordoba
38. Morgenster
39. Vergelegen

PAARL

40. Welgemeend
41. Glen Carlou
42. Fairview
43. Backsberg
44. Plaisir de Merle
45. KWV
46. Boschendal
47. Nederburg
48. La Motte
49. Boekenhoutskloof
50. Haute Cabrière

PAARL = WINE DISTRICT

— WINE DISTRICT BOUNDARY

Franschhoek = WINE WARD

•••• WINE WARD BOUNDARY

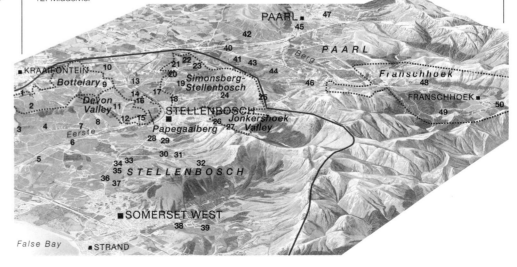

NORTH AFRICA

I T'S THE WASTED POTENTIAL that makes me want to cry. There are so many good vineyards here – or at least, vineyards that could be good, if anybody cared. Eighty per cent of the vines in Algeria are over forty years old. Anywhere else – like Australia or Burgundy, say – they'd be jumping up and down with resources like that. They'd be making incredibly concentrated, brooding, spicy red wines and they'd have buyers queueing down the street. What happens here? Very little. The majority just go on making rough, fruitless, baked wines without flavour or acidity. Yet there simply hasn't been a market for these wines since the French left in the 1950s and early 1960s. And as the French quit their colonies, the best winemakers left too, heading for France's Midi.

France was North Africa's biggest market for wine from the early 1900s onwards, and in the 1950s between a half and two-thirds of the entire international wine trade was in North African wines. When the wine arrived in France, it was mostly blended with rather smarter French stuff, in a way that would be illegal now. As the market fell away, so did the area under vine: Algeria, always the biggest producer of the three North African wine countries, had 400,000ha (988,387 acres) in 1938. By 1990, it hit a low of 102,000ha (252,040 acres). However, good news is coming through despite continuing problems: a replanting programme is underway and Algeria now has more than 150,000ha (370,645 acres). Three-quarters of Algeria's wine production is in the western coastal province of Oran, but much is still bottled and matured in France.

When the French left Morocco in 1956, the area under wine vines was about 55,000ha (135,900 acres); this had fallen to about 13,000ha (32,123 acres) by 1990. The phrase 'Moroccan wine' is no longer an oxymoron, though. Castel Frères' FF100 million development is instigating a rebirth. Nearly 1200ha (2965 acres), split between Boulaouane and Meknès, the main wine producing areas, have been planted, and two large wineries with a 100,000hl capacity are producing a range of decent offerings. Tunisia's vineyards have also shrunk, but the Italian Calatrasi operation in Khanguet, involving an $8million investment and the grafting of new varietals, coupled with New World expertise, promises better results.

So it's not all doom and gloom. The vines that have been uprooted were those on the hot plains: those that remain are on the cooler coastal ranges, where they are planted at up to 1200m (3937ft) above sea level – a relatively high altitude meaning cooler temperatures. Morocco benefits from an Atlantic coastline with its cooling breezes, although wind can be a problem: imagine being a vine in a near-desert country, with winds sweeping in from the Atlantic at 65km (40 miles) per hour. In Tunisia it's the hot, dry Scirocco wind that reduces the yields. What these countries need is advice on how to trellis and plant vines to protect them from wind. Because there's no reason why they couldn't be making brilliant wines. Sure, it's hot and dry – Algeria's vineyards only get 400–600mm (16–24in) of rain each year. But parts of Spain get less than that. Indeed, the 'Sahara Region' is now being officially extended to encompass southern Spain and Sicily.

GRAPE VARIETIES

Most of the grapes planted in North Africa are dull. Carignan is king, and shows over and over again just what reliably fruitless, tough red wine it can produce. Alicante Bouschet, Aramon and Cinsaut are equally uninspiring, though Cinsaut can do better if it's handled well. But Cabernet Sauvignon, Merlot, Mourvèdre and Syrah are becoming more widespread and growers should concentrate on these. Because sometimes when you taste the better reds, you get a glimpse – just a glimpse – of what they could achieve. Earthy, dusty, rustic (I'm not asking for miracles here), but with some ripe raspberry fruit. A bit of carbonic maceration could help no end in getting some juiciness and freshness into the wines.

As for whites, there's a fair bit of Clairette and Ugni Blanc, both contenders for the world's dullest wine grape, but Tunisia's sweet and dry Muscats are probably the best whites – pretty hefty, but at least they have perfume and fruit. Greater investment is the real key to improved quality. North Africans aren't great wine drinkers, and Islamic fundamentalism means attitudes to wine are ambiguous. The Koran forbids drinking alcohol, but the currency that can be earned from wine exports is an big attraction. Wine continues to be made and exported, so there must be a tiny ray of hope for the future.

WINE AREAS

▪ MOROCCO	▪ ALGERIA	▪ TUNISIA

APPELLATION D'ORIGINE GARANTIE WINE REGIONS	APPELLATION D'ORIGINE GARANTIE WINE REGIONS	APPELLATION D'ORIGINE CONTRÔLÉE WINE REGIONS
1. Doukkala	15. Côteaux de Tlemcen	22. Tibar
2. Sahel	16. Monts du Tessalah	23. 1er Cru Côteaux Tebourba
3. Zaer	17. Côteaux de Mascara	24. 1er Cru Côteaux d'Ultique
4. Zenata	18. Dahra	25. 1er Cru Muscat de Kelibia
5. Chellah	19. Côteaux du Zaccar	26. Mornag
6. Zemmour	20. Medéa	27. Sidi Salaam
7. Guerrouane	21. Ain Bessem-Bouira	28. Grand Cru Mornag
8. Beni M'tir		
9. Saiss		
10. Beni Sadden		
11. Zerhoun		
12. Rharb		
13. Angad		
14. Berkane		

ASIA

I WONDER, WOULD Cow's Nipple blend better with Cock's Heart or Dragon's Eye? And should I oak it? No, it's a serious question, and one which during the next generation, we might need to answer, because these are Asian grape varieties and they do produce wine. They sound unfamiliar: from the few examples I've had, they taste unfamiliar too, but the culture of wine is catching on in Asia. The economic boom at the end of the 20th century saw top quality European wine reach higher prices in markets like Singapore, Hong Kong and Shanghai than anywhere else. Add to this the widespread evidence that red wine is good for your heart, and a greatly increased awareness of all things Western as globalization continues on its remorseless path, and we could be looking at the birth – or rather rebirth, since both China and India have long, though largely lapsed, wine traditions – of a globally significant wine culture, which will not be satisfied merely by importing European wine, but will want to manufacture its own.

CHINA

China's wine industry is growing like a weed now that official policy promotes wine. There are already some 150,000ha (370,645 acres) under vine, and in the next 15 years output is expected to double, or even treble – who knows? Winery capacity is also expanding, but so far only 10 per cent of the grapes grown are crushed for wine. Inland regions, with their extreme climate, are best for dessert grapes or raisins, such as those grown in Xinjiang province in the north-west at 150m (492ft) below sea level. In the north-east, a maritime climate, moderate but for the occasional typhoon, produces the best wines, particularly in the coastal provinces of Shandong, Hebei and Tianjin. Many international varieties have been planted as well as traditional Chinese, German and Russian versions. And there are now a string of joint ventures between Western and Chinese companies, involving such companies as Rémy Martin and Pernod-Ricard of France, Torres of Spain and Sella & Mosca from Sardinia. I've had Chardonnays and Cabernet Francs, in particular from Shandong and Hebei, which were extremely good.

Western involvement has led to a major change in style. Chinese taste in wine (really the Chinese taste is for rice wine or, better still, brandy) is for something sweetish and oxidized. There's no point in planting Chardonnay for that sort of wine – but anyway, what's wanted is wines to appeal to Western wallets. This means that, just like everywhere else in the world, the newest wines aim to imitate classic European styles. So far they show promise.

INDIA

India has a long winemaking history, though its recent fame as a wine-producer is due entirely to Omar Khayyam, a Champagne-method sparkler launched by Château Indage in 1985, and made in collaboration with Piper-Heidsieck of Champagne. Grapes for it are grown in the Maharashtra hills above Bombay, and it is these highland areas that come nearest to escaping India's heat. Even so, massive irrigation is necessary, vines generally giving two crops a year; the monsoon crop is understandably less well regarded. Omar Khayyam is a blend of Chardonnay, Ugni Blanc, Pinot Noir, Pinot Blanc and Thompson Seedless: and while the white is good, the pink is fresh and excellent. There's also a sweeter fizz called Marquise de Pompadour, and red and white still wines. These bode well, as a Californian winemaker (ex-Bonny Doon) gets to grips with oak-aging Cabernet, Shiraz, Chardonnay and Ugni Blanc blends. Californian and French joint ventures are evidence of Indage's ambition, something Bangalore's Grover vineyards also show by employing Bordeaux superstar Michel Rolland as consultant.

Vinifera vines have to be be grafted in India, because phylloxera reached the subcontinent in the 1890s and wreaked as much havoc locally as it did elsewhere. The state of Maharashtra produces around 40 per cent of India's grapes, the rest coming from Karnataka, Andhra Pradesh and the Punjab, although less than one per cent of the total are made into wine.

JAPAN

In Japan, the problem is too much rain. There are spring and autumn monsoons, typhoons in summer, and icy winters. Land is either mountainous, or flat and waterlogged; there's little gently sloping terrain, beloved of vine growers. But a trellising system, called *tana-zukuri* spreads vines out along wires, so they can dry. The Mount Fuji area, west of Tokyo, especially Yamanashi, is proving the best producer so far. The east coast is more extreme. In all, wine is made in 46 out of 47 provinces, tropical Okinawa being the odd one out.

Japanese varieties and hybrids account for most of the vineyards, but only about ten per cent of grapes are used to make wine, much of it blended with bulk imports. The favourite *vinifera* vine is Koshu, giving big, juicy dessert grapes and light white wines. High rainfall and high vine yields tend to make Japanese wines light in body. Suntory make some exceptions with Bordeaux varieties, as well as impressive Sauternes-like sweet wine. The smaller producers now appearing are spearheading a drive towards quality home produce, but too much is still imported bulk wine bottled in Japan.

The imitation of European styles is the aim of China's new export-oriented wine industry. This Chardonnay, at Hua Dong Winery in Qingdao, is likely to be made into table wine, rather than grown for dried fruit or brandy.

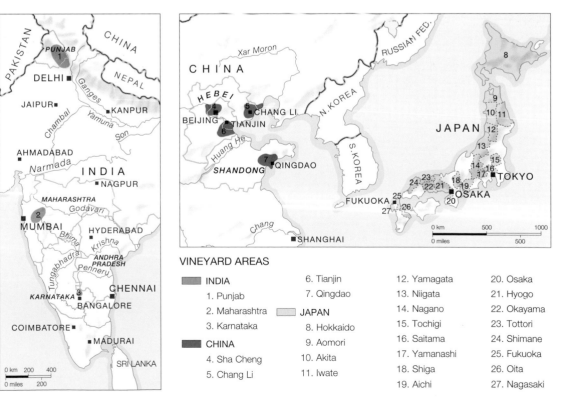

VINEYARD AREAS

INDIA
1. Punjab
2. Maharashtra
3. Karnataka

CHINA
4. Sha Cheng
5. Chang Li
6. Tianjin
7. Qingdao

JAPAN
8. Hokkaido
9. Aomori
10. Akita
11. Iwate
12. Yamagata
13. Niigata
14. Nagano
15. Tochigi
16. Saitama
17. Yamanashi
18. Shiga
19. Aichi
20. Osaka
21. Hyogo
22. Okayama
23. Tottori
24. Shimane
25. Fukuoka
26. Oita
27. Nagasaki

INDEX

ACKNOWLEDGMENTS

The publishers would like to thank the countless organisations and individuals all over the world who have given invaluable help and advice in preparing the maps and diagrams in this Atlas, and especially for the following sections:

FRANCE
Association Nationale Interprofessionelle des Vins de Table et des Vins de Pays (ANIVIT), Jean-Claude Audebert (Bourgueil), Domaine Baumard (Angers), Bureau Interprofessionel des Vins de Bourgogne, Bureau Interprofessionel des Vins du Centre, Cave de Tain l'Hermitage, Yves Chidaine (Montlouis), Comité Interprofessionel des Vins de Bordeaux, Comité Interprofessionel des Vins Côtes de Provence, Conseil Interprofessionelle des Vins d'Alsace, Georges Duboeuf (Beaujolais), GETEVAY (Chablis), Conseil Interprofessionnel des Vins du Languedoc, Olivier Humbrecht MW (Alsace), Institut National des Appellations d'Origine (INAO), Institut Technique du Vin, Inter Rhône, Maison du Vin (Saumur), Office International de la Vigne et du Vin, Alain Paret (St-Joseph), Lyn Parry (Rhône), René Renou (Bonnezeaux) Jean-Max Roger (Sancerre), Professor G. Seguin (Bordeaux University), SOPEXA (London) Syndicat Viticole d'Aloxe-Corton, Syndicat Viticole Médoc et Haut-Médoc, Syndicat Viticole de Pouilly, Syndicat Viticole St-Émilion, Union Interprofessionelle des Vins du Beaujolais, Les Vins du Val de Loire

GERMANY
Peter Anheuser (Nahe), Matthew Boucher, Bernard Breuer (Rheingau), Armin Diel (Nahe), German Wine Information Centre (London), Weingut Heyl von Herrnsheim (Rheinhessen), Karl-Heinz Johner (Baden), Weingut Juliusspital (Franken), Carl Koenen, Rainer Lingenfelder (Pfalz), Ernst Loosen (Mosel), Egon Müller Jr (Saar), Claus Piedmont (Saar), Rheinhessenwein, Dirk Richter (Mosel), Landwirtschaftskammer Rheinland-Pfalz, Verband Deutscher Prädikats und Qualitätsweingüter

SWITZERLAND
Swiss Wine Exporters' Association, Provins (Valais)

AUSTRIA
Arbeitsgemeinschaft Kartographie, Austrian Wine Marketing Board

ITALY
Richard Baudains, Dr Maurizio Castelli, Consorzio Bolgheri, Consorzio del Marchio Storico (Chianti Classico), Consorzio per la Tutela dei Vini (Valpolicella), Consorzio del Vino Brunello di Montalcino, Consorzio del Vino Nobile di Montepulciano, David Gleave MW, Alois Lageder (Alto Adige), Paul Merritt, Produttori del Barbaresco, Pietro Ratti (Barolo), Servizio della Vitivinicoltura (ERSA, Friuli).

SPAIN
Consejo Regulador DO Jerez, Consejo Regulador DO Penedès, Consejo Regulador DO Ribera del Duero, Consejo Regulador DOC Rioja, Fedejerez, Joachin Galvez, Instituto Nacional de Denominaciones de Origen (INDO), Rioja Wine Exporters Group, The Sherry Institute of Spain (London), Miguel Torres SA (Penedes), Wines from Spain (London)

PORTUGAL
Peter Cobb, Joanna Delaforce (Douro), Direcção Regional de Agricultura (Região Autónoma da Madeira), Bruce Guimaraens (Douro), Instituto do Vinho da Madeira, Madeira Wine Company, The Symington Family Port Companies

ENGLAND
Stephen Skelton, John Worontschak

EASTERN EUROPE
Association of the Czech Vine Growers and Winemakers (CMVVU), Boyar Estates (Hungary), Mike Frumosu (Romania), Hungarian Food & Wine Bureau (London), Poslovna Skupnost za Vinogradništvo in Vinarstvo Slovenije (Slovenia), Premium Brand Corporation (Black Sea States), Alena Vitkovska (Slovakia)

EASTERN MEDITERREAN
Chateau Musar (Lebanon), Cyprus High Commission Trade Centre, Doluca Winery, Nico Manessis (Greece)

USA
Alexander Valley Vineyards, Rod Berglund (Russian River), California North Coast Grape Growers Association, Carneros Quality Alliance, Central Coast Winegrowers' Association, Chalone Wine Group, Chemeketa Vineyard Management and Winemaking Program (Oregon), Stan Clarke (Washington State), Edna Valley Arroyo Grande Vintners Association, Catherine Fallis (California), Lake County Winegrape Commission, Landmark Vineyards (Sonoma), McDowell Valley Vineyards (Mendocino), Mendocino Winegrowers Association, Mill Creek Vineyard (Sonoma), Robert Mondavi Winery (Napa), Napa Valley Vintners Association, New York Wine & Grape Foundation, Oak Knoll (Oregon), Oregon Wine Advisory Board, Palmer Vineyards (Long Island), Paso Robles Vintners & Growers Association, David Petterson (cartographer, Oregon), Ponzi Vineyards (Oregon), Russian River Valley Winegrowers, Richard Sanford (Santa Barbara), Santa Barbara County Vintners' Association, Sonoma County Grape Growers Association, Sonoma Valley Vintners and Growers Alliance, Jonathan Swinchatt (EarthVision Inc., Napa), University of California at Davis, US Government Bureau of Alcohol, Tobacco and Firearms (BATF), Larry Walker, Dick Ward (Napa), Washington Wine Commission, Winegrowers of Dry Creek Valley, Wine Institute of California, Yamhill County Wineries Association

CANADA
British Columbia Wine Institute, Ontario Wine Institute

CHILE
Asociación de Exportadores y Embotelladores de Vinos A.G., Richard Neill, Alejandra Schultz, Christian Sotomayor, Patricio Tapia, Viñas de Colchagua, Viña Santa Rita (Maipo)

ARGENTINA
Catena Zapata (Mendoza), Familia Zuccardi (Mendoza), Instituto de Desarrollo Rural (Mendoza), Tom Pakenham, Pro Mendoza

AUSTRALIA
Australian Wine & Brandy Corporation, Australian Wine Bureau (London), Tony Brady (Clare), Clare Valley Winemakers Inc, Coonawarra Vignerons Association, Domaine Chandon (Yarra), Eden Valley Winemakers Association, Peter Forrestal (Margaret River), Hunter Valley Vineyard Association, Tony Keys, Tim Knappstein (Clare), Max and Stephen Lake (Hunter), Bob McLean (Barossa), Sally Marden (Barossa), Liz Morrison (Margaret River), Southcorp Wines, The Viticultural Council of the South East of South Australia, Wine Industry of Western Australia, Wynn's Coonawarra, Yarra Valley Winegrowers Association

NEW ZEALAND
Horticultural and Food Research Institute of New Zealand, Gus Lawson (Hawkes Bay), Montana Wines Ltd, Ollie Powrie (Hawkes Bay), John Stitchbury (Marlborough), Wine Institute of New Zealand, Wines of New Zealand (London)

SOUTH AFRICA
Dave Hughes, Dave Johnson, Angela Lloyd, South Africa Wine Industry Information & Systems (SAWIS)

NORTH AFRICA
Linda Domas, Tunisian Project Manager, Calatrasi

ASIA
Keith Grainger, Parmar Wines, Myoko Stevenson

GENERAL
Carpe Diem, The Royal Geographic Society Map Room, Westbury Communications

PICTURE CREDITS
Photographs of bottles by Nigel James.

Principal photo source by Cephas Picture Library. All photographs by Mick Rock except:
Kevin Argue 268 (below)
Nigel Blythe 47, 107, 118, 123, 184-5, 194
Stuart Boreham 80
Emma Borg 321
Andy Christodolo 5, 12, 14 (below right), 18, 21 (top row centre), 24, 139, 141, 143, 157, 255, 271, 279, 292
David Copeman 217
Chris Davies 309, 327
Jeffrey Drewitz 21 (third row right), 300
Bruce Fleming 247, 249
Kevin Judd 7, 9, 10 (above), 14 (below left), 15 (right), 16 (top left), 20 (top left and second right), 21 (third row centre), 22, 237, 242, 268 (above), 288, 304, 310, 313, 316
Char Abu Mansoor 231
R & K Muschenetz 1, 11, 250
Alain Proust 20 (bottom), 323
H Shearing 308
Ted Stefanski 21 (top row left and right)

Other photographs by
Michael Busselle 34, 41, 64, 74, 90
Charmaine Grieger 82, 275
Janet Price 21 (second row centre and right), 44, 50, 120, 129, 134, 280
Kristian Reynolds 263
Scope (Jean-Luc Barde) 77, 202, 205; (Bernard Galeron) 160, 163; (Jacques Guillard) 20 (top right), 145, 156; (Noel Hautemaniere) 104
David Williamson 220
Jon Wyand 54
Joco Znidarsic 16 (top row, left), 227